D0024786

Personality and Personal Growth

Fourth Edition

Robert Frager
James Fadiman

Institute of Transpersonal Psychology

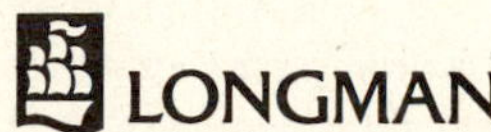

An imprint of Addison Wesley Longman, Inc.

New York • Reading, Massachusetts • Menlo Park, California • Harlow, England
Don Mills, Ontario • Sydney • Mexico City • Madrid • Amsterdam

To our Wives: Ayhan and Dorothy
and Children: Ariel, Eddie, John, Kenan, Renee, and Maria
and to our Teachers

Editor-in-Chief: Priscilla McGeehon
Acquisitions Editor: Eric Stano
Developmental Editor: James Strandberg
Supplements Editor: Cyndy Taylor
Marketing Manager: Jay O'Callaghan
Project Editor: Ann P. Kearns
Text and Cover Designer: Mary Archondes
Cover Painting: Jeanette Stobie, photographed by Francine Benard, from the collection of Eddy J. Louis
Art Studio: Academy Art, Ltd.
Photo Researcher: Karen Koblik
Production Manager: Alexandra Odulak
Desktop Coordinator: Joanne Del Ben
Manufacturing Manager: Hilda Koparanian
Electronic Page Makeup: Americomp
Printer and Binder: Courier/Kendallville, Inc.
Cover Printer: Coral Graphics Services, Inc.

For permission to use copyrighted material, grateful acknowledgement is made to the copyright holders on page 589, which is hereby made part of this copyright page.

Library of Congress Cataloging-in-Publication Data

Frager, Robert, Date.
Personality and personal growth/Robert Frager and James Fadiman.
— 4th ed.
p. cm.
Includes bibliographical references.
ISBN 0-321-01192-9
1. Personality. 2. Psychotherapy. 3. Self-actualization
(Psychology) I. Title.
BF698.F 1998
155.2—dc21 97-1064
CIP

ISBN 0-321-01192-9

12345678910—CRK—00999897

Brief Contents

Detailed Contents

Preface

Once again we have worked to improve a book that has succeeded as a useful and, above all, *readable* introduction to theories of personality.

Instead of holding to one viewpoint about personality and defending it throughout the text, we have organized each chapter so that it focuses more on the stronger aspects of the theory it presents—the reasons for the theory's continuing strength and popularity—than on its weaknesses. We encourage students to test the validity or utility of each theory against their own experience and common sense.

Every theory in this book has been tested on thousands of people. Each has helped individuals to resolve personal problems, improve child raising, enhance communication, or support personal growth and spiritual development. Behind every theory included here are active adherents, journals presenting research findings, and training programs; moreover, each theory has achieved wide application. None have been empirically proved, none have been empirically disproved; all have their supporters and critics.

Students have told us that this material is well worth their time. Even if they go no further in psychology, the ideas and issues raised in this book serve them and enrich their lives.

Expert proponents of each theory admit that all the available research does not merit inclusion in their own theoretical reviews. So, too, we have not stressed research in our presentation. Authors whose work we admire but did not cover, such as Gordon Allport, Henry Murray, Rollo May, Albert Bandura, and Walter Mischel, while relevant to current psychology, seem, to us, less relevant to student needs and concerns.

Overall, the changes in the fourth edition focused on making the book easier to teach from and to learn from. We've accomplished this goal without sacrificing the emphasis that we have maintained since the first edition: to write a textbook that encourages students to use themselves as the testing stone for each theory, to validate its insights in their own lives, and to come to their own conclusions about the utility and value of each set of ideas.

New to the Fourth Edition

The fourth edition has been entirely redesigned, with new graphics, new layout, and many new photos. In addition to the change in design, there are a number of major alterations in the text:

New Pedagogy: *Chapter Highlights and Key Concepts* are new pedagogical features we have added to each chapter for the fourth edition. Chapter Highlights, which provide a listed summary of the most important ideas in the chapter, appear after the Theory Firsthand. Key Concepts, near the end of every chapter, present full definitions of the most technical terms used by each theorist. Words defined there are boldfaced at the first major occurrence in the text.

New Introductory Chapter *Chapter One: Introduction* is a new chapter designed to help guide students into the chapters on theory that follow. Our approach is made clear: to honor the contributions of each theorist and to validate the unique ways in which each theory contributes to an understanding of human nature. This new chapter offers a detailed discussion of the book's structure and describes why we have organized the material as we have. We explain, too, why it is necessary to expand our awareness beyond white male psychology, and beyond American-European psychology, in order to more fully understand ourselves. Since students also continue to request help in framing their growing interests in Eastern disciplines, this new introductory chapter provides a preview of the extensive coverage of the Yoga, Zen, and Sufism traditions. We discuss the rationale for including transpersonal psychology and the different approaches to states of consciousness still neglected in other personality textbooks.

New Chapter on Anna Freud and the Post-Freudians *Chapter 5: Anna Freud and the Post-Freudians* is a new chapter that now covers Anna Freud's life and contributions and details her important work on defense mechanisms—the latter previously found in the chapter on Sigmund Freud. The discussion of Heinz Kohut has been intensively reworked and also appears in this new chapter, along with new coverage of the theorists Melanie Klein and Donald Winnicott by William Brater. Finally, what was, in the previous edition, an entire chapter on Fritz and Laura Perls and Gestalt therapy has been capsulated and placed in this chapter, which highlights only their most significant work.

Changes in the Fourth Edition

Complete Overhaul of the Horney Chapter by Bernard J. Paris *Chapter 6: Karen Horney and Humanistic Psychoanalysis* is a complete reworking of the coverage of Horney by her foremost biographer, Bernard J. Paris. Paris, the director of the International Karen Horney Society, is a gifted writer. He breaks down Horney's theory into three separate stages: feminine psychology, beyond the Freudian model, and new ways to understand the genesis and manifestation of neurosis. Paris also articulates the ways in which Horney's ideas have been utilized beyond the confines of psychology.

Revision of "The Psychology of Women" Chapter by Experts in the Field *Chapter 9: The Psychology of Women: A Relational Approach* was added to the third edition and has been revised by the same four clinician/scholars from the Stone Center in Wellesley, Massachusetts, who originally wrote this unique chapter. In their revision, a more comprehensive explanation is given on connection and joining as primary human needs. Class, color, and sexual orientation are now more fully considered in their effects on the development of women's personality structures. We regret, and are even dismayed, that ours is still the only textbook in this field to provide a complete chapter covering the psychology of women.

Revision of Other Chapters Each of the other chapters has been carefully worked over to improve the writing, strengthen the continuity, and make it easier for students to understand the ideas. A number of new biographies have given us better information and have led to changes in the Personal History sections of nearly every chapter. Topics and headings in several chapters have been reorganized, and many new examples are offered throughout. Several lengthy quotes within the text narrative have been pared down.

Changes by Chapter

- **Chapter 2: Sigmund Freud and Psychoanalysis.** Freud's personal history and his work on the ego have been expanded, and a cross-cultural critique on dreams is now included. The sections on the defense mechanisms and on Heinz Kohut have been revised and moved to Chapter 5.
- **Chapter 3: Carl Gustav Jung and Analytic Psychology.** More detail is now provided on Jung's theories of type, archetype, and individuation. We also updated coverage on Jung and Gnosticism, the shadow, spirituality, and aspects of the hero as archetype of mature masculinity. A new dream-analysis excerpt in the Theory Firsthand replaces the previous excerpt.
- **Chapter 4: Alfred Adler and Individual Psychology.** We have updated the information on Adlerian psychology in education, child therapy, and counseling. Additional exercises are included. The previous Theory Firsthand reading has been replaced with an excerpt from Adler's *Social Interest.*
- **Chapter 7: Erik Erikson and the Life Cycle.** New sources on Erikson's origins have been included, and his biography expanded to include the end of his life. More detail is now provided on Erikson's theory of old age. The lengthier excerpt in the Theory Firsthand has been cut, but the "Son of a Bombardier" selection is retained.
- **Chapter 8: Wilhelm Reich and Somatic Psychology.** This chapter has been significantly revised, and the somatic psychology material has been streamlined and more clearly integrated into Reichian theories. A fuller explanation of the various processes of armoring, including a new diagram, is also included.
- **Chapter 10: William James and the Psychology of Consciousness.** We have expanded the sections on James's intellectual antecedents, the spiritual self, and the characteristics of thought. Considerable reformatting of sections and headings has improved the flow of this chapter, and a new section has been added, "The Fringe," offering an alternative to Freud's theory of the unconscious.
- **Chapter 11: B. F. Skinner and Radical Behaviorism.** The Personal History section has been improved, and small clarifications and updates have been made throughout the chapter
- **Chapter 12: The Personal Construct Theory of George Kelly and Cognitive Psychology.** The chapter has been restructured, and Kelly's contributions to cognitive psychology are more fully described and integrated. Kaisa Puhakka, who revised the chapter, has added new sections on the philosophical assumptions underlying the computer model of human information processing. New excerpts from cognitive psychology theory have been added to the Theory Firsthand.
- **Chapter 13: Carl Rogers and the Person-Centered Perspective.** New biographies have enabled us to provide an expanded Personal History, especially in regard to the last ten years of his international work. Headings have been changed to make it easier to follow the development of Rogers's own shifting emphasis. The Theory Firsthand section has been streamlined to focus on one particularly interesting story.
- **Chapter 14: Abraham Maslow and Transpersonal Psychology.** Additional biographical information has been added on Maslow, and the diagram showing

Maslow's hierarchy of needs has been redesigned for clarity. Material on deficiency and being psychology is now included, and the latest research and theory based on Maslow's work is addressed. We also made extensive additions and edits of the transpersonal psychology section to incorporate results described in recent major publications. A new Personal Reflection, Transpersonal Experience, has been added.

- **Chapter 15: Yoga and the Hindu Tradition.** A new Personal Reflection, The Corpse Pose, has been added, as well as new material on the potential dangers of the role of the guru. The readings included in the Theory Firsthand in the previous edition have been replaced by an excerpt from *Radha: Diary of a Woman's Search.*
- **Chapter 16: Zen and the Buddhist Tradition.** Material has been added on Zen meditation and on the Buddhist concept of enlightenment as the highest human state. The Personal Reflection exercises have been revised, and a review of recent writings on Zen and Buddhism, as well as research and therapeutic techniques based on Zen principles and practice, is now included.
- **Chapter 17: Sufism and the Islamic Tradition.** We have significantly reworked this chapter. The history of Sufism is now clarified, far more detail on explicit Sufi psychology is provided, and the principles behind the role of spiritual guide, and its potential dangers to both practitioners and students of Sufism, are explored. The Theory Firsthand reading has been changed to an excerpt from *Forty Days: The Diary of a Traditional Solitary Sufi Retreat.*

Updates of Other Features

- **Personal Reflection Boxes.** These boxed exercises, included throughout the chapters of the text, have been retained and their design improved. The Personal Reflections are intended to challenge students to test the ideas of a theorist in their own lives and to address our interest in the personal growth dimension of the personality course. Four new Personal Reflections have been added to the fourth edition, including Transpersonal Experience in Chapter 14, and a number of those retained have been slightly reworded or reorganized for clarity.
- **The Theory Firsthand.** Excerpts from writings by the theorists themselves—case studies or revealing examples of their ideas—follow the text of every chapter and provide students with rich insight into both the theorist and the theory. We have changed some of these first-person readings to give clearer and more vivid examples of each theorist's point of view. New Theory Firsthand excerpts can be found in the chapters on Jung, Adler, Anna Freud and the Post-Freudians, Horney, Kelly, Yoga, and Sufism. We have dropped some excerpts this time, but are happy to retain the very popular and somewhat unusual Theory Firsthand in the Reich chapter, an excerpt from Orson Bean's *Me and the Orgone,* about the actor's experience in Reichian therapy.
- **Margin Quotes.** Throughout the text a number of quotations from theorists, their supporters, and, occasionally, their critics appear in the margins. This feature is retained in the fourth edition, with many new quotes incorporated.
- **Annotated Bibliography and References.** At the end of every chapter we have included an Annotated Bibliography of the most important books, to help students further understand a particular theory, and a References section. We have updated both of these features for this new edition.

Instructor's Guide

The *Instructor's Guide,* a book in itself, includes a greater variety of test questions than necessary. It has material we came across after this edition was completed that we thought valuable and pertinent. This guide has provocative quotes, research, commentaries, news clippings, ideas for parts of lectures, and additional points of view. We have included notes for an additional chapter on Shamanism by Professor Bryan Teixeira of Camosun College, Victoria, British Columbia. His students found it to be a valuable addition to other cross-cultural sections of the text. Teixeira summarizes theory and practices of the world's oldest attempt to describe human personality. Notes for another chapter on Ludwig Binswanger are provided by Professor George Bourne of Shippensburg University, Shippensburg, PA. Bourne offers a clear and engaging introduction to existential phenomenological psychology, in theory and practice. Any instructor may freely copy and distribute these materials as supplements. An outline of each chapter is included, along with media suggestions, additional Personal Reflections for individual or class use, and an extensive selection of true-false, multiple-choice, matching, and short essay questions. Be sure that you request a copy from Addison Wesley Longman. The test items are available on a diskette, with the software improved from the last edition.

Acknowledgments

For this edition we were joined by the gifted developmental editor James Strandberg, who rethought the entire text with fresh eyes and fresh ideas. The result was a good deal more work for us and a better text for you.

We have been fortunate to have had the help of Ann Kearns, project editor, Karen Koblik, photo researcher, Lisa Pinto, developmental manager, Marianne Terrero, marketing coordinator, Cyndy Taylor, supplements editor, Mary Archondes, the text and layout designer, Susan Joseph, our incredible copy editor, and Eric Stano, our benevolent editor.

Special thanks to William Brater, Ph.D., who wrote most of the new material in Chapter 5, and Susan Newton, Ph.D., who wrote the Chapter Highlights and Key Concepts sections and also updated and wrote the new material for the Instructor's Guide.

The manuscript was reviewed by

Michael Piechowski—Northland College
David W. Peterson—Mount Senario College
Dorothy Bianco—Rhode Island College
Donna Canavan—Boston College
George Boeree—Shippensburg University
Joan Cannon—University of Massachusetts
Jerome Small—Youngstown State University

whose suggestions and corrections strengthened major portions of the text and saved us from a number of scholarly gaffs. Any mistakes of fact or emphasis that remain are ours.

ROBERT FRAGER
JAMES FADIMAN

About the Authors

Robert Frager received his Ph.D. in social psychology from Harvard University, where he was a teaching assistant to Erik Erikson. He has taught psychology at UC Berkeley and UC Santa Cruz and is the founder and first president of the Institute for Transpersonal Psychology. He is also past president of the Association for Transpersonal Psychology. Author of several books and numerous articles in psychology and related fields, he is currently the chair of the doctoral program at the Institute of Transpersonal Psychology in Palo Alto, California.

I have been fortunate to have met and worked with many distinguished theorists and therapists whose work is featured in this text and have personally experienced Jungian analysis, gestalt therapy, Reichian and neo-Reichian therapy, and Rogerian group work. I have also lived in Zen temples, Yoga ashrams, and Sufi centers and studied and practiced these traditions.

In addition to teaching psychology, I teach the Japanese martial art of Aikido, which I have been practicing for over thirty years. I was a personal student of the founder of Aikido. He was the first of a series of wonderful teachers who have taught me what Maslow called "the farther reaches of human nature." I also teach Sufism and have recently completed a collection of Sufi stories, teachings, and poetry entitled *Essential Sufism.*

I am married to a wonderful, creative graphic artist and have four children, who are now 27, 24, 13, and 10.

James Fadiman received his Ph.D. in psychology from Stanford University and has taught at San Francisco State University, Brandeis University, and Stanford. He has his own consulting firm and offers seminars to executives and educators in the United States and abroad. He has written or edited books on holistic health, goal-setting, and abnormal psychology, is an editor for two journals, and sits on the board of several corporations concerned with the preservation of natural resources.

I have been fortunate in being able to use the psychological and clinical skills I learned in graduate school in a variety of areas beyond psychology. Although I was a college counselor for several years and continue to teach psychology, I have spent more time working as a consultant with scientists and business people. My early research into altered states of consciousness opened me up to discovering the profound wisdom in indigenous and non-Western cultures. My delight was in finding that that ancient wisdom has turned out to be immensely practical.

What I loved about writing this book is that it gave me a chance to put together different points of view that I've found personally useful, even when the creators of these ideas were at swords points with one another.

I'm currently developing a set of classes in creative-problem solving and invention for a major Silicon Valley electronics firm, starting a second novel, continuing to write a series of short stories, and continuing to be involved with several environmental start-up companies.

I've been married for thirty years to a documentary film-maker. We have two children.

CHAPTER 1

Introduction

This text is intended to provide students with a *worldwide, cross-cultural* body of knowledge that is of practical use in exploring human nature. Most students hope to find in psychology classes a set of structures, concepts, theories, and perspectives that will facilitate their own growth and their capacity to adjust to a rapidly changing, diverse society. In every chapter of this, our fourth, edition we present students with the tools to attain a greater understanding of their own and others' personalities.

A Constructive Approach to Personality Theory

We approach each theory in the text as positively and as sympathetically as possible. Each chapter has been read and evaluated by theorists and practitioners from each system to help us ensure that our treatment is relatively comprehensive and accurate. We have avoided, as much as possible, the tendency to criticize or belittle the accomplishments of any theory. Instead, we have tried to highlight the strengths and the effectiveness of each approach. We have sought to be neither partisan nor unthinkingly eclectic. However, we have been purposefully biased in our choice of theorists. We have included those theorists whose importance and utility are evident to us, and left out other well-known theorists who seemed less useful and less compatible with the overall aim of this book.

Each theorist in this book offers something of unique value and relevance, isolating and clarifying various aspects of human nature. We feel that each one is essentially "correct" in his or her own area of expertise. Nevertheless, we have presented certain crucial disagreements among personality theorists. These disputes often seem to resemble the famous tale of the blind men encountering an elephant. When each man touches a part of the elephant, he assumes that this one element is the key to the whole animal's appearance.

In the original version of this fable, the blind men were philosophers who were sent into a pitch-dark barn by a wise king (who was probably tired of their academic bickering). Each philosopher insisted that his or her limited experience and the theory based on that experience was the sum total of the truth. This tendency can still be found among personality theorists today. We wanted to take a different approach.

In our treatment of each theory, we assume that the theory has something of relevance to every one of us. For example, hourly wage earners may find that B. F. Skinner's concept of schedules of reinforcement is likely to shed light on their workplace behavior. However, it is doubtful that reading Skinner will help people understand why they attend religious services. Here, Carl Jung's writings on the power of symbols and the significance of the self are more likely to be useful. Thus, at different times or in different areas of our lives, each theory can provide us with guidance, enlightenment, or clarity.

You will probably also feel far more affinity for one or two theorists than for the others covered in this book. Each theorist is writing about certain basic patterns of human experience, most probably patterns that come from his or her own life. We find of greatest relevance those theories that focus on patterns that most match our own.

Each chapter discusses a theory or perspective that adds to our general knowledge of human behavior. We are convinced that, in addition to our innate biological pattern of growth and development, individuals possess a tendency for psychological growth and development. This tendency has been described by various psychologists as a striving for self-actualization: the desire to understand oneself, and the need to utilize one's capacities to the fullest.

Theories of Personality

Before Freud and the other major Western personality theorists, there was no real theory of personality. Mental disorders were considered to be the inexplicable results of "alien possession" of otherwise rational, logical individuals. In fact, the early physicians who specialized in treating mental patients were called "alienists."

One of Freud's greatest contributions was to insist that rules and a cause-and-effect structure govern mental events. He looked at the irrational and unconscious thoughts and behaviors of his patients and noted that they occurred according to certain patterns. In so doing, Freud founded a "science of the irrational." Furthermore, he recognized that behavior patterns found in neurotic and psychotic patients were basically intense versions of mental patterns observed in normal people.

Jung, Adler, and many others built on Freud's insights. In Jung's theory, the individual's unconscious includes not only personal memories (as Freud had stressed) but also material from the collective unconscious of all humanity. Alfred Adler and others focused their attention on the ego as a sophisticated mechanism of adaptation to the inner and outer environment.

Karen Horney explored ego psychology and also pioneered in the development of the psychology of women. In one sense, she expanded psychoanalytic theory to include women. Her work has been carried on by several generations of women theorists. Among the most highly regarded are the Stone Center group, who present their most recent theoretical work in Chapter 9, "The Psychology of Women."

William James, a contemporary of Freud and Jung, was more interested in consciousness itself than in the contents of consciousness. In his exploration of the way the mind operates, James was a precursor of the cognitive psychologists. He was also the founder of consciousness studies, a field in which researchers investigate such topics as altered states of consciousness, including dreams, meditation, and drug experiences.

Later American theorists, such as Carl Rogers and Abraham Maslow, concerned themselves with issues of psychological health and growth. As Maslow cogently wrote, "[I]t is as if Freud supplied to us the sick half of psychology and we must now fill it out with the healthy half" (Maslow, 1968, p. 5).

Expanding the Scope of Personality Theory

In recent years, four approaches to human nature and functioning have become increasingly important: cognitive psychology, the human potential movement, the psychology of women, and non-Western ideas. Our coverage of these forces is intended to expand the limits and range of traditional perspectives on personality theory.

Cognitive Psychology

Cognitive psychology has extended into many areas of psychology, including personality theory. Cognitive psychology provides a way of analyzing the functioning of the mind itself, and a way of appreciating the richness and complexity of human behavior. If we can better understand how we think, observe, attend, and remember, we will be able to understand more clearly how these cognitive building blocks lead to fears, illusions, creative works, and all the behaviors and mental events that make us who we are.

The pioneering cognitive psychologist George Kelly emphasized the importance of making intellectual sense out of our experience. For Kelly, all people are scientists, formulating theories and hypotheses about themselves and others and, like professional scientists, sometimes holding on to a favorite theory in spite of mounting evidence that it is invalid.

The Human Potential Movement

The human potential movement was founded in part at the Esalen Institute in California and at the National Training Laboratories in Maine in the 1950s and 1960s, and was based in great part on the theories of Rogers and Maslow. It is now a widely accepted cultural force. Growth, or training, centers exist in most major cities, generally offering intensive, often deeply moving weekend or weeklong workshops in various kinds of encounter groups, body-oriented work, meditation, and spiritual disciplines. These workshops also provide training in communication, time management, quality control, and stress reduction. At many colleges and universities, experientially oriented courses that stress personal involvement and emotional awareness are regular offerings, while corporations frequently send their executives to classes and seminars that are rooted in the human potential movement. Group leaders and participants, as well as government and corporate sponsors, generally believe that attendance at these sessions can result in beneficial, long-lasting changes.

Unfortunately, over a number of years, along with the emphasis on direct learning and immediate results, there developed an antitheoretical and anticonceptual bias, which sometimes was seen as a deliberate disregard for academic psychology. Conversely, academic psychologists tended to remain ignorant of the movement's very real and important achievements. We realized, however, that many of the theories and practices found in the human potential movement have a solid and cogent intellectual framework. In addition to Rogers and Maslow, the work of Wilhelm Reich, and Fritz and Laura Perls, has provided important theoretical foundations for this vital movement.

The Psychology of Women

A third major approach to human nature and functioning, still somewhat outside the academic beltway, acknowledges the differences between men and women. It sounds absurd, but most personality theories and most other textbooks still seem to sidestep this issue. When we wrote the first edition, in the early 1970s, we included a chapter called, "The Psychology of Women." At that time, there was a great deal of interest in the subject, but not much substantial research was available. For our second edition, we abandoned the chapter and integrated the question of sexual differences into the rest of the text. In our third and fourth editions, while still integrating the subject within many of the chapters, we have been privileged to work with a group of eminent scholars and therapists who generously took time away from their own cutting-edge research to write an original exposition of the unique contribution of women's studies to the field of personality. We have also completely revised our chapter on one of the most brilliant and underrated personality theorists, Karen Horney. Long before the modern women's movement unfolded, Horney provided the first cogent and comprehensive theory of women's psychology.

Eastern Theories of Personality

The final three chapters of this book are devoted to the models of personality developed in three Eastern psychospiritual disciplines: Yoga, Zen Buddhism, and Sufism. Chapters 15, 16, and 17 represent a broadening of the traditional limits of personality theory. This trend can be seen throughout psychology—recently it has become more of an international field of study, less dependent on U.S. and Western European intellectual and philosophical assumptions.

In these three chapters we add a richer, more diverse perspective to Western personality theory, which has been the province of white European-American men and, to a much lesser extent, women. These Eastern theories have been developed in societies and value systems that are often strikingly different from Europe and the United States. The beliefs and ideals emanating from these cultures enrich our ideas of what it is to be a human being.

The underlying religious traditions for these systems—Hinduism, Buddhism, and Islam—represent the perspectives of nearly three billion people today in over one hundred different countries. These three traditions are embraced by the majority of the world's population. They are living realities for their adherents, not academic, scholarly, or impractical abstractions.

Contemporary Concern with Eastern Systems Since the 1960s, interest in Eastern thought has increased throughout the United States. There has been a proliferation of courses, books, and organizations based on various Eastern disciplines. Many Westerners in search of new values and personal and spiritual growth are devoting themselves to the intensive study or practice of an Eastern system.

The Eastern theories include powerful concepts and effective techniques of personal and spiritual development. Both the research into and the practical application of these disciplines have increased in the West.

> There is growing recognition that Western psychologists may have underestimated the psychologies and therapies of other cultures. Certain Asian disciplines contain sophisticated therapies, and experimental studies have demonstrated their ability to induce psychological, physiological, and psychotherapeutic effects. An increasing number of Westerners, including mental health professionals, now use Asian therapies. Benefits include new perspectives on psychological functioning, potential, and pathology, as well as new approaches and techniques. In addition, the study of other cultures and practices often has the healthy effect of revealing unsuspected ethnocentric assumptions and limiting beliefs, thus leading to a broader view of human nature and therapy. . . .
>
> Asian psychologies focus primarily on existential and transpersonal levels and little on the pathological. They contain detailed maps of states of consciousness, developmental levels, and stages of enlightenment that extend beyond traditional Western psychological maps. Moreover, they claim to possess techniques for inducing these states and conditions. (Walsh, 1989, pp. 547–548)

These chapters are included to provide you with the opportunity to consider, evaluate, and, to some extent, experience these perspectives on personality in the context of a critical and comparative course within psychology. We have ample evidence of the interest and time that students are already devoting to these questions. Yet the degree of fundamental knowledge of the Eastern traditions is often very low in comparison to the amount of interest many people have in these pursuits, or even the amount of time they spend on them.

The Study of Eastern Psychologies Why study religions in a psychology textbook? The term *religion* has strong connotations of rigid dogma, conventional morality, and so on. These notions do not seem particularly compatible with psychology.

It is important to remember that we are dealing with Eastern *psychologies* rather than Eastern *religions.* Yoga, Zen, and Sufism originated in a common need to explain the relationship between religious practice and everyday life. Spiritual guides were among the earliest psychologists, in the West and in the East. They have had to understand the emotional and personal dynamics of their students, as well as the students' spiritual needs. In order to comprehend the issues their students faced, they turned first to their own experiences, a principle we find honored today in the training analysis that many psychotherapists undergo.

These systems do differ from most Western personality theories in their greater concern with values and moral considerations and in their stress on the advisability of living in accordance with certain spiritual standards. We should live within a moral code, they argue, because a morally codified life has definite, recognizable, and beneficial effects on our consciousness and overall well-being. However, all three psychologies view morals and values in a practical, even iconoclastic way. Each of these traditions stresses the futility and foolishness of valuing external form over inner function.

These psychologies, like their Western counterparts, are derived from careful observations of human experience. They are built on centuries of empirical observations of the psychological, physiological, and spiritual effects of a variety of ideas, attitudes, behaviors, and exercises.

Each system's ethos is based on the personal experiences and insights of its founders. The vitality and importance of these traditional psychologies rest on the continual testing, reworking, and modifying of their initial insights to fit new settings and interpersonal situations as well as different cultural conditions. In other words, these centuries-old psychologies are still relevant, still changing and developing.

Carl Jung wrote, "The knowledge of Eastern psychology . . . forms the indispensable basis for a critique and an objective consideration of Western psychology" (in Shamdasani, 1996, p. xlxi). Thus the development of a complete psychology rests on our study and understanding of Eastern thought.

Transpersonal Experience Each of these systems is focused on transpersonal growth, or growth beyond the ego and personality. They share with transpersonal psychology (see Chapter 14) the belief that it is possible, through meditation and other consciousness disciplines, to enter profound states of awareness beyond (*trans*) our everyday, personal experience. In contrast, Western psychologists generally discuss growth in terms of strengthening the ego: increased autonomy, self-determination, self-actualization, freedom from neurotic processes, and healthy-mindedness. Nevertheless, the concepts of transpersonal growth and ego strength may be more complementary than conflicting.

The pioneering personality theorist Andras Angyal discusses each of these viewpoints.

> Viewed from one of these vantage points [the full development of the personality] the human being seems to be striving basically to assert and to expand his self-determination. He is an autonomous being, a self-growing entity that asserts itself actively instead of reacting passively like a physical body to the impacts of the surrounding world. This fundamental tendency expresses itself in a striving of the person to consolidate and increase his self-government, in other words, to exercise his freedom and to organize the relevant items of his world out of the autonomous center of government that is his self. This tendency—which I have termed "the trend toward increased autonomy"—expresses itself in spontaneity, self-assertiveness, striving for freedom and for mastery. (Angyal, 1956, pp. 44–45)
>
> Seen from another vantage point, human life reveals a very different basic pattern from the one described above. From this point of view the person appears to seek a place for himself in a larger unit of which he strives to become a part. In the first tendency we see him struggling for centrality in his world, trying to mold, to organize, the objects and events of his world, to bring them under his own jurisdiction and government [as in ego growth]. In the second tendency he seems rather to surrender himself willingly to seek a home for himself in and to become an organic part of something

> that he conceives as greater than himself [as in transpersonal growth]. The super-individual unit of which one feels oneself a part, or wishes to become a part, may be variously formulated according to one's cultural background and personal understanding. (Angyal, 1956, pp. 45–46)

This second tendency would seem to be more applicable to those who have already achieved a certain degree of self-possession, maturity, and self-actualization. The development of a strong autonomous personality and sense of self seems to be a prerequisite for this second type of growth.

Chapters 15, 16, and 17 present comprehensive and practical theories of personality described in psychologically relevant terms. Each system is deeply concerned with questions of ultimate values, with transpersonal experience, and with the relationship of the individual self to a greater whole. Each theory has received considerable attention in the West, and many aspects of these systems are already being applied in different facets of psychology.

The evaluation of the Eastern systems is no different from the personal judgments we are asking you to make of the Western theories in this book: Do they help you understand yourself and others? Do they fit with your own experience?

The Structure of Each Chapter

Each chapter generally is divided into the following sections (Personal Reflection exercises, like the one on p. 14, are peppered throughout each chapter):

- Personal History
- Intellectual Antecedents
- Major Concepts
- Dynamics
  - Psychological Growth
  - Obstacles to Growth
- Structure
  - Body
  - Social Relationships
  - Will
  - Emotions
  - Intellect
  - Self
  - Therapist/Teacher
- Evaluation
- The Theory Firsthand
- Chapter Highlights
- Key Concepts
- Annotated Bibliography
- References

One of the great difficulties in comparing and contrasting different theories of personality is that not only has each major theory made its own discrete and unique contribution to the sum of human knowledge but each has its own approach, definitions, and dynamics. Often the same word, such as *self,* has widely varying meanings from theory to theory. (Some theorists have even used the same term differently within their own writings.) To make it easier, we have attempted to describe each theory in terms of its usefulness for human understanding. We approach each theory not as a researcher, not as a therapist, not as a patient but primarily as people trying to understand ourselves and other people. Fortunately, many of the theories do overlap and can be easily compared. Except where it was contrary to sense (for example Chapter 5, "Anna Freud and the Post-Freudians," and Chapter 9, "The Psychology of Women"), we have used this system of organization.

Personal History

Each chapter presents the personal history and the intellectual antecedents of the theorist. We outline the major influences on the theorist's thinking, influences rooted in childhood and in later life experiences.

We have learned that it is easier to understand a theory if we know more about the man or woman who created it. Thus the biographies we have for each chapter are extensive enough to allow you to develop a sense of the person before you begin to study his or her theory. You will find that Skinner's theory (or Freud's, or Rogers's, and so forth) makes much more sense if you can see how it arose from the theorist's life experience.

In this edition we have probably made more changes to the personal history sections than to any others because new biographies have corrected earlier errors and clarified the importance of hitherto unknown or poorly understood periods in the theorists' lives. For example, our discussion of Anna Freud, a major innovator in her own right, has been almost totally revised since our last edition.

Intellectual Antecedents

Every theory owes part of its genesis and its elaboration to the ideas of others. Every theory was developed within a particular society, at a particular time in history, a time in which certain other theories and concepts affected the thinking of virtually all writers and investigators. An idea is actually part of an ecosystem of related theories and concepts. It is often easier to appreciate the scope of a theory if we are aware of the major intellectual currents of the time. For example, most of the theories developed in the late nineteenth century were strongly influenced by Darwin's principles of evolution, natural selection, and survival of the fittest.

Major Concepts

The bulk of each chapter explores the theory, beginning with a summary of the major concepts. They are the foundation upon which each theory rests and are the elements most people would use to distinguish between theories. The concepts are also what each theorist would agree are his or her most important contributions to human understanding.

This section is called "Major Concepts," not "Major Facts." It would be encouraging to say that the major concepts covered in this book rest, after many years of research, on a factual base. Unfortunately, it is not so. There still is little objective evidence for the existence of the id, archetypes, sublimation, inferiority complex, or projection (major concepts from each of the next five chapters). However, there has been empirical confirmation of a number of important ideas, such as Erikson's concepts of identity and human development and Maslow's concept of self-actualization.

More than empirical data, the field of personality theory contains a vast amount of brilliant thinking, clear observation, innovative methods of therapy, and insightful expositions of concepts that help us grasp the complex reality of who we are.

As you will see, we rarely cite research. Virtually every theorist has been highly critical of the validity and usefulness of any of the research done on his or her theory (Corsini & Wedding, 1989). Instead, we use the limited pages we have for each theory to make it as clear, as vivid, and as understandable as possible.

Dynamics

We are living systems, not static ones. The ways in which we strive to achieve greater health and awareness we've called *psychological growth.* The ways in which growth is delayed, thwarted, turned aside, prevented, or perverted are described as *obstacles to growth.*

Every theory included has developed a set of interventions, variously called *therapy, counseling,* or *spiritual practices,* to help the person overcome the obstacles and return a person to normal personal growth. Although they are fascinating outgrowths of theory, we do not discuss these interventions in detail because this is a text on personality theory, not psychotherapy.

Structure

We have tried to be consistent in order to help you compare and contrast different theories, but not to be so rigid as to be unfair to the theories. While every theory in the book might say of itself that it includes every major aspect of human functioning, we have found that each one focuses most clearly on some areas and almost totally neglects others. Often we say no more under a given heading than, essentially, "This theory does not discuss this."

Body While this is a book of psychological theories, all of them are based on the study of embodied humans beings who breathe, eat, tense, and relax. Some theories pay close attention to how much the physical body influences psychological processes, others much less so.

Wilhelm Reich is probably the Western theorist most concerned with the body. Although, in his later work, Freud placed less emphasis on libido, Reich took Freud's concept of libido as his central principle. For Reich, the freeing of blocked bioenergy is the chief task of psychotherapy. Reich argued that mind and body are one; all psychological processes, he postulated, are a part of physical processes, and vice versa.

Social Relationships When we say that humans are social animals, we are suggesting that we derive meaning and satisfy our basic needs by being with each other—in families, in play groups, in friendships, in work groups, in couples, and in communities. Some theories consider these groups to be of primary importance, while others focus on the inner world of the individual and tend to ignore social relations. For example, Karen Horney, who was deeply interested in the cultural determinants of personality, defined neurosis in terms of social relationships. She analyzed three classic neurotic patterns: moving toward people, moving against people, and moving away from people.

Will Saint Paul said, "That which I would do, that I do not. That which I would not do, that I do." He was puzzling over the discrepancy between his intentions and his capacity to carry out those intentions.

Each of us has a similar interest in what inside us comes between our intentions ("I will finish all my reading on time for all my classes this week") and the results ("I saw two movies, went to a great party, did some of the reading, and skimmed some other stuff"). A number of the theories grapple with this fundamental human struggle—how to turn intention into action.

William James made the will a central concept in his psychology. For James, the will is a combination of attention and effort. It is an important tool for focusing consciousness, and, according to James, the will can be systematically strengthened and trained. In contrast, Skinner considered the will a confusing and unrealistic concept, because he assumed that all actions are determined, even if we may not know enough to understand how or why. There is no place for the will in Skinner's theory.

Emotions Descartes wrote, "I think, therefore I am." One might add, "I feel, therefore I am human." Psychological theory is rich in the many ways it considers the effects of emotions on all other mental and physical activities. In fact, thought that is divorced from emotion is both limited and ineffectual.

For Maslow and the Eastern psychologies, there are two basic kinds of emotions—positive and negative. Maslow included calmness, joy, and happiness as positive emotions. He wrote that they facilitated self-actualization. Similarly, the Yoga tradition distinguishes between emotions that lead to greater freedom and knowledge, and eventually enlightenment, and emotions that increase ignorance.

Intellect Personality theories often focus on the irrational aspects of the personality. It is of value to see how the theorists construe "rational" functioning in widely differing ways, and to discover that the theorists vary widely in the importance they place on rationality.

For cognitive theorist George Kelly, the intellect is a major element in constructing our conceptions of reality, the central concept in his theory. In Sufism, there are several levels of intellect, including curiosity, logic, and empirical understanding. There is also the developed intellect, which includes the heart as well as the head.

Self The self is an elusive concept, grappled with by many of the theorists but never completely captured. It is more than the ego, more than the sum total of the factors that make up the individual; it is less limited than the personality but contains it. The self is the concept that veers most defiantly away from the world of pure science, refusing to submit to objective measurement. Sounds confusing? It can be.

There is also a "felt sense" of self. You have a clear sense of who you are, no matter how ill you feel, how upset you might get, whatever your age. One of us asked his father, when the older man was 88, if he ever felt old. He said although he was acutely aware of how old his body was, the felt sense of himself seemed unchanged from childhood. His attitudes, opinions, behaviors, moods, and interests had all changed over the course of his life, but this elusive something was unchanged. Some theories avoid this slippery aspect of ourselves, while others wade in and make it a central concept.

One of the greatest differences between Yoga and Buddhism is how they define the self. In Yoga, the self is the eternal, unchanging essence of each individual. According to Buddhism, there is no unchanging, central self within the individual. The person is merely an impermanent collection of finite traits. The greater self, or Buddha-nature, is not individual but is as large as the entire universe.

Therapist/Teacher Each theory contains ideas to help people grow and gain more pleasure and integrity in their lives. And, in accordance with its major concepts, each theory establishes the type of training an individual would need in order to become a professional therapist or a skilled helper or guide. There is a wide range of what is considered acceptable preparation for such work. The psychoanalyst is generally a medical doctor who then undergoes an arduous training in psychoanalytic psychotherapy for several years, while the Zen monk learns through years of meditation and spiritual instruction. Each system makes specific demands on its practitioners and encourages the evolution of different skills.

Evaluation

There is a great temptation, in reviewing a theory, to take a strong position on the value of this or that concept. We have, instead, tried to stand aside and give you, our readers, the task of evaluating each theorist, not only according to traditional academic and psychological standards but also in terms of the usefulness of the theory for you personally, now or in the future. Our opinion is that every theory here can be of great value to all people at different points in their lives.

The Theory Firsthand

We include an extended passage, whenever possible, from the theorist's own writings, or a description of the system in operation. We feel it is important for you to be exposed to the style and the personality of each theorist. We want you to read for yourself something that each one has written, to get a sense of the "voice" of the theorist and to experience firsthand what made his or her work important and sought after. The style with which the theorists present their ideas is often as unique and meaningful as the ideas themselves. In addition to these excerpts, each chapter includes a number of margin quotes that provide useful, pithy insights into the theorists, their adherents, and, occasionally, their critics.

Chapter Highlights

As a new device to help students grasp the essential elements in every chapter, we have included a summary of the major points and central theoretical issues discussed in each theory.

Key Concepts

Another new pedagogical feature in this edition is the section "Key Concepts," which comes near the end of each chapter. In this glossarylike listing, we have provided definitions for the major terms used by each theorist.

Annotated Bibliography

Each chapter includes an annotated bibliography. The chapter is really only an introduction to an involved and complex system of thought. We *hope* you will pursue those theories that you find most interesting and valuable. We have facilitated this next step by suggesting those books that we have found most helpful in understanding each theory.

One of the kindest things a teacher can do for students is to steer them away from second-class readings and direct them to the most useful and/or best written books in a given area. (We have spent a tremendous amount of time going through the less useful books on each theory, and we don't feel that you have to do the same.) Each chapter includes a guide to where to start if you want to explore a subject in more depth.

References

We have put the references at the end of each chapter rather than interleaf them together in the back of the book. Students have told us that our text is a useful reference book for other classes, and for their personal self-study of particular theorists. It is because of their advice that we keep the references in this separated format.

Personal Reflections

In addition to this overall structure, each chapter contains, sprinkled throughout it, a series of Personal Reflections to give you a better feel for some aspects of the theory. Experiential learning and intellectual learning are complementary

Personal Reflection

Life History Questionnaire

Here is the first in a series of exercises in this text that are intended to bring you closer to the concepts presented. We are to some extent developed and conditioned by past experience; therefore, we approach any body of material already primed to accept or reject parts of it. Before reading this book, you might find it useful to review some of the major forces in your own development. Record your answers to the questions that follow. Answer the questions as freely and as fully as you can, as this exercise is designed for your own use.

1. What does your name mean? Are you named for a particular relative? Does your name have special significance for you or for your family?
2. What nickname(s) do you prefer? Why?
3. What is your ethnic and/or religious identification? If it is different from that of your family, comment on the difference.
4. Describe your siblings and your feelings about them.
5. Describe your parents (stepparents) and your feelings about them.
6. Who in your family do you most resemble? How?
7. What are the conditions of your life now—job, living situation, and so forth?
8. Do you have any recurring dreams/daydreams? What are they?
9. What men or women of the past or present do you appreciate and admire most? Why? Whom might you consider an ideal role model?
10. What books, poems, music, or other works of art have influenced you most? When and how?
11. What events or inner experiences give or have given you the greatest joy?
12. What events or inner experiences give or have given you the greatest sorrow?
13. What occupation would interest you the most if you could become whatever you wanted? Why?
14. What occupation would be the worst possible one for you, something you would just hate to do? Why?
15. Is there anything about yourself that you would like to change?
16. What is there about yourself that you especially like?

rather than contradictory processes. A personal encounter with a concept adds a dimension of immediacy to the theory that cannot be obtained by any other means. The exercises have all been tested, improved, and retested until our students pronounced them helpful.

We strongly advise you to try as many of the Personal Reflection exercises as possible. Our own students have found that doing so adds real depth to their understanding of the material, helps them remember the concepts, and adds to their knowledge of themselves and others.

References

Angyal, A. (1956). A theoretical model for personality studies. In C. Moustakas (Ed.), *The self.* New York: Harper & Row.

Corsini, R., & Wedding, D. (Eds.). (1989). *Current psychotherapies* (4th ed.). Itasca, IL: F. E. Peacock.

Maslow, A. (1968). *Toward a psychology of being* (2nd ed.). New York: Van Nostrand.

Shamdasani, S. (Ed.). (1996). *The psychology of kundalini yoga: Notes of the seminar given in 1932 by C. G. Jung.* Princeton, NJ: Princeton University Press.

Walsh, R. (1989). Asian psychotherapies. In R. Corsini & D. Wedding (Eds.), *Current psychotherapies* (4th ed.). Itasca, IL: F. E. Peacock.

CHAPTER 2

Sigmund Freud and Psychoanalysis

Sigmund Freud's work, originating in the disciplines of biology, neurology, and psychiatry, proposed a new understanding of personality that profoundly affected Western culture. His view of the human condition, striking violently against the prevailing opinions of his era, offered a complex and compelling way to understand normal and abnormal mental functioning. His ideas were like an explosion scattering the views of human nature held by the late Victorians in every direction. The dark sides of the human psyche that he explored helped people understand some of the horrors that occurred during World War I and the traumatic changes it made in every country involved in the conflict.

> Sigmund Freud, by the power of his writings and by the breadth and audacity of his speculations, revolutionized the thought, the lives, and the imagination of an age. . . . It would be hard to find in the history of ideas, even in the history of religion, someone whose influence was so immediate, so broad, or so deep. (Wollheim, 1971, p. ix)

Freud explored areas of the psyche that had been obscured by Victorian morality and philosophy. He devised new approaches to treat the mentally ill. His work challenged cultural, religious, social, and scientific taboos. His writings, his personality, and his determination to extend the boundaries of his work kept him at the center of an intense, shifting circle of friends, disciples, and critics. Freud was constantly rethinking and revising his earlier ideas. Interestingly, his harshest critics included those he had personally supervised at various stages in their careers.

It is not possible to discuss all of Freud's contributions in a single chapter. Therefore, what follows is a deliberate simplification of a complex and intricately constructed system. It is an overview intended to make later exposure to Freudian ideas more intelligible and to allow a better understanding of theorists whose works are heavily influenced by Freud.

Personal History

Sigmund Freud was born on May 6, 1856, in Freiberg in Moravia, now part of the Czech Republic. When he was 4 years old, his family suffered financial setbacks and moved to Vienna, where Freud remained most of his life. In 1938, he fled to England to escape from the German takeover of Austria.

During his childhood, Freud excelled as a student. Despite the limited financial position of his family, with all eight members living together in a crowded apartment, Freud, the eldest child, had his own room and even an oil lamp to study by while the rest of the family made do with candles. In *gymnasium* he continued his excellent academic performance. "I was at the top of my class for seven years. I enjoyed special privileges there and was required to pass scarcely any examinations" (Freud, 1925a, p. 9).

Such was the prevailing anti-Semitic climate of the time that, because Freud was Jewish, most professional careers, except medicine and law, were closed to him. He chose to enter the Faculty of Medicine at the University of Vienna in 1873.

> He was profoundly a Jew, not in a doctrinal sense, but in his conception of morality, in his love of the skeptical play of reason, in his distrust of illusion, in the form of his prophetic talent. (Bruner, 1956, p. 344)

His experiences at the University of Vienna, where he was treated as both an "inferior and an alien" because of being Jewish, strengthened his capacity to withstand criticism. "At an early age I was made familiar with the fate of being in the opposition and being put under the ban of the 'compact majority.' The foundations were thus laid for a certain degree of independence of judgement" (1935, p. 11). He remained a medical student for eight years, three more than was customary.

Neither at that time, nor indeed in my later life, did I feel any particular predilection for the career of a physician. I was moved, rather, by a sort of curiosity, which was, however, directed more towards human concerns than towards natural objects; nor had I grasped the importance of observation as one of the best means of gratifying it. (Freud, 1935, p. 10)

During these years, he worked in the physiological laboratory of Ernst Brücke, where he did independent research in histology, the study of the minute structure of animal and vegetable tissue, and published articles on anatomy and neurology. At the age of 26, Freud received his medical degree. He continued his work under Brücke for a year, while living at home. He aspired to fill the next open position in the laboratory, but Brücke had two excellent assistants ahead of Freud. He concluded, "The turning point came in 1882, when my teacher, for whom I felt the highest possible esteem, corrected my father's generous improvidence by strongly advising me, in view of my bad financial position, to abandon my theoretical career" (1925a, p. 13). In addition, Freud had fallen in love and realized that if he ever were to marry, he would need a better-paying position.

Although he moved reluctantly to a private practice, his primary interests remained in scientific exploration and observation. Working first as a surgeon, then in general medicine, he became a "house physician" at the principal hospital in Vienna. He took a course in psychiatry that furthered his interest in the relationships between mental symptoms and physical disease. By 1885, he had established himself in the prestigious position of lecturer at the University of Vienna. His career began to look promising.

From 1884 to 1887, Freud did some of the first research in cocaine. At first, he was impressed with its properties: "I have tested this effect of coca, which wards off hunger, sleep, and fatigue and steels one to intellectual effort, some dozens of times on myself" (1963, p. 11). He wrote about its potential therapeutic uses for both physical and mental disturbances. He later became concerned with its addicting properties and discontinued the research (Byck, 1975).

Even a superficial glance at my work will show how much I am indebted to the brilliant discoveries of Freud. (Jung in McGuire, 1974)

With Brücke's backing, Freud obtained a travel grant to work under Jean-Martin Charcot in Paris, where he studied hypnotic technique and served as Charcot's translator for his lectures (Carroy, 1991). Charcot saw Freud as a capable and understanding student and gave him permission to translate his papers into German upon Freud's return to Vienna.

His work in France increased his interest in hypnosis as a therapeutic tool. With the cooperation of the distinguished older physician Josef Breuer, Freud (1895) explored the dynamics of hysteria. Their findings were summarized by Freud: "The symptoms of hysterical patients depend upon impressive, but forgotten scenes of their lives (traumata). The therapy founded thereon was to cause the patients to recall and reproduce these experiences under hypnosis (catharsis)" (1914, p. 13). He found, however, that hypnosis was not as effective as he had hoped. It did not allow the patient or the therapist to work with the patient's resistance to recalling the traumatic memories. Eventually, Freud abandoned hypnosis altogether. Instead, he encouraged his patients to speak freely by reporting whatever thoughts came to mind, regardless of how these thoughts related to the patients' symptoms.

In 1896, Freud first used the term *psychoanalysis* to describe his methods. His own self-analysis began in 1897. Freud's interest in the unconsciousness insights provided by the dreams his patients described led to the publication, in 1900, of *The Interpretation of Dreams.* This serious treatment of the significance of dreams, radical at the time, received little attention but is now regarded by many to be his most important work. Freud followed it the next year with another major book, *The Psychopathology of Everyday Life,* which looked at the everyday moments in life when we reveal hidden wishes without being aware of what we are doing or saying. Eventually, Freud had a following of interested physicians, including Alfred Adler, Sandor Ferenczi, Carl Gustav Jung, Otto Rank, Karl Abraham, and Ernest Jones. The group established a society. Papers were written, a journal was published, and the psychoanalytic movement began to expand. Soon there were psychoanalytic groups in a dozen countries. By 1910, Freud was invited to the United States to deliver lectures at Clark University in Worcester, Massachusetts. His works were being translated into English. People were becoming interested in the theories of Dr. Sigmund Freud.

Freud spent the rest of his life developing, extending, and clarifying psychoanalysis. He tried to retain control over the psychoanalytic movement by ejecting members who disagreed with his views and by demanding an unusual degree of loyalty to his own position. Jung, Adler, and Rank, among others, left after repeated disagreements with Freud on theoretical issues. Each later founded a separate school of thought.

As I stepped on to the platform at Worcester to deliver my "Five Lectures" upon psychoanalysis it seemed like some incredible day-dream: psychoanalysis was no longer a product of delusion, it had become a valuable part of reality. (Freud, 1925a, p. 104)

Freud wrote extensively. His collected works fill 24 volumes and include essays concerning the fine points of clinical practice, a series of lectures outlining the theory in full, and specialized monographs on religious and cultural questions. He attempted to build a structure that would outlive him, one that might eventually reorient all of psychiatry. He was compelling and dogmatic in some areas and open to criticism and revision in others. He feared that analysts who deviated from the procedures he established might dilute the power and the possibilities of psychoanalysis. Above all, he wanted to prevent the distortion and misuse of psychoanalytic theory. When, for example, in 1931 Ferenczi suddenly changed his procedures, making the analytic situation one in which affection might be more freely expressed, Freud wrote him as follows:

> I see that the differences between us have come to a head in a technical detail which is well worth discussing. You have not made a secret of the fact that you kiss your patients and let them kiss you. . . .
>
> Now I am assuredly not one of those who from prudishness or from consideration of bourgeois convention would condemn little erotic gratifications of this kind. . . . We have hitherto in our techniques held to the conclusion that patients are to be refused erotic gratifications.
>
> Now picture what will be the result of publishing your technique. There is no revolutionary who is not driven out of the field by a still more radical one. A number of independent thinkers in matters of technique will say to themselves: why stop at a kiss? (Jones, 1955, pp. 163–164)

In spite of declining health, Freud maintained a private practice, a full writing schedule, and an ever-increasing correspondence, even answering letters from total strangers asking for help (Benjamin & Dixon, 1996). As Freud's work became more widely available, the criticisms increased. In 1933 the Nazis, offended by his frank discussion of sexual issues, burned a pile of Freud's books in Berlin. Freud commented on the event: "What progress we are making. In the Middle Ages they would have burnt me, nowadays they are content with burning my books" (Jones, 1957).

No one who, like me, conjures up the most evil of those half-tamed demons that inhabit the human breast, and seeks to wrestle with them, can expect to come through the struggle unscathed. (Freud, 1905b)

Perpetually embroiled in battles over the validity or utility of his work, he continued to write. His last book, *An Outline of Psycho-analysis* (1940), begins with a blunt warning to critics: "The teachings of psycho-analysis are based on an incalculable number of observations and experiences, and only someone who has repeated those observations on himself and others is in a position to arrive at a judgment of his own upon it" (p. 1).

Freud's last years were difficult. From 1923 on, he was in ill health, suffering from cancer of the mouth and jaws. He was in almost continual pain and had a total of 33 operations to halt the spreading cancer. When, in 1938, the Germans took over Austria and threatened Anna, his daughter, Freud left for London. He died there a year later.

Unfortunately, Freud's first biographer, Ernest Jones, also a close personal friend, wrote a sanitized account of his life, leaving the writing of a more balanced version to a later generation (Gay, 1988). Others have criticized Freud for a possible affair with his wife's sister (O'Brien, 1991), a lack of professional honesty (Masson, 1984), and a blatant disregard of confidentiality within psychoanalysis (Goleman, 1990; Hamilton, 1991). He has also been accused of possibly misrepresenting some of his most famous cases (Decker, 1991) and even of being "the false prophet of the drug world" (Thornton, 1984). Only the continuing importance of Freud's work supports the publication of these attacks.

Freud's ultimate importance can be judged not only by the ongoing interest in and debate over aspects of psychoanalytic theory but, to a greater extent, by the number of his ideas that have become part of the common heritage of the West. We are all in Freud's debt for partially illuminating the world that moves beneath conscious awareness.

Intellectual Antecedents

Freud's thinking was an original synthesis of his exposure to philosophical ideas, his training in scientific rigor, and his own contact with the unconscious.

Philosophy

While still a student at the University of Vienna, Freud was influenced by the German romantic poet Clemens Brentano and introduced to the ideas of Friedrich Nietzsche as well (Godde, 1991a). Nietzsche felt, for example, that moral convictions arose from internalized aggression. Freud agreed (Roazen, 1991). Freud's ideas are also close to those of Arthur Schopenhauer. They overlap in their view of the will, the importance of sexuality in determining behavior, the domination of reason by the emotions, and the centrality of repression—the nonacceptance of what one experiences (Godde, 1991b).

Biology

Some of Freud's faith in the biological origins of consciousness may be traced to Brücke's positions. Brücke once took a formal oath to abide by the following proposition, which was seen as open and optimistic for the time:

> No other forces than the common physical and chemical ones are active within the organism. In those cases which cannot at present be explained by these forces one either has to find the specific way or form of their action by means of the physical-mathematical method or to assume new forces equal in dignity to the chemical-physical forces inherent in matter, reducible to the force of attraction and repulsion. (Rycroft, 1972, p. 14)

Charcot demonstrated that it was possible to induce or relieve hysterical symptoms with hypnotic suggestion. Freud observed, as had others, that in hysteria patients exhibit symptoms that are physiologically impossible. For example, in *glove anesthesia* a person's hand is without feeling, while the sensations in the wrist and arm are normal. Because the nerves run continuously from the shoulder into the hand, there can be no physical cause for this symptom. It became clear to Freud that hysteria was a disorder whose genesis required a psychological explanation.

I sometimes come out of his lectures [Charcot's] . . . with an entirely new idea about perfection. . . . No other human being has ever affected me in the same way. (Freud in E. Freud, 1961, pp. 184–185)

The Unconscious

Freud did not discover the unconscious. The ancient Greeks, among others, recommended the study of dreams. Just before Freud's time, Johann Wolfgang von Goethe and Friedrich von Schiller "had sought the roots of poetic creation in the unconscious" (Gay, 1988, p. 128), as had many romantic poets and even Freud's contemporary, the novelist Henry James. Freud's contribution lies in his observing this part of the mind, its origins and its contents, with the emerging tools of scientific analysis. His work and the attention it attracted has made the unconscious a part of our public lexicon.

Freud's final attempt to develop a neurologically based psychology (1895) may have arisen from his own earlier and highly sophisticated personal explorations with cocaine (Fuller, 1992). This model, eventually cast aside by Freud, was revived and is seen by some to be a neglected but brilliant precursor to contemporary theories linking changes in brain chemistry to emotional states (Pribram, 1962).

Major Concepts

> One evening last week when I was hard at work, tormented with just that amount of pain that seems to be the best state to make my brain function, the barriers were suddenly lifted, the veil was drawn aside, and I had a clear vision from the details of the neuroses to the conditions that make consciousness possible. Everything seemed to connect up, the whole worked well together, and one had the impression that the thing was really a machine and would soon go by itself. . . . all that was perfectly clear, and still is. Naturally I don't know how to contain myself for pleasure. (Freud, letter to Fliess; in Bonaparte, 1954)

Many of the most puzzling and seemingly arbitrary turns of psychoanalytic theory . . . are either hidden biological assumptions, or result directly from such assumptions. (Halt, 1965, p. 94)

Underlying all of Freud's thinking is the assumption that the body is the sole source of all mental energy. He looked forward to the time when all mental phenomena might be explained with direct reference to brain physiology (Sulloway, 1979). In his attempt to create a theory that encompassed all mental activity, Freud worked from a biological model. His major concepts include a structural breakdown of the parts of the mind, its developmental stages, what its does with energy, and what drives it.

Psychic Determinism

Freud assumed that there were no discontinuities in mental life and that all thought and all behavior have meaning. He contended that *nothing* occurs randomly, least of all mental processes. There is a cause, even multiple causes, for every thought, feeling, memory, or action. Every mental event is brought about by conscious or unconscious intention and is determined by the events that have preceded it. It appears that many mental events occur spontaneously; however, Freud began to search out and describe the hidden links that join one conscious event to another.

Conscious, Unconscious, Preconscious

Freud described the mind as if it were divided into three parts, the conscious, the unconscious, and the preconscious.

There is no need to characterize what we call "conscious." It is the same as the consciousness of philosophers and of everyday opinion. (Freud, 1940, p. 16)

Conscious Consciousness is self-evident, and for that reason it is the part of the mind that science most concerned itself with—until Freud. However, the conscious is only a small portion of the mind; it includes only what we are aware of in any given moment. Although Freud was interested in the mechanisms of consciousness, he was far more interested in the less exposed and explored areas of consciousness, which he labeled the *preconscious* and the *unconscious* (Herzog, 1991).

Unconscious When a conscious thought or feeling seems to have no relation to the thoughts and feelings that preceded it, Freud suggested, the connections are present but unconscious. Once the unconscious links are found, the apparent discontinuity is resolved. "We call a psychical process unconscious whose existence we are obliged to assume—we infer it from its effects—but of which we know nothing" (1933, p. 70).

Within the unconscious are instinctual elements, which have never been conscious and which are never accessible to consciousness. In addition, there is material that has been barred—censored and repressed—from consciousness. This material is neither forgotten nor lost, but neither is it remembered. The thought or memory still affects consciousness, but indirectly.

Certain inadequacies of our psychic functions and certain performances which are apparently unintentional prove to be well motivated when subjected to psychoanalytic investigation. (Freud, 1901)

There is a liveliness and an immediacy to unconscious material. "We have found by experience that unconscious mental processes are in themselves 'timeless.' That is to say to begin with: they are not arranged chronologically, time alters nothing in them, nor can the idea of time be applied to them" (Freud in Fodor & Gaynor, 1958, p. 162). Memories that are decades old, when released into consciousness, have lost none of their emotional force.

Preconscious Strictly speaking, the preconscious is a part of the unconscious, but a part that can easily be made conscious. Those portions of memory that are accessible are part of the preconscious. This might include memories, for example, of everything a person did yesterday, a middle name, street addresses, the date of the Norman Conquest, favorite foods, the smell of fall leaves burning, and an oddly shaped birthday cake eaten during a tenth birthday party. The preconscious is like a holding area for the memories of a functioning consciousness.

Impulses

Impulse (**trieb** in German) is sometimes incorrectly translated in other textbooks as "instinct" (Bettelheim, 1982, pp. 87–88). Impulses or drives are pressures to act without conscious thought toward particular ends. Such impulses are "the ultimate cause of all activity" (Freud, 1940, p. 5). Freud labeled the physical aspects of impulses as needs and the mental aspects of impulses as wishes. These needs and wishes propel people to take action.

All impulses have four components: a *source,* an *aim,* an *impetus,* and an *object.* The source, where the need arises, may be a part or all of the body. The aim is to reduce the need until no more action is necessary; that is, to give the organism the satisfaction it now desires. The impetus is the amount of energy, force, or pressure that is used to satisfy or gratify the impulse. This is determined by the urgency of the underlying need. The object of an impulse is whatever thing or action allows satisfaction of the original desire.

There can be no question of restricting one or the other basic impulses to a single region of the mind. They are necessarily present everywhere. (Freud, 1940)

Consider the way in which these components appear in a thirsty person. The body gradually dehydrates until it needs more liquids; the source is the growing need for fluids. As the need becomes greater, thirst may be perceived. As this thirst is unsatisfied, it becomes more pronounced. As the intensity rises, so does the impetus or energy available to do something to relieve the thirst. The aim is to reduce the tension. The solution is not simply a liquid—milk, water, or beer—but all the acts that go toward reducing the tension. These might include getting up, going to the kitchen, choosing among various beverages, preparing one, and drinking it. A critical point to remember is that the impulse can be fully or partially satisfied in a number of ways, regardless of whether the initial seeking reactions are instinctual. The capacity to satisfy needs in animals is often limited by a pattern of stereotypical behavior. Human impulses only *initiate* the need for action; they do not predetermine the particular action or how it will be completed. The number of solutions open to an individual is a summation of his or her initial biological urge, the mental "wish" (which may or may not be conscious), and a host of prior ideas, habits, and available options.

Freud assumed that the normal, healthy mental and behavioral pattern is aimed at reducing tension to previously acceptable levels. A person with a need will continue seeking activities that can reduce the original tension. The complete cycle of behavior from relaxation to tension and activity and back to relaxation is called a *tension-reduction* model. Tensions are resolved by returning the body to the state of equilibrium that existed before the need arose.

Many seemingly helpful thoughts and behaviors, however, do not seem to reduce tension; in fact, they can create and maintain tension, stress, or anxiety.

To Freud, these thoughts and behaviors indicated that the direct expression of an impulse had been redirected or blocked.

Basic Impulses Freud developed two descriptions of basic impulses. The early model described two opposing forces: the sexual (more generally, the erotic or physically gratifying) and the aggressive, or destructive. Later he described these forces more globally as either life supporting or death (and destruction) encouraging. Both formulations presupposed a biological, ongoing, and unresolvable pair of conflicts. This basic antagonism is not necessarily visible in mental life, because most of our thoughts and actions are evoked not by one of these instinctual forces in isolation but by the two in combination.

Freud was impressed with the diversity and complexity of behavior that arises from the fusion of the basic drives. "The sexual impulses are remarkable for their plasticity, for the facility with which they can change their aims, for their interchangeability—for the ease with which they can substitute one form of gratification for another, and for the way in which they can be held in suspense" (1933, p. 97). What Freud noted is that the "object" can be a wide variety of things. Sexual desire, for example, can be released through sexual activity but also by watching erotic films, looking at images, reading about other people, fantasizing, and, so research studies would indicate, eating, drinking—even exercising. The impulses are the channels through which the energy can flow, but this energy obeys laws of its own.

Libido and Aggressive Energy

A person falls ill of a neurosis if his ego has lost the capacity to allocate his libido in some way. (Freud, 1916)

Each of these generalized impulses has a separate source of energy. **Libido** (from the Latin word for *wish* or *desire*) is the energy available to the life impulses. "Its production, increase or diminution, distribution and displacement should afford us possibilities for explaining the psychosexual phenomena observed" (Freud, 1905a, p. 118).

One characteristic of libido is its "mobility"—that is, the ease with which it can pass from one area of attention to another. Freud pictured the volatile nature of emotional responsiveness as a flow of energy, flowing in and out of areas of immediate concern.

Aggressive energy, or the death impulse, has no special name. It has been assumed to have the same general properties as libido, although Freud did not make this clear.

Cathexis

Cathexis is the process by which the available libidinal energy in the psyche is attached to or invested in a person, idea, or thing. Libido that has been cathected is no longer mobile and can no longer move to new objects. It is rooted in whatever part of the psyche has attracted and held it.

The German word Freud used, *Besetzung,* means both "to occupy" and "to invest." If you imagine your store of libido as a given amount of money, cathexis is the process of investing it. Once a portion has been invested or cathected, it remains there, leaving you with that much less to invest elsewhere.

For example, psychoanalytic studies of mourning interpret the lack of interest in normal pursuits and the excessive preoccupation with the recently deceased as a withdrawal of libido from usual relationships and as an extreme cathexis of the lost person.

Psychoanalytic theory is concerned with understanding where libido has been inappropriately cathected. Once released or redirected, this same energy is then available to satisfy other current needs. The need to release bound energies is also found in the ideas of Carl Rogers and Abraham Maslow, as well as in Buddhism and Sufism. Each of these theories comes to different conclusions about the source of psychic energy, but all agree with the Freudian contention that the identification and channeling of psychic energy is a major issue in understanding personality.

There are certain pathological conditions which seem to leave us no alternative but to postulate that the subject draws on a specific quantity of energy which he distributes in variable proportions in his relationships with objects and with himself. (LaPlanche & Pontalis, 1973, p. 65)

Structure of the Personality

Freud observed in his patients an endless series of psychic conflicts and compromises. He saw impulse pitted against impulse, social prohibitions blocking biological drives, and ways of coping often conflicting with one another. Only late in his career did he order, for himself, this seeming chaos by proposing three basic structural components of the psyche: the *id*, the *ego*, and the *superego*. These are now accepted English terms, but they are artificially abstract and leave a different impression from what Freud had intended. His words for each were simple and direct: *Das es* (id) simply means "it," *das Ich* (ego) means "I," and *das uber-Ich* (superego) means "above I." It is too late to correct the damage done by the initial translation of Freud's work into English. His writings were made deliberately obscure so as to sound more scientific, which appealed to the predominant American mind-set of the time (Bettelheim, 1982).

The Id

The **id** is the original core out of which the rest of the personality emerges. It is biological in nature and contains the reservoir of energy for all parts of the personality. Although the other parts of consciousness develop out of the id, the id itself is primitive and unorganized. "The logical laws of thought do not apply in the id" (Freud, 1933, p. 73). Moreover, the id is not modified as one grows and matures. The id is not changed by experience because it is not in contact with the external world. Its goals are to reduce tension, to increase pleasure, and to minimize discomfort. The id strives to do this through reflex actions (automatic reactions such as sneezing or blinking) and the psychological processes of the other portions of the mind.

The id may be likened to a blind king who has absolute power and authority but whose trusted counselors, primarily the ego, tell him how and where to use these powers.

The contents of the id are almost entirely unconscious. They include primitive thoughts that have never been conscious and thoughts that have been denied and found unacceptable to consciousness. According to Freud, experiences that have been denied or repressed still have the power to affect a

In the id there is nothing corresponding to the idea of time, no recognition of the passage of time, and (a thing which is very remarkable and awaits adequate attention in philosophic thought) no alteration of mental processes by the passage of time. . . . Naturally the id knows no values, no good and evil, no morality. (Freud, 1933, p. 74) person's behavior with undiminished intensity and without any conscious control.

The Ego

The **ego** is the part of the psyche that is in contact with external reality. It develops out of the id, as the infant becomes aware of its own identity, to serve and placate the id's repeated demands. In order to accomplish this, the ego, like the bark of a tree, protects the id but also draws energy from it. It has the task of ensuring the health, safety, and sanity of the personality. Freud postulated that the ego has several functions in relation both to the outside world and to the inner world, whose urges it strives to satisfy.

Its principal characteristics include control of voluntary movement and those activities that tend toward self-preservation. It becomes aware of external events, relates them to past events, then through activity either avoids the condition, adapts to it, or modifies the external world to make it safer or more comfortable. To deal with "internal events," it attempts to keep control over "the demands of the instincts, by deciding whether they shall be allowed to obtain satisfaction, by postponing that satisfaction to times and circumstances favorable in the external world or by suppressing their excitations completely" (1940, pp. 2–3). The ego's activities are to regulate the level of tension produced by internal or external stimuli. More tension is felt as discomfort, while a lowering of tension is felt as *pleasure*. Therefore, the ego pursues pleasure and seeks to avoid or minimize pain.

[We] might say that the ego stands for reason and good sense while the id stands for the untamed passions. (Freud, 1933)

Thus the ego is originally created by the id in an attempt to cope with stress. However, to do this, the ego must in turn control or modulate the id's impulses so that the individual can pursue realistic approaches to life.

The act of dating provides an example of how the ego controls sexual impulses. The id feels tension arising from unfulfilled sexual arousal and, without the ego's influence, would reduce this tension through immediate and direct sexual activity. Within the confines of a date, however, the ego can determine how much sexual expression is possible and how to establish situations in which sexual contact is most fulfilling. The id is responsive to needs, whereas the ego is responsive to opportunities.

The Superego

[The superego] is like a secret police department, unerringly detecting any trends of forbidden impulses, particularly of an aggressive kind, and punishing the individual inexorably if any are present. (Horney, 1939, p. 211)

This last part of the personality's structure develops not from the id but from the ego. The **superego** serves as a judge or censor over the activities and thoughts of the ego. It is the repository of moral codes, standards of conduct, and those constructs that form the inhibitions for the personality. Freud describes three functions of the superego: conscience, self-observation, and the formation of ideals. As conscience, the superego acts to restrict, prohibit, or judge conscious activity, but it also acts unconsciously. The unconscious restrictions are indirect, appearing as compulsions or prohibitions. "The sufferer . . . behaves as if he were dominated by a sense of guilt, of which he knows nothing" (1907, p. 123).

The superego develops, elaborates, and maintains the moral code of an individual. "A child's superego is in fact constructed on the model, not of its parents but of its parents' superego; the contents which fill it are the same and it becomes the vehicle of tradition and all the time resisting judgments of value which have propagated themselves in this manner from generation to generation" (1933, p. 39). The child, therefore, learns not only the real constraints in any situation but also the moral views of the parents before being able to act to obtain pleasure or to lower tension.

Relationship Between the Three Subsystems

The overarching goal of the psyche is to maintain—and when it is lost, to regain—an acceptable level of dynamic equilibrium that maximizes the pleasure of tension reduction. The energy that is used originates in the id, which has a primitive, instinctual nature. The ego, arising from the id, exists to deal realistically with the basic drives of the id. It also mediates between the forces that operate on the id, the superego, and the demands of external reality. The superego, arising from the ego, acts as a moral brake or counterforce to the practical concerns of the ego. It sets out a series of guidelines that define and limit the flexibility of the ego.

The id is entirely unconscious, whereas the ego and the superego are only partly so. "Certainly large portions of the ego and superego can remain unconscious, are, in fact, normally unconscious. That means to say that the individual knows nothing of their contents, and that it requires an expenditure of effort to make him conscious of them" (Freud, 1933, p. 69).

Psychoanalysis, in these terms, has a primary goal to strengthen the ego, to make it independent of the overly strict concerns of the superego, and to increase its capacity to deal with material formerly repressed or hidden in the id.

Psychosexual Stages of Development

As an infant becomes a child, a child an adolescent, and an adolescent an adult, there are marked changes in what is desired and how desires are satisfied. The shifting modes of gratification and the physical areas of gratification are the basic elements in Freud's description of the developmental stages. Freud uses the term **fixation** to describe what occurs when a person does not progress normally from stage to stage but remains overly involved with a particular stage. A person fixated in a particular stage will tend to seek gratification of needs in simpler or more childlike ways, rather than as an adult, which would result from normal development.

Psychoanalysis is the first psychology to take seriously the whole human body as a place to live in. . . . Psychoanalysis is profoundly biological. (Le Barre, 1968)

The Oral Stage

The **oral** stage begins at birth, when both needs and gratification primarily involve the lips, tongue, and somewhat later, the teeth. The basic drive of the infant is not social or interpersonal; it is simply to take in nourishment and to relieve the tensions of hunger and thirst. During feeding, the child is also soothed, cuddled, and rocked. The child associates both pleasure and the reduction of tension with the feeding process.

The mouth is the first area of the body that the infant can control; most of the libidinal energy available is directed or focused on this one area. As the child matures, other parts of the body develop and become important sites of gratification. However, some energy remains permanently affixed or cathected to the means for oral gratification. In adults, there are many well-developed oral habits and a continued interest in maintaining oral pleasures. Eating, sucking, chewing, smoking, biting, and licking or smacking one's lips are physical expressions of these interests. Constant nibblers, smokers, and those who often overeat may be partially fixated in the oral stage, people whose psychological maturation may be incomplete.

The late oral stage, after teeth have appeared, includes the gratification of the aggressive instincts. Biting the breast, which causes the mother pain and leads to the actual withdrawal of the breast, is an example of this kind of behavior. Adult sarcasm, tearing at one's food, and gossip have been described as being related to this developmental stage.

It is normal to retain some interest in oral pleasures. Oral gratification can be looked upon as pathological only if it is a dominant mode of gratification; that is, if a person is excessively dependent on oral habits to relieve anxiety or tension.

The Anal Stage

As the child grows, new areas of tension and gratification are brought into awareness. Between the ages of 2 and 4, children generally learn to control the anal sphincter and the bladder. The child pays special attention to urination and defecation. Toilet training prompts a natural interest in self-discovery. The rise in physiological control is coupled with the realization that such control is a new source of pleasure. In addition, children quickly learn that the rising level of control brings them attention and praise from their parents. The reverse is also true: the parents' concern over toilet training allows the child to demand attention both by successful control and by mistakes.

Adult characteristics that are associated with partial fixation at the **anal** stage are orderliness, parsimoniousness, and obstinacy. Freud observed that these three traits are usually found together. He speaks of the "anal character," whose behavior is closely linked to difficult experiences suffered during this time in childhood.

Part of the confusion that can accompany the anal stage is the apparent contradiction between lavish praise and recognition, on the one hand, and the idea that toilet behavior is "dirty" and should be kept a secret, on the other. The child does not initially understand that his or her bowel movements and urine are not valued. Small children love to watch the action of the toilet bowl as it flushes, often waving or saying good-bye to their evacuations. It is not unusual for a child to offer part of a bowel movement to a parent as a gift. Having been praised for producing it, the child may be surprised and confused if the parents react with disgust at the gift. Few areas of contemporary life are as saddled with prohibitions and taboos as toilet training and behaviors typical of the anal stage.

Personal Reflection

■ Psychosexual Stages

The following exercises and questions will give you a chance to experience feelings associated with each developmental stage. (If Freud is correct in his supposition that any remaining fixations from each stage will be linked to anxiety, the following could prove difficult or embarrassing.)

The Oral Stage

Buy a baby bottle with a nipple. Fill it with milk, water, or fruit juice. Either alone or with other members of the class, drink from the bottle. Does drinking, or even the thought of drinking, from a bottle bring up any memories or feelings? If you go ahead and do it, what postures are you most comfortable in? Allow yourself to experience your unfiltered reactions. Share these reactions with the class. Do you find there are responses that are specific to men or to women?

The Anal Stage

Notice to what extent privacy is a consideration in the architecture of public lavatories, as well as your bathroom at home. How does privacy play a role in how you behave in the lavatory? Do you avoid meeting anyone's eyes or even looking at anyone else when you enter a public rest room? Can you imagine urinating in public? In a park? By the side of the highway? In a forest?

Many people have strongly conditioned toilet behaviors. For example, some people must read while they are sitting on a toilet. What might be the purpose of this behavior?

Share some of your observations with others, and be aware of how it makes you feel to talk about aspects of this exercise. Joking or giggling could be a defense against some discomfort you might have with the topic.

The Phallic Stage

Can you recall what your parents said to you about your genitals when you were little? Can the women in the class recall any thoughts or ideas about boys and their penises? Can the men recall any fear of losing their penises? If you have no memories of these kinds of feelings, is this sufficient reason to assume that you had no such feelings at the time?

The Genital Stage

Write down any misinformation you have had about sexual matters that has been subsequently corrected. (Examples: You were brought by the stork or found at the supermarket. Every time a person has intercourse a pregnancy results.)

Do you think your early sexual experiences have affected your attitudes or beliefs about your own sexuality? Have those experiences reinforced previously held beliefs? How did you feel about your first sexual experience? Do you feel differently now? Can you relate your current attitudes about sexual matters to earlier attitudes or beliefs?

The Phallic Stage

Starting as early as age 3, the child moves into the **phallic** stage, which focuses on the genitals. Freud maintained that this stage is best characterized as phallic, because it is the period when a child becomes aware either of having a penis or of lacking one. This is the first stage in which children become conscious of sexual differences.

Freud tried to understand the tensions a child experiences during sexual excitement—that is, pleasure from the stimulation of the genital areas. This excitement is linked in the child's mind with the close physical presence of the parents. The craving for this contact becomes increasingly more difficult for the child to satisfy; the child is struggling for the intimacy that the parents share with each other. This stage is characterized by the child's wanting to get into bed with the parents and becoming jealous of the attention the parents give to each other. Freud concluded from his observations that during this period both males and females develop fears about sexual issues.

So you too are aware that the Oedipus complex is at the root of religious feeling. Bravo! (Freud, letter to Jung; in McGuire, 1974)

Freud saw children in the phallic stage reacting to their parents as potential threats to the fulfillment of their needs. Thus for the boy who wishes to be close to his mother, the father takes on some of the attributes of a rival. At the same time, the boy wants his father's love and affection, for which his mother is seen as a rival. The child is in the untenable position of wanting and fearing both parents.

In boys, Freud called this conflict the **Oedipus complex,** after the tragic hero in the plays by Greek dramatist Sophocles. In the most familiar version of the myth, Oedipus kills his father and later marries his mother (not knowing either parent). When he is eventually made aware of who he has killed and who he has married, Oedipus disfigures himself by tearing out both of his eyes. Freud believed that every male child reenacts a similar inner drama. He wishes to possess his mother and kill his father to achieve this goal. He also fears his father and is afraid that he, a child, will be castrated by him, reducing the youngster to a sexless being. The anxiety around castration, the fear and love for the father as well as the love and sexual desire for the mother, can never be fully resolved. In childhood, the entire complex is repressed. Among the first tasks of the developing superego are to keep this disturbing conflict out of consciousness and to protect the child from acting it out.

Every aspect of the female Oedipus complex has been effectively criticized, using empirical data and methods which did not exist in Freud's lifetime. (Emmanuel, 1992, p. 27)

For girls the problem is similar, but its expression and solution take a different turn. The girl wishes to possess her father, and she sees her mother as the major rival. Boys repress their feelings partly out of fear of castration. For girls it is different. The repression of their desires is less severe, less total. This lack of intensity allows the girl to "remain in the Oedipus situation for an indefinite period. She only abandons it late in life, and then incompletely" (Freud, 1933, p. 129). Freud's views about women and their psychological development have come under constant fire, as will be discussed in this chapter and in other chapters as well.

The Latency Period Whatever form the resolution of the struggle actually takes, most children seem to modify their attachment to their parents sometime after 5 years of age and turn to relationships with peers and to school activities, sports, and other skills. This phase, from age 5 or 6 until the onset of puberty, is called the **latency** period. It is a time when the unresolvable sexual desires of the phallic stage are not attended to by the ego and are successfully repressed by the superego.

> From then on, until puberty, . . . sexuality makes no progress; on the contrary, the sexual strivings diminish in strength, and much that the child practiced or knew before is given up and forgotten. In this period, after the early blooming of sexual life has withered, are built up such attitudes of the ego as shame, disgust, and morality, designed to stand against the later storms of puberty and to direct the paths of the freshly-awakened sexual desires. (1926, p. 216)

For both parents and children, this is a relatively calm and psychologically uneventful time.

The Genital Stage

The final period of biological and psychological development, the **genital** stage, occurs with the onset of puberty and the consequent return of libidinal energy to the sexual organs. Now boys and girls are made aware of their separate sexual identities and begin to look for ways to fulfill their erotic and interpersonal needs. Freud felt that homosexuality, at this stage, resulted from a lack of adequate development and that heterosexuality was characteristic of the healthy personality, a position still held in some quarters, in spite of contemporary understanding of the varieties of healthy sexual development.

Freud's Views About Women

Freud's ideas about women were based heavily on biological differences between men and women and have come under an ever-increasing volume of attack. Later chapters of this text, especially Chapter 6 ("Karen Horney and Humanistic Psychoanalysis") and Chapter 9 ("The Psychology of Women: A Relational Approach"), discuss current contrasting views. Here we are presenting only Freud's position so that you understand what other theorists are arguing about. Full-fledged, pointed rebuttals by feminist scholars, including books by Miller (1984) and Sagan (1988), leave few parts of Freud's theory standing upright.

Penis envy—the girl's desire for a penis and her related realization that she is "lacking" one—is a critical juncture in female development. "The discovery that she is castrated is a turning point in a girl's growth. Three possible lines of development diverge from it: one leads to sexual inhibition and to neurosis, the second to a modification of character in the sense of masculinity complex, and the third to normal feminity" (Freud, 1933, p. 126).

This theory has, according to Freud, substantial implications for the development of the female personality. The girl's penis envy persists as a feeling of inferiority and predisposes her to jealousy. Her perpetual desire for a penis, or "superior endowment," is, in the mature woman, converted to the desire for a child, particularly for a son, "who brings the longed-for-penis with him"

(1933). The woman is never decisively forced to renounce her Oedipal strivings out of castration anxiety. As a consequence, the woman's superego is less developed and internalized than the man's.

Freud asserts that women

> have the hope of someday obtaining a penis in spite of everything. . . . I cannot escape the notion (though I hesitate to give it expression) that for women the level of what is ethically normal is different from what it is in men. . . . We must not allow ourselves to be deflected from such conclusions by the denials of the feminists, who are anxious to force us to regard the two sexes equal in position and worth. (1925b, p. 258)

Freud viewed the little girl as a creature in whom phallic strivings were extremely important but inevitably unsatisfied, thus dooming the girl to feelings of perpetual deficiency and inferiority. Yet despite such assertions (which have, not surprisingly, received much criticism in feminist literature), Freud frequently stated that he never really felt that he understood women or the psychology of women. In fact, he reiterated time and again the tentative nature and value of his own portrayal of female sexuality and its vicissitudes.

Female sexuality is assumed by Freud to constitute disappointed *male* sexuality, rather than to represent the outcome of distinctly female tendencies. Today this view seems perhaps the weakest of suppositions in Freud's theory. Given this central bias, many of Freud's conclusions about the nature of female sexuality and female psychology seem questionable. In fact, some of the phenomena that Freud observed and attempted to describe appear a good deal more plausible when they are stripped of their disappointed-male bias.

Though anatomy, it is true, can point out the characteristics of maleness and femaleness, psychology cannot. For psychology the contrast between the sexes fades away into activity and passivity, in which we far too readily identify activity with maleness and passivity with femaleness. (Freud, 1930)

The assumption is made in most early psychoanalytic writing that a little girl's lack of a penis leads not only to envy of the boy's penis and *feelings of* inferiority but also to *actual* inferiority—that is, inferiority in terms of a woman's sense of justice, intellectual curiosity, capacity to implement her ideas independent of a man's approval, and so forth. The notion that penis envy may be a very real and commonly observed clinical phenomenon is dismissed, because it is so intimately connected, in the minds of many people, with the assumption of generalized female inferiority. This is unfortunate because, as Karen Horney (1926) has suggested, penis envy may be a natural experience for females in the same way that envy of pregnancy, childbirth, motherhood, and suckling is a natural experience for males. Even more important, *experiencing envy* does not doom the little girl to perpetual inferiority. Rather, its occurrence, says Horney, may present her with a complex set of feelings, the working through and mastery of which are central to her growth and development as a mature—certainly not inferior—human being.

Ernest Jones, Freud's early biographer, was one of the first psychoanalysts who argued that "the little girl's Oedipal attachment develops out of her intrinsic, innate femininity undergoing its own maturation processes" (Fliegel, 1973, p. 387). He also suggested that castration anxiety derives from a basic fear of loss of sexuality and that this fear poses as much threat to the little girl as to the little boy (Jones, 1927).

We may usefully reexamine a traditional psychoanalytic concept—one that has, in fact, received considerable feminist criticism. Instead of eliminating the whole notion of penis envy (which would not explain away its frequent clinical manifestations), we may reevaluate the idea that women feel inferior *as a result of penis envy,* to look more deeply into why some women do report feelings of inferiority, especially in their teenage years. The recurring criticism in the feminist literature suggests that Freud's observations about female feelings of inferiority might be reexamined but not dismissed, even if his idea of how these feelings originated does not seem realistic. Learning how to deal (in productive ways) with feelings of envy or of insecurity or of being different from other people is, after all, central to the challenge of growing up.

Dynamics: Psychoanalysis, Dreamwork, and Anxiety

The ideas that led to psychoanalysis arose out of years of treating clients. The theory, whose fundamental tenets brought about new ways of examining human behavior, was based on a few central premises. One of them was the key role of anxiety in the maintenance of neurosis, maladaptive, repetitive behavior.

Psychoanalysis: The Theory

Freud's intention, from his earliest writings, was to better understand those aspects of mental life that were obscure and apparently unreachable. He called both the theory and the therapy **psychoanalysis.**

> Psychoanalysis is the name (1) of a procedure for the investigation of mental processes which are almost inaccessible in any other way, (2) of a method (based upon that investigation) for the treatment of neurotic disorders and (3) of a collection of psychological information obtained along those lines, which is gradually being accumulated into a new scientific discipline. (1923, p. 234)

Freud believed that the unconscious material remains unconscious only with considerable and continual expenditure of libido. As this material is made accessible, energy is released that can be used by the ego for healthier pursuits. The release of blocked materials can minimize self-destructive attitudes. The need to be punished or the need to feel inadequate can be reevaluated by bringing into awareness those early events or fantasies that led to the need. People may then be freed from the suffering they perpetually bring upon themselves. For example, many Americans are concerned about their sexual attractiveness: penises are too short or too thin; breasts are too small, too large, or not well formed; and so forth. Most of these beliefs arise during the teenage years or earlier. The unconscious residues of these attitudes are visible in worries over sexual adequacy, desirability, premature ejaculation, frigidity, and a host of related concerns. If these unexpressed fears are explored, exposed, and relieved, there can be a rise in available sexual energy as well as a lowering of overall tension.

The more psychoanalysis becomes known, the more will incompetent doctors dabble in it and naturally make a mess of it. This will then be blamed on you and your theory. (Jung, letter to Freud; in McGuire, 1974)

The theory of psychoanalysis suggests that it is possible, but difficult, to come to terms with the recurring demands of the id. Analysis works to overcome the natural resistance and to bring the id's painful, repressed memories and ideas back into the conscious (Freud, 1906). "One of the tasks of psychoanalysis, as you know, is to lift the veil of amnesia which shrouds the earliest years of childhood and to bring the expressions of infantile sexual life which are hidden behind it into conscious memory" (1933, p. 28). The goals as described by Freud assume that if one is freed from the inhibitions of the unconscious, the ego establishes new levels of satisfaction in all areas of functioning. Thus the resolution of anxieties rooted in early childhood frees blocked or displaced energy for more realistic and complete gratification of one's needs.

Dreams and Dreamwork

In listening to the free associations of his patients, as well as in his own self-analysis, Freud began to scrutinize the reports and memories of dreams. In *The Interpretation of Dreams* (1900), he wrote how dreams help the psyche protect and satisfy itself. Obstacles and unmitigated desires fill daily life. Dreams are a partial balance, both physically and psychologically, between instinctual urges and real-life limitations. Dreaming is a way of channeling unfulfilled desires through consciousness without arousing the physical body.

> A structure of thoughts, mostly very complicated, which has been built up during the day and not brought to settlement—a day remnant—clings firmly even during night to the energy which it has assumed . . . and thus threatens to disturb sleep. This day remnant is transformed into a dream by the dream-work and in this way rendered harmless to sleep. (Freud in Fodor & Gaynor, 1958, pp. 52–53)

More important than the biological value of dreams are the psychological effects of **dreamwork.** Dreamwork is "the whole of the operations which transform the raw materials of the dream—bodily stimuli, day's residues, dream-thoughts—so as to produce the manifest dream" (LaPlanche & Pontalis, 1973, p. 125). A dream does not simply appear. It develops to meet specific needs, although these are not clearly described by the dream's manifest content.

We recognize the soundness of the wish-fulfillment theory up to a certain point, but we go beyond it. In our view it does not exhaust the meaning of the dream. (Jung, letter to Freud; in McGuire, 1974)

Almost every dream can be understood as a **wish fulfillment.** The dream is an alternative pathway to satisfy the desires of the id. While awake, the ego strives to increase pleasure and reduce tension. During sleep, unfulfilled needs are sorted, combined, and arranged so that the dream sequences allow additional satisfaction or tension reduction. For the id, it is unimportant whether satisfaction occurs in physical, sensory reality or in internal, imagined dream reality. In both cases, accumulated energies are discharged. The dream plays out, on at least two levels, current issues that are unresolved or that are part of larger, older patterns that have never been resolved.

A dream then, is a psychosis, with all the absurdities, delusions and illusions of a psychosis. No doubt it is a psychosis which has only a short duration, which is harmless and even performs a useful function. (Freud, 1940)

Repetitive dreams may occur when a daytime event triggers the same kind of anxiety that led to the original dream. For example, an active, happily married woman in her sixties may still dream, from time to time, of going to take a college exam. When she arrives at the classroom, she sees that the examination is over. She has arrived too late. She has this dream when she is anxious over some current difficulty; however, her anxiety is related neither to college nor to examinations, both of which she left behind many years ago.

Personal Reflection

■ Investigate Your Own Dreams

Make a dream journal by keeping a pad of paper by your bed. In the morning, before you do anything else, make a few notes about your dreams. Even if you have never remembered dreams before, this procedure will help you to recall them. It has been shown that groups of students given this assignment recall dreams regularly within a few days.

Later in the day, write out your dreams in as much detail as you can recall. What are your associations with particular aspects of your dreams? See if these associations point to possible meanings. For example, might your dreams be attempts at wish fulfillment? Try to guess what various segments might mean. Pay attention to those fragments that seem to be part of your "day residue." Do you notice anything that reflects your desires or attitudes toward others?

Keep this journal for several weeks. As you read other parts of this text, you will learn other ways to analyze dreams. From time to time, go over your dream journal, and see if you can make new interpretations. Notice especially any recurrent themes or patterns. (Chapters on Jung, Anna Freud, and the post-Freudians provide different approaches to recording dreams.)

Many dreams do not appear to be satisfying; some are depressing, some disturbing, some frightening, and many simply obscure. Many dreams seem to be the reliving of past events, whereas some appear to be prophetic. Through the detailed analysis of dozens of dreams, linking them to events in the life of the dreamer, Freud was able to show that dreamwork is a process of selection, distortion, transformation, inversion, displacement, and other modifications of an original wish. These changes render the modified wish acceptable to the ego even if the original wish is totally unacceptable to waking consciousness. Freud suggested reasons for the permissiveness in dreams in which we act beyond the moral restrictions of our waking lives. In dreams we kill, maim, or destroy enemies, relatives, or friends; we act out perversions and take as sexual partners a wide range of people. In dreams, we combine people, places, and occasions that would be an impossible mix in our waking world.

Dreams are not to be likened to the unregulated sounds that rise from a musical instrument struck by the blow of some external force instead of a player's hand; they are not meaningless, they are not absurd; . . . they can be inserted into the chain of intelligible waking mental acts; they are constructed by a highly complicated activity of the mind. (Freud, 1900)

Dreams attempt to fulfill wishes, but they are not always successful. "Under certain conditions, the dream can only achieve its end in a very incomplete way, or has to abandon it entirely; an unconscious fixation to the trauma seems to head the list of these obstacles to the dream functions" (Freud, 1933, p. 29).

Within the context of psychoanalysis, the therapist aids the patient in interpreting dreams to facilitate the recovery of unconscious material. Freud made certain generalizations about special kinds of dreams (e.g., falling dreams, flying dreams, swimming dreams, and dreams about fire), but he specified that the general rules are not always valid. An individual's own dream associations are more important than any preconceived set of rules of interpretation.

Dreams are the true interpreters of our inclinations, but art is required to sort and understand them. (Montaigne, 1580, *Essays*)

While some critics of Freud often suggest that he exaggerated the sexual components of dreams to conform to his overall theory, Freud's rejoinder is clear: "I have never maintained the assertion which has often been ascribed to

Dreams are real while they last—can we say more of life? (Havelock Ellis)

me that dream-interpretation shows that all dreams have a sexual content or are derived from sexual motive forces" (Freud, 1925a, p. 47). What he stressed was that dreams are neither random nor accidental but are a way to satisfy unfulfilled wishes.

A different kind of criticism is that Freud's ideas were severely limited by his lack of knowledge of non-European societies. In India, for example, "the self [and its dreams] are by no means so clearly limited as it is for us" (O'Flaherty, 1984, p. 22), and in Native American groups the function and the understanding of dreams stand outside Freud's speculations. "In most of the 16 Native American models, there is no distinct separation between the dreamed world and the lived world. . . . In contrast, Western models of dreaming sharply demarcate dreaming from waking, and see dreaming as a biologically-driven altered state of consciousness which, none-the-less, may produce useful information in the hands of a skilled interpreter" (Krippner and Thompson, 1996).

Freud had no good grounds for picking out repressed infantile wishes from the emerging glut of diverse unconscious dream thoughts as the principal motive forces for our dreams. (Grunbaum, 1994, p. 81)

Not at all outdated, Freud's penetration of the world of dreams is still vital and a matter of concern and debate (Kramer et al., 1994).

Anxiety

Anxiety makes repression and not, as we used to think, the other way round. (Freud, 1933, p. 69)

The major problem for the psyche is how to cope with **anxiety.** Anxiety is triggered by an expected or foreseen increase in tension or displeasure; it can develop in any situation (real or imagined) when the threat to some part of the body or psyche is too great to be ignored, mastered, or discharged.

Events with a potential to cause anxiety include, but are not limited to, the following:

1. Loss of a desired object—for example, a child deprived of a parent, a close friend, or a pet.
2. Loss of love—for example, rejection, failure to win back the love or approval of someone who matters to you.
3. Loss of identity—for example, castration fears, loss of face, or fear of public ridicule.
4. Loss of love for self—for example, superego disapproval of traits, as well as acts that result in guilt or self-hate.

There are two general ways to decrease the anxiety. The first is to deal with the situation directly. We overcome obstacles, either confront or run from threats, and resolve or come to terms with problems in order to minimize their impact. In these ways, we are working to eliminate difficulties, lowering the chances of their recurrence, and also decreasing the prospects of additional anxiety in the future. In Hamlet's words, we "take up arms against a sea of troubles and by opposing end them."

If the ego is obliged to admit its weakness, it breaks out into anxiety—realistic anxiety in regarding the face of the external world, moral anxiety regarding the super-ego, and neurotic anxiety regarding the strength of the passions in the id. (Freud, 1933)

The alternative approach defends against the anxiety by distorting or denying the situation itself. The ego protects the whole personality against the threat by falsifying the nature of the threat. The ways in which the distortions are accomplished are called *defense mechanisms.* These are fully described by Anna Freud (1936), in Chapter 5, and are treated as integral parts of the core concepts of psychoanalysis.

Structure

Freud considered almost every aspect of mental and social life. Important areas, including energy, the body, social relationships, emotions, intellect, self, and the special role of therapy, he treated in different ways at different times in his life. What follows here is an attempt to create some order out of enormous complexity.

Energy

At the center of Freud's theories is his concept of energy flow. Energy links his concepts of the unconscious, psychological development, personality, and neurosis. "His theories on impulses deal primarily with the *source* of mental energy; his theories on psychosexual development and the defenses deal with the *diversion* of energy; and his theories of the id, ego, and superego deal with *conflicts* of energy and the effects of such conflict" (Cohen, 1982, p. 4).

Body

Freud developed his theories based on physical and biological assumptions. Basic drives arise from somatic sources; libidinal energy is derived from physical energy; responses to tension are both mental and physical. The body is the core of experience. As Sulloway points out, "It was Freud's continued appeal to biological assumptions that justified his personal conviction that he had finally created a universally valid theory of human thought and behavior" (1979, p. 419).

The ego is first and foremost a body ego. (Freud, 1937)

Moreover, the primary focuses of energy are through the various forms of sexual expression (oral, anal, and genital). Maturity is partially defined as the capacity for achieving quality of expression in genital sexuality. Many of Freud's critics never looked at his entire theory but instead became obsessed with his reintroduction of physical and sexual concerns into the fields of so-called mental functioning.

In spite of Freud's recognition of the centrality of the body, his own writings on therapy almost totally ignore it. Perhaps the cultural denial of the body that characterized the age in which he lived colored his own apparent lack of interest in gestures, postures, and physical expressions exhibited by his patients. Many of the later Freudians, such as Erik Erikson and Frederick Perls, as well as those theorists who broke from Freud, such as Carl Jung and Wilhelm Reich, paid more attention to the actual physical body but less attention to biological theories.

The all-inclusive nature of sex energy has not yet been correctly understood by psychologists. In fact, the very term *reproductive* or *sex energy* is a misnomer. Reproduction is but one of the aspects of the life energy, of which the other theater of activity is the brain. (Krishna, 1974)

Social Relationships

Adult interactions and relationships are greatly influenced by early childhood experiences. The first relationships, those that occur within the nuclear family, are the defining ones. All later relationships are influenced by the ways those

Personal Reflection

■ Are There Patterns in Your Life?

Here is a way to look at your current relationships as they relate to your relationships with your parents.

Part 1

1. Make a list of some of the people you have liked or loved most in your life—excluding your parents. List men and women separately.
2. Describe desirable and undesirable aspects of each person.
3. Notice, reflect on, or record the similarities and differences in your lists. Are there certain traits common to the men and the women?

Part 2

1. Make a list of the desirable and undesirable characteristics of your parents.
2. List the desirable and undesirable characteristics of your parents as you saw them when you were a child. (The two lists may or may not overlap.)

Part 3

Compare and contrast the list of attributes of your parents with those of the other important people in your life.

initial relationships were formed and maintained. The basic patterns of child-mother, child-father, and child-sibling are the prototypes against which subsequent encounters are unconsciously measured. Later relationships are, to some degree, recapitulations of the dynamics, tensions, and gratifications that occurred within the original family.

Our choices in life—of lovers, friends, bosses, even our enemies—are derivatives of the parent-child bonds. The natural rivalries are recapitulated in our sex roles and in the way we accommodate the demands of others. Over and over again, we play out the dynamics begun in our homes, frequently picking as partners people who reawaken in us unresolved aspects of our early needs. For some, these are conscious choices. For others, choices are made without conscious knowledge of the underlying dynamics.

I confess that plunging into sexuality in theory and practice is not to my taste. But what have my taste and feeling about what is seemly and what is unseemly to do with the question of what is true? (Breuer in Sulloway, 1979, p. 80)

People shy away from this aspect of Freudian theory because it suggests that one's future choices are beyond one's control. The issue turns on the question of how much childhood experience determines adult choices. For example, one critical period in developing relationships occurs during the phallic stage, when both sexes first confront their growing erotic feelings toward their parents and the concomitant inability to gratify these urges. According to Freudian theory, even as the resulting Oedipal complications are resolved, these dynamics continue to affect the individual's relationships.

Relationships are built on a foundation of the residual effects of intense early experiences. Teenage, young adult, and adult dating, as well as friendship and marriage patterns, is a reworking of unresolved childhood issues.

Emotions

What Freud uncovered, in an age that had worshiped reason and denied the value and the power of emotion, was that we are not primarily rational animals but are driven by powerful emotional forces, the genesis of which is often unconscious. Emotions are the avenues for the release of tension and the appreciation of pleasure. Emotions may also serve the ego by helping it to keep certain memories out of awareness. Strong emotional responses may actually mask a childhood trauma. A feeling of disgust about a food that one has not even tasted in years, for example, may cover the memory of an unhappy time when that food was served. A phobic reaction effectively prevents a person from approaching an object or class of objects that might trigger a more threatening source of anxiety.

It was through observing both the appropriate and inappropriate expressions of emotion that Freud found the keys to uncovering and understanding the motivating forces within the unconscious.

Intellect

The intellect is one of the tools available to the ego. The person who is most free is able to use reason when it is expedient and whose emotional life is open to conscious inspection. Such a person is not driven by unfulfilled remnants of past events but can respond directly to each situation, balancing individual preferences against the restrictions imposed by the culture.

The most striking and probably the strongest emotional force in Freud was his passion for truth and his uncompromising faith in reason. For him, reason was the only human capacity that could help to solve the problem of existence or at least ameliorate the suffering that is inherent in human life.

Reason, so Freud felt, is the only tool—or weapon—we have to make sense of life, to dispense with illusions . . . to become independent of fettering authorities, and thus to establish our own authority. (Fromm, 1959)

For Freud, as for the age in which he lived, the impact of Darwin's work cannot be underestimated. An unquestioned goal of the time was to prove that rational thought placed human beings above the beasts. Much of the resistance to Freud's work arose from the evidence that people were in fact less reasonable, less in control of their emotions, and more like animals than anyone had suspected. Freud's own hope and personal belief was that reason was primary and that the intellect was the most, if not the only, important tool that consciousness possessed to control its darker side.

What Freud realized was that any aspect of unconscious existence, raised into the light of consciousness, might be dealt with rationally: "Where id is, there let ego be" (1933, p. 80). Where the irrational, instinctual urges dominate, let them be exposed, moderated, and dominated by the ego. If the original drive is not to be suppressed, it becomes the task of the ego, using the intellect, to devise safe and sufficient methods for satiation. The use of intellect depends entirely on the capacity and strength of the ego.

Self

The self is the total being: the body and the instincts, as well as the conscious and unconscious processes. To Freud, a self independent of the body or detached from it has no place in biological beliefs. When confronted with such a metaphysical (or spiritual) image of humankind, Freud asserted that this was not within his province as a scientist. Psychoanalysts have since moved past Freud's position and have written extensively about the self.

Therapist/Therapy

There is still no acceptable evidence to support the view that psychoanalysis is an effective treatment. (Rachman & Wilson, 1980, p. 76)

We have been chiefly concerned with Freud's general theory of personality. Freud himself, however, was involved in the practical applications of his work—the practice of psychoanalysis. The aim of psychoanalysis is to help the patient establish the best possible level of ego functioning, given the inevitable conflicts arising from the external environment, the superego, and the relentless instinctual demands of the id. Kenneth Colby, a former trainer of analysts, describes the goal of the analytic procedure:

> In speaking of the goal of psychotherapy, the term "cure" . . . requires definition. If by "cure" we mean relief of the patient's current neurotic difficulties, then that is certainly our goal. If by "cure" we mean a lifelong freedom from emotional conflict and psychological problems, then that cannot be our goal. Just as a person may suffer pneumonia, a fracture, and diabetes during his lifetime and require particular medication and separate treatment for each condition, so another person may experience at different times a depression, impotence, and a phobia, each requiring psychotherapy. . . . (1951, p. 4)

It is useful to keep in mind that therapy, as used by any of the theorists covered in this book, not only does not "cure" past problems but does not prevent future ones.

The Role of the Psychoanalyst

The therapist's task is to help the patient recall, recover, and reintegrate unconscious materials so that the patient's current life can become more satisfying. Freud says:

To stand firm against this general assault by the patient requires the analyst to have been fully and completely analyzed himself. . . . The analyst himself, on whom the fate of so many people depends, must know and be in control of even the most recondite weaknesses of his own character; and this is impossible without a fully completed analysis. (Ferenczi, 1955)

> We pledge him to obey the *fundamental rule* of analysis which is henceforward to govern his behavior towards us. He is to tell us not only what he can say intentionally and willingly, what will give him relief like a confession, but everything else as well that comes into his head, even if it is *disagreeable* for him to say it, even if it seems to him *unimportant* or actually *nonsensical.* (1940, p. 31)

The analyst is supportive of these disclosures, and neither critical nor approving of their content. The analyst takes no moral position but serves as a blank screen for the patient's opinions. The therapist presents as little as possible of his or her personality to the patient. This gives the patient the freedom to treat the analyst in a host of ways, transferring to the therapist attitudes, ideas, even physical characteristics that actually belong to persons in the patient's past. This **transference** is critical to the therapeutic process because it brings past events into a new context that fosters understanding. For example, if a female patient starts to treat a male therapist as she treats her father—outwardly submissive and deferential, but covertly hostile and disrespectful—the analyst can clarify these feelings for the patient. He can point out that he, the therapist, is not the cause of the feelings but that they originate within the patient herself and may reflect aspects of her relationship with her father that she has repressed.

Transference makes the therapy a living process. Rather than just talking about life, the patient forms a critical relationship with the therapist. To aid the patient in making these connections, the analyst interprets some of what the patient is saying, suggesting links that the patient may or may not have previously acknowledged. This process of interpretation is a matter of intuition and clinical experience.

The concept of Transference . . . contends that the observation, understanding and discussion of the patient's emotional reactions to the psychoanalytical situation constitute the most direct ways of reaching an understanding of his character structure and consequently of his difficulties. It has become the most powerful, and indeed the indispensable, tool of analytical therapy. (Horney, 1939, pp. 33–34)

As part of the psychoanalytic process, the patient is encouraged, never pressured, to uncover material. Freud saw analysis as a natural process; the energy that had been repressed emerges slowly into consciousness, where it can be used by the developing ego: "Whenever we succeed in analyzing a symptom into its elements, in freeing an impulse from one nexus, it does not remain in isolation, but immediately enters into a new one." The task of the therapist is to expose, explore, and isolate the component impulses that have been denied or distorted by the patient: "The psychosynthesis is thus achieved during analytic treatment without our intervention, automatically and inevitably" (1919, p. 161). Reforming old, unhealthy habits and establishing newer, healthier ones occurs without the intrusion of the therapist.

Limitations of Psychoanalysis

Analysis, as Freud and his immediate followers practiced it, was not for everyone. Freud said:

> The field of application of analytic therapy lies in the transference neuroses—phobias, hysteria, obsessional neurosis—and further, abnormalities of character which have been developed in place of these diseases. Everything differing from these, narcissistic and psychotic conditions, is unsuitable to a greater or less extent. (1933, p. 155)

Some analysts have said that people who are already functioning well, whose ego structure is healthy and intact, make the best candidates for psychoanalysis. Like any other form of treatment, it has inherent limitations that have been argued from every point of view. It has been compared favorably to Buddhism, because both provide ways to alleviate human suffering (Pruett, 1987). Psychoanalysis was scrutinized to see if it could stand up to a Marxist evaluation as well (Volosinov, 1927). Although Freud hoped that psychoanalysis could help explain all of human consciousness, he gently chided those who tended to believe that psychoanalytic psychotherapy was the ultimate cure.

It almost looks as if analysis were the third of those "impossible" professions in which one can be sure beforehand of achieving unsatisfying results. The other two . . . are education and government. (Freud, 1937)

Personal Reflection

■ Early Memories

Freud found that early memories were often indicative of current personal issues. You can try testing this assumption by doing the following exercise.

Find a partner. One of you will recall your earliest memory while the other records it on paper. (You will trade roles, so don't worry about who goes first.)

1. The speaker should sit so as not to be looking at the recorder. Recall your earliest memory or any very early memory. Tell it to the person who is the recorder. Talk no more than five minutes. The more clearly and vividly you can recall the memory, the more you may gain from this exercise. Other memories may emerge in addition to the one you are describing. Feel free to mention them as well. Remember, it's the recorder's task to take notes while the speaker talks about past events. Do not interrupt. Pay attention to the importance your partner puts on any aspect of a memory. In your notes, you can use the Freudian terms described in this chapter.
2. After five minutes, stop. Without any discussion, switch roles. The person who was the speaker is now writing down the partner's memories. At the end of another five minutes, stop. Silently, for a minute or so, think about what you have said and what you have heard.
3. Discuss your notes with each other. Point out any implications and connections you observe. Note differences in feelings expressed by your partner. Remember that defense mechanisms can and do distort or disguise memories. Try to relate aspects of these first memories to current events in your life.

Psychoanalysis is an intimate part of the decaying ideology of the bourgeoisie. (Volosinov, 1927, p. 132)

> Psychoanalysis is really a method of treatment like others. It has its triumphs and its defeats, its difficulties, its limitations, its indications. . . . I should like to add that I do not think our cures can compete with those of Lourdes. There are so many more people who believe in the miracles of the Blessed Virgin than in the existence of the unconscious. (1933, p. 152)

The post-Freudians, however, extended the range of clients and conditions that could be treated under the psychoanalytic umbrella in so many ways that their work merits a chapter of its own (see Chapter 5).

Evaluation

We have presented an overview of the vast and complex theoretical structure that Freud developed. We have not, in this chapter, attempted to include the numerous shadings and elaborations of his followers, disciples, detractors, critics, and clients. We have tried to organize and simplify the outlines of what was, at its inception, a radical and innovative point of view. Freud threw down a gauntlet that few thinkers have been able to leave unchallenged. Most of the theorists in this book acknowledge their debt to Freud, both those who agree with him and those who repeatedly oppose him.

Freud's ideas continue to influence psychology, literature, art, anthropology, sociology, and medicine. Many of his ideas, such as the importance of dreams and the vitality of the unconscious processes, are widely accepted. Other facets of his theory, such as the relationships among the ego, the id, and the superego, or the role of the Oedipus complex in adolescent development, are extensively debated. Still other parts of his work, including his analysis of female sexuality and his theories on the origins of civilization, have been widely criticized.

There continues to be a veritable torrent of books and articles about Freud's ideas, as well as a stream of journals and monographs about psychoanalytic therapy. More works are published on Freud each year than on all the other theorists in this book combined. A sampling of the publications from 1991 alone includes writings on almost every aspect of his work. Unpublished manuscripts were still being discovered and discussed (Bergeret, 1991; Nitzschke, 1991). Currently, Freud is being interpreted as far more humanistic, far more flexible, and far more open-minded in his analysis of human experience than had been originally thought. Aspects of his theories are intelligently criticized. For example, Horacek (1991) finds his observations on grieving wrong; van Dam (1991) attacks his description of the Oedipus complex, while Kerenyi and Hillman (1991) say his understanding of the Oedipus myth is flawed. Diller (1991) writes that all his other biographers have underplayed how Jewish Freud was. (Psychoanalysis was known for a time as the "Jewish science.") Warner (1991) lists reasons why Freud never liked the United States. One reason was its rule that psychoanalysts must be physicians. And on it goes. There is an international growth industry of Freudian journals, institutes, and presses, a world unto themselves. While most of this community is self-involved and self-contained, Freud's large presence still reasserts itself into the general culture from time to time. In 1993, for example, he was on the cover of *Time* magazine and a large exhibit of the impact of his ideas was scheduled by the Library of Congress. Shortly thereafter, however, that exhibit was shelved because of the amount of virulent criticism leveled against it.

It is not our intention to predict how Freudian theory will be judged historically. However, we maintain that his ideas are of no less urgent concern today than they were during his lifetime. Those who choose to study the mind or try to understand other human beings must make their peace with Freud's basic assertions through an examination of their own inner experience.

Our position is to recognize that there are times in a person's life when Freud's picture of the role of the conscious and unconscious seems like a personal revelation. The stunning impact of his thinking can illuminate an aspect of your own or someone else's character and send you scurrying after more of his books. There are other times when he does not seem to be of use, when his ideas seem distant, convoluted, and irrelevant.

At either time, Freud is a figure to be dealt with. His work evokes a personal response. As we looked through his books, accumulated over the years, we reread our own marginal notes in them, some of praise and some of damnation. He cannot be treated lightly, because he discussed and described issues that arise in everyone's life.

Whatever your response to Freud's ideas, Freud's advice would be to regard your response as an indicator of your own state of mind as well as a reasoned reaction to his work. In the words of the poet W. H. Auden about Freud: "If often he was wrong and at times absurd, to us he is no more a person now, but a whole climate of opinion" (1945).

Implications for Personal Growth

It is possible to examine your inner world for clues to your own behavior; however, it is an extremely difficult task because you have, with varying degrees of success, hidden these same clues from yourself.

Freud suggests that all behavior is linked together, that there are no psychological accidents—that your choice of persons, places, foods, and amusements stems from experiences you do not or will not remember. All thoughts and all behaviors have meaning.

If your memory for past events is actually a mixture of accurate remembrances and slanted, skewed, and distorted ones, how can you ever know what actually happened?

Here is an example of how two people can remember the same event differently:

> I recall with the clarity of personal suffering being forced to eat hot breakfast cereal for a lengthy period in my childhood. I recall it vividly and viscerally. I can evoke the dining room, my place, the table, the feeling of revulsion in my throat, the delaying strategies, waiting until the adults tired of me and left me in solitude with my half-completed bowl of now cold caking cereal; my attempts to kill the taste with all the sugar I could overpower it with are still clear. To this day I cannot look at a bowl of hot oatmeal without this rush of childhood memories. I *know* that I went through months of fighting with my mother over this issue. Several years ago, I discussed it with her. She recalled it clearly, but she *knew* that it was a brief set of events, a few days, perhaps a week or two at best, and she was surprised that I had any memory of it at all. I was left to decide—her memory against mine.

What emerges from reviewing this story is the realization that neither person was consciously lying, yet the stories were conspicuously different. There might be no way of ever knowing the actual events. The historical truth was not available; only the memories remained, and those were colored on both sides by selective repressions and distortions as well as elaborations and projections.

Freud does not suggest any way out of the dilemma. What he does open up is the realization that your memory or your version of your own past holds clues to how you behave and who you are. It is not simply a record of past events laid out neatly for objective examination.

Psychoanalysis uses a set of tools for personal analysis that includes lengthy self-examination, reflection, and dream analysis, while also noting recurrent patterns of thought and behavior. Freud has written of how he used the tools, what he discovered, and what he concluded from his discoveries. Although the conclusions are still a question of debate, the tools are at the core of a dozen other systems and may be the most lasting of his contributions to the study of personality.

The Theory Firsthand

Excerpt from *Studies in Hysteria*

The following material comes from one of Freud's early works. Most of it is self-explanatory. It is a glimpse of the way Freud pieced together a coherent picture of the cause of a single symptom from a few items of information.

In the summer vacation of the year 189— I made an excursion into the Hohe Tauern [one of the highest ranges in the Eastern Alps] so that for a while I might forget medicine and more particularly the neuroses. I had almost succeeded in this when one day I turned aside from the main road to climb a mountain which lay somewhat apart and which was renowned for its views and for its well-run refuge hut. I reached the top after a strenuous climb and, feeling refreshed and rested, was sitting deep in contemplation of the charm of the distant prospect. I was so lost in thought that at first I did not connect it with myself when these words reached my ears: "Are you a doctor, sir?" But the question was addressed to me, and by the rather sulky-looking girl of perhaps eighteen who had served my meal and had been spoken to by the landlady as "Katharina." To judge by her dress and bearing, she could not be a servant, but must no doubt be a daughter or relative of the landlady's.

Coming to myself I replied: "Yes, I'm a doctor: but how did you know that?"

"You wrote your name in the Visitors' Book, sir. And I thought if you had a few moments to spare . . . The truth is, sir, my nerves are bad. I went to see a doctor in L—— about them and he gave me something for them; but I'm not well yet."

So there I was with the neuroses once again—for nothing else could very well be the matter with this strong, well-built girl with her unhappy look. I was interested to find that neuroses could flourish in this way at a height of over 6,000 feet; I questioned her further therefore. I report the conversation that followed between us just as it is impressed on my memory and I have not altered the patient's dialect. [No attempt has been made in the English translation to imitate this dialect.]

"Well, what is it you suffer from?"

"I get so out of breath. Not always. But sometimes it catches me so that I think I shall suffocate."

This did not, at first sight, sound like a nervous symptom. But soon it occurred to me that probably it was only a description that stood for an anxiety attack: she was choosing shortness of breath out of the complex of sensations arising from anxiety and laying undue stress on that single factor.

"Sit down here. What is it like when you get 'out of breath'?"

"It comes over me all at once. First of all it's like something pressing on my eyes. My head gets so heavy, there's a dreadful buzzing, and I feel so giddy that I almost fall over. Then there's something crushing my chest so that I can't get my breath."

"And you don't notice anything in your throat?"

"My throat's squeezed together as though I were going to choke."

"Does anything else happen in your head?"

"Yes, there's a hammering, enough to burst it."

"And don't you feel at all frightened while this is going on?"

"I always think I'm going to die. I'm brave as a rule and go about everywhere by myself—into the cellar and all over the mountain. But on a day when that happens I don't dare to go anywhere; I think all the time someone's standing behind me and going to catch hold of me all at once."

So it was in fact an anxiety attack, and introduced by the signs of a hysterical "aura" [the premonitory sensations preceding an epileptic or hysterical attack] or, more correctly, it was a hysterical attack the content of which was anxiety. Might there not probably be some other content as well?

"When you have an attack do you think of something? and always the same thing? or do you see something in front of you?"

"Yes. I always see an awful face that looks at me in a dreadful way, so that I'm frightened."

Perhaps this might offer a quick means of getting to the heart of the matter.

"Do you recognize the face? I mean, is it a face that you've really seen some time?"

"No."

"Do you know what your attacks come from?"

"No."

"When did you first have them?"

"Two years ago, while I was still living on the other mountain with my aunt. (She used to run a refuge hut there, and we moved here eighteen months ago.) But they keep on happening."

Was I to make an attempt at analysis? I could not venture to transplant hypnosis to these altitudes, but perhaps I might succeed with a simple talk. I should have to try a lucky guess. I had found often enough that in girls anxiety was a consequence of the horror by which a virginal mind is overcome when it is faced for the first time with the world of sexuality.[1]

So I said: "If you don't know, I'll tell you how I think you got your attacks. At that time, two years ago, you must have seen or heard something that very much embarrassed you, and that you'd much rather not have seen."

"Heavens, yes!" she replied, "that was when I caught my uncle with the girl, with Franziska, my cousin."

"What's this story about a girl? Won't you tell me all about it?"

"You can say *anything* to a doctor, I suppose. Well, at that time, you know, my uncle—the husband of the aunt you've seen here—kept the inn on the--kogel [the name of the "other" mountain]. Now they're divorced, and it's my fault they were divorced, because it was through me that it came out that he was carrying on with Franziska."

"And how did you discover it?"

"This way. One day two years ago some gentlemen had climbed the mountain and asked for something to eat. My aunt wasn't at home, and Franziska, who always did

[1]I will quote here the case in which I first recognized this causal connection. I was treating a young married woman who was suffering from a complicated neurosis and, once again, was unwilling to admit that her illness arose from her married life. She objected that while she was still a girl she had had attacks of anxiety, ending in fainting fits. I remained firm. When we had come to know each other better she suddenly said to me one day: "I'll tell you now how I came by my attacks of anxiety when I was a girl. At that time I used to sleep in a room next to my parents'; the door was left open and a nightlight used to burn on the table. So more than once I saw my father get into bed with my mother and heard sounds that greatly excited me. It was then that my attacks came on."

the cooking, was nowhere to be found. And my uncle was not to be found either. We looked everywhere, and at last Alois, the little boy, my cousin, said: 'Why, Franziska must be in Father's room!' And we both laughed; but we weren't thinking anything bad. Then we went to my uncle's room but found it locked. That seemed strange to me. Then Alois said: 'There's a window in the passage where you can look into the room.' We went into the passage; but Alois wouldn't go to the window and said he was afraid.

So I said: 'You silly boy! I'll go. I'm not a bit afraid.' And I had nothing bad in my mind. I looked in. The room was rather dark, but I saw my uncle and Franziska; he was lying on her."

"Well?"

"I came away from the window at once, and leant up against the wall and couldn't get my breath—just what happens to me since everything went blank, my eyelids were forced together and there was a hammering and buzzing in my head."

"Did you tell your aunt that very same day?"

"Oh no, I said nothing."

"Then why were you so frightened when you found them together? Did you understand it? Did you know what was going on?"

"Oh no. I didn't understand anything at that time. I was only sixteen. I don't know what I was frightened about."

"Fräulein Katharina, if you could remember now what was happening in you at that time, when you had your first attack, what you thought about it—it would help you."

"Yes, if I could. But I was so frightened that I've forgotten everything."

(Translated into the terminology of our "Preliminary Communication" . . . , this means: "The affect itself created a hypnoid state, whose products were then cut off from associative connection with the ego-consciousness.")

"Tell me, Fräulein. Can it be that the head that you always see when you lose your breath is Franziska's head, as you saw it then?"

"Oh no, she didn't look so awful. Besides, it's a man's head."

"Or perhaps your uncle's?"

"I didn't see his face as clearly as that. It was too dark in the room. And why should he have been making such a dreadful face just then?"

"You're quite right."

(The road suddenly seemed blocked. Perhaps something might turn up in the rest of her story.)

"And what happened then?"

"Well, those two must have heard a noise, because they came out soon afterwards. I felt very bad the whole time. I always kept thinking about it. Then two days later it was a Sunday and there was a great deal to do and I worked all day long. And on the Monday morning I felt giddy again and was sick, and I stopped in bed and was sick without stopping for three days."

We (Breuer and I) had often compared the symptomatology of hysteria with a pictographic script which has become intelligible after the discovery of a few bilingual inscriptions. In that alphabet being sick means disgust. So I said: "If you were sick three days later, I believe that means that when you looked into the room you felt disgusted."

"Yes, I'm sure I felt disgusted," she said reflectively, "but disgusted at what?"

"Perhaps you saw something naked? What sort of state were they in?"

"It was too dark to see anything; besides they both of them had their clothes on. Oh, if only I knew what it was I felt disgusted at!"

I had no idea either. But I told her to go and tell me whatever occurred to her, in the confident expectation that she would think of precisely what I needed to explain the case.

Well, she went on to describe how at last she reported her discovery to her aunt, who found that she was changed and suspected her of concealing some secret. There followed some very disagreeable scenes between her uncle and aunt, in the course of which the children came to hear a number of things which opened their eyes in many ways and which it would have been better for them not to have heard. At last her aunt decided to move with her children and niece and take over the present inn, leaving her uncle alone with Franziska, who had meanwhile become pregnant. After this, however, to my astonishment she dropped these threads and began to tell me two sets of older stories, which went back two or three years earlier than the traumatic moment. The first set related to occasions on which the same uncle had made sexual advances to her herself, when she was only fourteen years old. She described how she had once gone with him on an expedition down into the valley in the winter and had spent the night in the inn there. He sat in the bar drinking and playing cards, but she felt sleepy and went up to bed early in the room they were to share on the upper floor. She was not quite asleep when he came up; then she fell asleep again and woke up suddenly "feeling his body" in the bed. She jumped up and remonstrated with him: "What are you up to, Uncle? Why don't you stay in your own bed?" He tried to pacify her: "Go on, you silly girl, keep still. You don't know how nice it is"—"I don't like your 'nice' things; you don't even let one sleep in peace." She remained standing by the door, ready to take refuge outside in the passage, till at last he gave up and went to sleep himself. Then she went back to her own bed and slept till morning. From the way in which she reported having defended herself it seems to follow that she did not clearly recognize the attack as a sexual one. When I asked her if she knew what he was trying to do to her, she replied: "Not at the time." It had become clear to her much later on, she said; she had resisted because it was unpleasant to be disturbed in one's sleep and "because it wasn't nice."

I have been obliged to relate this in detail, because of its great importance for understanding everything that followed.—She went on to tell me of yet other experiences of somewhat later date: how she had once again had to defend herself against him in an inn when he was completely drunk, and similar stories. In answer to a question as to whether on these occasions she had felt anything resembling her later loss of breath, she answered with decision that she had every time felt the pressure on her eyes and chest, but with nothing like the strength that had characterized the scene of discovery.

Immediately she had finished this set of memories she began to tell me a second set, which dealt with occasions on which she had noticed something between her uncle and Franziska. Once the whole family had spent the night in their clothes in a hay loft and she was woken up suddenly by a noise; she thought she noticed that her uncle, who had been lying between her and Franziska, was turning away, and that Franziska was just lying down. Another time they were stopping the night at the inn at the village of N——; she and her uncle were in one room and Franziska in an adjoining one. She woke up suddenly in the night and saw a tall white figure by the door, on the point of turning the handle: "Goodness, is that you, Uncle? What are you doing at the door?"—"Keep quiet. I was only looking for something."—"But the way out's by the *other* door."—"I'd just made a mistake" . . . and so on.

I asked her if she had been suspicious at that time. "No, I didn't think anything about it; I only just noticed it and thought no more about it." When I enquired whether she had been frightened on these occasions too, she replied that she thought so, but she was not so sure of it this time.

At the end of these two sets of memories she came to a stop. She was like someone transformed. The sulky, unhappy face had grown lively, her eyes were bright, she was lightened and exalted. Meanwhile the understanding of her case had become clear to me. The later part of what she had told me, in an apparently aimless fashion, provided an admirable explanation of her behaviour at the scene of the discovery. At that time she had carried about with her two sets of experiences which she remembered but did not understand, and from which she drew no inferences. When she caught sight of the couple in intercourse, she at once established a connection between the new impression and these two sets of recollections, she began to understand them and at the same time to fend them off. There then followed a short period of working-out, of "incubation," after which the symptoms of conversion set in, the vomiting as a substitute for moral and physical disgust. This solved the riddle. She had not been disgusted by the sight of the two people but by the memory which that sight had stirred up in her. And, taking everything into account, this could only be the memory of the attempt on her at night when she had "felt her uncle's body."

So when she had finished her confession I said to her: "I know now what it was you thought when you looked into the room. You thought: 'Now he's doing with her what he wanted to do with me that night and those other times.' That was what you were disgusted at, because you remembered the feeling when you woke up in the night and felt his body."

"It may well be," she replied, "that that was what I was disgusted at and that that was what I thought."

"Tell me just one thing more. You're a grown-up girl now and know all sorts of things . . ."

"Yes, now I am."

"Tell me just one thing. What part of his body was it that you felt that night?"

But she gave me no more definite answer. She smiled in an embarrassed way, as though she had been found out, like someone who is obliged to admit that a fundamental position has been reached where there is not much more to be said. I could imagine what the tactile sensation was which she had later learnt to interpret. Her facial expression seemed to me to be saying that she supposed that I was right in my conjecture. But I could not penetrate further, and in any case I owed her a debt of gratitude for having made it so much easier for me to talk to her than to the prudish ladies of my city practice, who regard whatever is natural as shameful.

Thus the case was cleared up.—But stop a moment! What about the recurrent hallucination of the head, which appeared during her attacks and struck terror into her? Where did it come from? I proceeded to ask her about it, and, as though *her* knowledge, too, had been extended by our conversation, she promptly replied: "Yes, I know now. The head is my uncle's head—I recognize it now—but not from *that* time. Later, when all the disputes had broken out, my uncle gave way to a senseless rage against me. He kept saying that it was all my fault: if I hadn't chattered, it would never have come to a divorce. He kept threatening he would do something to me; and if he caught sight of me at a distance his face would get distorted with rage and he would make for me with his hand raised. I always ran away from him, and always felt terrified that he would catch me some time unawares. The face I always see now is his face when he was in a rage."

This information reminded me that her first hysterical symptom, the vomiting, had passed away; the anxiety attack remained and acquired a fresh content. Accordingly, what we were dealing with was a hysteria which had to a considerable extent been abreacted. And in fact she had reported her discovery to her aunt soon after it happened.

"Did you tell your aunt the other stories—about his making advances to you?"

"Yes. Not at once, but later on, when there was already talk of a divorce. My aunt said: 'We'll keep that in reserve. If he causes trouble in the Court, we'll say that too.'"

I can well understand that it should have been precisely this last period—when there were more and more agitating scenes in the house and when her own state ceased to interest her aunt, who was entirely occupied with the dispute—that it should have been this period of accumulation and retention that left her the legacy of the mnemic symbol (of the hallucinated face).

I hope this girl, whose sexual sensibility had been injured at such an early age, derived some benefit from our conversation. I have not seen her since.[2] (Breuer & Freud, 1895, pp. 125–134)

Chapter Highlights

- The body is the sole source of all consciousness.
- Nothing occurs randomly—least of all, the individual's mental processes. All thoughts and all behaviors have meaning.
- The conscious is only a small part of the mind. The unconscious and the preconscious are the other components of consciousness, which are less exposed and explored. A psychic process is called unconscious when its existence is inferred from its effects. The preconscious is a part of the unconscious, the section that contains the available memories.
- Human impulses do not predetermine the outcome of an action. The two basic impulses are described as the sexual (life-supporting) and the aggressive, or destructive (death-encouraging).
- One's personality structure is composed of the id (it), the ego (I), and the superego (above I). The overarching goal of the psyche is to maintain an acceptable level of dynamic equilibrium that maximizes the pleasure felt as tension reduction.
- The primary goal of psychoanalysis is to strengthen the ego, to make it independent of the overly strict concerns of the superego, and to increase its capacity to deal with material formerly repressed or hidden.
- Freud proposed a psychosexual description of the developmental stages. Modes of gratification of desires and physical areas of gratification shift through each developmental stage. In his sequence, the individual would pass first through the oral, anal, and phallic stages. Issues of the Oedipal phase occur within the phallic stage. The latency period follows, until the individual emerges into the genital stage of development.

[2](*Footnote added, 1924*) I venture after the lapse of so many years to lift the veil of discretion and reveal the fact that Katharina was not the niece but the daughter of the landlady. The girl fell ill, therefore, as a result of sexual attempts on the part of her own father. Distortions like the one which I introduced in the present instance should be altogether avoided in reporting a case history. From the point of view of understanding the case, a distortion of this kind is not, of course, a matter of such indifference as would be shifting the scene from one mountain to another.

Fixation occurs when a person becomes overly involved in a particular stage.

- Freud, after acknowledging that he didn't fully understand women, proposed a biological reason for the feelings of inferiority reported by women undergoing psychoanalysis. His speculations, especially that female sexuality was "disappointed" male sexuality, have been roundly attacked since their first publication.
- Dreams are used in psychoanalysis as an aid to recover unconscious material. Neither random nor accidental, dreams are considered to be one way to satisfy unfulfilled wishes.
- Anxiety is the major coping problem for the psyche. If threats to the body or psyche are not dealt with directly, defense mechanisms come into play. The expenditure of energy necessary to maintain the defenses effectively limits the flexibility and strength of the ego.
- The concept of energy flow lies at the center of Freud's theories, linking concepts of the unconscious, psychological development, personality, and neurosis.
- Responses to tension are both mental and physical. Libidinal energy is derived from physical energy. Basic drives arise from somatic sources.
- Early childhood experiences greatly influence teenage, young adult, and adult patterns of interacting and relating. Relationships that occur in the nuclear family are the defining ones throughout an individual's later life.
- We are not primarily rational animals. Rather, we are often unconsciously driven by powerful emotional forces that may provide avenues for the release of tension and the appreciation of pleasure, and may serve to keep certain memories out of awareness.
- Given the conflicts inevitably arising from the external environment, the superego, and the relentless instinctual demands of the id, the aim of therapy is to help establish the best possible level of ego functioning.
- The therapist's role is to help a patient recall, recover, and reintegrate unconscious materials, so that the patient's life can become more satisfying.

Key Concepts

Aggressive energy Energy assumed to have the same general properties as libido. It is also termed the energy of the death impulse.

Anal Developmental stage from ages 2 to 4. Both the anal sphincter and the bladder are brought into awareness as areas of tension and gratification. A natural interest in self-discovery is prompted by toilet training.

Anxiety The major coping problem for the psyche. Anxiety is triggered by an expected or foreseen increase in tension or displeasure, real or imagined, when a threat to the body or psyche is too great to be ignored, discharged, or mastered.

Cathexis The process by which the available libidinal energy in the psyche is attached or invested in a person, idea, or thing. Once it is released this same energy may be redirected and become available for other current needs.

Dreamwork A process of distortion, selection, inversion, displacement, transformation, or other modifications of an original wish to render it acceptable to the ego, even if the original wish is not.

Impulses (drives) Pressures to act without conscious thought toward particular ends. Needs are the physical aspects and wishes are the mental aspects of impulses. There are four components to all impulses: source, aim, impetus, and object.

Ego (I) The part of the psyche that develops to ensure the health, safety, and sanity of the personality as it mediates between demands of the id and external reality. The ego is responsive to opportunities, whereas the id is responsive only to needs.

Fixation A response that occurs when there is excessive involvement in a particular developmental stage. In fixation, there is a tendency to seek gratification of needs in simpler or childlike ways, rather than as an adult.

Genital Developmental stage from puberty to adulthood. Libidinal energy returns to the genitals. Awareness of their separate sexual identities and the search for ways to satisfy erotic and interpersonal needs occurs for boys and girls.

Id (it) The original biological core out of which the rest of the personality emerges. Although primitive and unorganized, the id contains the reservoir of energy for all parts of the personality. It is not changed by experience, nor is it in contact with the external world. Its goals are to reduce tension, to increase pleasure, and to minimize discomfort. The id's contents are almost entirely unconscious.

Latency Developmental period from ages 5 to 6 until the onset of puberty. The individual's focus shifts from relationship with parents to relationships with peers, and to sports, school activities, and other skills. The superego successfully represses the unresolvable sexual desires of the phallic stage.

Libido The energy of the life impulses. Characterized as a flow of energy, it easily passes from one area of attention to another, moving with the volatile nature of emotional responsiveness. Aggressive energy, or the death impulse, is assumed to have the same properties as libido.

Neurosis Maladaptive, repetitive behaviors, formed as the product of dammed-up impulses in a restrictive environment.

Oedipus complex A conflict that occurs during the phallic stage of development. In boys, the father is seen as a rival for the mother's attention. Yet the boy still wants the father's love and affection, for which the mother is seen as a rival. The boy's feelings are repressed partly out of fear of castration. In girls, the problem is similar, but different in expression and solution. Because repression of desires is less total or severe, the girl is allowed to remain in this situation for an indefinite period.

Oral Developmental stage from birth to 2 to 4 years. Needs and gratification predominately involve lips, tongue, and, later, teeth. The basic drive is to take in nourishment, in order to relieve the tensions of hunger and thirst.

Penis envy In Freud's view, the feelings of inferiority that result from a girl's desire for a penis, and the related realization of its lack. In the mature woman, this ongoing desire for a penis is converted to the specific desire for a male child, who comes so equipped. In Horney's theory (Chapter 6), penis envy is viewed as the complement to a boy's envy of pregnancy, childbirth, and motherhood.

Phallic Developmental stage from ages 3 to 5. Focus is on the genitals, with an awareness of the presence or absence of a penis. Children become conscious of sexual differences.

Psychoanalysis A procedure for investigation, a method of treatment, and an accumulated collection of psychological information used to understand those aspects of mental life that are obscure and apparently unreachable. Psychoanalytic theory suggests that although it is a difficult process, one can come to terms with the recurring demands of the id.

Superego (above I) The part of the psyche that develops from the ego and serves as a repository of moral codes, standards of conduct, and inhibitions that function as conscience, self-observation, and formation of ideals. It develops, elaborates, and maintains the moral code of an individual, and also sets out a series of guidelines that define and limit the flexibility of the ego.

Transference Process in therapy whereby attitudes, ideas, and physical characteristics that belong to persons in the patient's past are brought forth into the relationship with the "blank screen" of the therapist. Transference brings past events into a new context that may foster understanding.

Wish fulfillment An aspect of dreams that may be considered as an alternate pathway to satisfy the desires of the id.

Annotated Bibliography

Books by Freud

Freud, S. The interpretation of dreams. In J. Strachey (Ed. and Trans.), *The standard edition of the complete psychological works of Sigmund Freud* (Vols. 4, 5 of 24). Hogarth Press, 1953–1966. (Originally published, 1900.)

Freud said of it in 1931: "It contains, even according to my present-day judgment, the most valuable of all the discoveries it has been my good fortune to make." We agree. The best of Freud. Read it to appreciate his intuitive genius and his writing style. Most of Freud's writings are available in a variety of inexpensive editions.

———. Introductory lectures on psycho-analysis. In *Standard edition* (Vols. 15, 16). (Originally published, 1916.)

Two courses of lectures given at the University of Vienna. The first part of the book assumes no knowledge of the subject; the second part assumes familiarity with the first. Lectures to and for students.

———. (1957). *A general selection from the works of Sigmund Freud* (John Rickman, Ed.). New York: Doubleday.

A good set of readings taken from different parts of Freud's work. Other collections may be as good. We like this one.

———. (1963). *Three case histories.* New York: Collier Books.

Three cases that Freud analyzed. He presents material from the cases, interweaving it with his developing theory. This is as close to seeing Freud in action as can be gleaned from his writings.

Books About Freud and His Ideas

Gay, P. (1988). *Freud: A life for our time.* New York: W. W. Norton.

The best biography of Freud available. Gay neither attacks nor defends Freud, avoiding the subjectivity that is the fault of most of the other biographies. He understands the era as well as the man.

Hall, C. S. (1954). *A primer of Freudian psychology.* New York: New American Library (Mentor Books).

A short, readable, and lucid exposition of the major features of Freud's theories. It is compact and accurate. The best easy introduction available.

Hall, C., & Lindzey, G. (1968). The relevance of Freudian psychology and related viewpoints for the social sciences. In G. Lindzey & E. Arronson (Eds.), *The handbook of social psychology* (2nd ed.). Menlo Park, CA: Addison-Wesley.

An intermediate-level summary of psychoanalytic thinking, with emphasis on its relevance to social psychology; a theoretical rather than clinical focus.

Rapaport, D. (1959). The structure of psychoanalytic theory. In S. Koch (Ed.), *Psychology: The study of a science: Vol. 3. Formulations of the person and the social context.* New York: McGraw-Hill.

Among the most sophisticated and complete theoretical statements of psychoanalytic thinking. Not for the fainthearted.

Roazen, P. (1993). *Meeting Freud's family.* Amherst: University of Massachusetts Press.

Good fun if you've become interested in the strange and often silly stories about the relationships at the center of the psychoanalytic world and those within Freud's household as well.

Sulloway, F. (1979). *Freud, biologist of the mind: Beyond the psychoanalytic legend.* New York: Basic Books.

Suggests that Freud was more aligned with biology than with psychology. A more human, less heroic view of him than usual, solidly based on historical documents. Disagrees with Ernest Jones on matters of fact and opinion. Endless references.

Books About Psychoanalysis

Bergman, M., & Hartman, F. (Eds.). (1976). *The evolution of psychoanalytic technique.* New York: Basic Books.

Collected papers from the first wave of movements and changes, arising out of Freud's original thinking. The work of those who felt that they stayed within the fold. Contributors include Erikson, Fenichel, Ferenczi, Alexander, and Reich.

———. (1972). *The fallacy of understanding. An inquiry into the changing structure of psychoanalysis.* New York: Basic Books.

A delightful musing about the way in which we see and interpret Freud's work from a vantage point years later and cultures apart. Their sensible rethinking of Freud's basic ideas and how they were first expressed and understood is a fresh look that stresses utility.

Levenson, E., & Mitchell, S. (1988). *Relational concepts in psychoanalysis: An integration.* Cambridge, MA: Harvard University Press.

A valiant and often compelling attempt to integrate a number of the successful offshoots from traditional psychoanalysis, including self psychology, existential psychoanalysis, object relations theories, and interpersonal psychoanalysis. Not for the fainthearted.

Schafer, R. (1983). *The analytic attitude.* New York: Basic Books.

An exploration of the inner workings of the mind of the analyst during therapy itself, by a professor of psychiatry at the Columbia University Medical Center for Psychoanalytic Training and Research. Widely read, used, and praised by professionals.

Psychoanalytic Books About Women

Jordan, J., Kaplan, A., Miller, J., Striver, I., & Surrey, J. (1991). *Woman's growth in connection.* New York: Guilford Press.

These authors are the best post-Freudian theorists writing about women. Not limited to psychoanalytic concerns.

Mitchell, J. (1974). *Psychoanalysis and feminism.* New York: Pantheon.

Mitchell explores at length the usefulness of psychoanalytic theory in contributing to an understanding of women's psychology in Western, male-dominated society. Mitchell is strongly and openly a feminist, and it is as a feminist that she examines psychoanalysis as put forth by Freud and various theorists since Freud. A critique of various feminist criticisms of these same theories—psychoanalysis in particular—is offered.

Ruitenbeck, H. (Ed.). (1966). *Psychoanalysis and female sexuality.* New Haven, CT: College and University Press.

A collection of psychoanalytic papers on female sexuality. Included are essays by Jones, Thompson, Horney, Freud, Greenacre, Riviere, and, somewhat surprisingly, Maslow.

References

Auden, W. H. (1945). *The collected poems of W. H. Auden.* New York: Random House.

Benjamin, L., & Dixon, D. (1996). Dream analysis by mail: An American woman seeks Freud's advice. *American Psychologist, 51*(5), 461–468.

Bergeret, J. (1991). 1983: The psychoanalytic glasnost. *Revue française de Psychanalyse, 55*(1), 111–116.

Bettelheim, B. (1982, March 1). Reflections: Freud and the soul. *The New Yorker,* pp. 52–93.

Bonaparte, M. (Ed.). (1954). *The origins of psychoanalysis: Letters to Wilhelm Fliess.* London: Imago.

Breuer, J., & Freud, S. (1953–1966). Studies in hysteria. In J. Strachey (Ed. and Trans.), *The standard edition of the complete psychological works of Sigmund Freud* (Vol. 2). London: Hogarth Press. (Originally published, 1895.)

Bruner, J. (1956). Freud and the image of man. *Partisan Review,* 23, 340–347.

Byck, R. (Ed.). (1975). *Cocaine papers by Sigmund Freud.* New York: New American Library.

Carroy, J. (1991). "My interpreter with German readers": Freud and the French history of hypnosis. *Psychanalyse à l'Université, 16*(62), 97–113.

Cohen, M. (1982). *Putting energy back into Freud.* Unpublished doctoral dissertation, California Institute of Transpersonal Psychology.

Colby, K. M. (1951). *A primer for psychotherapists.* New York: Ronald Press.

Decker, H. (1991). *Freud, Dora, and Vienna 1900.* New York: Free Press.

Diller, J. (1991). *Freud's Jewish identity: A case study in the impact of ethnicity.* Rutherford, England: Associated University Presses.

Emmanuel, D. (1992). A developmental model of girls and women. *Progress: Family Systems Research and Therapy, 1*(1), 25–40.

Farber, L. H. (1966). *The ways of the will: Essays toward a psychology and psycho-pathology of will.* New York: Harper & Row.

Fenichel, O. (1945). *The psychoanalytic theory of neurosis.* New York: Norton.

Ferenczi, S. (1955). *Final contributions to the problems and methods of psychoanalysis.* London: Hogarth Press/New York: Basic Books.

Fliegel, Z. O. (1973). Feminine psychosexual development in Freudian theory: A historical reconstruction. *The Psychoanalytic Quarterly, 42*(3), 385–408.

Fodor, N., & Gaynor, F. (1958). *Freud: Dictionary of psychoanalysis.* New York: Fawcett Books.

Freud, A. (1936). *The ego and the mechanisms of defense.* London: Hogarth Press.

Freud, E. (1961). *Letters of Sigmund Freud*. New York: Basic Books.

Freud, S. The neuro-psychoses of defense. In J. Strachey (Ed. and Trans.), *The standard edition of the complete psychological works of Sigmund Freud* (Vol. 3). London: Hogarth Press, 1953–1966. (Originally published, 1894.)

———. The interpretation of dreams. In *Standard edition* (Vols. 4, 5). (Originally published, 1900.)

———. The psychopathology of everyday life. In *Standard edition* (Vol. 6). (Originally published, 1901.)

———. Three essays on the theory of sexuality. In *Standard edition* (Vol. 7). (Originally published, 1905a.)

———. Fragment of an analysis of a case of hysteria. In *Standard edition* (Vol. 8). (Originally published, 1905b.)

———. Psycho-analysis and the establishment of the facts in legal proceedings. In *Standard edition* (Vol. 9). (Originally published, 1906.)

———. Obsessive actions and religious practices. In *Standard edition* (Vol. 9). (Originally published, 1907.)

———. Notes upon a case of obsessional neurosis. In *Standard edition* (Vol. 10). (Originally published, 1909.)

———. Five lectures on psycho-analysis. In *Standard edition* (Vol. 11). (Originally published, 1910.)

———. Formulations on the two principles of mental functioning. In *Standard edition* (Vol. 12). (Originally published, 1911.)

———. On the history of the psycho-analytic movement. In *Standard edition* (Vol. 14). (Originally published, 1914.)

———. Introductory lectures on psycho-analysis (Part III). In *Standard edition* (Vol. 16). (Originally published, 1916.)

———. On the transformations of instinct, as exemplified in anal eroticism. In *Standard edition* (Vol. 17). (Originally published, 1917.)

———. Lines of advance in psycho-analytic therapy. In *Standard edition* (Vol. 17). (Originally published, 1919.)

———. Beyond the pleasure principle. In *Standard edition* (Vol. 18). (Originally published, 1920.)

———. Two encyclopedia articles. In *Standard edition* (Vol. 18). (Originally published, 1923.)

———. An autobiographical study. In *Standard edition* (Vol. 20). (Originally published, 1925a.) (Also, *Autobiography*. New York: Norton, 1935.)

———. Some psychical consequences of the anatomical distinctions between the sexes. In *Standard edition* (Vol. 19). (Originally published, 1925b.)

———. The question of lay analysis. In *Standard edition* (Vol. 20). (Originally published, 1926.)

———. Civilization and its discontents. In *Standard edition* (Vol. 21). (Originally published, 1930.)

———. New introductory lectures on psycho-analysis. In *Standard edition* (Vol. 22). (Originally published, 1933.) (Also, New York: Norton, 1949.)

———. Analysis terminable and interminable. In *Standard edition* (Vol. 23). (Originally published, 1937.)

———. An outline of psycho-analysis. In *Standard edition* (Vol. 23). (Originally published, 1940.) (Also, New York: Norton, 1949.)

———. (1950). *The origins of psycho-analysis* (including 1895, A project for a scientific psychology). London: Hogarth Press.

———. (1963). *The cocaine papers*. Zurich: Duquin Press. (Papers not reprinted in *The Standard edition;* originally published, 1884–1887.)

Fromm, E. (1959). *Sigmund Freud's mission: An analysis of his personality and influence*. New York: Harper & Row.

Fuller, R. (1992). Biographical origins of psychological ideas: Freud's cocaine studies. *Journal of Humanistic Psychology, 32*(3), 67–86.

Gay, P. (1988). *Freud: A life for our time*. New York: W. W. Norton.

Godde, G. (1991a). Freud's philosophical discussion circles in his student years. *Jahrbuch der Psychoanalyse, 27,* 73–113.

———. (1991b). Schopenhauer's anticipation of Freudian metapsychology. *Psyche Zeitschrift für Psychoanalyse und ihre Anwendungen, 45*(11), 944–1033.

Goleman, D. (1990, February 7). Freud's reputation shrinks a little. *The New York Times,* (c) 1, 4.

Grunbaum, A. (1994). A brief appraisal of Freud's dream theory. *Dreaming, 4*(1), 80–82.

Halt, R. R. (1965). A review of some of Freud's biological assumptions and their influence on his theories. In N. S. Greenfield & W. C. Lewis (Eds.), *Psychoanalysis and current biological thought*. Madison: University of Wisconsin Press.

Hamilton, J. (1991). A reconsideration of the Freud-Tausk-Deutch relationship. *Psychoanalytic Review, 78*(2), 267–278.

Herzog, P. (1991). *Conscious and unconscious: Freud's dynamic distinction reconsidered*. Madison, CT: International Universities Press.

Horacek, B. J. (1991). Toward a more viable model of breathing: Consequences for older persons. *Journal of Death Studies, 15*(5), 459–472.

Personal Reflection

■ The Persona

List your favorite articles of clothing, jewelry, or other possessions that you generally carry, a purse or backpack, for example. Choose the one article that you feel most represents *you,* that somehow is an integral part of your self-image. Choose something that you wear or carry most of the time.

1. Go without the item for a week and note your reactions to its absence.
2. Lend the item to a friend. How does it feel to you to see a favorite possession worn or used by someone else?

tudes that impinge on them. The persona is, in addition, a valuable tool for communication. In Roman drama the actors' boldly drawn masks informed the entire audience clearly, if somewhat stereotypically, of the personality and attitudes of the role each actor was playing. The persona can often be crucial to our positive development. As we begin to play a certain role, our ego gradually comes to identify with it. This process is central to personality development.

This process is not always positive, however. As the ego identifies with the persona, people start to believe that they are what they pretend to be. According to Jung, we eventually have to withdraw this identification and learn who we are in the process of self-realization, or individuation. Minority group members and other social outsiders in particular are likely to have problems with their identities, because of cultural prejudice and social rejection of their personas (Hopcke, 1995).

The persona may be expressed by objects we use to cover ourselves (clothing or a veil) and by the tools of an occupation (shovel or briefcase). Thus ordinary items become symbols of the individual's identity. The term *status symbol* (car, house, or diploma) conveys society's understanding of the importance of image. All of these symbols can be found in dreams as representations of the persona. For example, someone with a strong persona may appear in a dream as overdressed, or constricted by too much clothing. A person with a weak persona might appear naked and exposed. One possible expression of an inadequate persona would be a figure that has no skin.

The Shadow

How can I be substantial without casting a shadow? I must have a dark side too if I am to be whole; and by becoming conscious of my shadow I remember once more that I am a human being like any other. (Jung, 1931c, p. 59)

The **shadow** is an archetypal form that serves as the focus for material that has been repressed from consciousness; its contents include those tendencies, desires, memories, and experiences that are rejected by the individual as incompatible with the persona and contrary to social standards and ideals. The shadow contains all the negative tendencies the individual wishes to deny, including animal instincts, as well as undeveloped positive and negative qualities.

The stronger our persona is and the more we identify with it, the more we deny other parts of ourselves. The shadow represents what we consider to be inferior in our personality and also that which we have neglected and never developed in ourselves. In dreams, a shadow figure may appear as an animal, a dwarf, a vagrant, or any other low-status figure.

In his work on repression and neurosis, Freud focused primarily on aspects of what Jung calls the shadow. Jung found that the repressed material is organized and structured around the shadow, which becomes, in a sense, a negative self, or the shadow of the ego. The shadow is often experienced in dreams as a dark, primitive, hostile, or repellent figure, because the contents of the shadow have been forcibly pushed out of consciousness and appear antagonistic to the conscious outlook. If the material from the shadow is allowed back into consciousness, it loses much of its primitive and frightening quality.

The shadow is most dangerous when unrecognized. Then the individual tends to project his or her unwanted qualities onto others or to become dominated by the shadow without realizing it. Images of evil, the devil, and the concept of original sin are all aspects of the shadow archetype. The more the shadow material is made conscious, the less it can dominate. But the shadow is an integral part of our nature, and it can never be simply eliminated. A person who claims to be without a shadow is not a complete individual but a two-dimensional caricature, denying the mixture of good and evil that is necessarily present in all of us.

The Jungian approach to the shadow has been the subject of many popular books and articles (see Abrams & Zweig, 1991, and Abrams, 1994, for a look at the shadow in America).

The ancient Chinese sage Chuang-tzu (369–286 B.C.) provides an approach to dealing with the shadow that is remarkably similar to Jung's approach:

> There was a man
> who was so disturbed
> by the sight of his own shadow
> and so displeased with his own footsteps
> that he determined to get rid of both.
> The method he hit upon was to run away from them.
> So he got up and ran.
> But every time he put his foot down
> there was another step,
> while his shadow kept up with him
> without the slightest difficulty.
> He attributed his failure
> to the fact that he was not running fast enough.
> So he ran faster and faster, without stopping,
> until he finally dropped dead.
> He failed to realize
> that if he merely stepped into the shade,
> his shadow would vanish,
> and if he sat down and stayed still,
> there would be no more footsteps. (In Merton, 1965, p. 155)

Each repressed portion of the shadow represents a part of ourselves. To the extent that we keep this material unconscious, we limit ourselves. As the shadow is made more conscious, we regain previously repressed parts of ourselves. Also, the shadow is not simply a negative force in the psyche. It is a storehouse for considerable instinctual energy, spontaneity, and vitality, and it is a major source of our creative energies. Like all archetypes, the shadow is rooted in the collective unconscious, and it can allow the individual access to much of the valuable unconscious material that is rejected by the ego and the persona.

The following passage from one of Jung's letters provides a clear illustration of Jung's concept of the shadow and of the unconscious in general:

> It is a very difficult and important question, what you call the technique of dealing with the shadow. There is, as a matter of fact, no technique at all, inasmuch as technique means that there is a known and perhaps even prescribable way to deal with a certain difficulty or task. It is rather a dealing comparable to diplomacy or statesmanship. There is, for instance, no particular technique that would help us to reconcile two political parties opposing each other. . . . If one can speak of a technique at all, it consists solely in an attitude. First of all, one has to accept and to take seriously into account the existence of the shadow. Secondly, it is necessary to be informed about its qualities and intentions. Thirdly, long and difficult negotiations will be unavoidable. . . .
>
> Nobody can know what the final outcome of such negotiations will be. One only knows that through careful collaboration the problem itself becomes changed. Very often certain apparently impossible intentions of the shadow are mere threats due to an unwillingness on the part of the ego to enter upon a serious consideration of the shadow. Such threats diminish usually when one meets them seriously. (1973, p. 234)

Just when we think we understand it, the shadow will appear in another form. Dealing with the shadow is a lifelong process of looking within and honestly reflecting on what we see there. It is also important to remain grounded in our central, authentic core, our innermost self (von Franz, 1995).

Anima and Animus

Jung postulated an unconscious structure that is the complement of the persona. Jung calls this the **anima** in man and the **animus** in woman. This basic psychic structure serves as a focus for all the psychological material that does not fit with an individual's conscious self-image as a man or as a woman. Thus to the extent that a woman consciously defines herself in feminine terms, her animus will include those unrecognized tendencies and experiences that she has defined as masculine.

For a woman the process of psychological development entails entering into a dialogue between her ego and her animus. The animus may be pathologically dominated by identification with archetypal images (for example, the bewitched prince, the romantic poet, the ghostly lover, or the marauding pirate) and/or by an extreme father fixation.

The animus is initially viewed as a wholly separate personality. As the animus and its influence on the individual is recognized, the animus assumes the role of liaison between conscious and unconscious until it gradually becomes

Personal Reflection

The Shadow

One aspect of the shadow can be personified by a small demon, an imp dedicated to harming you or foiling your best-laid plans. It may appear as an implacable inner critic or as a demanding judge. The following is intended to help you better understand this aspect of your shadow.

1. Think about how you would describe *in detail* your personal demon and how it operates in your life. When does it appear? Do any triggers seem to bring it out?
2. If you were to personify this aspect of the shadow, what would it look like? Does it have a name? How would it dress? What would some of its favorite expressions be?
3. Communicate with this figure. Discuss its good qualities. How has it helped you? Also examine how it has fostered or arrested your personal change or growth.
4. What inner figure would be the opposite of the personal demon? With this opposite figure in mind, review steps 1 to 3.

integrated into the self. Jung views the quality of this union of opposites (in this case, masculine and feminine) as the major determinant of female personality functioning.

A similar process occurs between the anima and the masculine ego in the male. As long as our anima or animus is unconscious, not accepted as part of our self, we will tend to project it outward onto people of the opposite sex:

> Every man carries within him the eternal image of woman, not the image of this or that particular woman, but a definitive feminine image. This image is . . . an imprint or "archetype" of all the ancestral experiences of the female, a deposit, as it were, of all the impressions ever made by woman. . . . Since this image is unconscious, it is always unconsciously projected upon the person of the beloved, and is one of the chief reasons for passionate attraction or aversion. (Jung, 1931b, p. 198)

According to Jung, the child's opposite-sex parent is a major influence on the development of the anima or animus. All relations with the opposite sex, including parents, are strongly affected by the projection of anima or animus fantasies. This archetype is one of the most influential regulators of behavior. It appears in dreams and fantasies as figures of the opposite sex, and it functions as the primary mediator between unconscious and conscious processes. It is oriented primarily toward inner processes, just as the persona is oriented to the outer. It is a source of projections, a source of image making, and a door to creativity in the psyche. (The creative influence of the anima can be seen in artists who have depicted their muses as female goddesses.) Jung also called this

Personal Reflection

■ Seeing Ourselves in Others

List all the qualities you admire in the person you love or respect most. Then list all the qualities you dislike in the person you respect the least.

The first list most likely contains your anima or animus projections—those qualities you have inside you that you can develop. The second list contains your shadow projections—those qualities that you must confront within yourself.

archetype the "soul image." Because it has the capacity to bring us in touch with our unconscious forces, it is often the key to unlocking our creativity.

The Self

The archetype of the individual is the Self. The Self is all-embracing. God is a circle whose center is everywhere and whose circumference is nowhere. (Jung in McGuire & Hull, 1977, p. 86)

The **self** is the most important archetype and also the most difficult to understand. Jung has called the self the *central archetype,* the archetype of psychological order and the totality of the personality. The self is the archetype of centeredness. It is the union of the conscious and the unconscious that embodies the harmony and balance of the various opposing elements of the psyche. The self directs the functioning of the whole psyche in an integrated way. According to Jung, "[C]onscious and unconscious are not necessarily in opposition to one another, but complement one another to form a totality, which is the *self*" (1928b, p. 175). Jung discovered the self archetype only after his investigations of the other structures of the personality.

The self is depicted in dreams or images impersonally (as a circle, mandala, crystal, or stone) or personally (as a royal couple, a divine child, or some other symbol of divinity). Great spiritual teachers, such as Christ, Muhammed, and Buddha, are also symbols for the self. These are all symbols of wholeness, unification, reconciliation of polarities, and dynamic equilibrium—the goals of the individuation process (Edinger, 1996). Jung explains the function of the self:

> The ego receives the light from the Self. Though we know of this Self, yet it is not known. . . . Although we receive the light of consciousness from the Self and although we know it to be the source of our illumination, we do not know whether it possesses anything we would call consciousness. . . . If the Self could be wholly experienced, it would be a limited experience, whereas in reality its experience is unlimited and endless. . . . If I were one with the Self I would have knowledge of everything, I would speak Sanskrit, read cuneiform script, know the events that took place in pre-history, be acquainted with the life of other planets, etc. (1975, pp. 194–195)

The self is a deep, inner, guiding factor, which can seem to be quite different, even alien, from the ego and consciousness. "The self is not only the centre, but also the whole circumference which embraces both conscious and unconscious; it is the centre of this totality, just as the ego is the centre of consciousness" (1936b, p. 41). It may first appear in dreams as a tiny, insignificant image, because the self is so unfamiliar and undeveloped in most people. The development of the self does not mean that the ego is dissolved. The ego remains the center of consciousness, an important structure within the psyche. It becomes linked to the self as the result of the long, hard work of understanding and accepting unconscious processes.

Symbols

According to Jung, the unconscious expresses itself primarily through symbols. Although no specific symbol or image can ever fully represent an archetype (which is a form without specific content), the more closely a symbol conforms to the unconscious material organized around an archetype, the more it evokes a strong, emotionally charged response.

> The symbol has a very complex meaning because it defies reason; it always presupposes a lot of meanings that can't be comprehended in a single logical concept. The symbol has a future. The past does not suffice to interpret it, because germs of the future are included in every actual situation. That's why, in elucidating a case, the symbolism is spontaneously applicable, for it contains the future. (Jung in McGuire & Hull, 1977, p. 143)

As a plant produces its flower, so the psyche creates its symbols. (Jung, 1964, p. 64)

Jung is concerned with two kinds of symbols: individual and collective. By individual symbols Jung means "natural" symbols that are spontaneous productions of the individual psyche, rather than images or designs created deliberately by an artist. In addition to the personal symbols found in an individual's dreams or fantasies, there are important collective symbols, which are often religious images, such as the cross, the six-pointed Star of David, and the Buddhist wheel of life.

Symbolic terms and images represent concepts that we cannot completely define or fully comprehend. Symbols always have connotations that are unclear or hidden from us. For Jung, a sign *stands for* something else, but a symbol, such as a tree, *is* something in itself—a dynamic, living thing. A symbol may represent the individual's psychic situation, and it *is* that situation at a given moment.

Active Imagination Jung valued the use of active imagination as a means of facilitating self-understanding through work with symbols. He encouraged his patients to paint, sculpt, or employ some other art form as a way to explore their inner depths. Active imagination is not passive fantasy but an attempt to engage the unconscious in a dialogue with the ego, through symbols.

Active imagination refers to any conscious effort to produce material directly related to unconscious processes, to relax our usual ego controls without allowing the unconscious to take over completely. The process of active imagination differs for each individual. Some people use drawing or painting most profitably, whereas others prefer to use conscious imagery, or fantasy, or some other form of expression.

Jung himself used a variety of outlets to explore his unconscious. He designed his retreat house in Bollingen according to his inner needs, and, as he himself developed, he added wings to the house. Jung also painted murals on

is based on a more complex theory of the psyche than Maslow's. "Individuation means becoming a single, homogeneous being, and, insofar as 'individuality' embraces our innermost, last, and incomparable uniqueness, it also implies becoming one's own self. We could therefore translate individuation as 'coming to selfhood' or 'self-realization' " (Jung, 1928b, p. 171).

Individuation is a natural, organic process. It is the unfolding of our basic nature, and is a fundamental drive in each of us. As Jung has written, "it is what makes a tree turn into a tree" (in McGuire & Hull, 1977, p. 210). Like any natural process, it can become blocked or interfered with, just as the growth of a tree may become stunted in an unfavorable environment.

Individuation is a process of achieving wholeness and thus moving toward greater freedom. The process includes development of a dynamic relationship between the ego and the self, along with the integration of the various parts of the psyche: the ego, persona, shadow, anima or animus, and the other unconscious archetypes. As people become more individuated, these archetypes may be seen as expressing themselves in more subtle and complex ways.

> The more we become conscious of ourselves through self-knowledge, and act accordingly, the more the layer of the personal unconscious that is superimposed on the collective unconscious will be diminished. In this way there arises a consciousness which is no longer imprisoned in the petty, oversensitive, personal world of objective interests. This widened consciousness is no longer that touchy, egotistical bundle of personal wishes, fears, hopes, and ambitions. . . . [I]nstead, it is a function of relationship to the world of objects, bringing the individual into absolute, binding, and indissoluble communion with the world at large. (Jung, 1928b, p. 176)

Everything that happens to us, properly understood, leads us back to ourselves; it is as though there were some unconscious guidance whose aim it is to deliver us from all this and make us dependent on ourselves. (Jung, 1973, p. 78)

As an analyst, Jung found that those who came to him in the first half of life were relatively uninvolved with the inner process of individuation; they were concerned primarily with emergence as an individual, external achievement, and the attainment of the goals of the ego. Older patients, who had fulfilled such goals reasonably well, tended to develop different aims: to strive for integration rather than achievement and to seek harmony with the totality of the psyche.

From the point of view of the ego, growth and development consist of integrating new material into one's consciousness; this process includes the acquisition of knowledge of the world and of oneself. Growth, for the ego, is essentially the expansion of conscious awareness. Individuation, by contrast, is the development of the self, and from the point of view of the self, the goal is the union of consciousness and the unconscious.

Unveiling the Persona Early in the individuation process, we must begin the unveiling of the persona and view it as a useful tool rather than as a permanent part of ourselves. Although the persona has important protective functions, it is also a mask that hides the self and the unconscious.

> When we analyze the persona we strip off the mask, and discover that what seemed to be individual is at bottom collective; in other words, that the persona was only a mask for the collective psyche. Fundamentally the per-

> sona is nothing real: it is a compromise between individual and society as to what a man should appear to be. He takes a name, earns a title, represents an office, he is this or that. In a certain sense all this is real, yet in relation to the essential individuality of the person concerned it is only secondary reality, a product of compromise, in making which others often have a greater share than he. (Jung, 1928b, p. 156)

In becoming aware of the limitations and distortions of the persona, we become more independent of our culture and our society.

Confronting the Shadow When we look beyond mere appearances, we are forced to confront the shadow. We can become free of the shadow's influence to the extent that we accept the reality of the dark side in each of us and simultaneously realize that we are more than the shadow.

Confronting the Anima or Animus A further step is to confront the anima or animus. We must deal with this archetype as a real person or persons that we can communicate with and learn from. For example, Jung would ask the anima figures that appeared to him about the interpretation of dream symbols, like an analysand consulting an analyst. We also become aware that the anima or animus figures have considerable autonomy and that they are likely to influence or even dominate us if we ignore them or blindly accept their images and projections as our own personal productions.

Developing the Self The goal and culmination of the individuation process is the development of the self. "The self is our life's goal, for it is the completest expression of that fateful combination we call individuality" (Jung, 1928b, p. 238). The self replaces the ego as the midpoint of the psyche. Awareness of the self brings unity to the psyche and helps to integrate conscious and unconscious material: "The aim of individuation is nothing less than to divest the self of the false wrappings of the persona on the one hand, and of the suggestive power of primordial images on the other" (Jung, 1945, p. 174). The ego is still the center of consciousness, but it is no longer seen as the nucleus of the entire personality.

The unconscious mind of man sees correctly even when conscious reason is blind and impotent. (Jung, 1952b, p. 386)

Jung wrote that

> one must be what one is; one must discover one's own individuality, that centre of personality, which is equidistant between the conscious and the unconscious; we must aim for that ideal point towards which nature appears to be directing us. Only from that point can one satisfy one's needs. (In Serrano, 1966, p. 91)

Although it is possible to describe individuation in terms of stages, the process is considerably more complex than the simple progression outlined here. All of the steps listed overlap, and each of us continually returns to old problems and issues (hopefully from a different perspective). Individuation might be represented as a spiral in which we keep confronting the same basic questions, each time in a more precise form. (This concept is closely related to

Mohandas Gandhi: An individuated leader

the Zen Buddhist conception of enlightenment, in which an individual never solves a personal *koan,* or spiritual problem, and the searching is seen as a goal in itself.)

Obstacles to Growth

Individuation, consciously undertaken, is a difficult task, and the individual must be relatively psychologically healthy to handle the process. The ego must be strong enough to undergo tremendous changes, to be turned inside out in the process of individuation:

> One could say that the whole world with its turmoil and misery is in an individuation process. But people don't know it, that's the only difference. . . . Individuation is by no means a rare thing or a luxury of the few, but those who know that they are in such a process are considered to be lucky. They get something out of it, provided they are conscious enough. (Jung, 1973, p. 442)

This process is especially difficult because it is an individual enterprise, often carried out in the face of the rejection or, at best, indifference of others. Jung writes that

> nature cares nothing whatsoever about a higher level of consciousness; quite the contrary. And then society does not value these feats of the psyche very highly; its prizes are always given for achievement and not for personality, the latter being rewarded for the most part posthumously. (1931a, p. 394)

Each stage in the individuation process is accompanied by difficulties. First is the danger of identification with the persona. Those who identify with the persona may try to become "perfect," unable to accept their mistakes or weaknesses as well as any deviations from their idealized self-concepts. Individuals who *fully* identify with the persona tend to repress any tendencies that do not fit the self-image and attribute such behaviors to others; the job of acting out aspects of the repressed, negative identity is assigned to other people.

The shadow can also become a major obstacle to individuation. People who are unaware of their shadows can easily act out harmful impulses without ever recognizing them as wrong or without any awareness of their own negative feelings. In such people, an initial impulse to harm or do wrong is instantly rationalized as they fail to acknowledge the presence of such an impulse in themselves. Ignorance of the shadow may also result in an attitude of moral superiority and projection of the shadow onto others. For example, some of those loudly in favor of the censorship of pornography seem to be fascinated by the materials they want to ban; they may even convince themselves of the need to study carefully all the available pornography in order to be effective censors.

> Filling the conscious mind with ideal conceptions is a characteristic feature of Western theosophy. . . . One does not become enlightened by imagining figures of light, but by making the darkness conscious. (Jung, 1954a, pp. 265–266)

Confronting the anima or animus brings with it the problem of relating to the collective unconscious. In the man, the anima may produce sudden emotional changes or moodiness. In the woman, the animus may manifest itself as irrational, rigidly held opinions. Jung's discussion of anima and animus is not a description of masculinity and femininity in general. The content of the anima or animus is the complement of our conscious conception of ourselves as masculine or feminine—which, in most people, is strongly determined by cultural values and socially defined sex roles.

An individual who is exposed to collective material faces the danger of becoming engulfed by it. According to Jung, this outcome can take one of two forms. First, there is the possibility of ego inflation, in which the individual claims all the virtues and knowledge of the collective psyche. The opposite reaction is that of ego impotence; the person feels that he or she has no control over the collective psyche and becomes acutely aware of unacceptable aspects of the unconscious—irrationality, negative impulses, and so forth.

As in many myths and fairy tales, the greatest obstacles are those found closest to the goal (von Franz, 1995). When the individual deals with the anima and animus, tremendous energy is unleashed. This energy can be used to build up the ego instead of developing the self. Jung has referred to this as identification with the archetype of the mana-personality. (*Mana* is a Melanesian word for the energy or power that emanates from people, objects, or supernatural beings; it is energy that has an occult or bewitching quality.) The ego identifies with the archetype of the wise man or wise woman, the sage who knows everything. (This syndrome is not uncommon among older university professors, for example.) The mana-personality is dangerous because it is a false exaggeration of power. Individuals stuck at this stage try to be both more and less than they really are: more, because they tend to believe they have become perfect, holy, or even godlike; but actually less, because they have lost touch with their essential humanity and the fact that no one is infallible, flawless, and perfectly wise.

Not perfection, but completeness is what is expected of you. (Jung, 1973, p. 97)

Jung sees temporary identification with the archetype of the self or the mana-personality as being almost inevitable in the individuation process. The best defense against the development of ego inflation is to remember one's essential humanity and to stay grounded in the reality of what one can and must do, not what one *should* do or be.

Structure

Body

Psyche and body are not separate entities, but one and the same life. (Jung, 1917, p. 113)

In his voluminous writings, Jung did not deal explicitly with the role of the body but chose to direct his efforts to analyzing the psyche. He has argued that physical processes are relevant to us only to the extent that they are represented in the psyche. The physical body and the external world can be known only as psychological experiences: "I'm chiefly concerned with the psyche itself, therefore I'm leaving out body and spirit. . . . Body and spirit are to me mere aspects of the reality of the psyche. Psychic experience is the only immediate experience. Body is as metaphysical as spirit" (1973, p. 200). For Jung, it is the *experience* of the body that is all-important (Conger, 1988).

Social Relationships

Jung stresses that individuation is essentially a personal endeavor; however, it is also a process that develops through relationships with other people:

> As nobody can become aware of his individuality unless he is closely and responsibly related to his fellow beings, he is not withdrawing to an egoistic desert when he tries to find himself. He only can discover himself when he is deeply and unconditionally related to some, and generally related to a great many, individuals with whom he has a chance to compare, and from whom he is able to discriminate himself. (Jung in Serrano, 1966, pp. 83–84)

Individuation does not isolate, it connects. I never saw relationships thriving on unconsciousness. (Jung, 1973, p. 504)

Social interaction is important in the formation and development of the major personality structures: persona, shadow, and anima or animus. The contents of social experiences help determine the specific images and symbols associated with each structure; at the same time, these basic archetypal structures mold and guide our social relationships.

Will

Jung felt that individual will is a relatively recent human development. In primitive cultures, rituals (such as hunting dances) work tribal members into a state of action, a state that substitutes for our modern willpower:

> The will was practically nonexistent and it needed all the ceremonial which you observe in primitive tribes to bring up something that is an equivalent to our word "decision." Slowly through the ages we have acquired a certain amount of willpower. We could detach so much energy from the energy of nature, from the original unconsciousness, from the original flow of events, an amount of energy we could control. (Jung in McGuire & Hull, 1977, p. 103)

Jung defines the will as the energy that is at the disposal of consciousness or the ego. The development of the will is associated with learning cultural values, moral standards, and the like. Will has power only over conscious thought and action and cannot directly affect instinctual or other unconscious processes, although it has substantial, indirect power over them through conscious processes.

Emotions

Jung stresses the central role that the study of the emotions must play in psychology:

> Psychology is the only science that has to take the factor of value (i.e., feeling) into account, because it is the link between psychical events and life. Psychology is often accused of not being scientific on this account; but its critics fail to understand the scientific and practical necessity of giving due consideration to feeling. (1964, p. 99)

In my medical experience as well as in my own life I have again and again been faced with the mystery of love, and have never been able to explain what it is. (Jung, 1961, p. 353)

Psychic material that is directly related to the archetypes tends to arouse strong emotions and often has an awe-inspiring quality. When Jung discusses symbols, he is not writing about lifeless words or empty forms but about powerful, living realities by which men and women live their lives and for which many have died. According to Jung, emotion is the force behind the process of individuation; "Emotion is the chief source of consciousness" (1954b, p. 96). All real, inner change has an emotional component.

Intellect

For Jung, the intellect refers to directed, conscious thought processes. Jung distinguishes intellect from intuition, which draws strongly on unconscious material. The intellect has an important, but limited, role in psychological functioning. Jung stresses that a purely intellectual understanding cannot be complete: "A psychology that satisfies the intellect alone can never be practical, for the totality of the psyche can never be grasped by intellect alone" (1917, p. 117). The intellect works best in conjunction with intuition and feeling.

Therapist

A therapist who has a neurosis does not deserve the name, for it is not possible to bring the patient to a more advanced stage than one has reached oneself. (Jung, 1973, p. 95)

According to Jung, therapy is a joint effort between analyst and analysand working together as equals. Because the two form a dynamic unit, the analyst must also be open to change as a result of the interaction. Jung felt that therapy involves primarily the interaction of the analyst's unconscious with that of the analysand, who can advance in therapy only as far as the analyst has:

> It is a remarkable thing about psychotherapy: you cannot learn any recipes by heart and then apply them more or less suitably, but can cure only from one central point; and that consists in understanding the patient as a psychological whole and approaching him as a human being, leaving aside all theory and listening attentively to whatever he has to say. (1973, p. 456)

Any of my pupils could give you so much insight and understanding that you could treat yourself if you don't succumb to the prejudice that you receive healing through others. In the last resort every individual alone has to win his battle, nobody else can do it for him. (Jung, 1973, p. 126)

Jung tried to avoid reliance on theory and on specific techniques in the process of therapy. He believed that such reliance tends to make the analyst mechanical and out of touch with the analysand. The therapist does not merely treat parts of the psyche like a mechanic patching up an old car that needs a new carburetor or muffler. The aim of therapy is to approach the analysand as a whole individual through a genuine relationship.

Jung generally saw people only once or twice a week. To foster a sense of autonomy in analysands, he would often give them homework—for example, he might ask them to analyze their own dreams. At his insistence, his clients would take occasional vacations from analysis in order to avoid becoming dependent on him and on the analytic routine.

Jung has outlined two major stages of the therapeutic process, each of which has two parts. First comes the *analytic stage*. It consists initially of *confession,* in which the individual begins to recover unconscious material. Ties of dependency on the therapist tend to develop at this stage. Next comes *elucidation* of the confessional material, in which greater familiarity and understanding of psychic processes develops. The patient remains dependent on the therapist.

The serious problems in life, however, are never fully solved. If ever they should appear to be so it is a sure sign that something has been lost. The meaning and purpose of a problem seem to lie not in its solutions but in our working at it incessantly. (Jung, 1931a, p. 394)

The second stage of therapy is the *synthetic*. First comes *education,* in which Jung stressed the need to move from psychological insight to actual new experiences that result in individual growth and the formation of new habits. The final part is the *transformation*. The analysand-analyst relationship is integrated, and dependency is reduced as the relationship becomes transformed. The individual experiences a highly concentrated individuation process, though archetypal material is not necessarily confronted. This is the stage of self-education, in which the individual takes more and more responsibility for his or her own development.

Evaluation

Jung has often been criticized for his lack of a coherent, clearly structured system of thought. His writing sometimes seems to go off on tangents, rather than present ideas in a formal, logical, or even systematic fashion. Also, at different times Jung may use varying definitions for the same term. He was aware of this difficulty in his writing but did not see it as necessarily a drawback. Jung believed that life rarely follows the logical, coherent pattern that has become the standard for scientific and academic writing, and his own style may be closer to the rich complexity of psychological reality.

Jung deliberately developed an open system, one that could admit new information without distorting it to fit an inclusive, theoretical framework. He never believed that he knew all the answers or that new information would merely confirm his theories. Consequently, his theorizing lacks a tight, logical structure that categorizes all life in terms of a small number of theoretical constructs.

Religion and Mysticism

Because he dealt with religion, alchemy, spirituality, and the like, some critics have labeled Jung a mystic rather than a scientist. But it is clear that Jung's attitude was always that of an investigator rather than that of a believer or a disciple. To him, mystical belief systems were important expressions of human ideals and aspirations. Jung treated spiritual experiences as data that no one concerned with the full range of human thought and behavior should ignore.

I am a researcher and not a prophet. What matters to me is what can be verified by experience. But I am not interested at all in what can be speculated about experience without any proof. (Jung, 1973, p. 203)

> I am and remain a psychologist. I am not interested in anything that transcends the psychological content of human experience. . . . But on the psychological level I have to do with religious experiences which have a structure and a symbolism that can be interpreted. For me, religious experience is real, is true. I have found that through such religious experiences the soul may be "saved," its integration hastened, and spiritual equilibrium established. (Jung in McGuire and Hull, p. 229)

Jung saw clearly that a religious approach to life was closely related to psychological health:

> Among all my patients in the second half of life—that is to say, over thirty-five—there has not been one whose problem in the last resort was not that of finding a religious outlook on life. It is safe to say that every one of them fell ill because he had lost what the living religions of every age have given to their followers, and none of them has been really healed who did not regain his religious outlook. (1932, p. 334)

Jung's stress on the practical importance of spirituality is evident in a letter that he wrote to Bill Wilson, the cofounder of Alcoholics Anonymous. In the letter, Jung wrote about an alcoholic patient, Roland H., saying that Roland's addiction to alcohol was hopeless unless "he could become the subject of a spiritual or religious experience—in short a genuine conversion." Jung greatly influenced Wilson in his own conversion and cure as well as in his cofounding AA in 1934. The following is an excerpt from the letter Jung wrote to Wilson:

The main interest of my work is not concerned with the treatment of neuroses but rather with the approach to the numinous [a sense of the holy]. But the fact is that the approach to the numinous is the real therapy and inasmuch as you attain to the numinous experiences you are released from the curse of pathology. (Jung, 1973, p. 377)

> I had no news from Roland H. and often wondered what has been his fate. . . . His craving for alcohol was the equivalent, on a low level, of the spiritual thirst of our being for wholeness, expressed in medieval language: the union with God.
>
> How could one formulate such an insight in a language that is not misunderstood in our days?
>
> The only right and legitimate way to such an experience is that it happens to you in reality, and it can only happen to you when you walk on a path which leads you to higher understanding. You might be led to that goal by an act of grace or through a personal and honest contact with friends, or through a higher education of the mind beyond the confines of mere rationalism. . . .

> You see, "alcohol" in Latin is *spiritus,* and you use the same word for the highest religious experience as well as for the most depraving poison. The helpful formula therefore is: *spiritus contra spiritum.* (1984, pp. 197–198)

Jung's inspiration in the founding of Alcoholics Anonymous and the 12-step movement may have been one of his greatest contributions to modern society.

The Analysis of Symbols

Psychic development cannot be accomplished by intention and will alone; it needs the attraction of a symbol. (Jung, 1928a, p. 25)

Jung's recognition of the importance of symbols and his detailed analysis of symbols and their interpretations are his most important contributions to psychology. Jung was deeply aware of the complexity of symbolism and of the need to analyze symbols without oversimplifying. He was drawn to mythology, folklore, and alchemy because they provided various contexts that shed light on the complex symbolic productions he encountered in analysis.

Although Jung's writing is difficult to comprehend, it is perhaps more valuable than simpler or more logical prose because it conveys the richness of his thinking. His flexibility and open-mindedness, and his concern for the deeper truths of human existence, give Jung's work a breadth and complexity virtually unmatched in psychology.

Recent Developments: Jung's Influence

I can only hope and wish that no one becomes "Jungian." . . . I proclaim no cut-and-dried doctrine and I abhor "blind adherence." I leave everyone free to deal with the facts in his own way, since I also claim this freedom for myself. (Jung, 1973, p. 405)

Jung's ideas have been growing steadily in popularity and influence. The Jung Institute in Zurich still trains analysts from around the world. Jungian institutes in several countries and in major U.S. cities provide extensive research materials, lecture series, weekend workshops, and long-term training in Jungian analysis. The practice of Jungian analysis has continued to develop since Jung's death (see Stein, 1995).

The Myers-Briggs Type Indicator, based on Jung's theory of types, has become one of the most popular psychological tests in the world (Myers, 1980). Widely used today in business and in education, it has been taken by millions of people. Each individual is scored on introversion versus extraversion, thinking versus feeling, intuition versus sensation, and also perception versus judgment. This final category was added to Jung's basic scheme. *Perception* refers to an openness to new evidence and new experience. *Judgment* refers to the shutting out of new perceptions and coming to a quick decision.

Among the many prominent writers and scholars who have elaborated on Jung's ideas, Joseph Campbell applied Jungian concepts to topics including myth (1985, 1988) and the hero archetype (1949). James Hillman (1975, 1989), strongly influenced by Jung, developed an approach he calls *archetypal psychology.* Jean Shinoda Bolen (1984, 1989) has written two best-selling books on the archetypes of the goddesses in women and the gods in men. In their book *King, Warrior, Magician, Lover,* Robert Moore and Douglas Gillette (1990) describe the "archetypes of mature masculinity." One of the founders of the men's movement, Robert Bly (1990), has been strongly influenced by Jung's ideas.

There is a whole literature relating Jungian psychology and spirituality, primarily from a Christian perspective. This literature includes writings by Kelsey (1974, 1982) and by Sanford (1968, 1981). Caprio and Hedberg's (1986) *Coming Home: A Handbook for Exploring the Sanctuary Within* is a practical guide for spiritual work in the Christian tradition. It contains striking personal stories, excellent illustrations, and useful exercises.

Everything men assert about God is twaddle, for no man can know God. (Jung, 1975, p. 377)

For a fine look at the relationship between Jungian psychology and Buddhism, see Spiegelman and Miyuki (1985). Spiegelman (1982) has also written on the links between Jungian psychology and Jewish mysticism, as well as on the relationship between Jungian psychology and Hinduism (Spiegelman & Vasavada, 1987).

Jung's rich, complex, and sophisticated ideas are gradually gaining the widespread acceptance they so well deserve.

The Theory Firsthand

Excerpts from *Analytical Psychology*

Word Association

Jung's first introduction to depth *psychology came with his experiments in word association. He developed great expertise at interpreting associations. His intuitive abilities were often astonishing.*

Many years ago, when I was quite a young doctor, an old professor of criminology asked me about the experiment [in word association] and said he did not believe it. I said: "No, Professor? You can try it whenever you like." He invited me to his house and I began. After ten words he got tired and said: "What can you make of it? Nothing has come of it." I told him he could not expect a result with ten or twelve words; he ought to have a hundred and then we would see something. He said: "Can you do something with these words?" I said: "Little enough, but I can tell you something. Quite recently you have had worries about money, you have too little of it. You are afraid of dying of heart disease. You must have studied in France, where you had a love affair, and it has come back to your mind, as often, when one has thoughts of dying, old sweet memories come back from the womb of time." He said: "How do you know?" Any child could have seen it! He was a man of 72 and he had associated *heart* with *pain*—fear that he would die of heart failure. He associated *death* with *to die*—a natural reaction—and with *money* he associated *too little,* a very usual reaction. Then things became rather startling to me. To *pay,* after a long reaction time, he said *La Semeuse,* though our conversation was in German. That is the famous figure on the French coin. Now why on earth should this old man say *La Semeuse?* When he came to the word *kiss* there was a long reaction time and there was a light in his eyes and he said: *Beautiful.* Then of course I had the story. He would never have used French if it had not been associated with a particular feeling, and so we must think why he used it. Had he had losses with the French franc? There was no talk of inflation and devaluation in those days. That could not be the clue. I was in doubt whether it was money or love, but when he came to *kiss/beautiful* I knew it was love. He was not the kind of man to go to France in later life, but he had been a student in Paris, a lawyer, probably at the Sorbonne. It was relatively simple to stitch together the whole story. (Jung, 1968, p. 57)

Dream Analysis

The following excerpt illustrates Jung's approach to dream analysis:

I remember the case of a young girl who had been with two analysts before she came to me, and when she came to me she had the identical dream she had had when she was with those analysts. Each time at the very beginning of her analysis she had a particular dream: *She came to the frontier and she wanted to cross it, but she could not find the custom-house where she should have gone to declare whatever she carried with her.* In the first dream she was seeking the frontier, but she did not even come to it. That dream gave her the feeling that she would never be able to find the proper relation to her analyst; but because she had feelings of inferiority and did not trust her judgment, she remained with him, and nothing came of it at all. She worked with him for two months and then she left. [Then, she worked with another analyst for three months and left him as well.] . . .

When she came to me—she had seen me before at a lecture and had made up her mind to work with me—she dreamed that *she was coming to the Swiss frontier. It was day and she saw the custom-house. She crossed the frontier and she went into the custom-house, and there stood a Swiss customs official. A woman was in front of her and he let that woman pass, and then her turn came. She had only a small bag with her, and she thought she would pass unnoticed. But the official looked at her and said: "What have you got in your bag?" She said: "Oh, nothing at all," and opened it. He put his hand in and pulled out something that grew bigger and bigger, until it was two complete beds.* Her problem was that she had a resistance against marriage; she was engaged and would not marry for certain reasons, and those beds were the marriage-beds. I pulled that complex out of her and made her realize the problem, and soon after she married.

These initial dreams are often most instructive. Therefore I always ask a new patient when he first comes to me: "Did you know some time ago that you were coming? Have you met me before? Have you had a dream lately, perhaps last night?—because if he did, it gives me most valuable information about his attitude. And when you keep in close touch with the unconscious you can turn many a difficult corner. (Jung, 1968, pp. 168–169)

Chapter Highlights

- Establishing and encouraging the relationship between the conscious and the unconscious processes is essential to achieving individual wholeness.
- Individuation is the process of personal development toward wholeness. It involves establishing a connection between the ego and the self, and integrating the various parts of the psyche.

- The ego is the center of consciousness, and the self is the center of the total psyche, including both the conscious and the unconscious processes.
- Thinking, feeling, sensation, and intuition are the four fundamental psychological functions. Each is available to experience in either introverted or extraverted fashion. The superior function is more conscious, more developed. The inferior function is the most primitive, and the least conscious, function. The inferior function may also serve as a way into the unconscious. A well-rounded approach to the world results from a combination of all four functions.
- Forgotten memories, repressed experiences, and subliminal perceptions make up the personal unconscious. The contents of the collective unconscious are not rooted in personal experience but are universal across time and cultures.
- Archetypal imagery may be seen in many cultures and during many historical eras, as evidenced by common themes in world myths, folktales, and legends.
- The major structures of the personality are archetypes: the persona, the ego, the shadow, the anima and the animus, as well as the self.
- Symbols are the primary form of expression of the unconscious. As with the unconscious processes, there are two forms of symbols, the individual and the collective.
- Dreams function to restore psychological balance, to reestablish one's total psychic equilibrium. Dreams should be approached as living entities that must be observed carefully and experienced fully to be understood.
- The psyche has an innate urge toward wholeness, and every individual has a tendency toward self-development or individuation.
- Jung considered the full range of human thought and behavior to contain data from spiritual experiences. He viewed mystical belief systems as important expressions of human aspirations and ideals.
- Jung's most important contributions to psychology are his recognition of the psychological importance of symbols and his detailed analysis of their interpretations.

Key Concepts

Active imagination Drawing, painting, sculpting, conscious imagery, fantasy, and other forms of expression. It is an attempt, through the use of symbols, to engage the unconscious in dialogue with the ego.

Anima/Animus A basic psychological structure in the unconscious. The complement to the persona, the anima or animus focuses all the psychological material that does not fit with an individual's conscious self-image as man or woman. Initially present as a separate personality of the opposite sex, it becomes a liaison between the conscious and the unconscious, and gradually becomes integrated into the self.

Archetypes Formless and primordial a priori structures of the psyche that act as structure-forming elements in the unconscious.

Collective unconscious The center of all the psychic material that does not come from personal experience. It extends across cultures and across time.

An inborn psychological entity that structures the individual's development, the collective unconscious contains the heritage of humankind's spiritual evolution.

Extraversion The preferred attitude of one whose primary orientation is outward, who is more at ease with the world of other people and objects.

Individuation The process of developing a dynamic relationship between the ego and the self, along with the integration of the various parts of the psyche. The union of consciousness and the unconscious is the goal of individuation.

Introversion The preferred attitude of one whose primary orientation is inward, who is more comfortable with the world of feelings and thoughts.

Persona The character we assume in relating to others. It includes the clothing we wear and our individual style of expression.

Self The archetype of centeredness and psychological order. It directs the functioning of the whole psyche in an integrated way. The self embodies the balance and harmony of the various opposing elements of the psyche.

Shadow The archetype that serves as focus for material that has been repressed from consciousness. It may include material contrary to social standards, as well as those desires, tendencies, memories, and experiences rejected by the individual. The shadow is also a storehouse of creative and instinctual energy, spontaneity, and vitality.

Annotated Bibliography

Primary Sources

Jung, C. G. (1961). *Memories, dreams, reflections.* New York: Random House (Vintage Books).

An autobiography that helps place Jung's multifaceted thinking in perspective and provides an excellent introduction to Jung's thought. Includes a glossary with discussions of Jung's major concepts.

———. (Ed.). (1964). *Man and his symbols.* New York: Doubleday.

Contains an extremely clear essay by Jung called "Approaching the Unconscious." The book is amply illustrated, one of the best integrations of text and pictures in psychology. There is an inexpensive Dell paperback edition, but the Doubleday hardcover edition has more photos, many in color.

———. *Collected works of C. G. Jung* (H. Read, M. Fordham, & G. Adler, Eds.). Princeton, NJ: Princeton University Press, 1967. (Published under the sponsorship of the Bollingen Foundation; English edition, London: Routledge & Kegan Paul; American edition, volumes issued 1953–1967, Pantheon Books.)

For those seriously interested in exploring Jung in depth, this work includes virtually all of Jung's writings.

———. (1968). *Analytical psychology, its theory and practice.* New York: Pantheon Books.

A clear account of Jung's theories, containing transcripts of a series of lectures he gave in London.

Many of Jung's essays are now available in paperback editions. Of special interest are *Two Essays on Analytical Psychology,* an overview of the entire theoretical system, and *Psychological Types,* especially Chapter 10, "General Descriptions of Types," and Chapter 11, "Definitions," both of which discuss the major Jungian concepts.

Secondary Sources

Dry, A. (1961). *The psychology of Jung.* New York: Wiley.

Fordham, F. (1953). *An introduction to Jung's psychology.* London: Penguin Books.

Hall, C., & Nordby, V. (1973). *A primer of Jungian psychology.* New York: New American Library (Mentor Books).

Clear and well-written overview of Jungian psychology.

Jacoby, J. (1959). *Complex, archetype, symbol in the psychology of C. G. Jung.* New York: Pantheon Books.

Serrano, M. (1966). *C. G. Jung and Hermann Hesse: A record of two friendships.* London: Routledge & Kegan Paul.

It includes some fascinating conversations between Jung and Serrano, a Chilean poet and novelist who lived in India for several years.

Singer, J. (1972). *Boundaries of the soul: The practice of Jung's psychology.* New York: Doubleday.

A clear account of the dynamics of Jungian theory and therapy, by a modern Jungian analyst.

References

Abrams, J., & Zweig, C. (Eds.). (1991). *Meeting the shadow.* Los Angeles: Tarcher.

Abrams, J. (Ed.). (1994). *The shadow in America.* Novato, CA: Nataraj.

Adler, G. (1918). *Studies in analytical psychology.* New York: Norton.

Bly, R. (1990). *Iron John.* Menlo Park, CA: Addison-Wesley.

Bolen, J. (1984). *The goddesses in everywoman.* San Francisco: Harper & Row.

———. (1989). *The gods in everyman.* San Francisco: Harper & Row.

Brookes, C. (1991). Jung's concept of individuation. *Journal of the American Academy of Psychoanalysis, 19,* 307–315.

Campbell, J. (1949). *Hero with a thousand faces.* New York: Harcourt Brace Jovanovich.

———. (1985). *The inner reaches of outer space: Metaphor as myth and as religion.* New York: A. van der Marck.

———. (1988). *The power of myth.* New York: Doubleday.

———. (Ed.). (1971). *The portable Jung.* New York: Viking Press.

Caprio, B., & Hedberg, T. (1986). *Coming home: A handbook for exploring the sanctuary within.* New York: Paulist Press.

Conger, J. (1988). *Jung and Reich: The body as shadow.* Berkeley, CA: Atlantic Books.

Dry, A. (1961). *The psychology of Jung.* New York: Wiley.

Edinger, E. (1996). *The Aion lectures.* Toronto: Inner City Books.

Evans, R. (1964). *Conversations with Carl Jung.* New York: Van Nostrand.

Feuerstein, G. (1989). *Yoga: The technology of ecstasy.* Los Angeles: Tarcher.

Fordham, F. (1953). *An introduction to Jung's psychology.* London: Penguin Books.

Freud, S. The interpretation of dreams. In J. Strachey (Ed. and Trans.), *The standard edition of the complete psychological works of Sigmund Freud* (Vols. 4, 5). London: Hogarth Press, 1953–1966. (Originally published, 1900.)

———. (1964). An outline of psychoanalysis. *Standard edition* (Vol. 23). London: Hogarth Press and Institute of Psychoanalysis.

Glover, E. (1950). *Freud or Jung?* New York: Norton.

Hall, C., & Nordby, V. (1973). *A primer of Jungian psychology.* New York: New American Library (Mentor Books).

Harding, M. E. (1965). *The "I" and the "Not-I."* New York: Bollingen.

———. (1970). *The way of all women.* New York: C. G. Jung Foundation for Analytical Psychology.

Hillman, J. (1975). *Re-visioning psychology.* New York: Harper & Row.

———. (1989). *A blue fire: Selected writings by James Hillman.* New York: Harper & Row.

Hopcke, R. (1995). *Persona: Where sacred meets profane.* Boston: Shambhala.

Jacobs, H. (1961). *Western psychotherapy and Hindu-sadhana.* London: Allen & Unwin.

Jacoby, J. (1959). *Complex, archetype, symbol in the psychology of C. G. Jung.* New York: Pantheon Books.

Jung, C. G. The psychology of dementia praecox. In H. Read, M. Fordham, & G. Adler (Eds.), *Collected works of C. G. Jung* (Vol. 3). Princeton, NJ: Princeton University Press, 1967. (Published under the sponsorship of the Bollingen Foundation; English edition, London: Routledge & Kegan Paul; American edition, volumes issued 1953–1967, Pantheon Books.) (Originally published, 1907.)

———. Symbols of transformation. In *Collected works* (Vol. 5). (Originally published, 1912.)

———. The transcendent function. In *Collected works* (Vol. 8). (Originally published, 1913.)

———. The psychology of the unconscious. In *Collected works* (Vol. 7). (Originally published, 1917.)

———. Psychological types. In *Collected works* (Vol. 6). (Originally published, 1921.)

———. On psychic energy. In *Collected works* (Vol. 8). (Originally published, 1928a.)

———. The relations between the ego and the unconscious. In *Collected works* (Vol. 7). (Originally published, 1928b.)

———. The stages of life. In *Collected works* (Vol. 8). (Originally published, 1931a.)

———. Marriage as a psychological relationship. In *Collected works* (Vol. 17). (Originally published, 1931b.)

———. Problems of modern psychotherapy. In *Collected works* (Vol. 16). (Originally published, 1931c.)

———. Psychotherapists or the clergy. In *Collected works* (Vol. 11). (Originally published, 1932.)

———. (1933). *Modern man in search of a soul.* New York: Harcourt Brace Jovanovich.

———. The practical use of dream analysis. In *Collected works* (Vol. 16). (Originally published, 1934.)

———. The concept of the collective unconscious. In *Collected works* (Vol. 9, Part 1). (Originally published, 1936a.)

———. Individual dream symbolism in relation to alchemy. In *Collected works* (Vol. 12). (Originally published, 1936b.)

———. The archetypes and the collective unconscious. In *Collected works* (Vol. 9, Part 1). (Originally published, 1936c.)

———. Psychology and religion. In *Collected works* (Vol. 2). (Originally published, 1938.)

———. Conscious, unconscious, and individuation. In *Collected works* (Vol. 9, Part 1). (Originally published, 1939.)

———. A psychological approach to the dogma of the Trinity. In *Collected works* (Vol. 11). (Originally published, 1942.)

———. The relations between the ego and the unconscious. In *Collected works* (Vol. 7). (Originally published, 1945.)

———. Instinct and the unconscious. In *Collected works* (Vol. 8). (Originally published, 1948.)

———. A study in the process of individuation. In *Collected works* (Vol. 9, part 1). (Originally published, 1950.)

———. Aion. In *Collected works* (Vol. 9, Part 2). (Originally published, 1951a.)

———. The psychology of the child archetype. In *Collected works* (Vol. 9, Part 1). (Originally published, 1951b.)

———. Symbols of transformation. In *Collected works* (Vol. 5). (Originally published, 1952a.)

———. Answer to Job. In *Collected works* (Vol. 12). (Originally published, 1952b.)

———. The philosophical tree. In *Collected works* (Vol. 13). (Originally published, 1954a.)

———. Psychological aspects of the mother archetype. In *Collected works* (Vol. 9, Part 1). (Originally published, 1954b.)

———. The undiscovered self (present and future). In *Collected works* (Vol. 10). (Originally published, 1957.)

———. (1961). *Memories, dreams, reflections.* New York: Random House (Vintage Books).

———. (1968). *Analytical psychology, its theory and practice.* New York: Pantheon.

———. (Ed.). (1964). *Man and his symbols.* New York: Doubleday.

———. (1973). *Letters* (G. Adler, Ed.). Princeton, NJ: Princeton University Press.

———. (1975). *Letters, Vol. II: 1951–61.* (G. Adler, Ed.). Princeton, NJ: Princeton University Press.

———. (1984). *Selected letters of C. G. Jung, 1909–1961.* (G. Adler, Ed.). Princeton, NJ: Princeton University Press.

Kakar, S. (1994). Encounters of the psychological kind: Freud, Jung, and India. In L. Boyer, R. Boyer, & H. Stein (Eds.), *Essays in honor of George A. DeVos.* Hillsdale, NJ: Analytic Press.

Kelsey, M. (1974). *God, dreams, and revelation: A Christian interpretation of dreams.* Minneapolis: Augsburg.

———. (1982). *Christo-psychology.* New York: Crossroad.

McGuire, W. (Ed.). (1974). *The Freud-Jung letters: The correspondence between Sigmund Freud and C. G. Jung.* Princeton, NJ: Princeton University Press.

McGuire, W., & Hull, R. F. C. (Eds.). (1977). *C. G. Jung speaking.* Princeton, NJ: Princeton University Press.

Merton, C. (Trans.). (1965). *The way of Chuang Tzu.* New York: New Directions.

Moore, R., & Gillette, D. (1990). *King, warrior, magician, lover: Rediscovering the archetypes of mature masculinity.* San Francisco: HarperCollins.

Myers, I. (1980). *Gifts differing.* Palo Alto, CA: Consulting Psychologists Press.

Neumann, E. (1954). *The origins and history of consciousness.* Princeton, NJ: Princeton University Press.

Pearson, C. (1989). *The hero within: Six archetypes we live by.* New York: Harper & Row.

———. (1991). *Awakening the heroes within.* San Francisco: HarperSanFrancisco.

Progoff, I. (1953). *Jung's psychology and its social meaning.* New York: Julian Press.

Riesman, D. (1950). *The lonely crowd.* New Haven, CT: Yale University Press.

Sanford, J. A. (1968). *Dreams: God's forgotten language.* Philadelphia: Lippincott.

———. (1981). *The man who wrestled with God: Light from the Old Testament on the psychology of individuation.* Ramsey, NY: Paulist Press.

Segal, R., Singer, J., & Stein, M. (Eds.). (1995). *The allure of Gnosticism: The Gnostic experience in Jungian psychology and contemporary culture.* Chicago: Open Court.

Serrano, M. (1966). *C. G. Jung and Hermann Hesse: A record of two friendships.* London: Routledge & Kegan Paul.

Singer, J. (1972). *Boundaries of the soul: The practice of Jung's psychology.* New York: Doubleday.

Spiegelman, J. (1982). *Jungian psychology and the tree of life.* Phoenix, AZ: Falcon Press.

Spiegelman, J., & Miyuki, M. (1985). *Buddhism and Jungian psychology.* Phoenix, AZ: Falcon Press.

Spiegelman, J., & Vasavada, A. (1987). *Hinduism and Jungian psychology.* Phoenix, AZ: Falcon Press.

Stein, M. (Ed.) (1995). *Jungian analysis.* Chicago: Open Court.

Suzuki, D. T. (1964). *An introduction to Zen Buddhism.* New York: Grove Press.

Taylor, J. (1992). *Where people fly and water runs uphill: Using dreams to tap the wisdom of the unconscious.* New York: Warner Books.

von Franz, M. (1975). *C. G. Jung: His myth in our time.* New York: Putnam.

———. (1991). *Dreams.* Boston: Shambhala.

———. (1995). *Shadow and evil in fairy tales.* Boston: Shambhala.

Whitmont, E. (1969). *The symbolic quest.* New York: Putnam.

Wilhelm, R., & Jung, C. G. (1962). *The secret of the golden flower.* London: Routledge & Kegan Paul.

CHAPTER 4

Alfred Adler and Individual Psychology

Alfred Adler is the founder of the holistic system of individual psychology, which seeks to understand each person as an integrated totality within a social system. He called his approach *Individual Psychology* because it stresses the uniqueness of the individual rather than the universalities of behavior described by Freud.

Adler's followers established centers throughout Europe, England, and the United States, and many of his original ideas have become widely accepted in psychology and psychotherapy today. Probably more people have heard of Adler's concept of the *inferiority complex* than of any other single idea in psychology.

The four major principles of Adler's system are holism, the unity of the individual's style of life, social interest or community feeling, and the importance of goal-directed behavior. Adler's argument that goals and expectations have a greater influence on behavior than do past experiences was a major cause of his break with Freud. Adler also believed that individuals are motivated primarily by the goal of superiority, or conquest of their environment. He stressed both the effect of social influences on individuals and the importance of social interest: a sense of community, cooperation, and concern for others. For Adler, life is essentially a movement toward more successful adaptation to the environment, greater cooperation, and altruism.

Adler's individual psychology is similar to behaviorism in its stress on overt behaviors and their consequences as well as in its assertion that concepts must be concrete and related to actual behavior. In contrast to most of the other psychological theories covered in this text, individual psychology is not a *depth psychology;* that is, it does not postulate intangible forces and constructs deep within the psyche. Rather, Adler developed a context psychology in which behavior is understood in terms of the physical and social environment, a context that the individual generally is not aware of. Adler was the first to practice family therapy, which he introduced in 1920. Adlerians have made important contributions to group therapy, to *brief therapy,* and to applications of psychology in education.

Personal History

Alfred Adler was born in a suburb of Vienna on February 7, 1870, the son of a middle-class Jewish merchant. The Adler family was extremely musical. Alfred's sister was an excellent pianist, one brother became a violin teacher, and Alfred himself had such a beautiful voice that he was often encouraged to seek a career in the opera. As a child, he suffered from a number of serious illnesses, including rickets. He also suffered from a jealous rivalry with his older brother. He once commented, "My elder brother . . . was always ahead of me—he is *still* ahead of me!" (Adler in Bottome, 1957, p. 27).

Adler struggled hard to overcome his physical weakness. Whenever possible, young Alfred ran and played with other children, with whom he was popular. He seemed to gain a sense of equality and self-esteem from his friends that he did not find at home. These experiences can be seen later in Adler's work, in his stress on the community sharing of feelings and values, which he called *social interest* and through which, he believed, individuals can achieve their potential as productive members of society.

During his sickly youth, Adler read voraciously. In his adult years, his familiarity with literature, the Bible, psychology, and German philosophy made him popular in Viennese society and later as a lecturer throughout the world.

The hardest things for human beings to do is to know themselves and change themselves. (Adler, 1928, p. 11)

As a child, Adler was confronted by death on several occasions. When Alfred was 3 years old, his younger brother died in the bed they shared. In addition, Adler twice narrowly escaped being killed in street accidents; and, at the age of 5, he contracted a severe case of pneumonia. The family physician believed the case to be hopeless, but another doctor managed to save him. As a result of this experience, Adler decided that he wanted to be a doctor.

At the age of 18, Adler entered the University of Vienna to study medicine. He was deeply interested in socialism and attended a number of political meetings. It was at one of these meetings that he met his future wife, Raissa, a Russian student, who was attending the university.

Adler received his medical degree in 1895. He established a practice first in ophthalmology and then in general medicine. Because of his growing interest in nervous system functioning and adaptation, Adler's professional interests later shifted to neurology and psychiatry. In 1901, Adler, a rising young physician, strongly defended in print Freud's new book, *The Interpretation of Dreams.* Although Freud had never met Adler, he was deeply touched by Adler's courageous defense of his work, and he wrote to thank Adler and invite him to join a newly formed discussion group on psychoanalysis.

Adler entered this group (which later became the Vienna Psychoanalytic Society) as an accomplished young professional who was already developing his own theoretical orientation. He was not a follower of Freud. He was never Freud's "pupil" and never underwent a training analysis. Nevertheless, in 1910, Adler became president of the psychoanalytic society and coeditor of one of its journals.

Just one year later, Adler's increasingly divergent theoretical orientation had become unacceptable to Freud and to many other members of the society. Two major differences were Adler's emphasis on power rather than on sexuality as a central human drive, and Adler's focus on the social environment and his deemphasis on unconscious processes. Adler resigned as president and left the society along with 9 like-minded colleagues who also felt that psychoanalysis was too rigid and intolerant of independent thinking. The rest, a group of only 14, remained with Freud. Adler founded his own organization, the Association for Individual Psychology, which gradually spread throughout Europe.

Adler and his followers became active in the field of education, especially in teacher training, because of their belief in the importance of working with those who shaped the minds and characters of the young. Endorsed by the minister of education, Adler and his associates established child guidance centers in the public schools, where children and their families could receive counseling. By the 1930s, there were 30 such clinics in Vienna alone. From 1921 until 1927, when he went to teach in the United States, Adler lectured and took demonstration cases twice a month to colleagues, parents, and teachers alike. He would often explain someone's life pattern after hearing only a few basic facts about the individual, as well as his or her earliest memories or dreams.

An eminent medical colleague stated, "The whole approach of the Viennese

School of Medicine to their patients was altered . . . by Adler's teaching. I do not believe a single doctor of any standing in Vienna failed to attend, at one time or another, Adler's lectures and to profit by them" (Bottome, 1957, p. 209).

Adler's wisdom and deep understanding of human nature were evident to virtually everyone who came in contact with him. The desk clerk at a hotel in which Adler often stayed mentioned to one of Adler's colleagues, "You can hardly keep the bell-boys or the porter out of his room. They'll take any excuse to talk to him, and as far as that goes, I'm not much better myself!" (Bottome, 1957, p. 54).

Adler published numerous papers and monographs and also devoted a great deal of time to lecture tours throughout Europe and the United States. Between the first and second world wars, Adlerian groups were formed in 20 European countries and in the United States. In 1927, Adler was appointed lecturer at Columbia University. In 1928, he lectured at the New School for Social Research in New York, and a year later returned to give a series of lectures and clinical demonstrations. Adler left Vienna permanently in 1932 because of the rise of Nazism. He settled in the United States and accepted a visiting professorship in medical psychology at the Long Island Medical College. Adler died in Scotland in 1937, at the age of 67, while on a European lecture tour.

Intellectual Antecedents

Adler's theories are based on a variety of sources, but especially significant were Darwinian evolution, Freud's psychoanalytic theories, Nietzsche's will to power, Vaihinger's fictional goals, and the theory of holism.

Evolution

Adler was strongly influenced by Darwin's theory of evolution, as were most of his contemporaries. His concept of individual psychology is based on the premise that adaptation to the environment is the fundamental aspect of life.

Individual Psychology stands firmly on the ground of evolution and in the light of evolution regards all human striving as a struggle for perfection. (Adler, 1964a, pp. 36–37)

Most psychological theorists are primarily concerned with intrapsychic dynamics. Adler was not. He was an *ecological psychologist,* focusing on the relations between individual and environment. Adler's early book on organ inferiority and compensation was largely an application of the Darwinian view of medicine. It was considered a medical complement to psychoanalytic theory and was well received by Freud. Adler's later work can be viewed as a refutation of social Darwinism, which emphasizes the survival of the fittest and the elimination of the unfit. According to Adler, organic inferiority can stimulate us to superior attainments, instead of necessarily causing defeat in the struggle of life. Also, Adler argued, cooperation and community feeling are more important than competition in the process of human evolution.

Psychoanalysis

Adler had begun his own theoretical work and had already published papers in the areas of social medicine and education before he met Freud. Although he never really accepted the concepts of libido or the Oedipus complex, Adler was profoundly influenced by psychoanalytic theory, especially the importance of early childhood experiences and the mother-child relationship, the purposefulness of neurotic symptoms, and the meaningfulness of dreams.

All neurotic symptoms are safeguards of persons who do not feel adequately equipped or prepared for the problems of life. (Adler, 1964b, p. 95)

Freud considered Adler to have been his pupil, an assertion that Adler consistently denied. Rather than building upon psychoanalytic theory, Adler developed an independent theoretical position, often in response to Freud's views. The two men had fundamentally different approaches to the exploration of human nature. Freud was interested in the analysis of parts and stressed division, whereas Adler insisted that the individual's "wholeness" was the key to understanding that person. Symptoms had significance only as an aspect of the individual personality.

Adler disagreed with Freud on several major points. He could never accept Freud's theory that the repressed, unconscious, sexual material of childhood was the core of all neuroses. Adler, who viewed sexuality as an expression of one's personality and not as its fundamental motivator, opposed Freud's assertion of the primacy of the libido. Adler suggested a different fundamental drive, the drive for power. The child, Adler explained, strives to become strong and exert power over others. The major biological fact for Adler was not the child's instinctive sexual behavior but the child's smallness and helplessness in relation to the surrounding adult world. According to Adler, children's early attempts to adapt to their environment may result in their choosing to dominate others as a means of gaining self-esteem and of achieving success.

Adler would always say to new patients, "The Doctor sits in your chair." (Adler in Bottome, 1957, p. 217)

Adler was highly critical of Freudian analysis, which he felt was without moral orientation and produced antisocial, selfish individuals: "It is a spoilt child psychology, but what can be expected from a man who asks, 'Why should I love my neighbor?'" (Adler in Bottome, 1957, p. 256). Adler felt strongly that psychological health must be built on healthy social relationships.

Friedrich Nietzsche

Like virtually all intellectuals of his generation, Adler was affected by Friedrich Nietzsche's influential writings. However, he was not a superficial imitator of Nietzsche, as some critics have maintained. Although his earliest conceptualization of the aggressive instincts did have much in common with Nietzsche's will to power, Adler's later formulation of the striving for superiority is a much broader concept than the striving for power; it emphasizes the role of creative growth and development. In addition, Adler's concept of social interest stands in diametric opposition to Nietzsche's individualistic perspective.

Fictional Goals

Adler was significantly influenced by the writings of Hans Vaihinger, a philosopher who proposed the concept of social *fictions,* which have no basis in reality but become critical determinants of human behavior. Vaihinger believed that people, confronted by a welter of facts and experiences, create systems to organize their experiences. They then assume that these mere systems are the truth. These fictions become some of the most important influences on our behavior.

According to Vaihinger, people are more affected by their *expectations* than by their actual experiences. He called this approach *fictionalism,* or the *philosophy of "as if."* In *The Neurotic Constitution* (1912), Adler suggests that all human behavior, thought, and feeling proceed along *as if* lines. Beginning in childhood, we attempt to adapt to our environment and overcome any felt weakness. We create for ourselves an idealized goal of perfect adaptation, then struggle toward it *as if* the goal equals success, happiness, and security.

Holism

Fifteen years after his exposure to Vaihinger, Adler's thinking was affected by the holistic philosophy of Jan Smuts. Smuts was a South African military leader, statesman, and philosopher, whose work on holism influenced many contemporary thinkers. The two men corresponded, and Adler was instrumental in having Smuts's work published in Europe. Smuts believed that whole systems often have properties that are distinct from the properties of their parts—that there is an impulse toward increasing organization, toward wholeness in every individual. Adler used to say, "You must not only ask yourself what effect a bacillus has on a body—it is also important to know what is the effect of the body on the bacillus!" (Adler in Bottome, 1957, p. 72). He found in holistic philosophy a confirmation of many of his own ideas and an important philosophical basis for individual psychology.

There is a logic from the head; there is also a logic from the heart; and there is an even deeper logic from the whole. (Adler in Bottome, 1957, p. 80)

Major Concepts

One of Adler's greatest contributions to psychology was his postulation of the inferiority complex and of our need to compensate for our feelings of inferiority. In the Adlerian system, the process of striving for superiority was a significant reformulation of Nietzsche's concept of will to power. The concepts of life goals, lifestyle, and the creative power of the individual are important holistic contributions to psychology. Adler's emphasis on social interest, cooperation, and the effects of society on gender differences keeps his theory rooted in a social context.

Inferiority and Compensation

In his monograph on **organ inferiority** which first appeared in 1907, Adler attempted to explain why illness affects different people in different ways. At the time, Adler wrote as a physician concerned primarily with physiological processes. He suggested that in each individual, certain weaker organs are particularly susceptible to diseases. Adler also noted that organic weaknesses can be overcome through diligent training and exercise. In fact, a weak organ can be developed to such a degree that it becomes a person's greatest strength. Adler wrote, "In almost all outstanding people we find some organ imperfection; and we gather the impression that they were sorely confronted at the beginning of life but struggled and overcame their difficulties" (1931, p. 248).

The important thing is not what one is born with, but what use one makes of that equipment. (Adler, 1964b, p. 86)

Adler extended his investigation of organ inferiority to the study of the psychological sense of inferiority. He coined the term **inferiority complex.** According to Adler, children are deeply affected by a sense of inferiority, which is an inevitable consequence of the child's size and lack of power. Adler's own childhood experiences led him to stress the importance of this concept:

> One of my earliest recollections is of sitting on a bench, bandaged up on account of rickets, with my healthy elder brother sitting opposite me. He could run, jump and move about quite effortlessly, while for me movement of any sort was a strain and an effort. (Adler in Bottome, 1957, p. 30)

Adler believed that the life experiences of all children involve feelings of weakness, inadequacy, and frustration.

Children are relatively small and helpless in the world of adults. For children, controlling their own behavior and breaking free from adult domination is a primary concern. From this perspective, power is seen as the first good and weakness as the first evil. The struggle to attain power is the child's earliest compensation for a sense of inferiority.

Inferiority feelings are not in themselves abnormal. They are the cause of all improvements in the position of mankind. (Adler, 1956, p. 117)

Moderate feelings of inferiority can motivate the individual to constructive achievements. However, a deep sense of inferiority impedes positive growth and development:

> He [the child] realizes at an early age that there are other human beings who are able to satisfy their urges more completely, and are better prepared to live. . . . [H]e learns to over-value the size and stature which enable one to open a door, or the ability to move heavy objects, or the right of others to give commands and claim obedience to them. A desire to grow, to become as strong or even stronger than all others, arises in his soul. (Adler, 1928, p. 34)

For Adler, virtually all progress is the result of our attempts to compensate for inferiority feelings. These feelings motivate us in our most significant achievements.

Aggression and Striving for Superiority

In his early writings, Adler emphasized the importance of aggression and the striving for power. He did not equate aggression with hostility, however, but with a sense of initiative in overcoming obstacles—for example, as in aggressive sales tactics. Adler asserted that aggressive tendencies in humans have been crucial in individual and species survival. Aggression may manifest itself in the individual as the *will to power,* a phrase of Nietzsche's that Adler used. Adler pointed out that both men and women often use sexuality to satisfy the urge for power.

In his later theorizing, Adler viewed aggression and the will to power as manifestations of a more general motive, the goal of superiority or perfection—that is, motivation to improve ourselves, to develop our capacities and potential. Adler believed that all healthy individuals are motivated to strive for perfection, to seek continuous improvement: "The striving for perfection is innate in the sense that it is a part of life, a striving, an urge, a something without which life would be unthinkable" (1956, p. 104).

The goal of superiority can take either a positive or a negative direction. When the goal includes social concerns and an interest in the welfare of others, it develops in a constructive and healthy direction. Individuals motivated by such a goal strive to grow, to develop their skills and abilities, and to work for a constructive way of living. However, some people seek *personal* superiority—to achieve a sense of superiority by dominating others rather than by becoming more useful to others. For Adler, striving for personal superiority is a neurotic perversion, the result of a strong sense of inferiority and a lack of social interest. Personal superiority generally fails to bring the recognition and personal satisfaction that the individual is seeking.

The feeling of personal worth can only be derived from achievement, from the ability to overcome. (Adler, 1964b, p. 91)

The goal of superiority has its roots in the evolutionary process of continuous adaptation to the environment. All species must evolve toward more effective adaptation or else suffer extinction, and thus individuals are driven to seek a more harmonious relationship with the environment: "If this striving were not innate to the organism, no form of life could preserve itself. The goal of mastering the environment in a superior way, which one can call the striving for perfection, consequently also characterizes the development of man" (1964b, p. 39).

To live means to develop. (Adler, 1964b, p. 31)

Adler once said to a patient:

> What do you first do when you are learning to swim? You make mistakes, do you not? And then what happens? You make other mistakes, and when you have made *all* the mistakes you possibly can without drowning—and some of them many times over—what do you find? That you can swim? Well—life is just the same as learning to swim! Do not be afraid of making mistakes, for there is no other way of learning how to live! (Adler in Bottome, 1957, p. 37)

According to Adler, the "supreme law" of life is that "the sense of worth of the self shall not be allowed to be diminished" (Adler, 1956, p. 358). Individuals want to have a sense of success and self-worth.

Life Goals

To Adler, the goal of mastering the environment was too broad a concept to explain logically how people choose a direction in life. Therefore, Adler turned to the idea that individuals develop a specific **life goal** that serves as a focus for achievement. The individual's life goal is influenced by personal experiences, values, attitudes, and personality. The life goal is not a clear and consciously chosen aim.

The goal of superiority with each individual is personal and unique. It depends upon the meaning he gives to life. This meaning is not a matter of words. It is built up in his style of life and runs through it. (Adler, 1956, p. 181)

Man is but a drop of water . . . but a very conceited drop. (Adler in Way, 1950, p. 167)

The formation of life goals begins in childhood as compensation for feelings of inferiority, insecurity, and helplessness in an adult world. Life goals generally serve as a defense against feelings of impotence, as a bridge from the unsatisfying present to a bright, powerful, and fulfilling future. As adults, we may have definite, logical reasons for our career choices. However, the life goals that guide and motivate us were formed early in childhood and remain somewhat obscured from consciousness. For example, Adler mentions that many physicians chose their careers in childhood, as he did, as a means of coping with their insecurity concerning death.

Personal Reflection

■ Power

Adler wrote a great deal about having a sense of power and mastery in one's environment.

1. Where and when have you felt powerless in your life? What was it like? Are there any areas in which you still feel powerless? How might you change that?
2. Give a specific example of a time you sought personal superiority instead of constructive self-improvement. What were the results? How did you feel?
3. Imagine that you had the power to accomplish almost anything. What would you do? How would having real power affect your life? Would you be likely to have more friends or fewer friends? Would you be happier or sadder—in what ways?

Life goals are always somewhat unrealistic and may become neurotically overinflated if inferiority feelings are too intense. For the neurotic, there is generally a wide gap between conscious aims and unconscious, self-defeating life goals. Fantasies of personal superiority and self-esteem are given more attention than goals involving real achievement. Adler's favorite question to his patients was, "What would you do if you had not got this trouble?" In their answers, he usually discovered what his patients' symptoms helped them to avoid.

Life goals provide direction and purpose for our activities; they enable an outside observer to interpret aspects of our thought and behavior in terms of these goals. Adler points out that our character traits are neither innate nor unalterable but are adopted as integral facets of our goal orientation: "They are not primary but secondary factors, forced by the secret goal of the individual, and must be understood teleologically" (1956, p. 219). For example, someone who strives for superiority by seeking personal power will develop various character traits necessary to attain this goal—traits such as ambition, envy, and distrust.

Style of Life

Adler emphasized the need to analyze individuals as a unified totality. **Lifestyle** is the unique way that an individual chooses to pursue his or her life goal. It is an integrated means of adapting to and interacting with life in general.

The foremost task of Individual Psychology is to prove this unity in each individual—in his thinking, feeling, acting; in his so-called conscious and unconscious—in every expression of his personality. (Adler, 1964b, p. 69)

According to Adler, the key to understanding a person's behavior is found in the hidden purposes to which all his or her energies are directed. These purposes reveal far more than external facts or situations. For example, if I believe that my father mistreated me as a child and blame a life of failure on this construction of events, then I have orchestrated my own failure. How I was actually treated is immaterial. My belief that I was abused is true psychologically. Further, I have made the mistreatment a reality to fit my chosen style of life, a life of failure:

Personal Reflections

Understanding Goals

Adler emphasized more the pull of the future than the pressure of the past. For Adler, where we hope to *go* is more important than where we have *been*. In order to discover the relationship between your life goals and daily activities, try the following exercises.

Set aside 15 minutes for this exercise. Sit down with four sheets of paper and a pen or pencil. Write at the top of the first sheet, "What are my lifetime goals?" Take 2 minutes to answer this question. Write down whatever comes into your mind, no matter how general, abstract, or trivial it may seem. You may want to include personal, family, career, social, community, or spiritual goals. Then give yourself an additional 2 minutes to go over your list and make any additions or alterations. Set aside this first sheet.

Take your second sheet and write at the top, "How would I like to spend the next three years?" Take 2 minutes to answer this question. Then take 2 more minutes to go over your list. This question should help you pinpoint your goals more specifically than you did with the first question. Again, set aside this list.

For a different perspective on your goals, write on your third sheet, "If I knew my life would end six months from today, how would I live until then?" The purpose of this question is to find out if there are things that are important to you that you are not doing or even considering now. Again, write for 2 minutes; go back over your answers for another 2 minutes, and set this sheet aside.

On your fourth sheet of paper, write down the three goals you consider most important out of all the goals you have listed. Compare all four lists. Are there any themes running through the various goals you have given? Are most of your goals in one category, such as social or personal? Do some goals appear on the first three lists? Do the goals you have chosen as most important differ in some way from the other goals on your lists?

Although this method does not fully uncover the unconscious life goals that Adler discussed, it can be a powerful way of discovering the relationship between your goals and your daily activities. It is also a useful exercise to repeat every six months or so in order to see what changes may have occurred. (Adapted from Lakein, 1974)

It is, as we have already seen, in the first four or five years of life that the individual is establishing the unity of his mind and constructing the relationship between mind and body. He is taking his hereditary material and the impressions he receives from the environment and is adapting them to his pursuit of superiority. By the end of the fifth year his personality has crystallized. The meaning he gives to life, the goal he pursues, his style of approach, and his emotional disposition are all fixed. They can be changed later; but they can be changed only if he becomes free from the mistake involved in his childhood crystallization. Just as all his previous expressions were coherent with his interpretation of life, so now, if he is able to correct

> the mistake, his new expressions will be coherent with his new interpretation. (Adler, 1931, p. 34)

Seemingly isolated habits and behavior traits gain meaning as an element of the individual's lifestyle and goals, and thus psychological and emotional problems must be treated within this context. The whole style of life must be addressed in treatment, because a given symptom or trait is but an expression of the unified lifestyle of the individual.

Mosak (1989) has listed the following dimensions of lifestyle:

1. The *self-concept*—conceptions about oneself, who one is.
2. The *self-ideal*—notions of what one *should* be. (Adler developed this concept in 1912.)
3. The *image of the world*—convictions about such things as the world, people, and nature as well as about what the world demands.
4. *Ethical convictions*—a personal ethical code.

The Schema of Apperception

As part of the lifestyle, individuals develop a conception of self and of the world. Adler called this the **schema of apperception. Apperception** is a psychological term that refers to perception involving a subjective interpretation of what is received by the senses.

You find what you planned to find. (Adler, 1964b, p. 100)

Adler emphasized that it is one's conception of the world that determines behavior. If someone believes that a coil of rope in a dark corner is a snake, his or her fear can be as intense as if a snake were actually present. Adler reminds us that "our senses do not receive actual facts, but merely a subjective image of them, a reflection of the external world" (1956, p. 182). The schema of apperception is generally self-reinforcing. For example, when we are afraid, we are more likely to perceive threats in the environment, which reinforces our original belief that the environment is a threatening one. Adler's work on the schema of apperception is an important precursor to cognitive psychology and cognitive therapy. (See Chapter 11.)

Adler knew how to use this principle in therapy with great effectiveness. One patient came to him with a long history of failure. He was a man of considerable ability who had no self-confidence. Adler pointed out that his "ability" at failure could be used to his advantage. "A success is very important for you, I admit; then why not try to fail, since according to your own evidence, you would be almost certain to succeed in bringing it off?" (Adler in Bottome, 1957, p. 100). This was a real turning point for the individual, who could not help laughing at himself.

The Creative Power of the Individual

Adler pointed out that we respond actively and creatively to the various influences affecting our lives. We are not inert objects, passively accepting all outside forces; we actively seek out certain experiences and reject others. We selectively codify and interpret experience, developing an individualized schema of apperception and forming a distinct pattern of relating to the world:

Personal Reflection

■ Three Wishes

You have found an old sealed bottle that has washed up on shore. When you open it, a genie appears and grants you three wishes. As you contemplate your wishes, remember that they should be within the realm of the humanly attainable. They should be exciting yet believable.

1. Write out your three wishes.
2. Choose the one that is the most important to you.
3. Write out your wish clearly and in detail, as a central life goal.
4. What are you doing or planning to do in order to attain this goal?
5. What are the obstacles to your attaining your goal?
6. What feelings come up when you write out your goals and take them seriously?
7. If you wish, repeat steps 3–6 for your other two wishes.

> The science of Individual Psychology developed out of the effort to understand that mysterious creative power of life which expresses itself in the desire to develop, to strive, to achieve. . . . This power is *teleological,* it expresses itself in the striving after a goal, and, in this striving, every bodily and psychological movement is made to cooperate. It is thus absurd to study bodily movements and mental conditions abstractly without relation to an individual whole. (Adler, 1956, p. 92)

Each individual, Adler believed, has a center where he or she is free. Since we are free, we are responsible for our actions and for our lives.

It is futile to attempt to establish psychology on the basis of drives alone, without taking into consideration the creative power of the child which directs the drive, molds it into form, and supplies it with a meaningful goal. (Adler, 1956, p. 177)

Adler always stressed the individual's positive, creative, healthy capacities. When a patient came to see him, Adler did not ask himself, "How ill is she?" but always "How much in her is healthy?" He believed that the basis of any cure lay not in the strength of the illness but in the individual's power of resistance (Bottome, 1957).

At the core of Adler's model of human nature is creativity—the capacity to formulate (consciously or unconsciously) goals and the means of achieving them. This culminates in the development of a life plan, which organizes one's life into a self-consistent lifestyle.

Each individual arrives at a concrete goal of overcoming through his creative power, which is identical with the self. (Adler, 1956, p. 180)

For Adler, the formation of a life goal, lifestyle, and schema of apperception is essentially a creative act. It is the creative power of the personality, or of the self, that guides and directs the individual's response to the environment. Adler attributes to the individual uniqueness, awareness, and control over his or her own destiny—qualities he felt that Freud did not sufficiently stress in his conception of human nature. "Every individual represents both a unity of personality and the individual fashioning of that unity. The individual is thus both the picture and the artist. He is the artist of his own personality" (Adler, 1956, p. 177). Adler emphasized that we are not powerless pawns of external forces. We mold our own personalities.

Social Interest

Adler's theories regarding aggression and the striving for power have been oversimplified and overemphasized by many critics. Adler's concept of **social interest** is central to his later writing. (A better translation of his original German term, *Gemeinschaftsgefühl,* might be "community feeling.") By social interest, Adler means "the sense of human solidarity, the connectedness of man to man . . . the wider connotation of a 'sense of fellowship in the human community' " (Wolfe in Adler, 1928, p. 32n). *Community feeling* refers to the interest we take in others not simply to serve our own purposes but to develop "an interest in the interests" of others.

All failures . . . are products of inadequate preparation in social interest. They are all non-cooperative, solitary beings who run more or less counter to the rest of the world; beings who are more or less asocial if not anti-social. (Adler, 1964b, p. 90)

From his holistic perspective, Adler saw the individual not only as a unified whole but as a part of larger wholes—family, community, society, and humanity. Our lives and all our activities are carried out within a social context:

> Any man's value is determined by his attitude toward his fellow man, and by the degree in which he partakes of the division of labor which communal life demands. His affirmation of this communal life makes him important to other human beings, makes him a link in a great chain which binds society, the chain which we cannot in any way disturb without also disturbing human society. (Adler, 1928, p. 121)

In one sense, all human behavior is social because, as Adler argued, we develop in a social environment and our personalities are socially formed. Social interest is more than concern for our immediate community or society. In its broadest sense it refers to concern for "the ideal community of all mankind, the ultimate fulfillment of evolution" (Adler, 1964b, p. 35). Social interest includes feelings of kinship with all humanity and relatedness to the whole of life.

Cooperation

One important aspect of social interest is the development of cooperative behavior. From an evolutionary point of view, the ability to cooperate in food gathering, hunting, and defense against predators has been a vital factor in the survival of the human race and the most effective form of adaptation to the environment.

The only individuals who can really meet and master the problems of life, however, are those who show in their striving a tendency to enrich all others, who go ahead in such a way that others benefit also. (Adler, 1956, p. 255)

Adler believed that only by functioning as cooperative, contributing members of society can we overcome our actual inferiorities or our sense of inferiority. On the other hand, lack of cooperation and the resulting sense of inadequacy and failure are at the root of all neurotic or maladaptive styles of life. "If a person cooperates," Adler wrote, "he will never become a neurotic" (1964b, p. 193). Those who have made the most valuable contributions to humanity have been the most cooperative individuals, and the works of the great geniuses have always been oriented in a social direction (Adler, 1931).

Adler on Women

Alfred Adler took the somewhat radical position that psychological differences between the sexes are entirely the result of cultural attitudes. He condemned

Personal Reflection

■ Practicing Cooperation

In order to understand more clearly what Adler meant by cooperation and social interest, devote as much time in one week as you can to helping others. Keep a record of your behavior and of your feelings. Resolve that you will not refuse any reasonable requests from others, even if these requests take up some of your valuable time, energy, or even money. (If you want to make the exercise more demanding, let all your friends know that you are carrying out this exercise and that you will be available to serve them for a week!) Don't simply wait for someone to ask you, but actively look for opportunities to offer your help to others.

At the end of the week, review your experiences. How did other people react to you? What were your reactions to helping others? What did you learn from the exercise?

society's conception of women in which they are viewed as inferior in order to perpetuate cultural systems of male domination and male privilege. He suggested that a

> girl comes into the world with a prejudice sounding in her ears which is designed only to rob her of her belief in her own value, to shatter her self-confidence, and destroy her hope of ever doing anything worthwhile. . . . The obvious advantages of being a man (in our society) have caused severe disturbances in the psychic development of women. (1973, pp. 41–42)

Adler also pointed out that a society's attitude toward gender differences affects an individual's development from birth more profoundly than most other cultural attitudes.

The life of the human soul is not a "being" but a "becoming." (Adler, 1929, p. ix)

Basic Principles of Adlerian Theory

Mosak (1989) has outlined the basic assumptions of Adlerian psychology. They are summarized as follows:

1. All behavior occurs in a social context. People cannot be studied in isolation.
2. The focus is on interpersonal psychology. Most important for the individual is the development of a feeling of being an integral part of a larger social whole.
3. Individual psychology stresses holism rather than reductionism. All functions are subordinate to the person's goals and style of life.
4. In Adlerian psychology, the term *unconscious* is an adjective rather than a noun. Unconscious processes are purposeful and serve the individual's goals, as do conscious processes.

5. To understand the individual, you must understand his or her style of life, or cognitive organization. This is the lens through which people view themselves and their lives.
6. Although behavior may change, the style of life and long-range goals of the individual remain relatively constant, unless the individual's fundamental convictions are transformed. Such transformation is one of the main tasks of therapy.
7. Behavior is not determined by the past but by either heredity or the environment. Individuals are motivated by self-selected goals, which they feel will bring them success and happiness.
8. The central motivation for each individual is to strive for perfection or for superiority. (This point is comparable to Horney's concept of self-realization and Maslow's self-actualization.)
9. The individual is confronted by many different life choices. He or she may choose healthy, socially useful goals or neurotic, socially useless ones.
10. Adlerian psychology focuses primarily on process. Relatively little attention is paid to the labeling of individuals.
11. Whatever meaning life has derives from what we attribute to it ourselves. A healthy conception of life includes a sense of the importance of helping others and contributing to society.

Dynamics

Psychological Growth

Psychological growth is primarily a matter of moving from the self-centered goal of personal superiority to an attitude of constructive mastery of the environment and socially useful development. Constructive striving for superiority, plus strong social interest and cooperation, is the basic trait of the healthy individual.

Life Tasks Adler discussed three major life tasks that confront the individual: work, friendship, and love. They are determined by the basic conditions of human existence:

> These three main ties are set by the facts that we are living in one particular place in the universe and must develop with the limits and possibilities which our circumstances set us; that we are living among others of our own kind to whom we must learn to adapt ourselves; and that we are living in two sexes with the future of our race dependent on the relations of these two sexes. (Adler, 1931, p. 264)

Work includes those activities that are useful to the community, not simply those occupations for which we receive an income. For Adler, work provides a sense of satisfaction and self-worth only to the extent that it benefits others. The importance of our work is ultimately based on our dependence on the physical environment:

> We are living on the surface of this planet, with only the resources of this planet, with the fertility of its soil, with its mineral wealth, and with its cli-

> mate and atmosphere. It has always been the task of mankind to find the right answer to the problem these conditions set us. . . . [I]t has always been necessary to strive for improvement and further accomplishments. (Adler, 1956, p. 131)

Friendship is an expression of our membership in the human race and of our constant need to adapt to and interact with others of our species. Our specific friendships provide essential links to our communities because no individual relates to society in the abstract. Friendly, cooperative endeavor is also an important element in constructive work.

Love is discussed by Adler in terms of heterosexual love. It involves a close union of mind and body and the utmost cooperation between two people of the opposite sex. Love comes from intimacy, which is essential to the continuance of our species. Adler writes that the close bond of marriage represents the greatest challenge to our ability to cooperate with another human being, and a successful marriage creates the best environment for promoting cooperation and social interest in children.

To Adler, these three tasks (work, friendship, and love) are interrelated. Success at one leads to success at the others. In fact, these three tasks are all aspects of the same problem—how to live constructively in our environment.

Obstacles to Growth

In discussing the major obstacles to human growth and development, Adler first stressed three negative childhood conditions—organ inferiority, pampering, and neglect. He emphasized that adult neurosis is rooted in an attempt to overcome a feeling of inferiority that results in increasing isolation and estrangement from society. Neurosis and virtually all other psychological problems occur when we strive for personal superiority instead of for healthy, constructive achievement.

Organ Inferiority, Pampering, and Neglect The childhood situations that tend to result in a lack of social interest, isolation, and a noncooperative lifestyle, based on the unrealistic goal of personal superiority, are organ inferiority, pampering, and neglect.

Children who suffer from illnesses often become highly self-centered. They withdraw from social interaction out of a sense of inferiority and inability to compete successfully with other children. However, those children who overcome their difficulties may overcompensate for their original weakness and develop their abilities to an unusual degree.

Pampered or spoiled children also have difficulties in developing a sense of social interest and cooperation. They lack confidence in their own abilities because others have always done for them what they could have done for themselves. Rather than cooperate with others, they tend to make one-sided demands on friends and family. Social interest is usually minimal, and Adler found that pampered children usually have little genuine feeling for the parents they manipulate so well.

Neglect is the third situation that may impede a child's development. A neglected or unwanted child has never known love and cooperation in the home and therefore finds it extremely difficult to develop these capacities. Such children have no confidence in their ability to be useful and to gain affection and esteem from others. They tend to become cold and hard as adults.

> The traits of unloved children in their most developed form can be observed by studying the biographies of all the great enemies of humanity. Here the one thing that stands out is that as children they were badly treated. Thus they developed hardness of character, envy and hatred; they could not bear to see others happy. (Adler, 1956, p. 371)

As a result of organ inferiority, pampering, and neglect, children often have distorted worldviews, which lead to faulty lifestyles. Again, Adler stressed that it is not the children's "experience" but their perceptions and conclusions about their experience that determine the way they pursue their lives.

The Basic Dynamics of Neurosis In 1913, Adler and his group published an Adlerian approach to neurosis (Bottome, 1957). The main points are summarized as follows:

1. Every neurosis can be understood as an attempt to overcome a feeling of inferiority and to gain a feeling of competence.
2. Neurosis tends to isolate the individual because it leads away from social functioning and the solving of real-life problems.
3. The neurotic individual's relations with others are severely limited by a combination of hypersensitiveness and intolerance.
4. Estranged from reality, the neurotic tends to live a life of imagination and fantasy, avoiding responsibilities and service to society.
5. Illness and suffering become a substitute for the original, healthy goal of superiority.
6. The neurosis represents an attempt to be free of all the constraints of society by establishing a *counter-compulsion*. This may take the form of anxiety attacks, sleeplessness, compulsions, hallucinations, hypochondria, and so forth.
7. Even logical thinking becomes dominated by the counter-compulsion.
8. Logic, love, compassion, and the will to live all arise from social life. Neurotic isolation and striving for power are directed against this.
9. The neurotic is constantly seeking personal power and prestige, looking for excuses to leave real-life problems unsolved, and consequently never develops social interest.
10. To cure a neurosis, the therapist helps to change completely the individual's orientation, which results from his or her whole upbringing, and enable the patient to become an active, involved member of society.

No act of cruelty has ever been done which has not been based upon a secret weakness. The person who is really strong has no inclination to cruelty. (Adler, 1956, p. 390)

This list illustrates how Adler's main ideas can be applied to understanding and working with human problems. He clearly emphasizes the importance of living constructively and cooperatively in society.

Striving for Personal Superiority When inferiority feelings predominate or when social interest is underdeveloped, individuals tend to seek personal superiority, because they lack confidence in their ability to function effectively and to work constructively with others. The trappings of success, prestige, and esteem become more important than concrete achievements. "They have turned away from the real problems of life and are engaged in shadow-fighting to reassure themselves of their strength" (Adler, 1956, p. 255). Such individuals contribute nothing of real value to society and become fixed in self-centered behavior patterns that inevitably lead to a sense of failure.

Structure

Body

To Adler, the body is a major source of inferiority feelings in the child, who is surrounded by those who are bigger and stronger and who function more effectively physically. However, what is most important is our attitude toward our bodies (Adler, 1964b). Many attractive men and women have never resolved childhood feelings of ugliness and unacceptability, and they still behave as if they were unattractive. On the other hand, those who have physical deficiencies may, through compensation, strive hard and develop their bodies to a greater than average extent.

Social Relationships

Social relationships are of central importance in Adler's theories. They are a direct expression of social interest and are essential in developing a fulfilling, constructive lifestyle. Adler never forgot that we are social beings. Without society and social relationships, the individual would have no language and would enjoy extremely limited thinking and functioning.

Will

For Adler, *will* is another name for the striving for superiority and the actualizing of life goals. As such, it is a central element in his theory. What is crucial for Adler is that the will be used constructively for individual growth and social cooperation. The will is misused when it is directed toward self-centered, self-aggrandizing goals.

Emotions

Adler writes of two kinds of emotions: socially disjunctive emotions, which are related to individual goal attainment, and socially conjunctive emotions, which promote social interaction. Disjunctive emotions, such as anger, fear, or disgust, are intended to bring about a positive change in the life situation of the individual, although sometimes at the expense of others. They result from a sense of failure or inadequacy and serve to mobilize the individual's strength to make fresh efforts (Adler, 1956). Conjunctive emotions tend to be socially oriented, as in the desire to share our joy and laughter with others. The emotion of sympathy is "the purest expression of social interest" and reveals the extent to which we can relate to others (1956, p. 228).

Arnold Schwarzenegger during his body-building career

Intellect

Adler distinguishes between reason and intelligence. Neurotics, criminals, and others who do not function successfully in society are often quite intelligent. Frequently, they give perfectly logical arguments and justifications for their behavior. However, Adler has called this kind of intelligence *personal intelligence,* or thinking that is bound by the individual's goal of personal superiority rather than by socially useful considerations. Reason is "the kind of intelligence which contains social interest and which is thus limited to the generally useful" (1956, p. 150). Reason is in accord with common sense, which comes out of basic cultural attitudes and values.

Self

The *self* is the individual's style of life. It is the personality viewed as an integrated whole.

> In real life we always find a confirmation of the melody of the total self, of the personality, with its thousandfold ramifications. If we believe that the foundation, the ultimate basis of everything has been found in character traits, drives, or reflexes, the self is likely to be overlooked. Authors who emphasize a part of the whole are likely to attribute to this part all the aptitudes and observations pertaining to the self, the individual. They show "something" which is endowed with prudence, determination, volition, and creative power without knowing that they are actually describing the self, rather than drives, character traits, or reflexes. (Adler, 1956, p. 175)

For Adler, the self is a dynamic, unitary *principle* rather than a structure to be found within the psyche. "[In Adlerian psychology] the self is not considered as an entity. . . . There is literally no self to actualize but through transactions with its world" (Ansbacher, 1971, p. 60). Adler's position concerning the self strongly resembles the concept of *selflessness* in Buddhist psychology.

Therapist

The aim of Adlerian psychotherapy is to help the individual reconstruct assumptions and goals in accord with greater social usefulness. Adler defines three major aspects of therapy: understanding the specific lifestyle of the patient, helping patients understand themselves, and strengthening social interest.

> There must be uncovered, step by step, the unattainable goal of superiority over all; the purposive concealment of this goal; the all-dominating, direction-giving power of the goal; the patient's lack of freedom and his hostility toward mankind, which are determined by the goal. (Adler, 1956, p. 333)

Understanding the Lifestyle Therapy requires cooperation. One of the first tasks is to address the goals and expectations of each patient. Patients often expect from the therapist the kind of response they have gotten from everyone else. The patient may feel misunderstood, unloved, or unfairly treated. The therapist must carefully avoid meeting these unconscious expectations.

Because the lifestyle forms a basically consistent whole, the therapist looks for themes that run through the individual's behavior. In order to determine their lifestyles, Adler asked patients for their earliest memories, the most salient events from early childhood: "There are no 'chance memories'; out of the incalculable number of impressions which meet an individual, he chooses to remember only those which he feels, however darkly, to have a bearing on his situation" (1931, p. 73).

Adler also emphasized the importance of expressive behavior, including posture and intonation: "I have found it of considerable value to conduct myself as during pantomime, that is, for a while not to pay any attention to the words of the patient, but instead to read his deeper intention from his bearing and his movements within a situation" (1956, p. 330).

> Even when a patient lies it is of value to me. . . . [I]t is his lie and nobody else's! What he cannot disguise is his own originality. (Adler in Bottome, 1957, p. 162)

Adler assumed that the patient's life plan had developed under negative conditions, so the therapist should be sensitized to look for organ inferiority, pampering, or neglect in childhood.

Promoting Self-understanding Adler viewed the major problem of most patients as being their erroneous schema of apperception, determined by an unattainable and unrealistic goal of superiority over others. One of the major tasks of the therapist is to help patients understand their own lifestyles, including their basic approaches to life. Only after self-understanding is reached can people correct their nonadaptive style of life: "A patient has to be brought into such a state of feeling that he likes to listen, and wants to understand. Only then can he be influenced to live what he has understood" (1956, p. 335). Self-understanding means learning to see the mistakes we make in coping with daily situations. It involves gaining a better understanding of the world and of our place in it.

According to Adler, success in therapy is always up to the patient.

> The actual change in the nature of the patient can only be his own doing. . . . One should always look at the treatment and the cure not as the success of the consultant but as the success of the patient. The adviser can only point out the mistakes, it is the patient who must make the truth living. (1956, p. 336)

Adler placed greater value on learning to understand the consequences of our behavior than on learning more about our inner experience. For Adler, insight is not merely intellectual understanding. It is understanding translated into constructive action.

Psychotherapy is an exercise in cooperation and a test of cooperation. We can succeed only if we are genuinely interested in the other. (Adler, 1956, p. 340)

Strengthening Social Interest Therapy is a cooperative enterprise between therapist and patient, a supportive relationship that helps the patient develop a sense of cooperation and social interest: "The task of the physician or psychologist is to give the patient the experience of contact with a fellow man, and then to enable him to transfer this awakened social interest to others" (Adler, 1956, p. 341).

> We can succeed only if we are genuinely interested in the other. We must be able to see with his eyes and listen with his ears. He must contribute his part to our common understanding. . . . Even if we felt we'd understood him we should have no witness that we were right unless he also understood. (Adler, 1929, p. 340)

Adler pointed out that the therapist often has to provide the care, support, and sense of cooperation that the patient never received from his or her parents. Adler was convinced that concern for self rather than for others is at the core of most psychological problems. He felt that the major task of the therapist is gradually to guide the patient away from exclusive interest in self toward working constructively for others as a valuable member of the community. In caring for the patient, the therapist serves as a role model for social interest.

The Role of the Therapist As a therapist, Adler worked to establish a sense of equality between patient and therapist. He preferred facing the patient to sitting behind the reclining patient, as was Freud's practice. Adler would also engage in a free discussion, not free association. His beliefs and attitudes concerning the therapeutic relationship seem to foreshadow the work of Carl Rogers.

Adler strongly believed in empowering others. He felt that patients had to work to change themselves. The therapist could provide only insight and support. "A patient is like a person in a dark room. He complains to me, 'I cannot get out.' I switch on the light and point out the door-handle. If he still says that he cannot get out—I know that he does not wish to get out!" (Adler in Bottome, p. 101).

I tell [patients] "You can be cured in fourteen days if you follow this prescription. Try to think every day how you can please someone." (Adler, 1956, p. 347)

Adlerian psychology distinguishes between psychotherapy and counseling. Therapy seeks to bring about a fundamental change in an individual's unhealthy lifestyle. Counseling is aimed at changing behavior within an existing lifestyle.

Evaluation

Adler's theories have had a great impact on humanistic psychology, psychotherapy, and personality theory. Many of his concepts have been integrated into other schools of thought. Adler's stress on social interest has made psychotherapy much more social in orientation. Also, his concern with conscious, rational processes has created the first ego psychology. In fact, it has been suggested that neo-Adlerian is a more accurate term than *neo-Freudian* for theorists such as Erich Fromm, Karen Horney, and Harry Stack Sullivan (Wittels, 1939). In the words of one writer, "most observations and ideas of Alfred Adler have subtly and quietly permeated modern psychological thinking to such a degree that the proper question is not whether one is Adlerian but how much of an Adlerian one is" (Wilder, 1959, p. xv). Adler's thoughts have had a major influence on many other eminent psychologists, yet, astonishingly, he is relatively unknown outside the field.

Viktor Frankl and Rollo May, noted existential analysts, have regarded Adler's psychology as an influential precursor to existential psychiatry (Frankl, 1970; May, 1970), and Adler's interest in holism, goal-directedness, and the role of values in human behavior anticipated many of the developments of humanistic psychology. Abraham Maslow writes:

> For me Alfred Adler becomes more and more correct year by year. As the facts come in, they give stronger and stronger support to his image of man. . . . [I]n one respect especially the times have not yet caught up with him. I refer to his holistic emphasis. (1970, p. 13)

However, Adler has failed to receive the credit he really deserves. Concepts original to Adler are often seen as derivatives of psychoanalytic theory or as self-evident or trivial. In his survey of major psychiatric schools of thought, Ellenberger argues:

> It would not be easy to find another author from which so much has been borrowed from all sides without acknowledgment than Alfred Adler. His teaching has become . . . a place where anyone and all may come and draw anything without compunction. An author will meticulously quote the source of any sentence he takes from elsewhere, but it does not occur to

> him to do the same whenever the source is individual psychology; it is as if nothing original could ever come from Adler. (1970, p. 645)

Albert Ellis, the founder of rational-emotive therapy, goes even further in his assessment of Adler's contributions:

> Alfred Adler, more even than Freud, is probably the true father of modern psychotherapy. Some of the reasons are: He founded ego psychology, which Freudians only recently rediscovered. He was one of the first humanistic psychologists. . . . He stressed holism, goal-seeking, and the enormous importance of values in human thinking, emoting, and acting. He correctly saw that sexual drives and behavior, while having great importance in human affairs, are largely the result rather than the cause of man's non-sexual philosophies.
>
> It is difficult to find any leading therapist today who in some respect does not owe a great debt to the Individual Psychology of Alfred Adler. (1970, p. 11)

One reason for Adler's relative lack of popularity lies in his writing style. He was an excellent speaker and much preferred lecturing to writing. His writing is not always precise, and his theorizing tends to be phrased in a simple, commonsensical manner that often seems superficial or shallow. Adler was more interested in practice than in theory. He was at his best in dealing with actual case materials; thus his work has tended to be most popular among teachers, social workers, clinical practitioners, and others who require practical psychological skills in their professional work. Adler's seminal contributions to the development of modern psychology include the idea of the inferiority complex, examination of the role of power and aggression in human behavior, the concept of unity of the personality, and stress on the significance of nonsexual factors in development.

Recent Developments: Adler's Influence

Many of Adler's pioneering ideas have become so well accepted that they are taken for granted today. His work on the interaction of psychological and physical elements in organ inferiority was instrumental in establishing psychosomatic medicine, and his writings laid the foundations of the increasingly popular field of parenting. Almost every modern book on parenting makes use of Adler's principles of child discipline, generally without giving him much credit. Adler's student Rudolf Dreikurs has had a powerful influence on this field. His book *Children: The Challenge* (1964) has become a classic.

Adlerian training institutes, family education centers, study groups, and professional societies are growing in size and influence (Mosak, 1989). The first Adlerian psychology textbook written in English, *Individual Psychology* (Manaster & Corsini, 1982), has generated widespread interest. *A Bibliography of Adlerian Psychology,* in two volumes, covers over ten thousand references to the literature of Adlerian psychology (Mosak & Mosak, 1975a, 1975b).

Adlerian psychology is flourishing. Adler's influence on leading psychologists, such as Abraham Maslow, Carl Rogers, and Rollo May, has been well documented (Ansbacher, 1990). A major biography of Adler appeared in 1994 (Hoffman). Adlerian theory has been shown to be a precursor to cognitive theory in many ways (Scott, Kelly, & Tolbert, 1995) and continues to influence educational psychology (Carlson, 1995), counseling (Kern, 1993; Nystul, 1995), and child therapy (Mosak & Maniacci, 1993; Kottman, 1995).

The Theory Firsthand

Excerpt from *Social Interest*

The following passage provides an example of Adler's analytic methods.

A woman thirty-two years of age complained of a violent pain around the left side of her left eye and of double vision which compelled her to keep her left eye closed. The patient had had attacks like that for eleven years; the first occurred when she became engaged to her husband. . . . She blamed a cold bath for her last attack and believed that her former attacks were caused by cold draughts. . . .

Before her marriage she had taught the violin, had also appeared at concerts, and liked her work; but she had given it up after her marriage. She was now living with her brother-in-law's family, to be nearer to the doctor, as she said, and she was quite happy there. . . .

She is undoubtedly the ruling partner in her marriage, but she comes up against her husband's indolence and his desire for peace. He works hard, comes home tired late in the evening, and is not inclined to go out with his wife or carry on a conversation with her. If she has to play in public she suffers from violent stage-fright. The question introduced by me as an important one, What would she do if she were in good health?—a question the answer to which shows clearly the reason for the patient's timid retreat—she answers evasively with a reference to her perpetual headaches. . . . The patient persists in asserting that cold in any form hurts her and brings about all sorts of attacks. Nevertheless, before her last attack she took a cold bath, which, as she says, promptly caused the attack. . . .

It appeared that the patient ever since she had witnessed with the utmost horror the birth of a younger sister had had an insane anxiety about child-bearing. . . . When she was eleven years old her father had accused her unjustly of having sexual intercourse with a neighbor's son. This premature contact with the sexual relationship, closely associated with terror and anxiety, made her protest against love more vigorous, and this protest appeared during her marriage as frigidity. Before entering into the marriage she asked a binding declaration from her bridegroom that he would permanently deny himself any children. Her attacks of migraine and the fear of them that constantly possessed her made it easier for her to assume a relationship that reduced conjugal intercourse to a minimum. . . .

She certainly esteems her husband highly, but she is far from being in love with him; indeed she has never really been in love. When asked repeatedly what she would do if she were permanently cured she answered at length that she would remove to the capital, give violin lessons there, and play in an orchestra. Any one who has acquired the art of guessing taught by Individual Psychology would have no difficulty in understanding that this meant separation from her husband, who was tied to the provincial town. . . . Since her husband has a great admiration for her and gives her incomparably the best opportunity to ride her craving for power at full gallop, it is naturally very difficult for her to separate from him. . . .

A complete cure was effected within a month. Previous to that came the explanation of the exogenous factor that had led to the last attack. She found in her husband's coat pocket a letter from a girl containing merely a few words of greeting. Her husband was able to allay her suspicion. None the less she continued to be suspicious and entertained a jealousy of her husband she had never felt before. From that time she kept watch on him. It was during this period that she took the cold bath and her attack began. . . . In explanation she says that she has never been jealous, that her pride has forbidden her that vice, but that since the discovery of the letter she had considered the possibility of her husband's being unfaithful to her. When she thought of the likelihood of this her wrath increased—against the assumed dependence of the wife on the husband. Her cold bath was therefore really the revenge of her style of life for what she imagined to be the unquestionable dependence of her worth upon her husband, and for his failure to appreciate that worth. Had she not had her attack of migraine—the result of her shock—then she would have had to admit that she was worthless. This however would have been the worst that could have happened to her. (Adler, 1964a, pp. 75–85)

Chapter Highlights

- Adler's main contributions to modern psychology are the significance of nonsexual factors in the environment, the concept of the unity of the personality, the role of power and aggression in human behavior, and the concept of the inferiority complex.
- Adler stressed the uniqueness of the individual, the importance of understanding the unity of the person, and the context of a social system.
- For the individual, conquest of the environment is a primary goal, but this drive is balanced by the importance of social interest, or community feeling and cooperation.
- As in behaviorism, concepts in Adlerian psychology are related to actual, concrete behavior. Stress is placed on overt behaviors and their consequences.
- Individual psychology focuses on the relations between the environment and the individual rather than on intrapsychic dynamics.
- The individual's attempts to compensate for organ inferiority or inferiority feelings result in virtually all progress and underlie humankind's most significant achievements.
- The drive for power is fundamental. A later formulation of this principle is the concept of striving for superiority, which includes the role of development and creative growth.
- The evolutionary process of conscious adaptation to the environment is the foundation for the individual's striving for perfection, or mastering of the environment in a superior way.
- The goal of superiority or perfection motivates healthy individuals to seek continuous improvement and growth. Such striving is positive if it

includes social concerns and interest in the welfare of others. It is negative if the focus is on personal superiority through domination of others.

- To become a worthy human being is a goal of the individual. Life's supreme law is that diminishment of the sense of self-worth is not to be allowed.
- Behavior is determined by the individual's conception of the world.
- Psychological and emotional problems must be considered and treated in the context of the individual's life goals and lifestyle. The unified lifestyle of the individual is manifest in every trait or symptom.
- Creativity—the capacity to formulate both goals and the means of achieving them—is at the core of the individual. The life goal provides self-consistent organization of one's life; it is a creative response to the environment.
- Community feeling, or social interest, is the sense of the larger social context and of the connectedness of the individual to family, community, society, and humanity.
- Cooperation is a key facet in social interest. Feelings of inferiority can be overcome only through the individual's active participation as a contributing and valuable member of society.
- At the root of maladaptive or neurotic styles of life are a lack of cooperation and the resulting sense of failure and inadequacy.
- The healthy individual is cooperative, has strong social interest, and constructively strives for superiority.
- Every neurosis is an attempt to gain a feeling of competence and to overcome feelings of inferiority. Neurosis isolates the individual; it leads away from social functioning and the solving of real-life problems. To cure a neurosis, the therapist helps the patient completely change his or her orientation, to direct the patient back into society.
- Personal superiority is sought by individuals who are lacking in the confidence that they can function effectively and constructively with others. Feelings of inferiority predominate.
- It is more important to understand the consequences of behavior than to focus on one's inner experience. Insight is not simply intellectual understanding but understanding translated into constructive action.
- At the core of most psychological problems is concern for self rather than concern for others.

Key Concepts

Apperception Perception involving a subjective interpretation of what the senses perceive.

Inferiority complex The feeling of inadequacy that results from children's sense of their small size and powerlessness. Adler looked at the psychological aspects of inferiority, which he believed touched the life experiences of all children. (See *Organ inferiority*.)

Life goal An individual's focus for achievement. Formation begins in childhood as a compensation for inferiority feelings, and continues as a defense against feelings of impotence.

Lifestyle The individual's unique manner of interacting with and adapting to life in general, in pursuit of his or her life goal.

Organ inferiority The concept that in each person's biological structure, some organs are weaker, more susceptible to disease than others. Through training and exercise, the individual can make the weak organ become his or her greatest strength or asset. (See *Inferiority complex.*)

Schema of apperception An individual's conception of the world and of self, developed as part of the lifestyle and generally self-reinforcing.

Social interest The community sharing of values and feelings. In its broadest sense, the term refers to feelings of relatedness and kinship with all humanity as well as to the whole of life.

Annotated Bibliography

Adler, A. (1929). *The practice and theory of individual psychology.* London: Routledge & Kegan Paul.

A collection of essays and discussions on neurosis and psychological problems, including considerable case material.

———. (1931). *What life should mean to you.* Boston: Little, Brown.

A clearly written exposition of Adler's basic concepts, for the layperson.

———. (1956). *The individual psychology of Alfred Adler: A systematic presentation in selections from his writings* (H. L. Ansbacher & R. R. Ansbacher, Eds.). New York: Harper & Row.

The best introduction to Adler's work; it includes materials that are not available elsewhere in English. Two major sections: personality theory and abnormal psychology.

———. (1964). *Superiority and social interest: A collection of later writings* (H. L. Ansbacher & R. R. Ansbacher, Eds.). New York: Viking Press.

Includes sections on theory, case studies, religion, and various applications of individual psychology. Also contains an essay on the increasing recognition of Adler, a biography, and a definitive bibliography of Adler's writings.

Dreikurs, R. (1957). *Psychology in the classroom: A manual for teachers.* New York: Harper & Row.

An application of Adler's theories to education, including extensive case material.

Manaster, G. J., & Corsini, R. J. (1982). *Individual psychology.* Itasca, IL: F. E. Peacock.

The first textbook of Adlerian psychology written in English. It includes a complete Adlerian psychotherapy case summary and also a section on research in Adlerian psychology.

References

Ackerknecht, L. (n.d.). *Recent influences of Adlerian psychology on general psychology.* Unpublished manuscript.

Adler, A. (1912). *The neurotic constitution.* New York: Moffat, Yard.

———. (1928). *Understanding human nature.* London: Allen & Unwin.

———. (1929). *The practice and theory of individual psychology.* London: Routledge & Kegan Paul.

———. (1930). *The science of living.* London: Allen & Unwin.

———. (1931). *What life should mean to you.* Boston: Little, Brown.

———. (1956). *The individual psychology of Alfred Adler: A systematic presentation in selections from his writings* (H. L. Ansbacher & R. R. Ansbacher, Eds.). New York: Harper & Row.

———. (1964a). *Social interest: A challenge to mankind.* New York: Capricorn Books.

———. (1964b). *Superiority and social interest: A collection of later writings* (H. L. Ansbacher & R. R. Ansbacher, Eds.). New York: Viking Press.

———. (1973). Sex. In J. Miller (Ed.), *Psychoanalysis and women.* Baltimore: Penguin Books.

Adler, K., & Deutsch, D. (Eds.). (1959). *Essays in individual psychology.* New York: Grove Press.

Ansbacher, H. L. (1971). Alfred Adler and humanistic psychology. *Journal of Humanistic Psychology, 2,* 53–63.

———. (1974). The Adlerian and Jungian schools. [Part] A: Individual psychology. In S. Arieti (Ed.), *American handbook of psychiatry.* New York: Basic Books.

———. (1990). Alfred Adler's influence on the three leading cofounders of humanistic psychology. *Journal of Humanistic Psychology, 30,* 45–53.

Bottome, P. (1957). *Alfred Adler: A portrait from life.* New York: Vanguard Press.

Carlson, J. (1995). Adlerian parent consultation. In A. Dougherty (Ed.), *Case studies in human services consultation.* Pacific Grove, CA: Brooks/Cole.

Dreikurs, R. (1950). *Fundamentals of Adlerian psychology.* New York: Greenberg.

———. (1957). *Psychology in the classroom: A manual for teachers.* New York: Harper & Row.

———. (1964). *Children: The challenge.* New York: Dutton.

Ellenberger, H. (1970). *The discovery of the unconscious: The history and evolution of dynamic psychiatry.* New York: Basic Books.

Ellis, A. (1970). Tributes to Alfred Adler on his hundredth birthday. *Journal of Individual Psychology, 26,* 11–12.

Frankl, V. (1970). Tributes to Alfred Adler on his hundredth birthday. *Journal of Individual Psychology, 26,* 12.

Hall, C., & Lindzey, G. (1957). *Theories of personality.* New York: Wiley.

Hoffman, E. (1994). *The drive for self: Alfred Adler and the founding of individual psychology.* Reading, MA: Addison Wesley.

Kern, C. (1993). Adlerian counseling. *TCA Journal, 21,* 85–95.

Kottman, T. (1995). *Partners in play: An Adlerian approach to play therapy.* Alexandria, VA: American Counseling Association.

Lakein, A. (1974). *How to get control of your time and your life.* New York: New American Library.

Manaster, G. J., & Corsini, R. J. (1982). *Individual psychology.* Itasca, IL: F. E. Peacock.

Maslow, A. (1970). Tributes to Alfred Adler on his hundredth birthday. *Journal of Individual Psychology, 26,* 13.

May, R. (1970). Tributes to Alfred Adler on his hundredth birthday. *Journal of Individual Psychology, 26,* 13.

Mosak, H. (1989). Adlerian psychotherapy. In R. Corsini & D. Wedding (Eds.), *Current psychotherapies* (4th ed.). Itasca, IL: F. E. Peacock.

Mosak, H., & Maniacci, M. (1993). Adlerian child psychotherapy. In R. Kratochwill & J. Morris (Eds.), *Handbook of psychotherapy with children and adolescents.* Boston: Allyn & Bacon.

Mosak, H., & Mosak B. (1975a). *A bibliography of Adlerian psychology* (Vol. 1). Washington, DC: Hemisphere.

———. (1975b). *A bibliography of Adlerian psychology* (Vol. 2). Washington, DC: Hemisphere.

Nystul, M. (1995). A problem solving approach to counseling. *Elementary School Guidance and Counseling, 29,* 297–302.

Orgler, H. (1939). *Alfred Adler: The man and his work.* London: Daniel.

Scott, C., Kelly, F., & Tolbert, B. (1995). Realism, constructivism, and the individual psychology of Alfred Adler. *Individual Psychology Journal of Adlerian Theory, Research and Practice, 51,* 4–20.

Way, L. (1950). *Adler's place in psychology.* London: Allen & Unwin.

Wilder, J. (1959). Introduction. In K. Adler & D. Deutsch (Eds.), *Essays in individual psychology.* New York: Grove Press.

Wittels, F. (1939). The neo-Adlerians. *American Journal of Sociology, 45,* 433–445.

CHAPTER 5

Anna Freud and the Post-Freudians

Melanie Klein, Donald Winnicott, Heinz Kohut, and the Gestalt Therapy of Fritz and Laura Perls

While Sigmund Freud and many others surmised that the theory of psychoanalysis could be applied to the understanding of every individual, the therapeutic method was acknowledged by most practitioners, including Freud himself, to be severely limited in the kinds of patients and the range of pathology for which it was suited.

A number of the early followers of Freud quarreled with him about the theory and the practice and left to form their own dissident movements. Several of the theories associated with those movements are described in Chapters 3 and 4. However, a number of important theorists and therapists stayed within the Freudian overview, extending psychoanalysis to include new conditions and populations as well as adding new approaches to the practice of psychoanalysis. These followers included his daughter Anna, a number of analysts who knew Freud late in his life, and some whose contributions came from outside the central circle of influence.[1]

Anna Freud

Personal History

Freud's staunchest supporter was his daughter Anna, who not only made major theoretical contributions to psychoanalysis but also developed, taught, and encouraged the use of this type of treatment with disturbed young children. Perhaps even more important, she pioneered the use of psychoanalytic insights to teaching and helping normal children in difficult life situations. Many textbooks and histories underplay her contributions, for several reasons:

- She had the same last name as her famous father.
- She lived in his home, and was his constant companion, aide, and colleague until his death.
- She did not seek special recognition but did her work quietly with the hundreds of child analysts she trained and with the children she loved.

Anna Freud, the last of Freud's six children, was born in 1895, in a large, comfortable house in a good neighborhood in Vienna, where she stayed until the age of 43, when she and her father both fled to London to escape the Nazi takeover.

In 1914, at age 18, just out of high school, Anna Freud was courted by Ernest Jones, a staunch Freudian who would later be Freud's first major biographer (Jones, 1953, 1955, 1957). This potential match did not suit the senior Freud at all. He found Jones too old (he was 35) and thought his motivations dubious. Anna said later, "Naturally I was flattered and impressed, though not without a lurking suspicion that his interest was directed more to my father than to myself" (in Young-Bruehl, 1988). Shortly thereafter, she trained in an elementary school to be a teacher and taught in a small private school for five years. She says, "As I look back . . . I realize how important those years were.

[1]Several reviewers correctly complained that Fritz and Laura Perls would not be seen by the other post-Freudians as one of their number. However, the Perlses, like the others, saw their own work initially as an extension of Sigmund Freud's and only later acknowledged a greater independence.

They offered me a chance to know 'normal' children before I started seeing children who were in trouble for one reason or another" (A. Freud in Coles, 1992, p. 5).

When she was 23 years old, she underwent two years of psychoanalysis with her father. Today such an event would be unthinkable, because of the private nature of psychoanalysis as well as the considerations given to the role of sexual issues said to occur between parents and children. But in the beginning, when Freud's work was experimental, analysis of a daughter by her father was noted as unusual but not inappropriate.

Concerning the analysis of your son, that certainly is a ticklish business. . . . With my own daughter I succeeded well. . . . [However,] I would not advise you to do it and have no right to forbid it. (S. Freud in a letter to psychoanalyst Eduardo Weiss, 1935)

Whatever else occurred during the therapy, it sharpened Anna's interest in psychoanalysis, which became the focus of her subsequent career. By 1926, she was a practicing psychoanalyst, working with children and lecturing to teacher and parents on how the insights of psychoanalytic theory could be useful in their normal interactions with children. Her early lectures were published as *The Psychoanalytic Treatment of Children* (1964, Vol. 1). A year later she lectured at the Tenth International Psychoanalytic Congress on the different ways to work with adults and children. These ideas were later expanded into *Psychoanalysis for Teachers and Parents* (1964, Vol. 1).

While the fact that she worked with small children was in itself a radical extension of her father's original investigations, it was overshadowed by the publication, in 1936, of her most important book, *The Ego and the Mechanisms of Defense.* Before this book appeared, psychoanalytic thinking focused primarily on the id and instinctual drives. After it, both theory and treatment included more attention to the daily activities directed by or in the domain of the ego.

On March 22, 1938, nine days after German troops crossed the Austrian border, Anna was detained and interrogated by the Gestapo. Shortly thereafter, Anna and her father, then 82 years old and not at all well, left for England. He died 18 months later, in the first few weeks of World War II.

During the war, Anna helped organize and run the Hampstead Nursery in London, which consoled and supported families whose lives were disrupted by the war and, more especially, by the bombings of London itself. In two books, *War and Children* and *Infants Without Families* (1964–1981, Vol. 3), she described the mental and emotional damage that happens to ordinary people in terrible circumstances.

In sharp distinction to the conventional wisdom that sent thousands of children out of London to institutions in the countryside, she found that

> war acquires comparatively little significance for children as long as it only threatens their lives, disturbs their material comfort or cuts their food rations. It becomes enormously significant the moment it breaks up family life and uproots the first emotional attachments of the child within the family group. London children were, therefore, much less upset by bombing than by evacuation to the country as a protection against it. (Vol. 3)

In 1947, while maintaining a private practice, Freud established the Hampstead Clinic, a training center to educate those who wished to be child analysts. Until the end of her life she continued to work there with children, to train teachers, and to extend the domain and scope of psychoanalysis.

She lived in England—in the house where she and her father had settled—with a good friend, the psychoanalyst (and former analysand of Sigmund Freud's) Dorothy Burlingham, until Anna's own death in 1979. (See Burlingham, 1989.)

Anna Freud's most important intellectual influences were the ideas of her father, followed by the works of other analysts—both those favorable to his views and those deeply opposed. Beyond the psychoanalytic world, Anna Freud's decision to become a teacher of children and her subsequent career working with children owed much to the work of Maria Montessori and the schools she and her followers developed, which saw the child as capable of insight, discipline, and self-awareness at an early age. In addition, Freud had a fondness for nonanalytic writers whose capacity to describe the contradictions in the lives and minds of individuals were sources of her own lifelong self-instruction. She knew the works of Goethe and Rilke well and said that both had been strong influences on her own thinking.

Asked what she would do in her later years (she was over 70 at that time) Anna Freud replied, "I don't know anything else to do but be with children—and those [adults] who also choose to be with children." (in Coles, 1992, p. 27)

She loved poetry, and I heard she wrote it; and she had memorized a number of poems. She loved to encourage the children to make music and art. (E. Erikson in Coles, 1992, p. 14)

Principal Contributions: The Defense Mechanisms

Anna Freud's descriptions of ego defenses passed into the therapeutic literature and from there into general use with little dissent. According to Freud, each of us wards off anxieties with a combination of strategies that arise from our genetic predisposition, external difficulties, and the microculture of our family and community.

Defenses used with awareness and self-understanding make life more endurable and more successful. However, when defenses obscure reality and impede our ability to function, they become neurotic and their effects are damaging.

The **defense mechanisms** described here are repression, denial, rationalization, reaction formation, projection, isolation, regression, and sublimation. All the defenses except sublimation block the direct expression of instinctual needs. Although any of these mechanisms can be and are found in healthy individuals, their very presence is an indication of possible neurosis.

Repression

Repression forces a potentially anxiety-provoking event, idea, or perception away from consciousness, thus precluding any possible resolution. "The essence of repression lies simply in turning something away, and keeping it at a distance, from the consciousness" (S. Freud, 1915, p. 147). Unfortunately, the repressed element is still part of the psyche, though unconscious, and remains active. "Repression is never performed once and for all but requires a constant expenditure of energy to maintain the repression, while the repressed constantly tries to find an outlet" (Fenichel, 1945, p. 150).

Hysterical symptoms are often found to have originated in earlier repression. Some psychosomatic ailments, such as asthma, arthritis, and ulcers, may be linked to repression. Excessive lassitude, phobias, and impotence or frigidity may also be derivatives of repressed feelings. For example, if you have strongly ambivalent feelings about your father, you might love him and at the same time wish he were dead. The desire for his death, the accompanying fantasies, and your resulting feelings of guilt and shame might all be unconscious because both your ego and your superego would find the idea unacceptable. Should your father actually die, these conflicting feelings would be still more rigidly repressed. To admit to your ambivalence would mean you felt pleasure at

If the ego employs repression the formation of symptoms relieves it of the task of mastering its conflicts. (A. Freud, 1946, p. 52)

his death, a reaction even more unacceptable to your superego than the original resentment or hostility. In this situation, you might appear unaffected or unmoved by his death, the repression withholding your genuine and appropriate grief and sense of loss as well as your inexpressible hostility.

There are times in life when you must face reality directly and then deny it. (Garrison Keillor, 1995)

Denial **Denial** is the unwillingness to accept an event that disturbs the ego. Adults have a tendency to "daydream" that certain events are not so, that they didn't really happen. This flight into fantasy can take many forms, some of which seem absurd to the objective observer. The following traditional story is an illustration:

> A woman was brought into court at the request of her neighbor. This neighbor charged that the woman had borrowed and damaged a valuable vase. When it came time for the woman to defend herself, her defense was threefold: "In the first place, I never borrowed the vase. Second, it was chipped when I took it. Finally, your honor, I returned it in perfect condition."

People are in general not candid over sexual matters. They do not show their sexuality freely, but to conceal it they wear a heavy overcoat woven of a tissue of lies, as though the weather were bad in the world of sexuality. (S. Freud in Malcolm, 1980)

The form of denial found most often in psychotherapy is the remarkable tendency to remember events incorrectly. An example is the patient who vividly recalls one version of an incident, then at a later time may recall the incident differently and become suddenly aware that the first version was a defensive fabrication.

Sigmund Freud did not claim that his clinical investigations, which led to his theories, were entirely original. In fact, he quotes Charles Darwin's and Friedrich Nietzsche's observations about themselves. Darwin, in his autobiography, noted:

> I had during years followed a golden rule, namely, whenever I came across a published fact, a new observation or idea, which ran counter to my general results, I made a memorandum of it without fail and at once; for I had found by experience that such facts and ideas were far more apt to slip the memory than favorable ones. (Darwin in S. Freud, 1901, p. 148)

Nietzsche commented on a different aspect of the same process:

> "I have done that," says my memory. "It is impossible that I should have done it," says my pride, and it remains inexorable. Finally my memory yields. (Nietzsche in S. Freud, 1901, p. 148)

Rationalization **Rationalization** is the process of finding acceptable reasons for unacceptable thoughts or actions. It is a process whereby a person presents an explanation that is either ethically acceptable to others or logically consistent with an attitude, action, idea, or feeling that actually arises from other motivating sources. We use rationalization to justify our behavior when in fact the reasons for our actions are not commendable or not even understood by us. The following statements might be rationalizations (the statements in parentheses are possible unexpressed feelings):

> "I'm doing this for your own good." (I want to do this to you. I don't want it done to me. I even want you to suffer a little bit.)
>
> "The experiment was a logical continuation of my prior work." (It started as a mistake; I was lucky that it worked out.)

Personal Reflection

■ Defense Mechanisms

Recall a time or an event that was psychologically painful—for example, the death of a close friend or relative—or a time when you were deeply humiliated, beaten up, or caught in a crime. Notice first of all your lack of interest in recalling the event clearly and, further, your resistance even to thinking about it. Your tendency may be to say, "I don't want to do this. I can skip this exercise. Why should I think about that again?" If you can, overcome your initial defenses with an act of will and try to recall the event. You may be aware of strong feelings all over again. If it is too difficult to stay focused on the memory, notice instead the ways your mind keeps diverting your attention. Can you begin to see the mechanisms people use to avoid psychic tension?

Rationalization is a way of accepting pressure from the superego; it disguises our motives, rendering our actions morally acceptable. As an obstacle to growth, it prevents the person who is rationalizing (or anyone else!) from working with, observing, and understanding the genuine, less-commendable motivating forces. When a rationalization is viewed from the outside, as in the following story, its foolish aspect is obvious:

> "I have chosen," said the mouse, "to like cheese. Such an important decision, needless to say, cannot be arrived at without a sufficient period of careful deliberation. One does not deny the immediate, indefinable aesthetic attraction of the substance. Yet this in itself is possible only to the more refined type of individual—as an example, the brutish fox lacks the sensitive discrimination even to approach cheese.
>
> "Other factors in the choice are not less susceptible to rational analysis: which is, of course, as it should be.
>
> "The attractive colour, suitable texture, adequate weight, interestingly different shapes, relatively numerous places of occurrence, reasonable ease of digestion, comparative abundance of variety in nutritional content, ready availability, considerable ease of transport, total absence of side-effects—these and a hundred other easily defined factors abundantly prove my good sense and deep insights, consciously exercised in the making of this wise and deliberate choice." (Shah, 1972, p. 138)

Reaction Formation **Reaction formation** substitutes behaviors or feelings that are diametrically opposed to the actual wish; it is an explicit and usually unconscious inversion of the wish.

Like other defense mechanisms, reaction formations are developed first in childhood. "As the child becomes aware of sexual excitement which cannot be fulfilled, the sexual 'excitations' evoke opposing mental forces which, in order to suppress this unpleasure effectively, build up the mental dams of disgust, shame and morality" (S. Freud, 1905, p. 178). Not only is the original idea repressed, but any shame or self-reproach that might arise by admitting such thoughts is also excluded from awareness.

Unfortunately, the side effects of reaction formation may cripple social relationships. The principal identifying characteristics of reaction formation are its excessiveness, its rigidity, and its extravagance. The urge being denied must be repeatedly obscured.

The person who has built up reaction formations does not develop certain defense mechanisms for use when an instinctual danger threatens; he has changed his personality structure as if this danger were continually present, so that he may be ready whenever the danger occurs. (Fenichel, 1945)

The following letter was written to a researcher from an antivivisectionist. It is a clear example of one feeling—compassion toward all living things—used to disguise another feeling—a desire to harm and torture:

> I read [a magazine article] . . . on your work on alcoholism. . . . I am surprised that anyone who is as well educated as you must be to hold the position that you do would stoop to such a depth as to torture helpless little cats in the pursuit of a cure for alcoholics. . . . A drunkard does not want to be cured—a drunkard is just a weak-minded idiot who belongs in the gutter and should be left there. Instead of torturing helpless little cats why not torture the drunks or better still exert your would-be noble effort toward getting a bill passed to *exterminate* the drunks. . . . My greatest wish is that you have brought home to you a torture that will be a thousand fold greater than what you have, and are doing to the little animals. . . . If you are an example of what a noted psychiatrist should be I'm glad I am just an ordinary human being without letters after my name. I'd rather be just myself with a clear conscience, *knowing I have not hurt any living creature,* and can sleep without seeing frightened, terrified dying cats—because I know they must die after you have finished with them. No punishment is too great for you and I hope I live to read about your mangled body and long suffering before you finally die—and I'll laugh long and loud. (Masserman, 1961, p. 38)

Reaction formations may be evident in any excessive behavior. The homemaker who is continually cleaning her house may, in reality, be concentrating her awareness on being with and examining dirt. The parent who cannot admit his or her resentment of the children "may interfere so much in their lives, under the pretext of being concerned about their welfare and safety, that [the] overprotection is really a form of punishment" (Hall, 1954, p. 93). Reaction formation masks parts of the personality and restricts a person's capacity to respond to events; the personality may become relatively inflexible.

Projection The act of attributing to another person, animal, or object the qualities, feelings, or intentions that originate in oneself is called **projection.** It is a defense mechanism in which the aspects of one's own personality are displaced from within the individual onto the external environment. The threat is treated as if it were an external force. A person can therefore deal with actual feelings, but without admitting or being aware of the fact that the feared idea or behavior is his or her own. The following statements might be projections (the statement in parentheses could be the actual unconscious feeling):

1. "All that men/women want is one thing." (I think about sex a lot.)
2. "You can never trust a wop/spic/nigger/WASP/honky/college boy/woman/priest." (I want to take unfair advantage of others.)
3. "You're mad at me." (I'm mad at you.)

Whenever we characterize something "out there" as evil, dangerous, perverted, and so forth, without acknowledging that these characteristics might also be true for us, we are probably projecting. It is equally true that when we see others as being powerful, attractive, capable, and so forth, without appreciating the same qualities in ourselves, we are also projecting. The critical variable in projection is that we do not see in ourselves what seems vivid and obvious in another.

Research into the dynamics of prejudice has shown that people who tend to stereotype others also display little insight into their own feelings. People who deny having a specific personality trait are more critical of that trait when they see it in, or project it onto, others (Sears, 1936).

Isolation **Isolation** separates the anxiety-arousing parts of a situation from the rest of the psyche. It is the act of partitioning off, so that little or no emotional reaction remains connected to the event.

When a person discusses problems that have been isolated from the rest of the personality, the events are recounted without feeling, as if they had happened to a third party. This stoic approach can become a dominant style of coping. A person may withdraw more and more into ideas, having less and less contact with his or her own feelings.

Children sometimes play at isolation, dividing their identities into good and bad aspects. They may take a toy animal and have it say and do all kinds of forbidden things. The animal's personality may be tyrannical, rude, sarcastic, and unreasonable. Thus a child may be able to display, through the animal, these "splitting" behaviors that parents would not tolerate under normal circumstances.

Freud felt that the normal prototype of isolation is logical thinking, which also tries to detach the content from the emotional situation in which it is found. Isolation becomes a defense mechanism only when it is used to prevent the ego from accepting anxiety-ridden aspects of situations or relationships (S. Freud, 1926).

Regression **Regression** is a reversion to an earlier level of development or to a mode of expression that is simpler and more childlike. It is a way of alleviating anxiety by withdrawing from realistic thinking into behaviors that have reduced anxiety in the past. Linus, in the "Peanuts" comic strip, always returns to a safe psychological situation when he is under stress; he feels secure when he is holding his blanket. A person who is regressing may prefer the ice-cream flavor he or she was given as a child, or may reread a favorite book, as ways to withdraw from the present.

Sublimation **Sublimation** is the process whereby energy originally directed toward sexual or aggressive goals is redirected toward new aims—often artistic, intellectual, or cultural. Sublimation has been called the "successful defense" (Fenichel, 1945). If the original energy can be thought of as a river that periodically floods, destroying homes and property, sublimation is the building of dams and diversionary channels. These, in turn, may be used to generate electric power, irrigate formerly arid areas, create parks, and open up other recreational opportunities. The original energy of the river is successfully diverted into socially acceptable or culturally sanctioned channels. Sublimation, unlike the other defenses, actually resolves and eliminates the tension.

Personal Reflection

■ Regressive Behaviors

Regression is a primitive way of coping. Although it reduces anxiety, it often leaves the source of the anxiety unresolved. Consider the following extensive list of regressive behaviors suggested by Calvin Hall. See if it includes any of your own behaviors.

> Even healthy, well-adjusted people make regressions from time to time in order to reduce anxiety, or, as they say, to blow off steam. They smoke, get drunk, eat too much, lose their tempers, bite their nails, pick their noses, break laws, talk baby talk, destroy property, masturbate, read mystery stories, go to the movies, engage in unusual sexual practices, chew gum and tobacco, dress up as children, drive fast and recklessly, believe in good and evil spirits, take naps, fight and kill one another, bet on the horses, daydream, rebel against or submit to authority, gamble, preen before the mirror, act out their impulses, pick on scapegoats, and do a thousand and one other childish things. Some of these regressions are so commonplace that they are taken to be signs of maturity. Actually they are all forms of regression used by adults. (1954, pp. 95–96)

Do you agree with Hall that all the behaviors on his list are truly regressive?

The forces that can be employed for cultural activities are thus to a great extent obtained through the suppression of what are known as the "perverse" elements of sexual excitation. (S. Freud, 1908)

Sigmund Freud argued that the enormous energy and complexity of civilization results from the desire to find acceptable and sufficient outlets for suppressed energy. Civilization encourages the transcendence of the original drives and, in some cases, creates alternative goals that can be more satisfying to the id than the satisfaction of the original urges. This transformation "places extraordinarily large amounts of force at the disposal of civilized activity, and it does this in virtue of its especially marked characteristic of being able to displace its aim without materially diminishing its intensity" (S. Freud, 1908, p. 187).

Summary of the Defense Mechanisms The defenses described here are ways the psyche has to protect itself from internal or external tension. The defenses avoid reality (repression), exclude reality (denial), redefine reality (rationalization), or reverse reality (reaction formation). These mechanisms place inner feelings on the outer world (projection), partition reality (isolation), cause a withdrawal from reality (regression), or redirect reality (sublimation). In every case, libidinal energy is necessary to maintain the defense, indirectly limiting the flexibility and strength of the ego.

The defensive methods so far discovered by analysis all serve a single purpose—that of assisting the ego in its struggle with the instinctual life. . . . [I]n all these situations of conflict the ego is seeking to repudiate a part of its own id." (A . Freud, 1946, p. 73)

"When a defense becomes very influential, it dominates the ego and curtails its flexibility and its adaptability. Finally, if the defenses fail to hold, the ego has nothing to fall back upon and is overwhelmed by anxiety (Hall, 1954, p. 96). Each defense takes psychological energy away from more satisfying ego activities.

Further Developments in Psychoanalytic Theory: Melanie Klein, Donald Winnicott, and Heinz Kohut[2]

The psychoanalytic tradition has evolved in several directions since its revolutionary beginning in the first quarter of the twentieth century. These developments have effectively extended theory and psychotherapeutic technique to psychological conditions that Freud thought were untreatable. For Sigmund Freud, the central concern of psychoanalytic theory was the internal neurotic conflicts that arise in the Oedipal period, at 3 to 6 years of age, and the primary intervention was the interpretation and illumination, in psychoanalysis, of these now-unconscious conflicts. Interpretation proved effective in part because the conflicts themselves arose when the child was starting to have verbal memory. However, in the 1930s, psychoanalysts began to encounter patients whose difficulties seemed to have arisen much earlier and therefore were much more deeply buried in the unconscious. Such conflicts, the therapists realized, were pivotal in the early organization of the mind and were often responsible for more severe pathological conditions, such as the borderline conditions (the lack of a stable sense of self), narcissistic conditions (an inflated and unreal sense of self), and even the psychoses. Equally important, these early conflicts seemed to be the cause of the common situation in which normal people suffered from feelings of unreality, emptiness, and a loss of meaning, situations that could not be relieved through classical interpretive techniques. In sum, the theoretical advances made after Freud and the new psychotherapeutic techniques that resulted rounded out psychoanalytic theory so that the psychoanalyst of today has the tools and the understanding to work with all but the most severe mental disorders.

As things stand today, the student who wishes to comprehend the significant elaborators of Freud's original theory is confronted with a huge body of literature. In addition, each theorist approached psychoanalytic problems in his or her own way and thus developed different definitions and different ways of explaining the major concepts of the field. The result is tremendous theoretical diversity. Melanie Klein, for example, in her penetrating studies of the forces that split and organize the mind, developed a description of the ego that is significantly different from that established by Anna Freud as she examined the mechanism of ego defenses. Also, the understanding of the self based on an inherent sense of being as developed by Donald Winnicott differs from the self as conceived by Heinz Kohut, who considered idealization and ambition as fundamental. In the following discussion, we will not attempt to cover a theorist's entire work or impose a consistency of our own but will describe and illustrate those ideas that have had lasting impact in the psychoanalytic tradition. Most of these ideas, fortunately, have a strong element of common sense to them. As you read, try to imagine how you experience the states of mind that each theorist describes. That will make it easier to resolve the different approaches and definitions.

It is the task of the analyst to bring into consciousness that which is unconscious, no matter to which psychic institution it belongs. (A. Freud, 1946, p. 30)

We cannot help noticing when we meet to discuss human nature that we are apt to use the same terms with meanings that are not only different from each other but seem irreconcilable. The worst offenders are the words "unconscious" and "self." (Winnicott, 1989, p. 488)

[2]Suggested, conceived, and developed by William Brater.

Melanie Klein (1882–1960)

Melanie Klein (1882–1960) was a key figure within the psychoanalytic movement during the time when its intellectual center shifted from Vienna to London. Early in her career she became associated with and gained the respect of several men in what was called Freud's "inner circle."

Klein was born in Vienna but moved, first to Prague, where she was analyzed by Freud's close associate and friend Sandor Ferenczi, and then to Berlin, where she continued her analysis with Karl Abraham, the originator of the early childhood psychosexual stages, and finally to London in 1926, at the request of Ernest Jones, Freud's closest associate and biographer in England. Each of these men encouraged her in unique ways: Ferenczi saw her as a person with exceptional psychoanalytic insights and inspired her to deeply engage the emotional world of her patients; Abraham supported her original work even when it diverged from Sigmund Freud's and inspired her to analyze children; and Jones gave her a forum to express her original ideas (Grosskurth, 1986). She was in the midst of her most innovative work when Freud, fleeing the Nazi invasion, arrived in London accompanied by his adult daughter Anna. From that time on, there were debates and disagreements between Anna Freud and Klein as to what were the correct ways to understand and use psychoanalysis.

Despite her early acceptance as an extraordinarily brilliant new theorist, Klein became controversial as she expanded the study of the unconscious. For example, she made central to her thinking the "death instinct," an idea of Freud's that had otherwise found little favor in the psychoanalytic community. To Klein, the death instinct functioned in complex and often highly destructive fantasies of young children. The innate aggression she observed in children's play was, according to Klein, the manifestation of the death instinct as well. This innate aggression she considered to be as important as the sexual drive (or even more so) in organizing the psyche. She even suggested that the superego, which Freud had described as arising in the Oedipal period, actually appears in a primitive form in the first months of life (Segal, 1973). Anna Freud, in particular, found Klein's emphasis on pre-Oedipal processes as grossly unorthodox, and this difference in viewpoint was part of the bitter personal and theoretical conflict that arose between them. Klein's theories and observations seemed to run counter to the more commonly accepted idea that the sexual conflicts in the Oedipal period are the most important organizing factors of the psyche. Freud himself remained neutral, publicly, in the controversy, thereby giving tacit blessing to the tremendously different but important work of both women. In private correspondence, however, he considered that Jones's support of Klein against his own daughter's position was a long-delayed act of "revenge for Anna's having refused in 1914 to let Jones court her" (Young-Bruehl, 1988, p. 172).

> If we have become able, deep in our unconscious minds, to clear our feelings to some extent towards our parents of grievances, and have forgiven them for the frustrations we had to bear, then we can be at peace with ourselves and are able to love others in the true sense of the word. (Klein, 1975, Vol. I, p. 343)

Klein was unflinching in her descriptions and interpretations of those experiences that many mentally ill people live with all the time and that all people live with some of the time—namely, violent, hateful, and destructive fantasies toward persons who are needed and even loved. Klein explained the common experience of suddenly hating and rejecting a person that a moment ago had been cherished. A mother, for example, can be driven to hurt her own infant when it is inconsolably fussy. Children (as well as teenagers or adults) can suddenly reject a beloved person—their mother, a boyfriend or girlfriend, or a spouse—because that person is not responding to them as they wish. Perhaps because Klein understood hate so well, she also understood love. She was the first analyst to describe love not just as erotic fulfillment but as true kindness and authentic caring for another. The emergence of conscious love, she realized, was inherently connected to our remorse over destructive hate. That is, once we realize how internally violent we can be toward those we love, we also realize how necessary it is to care for the relationships we value. She thus explained one of the great mysteries that all people face, that love and hate—our personal heaven and hell—cannot be separated from one another.

One of Klein's most important ideas is that aggression and love act as fundamental organizing forces in the psyche. Aggression splits the psyche while love unites it. A child (or adult) will aggressively "split" the world in order to reject what it hates and keep what it desires. What a child seeks is always to have the good and full breast and to reject the empty, intrusive, or unresponsive breast. Therefore, Klein postulated, the first organizer of the mind is a separation process. Standing in contrast to this destructive splitting process is another organizational process, which integrates and allows for wholeness and love. Klein observed that the child who is hateful toward its mother (at least in fantasy) will in time try to repair the damage that the child thinks has been done. A common example is a toddler who offers a favorite toy or teddy bear as a gift in order to console the mother for the damage inflicted in fantasy. In this way, the mother, who, in the child's mind, was split, will be joined into one image combining both good and bad (Klein, Vol. I, 1975).

Klein described these two processes as fundamental positions within the psyche. The first she called the paranoid-schizoid position because the child splits (*schizoid*) the breast into good and bad out of fear (*paranoid*). The second she called the depressive position because, after splitting and destroying the mother (in fantasy), the child, in a state of depressive reverie, imagines a whole mother that includes both good and bad qualities. These positions form two poles of psychological functioning that occur over and over again as new experiences are integrated into the psyche. While Klein has been criticized for the cumbersomeness of these terms, it is evident that they describe real experiences, observed in children and felt by adults. Klein's ideas have had a profound influence on the field of psychoanalytic thought called *object relations theory,* perhaps the most popular area of psychoanalytic thought today. Fundamental to her theory is the idea that our relations to loved and hated "objects" (or significant people in our lives) are the building blocks for how we think and experience the world (Greenberg & Mitchell, 1983). Our experiences with important persons, such as our parents or first romantic partners, become internalized and then structure our experience not only of others but also of our own identity. For example, when we "split" the world into good and bad, we also split our own sense of self into fearful and longing aspects. Or if we have achieved a certain integration and can consistently maintain a unified internal image of those we love, then we experience ourselves as whole and at peace.

The baby feels that what he desires in his phantasies has really taken place; that is to say he feels that he *has really destroyed* the object of his destructive impulses, and is going on destroying it: this has extremely important consequences for the development of his mind. (Klein, 1975, Vol. I, p. 308)

Klein's influence on psychoanalytic technique has also been considerable. She introduced an effective style of forceful interpretation of aggressive and sexual drives still used by many analysts. Because she looked at the earliest and most painful processes of the human psyche—including hateful love, intense fearful longing, demanding closeness, needy reparations, envious attachment, grateful kindness, and real love—her work has allowed psychoanalysis to examine modes of human behavior that had been ignored. Schools of Kleinian psychoanalytic theory and technique are found throughout the Western world.

Donald Winnicott (1896–1971)

Donald Winnicott worked in England contemporaneously with Klein. He was a brilliant clinician whose insights have increasingly influenced not only psychoanalytic theory but also child and adult psychotherapists of nearly all schools. The reason for this wide success is that, despite his often radical insights and innovations in theory and practice, Winnicott's work, more than that of any other psychoanalytic thinker, resonates with common sense. He never loses sight of the fact that he is describing real people (Goldman, 1993). It is impossible for a baby to live, either physically or psychologically, without its mother or other primary caretaker. Psychologically, the developing self of the baby thrives only in the loving, playful, and, above all, mirroring environment of the mother's attention. This leads to the theoretical premise that no psyche can be understood as existing in isolation. This idea profoundly influenced the emerging field of object relations theory.

Winnicott had plenty of opportunity to observe infants and their mothers, because he was a pediatrician before he became a psychoanalyst. He said that he saw as many as sixty thousand babies and their mothers during a lifetime of work in a London hospital (Goldman, 1993). Most of Winnicott's psychoanalytic formulations and innovations in psychoanalytic technique developed out of the realization that the mother-infant relation shared many of the qualities of the analyst-patient relation. Arrested development in adults can be understood in terms of deficiencies of mothering in infancy. The analyst, by recreating the conditions of good mothering, can help effect a cure.

Winnicott took a radical step when he observed that personal identity rests primarily on the sense of being. In other words, the sense of personal existence is more fundamental than sexual or aggressive drives in personality formation: "After being—doing and being done to. But first, being" (Winnicott, 1971, p. 85). The *capacity to be* begins with the baby's relation to its mother and specifically to the breast. If the hungry infant finds a continuity of loving care—meaning that the mother offers the breast in an attuned and loving fashion—then the baby will begin to sense its own continuity of existence. But if the mother resents or holds back the breast and thus causes frustration in the child, traumatic breaks in the child's primary reality will occur. As the personal sense of being becomes strong, it forms a foundation for all later functions of the personality.

Either the mother has a breast that is, so that the baby can also be when the baby and mother are not yet separated out in the infant's rudimentary mind; or else the mother is incapable of making this contribution, in which case the baby has to develop without the capacity to be, or with a crippled capacity to be. (Winnicott, 1971, p. 82)

Winnicott is also known for the phrase the **good enough mother** (1971). He realized that there is a great burden on the mother to provide an environment in which the child can develop a sense of self—that is, an unquestioned sense of its own existence. He also realized that, paradoxically, it is best if the mother is not perfect. Indeed, she only has to be good enough (a reality that also applies to the psychotherapist). If she were perfect in her responses, the child would remain dependent. Because of regular but not excessive lapses in maternal attunement and care, the child (or client in psychotherapy) must fall back on his or her own resources and develop the capacity to fulfill his or her own needs. The mother's responsibility is to provide an environment in which the child can develop, over time, a true and authentic sense of itself; for this to occur, a good enough but not perfect mother is called for.

To be good enough, however, the mother must meet the needs of the child most of the time. The child, Winnicott says, has no sense of its own limitations; it feels itself to be omnipotent. This sense of omnipotence is essential for the development of a self. If the baby desires to be fed and the mother supplies the breast or bottle at the right moment; if the baby smiles and the mother smiles back in validation; if the baby has wet itself and cries and the mother responds with a change of diaper, then the baby will build up a sense that its spontaneous expressions are effective. In time, the child's sense of omnipotence gives way to feelings of relative independence as it learns to satisfy its own needs. Nevertheless, it is the child's early success in expressing itself within the mother-infant relationship that sets in motion the sense of effectiveness and authenticity as an adult.

Winnicott makes a distinction between a **true self** and a **false self.** When the baby's omnipotence is respected, a true self develops; however, when the child does not feel effective, he or she will feel helpless and tend to adapt to the mother's needs in order to get what it desires. In this case it develops a false self. Many of the patients who came to Winnicott as a psychoanalyst felt empty and ineffective because they lived for the most part as a false self, gauging all desires and actions through the response of others. Winnicott saw the task of psychoanalysis as creating an environment in which the spontaneous expressions of the true self could emerge. He was famous for devising playful strategies and environments in which this could most easily happen (Winnicott, 1971).

Until very late in his life, he would ride his bicycle with his feet on the handlebars and drive his car with his head through the roof and a walking stick on the accelerator. In fact, when he was 71 years old, his cycling behavior brought a warning from the police. (Goldman, 1993, p. 20)

Another concept of Winnicott's that is widely accepted is what he called **transitional objects** or **transitional phenomena.** This concept is based on observations that we all have made and experiences that we may even remember from our childhood. It is the observation that for babies and children (even adults), certain objects take on special importance. The blanket or teddy bear that a child is often passionately attached to are common examples. Winnicott saw that these objects have a special role, imbued with power from inside the child while at the same time being real objects in an objective world. Winnicott realized that we do not go from a completely unformed sense of self to a fully formed self. Transitions are necessary. These occur in an area between the "real" external world and the purely subjective internal world composed of a sense of being and fantasy. The transitional object is the point where these two worlds meet, where the internal subjective world finds external form. These objects and the world of inner images in which they exist are the first tender expressions of the self and must be valued and guarded by the mother (and later by the psychotherapist).

Winnicott's observations are especially pertinent to the psychotherapeutic relation between therapist and patient. He saw that the psychoanalytic relationship was a replay of the child's first relationship—that is, with its mother—and thus analyst = mother and patient = child. The psychotherapeutic environment was like the maternal environment, a facilitating environment in which the analyst (mother) provides a container for the emerging psychological growth of the patient (child). For the treatment to be successful, the analyst must maintain tremendous respect for the client.[3]

Winnicott believed that play could be extremely useful in allowing the true self to emerge. In play, a person can regress to the time when the original wounds occurred. Winnicott permitted a great deal of unconventionality in his psychoanalytic practice. It was necessary, he thought, to meet the needs of the patient rather than force the patient to accommodate the schedule and needs of the analyst. That would only further develop a false self in the patient. Winnicott would, for example, schedule open-ended sessions that might last two or three hours if the usual "50-minute hour" was felt by the patient to be coercive or unattuned. Above all, it is the empathic attunement and meeting of the needs of the patient's true self that is the goal during psychoanalysis.

The mother's adaptation to the infant's needs, when good enough, gives the infant the illusion that there is an external reality that corresponds to the infant's own capacity to create. (Winnicott, 1971, p. 12f)

More than most theorists, Winnicott always began with observations and then went on to develop a conceptual framework. He saw, for example, that the child develops from absolute dependence on its mother, to relative dependence, to a state "toward independence." The concepts of the *good enough mother,* the *facilitating environment,* the *true self,* and the *false self,* as well as many other of Winnicott's terms and phrases, are all based on common sense. In fact, one of the greatest benefits imparted to many readers of Winnicott is the inspiration to seek one's own commonsense approach to psychological matters. By displaying his own spontaneous creativity, Winnicott continues to inspire many psychotherapists to trust their intuition and capacity to help others.

Heinz Kohut (1913–1981)

Heinz Kohut originated the psychoanalytic school of thought called *self psychology.* Raised and educated in Vienna, he, like the Freuds, was forced by the Nazis to leave Austria in 1939. He finished medical school and did his psychoanalytic training in the United States. His work at the beginning was understood to be a extension of the Freudian model, and he strove to integrate drive forces into his newly developing theory of the self (St. Clair, 1986). However, he eventually came to see the personality as progressing along two lines of development, one leading to ego maturity as Freud understood the term and the other leading to self maturity, an area not well defined (Kohut, 1977). In fact, several others, including Winnicott and Jung, had undertaken a psychological study of the self from their own points of view. However, Kohut added a key element to this study. He recognized that our innate narcissism is an essential part of development of the self and described it as a separate line of development within the personality. His influence has been widespread, spawning associations, training institutes, and journals.

Like the Freuds, Klein, and Winnicott, Kohut based his innovative thinking on observation within the psychoanalytic setting. He often worked with patients who reported the sensation of falling apart or of desperately coping with inner emptiness. He was not satisfied with a Freudian psychoanalytic diagnosis of repressed sexual and aggressive energies. Rather, he concluded, these pa-

[3]Note how close this is to Rogers's person-centered therapy.

tients suffered from lack of development of the self and of an inner sense of substantiality. The *self* became a term that gathered together, for Kohut, one's basic sense of reality and purpose, one's ambitions and ideals. It was the core of a person's sense of meaning. In addition to diagnosing the malady of inner emptiness, Kohut noticed how this condition was cured: those patients who recovered did so when they felt profoundly understood by the analyst over an extended period of time. He found that deep empathic listening, and not interpretation, was the key to cure. Indeed, interpretation, the traditional psychoanalytic intervention, only made matters worse.

Many of these observations on the symptoms of emptiness and meaninglessness, as well as the effectiveness of empathy as a therapeutic tool, had already been made by Winnicott, but Kohut developed theoretical models for a systematic understanding and treatment of these difficult conditions.

Kohut developed an aspect of Freud's concept of narcissism that allowed him to bypass drive theory altogether and directly propound a theory of the self. Until Kohut, narcissism had been considered a pathological condition wherein a person—like the mythical Narcissus looking at his reflection in the forest pool—takes his or her body and sense of identity to be the center of the world and the sole criterion of what is valuable. We are all familiar with people who talk only about themselves or their experiences, while placing no significance on the thoughts or feelings of others. Kohut realized that such a condition is an aberration of an essentially normal process and that going through a narcissistic period is a necessary and healthy part of growing up. Every baby and young child needs to feel itself to be the center of the universe, at least some of the time. Only when this is denied does the resulting emptiness draw forth a narcissistic hunger for attention that later becomes a personality defect. Indeed, he saw that normal narcissism forms the core of the self.

Kohut focused his attention on two normal narcissistic processes that are crucial in the development of the self. The first is **mirroring,** in which the baby looks to its mother and sees its own self reflected in her delighted gaze. In the mirroring relationship, it is as if the baby says to itself: "You see the wonderful me. Therefore, I am wonderful." By seeing its own goodness in the gleam of its mother's eyes, the child feels full of self-worth. The second normal narcissistic process is **idealizing,** which begins as the child recognizes its parent or other special person. Here internal qualities of its own self—goodness, perfection, omnipotence, meaning, a feeling of reality, etc.—are projected onto this person so that the child can (as if) say: "I see and am close to the wonderful you; therefore, I exist and am wonderful too." In both the mirroring and the idealizing object relation, the child knows its self with the help of another.

Kohut called these mirroring and idealizing persons **selfobjects** (Kohut, 1977) because the child feels them to be an extension of itself. Over time, the child will internalize the relations with selfobjects so that he or she can perform the functions of mirroring and idealizing internally. When successful, these two internalized processes form the basis of a bipolar self. The internal process of mirroring leads to realistic ambitions in the world supported by the internalized mother's encouraging praise. Similarly, when the idealized father has been internalized, the child can strive for realistic ideals. These two poles constitute the core of a healthy self and generate the heartfelt ambitions and ideals that provide a sense of purpose and meaning.

[Kohut linked] the two poles in a "tension arc" of basic skills and talents with which the individual attempts to perform the life-long balancing act of striving for individual goals while, at the same time, living in conformity with ideals and values which make life meaningful. (Tobin, 1991, p. 15)

The successful end of the analysis . . . has been reached when the analysand's formerly enfeebled or fragmented nuclear self . . . has been sufficiently strengthened and consolidated to be able to function as a more or less self-propelling, self-directed, and self-sustaining unity which provides a central purpose to his or her personality and gives a sense of meaning to his or her life. (Kohut, 1977, pp. 138–139)

Kohut observed that either of these processes would allow for the successful development of the self. For example, if the mother failed to mirror properly then the healthy idealizing process with the father could still allow for a sufficient emergence of a sense of self for a feeling of realness and motivation to occur. If one pole functions well, then deficiencies in the other pole can be made up later. However, if both fail, then the symptoms Kohut was concerned with—feeling unreal, empty, and without meaning—will ensue, because there is no internal self structure that can produce feelings of self-worth.

In addition to the theory, Kohut developed practical means for treating the disorders of the self. He found that deficiencies in self structure are made visible in three transference situations, or ways of seeing one's psychoanalysis. In a *mirroring transference,* the patient attempts to make up for the deficiencies by experiencing the therapist as being totally fascinated and delighted with the patient. The patient feels an insatiable need to talk about every aspect of his or her life. In an *idealizing transference,* the patient makes the analyst into a special person worthy of awe and admiration and then feels important and meaningful through their association. In a *twinship transference,* the patient builds a fantasy that he or she and the analyst are somehow companions, equals on the journey of life. In this case the patient no longer feels alone or empty. In all three transference modes, the psychotherapeutic intervention is generally the same: profound empathic understanding on the part of the analyst. The transference and the particular relationship it engenders is accepted and understood by the analyst and, as a result, the patient can gradually internalize the person of the analyst. Thus the mental organization that the patient could not attain with the parents is now successfully structured so that his or her health has been restored (Kohut, 1977).

Further Developments in Psychoanalytic Therapy: The Gestalt Therapy of Fritz and Laura Perls

In contrast to Anna Freud, Klein, Winnicott, and Kohut, Frederick (Fritz) and Laura Perls saw their contributions to the psychology of personality chiefly in the practice of psychotherapy, rather than in the creation of theory. In fact, the lack of a strictly theoretical emphasis in much of the Perlses' later work reflects the direction in which they were trying to take psychology. Fritz took the theoretical model outside the therapy office into the mainstream of the human potential movement. His aggressive, confrontational style and his decision to work with individuals in front of large groups made the therapy well-known and accessible. More recently, Gestalt therapy has become less dramatic in its execution but more widely understood and applied by therapists of many different persuasions.

Frederick S. Perls was born in Berlin in 1893, the son of lower-middle-class Jewish parents. In trouble with authorities throughout his adolescence, he managed nonetheless to receive a medical degree, specializing in psychiatry. While finishing his medical training, he served as a medic during World War I. After the war, Fritz worked in Frankfurt, where he met Laura. The two of them, along with many of their friends, were in psychoanalysis with early disciples of Freud.

Laura Perls was born in 1905. Early in life she was attracted by psychoanalysis, reading Freud's *The Interpretation of Dreams* when she was 16. She later studied with the theologians Paul Tillich and Martin Buber (Humphrey, 1986).

In 1927 the Perlses moved to Vienna, where Fritz began psychoanalytic training. He was in analysis with Wilhelm Reich and was supervised by several other early, important psychoanalysts: Karen Horney, Otto Fenichel, and Helene Deutsch. Fritz and Laura were married in 1930. Threatened by Hitler's rise to power, the Perlses fled to Holland in 1933 and then to South Africa. Already innovative, Laura had begun to sit facing her clients and to pay attention to bodily postures and gestures, drawing from her background in body work and modern dance (Serlin, 1992).

None of us, probably with the exception of Freud himself, realized the prematurity of applying psychoanalysis to treatment. . . . We did not see it for what it actually was: a *research project.* (F. Perls, 1969c, p. 142)

Fritz and Laura emigrated to the United States in 1946 and proceeded to develop what became Gestalt therapy. In 1952 they established, at first in their apartment, the New York Institute for Gestalt Therapy. Later, Fritz moved to Los Angeles and then, in the early 1960s, to the Esalen Institute in Big Sur, California. There he offered workshops, taught, and became well-known as the exponent of a viable new philosophy and method of psychotherapy. He died in 1970 on Vancouver Island, the site of the first Gestalt therapeutic community (Gaines, 1979; Shepard, 1975). While Fritz lived, for his students there was a confusion between his personal style, often abrasive, and Gestalt therapy, which, although confrontational, offered support.

Laura, separated from Fritz, remained in New York, ran the New York institute for many years, and trained therapists. Her opinions often contrasted sharply with what Fritz espoused in his later writings (Rosenfeld, 1978). Laura died on a visit to her hometown in Germany in 1990.

The practical focus on body awareness, however, became part of Gestalt therapy not only through Reich, but through my lifelong experience with modern dance . . . and my awareness of Alexander and Feldenkrais and other body therapies. (L. Perls, 1992, pp. 52–53)

A Note on Gestalt Psychology

The word *Gestalt,* as used by the Perlses, refers to the work done primarily with the psychology of perception beginning in the late 1800s in Germany and Austria. Although there is no precise English equivalent for the German word *Gestalt,* the general meaning is "pattern or configuration—a particular organization of parts that makes up a particular whole." The chief principle of the Gestalt approach is that the analysis of parts can never provide an understanding of the whole, because the whole consists of the parts *plus* the interactions and interdependencies of the parts.

One aspect of this idea can be understood by noticing how a person, in a given situation, makes his or her perceptions meaningful, how he or she distinguishes between *figure* and *ground.* Figure 5.1 (p. 142) is an example: a stimulus whose interpretation depends on what is perceived as figure and what is perceived as ground. If the white is seen as figure and the black as ground, a white chalice appears; if the black is viewed as figure and the white as ground, two heads in silhouetted profile emerge. According to Gestaltists, the phenomenon represented by this picture shows how an organism selects what is of interest to it at any particular moment. To a thirsty person, a glass of water placed in the

I feel rather desperate about this manuscript. I've got a view looking at a tapestry, nearly completely woven, yet unable to bring across the total picture, the total gestalt. (F. Perls, 1969b)

FIGURE 5.1 An Example of the Figure-Ground Phenomenon

midst of favorite foods emerges as figure against the background of the food, while to a hungry person food is the foreground.

The Gestalt therapists, drawing from this kind of data, opposed the notion that the study of human beings could be encompassed by an entirely rational, mechanistic, natural-scientific approach. They insisted that the experiential world of an individual can be understood only through that individual's direct description. The world that the individual encounters *cannot* be separated from his or her personal experience.

Mind-Body Unity

To the Perlses, the mind-body split of many psychologies is arbitrary and misleading. Thus they viewed people as operating as a totality and described behavior in terms that stressed unity rather than division into parts. They believed strongly in the **wisdom of the organism** and saw the healthy, mature person as a self-supporting, self-regulating individual. As a result, they sought, in their therapeutic approach, to help their patients gain awareness of and direct contact with themselves and the world. They emphasized the organism as a whole, being in the here and now, and *how* over *why,* as critical aspects of living with more awareness.

The Organism as a Whole Fritz Perls suggested that any aspect of an individual's behavior may be viewed as a manifestation of the whole—the person's being (F. Perls, 1978). In therapy, for example, what the patient does—how he or she moves, speaks, and so on—provides as much information as what he or she thinks and says. Our bodies are direct representations of who we are. By simply observing our most readily apparent physical behaviors—posture, breathing, movements—we can learn an immense amount about ourselves.

Nothing is ever really repressed. All relevant gestalten are emerging, they are on the surface, they are obvious like the emperor's nakedness. (F. Perls, 1969b, p. 272)

Here-and-Now Emphasis The Perlses' holistic view places particular emphasis on an individual's immediate self-perception in relation to his or her environment. For example, neurotics are unable to live in the present. They chronically carry with them "unfinished business" from the past. Because their attention is focused on what remains unresolved, they have neither the awareness nor the energy to deal fully with the present. They experience themselves as unable to live successfully in the present. The Gestalt approach does not examine the past for memories of trauma but asks the patient simply to focus on becoming aware of his or her *present* experience. The bits and pieces of unresolved conflicts from the past will inevitably emerge, the Perlses felt, as part of that present experi-

Personal Reflection

Continuum of Awareness

This exercise in awareness requires much practiced discipline, yet, paradoxically, it serves to develop one's spontaneity.

Part 1. Begin by noticing your breathing. Is it regular or not? Deep or shallow? Notice the room around you, the temperature, the light, the furniture, and the other people. Just be aware, from second to second, of what you are experiencing, how you experience your existence. Now. And now. And now.

Observe the progress of your awareness. Do you interrupt yourself with planning, rehearsing, fantasizing, remembering? Do you evaluate rather than permit pure awareness? What does awareness feel like?

Pay particular attention to the ways in which you sabotage your own attempts at sustained awareness. Are these ways in which you often prevent yourself from fully contacting your own experience?

Part 2. This is more difficult. Try to prolong and stay in contact with the moment at which you want to avoid continued awareness. Can you get a sense of what you are avoiding? Does a situation emerge that you feel is unfinished?

ence. As those unfinished situations appear, the patient reexperiences them in order to complete and assimilate them into the present.

Anxiety is the gap, the tension between the *now* and the *then*. Fritz Perls gives the following example: If I were to ask, "Who wants to come up here [in front of a group] to work?" you probably would quickly start to rehearse "What shall I do there?" and so on. And of course you might get stage fright as you leave the secure reality of the now and jump into the future (1969a). Inability to tolerate this tension causes individuals to fill the gap with planning, rehearsing, and attempts at making the future secure. These activities not only absorb energy and attention away from the present (thereby perpetually creating unfinished situations); they also prevent the kind of openness to the future that growth and spontaneity imply.

Importance of *How* over *Why* A natural outcome of the here-and-now orientation is a stress on understanding experience in a descriptive fashion. An individual who understands how he or she does something is in a position to understand the action itself. Because every action may be the result of many different causes, to focus on one or another of the causes can lead a person further and further away from observing the action itself. Preoccupation with asking *why* things happen prevents people from experiencing *how* they happen; thus genuine emotional awareness is blocked in the interest of providing explanations.

I believe that this is a great thing to understand: that awareness per se—by and of itself—can be curative. (F. Perls, 1969a, p. 16)

The Centrality of Awareness The view of the organism as a whole, the here-and-now emphasis, and the importance of *how* over *why* constitute a foundation for examining awareness, the focal point of the Perlses' approach. The process of growth is, in Gestalt terms, a process of expanding self-awareness, while the major factor inhibiting psychological growth is avoidance of awareness.

With full awareness you become aware of this organismic self-regulation, you can let the organism take over without interfering, without interrupting. (F. Perls, 1969b)

Neurosis and Health

Emotions are the very life of us. . . . [E]motions are the very language of the organism; they modify the basic excitement according to the situation which has to be met. (F. Perls, 1973, p. 23)

The Perls believed that emotional constriction is the root cause of all neurotic behavior. If emotional expression is prevented, anxiety builds upon anxiety. Once anxious, people try to desensitize their sensory systems in order to reduce the built-up tension. At this point, symptoms, such as frigidity or a phobic reaction—what Fritz Perls called the "holes in our personalities"—develop. This emotional desensitizing leads to the avoidance of awareness that in turn creates layers of neurosis that are maintained by several kinds of neurotic mechanisms.

Layers of Neurosis Fritz Perls suggested that neurosis may be loosely viewed as a five-layered structure, and that growth and eventual freedom from neurosis occurs by passing through these five layers.

The first of the **layers of neurosis** is the *cliché layer,* or the *layer of token existence.* It includes such tokens of contact as the rather empty expressions *good morning, hello,* and *nice weather, isn't it?* The second layer is the *role layer,* or *game-playing layer.* This is the *as if* layer, where we pretend to be the person we would most like to be—for example, the always competent business executive, the perpetually nice little girl, or the very important person.

After we have reorganized these two layers, Perls believed, we reach the *impasse layer,* also called the *antiexistence layer* or *phobic avoidance layer.* Here we experience emptiness, nothingness. By avoiding the nothingness, we generally cut off our awareness and retreat to the game-playing layer. If, however, we are able to maintain awareness of ourselves in this emptiness, we reach the *death* or *implosive* layer. This layer appears as death or as fear of death, because it consists of a paralysis of opposing forces. But if we can stay in contact with this deadness, we reach the last layer, the *explosive layer.* He suggests that becoming aware of this level constitutes the development of the authentic person, the true self, the person capable of experiencing and expressing emotion.

There are four basic kinds of explosions that an individual may experience when emerging from the death layer. There is the explosion of *grief* that involves the working through of a loss or death that was previously unassimilated. There is the explosion into *orgasm* in people who are sexually blocked. There is the explosion into *anger* when the expression of this feeling has been repressed. And, finally, there is the explosion into what Perls called *joie de vivre*—joy and laughter, the joy of life.

There are a couple of points absolutely crucial to Gestalt. One is that you already know everything you need to know to lead a fully satisfying, happy, effective life. (Enright, 1980, p. 17)

The basic misconception that this energy needs to be controlled derives from our fear of emptiness and nothingness (the third layer). The Perlses saw that Eastern philosophies, particularly Zen, have a good deal to teach us about the life-affirming, positive aspect of nothingness and about the importance of permitting the experience of nothingness without interrupting it. They maintained the notion that change cannot be forced and that psychological growth is a natural, spontaneous process.

Neurotic Mechanisms Fritz Perls described four neurotic mechanisms that impede growth. They are *introjection, confluence, retroflection,* and *projection.*

Introjection **Introjection,** or "swallowing whole," is the mechanism by which individuals incorporate standards, attitudes, and ways of acting and thinking that are not their own and that they do not assimilate or digest sufficiently to make their own. Introjecting individuals find it difficult to distinguish between what they really feel and what others want them to feel—or simply what others feel. Because the concepts or attitudes they swallow are incompatible with one another, introjecting individuals find themselves conflicted.

Confluence In **confluence,** individuals experience no boundary between themselves and the environment. Confluence makes a healthy rhythm of contact and withdrawal impossible because both contact and withdrawal presuppose the capacity to have an accurate experience of the *other* as other.

Retroflection The term **retroflection** means, literally, "turning back sharply against." Retroflecting individuals turn against themselves, and instead of directing their energies toward changing and manipulating their environment, they direct these energies toward themselves. They split themselves and become both subject and object of all their actions; they are the target of all their behavior.

Projection **Projection** is the tendency to make others responsible for what originates in the self. It involves a disowning of one's impulses, desires, and behaviors, as one places what belongs to the self outside the self.

Fritz Perls describes the interaction between the four mechanisms:

> The introjector does as others would like him to do, the projector does unto others what he accuses them of doing to him, the man in pathological confluence doesn't know who is doing what to whom, and the retroflector does to himself what he would like to do to others. . . . As introjection displays itself in the use of the pronoun " I" when the real meaning is "they"; as projection displays itself in the use of the pronouns "it" and "they," when the real meaning is "I"; as confluence displays itself in the use of the pronoun "we" when the real meaning is in question; so retroflection displays itself in the use of the reflective [sic] "myself." (F. Perls, 1973, pp. 40–41)

Projection is crucial in the formation and understanding of dreams. In Fritz Perls's view, all the parts of a dream are projected, disowned fragments of ourselves. Every dream contains at least one unfinished situation that involves these projected fragments. To work on the dream is to reown those projected elements, thereby bringing closure to the unfinished gestalt.

> Any disturbance of the organismic balance constitutes an incomplete gestalt, an unfinished situation forcing the organism to become creative, to find means and ways to restore that balance. (F. Perls, 1969b, p. 79)

Health Psychological health and maturity is defined by the Perlses as the capacity to exchange *external* support and regulation for *self*-support and *self*-regulation. A basic proposition of Gestalt theory is that every organism possesses the capacity to achieve an optimum balance within itself and in relation to its environment. Self-regulating, self-supporting individuals recognize their own capacity to choose the means of fulfilling needs as the needs emerge.

> It is not necessary deliberately to schedule, to encourage or inhibit, the promptings of appetite, sexuality, and so forth. . . . If these things are let be, they will spontaneously regulate themselves." (F. Perls, R. Hefferline, & P. Goodman in Stoehr, 1994, p. 44)

In stressing the *self*-supporting, *self*-regulating nature of psychological well-being, the Perlses do not suggest that an individual can exist in any sense separate from his or her environment. In fact, organismic balance presumes a constant interaction with the environment. The crucial point is that we can choose

Personal Reflection

■ Projection

Try doing this exercise on projection in a small group, and listen to and reflect on one another's descriptions. Look around the room; choose an object that stands out vividly for you. Try identifying with the object; describe yourself in terms of the object. Describe the object, but instead of "it," say "I." After several minutes, discuss with the group what your descriptions might be saying about you.

For example, a woman who identified with a beam in the ceiling described it partly as follows: "I'm very old-fashioned and uselessly ornate. . . . I have a heavy load to bear." (Adapted from Enright, 1977)

how we relate to the environment; we are self-supporting and self-regulating because we recognize our own capacity to determine how we support and regulate ourselves in a world that includes much more than just ourselves.

Therapy and Dreamwork

The Perlses found, in working with clients, that their theoretical ideas began to drift from the Freudian center. As they moved away from Freud, their practice as therapists changed, and they eventually developed a novel way to work with and understand dreams.

Not Freud's discoveries but his philosophy and technique have become obsolete. (F. Perls, 1969b, p. 14)

Beyond Freudian Psychoanalysis Fritz Perls's first book, *Ego, Hunger and Aggression* (1947), was intended to provide extensions of Freud's work, not to offer a new theory of personality. The Perlses' disagreements with Freud had primarily to do with Freud's psychotherapeutic treatment methods rather than with his more theoretical expositions.

Initially, the Perlses' departures concerned Freud's theory of impulses and libido. For them, impulses were not basic drives that dictate human behavior but expressions of biological and emotional needs. The Perlses suggested that the psychoanalytic methods of interpretation and free association allowed avoidance of direct experience and were, therefore, inefficient and often ineffective methods of self-exploration.

They also disagreed with Freud's supposition that the most important therapeutic task is the freeing of repressions, following which the working through or assimilation of the material can occur naturally. The Perlses thought that every individual, simply by existing, has plenty of material with which to work in therapy. The difficult and vital task is the assimilation process itself, the integrating of previously introjected traits, habits, attitudes, and patterns of behavior.

When I work, I am not Fritz Perls. I become nothing—no thing, a catalyst, and I enjoy my work. I forget myself and surrender to your plight. And once we have closure I come back to the audience, a prima donna demanding appreciation. I can work with everybody. I cannot work successfully with everybody. (F. Perls, 1969b, pp. 228–229)

The Role of the Therapist The Perlses felt that the therapist is basically a screen on which the patient sees his or her own missing potential. The therapist is, above all, a skillful frustrator. The patient has the therapist's attention and

Personal Reflection

■ Dreamwork

Part 1. Write the dream down and make a list of *all* the details in the dream. Get every person, every thing, every mood, and then work on these to become each one of them. Ham it up, and really transform yourself into each of the different items. Really *become* that thing—whatever it is in a dream—*become* it. Use your magic. Turn into that ugly frog or whatever is there—the dead thing, the live thing, the demon—and stop thinking. Lose your mind and come to your senses. Every little bit is a piece of the jigsaw puzzle, which together will make up a much larger whole—a much stronger, happier, more completely *real* personality.

Part 2. (Note: this is much more demanding).

Next, take each one of these different items, characters, and parts, and let them have encounters between them. Write a script. Have a dialogue between the two opposing parts and you will find—especially if you get the correct opposites—that they always start out fighting each other. All the different parts—any part in the dream is yourself, is a projection of yourself, and if there are inconsistent sides, and you use them to fight each other, you have the eternal conflict game, the self-torture game. As the process of encounter goes on, there is a mutual learning until we come to a oneness and integration of the two opposing forces. Then the civil war is finished, and your energies are ready for your struggles with the world.

acceptance. At the same time, the therapist must frustrate the patient by refusing to provide the support that the patient lacks within. The therapist acts as a catalyst in helping the patient break through avoidance and impasse points (Wheeler, 1991). The therapist's primary catalytic tool is to help the patient see *how* he or she consistently interrupts himself or herself, avoids awareness, plays roles, and so forth (Wheeler, 1993).

According to Fritz Perls, individual therapy was obsolete, both inefficient and often ineffective. He suggested that work in groups had a good deal more to offer, whether the work actually involved the entire group or became an interaction between the therapist and one member of the group. For example, current Gestalt theorists are expanding their practices to include couples (Wheeler and Backman, 1994).

Gestalt Dreamwork Fritz Perls saw dreams as messages about our unfinished situations, including what we are missing in our lives, what we are avoiding doing, and how we are avoiding and disowning parts of ourselves. This approach is very different from the way Freud worked with dreams.

> I especially prefer to work with dreams. I believe that in a dream we have a clear existential message of what's missing in our lives, what we avoid doing and living. (F. Perls, 1969a, p. 76)

> In Gestalt Therapy we don't interpret dreams. We do something more interesting with them. Instead of analyzing and further cutting up the dream, we want to bring it back to life. And the way to bring it back to life is to relive the dream as if it were happening now. Instead of telling the dream as if it were a story in the past, act it out in the present, so that it becomes a part of yourself, so that you are really involved.

> If you understand what you can do with dreams, you can do a tremendous lot for yourself on your own. Just take any old dream or dream fragment, it doesn't matter. As long as a dream is remembered, it is still alive and available, and it still contains an unfinished, unassimilated situation. . . . And if you understand the meaning of each time you identify with some bit of a dream, each time you translate an *it* into an *I*, you increase in vitality and in your potential. (F. Perls, 1969a, pp. 68–70)

The novel way that Perls clarified and expanded on dreams made working with him or observing others working with him an often disturbing, yet clarifying, experience.

Evaluation

If you see the events of your life clearly, then your living goes well, without confusion and unnecessary misery. . . . [W]ith awareness, you can minimize the pain and maximize the joys and satisfactions. (Stevens & Stevens, 1977, p. x)

Gestalt therapy is, above all, a synthesis of approaches to understanding human psychology and behavior. As such a synthesis, Gestalt therapy has usefully incorporated a great deal from psychoanalytic and existential psychology, as well as bits and pieces from behaviorism (the emphasis on behavior and the obvious), psychodrama (the enacting of conflicts), group psychotherapy (work in groups), and Zen Buddhism (the emphasis of wisdom over intellectualization and the focus on present awareness). The spirit of Gestalt therapy is a humanistic, growth-oriented one, which, in addition to Fritz Perls's associations with the Esalen Institute, made Gestalt therapy a major force in the human potential movement. The commonsense, conversational nature of the literature of Gestalt therapy, as well as the attitudes of many Gestalt therapists, has contributed to a welcome demystification of psychotherapy.

Because of Gestalt's strong stand against many prevailing ideas and partly because of Fritz Perls's personality (F. Perls, 1989), it never lacked for critics. Gestalt's emphasis on feelings over thoughts and process over content was criticized (Jurjevich, 1978; Becker, 1982). Some singled out the Gestalt prayer as irrational (Morris & Ellis, 1975), while others questioned Gestalt's most fundamental assumptions. "[Some of Gestalt's] theses are not only false, but dangerous. [Among them are these:] A human being functions best when left alone. Human nature is itself good. . . . All thinking is neurotic and immature" (Cadwallader, 1984, p. 193).

By the early 1990s, there were 62 Gestalt training centers worldwide.

Summary

In the period after Freud's death, at least three important subschools emerged in addition to the more distinct Gestalt position. The first of these, ego psychology, associated with Anna Freud (along with many others, most notably Heinz Hartmann), developed the concept of ego defenses—the processes whereby the ego defends itself against the knowledge of id-superego conflicts—and the means for interpreting them, thus making traditional psychoanalytic technique even more effective. Second, theorists examined pre-Oedipal development and conflicts. Melanie Klein, Donald Winnicott, and others propounded ideas that form the basis of what has come to be called object relations theory. These theorists observed that many of the conflicts that appear in the Oedipal period can also be seen in very young children whose primary relationship is not represented by a triangle (mother, father, child) but by a simple dyad with the mother. For this reason, the relationship with the mother, called the *love object*, became the focus of observation. Yet another school, based on Kohut's work, developed the idea that it is not the ego but a more fundamental expression of identity, the self, that is the most important aspect of identity. Kohut called his body of work self psychology and was concerned with how psychoanalysis could melt these early wounds.

In addition, Fritz and Laura Perls developed Gestalt therapy, which emphasizes the energy of the emotions, the primacy of the here and now rather than of past events, and an approach and treatment that employs a confrontational style instead of the more indirect, supportive styles favored by the other post-Freudian innovators.

The Theory Firsthand

Three Excerpts from Anna Freud

On Adolescents

Adolescents are excessively egoistic, regarding themselves as the center of the universe and the sole object of interest, and yet at no other time in later life are they capable of so much self-sacrifice and devotion. They form the most passionate love relations, only to break them off as abruptly as they began them. On the one hand, they throw themselves enthusiastically into the life of the community and, on the other, they have an overpowering longing for solitude. They oscillate between blind submission to some self-chosen leader and defiant rebellion against any and every authority. They are selfish and materially minded and at the same time full of lofty idealism. They are ascetic but will suddenly plunge into instinctual indulgence of the most primitive character. At times their behavior to other people is rough and inconsiderate, yet they themselves are extremely touchy. Their moods veer between lighthearted optimism and the blackest pessimism. Sometimes they will work with indefatigable enthusiasm and at other times they are sluggish and apathetic. (A. Freud in Coles, 1992, p. 164)

On the Defenses

When I speak of successful defense I look at it from the point of view of the ego. If the ego defends itself successfully, it means that it achieves its aim of not allowing the forbidden impulse to enter into consciousness and that it does away with the anxiety connected with it and escapes unpleasure of any kind. That is a successful defense although it may have disastrous consequences for health and for later development. But from the point of view of defending oneself it is successful. You know if someone attacks you and you kill that person, the defense has been immensely successful, but it may not be approved of and may have disagreeable consequences. It all depends on your viewpoint. (A. Freud in Sandler, 1985, p. 194)

The Effects of Changes in Psychoanalytic Thinking

A psychoanalytic education, one that would prevent neurosis, was our goal. The attempts to reach this aim have never been abandoned, difficult and bewildering as their results turned out to be at times. . . . [A]t the time when psychoanalysis laid great emphasis on the seductive influence of sharing the parents' bed and the traumatic consequences of witnessing parental intercourse, parents were warned against bodily intimacy with their children and against performing the sexual act in the presence of even their youngest infants. When it was proved in the analyses of adults that the withholding of sexual knowledge was responsible for many intellectual inhibitions, full sexual enlightenment at an early age was advocated. When hysterical symptoms, frigidity, impotence, etc., were traced back to prohibitions and the subsequent repressions of sex in childhood, psychoanalytic upbringing put on its program a lenient and permissive attitude toward the manifestations of infantile, pregenital sexuality. When the new instinct theory gave aggression the status of a basic drive, tolerance was extended also to the child's early and violent hostilities, his death wishes against parents and siblings, etc. When anxiety was recognized as playing a central part in symptom formation, every effort was made to lessen the children's fear of parental authority. When guilt was shown to correspond to the tension between the inner agencies, this was followed by the ban on all educational measures likely to produce a severe super-ego. When the new structural view of the personality placed the onus for maintaining an inner equilibrium on the ego, this was translated into the need to foster in the child the development of ego forces strong enough to hold their own against the pressure of the drives. Finally, in our time, when analytic investigations have turned to earliest events in the first year of life and highlighted their importance, these specific insights are being translated into new and in some respects revolutionary techniques of infant care.

(From *Normality and Pathology in Childhood,* Vol. 6 of *The Writings of Anna Freud;* quoted in Coles, 1992, pp. 192–193)

The Theory Firsthand

Excerpt from Fritz Perls, *Gestalt Therapy Verbatim*

This is a cogent example of Fritz Perls's style and point of view.

I want to talk about the present development of humanistic psychology. It took us a long time to debunk the whole Freudian crap, and now we are entering a new and more dangerous phase. We are entering the phase of the turner-onners: turn on to instant cure, instant joy, instant sensory-awareness. We are entering the phase of the quacks and the con-men, who think if you get some breakthrough, you are cured—disregarding any growth requirements, disregarding any of the real potential, the inborn genius in all of you. If this is becoming a faddism, it is as dangerous to psychology as the year-decade-century-long lying on the couch. At least the damage we suffered under psychoanalysis does little to the patient except for making him deader and deader. This is not as obnoxious as this quick-quick-quick thing. . . .

The stopping block seems to be anxiety. Always anxiety. Of course you are anxious if you have to learn a new way of behavior, and the psychiatrists usually are afraid of anxiety. They don't know what anxiety *is.* Anxiety is the excitement, the *élan vital* which we carry with us, and which becomes stagnated if we are unsure about the role we have to play. If we don't know if we will get applause or tomatoes, we hesitate, so the heart begins to race and all the excitement can't flow into activity, and we have stage fright. So the formula of anxiety is very simple: anxiety is the gap between the *now* and the *then.* If you are in the now, you can't be anxious, because the excitement flows immediately into ongoing spontaneous activity. If you are in the now, you are creative, you are inventive. If you have your senses ready, if you have your eyes and ears open, like every small child, you find a solution.

A release to spontaneity, to the support of our total personality—yes, yes, yes. . . . (1969a, pp. 1–4)

Chapter Highlights

- Anna Freud was the staunchest supporter of her famous father. She developed, taught, and encouraged the use of psychoanalysis with disturbed young children, and used insights gained from its practice in working with normal children in difficult life situations.
- In *The Ego and the Mechanisms of Defense,* Anna Freud illuminated the place of daily activities directed by and in the domain of the ego. Her work played down the primacy of the role of the id and instinctual drives, both in theory and in practice.
- The individual uses a combination of strategies as defense mechanisms to ward off anxieties of all kinds. These strategies arise from a mixture of external difficulties, genetic predisposition, and the microculture of the individual's family and community.
- Life may be more endurable and more successful when the defenses are used with awareness and self-understanding. They become neurotic and have damaging effects when they hamper the individual's ability to function and when they obscure reality.
- Beginning in the 1930s, psychoanalysts who were expanding Freudian theory and practice looked at the less verbal or conscious conflicts in the young child. Those very early conflicts were pivotal in the organization of the mind, and often responsible for more severe pathology—borderline and narcissistic conditions, and psychosis.
- Classical interpretive techniques provided no relief from the common situation in which normal people suffered from feelings of emptiness,

unreality, and a loss of meaning. Such emotions seemed rooted in early conflicts.

- Melanie Klein extended the study of the unconscious. Central to her theorizing was a concept of the death instinct as it manifests itself in the aggressive fantasies and play of children. She considered this innate aggression to be equal to, if not more important than, the sexual drive in organizing the psyche.
- According to Klein, the emergence of conscious love is inherently connected to the remorse over destructive hate. Once we realize how internally violent we can be toward those we love, we also realize how necessary it is to care for the relationships we value.
- In Klein's theory, aggression and love act as organizing forces in the psyche, with aggression splitting it, and love uniting it again. Our experiences in relating to the most loved and hated "objects" (or significant others) determine how we think and experience the world.
- Donald Winnicott's psychoanalytic thinking rested on the premise that no psyche can be understood as existing in isolation. The infant's developing self thrives only in the playful, loving, and, above all, mirroring environment of the mother's (or primary caregiver's) attention.
- Winnicott observed that personal identity rests primarily on the sense of being. More fundamental than sexual or aggressive drives in personality formation is the sense of personal existence. He believed that the foundation for all later functions of the personality is formed as the personal sense of being becomes strong.
- The psychoanalytic school of self psychology grew from the observations and practice of Heinz Kohut. The term *self* encompassed, for Kohut, the individual's sense of reality and purpose, ambitions, and ideals.
- To develop practical ways of working with deficiencies in self structure, Kohut proposed three approaches to transference, or ways of seeing one's psychoanalysis: mirroring transference, idealizing transference, and twinship transference. The intervention is the same in all three—profound empathic understanding on the part of the analyst.
- In Gestalt therapy, an analysis of the parts can never provide an understanding of the whole, because the whole consists of the parts plus the interactions and interdependencies of the parts. An individual's direct description is necessary for an understanding of that person's experiential world. That world cannot be separated from personal experience.
- In Gestalt therapy, any aspect of a person's behavior may be viewed as a manifestation of the whole. Information is provided by what is done, as well as how one moves and speaks, or what is thought and said. The importance of understanding experience in a descriptive fashion focuses attention on understanding *how* rather than *why* something occurs.
- Dreams are considered messages about unfinished situations, in the Gestalt view, including what we avoid doing, what we are missing in our lives, and how we are avoiding and disowning parts of ourselves. In this approach, a dream is acted out, brought back to life as though it were happening now.
- Gestalt therapy was developed by Fritz and Laura Perls. It emphasizes the role of the here and now instead of past events, the energy of the emotions, and the usefulness of a more confrontational style.

Key Concepts

Confluence A neurotic mechanism in which individuals experience no boundary between the environment and themselves. The response, as postulated by Gestalt therapy, precludes having an accurate experience of the *other* as other.

Defense mechanisms Ways in which the ego attempts to protect the whole personality against threat, in the Freudian model. Repression, denial, rationalization, reaction formation, projection, isolation, regression all block direct expression of instinctual needs. Sublimation rechannels that expression.

Denial Defense mechanism comprised of the unwillingness to accept an event that disturbs the ego.

False self For Winnicott, a response that develops when a child does not feel effective and adapts to the mother's needs in order to get what it wants. The false self may also show up in later life as the individual gauges all desires and actions through the reactions of others.

Good enough mother In Winnicott's view, the responsibility of the mother to provide an environment in which the child can develop, over time, a true and authentic sense of itself. This responsibility calls for a good enough, but not perfect, mother, who can meet the needs of the child most of the time.

Idealizing For Kohut, the second normal narcissistic process, wherein the child projects onto its parent or other special person qualities of its own self—goodness, meaning, omnipotence, perfection, feeling of reality.

Introjection Defense mechanism in Gestalt therapy, in which individuals incorporate attitudes, standards, and modes of thinking and acting that are not their own, nor are they sufficiently assimilated or digested to be made so.

Isolation Defense mechanism of partitioning, or separating, the anxiety-arousing parts of a situation from the rest of the psyche. Little or no emotional reaction remains connected to the event.

Layers of neurosis A five-layered structure of neurosis. As described by Fritz Perls, growth comes from passing through these layers. First is the cliché, or layer of token existence. Next is the role layer, or game-playing layer. Then comes the impasse layer, or antiexistence or phobic layer. Fourth is the death or implosive layer. The last layer is the explosive layer.

Mirroring For Kohut, the normal narcissistic process in which the baby looks to its mother (or primary caregiver) and sees itself reflected in a delighted gaze. By seeing its own goodness reflected, the child feels full of self-esteem. This process leads, over time, to realistic ambitions supported by the internalized mother's praise.

Projection In the Gestalt view, the disowning of one's impulses, along with one's desires and behaviors. Projection also appears as a tendency to make others responsible for what is self-originated. It is crucial in the formation and understanding of dreams.

Projection Defense mechanism in which a person attributes to another person, animal, or object the qualities, feelings, or intentions that originate in the self. The projection is then treated as if it were an external force.

Rationalization Defense mechanism in which the individual finds acceptable reasons for unacceptable thoughts or actions. It disguises motives, rendering our actions morally justifiable, thus bowing to pressure from the superego.

Reaction formation Defense mechanism that replaces behaviors or feelings with those that are diametrically opposite. The result is an explicit and usually unconscious inversion of the wish.

Regression Defense mechanism that is manifested as reversion to an earlier level of development, or to a mode of expression that is simpler or more childlike.

Repression Defense mechanism that forces a potentially anxiety-provoking idea, event, or perception away from consciousness, precluding possible resolution.

Retroflection A neurotic process in Gestalt theory, in which individuals become both subject and object of their actions. By splitting themselves, they become their own target.

Selfobjects In Kohut's theory, the mirroring and idealizing persons that are felt by the child to be an extension of itself. Over time, these two functions are internalized and form the basis of a bipolar self.

Sublimation A defense mechanism in the Freudian model. It differs from the other Freudian defenses in that the tension may actually be resolved and eliminated by redirecting it to other channels. Intellectual, artistic, or cultural goals may receive the energies that had been directed toward sexual or aggressive ends.

Transitional objects or **transitional phenomena** For Winnicott, objects that have a special role, imbued with power from within the child. At the same time, they are actual objects in the real world.

True self In Winnicott's formulation, what develops when the baby's omnipotence is respected. In therapy, play allows the true self to emerge.

Wisdom of the organism In the view of Fritz Perls, a kind of intuition based more in emotion than in intellect, and more in nature than in conceptual systems. He also suggested that the intellect is vastly overvalued in our society, at the expense of genuine emotional awareness.

Annotated Bibliography

Greenberg, J., & Mitchell, S. (1983). *Object relations theory and clinical psychoanalytic theory.* Cambridge, MA: Harvard University Press.

Lays out clearly the different points of view of the major living theorists. Excellent early chapters on Freud's initial descriptions of the nature of the analytic relationship.

Kohut, H. (1977). *The restoration of the self.* New York: International Universities Press.

Hard reading; however, it is the best introduction to his thinking.

Peltzman, B. (1990). *Anna Freud: A guide to research.* New York: Garland.

Annotated companion to the collected works. Descriptions of her most interesting and important papers.

Perls, F. S. (1947). *Ego, hunger and aggression.* New York: Random House.

Perls's most intellectually oriented work, it explains in detail the theory of Gestalt therapy in its development from psychoanalysis and Gestalt psychology. The work includes several chapters by Laura Perls as well.

———. (1969a). *Gestalt therapy verbatim.* Lafayette, CA: The Real People Press.

An excellent discussion of the basics of Gestalt therapy, including transcripts of therapy sessions.

———. (1969b). *In and out of the garbage pail.* Lafayette, CA: The Real People Press.

Perls's autobiography, full of anecdotes and written in a casual, humorous style; an experience in Gestalt writing that describes the origins and development of Gestalt therapy.

———. (1973). *The Gestalt approach: Eyewitness to therapy.* Ben Lomond, CA: Science and Behavior Books; New York: Bantam, 1976.

Perls's last manuscripts, published together and posthumously. *The Gestalt Approach* offers an excellent, readable, and theoretical exposition of Gestalt therapy, while *Eyewitness to Therapy* includes the transcripts from a series of films of therapy sessions, which Perls had planned to use as teaching material.

Pine, F. (1990). *Drive, ego, object, and self: A synthesis for clinical work.* New York: Basic Books.

Brings together in a well-written, flowing narrative different perspectives used in clinical practice, followed by a series of case examples.

Segal, H. (1973). *Introduction to the work of Melanie Klein.* London: Hogarth Press and the Institute of Psychoanalysis.

A clear, readable, and compact presentation of Klein's theory. Segal makes Klein's very difficult concepts accessible.

St. Clair, M. (1986). *Object relations and self psychology: An introduction.* Monterey, CA: Brooks/Cole.

An overview of the major theorists in the fields of object relations theory and self psychology. Assumes no prior knowledge of the subjects. It is short and clear.

Winnicott, D. W. (1971). *Playing and reality.* New York: Penguin.

Winnicott wrote a lot, but this short, readable book gives his most important ideas, including the true self and the false self, transitional objects, and the good enough mother.

References

Becker, E. (1982). Growing up rugged: Fritz Perls and Gestalt therapy. *ReVISION,* 5(2), 6–14.

Burlingham, M. (1989). *The last Tiffany: A biography of Dorothy Tiffany Burlingham.* New York: Atheneum.

Cadwallader, E. (1984). Values in Fritz Perls's Gestalt therapy: On the dangers of half-truths. *Counseling and Values, 28*(4), 192–201.

Coles, R. (1992). *Anna Freud: The dream of psychoanalysis.* Reading, MA: Addison-Wesley (Mentor Books).

Enright, J. (1977). Thou art that: Projection and play. In J. Stevens (Ed.), *Gestalt is.* New York: Bantam, 152–159.

———. (1980). *Enlightening Gestalt: Waking up from the nightmare.* Mill Valley, CA: Pro Telos.

Fenichel, O. (1945). *The psychoanalytic theory of neurosis.* New York: Norton.

Freud, A. (1946). *The ego and the mechanisms of defense.* New York: International Universities Press. (Originally published, 1936.)

———. (1964–1981). *The writings of Anna Freud.* New York: International Universities Press. (8 vols.)

Freud, S. The psychopathology of everyday life. In J. Strachey (Ed. and Trans.), *The standard edition of the complete psychological works of Sigmund Freud* (Vol. 6). London: Hogarth Press, 1953–1966. (Originally published, 1901.)

———. Three essays on the theory of sexuality. In *Standard edition* (Vol. 7). (Originally published, 1905.)

———. "Civilized" sexual morality and modern nervous illness. In *Standard edition* (Vol. 9). (Originally published, 1908.)

———. Repression. In *Standard edition* (Vol. 14). (Originally published, 1915.)

———. Inhibitions, symptoms, and anxiety. In *Standard edition* (Vol. 14). (Originally published, 1926.)

Gaines, J. (1979). *Fritz Perls: Here and now.* Millbrae, CA: Celestial Arts.

Goldman, D. (1993). *In search of the real: The origins and originality of D. W. Winnicott.* Northvale, NJ: Jason Aronson.

Gordon, D. (1987). Gestalt therapy: The historical influences of Frederick S. Perls. *Gestalt Journal, 9*(10), 28–39.

Greenberg, J., & Mitchell, S. (1983). *Object relations theory and clinical psychoanalytic theory.* Cambridge, MA: Harvard University Press.

Grosskurth, P. (1986). *Melanie Klein.* London: Hodder and Stroughton.

Hall, C. S. (1954). *A primer of Freudian psychology.* New York: New American Library.

Humphrey, K. (1986). Laura Perls: A biographical sketch. *Gestalt Journal,* (1), 5–11.

Jones, E. (1953, 1955, 1957). *The life and work of Sigmund Freud* (3 vols.). New York: Basic Books.

Jurjevich, R. (1978). Emotionality and irrationality in psychotherapeutic fads. *Psychotherapy Theory, Research, and Practice, 15*(2), 168–179.

Keillor, G. (1995, April 19). *A prairie home companion.* National Public Radio.

Klein, M. (1975). *The writings of Melanie Klein,* 4 vols. Vol. I: *Love, guilt and reparation and other works 1921–1945.* Vol. II: *The psychoanalysis of children.* Vol. III: *Envy and gratitude and other works 1946–1963.* Vol. IV: *Narrative of a child analysis. The conduct of the psychoanalysis of children as seen in the treatment of a ten-year-old boy.* London: Hogarth Press and the Institute of Psychoanalysis.

Kohut, H. (1959). Introspection, empathy and psychoanalysis: An examination of the relationship between modes of observation and theory. *Journal of the American Psychoanalytic Association, 7,* 459–483.

———. (1971). *The analysis of the self.* New York: International Universities Press.

———. (1977). *The restoration of the self.* New York: International Universities Press.

———. (1982). Introspection, empathy, and the semicircle of mental health. *International Journal of Psychoanalysis, 63,* 395–407.

———. (1984). *How does analysis cure?* Chicago: University of Chicago Press.

Kriegman, D. (1990). Compassion and altruism in psychoanalytic theory: An evolutionary analysis of self psychology. *Journal of the American Academy of Psychoanalysis, 18*(2), 342–367.

Malcolm, J. (1980, November 24 & December 1). The impossible profession. *The New Yorker.*

Masserman, J. H. (1961). *Principles of dynamic psychiatry* (2nd ed.). Philadelphia: Saunders.

Morris, K., & Ellis, A. (1975). The Perls' perversion. *Personnel and Guidance Journal, 54*(2), 90–93.

Pauchant, T., & Dumas, C. (1991). Abraham Maslow and Heinz Kohut. *Journal of Humanistic Psychology, 31*(2), 49–71.

Perls, F. S. (1969a). *Ego, hunger and aggression*. New York: Random House. (Originally published, 1947.)

———. (1969b). *Gestalt therapy verbatim*. Lafayette, CA: The Real People Press.

———. (1969c). *In and out of the garbage pail*. Lafayette, CA: The Real People Press.

———. (1973). *The Gestalt approach: Eyewitness to therapy*. Ben Lomond, CA: Science and Behavior Books; New York: Bantam, 1976.

———. (1977). Resolution. In J. Stevens (Ed.), *Gestalt is*. New York: Bantam, 70–75.

———. (1978). Psychiatry in a new key. *Gestalt Journal, 1*(1), 32–53.

———. (1979). Planned psychotherapy. *Gestalt Journal, 2*(2), 5–23.

———. (1989). Theory and technique of personality integration. *TACD Journal, 17*(1), 35–52.

Perls, F. S., Hefferline, R. F., & Goodman, P. (1951). *Gestalt therapy*. New York: Dell.

Perls, L. (1986). Opening address: 8th annual conference on the theory and practice of Gestalt therapy—May 17, 1985. *Gestalt Journal, 9*(1), 12–15.

———. (1992). Concepts and misconceptions of Gestalt therapy. *Journal of Humanistic Psychology, 32*(3), 50–56. (Originally published in *Voices, 14*[3]).

Rogers, C. (1986). Rogers, Kohut, and Erikson. *Person-Centered Review, 1*, 125–140.

Rosenfeld, E. (1978). An oral history of Gestalt therapy. Part I: A conversation with Laura Perls. *Gestalt Journal, 1*(1), 8–31.

Sandler, J., with Anna Freud. (1985). *The analysis of defenses: The ego and the mechanisms of defence revisited*. New York: International Universities Press.

Sears, R. T. (1936). Experimental studies of projection. I: Attributions of traits. *Journal of Social Psychology, 7*, 151–163.

Segal, H. (1973). *Introduction to the work of Melanie Klein*. London: Hogarth Press and the Institute of Psychoanalysis.

Serlin, I. (1992). Tribute to Laura Perls. *Journal of Humanistic Psychology, 32*(3), 57–66.

Shah, I. (1972). *The magic monastery*. New York: Dutton.

Shepard, M. (1975). *Fritz: An intimate portrait of Fritz Perls and Gestalt therapy*. New York: Dutton–Saturday Review Press.

Smith, E. (1975). The role of early Reichian theory in the development of Gestalt therapy. *Psychotherapy Theory, Research, and Practice, 12*(3), 268–272.

St. Clair, M. (1986). *Object relations and self psychology: An introduction*. Monterey, CA: Brooks/Cole.

Stevens, J., & Stevens, B. (1977). Introduction. In J. Stevens (Ed.), *Gestalt is*. New York: Bantam, vii–xi.

Stoehr, T. (1994). *Here now next: Paul Goodman and the origins of Gestalt therapy*. San Francisco: Jossey-Bass.

Tobin, S. (1990). Self psychology as a bridge between existential-humanistic psychology and psychoanalysis. *Journal of Humanistic Psychology, 30*(1), 14–63.

———. (1991). A comparison of psychoanalytic self psychology and Carl Rogers' person-centered therapy. *Journal of Humanistic Psychology, 31*(1) 9–33.

Wheeler, G. (1991). *Gestalt reconsidered: A new approach to contact and resistance*. New York: Gardner Press.

———. (1993). Translator's introduction. In B. Heimannsberg & C. Schmidt (Eds.), *The collective silence: German identity and the legacy of shame*. San Francisco: Jossey-Bass, xv–xxviii.

Wheeler, G., & Backman, S. (1994). *On intimate ground: A Gestalt approach to working with couples*. San Francisco: Jossey-Bass.

Winnicott, D. W. (1960). The theory of the parent-infant relationship. In *The maturational process and the facilitating environment*. London: Hogarth Press, 1975.

———. (1971). *Playing and reality*. New York: Penguin Books.

———. (1989). *Psycho-analytic explorations*. Ed. C. Winnicott, R. Shepherd, & M. Davis. Cambridge, MA: Harvard University Press.

Young-Bruehl, E. (1988). *Anna Freud*. New York: Summit.

CHAPTER 6

Karen Horney and Humanistic Psychoanalysis

Bernard J. Paris

Because her thought went through three distinct phases, Karen Horney has come to mean different things to different people. Some think of her primarily in terms of her essays on feminine psychology, written in the 1920s and early 1930s, in which she tried to modify Freud's ideas about penis envy, female masochism, and feminine development while remaining within the framework of orthodox theory. These essays were too far ahead of their time to receive the attention they deserved, but they have been widely read since their republication in *Feminine Psychology* in 1967, and there is a growing consensus that Karen Horney was the first great psychoanalytic feminist.[1]

[David Letterman's] neurosis has achieved classical dimensions. I happened to be reading Dr. Karen Horney's "The Neurotic Personality of Our Time" recently, and (except for the pages that reminded me of me) almost every chapter cried out, *Dave, Dave, Dave. . . .* As Horney writes of this kind of highfalutin' defeatist, "He tends to feel that he is nothing, but is irritated when he is not taken for a genius." (James Wolcott, "Letterman Unbound: Dave's No. 2 and Trying Harder," *The New Yorker,* June 3, 1996, p. 82)

Those who are attracted to the second stage of Horney's thought identify her primarily as a neo-Freudian member of the cultural school, which also included Erich Fromm, Harry Stack Sullivan, Clara Thompson, and Abraham Kardiner. In *The Neurotic Personality of Our Time* (1937) and *New Ways in Psychoanalysis* (1939), Horney broke with Freud and developed a psychoanalytic paradigm in which culture and disturbed human relationships replaced biology as the most important causes of neurotic development. *The Neurotic Personality of Our Time* made Horney famous in intellectual circles. It created a heightened awareness of cultural factors in mental disturbance and inspired studies of culture from a psychoanalytic perspective. Because of its criticism of Freud, *New Ways in Psychoanalysis* made Horney infamous among orthodox analysts and led to her ostracism from the psychoanalytic establishment. Although it paid tribute to Freud's genius and the importance of his contribution, it rejected many of his premises and tried to shift the focus of psychoanalysis from infantile origins to the current structure of the personality. It laid the foundations for the development of present-oriented therapies, which have become increasingly important in recent years (Wachtel, 1977).

In the 1940s, Horney developed her mature theory, which many feel to be her most distinctive contribution. In *Our Inner Conflicts* (1945) and *Neurosis and Human Growth* (1950), she argued that individuals cope with the anxiety produced by feeling unsafe, unloved, and unvalued by disowning their real feelings and developing elaborate strategies of defense. In *Our Inner Conflicts,* she concentrated on the interpersonal defenses of moving toward, against, and away from other people and the neurotic solutions of compliance, aggression, and detachment to which they give rise. In *Neurosis and Human Growth,* she emphasized intrapsychic defenses, showing how self-idealization generates a search for glory and what she called the pride system, which consists of neurotic pride, neurotic claims, tyrannical shoulds, and self-hate. The range and power of Horney's mature theory have been shown not only by the theory's clinical applications but also by its use in such fields as literary criticism, biography, and the study of culture and gender.

The object of therapy for Horney is to help people relinquish their defenses—which alienate them from their true likes and dislikes, hopes, fears, and desires—so that they can get in touch with what she called the real self. Because

[1]Some material in this chapter is adapted from *Karen Horney: A Psychoanalyst's Search for Self-Understanding,* by Bernard J. Paris (1994).

of her emphasis on self-realization as the source of healthy values and the goal of life, Horney is one of the founders of humanistic psychology.

Personal History

Karen Horney was born Karen Danielsen in a suburb of Hamburg on September 15, 1885. Her father was a sea captain of Norwegian origin; her mother was of Dutch-German extraction. Karen had a brother, Berndt, who was 4 years older than she. Karen sided with her mother in the fierce conflicts between her parents, who were ill-matched in age and background, and her mother supported Karen's desire for an education, against her father's opposition.

When she was 13, Karen decided that she wanted to be a physician, and she was one of the first women in Germany to be admitted to medical school. She received her medical education at the universities of Freiburg, Göttingen, and Berlin. In 1909 she married Oskar Horney, a social scientist she had met while they were both students in Freiburg. In 1910 she entered analysis with Karl Abraham, a member of Freud's inner circle and the first psychoanalyst to practice in Germany. Karen decided to become an analyst herself and in 1920 was one of the six founding members of the Berlin Psychoanalytic Institute. She taught there until 1932, when Franz Alexander invited her to become associate director of the newly formed Chicago Psychoanalytic Institute. She joined the faculty of the New York Psychoanalytic Institute in 1934 but was driven out in 1941 as a result of the publication of *New Ways in Psychoanalysis.* She founded the American Institute for Psychoanalysis the same year and was dean until her death in 1952. She was also founding editor of *The American Journal of Psychoanalysis.*

[Horney writes at the age of 17:] I asked this morning whether I might join a class in animal dissection, and I was turned down. . . . *Et voilà* a substitute: I shall take myself to pieces. That will probably be more difficult, but also more interesting. (Horney, 1980, p. 58)

Karen Horney was introspective and self-analytical in her youth, partly because of her temperament and partly because of her unhappy childhood. She felt that she had been unwanted and that her brother was much more highly valued than she, principally because he was a male. Since she disliked her father, whom she regarded as a religious hypocrite, and her mother confided in her brother, she felt alone and unsupported in the family. To compensate for this, she tried to attach herself to her brother, with whom she seems to have engaged in some kind of sex play between the ages of 5 and 9. When her brother distanced himself from her on reaching puberty, Karen felt rejected and tried to gain a sense of worth by becoming fiercely competitive in school.

As a child, Karen was bitter, angry, and rebellious, but when she reached puberty, she could no longer tolerate her isolation and won a position in the family by joining the circle of her mother's admirers. At the age of 13, she began keeping a diary (Horney, 1980) in which she expressed adoration of her mother and brother. Her buried hostility toward them erupted when she was 21, however, and her relations with them were strained thereafter. The diaries that were written while Karen was repressing her anger give a misleading picture of her relations with her family and must be read in light of the Clare case in *Self-Analysis* (1942), which is highly autobiographical and explains her behavior during adolescence.

If she, too, admired the mother she need no longer feel isolated and excluded but could hope to receive some affection, or at least be accepted. . . . [She] was no longer the disregarded ugly duckling, but became the wonderful daughter of a wonderful mother. . . . [But] by admiring what in reality she resented, she became alienated from her own feelings. She no longer knew what she herself liked or wished or feared or resented. (From the Clare case, Horney, 1942, pp. 50–51)

Although Karen's diaries are misleading about her relations with her family, they reveal her emotional problems quite clearly. She suffered from depression, timidity, and paralyzing fatigue, could not bear being without a boyfriend, was insecure about her mental abilities, and felt like an ugly duckling who could not compete with her beautiful mother. She had great difficulty focusing on her work and was able to succeed academically only because of her exceptional intelligence.

Neurotic girls cannot love a "weak" man because of their contempt for any weakness; but neither can they cope with a "strong" man because they expect their partner always to give in. Hence what they secretly look for is the hero, the superstrong man, who at the same time is so weak that he will bend to all their wishes. . . . (Horney, 1937, p. 170)

Karen's diaries were mostly devoted to her relationships with males, from whom she desperately needed attention. The typical pattern of her relationships was first idealization of the male, followed by disappointment, depression, and efforts to comprehend why the relationship failed. Because of her disappointments, she moved from man to man, often trying to hold on to several at once because each satisfied different demands. She hoped to find a great man who could fulfill her conflicting needs for dominance and submission, crude force and refined sensibility, but she was perpetually disappointed. Deeply unhappy, she tried to understand the sources of her misery, first in her diaries and then in her psychoanalytic writings, many of which are covert autobiography.

Won't I ever be getting well, completely well? I am beginning to despair of it. . . . I often feel as though I were paralyzed. . . . When I waken in the morning, I wish the day were already over. (Letter to Karl Abraham, after two courses of analysis—Horney, 1980, p. 270)

At first, Karen thought that Oskar Horney was the great man for whom she had been looking, but he was not forceful enough, and the marriage was soon in trouble. She sought help in her analysis with Karl Abraham, but her symptoms were the same after two years of treatment as they had been when she began. The failure of her analysis is one reason why she began to question orthodox theory, especially with respect to the psychology of women. After having three children, Karen and Oskar separated in 1926 and divorced in 1938. Karen never remarried, but she had many troubled relationships of the kind she describes in her essays on feminine psychology and the Clare case in *Self-Analysis.*

Although she had begun to emphasize culture in her writings of the 1920s, it was her move to the United States in 1932 that convinced her that Freud had given too much importance to biology and too little to social factors. First in Chicago and then in New York, she found patients whose problems were very different from those she had encountered in Germany. This experience, combined with her reading in the burgeoning sciences of sociology and anthropology, made her doubt the universality of the Oedipus complex and led her to explore the impact of culture on individual psychology. In 1935 she lectured on this topic at the New School for Social Research and was invited by W. W. Norton to write the book that became *The Neurotic Personality of Our Time.* As Horney's disagreements with Freud deepened, she felt it important to contrast her thinking with his in a systematic way, and this she did in *New Ways in Psychoanalysis.*

Horney's third book, *Self-Analysis* (1942), was an outgrowth of the breakdown of her relationship with Erich Fromm. She had known Fromm when he was a student at the Berlin Psychoanalytic Institute (he was 15 years younger than she), and she met him again when he lectured at the University of Chicago in 1933. They became lovers when both moved to New York in 1934. Their relationship was intellectual as well as emotional, with Fromm teaching Horney sociology and Horney teaching Fromm psychoanalysis. The relationship deteriorated in the late 1930s, after Horney sent her daughter Marianne, who was specializing in psychiatry, to Fromm for a training analysis. When Marianne's hostilities toward her mother emerged in the course of analysis, as was to be expected, Horney blamed Fromm. The breakdown of the relationship was extremely painful to Horney and led to a period of intense Self-Analysis. This issued in the writing of *Self-Analysis,* in which the story of Clare and Peter is a fictionalized account of what happened between Horney and Fromm. Despite their estrangement, Fromm became a member of the American Institute for Psychoanalysis when it was founded in 1941, but Horney drove him out in 1942, using his status as a lay analyst (he had a Ph.D. rather than an M.D.) as a pretext.

The 1930s were a turbulent period for Horney, culminating in the hostile reaction of her colleagues at the New York Psychoanalytic Institute to her criticisms of Freud and her split with Erich Fromm. The 1940s were equally turbulent, since many of Horney's most distinguished colleagues left the American Institute, one group (including Fromm, Harry Stack Sullivan, and Clara Thompson) to form the William Alanson White Institute and another to join the New York Medical College. These splits were partly the result of Horney's need for dominance and her inability to grant others the kind of academic freedom she had demanded for herself at the New York Psychoanalytic Institute. Horney continued to have difficulties in her love life, and these often contributed to dissention at her institute, since she tended to place men with whom she was having relationships in positions of power. Despite the political turmoil it involved, heading her own institute enabled Horney to flourish. It gave her the intellectual freedom she had always sought and facilitated the development of her mature theory. Toward the end of the decade, Horney became interested in Zen, and not long before her death in 1952, she traveled to Japan with D. T. Suzuki, who had written and lectured about Zen in the United States, to visit Zen monasteries.

[S]he was described [by people whom her biographer interviewed] variously—and contradictorily—as both frail and strong, open and reticent, aloof and "with you," distant and close, caring, motherly and uncaring, unsympathetic, loving and unloving, dominating and self-effacing, manipulative and compliant, a leader and a follower, fair and mean. . . . The impression emerged that she . . . needed to encompass and unify many diverse and conflicting traits, apparently with constant struggle. (Rubins, 1978, pp. xiii–xiv)

Although Horney was a brilliant clinician, she suffered all her life from not having had an analyst who could really help her. After her disappointing experiences, first with Karl Abraham and then with Hanns Sachs in the early 1920s, she turned to Self-Analysis in an effort to gain relief from her emotional difficulties. Combined with her clinical experience, her Self-Analysis generated many of her psychoanalytic ideas. Her constant struggle to obtain relief from her problems was largely responsible for the continual evolution of her theory and the deepening of her insights. Horney had a remarkable ability to see herself clearly and to be brutally honest about her own problems. With the exception of her earliest essays, she did not construct a theory that universalized or normalized her difficulties.

She created in spite of her problems, because of her problems, and through her problems. (Harold Kelman in Paris, 1994, p. 176)

Although Horney made little progress with some of her problems, she was remarkably successful with others. As a young woman, she had suffered severely from depression, fatigue, and inability to work, but she became extraordinarily creative, energetic, and productive. Like Clare in *Self-Analysis,* she was a late bloomer, since she did not write very much until she was in her forties. The last 15 years of her life were remarkable: she published five groundbreaking books; she was in great demand as an analyst, supervisor, and speaker; she founded and directed the American Institute for Psychoanalysis; she founded and edited *The American Journal of Psychoanalysis;* she taught at the New School on a regular basis; she read widely; she learned how to paint; she had many eminent friends and a busy social life; she spent much time in the summers with her daughters; and she traveled a great deal. Her failure to overcome some of her problems

It is probably fair to say that she poured all her creative energy into work, into search, in part as a genuine creative effort and in part as a rescue . . . from interpersonal difficulties. She was a tremendously conflicted person who found a successful, eminently satisfying creative way of life. I think she would always want her books to speak for her, as justifying her existence. (Marianne Eckardt, Horney's daughter, in Paris, 1994, p. 178) made her realistic, while her successes were the source of her famous optimism. Her belief both in the human potential for growth and in the difficulty of achieving it was based on her own experience.

Intellectual Antecedents

Sigmund Freud and Psychoanalysis

Although a reviewer described *New Ways in Psychoanalysis* as "a fourteen-round ring battle between the 'new ways' (Horney) and the 'old ways' (Freud)" (Brown, 1939, p. 328), Horney acknowledged that she was deeply indebted to Freud, who had provided the foundation for all subsequent psychoanalytic thought. It is not difficult to see why the young Karen Horney was attracted to psychoanalysis. She suffered from many mysterious complaints, and her ability to function was impaired. Of an introspective temperament, she had been in the habit of seeking relief by scrutinizing her feelings and motivations. Psychoanalysis offered the most powerful tools available for such an enterprise. She frequently recognized herself, moreover, in Freud's description of women's problems. Given her suffering, her temperament, and her craving for self-understanding, psychoanalysis as a theory and a therapy must have seemed to be exactly what she was looking for.

As psychology has been until now mostly worked at from the side of men, it seems to me to be the given task for a woman psychologist—or at least I think it to be mine—to work out a fuller understanding for specifically female trends and attitudes in life. (Horney in Paris, 1994, p. 55)

While some aspects of Freudian theory fit Horney's experience well, others did not. By the early 1920s she began to propose modifications in the light of her observations of her female patients and her own experiences as a woman. Perhaps the most important factor in Horney's initial dissent was that she came to see psychoanalytic theory as reproducing and reinforcing the devaluation of the feminine from which she had suffered in childhood. Disturbed by the male bias of psychoanalysis, she dedicated herself to proposing a woman's view of the differences between men and women and the disturbances in the relations between the sexes. This eventually led to the development of a psychoanalytic paradigm that was quite different from Freud's. However, Horney always paid tribute to what she regarded as Freud's enduring contributions. These included the doctrines "that psychic processes are strictly determined, that actions and feelings may be determined by unconscious motivations, and that the motivations driving us are emotional forces" (1939, p. 18). She valued Freud's accounts of repression, reaction formation, projection, displacement, rationalization, and dreams; and she felt that Freud had provided indispensable tools for therapy in the concepts of transference, resistance, and free association (1939, p. 117).

Alfred Adler

Fritz Wittels (1939) argued that neo-Freudians like Horney were really closer to Adler than to Freud and should really be called neo-Adlerians. Horney began reading Adler as early as 1910, and despite the fact that she did not give him a great deal of credit as an intellectual antecedent, there are important similarities between her later thinking and his.

Adler's influence first appears in a diary entry in 1911. In her work with Karl Abraham, Horney struggled to understand her fatigue, and in her diary she recorded the numerous explanations he proposed, most of which had to do with unconscious sexual desires. In one entry, however, she looked at herself from an Adlerian perspective and arrived at an explanation that sounds very much like her own analysis of Clare, written 30 years later. She wondered whether her fear of productive work derives not only from her mistrust of her own capacity but also from the need to be first that Adler considered characteristic of neurotics.

[F]rom a feeling of uncertainty and inferiority, I am afraid that I will not be able to do anything first class, above average, and therefore prefer not to attempt it at all, perhaps trying to create a special position for myself through this exaggerated refusal. (Horney, 1980, p. 250)

Horney was especially intrigued by Adler's account of the *masculine protest* that develops in every woman in response to her sense of physical inferiority to men. She had no difficulty in identifying the masculine protest in herself. She "envied Berndt because he could stand near a tree and pee" (Horney, 1980, p. 252), she liked wearing pants, she played the prince in charades, and at the age of 12 she cut off her hair to the neckline. She compensated for her physical inferiority to males by excelling in school, taking great pride that she was a better student than her brother. In the terms of her culture, she was behaving like a man by studying medicine and believing in sexual freedom.

According to Horney's Adlerian Self-Analysis, she needed to feel superior because of her lack of beauty and her feminine sense of inferiority, which led her to try to excel in a male domain. But her low self-esteem made her afraid she would fail, so she avoided productive work, as do "women in general" (Horney, 1980, p. 251), and experienced disproportionate anxiety over exams. Her fatigue was at once a product of her anxiety, an excuse for withdrawing from competition with men, and a means of concealing her inferiority and gaining a special place for herself by arousing concern.

Horney did not pursue this Adlerian way of thinking for the next two decades, but she returned to it in the 1930s and 1940s, when it became highly congruent with her own approach to psychoanalysis. Although she tended to characterize Adler as superficial, she recognized his importance as an intellectual antecedent, acknowledging that he was the first to see the search for glory "as a comprehensive phenomenon, and to point out its crucial significance in neurosis" (1950, p. 28).

Other Intellectual Influences

While still in Germany, Horney began to cite ethnographic and anthropological studies, as well as the writings of the philosopher and sociologist Georg Simmel, with whom she developed a friendship. After she moved to the United States, her sense of the differences between central Europe and America made her receptive to the work of such sociologists, anthropologists, and culturally oriented psychoanalysts as Erich Fromm, Max Horkheimer, John Dollard, Harold Lasswell, Edward Sapir, Ruth Benedict, Ralph Linton, Margaret Mead, Abraham Kardiner, and Harry Stack Sullivan, with most of whom she had personal relationships. In response to these influences, Horney argued not only that culture is more important than biology in the generation of neuroses but also that pathogenic conflict between the individual and society is the product

Georg Simmel says . . . that historically the relations of the sexes may be crudely described as that of master and slave. Here, as always, it is "one of the privileges of the master that he has not constantly to think that he is master, while the position of the slave is such that he can never forget it." (Horney, 1967, p. 69)

[I]n the terms of William James: [the real self] . . . is the source of spontaneous interest and energies, "the source of effort and attention from which emanate the fiats of will"; . . . it is the part of ourselves that wants to expand and grow and to fulfill itself. It produces the "reactions of spontaneity" to our feelings or thoughts, "welcoming or opposing, appropriating or disowning, striving with or against, saying yes or no." (Horney, 1950, p. 157)

[Despite his despair, a man may] be perfectly well able to live on . . . and perhaps no one notices that in a deeper sense he lacks a self . . . for a self is a thing the world is least apt to inquire about. . . . The greatest danger, that of losing one's own self, may pass off as quietly as if it were nothing; every other loss, that of an arm, a leg, five dollars, a wife, etc., is sure to be noticed. (Kierkegaard in Horney, 1945, p. 185)

of a bad society rather than being inevitable, as Freud had contended. Following Bronislaw Malinowski, Felix Boehm, and Erich Fromm, Horney regarded the Oedipus complex as a culturally conditioned phenomenon; and following Harry Stack Sullivan, she saw the needs for "safety and satisfaction" as more important than sexual drives in accounting for human behavior.

Although at first she saw conceptions of psychological health as relative to culture, in the late 1930s she developed a definition of health that was universal in nature. Drawing on W. W. Trotter's *Instincts of the Herd in Peace and War* (1916), she described emotional well-being as "a state of inner freedom in which 'the full capacities are available for use' " (1939, p. 182). The central feature of neurosis was now self-alienation, loss of contact with "the spontaneous individual self" (1939, p. 11). Horney gave Erich Fromm primary credit for this new direction in her thinking, but other important influences were William James and Søren Kierkegaard. In her descriptions of the "real self," she was inspired by James's account of the "spiritual self" in *Principles of Psychology* (1890), and in her discussions of loss of self, she drew on Kierkegaard's *The Sickness unto Death* (1949). Horney also cited Otto Rank's concept of "will" as an influence on her ideas about the real self, and in her later work she invoked the Zen concept of "wholeheartedness."

It is difficult to determine why Horney shifted from an emphasis on the past to one on the present, but she acknowledged the influence of Harald Schultz-Henke and Wilhelm Reich, analysts whom she knew from her days in Berlin. The Adlerian mode of analysis she had employed in her diary and to which she returned also focused on the present.

Major Concepts

Since Horney's thought went through three phases, it will be best to discuss the major concepts of each phase separately. We shall look first at her ideas about feminine psychology, then at the new psychoanalytic paradigm she developed in the 1930s, and finally at her mature theory.

Feminine Psychology

[T]he psychology of women has hitherto been considered only from the point of view of men. It is inevitable that the man's position of advantage should cause objective validity to be attributed to his subjective, affective relations to the woman, and according to Delius the psychology of women hitherto actually represents a deposit of the desires and disappointments of men. (Horney, 1967, p. 56)

Nancy Chodorow locates the "political and theoretical origins" of psychoanalytic feminism with Karen Horney, whose theories form the basis "for most of the recent revisions of psychoanalytic understandings of gender and for most psychoanalytic dissidence on the question of gender in the early period as well" (1989, pp. 2–3). Horney's ideas were ignored for many years but now seem remarkably astute.

The Male View of Women In her earliest essays on feminine psychology, Horney strove to show that girls and women have intrinsic biological constitutions and patterns of development that are to be understood in their own terms and not just as products of their difference from and presumed inferiority to men. She argued that psychoanalysis regards women as defective men because it is the product of a male genius (Freud) and a male-dominated culture. The male view of the female has been incorporated into psychoanalysis as a scientific picture of woman's essential nature.

An important question for Horney is why men see women as they do. She contended that male envy of pregnancy, childbirth, and motherhood, and of the breasts and suckling, gives rise to an unconscious tendency to devalue women and that men's impulse toward creative work is an overcompensation for their small role in procreation. The **womb envy** of the male must be stronger than the so-called **penis envy** of the female, since men need to depreciate women more than women need to depreciate men.

In later essays, Horney continued to analyze the male view of woman in order to expose its lack of scientific foundation. In "The Distrust Between the Sexes" (1931), she argued that woman is seen as "a second-rate being" because "at any given time, the more powerful side will create an ideology suitable to help maintain its position. . . . In this ideology the differentness of the weaker one will be interpreted as inferiority, and it will be proven that these differences are unchangeable, basic, or God's will" (1967, p. 116). In "The Dread of Woman" (1932), Horney traced the male dread of woman to the boy's fear that his genital is inadequate in relation to the mother. The threat posed by woman is not castration but humiliation; the threat is to his masculine self-regard. As he grows up, the male continues to have a deeply hidden anxiety about the size of his penis or his potency, an anxiety that has no counterpart for the female, who "performs her part by merely *being*" (1967, p. 145) and is not obliged to go on proving her womanhood. There is, therefore, no corresponding female dread of men. The male deals with his anxiety by erecting an ideal of efficiency, by seeking sexual conquests, and by debasing the love object.

She is said to be at home only in the realm of eros. Spiritual matters are alien to her innermost being, and she is at odds with cultural trends. She therefore is, as Asians frankly state, a second-rate being. . . . [She is] prevented from real accomplishment by the deplorable, bloody tragedies of menstruation and childbirth. And so every man silently thanks his God, just as the pious Jew does in his prayers, that he was not created a woman. (Horney, 1967, p. 114)

Cultural Factors In her essays on feminine psychology, Horney moved steadily away from Freud's belief that "anatomy is destiny" and toward a greater emphasis on cultural factors as a source of women's problems and of gender identity. She acknowledged that little girls envy the male plumbing but regarded this as psychologically insignificant. What women chiefly envy is male privilege, and what they need is greater opportunity to develop their human capacities. The patriarchal ideal of woman does not necessarily correspond to her inherent character, but the cultural power of that ideal often makes women behave in accordance with it.

In "The Problem of Feminine Masochism" (1935), Horney challenged the idea that "masochistic trends are inherent in, or akin to, the very essence of female nature" (1967, p. 214). This is the position of psychoanalysis, which reflects the stereotypes of male culture, but Horney identified a number of social conditions that have made women more masochistic than men. Moreover, comparative studies show that these conditions have not been universal and that some societies have been more unfavorable to women's development than have been others.

Our culture, as is well known, is a male culture, and therefore by and large not favorable to the unfolding of woman and her individuality. . . . [N]o matter how much the individual woman may be treasured as a mother or as a lover, it is always the male who will be considered more valuable on human and spiritual grounds. The little girl grows up under this general impression. (Horney, 1967, p. 82)

The Masculinity Complex Horney did not deny that women often envy men and are uncomfortable with their feminine role. Indeed, many of her essays deal with the **masculinity complex** (similar to Adler's *masculine protest*), which she defined as "the entire complex of feelings and fantasies that have for their content the woman's feeling of being discriminated against, her envy of the male, her wish to be a man and to discard the female role" (1967, p. 74). Although she initially argued that women are bound to have a masculinity complex because of their need to escape the guilt and anxiety that result from their Oedipal situation, Horney soon came to feel that the masculinity complex is not inevitable but is the product of a male-dominated culture and of particular kinds of family dynamics. The fact that "a girl is exposed from birth onward to the suggestion—inevitable, whether conveyed brutally or delicately—of her inferiority" is an experience "that constantly stimulates her masculinity complex" (1967, p. 69).

In discussing family dynamics, Horney focused at first on the girl's relationship with male members of the family, but later she derived the masculinity complex and all the phenomena traditionally associated with penis envy—such as feelings of inferiority, vindictiveness, and competitiveness toward men—from the girl's relationship with females in the family, particularly the mother. In "Maternal Conflicts" (1933), she brought together the separate features of childhood to which she had attributed the masculinity complex in previous essays: "A girl may have reasons to acquire a dislike for her own female world very early, perhaps because her mother has intimidated her, or she has experienced a thoroughly disillusioning disappointment from the side of the father or brother; she may have had early sexual experiences that frightened her; or she may have found that her brother was greatly preferred to herself" (1967, p. 179). All of these features were present in Karen Horney's childhood.

The Overvaluation of Love "The Overvaluation of Love" (1934) is the culmination of Horney's attempt to analyze herself in terms of feminine psychology. The essay draws on the cases of seven women whose family histories, symptoms, and social backgrounds are similar to Horney's, and she may well have included herself in her clinical sample. Most of the essay is devoted to trying to explain why these women have an obsessive need for a male but are unable to form satisfactory relationships. Their obsession is traced to a childhood situation in which each "had come off second best in the competition for a man" (1967, p. 193). It is the typical fate of the girl to be frustrated in her love for her father, but for these women the consequences are unusually severe because of the presence of a mother or sister who dominates the situation erotically.

The girl responds to her sense of defeat either by withdrawing from the competition for a male or developing a compulsive rivalry with other women in which she tries to demonstrate her erotic appeal. The conquest of men provides not only what Horney would later call a "vindictive triumph" but is also a way of coping with anxiety and self-hate. The insecure girl develops an anxiety about being abnormal that often manifests itself as a fear that something is wrong with her genitals or that she is ugly and cannot possibly be attractive to men. As a defense, she may pay an inordinate amount of attention to her ap-

Personal Reflection

■ A Matter of Philosophy

In the beginning of *Neurosis and Human Growth* (1950, pp. 14–15), Horney distinguishes three concepts of morality that rest on three views of human nature:

1. If the human being is by nature sinful or ridden by primitive impulses, the goal of morality must be to curb them, tame them, overcome them.
2. If there is something inherently "good" in human nature and something inherently "bad," the goal of morality must be to ensure the eventual victory of the good by suppressing the bad and directing or reinforcing the good elements, using will, reason, and strength.
3. If human nature is seen as inevitably evolving toward self-realization by an intrinsic tendency, not by will, then the goal of morality becomes one of removing obstacles in the way of that evolution, in order to provide maximum opportunity for the spontaneous forces of growth to manifest.

Having read Horney's three concepts, you can try the following exercise.

1. In a group of at least three students, discuss the three positions and tentatively choose one to support.
2. Horney embraced the third concept of morality. Discuss what implications this philosophy had on her attitude toward psychotherapy.
3. Whichever position you have chosen, ask yourself whether you actually live by this position. How do you behave that shows your response to be true? Share your answers with the group.

pearance or may wish to be a male. The most important defense is proving that, despite her disadvantages, she *can* attract a man. To be without a man is a disgrace, but having one proves that she is "normal": "Hence the frantic pursuit" (1967, pp. 197–198).

The situation of these women is sad because although their relationships with men are paramount, they are never satisfactory. They tend to lose interest in a man as soon as he is conquered, because they have "a profound fear of the disappointments and humiliations that they expect to result from falling in love" (1967, p. 205). Having been rejected by father or brother in childhood, they simultaneously need to prove their worth through erotic conquests and to make themselves invulnerable by avoiding deep emotional bonds. They tend to change partners frequently, since, after securing a man, they need to get out of the relationship before they get hurt. However attractive they are, they do not believe that a man can actually love them. Moreover, they have a "deep-seated desire for revenge" because of their original defeat: "[T]he desire is to get the better of a man, to cast him aside, to reject him just as she herself once felt cast aside and rejected" (1967, p. 206).

The experience [of childhood sexual excitation] left certain traces in its wake . . . of a pleasure far in excess of that from any other source, and of something strangely vitalizing to the whole organism. I am inclined to think that these traces cause these particular women . . . to conceive of sexual gratification as a kind of elixir of life that only men are able to provide and without which one must dry up and waste away. . . . (Horney, 1967, p. 204)

[W]e should stop bothering about what is feminine. . . . Standards of masculinity and femininity are artificial standards. . . . Differences between the two sexes certainly exist, but we shall never be able to discover what they are until we have first developed our potentialities as human beings. Paradoxical as it may sound, we shall find out about these differences only if we forget about them. (Horney, 1935, in Paris, 1994, p. 238)

Gender Neutrality Although Horney had devoted most of her professional life to writing about feminine psychology, she abandoned the topic in 1935 because she felt that the role of culture in shaping the female psyche makes it impossible to determine what is distinctively feminine. In a lecture entitled "Woman's Fear of Action" (1935), she argued that only when women have been freed from the conceptions of femininity fostered by male-dominated cultures can we discover how they really differ from men psychologically. Our primary objective must not be to identify what is essentially feminine but to foster "the full development of the human personalities of all" (Paris, 1994, p. 238). After this, Horney developed a theory that she considered to be gender-neutral, one that applied equally to males and to females.

Horney's New Paradigm

In *The Neurotic Personality of Our Time* and *New Ways in Psychoanalysis,* Horney subjected Freud's theories to a systematic critique and developed her own version of psychoanalysis. Its distinguishing features were a greater emphasis on culture, the conception of neurosis as a set of defenses devised to cope with basic anxiety, and a focus on present character structure rather than on infantile origins.

It seems that the person who is likely to become neurotic is one who has experienced the culturally determined difficulties in an accentuated form, mostly through the medium of childhood experiences, and who has consequently been unable to solve them, or has solved them only at great cost to his personality. We might call him a stepchild of our culture. (Horney, 1937, p. 290)

The Role of Culture Horney argued that because of his overemphasis on the biological sources of human behavior, Freud had incorrectly assumed the universality of the feelings, attitudes, and kinds of relationships that were common in his culture. Not recognizing the importance of social factors, he attributed neurotic egocentricity to a narcissistic libido, hostility to a destruction instinct, an obsession with money to an anal libido, and acquisitiveness to orality. But anthropology shows that cultures vary widely in their tendency to generate these characteristics, and the Oedipus complex as well, and Horney's own experience of cultural difference after she moved to the United States confirmed this point of view.

Horney rejected Freud's derivation of neurosis from the clash between culture and instinct. In Freud's view, we must have culture in order to survive, and we must repress or sublimate our instincts in order to have culture. Horney did not believe that collision between the individual and society is inevitable but rather that it occurs when a bad environment frustrates our emotional needs and inspires fear and hostility. Freud depicts human beings as inherently insatiable, destructive, and antisocial; according to Horney, these are not expressions of instinct but neurotic responses to adverse conditions.

[Basic anxiety develops when] the environment is dreaded as a whole because it is felt to be unreliable, mendacious, unappreciative, unfair, unjust, begrudging, and merciless. . . . The child . . . feels the environment as a menace to his entire development and to his most legitimate wishes and strivings. He feels in danger of his individuality being obliterated, his freedom taken away, his happiness prevented. In contrast to the fear of castration this fear is not fantasy, but is well-founded on reality. (Horney, 1939, p. 75)

The Structure of Neurosis Horney did not reject the significance of childhood in emotional development, as is sometimes thought, but she emphasized pathogenic conditions in the family that make children feel unsafe, unloved, and unvalued rather than the frustration of libidinal desires. As a result of these conditions, children develop **basic anxiety,** a feeling of helplessness in a potentially hostile world, which they try to reduce by adopting such strategies of defense as the pursuit of love, power, or detachment.

Horney felt that these defensive strategies are doomed to failure because they generate **vicious circles** in which the means employed to allay anxiety tend to increase it. For example, the frustration of the need for love makes that need insatiable, and the demandingness and jealousy that follow make it less likely than ever that the person will receive affection. People who have not been loved develop a feeling of being unlovable that leads them to discount any evidence to the contrary. Being deprived of affection has made them dependent on others, but they are afraid of that dependency because it makes them too vulnerable. Horney compared the situation created in this way with that "of a person who is starving for food yet does not dare to take any for fear that it might be poisoned" (1937, p. 114).

Although Horney devoted much of *The Neurotic Personality of Our Time* to the neurotic need for love, she gave a good deal of space to the quest for power, prestige, and possession that develops when a person feels hopeless about gaining affection.

Horney's paradigm for the structure of neurosis is one in which disturbances in human relationships generate a basic anxiety that leads to the development of strategies of defense that are not only self-defeating but in conflict with each other, since people adopt not just one but several of them. This paradigm formed the basis of Horney's mature theory.

Structure Versus Genesis Perhaps the most significant aspect of Horney's new version of psychoanalysis was her shift in emphasis, both in theory and in clinical practice, from the past to the present. She replaced Freud's focus on genesis with a structural approach, arguing that psychoanalysis should be less concerned with infantile origins than with the current constellation of defenses and inner conflicts. This feature of her theory sharply differentiated it from classical psychoanalysis, which seeks to explain the present by trying to recover the past.

My conviction, expressed in a nutshell, is that psychoanalysis should outgrow the limitations set by its being an instinctivistic and a genetic psychology. (Horney, 1939, p. 8)

In *New Ways in Psychoanalysis,* Horney distinguished between her own "evolutionistic" thinking and what she called Freud's "mechanistic-evolutionistic" thought. Evolutionistic thinking presupposes "that things which exist today have not existed in the same form from the very beginning, but have developed out of previous stages. These preceding stages may have little resemblance to the present forms, but the present forms would be unthinkable without the preceding ones." Mechanistic-evolutionistic thinking holds that "nothing really new is created in the process of development," that "what we see today is only the old in a changed form" (1939, p. 42). For Horney, the profound influence of early experiences does not preclude continued development, whereas for Freud nothing much new happens after the age of 5, and later reactions or experiences are to be considered as a repetition of earlier ones.

In short, then, libido theory in all its contentions is unsubstantiated. . . . What is offered as evidence are unwarranted and often gross generalizations of certain good observations. Similarities existing between physiological functions and mental behavior or mental strivings are used to demonstrate that the former determine the latter. Peculiarities in the sexual sphere are off-hand assumed to engender similar coexisting peculiarities in character traits. (Horney, 1939, p. 68)

At the heart of Freud's conception of the relation between childhood experiences and the behavior of the adult is the doctrine of the timelessness of the unconscious. Fears and desires, or entire experiences, that are repressed in childhood remain uninfluenced by further experiences or growth. This gives rise to the concept of *fixation,* which may pertain to a person in the early environment, such as father or mother, or to a stage of libidinal development. Because of the concept of fixation, it is possible to regard later attachments or

bargain with fate in which obedience to the dictates of that solution is supposed to be rewarded.

. . . our friend William Dobbin, who was personally of so complying a disposition that if his parents had pressed him much, it is probable he would have stepped down into the kitchen and married the cook, and who, to further his own interests, would have found the most insuperable difficulty in walking across the street . . . (Thackeray, *Vanity Fair,* Chapter 23)

The Compliant Solution People in whom the **compliant solution** is dominant try to overcome their basic anxiety by gaining affection and approval and controlling others through their dependency. Their values "lie in the direction of goodness, sympathy, love, generosity, unselfishness, humility; while egotism, ambition, callousness, unscrupulousness, wielding of power are abhorred" (1945, p. 54). They embrace Christian values, but in a compulsive way, because they are necessary to their defense system. They must believe in turning the other cheek, and they must see the world as displaying a providential order in which virtue is rewarded. Their bargain is that if they are good, loving people who shun pride and do not seek their own gain or glory, they will be well treated by fate and other people. If their bargain is not honored, they may despair of divine justice, they may conclude that they are at fault, or they may have recourse to belief in a justice that transcends human understanding. They need to believe not only in the fairness of the world order but also in the goodness of human nature, and here, too, they are vulnerable to disappointment. Self-effacing people must repress their aggressive tendencies in order to make their bargain work, but they are frequently attracted to expansive people through whom they can participate vicariously in the mastery of life. They often develop a "morbid dependency" on their partner.

Expansive Solutions: Narcissistic, Perfectionistic, and Arrogant-Vindictive People in whom the **expansive solutions** are predominant have goals, traits, and values that are opposite to those of the self-effacing solution. What appeals to them most is not love but mastery. They abhor helplessness, are ashamed of suffering, and need to achieve success, prestige, or recognition. In *Neurosis and Human Growth,* Horney divided the expansive solutions into three distinct kinds—narcissistic, perfectionistic, and arrogant-vindictive. There are thus five major solutions in all.

When the rain came to wet me once, and the wind to make me chatter; when the thunder would not peace at my bidding; there I found 'em, there I smelt 'em out. Go to, they are not men o' their words! They told me I was everything. 'Tis a lie—I am not ague-proof. (King Lear in Shakespeare, *King Lear,* Act 4, scene 6)

People who are drawn to the **narcissistic solution** seek to master life "by self-admiration and the exercise of charm" (1950, p. 212). They were often favored and admired children, gifted beyond average, who grew up feeling the world to be a fostering parent and themselves to be favorites of fortune. They have an unquestioned belief in their abilities and feel that there is no game they cannot win. Their insecurity is manifested in the fact that they may speak incessantly of their exploits or wonderful qualities and need endless confirmation of their estimate of themselves in the form of admiration and devotion. Their bargain is that if they hold on to their dreams and their exaggerated claims for themselves, life is bound to give them what they want. If it does not, they may experience a psychological collapse, since they are ill equipped to cope with reality.

The idea of undeserved fortune, whether good or bad, is alien to [the perfectionist]. His own success, prosperity, or good health is therefore less something to be enjoyed than a proof of his virtue. Conversely, any misfortune befalling him . . . may bring this seemingly well-balanced person to the verge of collapse. (Horney, 1950, p. 197)

The **perfectionistic solution** is the refuge of people with extremely high standards, moral and intellectual, on the basis of which they look down upon others. They take great pride in their rectitude and aim for a "flawless excellence" in the whole conduct of life. Because of the difficulty of living up to their standards, they tend to equate knowing about moral values with being a good person. While they deceive themselves in this way, they may insist that others live up to their standards of perfection and may even despise them for failing to do so, thus externalizing their self-condemnation. Perfectionists have a legalistic bargain in which being fair, just, and dutiful entitles them "to fair treatment by others and by life in general. This conviction of an infallible justice operating in life gives [them] a feeling of mastery" (1950, p. 197). Through the height of their standards, they compel fate. Ill-fortune or errors of their own making threaten their bargain and may overwhelm them with feelings of helplessness or self-hate.

The **arrogant-vindictive solution** suits people who are motivated chiefly by a need for vindictive triumphs. Whereas narcissists received early admiration and perfectionists grew up under the pressure of rigid standards, arrogant-vindictive people were harshly treated in childhood and have a need to retaliate for the injuries they have suffered. They feel "that the world is an arena where, in the Darwinian sense, only the fittest survive and the strong annihilate the weak" (1945, p. 64). The only moral law inherent in the order of things is that might makes right. In their relations with others they are competitive, ruthless, and cynical. They want to be hard and tough, and they regard all manifestation of feeling as a sign of weakness. Their bargain is essentially with themselves. They do not count on the world to give them anything but are convinced that they can reach their ambitious goals if they remain true to their vision of life as a battle and do not allow themselves to be influenced by traditional morality or their softer feelings. If their expansive solution collapses, self-effacing trends may emerge.

Others there are
Who, trimmed in forms and visages of duty,
Keep yet their hearts attending on themselves,
And throwing but shows of service on their lords,
Do well thrive by them, and when they have lined their coats,
Do themselves homage. These fellows have some soul;
And such a one do I profess myself. (Iago in Shakespeare, *Othello,* Act 1, scene 1)

Detachment Those in whom **detachment** is the predominant solution pursue neither love nor mastery but rather worship freedom, peace, and self-sufficiency. They disdain the pursuit of worldly success and have a profound aversion to effort. They have a strong need for superiority and usually look on their fellows with condescension, but they realize their ambition in imagination rather than through actual accomplishments. They handle a threatening world by removing themselves from its power and shutting others out of their inner lives. In order to avoid being dependent on the environment, they try to subdue their inner cravings and to be content with little. They do not usually rail against life but resign themselves to things as they are and accept their fate with ironic humor or stoical dignity. Their bargain is that if they ask nothing of others, others will not bother them; that if they try for nothing, they will not fail; and that if they expect little of life, they will not be disappointed.

[M]y lodging was my private solitude, my shell, my cave, in which I concealed myself from all mankind. . . . (Dostoevski, "Notes from the Underground," Part 2, section 8)

Intrapsychic Strategies of Defense While interpersonal difficulties are creating the moves toward, against, and away from people, and the conflicts between them, concomitant intrapsychic problems are producing their own defensive strategies. Self-idealization generates what Horney calls the pride system, which includes neurotic pride, neurotic claims, tyrannical shoulds, and increased self-hate.

The Idealized Image and the Search for Glory To compensate for feelings of weakness, worthlessness, and inadequacy, we create, with the aid of our imagination, an **idealized image** of ourselves that we endow with "unlimited powers and exalted faculties" (1950, p. 22). The process of self-idealization must be understood in relation to the interpersonal strategies, since the idealized image is based on our predominant defense and the attributes it exalts. The idealized image of self-effacing people "is a composite of 'lovable' qualities, such as unselfishness, goodness, generosity, humility, saintliness, nobility,

"You know, it was like this! This was it: I wanted to make myself a Napoleon, and that is why I killed her. . . . Now do you understand?" (Raskolnikov in Dostoevski, *Crime and Punishment,* Part 5, Chapter 4)

sympathy." It also glorifies "helplessness, suffering, and martyrdom" and deep feelings for art, nature, and other human beings (1950, p. 222). Arrogant-vindictive people see themselves as invincible masters of all situations. They are smarter, tougher, more realistic than other people and therefore can get the better of them. They take pride in their vigilance, foresight, and planning and feel that nothing can hurt them. The narcissistic person is "the anointed, the man of destiny, the prophet, the great giver, the benefactor of mankind" (1950, p. 194). Narcissists see themselves as having unlimited energies and as being capable of great achievements, effortlessly attained. Perfectionists see themselves as models of rectitude whose performance is invariably excellent. They have perfect judgment and are just and dutiful in their human relationships. The idealized image of detached or resigned people "is a composite of self-sufficiency, independence, self-contained serenity, freedom from desires and passions," and stoic indifference to the slings and arrows of outrageous fortune (1950, p. 277). They aspire to be free from restraint and impervious to pressure. In each solution, the idealized image may be modeled in whole or in part on a religious or cultural ideal or an example from history or personal experience.

One patient was, in his image, a benefactor of mankind, a wise man who had achieved a self-contained serenity, and a person who could without qualms kill his enemies. These aspects—all of them conscious—were to him not only uncontradictory but also even unconflicting. In literature this way of removing conflicts by isolating them has been presented by Stevenson in *Doctor Jekyll and Mr. Hyde.* (Horney, 1950, p. 22)

The idealized image does not ultimately make us feel better about ourselves but rather leads to increased self-hate and additional inner conflict. Although the qualities with which we endow ourselves are dictated by our predominant interpersonal strategy, the subordinate solutions are also represented; and since each solution glorifies a different set of traits, the idealized image has contradictory aspects, all of which we must try to actualize. Moreover, since we can feel worthwhile only if we *are* our idealized image, everything that falls short is deemed worthless, and there develops a *despised image* that becomes the focus of self-contempt. A great many people shuttle, said Horney, between "a feeling of arrogant omnipotence and of being the scum of the earth" (1950, p. 188).

We have reason to wonder whether more human lives—literally and figuratively—are not sacrificed on the altar of glory than for any other reason. (Horney, 1950, pp. 29–30)

With the formation of the idealized image, we embark on a **search for glory,** the object of which is to actualize our idealized self. What is considered to be glorious will vary with each solution. The search for glory constitutes a private religion the rules of which are determined by our particular neurosis, but we may also participate in the glory systems that are a prominent feature of every culture. These include organized religions, various forms of group identification, wars and military service, and competitions, honors, and hierarchical arrangements of all kinds.

The Pride System The creation of the idealized image produces not only the search for glory but also the **pride system:** neurotic pride, neurotic claims, tyrannical shoulds, and self-hate, all of which will vary with our predominant solution.

Neurotic pride substitutes a pride in the attributes of the idealized self for realistic self-confidence and self-esteem. Threats to pride produce anxiety and hostility; its collapse results in self-contempt and despair. On the basis of our pride, we make **neurotic claims** on the world, demanding to be treated in accordance with our grandiose conception of ourselves. The claims are "pervaded by expectations of magic" (1950, p. 62). They intensify our vulnerability, for their frustration deflates our pride and confronts us with the sense of powerlessness and inadequacy from which we are fleeing.

energies shift from developing
grandiose conception of ourselve
tem, which becomes a kind of F
destroy its creator. Neurosis is a
others but also in our relationshi

The disturbance in the relati
ble for us to form better relatio
such relationships, they would n
is the logical outgrowth of early
Once in existence, it has a dynam
dent of external events. Since the
ers, it poisons all our relationshi
be a source of healing or growth.
alysts must recognize its manifes
structure and function.

The Central Inner Con

In the course of successful thera
the pride system and the emergin
hate. Horney calls this the **centr**
volves accepting a world of uncer
up the search for glory and settli
therefore senses the real self as a
with scorn.

Although the central inner c
logical growth, it is extremely c
their lives on dreams of glory m
the habit of self-idealization. If t
seize on their improvement as "t
in the shining glory of perfect he
others for being neurotic, drive t
be healthy ways, and rage at the
have problems and imperfections
pathetic" toward themselves and
ticularly wonderful nor despicabl
man beings they are (1950, p. 35

The Process of Psyc

Horney said that her desire to ree
"a dissatisfaction with therapeuti
analysis she redefined *transferen*
apy, and in *Self-Analysis* she deve
cordance with her new paradigm
therapy in subsequent writings (
sent rather than on the past, on s
same.

Personal Reflection

■ Do I Make Neurotic Claims?

Horney suggested that studying your own reactions can lead you to observe your own neurotic patterns. She said, "It is in our real interest to examine our own reactions when we become preoccupied with a wrong done to us, or when we ponder the hateful qualities of somebody or when we feel the impulse to get back at others" (1950, p. 57).

The following questions may help you to explore your own patterns:

1. Can you recall a time when you asked for something that was unrealistic and you became upset because you did not get what you wanted?
2. Can you recall a time when you agreed to do something that you really did not want to do?
3. Can you recall a time when you were highly critical of someone else because that person did not meet your *own* standards of right and wrong?
4. Can you recall a time when your pride was hurt?

The idealized image generates not only pride and claims but also what Horney calls the **tyranny of the shoulds.** The function of the shoulds is to compel us to live up to our grandiose conception of ourselves. The shoulds are determined largely by the character traits and values associated with our predominant solution, but since our subordinate trends are also represented in the idealized image, we are often caught in a "crossfire of conflicting shoulds." For example, the self-effacing person wants to be good, noble, loving, forgiving, generous; but he has an aggressive side that tells him to "go all out for his advantage" and to "hit back at anybody who offends him. Accordingly he despises himself at bottom for any trace of 'cowardice,' or ineffectualness and compliance. He is thus under a constant crossfire. He is damned if he does do something, and he is damned if he does not" (1950, p. 221). This is a good description of Hamlet (see Paris, 1991a). "It is the threat of a punitive self-hate that lurks behind [the shoulds]," observed Horney, that "truly makes them a regime of terror" (1950, p. 85).

The shoulds are in fact self-destructive in their very nature. . . . They put a person into a strait jacket and deprive him of inner freedom. Even if he manages to mold himself into a behavioristic perfection, he can do so only at the expense of his spontaneity and the authenticity of his feelings and beliefs. The shoulds aim in fact, like any political tyranny, at the extinction of individuality. (Horney, 1950, p. 118)

The shoulds are the basis of our **bargain with fate.** No matter what the solution, our bargain is that our claims will be honored if we live up to our shoulds. We seek magically to control external reality by obeying our inner dictates. We do not see our claims as unreasonable, of course, but only as what we have a right to expect, given our grandiose conception of ourselves, and we will feel that life is unfair if our expectations are frustrated. Our **sense of justice** is determined by our predominant solution and the bargain associated with it.

I love little pussy, her coat is so warm
And if I don't hurt her, she'll do me no harm.
I'll sit by the fire and give her some food,
And pussy will love me because I am good. (Mother Goose)

Self-hate is the end product of the intrapsychic strategies of defense, each of which tends to magnify our feelings of inadequacy and failure. Self-hate is essentially the rage the idealized self feels toward the self we actually are for not being what it "should" be. Horney sees self-hate as "perhaps the greatest tragedy of the human mind. Man in reaching out for the Infinite and Absolute also starts destroying himself. When he makes a pact with the devil, who

[T]he easy way to infinite glory is inevitably also the way to an inner hell of self-contempt and self-torment. By taking this road, the individual is in fact losing his soul—his real self. (Horney, 1950, p. 39)

Literary Study

> While arguing that [*Vanity Fair*] is full of contradictions and is thematically unintelligible, I suddenly remembered Karen Horney's statement that "inconsistencies are as definite an indication of the presence of conflicts as a rise in body temperature is of physical disturbance," and in the next instant I realized that the novel's contradictions become intelligible if we see them as part of a system of inner conflicts. . . . I have been unfolding the implications of that "aha" experience ever since. (Paris, 1991a, p. 6)

Bernard Paris has argued that Horney's theories are especially appropriate for the analysis of literary characters. One of the chief objections to the psychoanalytic study of character has been its reliance on infantile experience to account for the behavior of the adult, since such experience is rarely, if ever, presented in literature. But Horney's theories focus on the kinds of adult defenses and inner conflicts about which literature often provides a great deal of information. In addition to being used in character study, Horney's theories have been employed in the analysis of thematic inconsistencies, tensions between theme and characterization, the relation between authors and their works, and the psychology of reader response (see Paris, 1974, 1978, 1986, 1989, 1991a, 1991b, 1991c). They have helped to illuminate works and authors not only from most periods of British and American literature but also from ancient Greece and Rome, and from France, Russia, Germany, Spain, Norway, and Sweden, in a variety of centuries. They have been employed in the study of Chinese, Japanese, and Indian literature as well.

Psychobiography

> Suddenly the thought occurred to me: What if the idealized image of Stalin appearing day by day in the party-controlled, party-supervised Soviet press was *an idealized self in Horney's sense?* If so, [Stalin] must be the most self-revealed disturbed person of all time. To find out what was most important about him there would be no need to get him onto a couch; one could do it by reading *Pravda* while rereading Horney! (Tucker, 1985, p. 251)

Horney's emphasis on the present structure of the psyche has also proved to be valuable in psychobiography. Like the literary critic approaching a character or an author, the biographer usually has much information about youth and adulthood but little or none about very early experience. Biographical studies of Robert Frost (Thompson, 1966, 1970; Thompson & Winnick, 1976), Charles Evans Hughes (Glad, 1966), the Kennedys (Clinch, 1973), Stalin (Tucker, 1973, 1985, 1990), Woodrow Wilson (Tucker, 1977), Jimmy Carter (Glad, 1980; see also 1973), Felix Frankfurter (Hirsch, 1981), and Lyndon Johnson (Huffman, 1989) have fruitfully employed Horneyan analysis.

The biography of Frost exemplifies how Horney can be used. Named official biographer 24 years before Frost died, Lawrence Thompson became aware of the poet's many cruelties, self-contradictions, and inner conflicts. After completing a draft of his first volume, he read *Neurosis and Human Growth* and found in it the analytic concepts he needed to make sense of his bewildering subject. Had Horney's book mentioned Frost on every page, Thompson wrote in his notebook, "it couldn't have come closer to giving a psychological framework to what I've been trying to say" (Sheehy, 1986, p. 398). Thompson revised what he had written to reflect his new understanding of Frost as a man who developed a search for glory in response to early humiliations and who longed to triumph over and retaliate against those who had hurt him. Frost's contradictory accounts of his life were a product of both his inner conflicts and his need to confirm his idealized image by mythologizing himself. Frost sometimes used his poetry to "escape from his confusions into idealized postures," while at other times it served "as a means of striking back at, or of punishing" those he considered his enemies (Thompson, 1966, p. xix).

Cultural Study

Several writers have used Horney in the analysis of culture. David M. Potter (1954) was particularly struck by Horney's analysis of the character traits, inner conflicts, and vicious circles created by the competitiveness of American culture. We trade security for opportunity and then feel anxious and insecure. Paul Wachtel (1989, 1991) also argues that there is something compulsive, irrational, and self-defeating in the way Americans pursue an ever-increasing wealth. We promote competition rather than mutual support, and we behave aggressively in order to avoid being perceived as weak. James Huffman (1982) emphasizes the sense of threat and feelings of inferiority that have influenced the American character from the beginning of our history, resulting in a compensatory self-idealization and a search for national glory. We make exaggerated claims for ourselves and are outraged when they are not honored by other nations. Like Potter and Wachtel, Huffman sees the American character as predominantly aggressive. We like our leaders to be belligerent, and we glorify people who fight their way to the top. Bernard Paris (1986) has discussed Victorian culture from a Horneyan perspective and has correlated conflicting cultural codes found in Elizabethan culture (as reflected in Shakespeare's plays) with Horney's strategies of defense (Paris, 1991a).

Gender Study

Horney has been rediscovered in recent years by feminists, many of whose positions she anticipated. Although most attention has been given to her early essays, her mature theory also has important implications for understanding gender identity and masculine and feminine psychology. Impressive work has been done along these lines by Alexandra Symonds, a Horneyan analyst, and Marcia Westkott, a social psychologist. Horney's mature theory has also been used to address gender issues in popular books by Helen De Rosis and Victoria Pelligrino (1976) and Claudette Dowling (1981).

Symond's essays (1974, 1976, 1978, 1991) are based largely on her clinical experience with women who were suffering from their feminine role, or who were trying to escape that role but finding it difficult, or who seemed to have escaped but were having trouble dealing with the consequences. In every case, the starting point was a culture that conditioned girls to be self-effacing and dependent, while boys were encouraged to be autonomous and aggressive. While focusing on the plight of girls, Symonds recognized that boys develop difficulties of their own as a result of cultural stereotyping.

In *The Feminist Legacy of Karen Horney* (1986), Marcia Westkott explored the implications of Horney's mature theory for feminine psychology, with chapters on the sexualization and devaluation of women and the dependency, anger, and detachment they feel as a consequence. In addition, she developed a Horneyan critique of a major strand of feminist theory. Jean Baker Miller, Nancy Chodorow, Carol Gilligan, and the Stone Center group have associated an array of personality traits specifically with women. These include a need for affiliation, a nurturing disposition, a sense of responsibility for other people, and a relational sense of identity. Westkott observed that although these traits

[Female altruism emerges] not out of an extended attachment between mother and daughter but out of the . . . mother's devaluation of the daughter's needs, expressed in imposing her own needs to be nurtured. . . . Female altruism, from this perspective, is a contradiction in which the undernurtured nurturer gives what she does not have in order to be "loved" by those who have disregard or even contempt for her true self and needs. (Westkott, 1986, pp. 134–135, 139–140) are regarded in a positive way, they emerged from "a historical setting in which women are less highly valued than men" (Westkott, 1986, p. 2). She proposed that these traits are defensive reactions to subordination, devaluation, and powerlessness and that, however desirable they may seem from a social point of view, they are inimical to women's self-actualization. Westkott thus demythified the celebration of female relationality, arguing that it has provided "a contemporary theoretical justification for traditionally idealized femininity" (1989, p. 245). She contended, with Horney, that being deprived is not ennobling but damaging and that the self-effacing qualities many women develop in order to cope with devaluation are destructive.

Evaluation

Horney was the first, and perhaps the best, critic of Freud's ideas about women. Her early essays on female psychology have an astonishing immediacy. . . . Many of Horney's other ideas, which so enraged the New York Society in 1941, have since been incorporated into psychoanalytic thinking. . . . (Quinn, 1987, p. 14)

Karen Horney is important for her contributions to feminine psychology, which were forgotten for many years but have been highly influential since their republication in *Feminine Psychology* in 1967. They are especially notable for their exploration of female development from a woman's point of view and for their emphasis on the cultural construction of gender. Unlike her essays on feminine psychology, Horney's first two books had a great impact in their day, and their case for the importance of culture and for a structural model of neurosis continues to have an influence. The growing emphasis on present-oriented therapies owes something to Horney's teachings. Her third book, *Self-Analysis* (1942), inspired the Institute for Self-Analysis in London and is still the most thorough discussion of the possibilities and techniques of successful self-exploration. It should be noted that Horney felt that Self-Analysis has the best chance of success when it is employed in conjunction with therapy or as a way of continuing to work on oneself after termination.

While each stage of Horney's thought is important, her mature theory represents her most significant contribution. Most of Horney's early ideas have been revised or enriched—by Horney herself or by others—or have been absorbed or discovered anew by later writers. This is not the case with her mature theory. *Our Inner Conflicts* (1945) and *Neurosis and Human Growth* (1950) provide explanations of human behavior in terms of currently existing constellations of defenses and inner conflicts that can be found nowhere else. Horney does not account for the whole of human psychology, since, like every theorist, she describes only part of the picture, but her mature theory is highly congruent with frequently occurring patterns of behavior. Although Horney objected to the instinctivistic nature of Freudian theory, her own theory has a biological basis, since the movements against, away from, and toward other people are human elaborations of the basic defenses of the animal kingdom—fight, flight, and submission. All the strategies are encoded in almost every culture; but each culture has its characteristic attitudes toward the different strategies, its own formulations of and variations upon them, and its own structure of inner conflicts. Horney is often thought of as having described the neurotic personality of her time, but, as its interdisciplinary uses show, her mature theory has wide applicability.

Conclusion

Most psychoanalytic theory has followed Freud in focusing on early origins as a means of explanation and therapy. Well in advance of many recent critics of psychoanalysis, Karen Horney felt that this practice results in circular reasoning, in the conversion of analogies into causes, and in a variety of other epistemological problems. She also felt it to be therapeutically ineffective. Horney doubted that early childhood could ever be accurately recovered, since we are bound to reconstruct it from the perspective of our present needs, beliefs, and defenses. We have a natural desire to explain things in terms of their origins, but Horney felt that there are as many myths of origin as there are psychoanalytic theories. It is more profitable, she argued, "to focus on the forces which actually drive and inhibit a person; there is a reasonable chance of understanding these, even without much knowledge of childhood" (1939, p. 146). Horney tried to explain behavior in terms of its function within the current constellation of defenses and to account for contradictory attitudes, actions, and beliefs by seeing them as part of a structure of inner conflicts.

Karen Horney is perhaps the first humanistic psychoanalyst. Her theories are entirely compatible with those of Abraham Maslow, who was influenced by her. Both theories are based on the idea of a *real self* that it is the object of life to actualize. Horney focused on what happens when we become alienated from our real selves as a result of a pathogenic environment, while Maslow focused on what we require for healthy growth and the characteristics of self-actualizing people. Horney described the defensive strategies we employ when our healthy basic needs for safety, love and belonging, and esteem have been turned into insatiable neurotic needs as a result of having been thwarted. The theories of Horney and Maslow are complementary and, taken together, provide a more comprehensive picture of human behavior than either provides by itself.

Albert Schweitzer uses the terms "optimistic" and "pessimistic" in the sense of "world and life affirmation" and "world and life negation." Freud's philosophy, in this deep sense, is a pessimistic one. Ours, with all its cognizance of the tragic element in neurosis, is an optimistic one. (Horney, 1950, p. 378)

The Theory Firsthand

Excerpt from *Self-Analysis*

The following excerpt is from Horney's account of the Self-Analysis of her "patient" Clare, who is a fictionalized version of herself. It deals with Clare's efforts to free herself from her "morbid dependency" on her lover, Peter, a fictionalized version of Erich Fromm, who has left her.

She wavered between times in which the experience with Peter and all that it entailed appeared as part of a far-distant past, and others in which she desperately longed to win him back. Solitude, then, was felt as an unfathomable cruelty perpetrated on her.

In one of these latter days, going home alone from a concert, she found herself thinking that everyone was better off than she. . . . She recognized that a tendency must be at work which made her talk herself into an exaggerated misery. . . . She had an expectation that great distress would bring about help. And for the sake of this unconscious belief she made herself more miserable than she was. It was shockingly silly, yet she had done it, and had done it frequently. . . . She remembered any number of occasions when she had felt herself the most abused of mortals, only to realize some time later that she had made matters much worse than they actually were. When she had been in the spell of such unhappiness, however, the reasons for it looked, and even felt, real. . . .

Yes, there was a clear pattern that repeated itself—exaggerated misery and at the same time an expectation of help, consolation, encouragement, from her mother, from God, from Bruce [her first love], from her husband, from Peter. Her playing the martyr role, apart from everything else, must have also been an unconscious plea for help.

Clare was thus on the verge of recognizing another important clue to her dependency. . . . She recognized that a belief that she could command help through misery actually had a strong hold upon her.

Within the next months she saw with a gradually increasing measure of lucidity and in great detail what this belief did to her. She saw that she unconsciously tended to make a major catastrophe out of every difficulty that arose in her life, collapsing into a state of complete helplessness, with the result that despite a certain front of bravery and independence her prevailing feeling toward life was one of helplessness in the face of overwhelming odds. She recognized that this firm belief in forthcoming help had amounted to a kind of private religion, and that not unlike a true religion it had been a powerful source of reassurance.

Clare also acquired a deepened insight as to the extent to which her reliance on someone else had taken the place of reliance on herself. If she always had someone who taught her, stimulated her, advised her, helped her, defended her, gave her affirmation of her value, there was no reason why she should make any effort to overcome the anxiety involved in taking her life into her own hands. . . . The dependency had not only perpetuated her weakness by stifling her incentive to become more self-reliant but it had actually created an interest in remaining helpless. If she remained humble and self-effacing all happiness, all triumph would be hers. Any attempt at greater self-reliance and greater self-assertion was bound to jeopardize these expectations of a heaven on earth. . . . The compulsive modesty had not only given her the sheltering cloak of inconspicuousness, but it had also been the indispensable basis for her expectations of "love."

She realized it was merely a logical consequence, then, that the partner to whom she ascribed the godlike role of magic helper—to use a pertinent term of Erich Fromm's—became all important, and that to be wanted and loved by him became the only thing that mattered. . . . [Peter's] importance lay in the fact that he was an instrument whose services she could demand by making her need for them sufficiently great.

As a result of these insights she felt much more free than ever before. The longing for Peter, which at times had been excruciatingly strong, started to recede. More important, the insight brought about a real change in her objectives in life. She had always consciously wanted to be independent, but in her actual life had given this wish mere lip service and had reached out for help in any difficulty that arose. Now to become able to cope with her own life became an active, alive goal. (pp. 233–238)

Chapter Highlights

- There were three distinct phases in the development of Karen Horney's thought: (1) Her early essays on feminine psychology. (2) Her recognition that culture and disturbed human relationships are more important than biology as causes of neurotic development. (3) Her study of the interpersonal defenses and the intrapsychic defenses developed to cope with anxiety.
- Horney was one of the founders of humanistic psychology, which is based on her emphasis that healthy values and the goals of life grow from self-realization. Drawing on her own experience, she believed in the human potential for growth and recognized the difficulty of achieving it.
- Horney acknowledged that she was deeply indebted to the foundation Freud provided. However, she came to see the male bias in psychoanalysis as reinforcing and reproducing the devaluation of the feminine.
- She proposed a women's view of the disturbances in the relations between the sexes and the differences between women and men, and suggested that girls and women have patterns of development that are to be understood in their own terms, not simply in relation to those of men.
- Horney saw that it was male privilege more than the penis that women envied, and that greater opportunity to develop their human capacities is needed for both men and women.
- Horney's version of psychoanalysis looks at neurosis as a set of defenses against basic anxiety. It places a greater emphasis on the role of culture, and shifts the focus from the infantile origins of character structure, as described by Freud.
- Her emphasis on a structural approach, in both theory and practice, looks to the individual's current constellation of inner conflicts and defenses to explain the present, rather than trying to recover the past in order to explain the present.
- In contrast to Freud's view that nothing much new happens after the age of 5, Horney suggested that development does not stop at that point and that the individual's later reactions or experiences evolve from the preceding ones.
- It is through a developmental process rather than through repetition that past events are contained in the present. Early experiences affect us profoundly by determining the direction of development and by conditioning the ways in which we respond to the world, rather than by producing fixations that cause us to repeat earlier patterns.
- Horney suggests that there are three basic strategies people use to cope with basic anxiety: by moving toward people and adopting a self-effacing or compliant solution; moving against people and adopting an aggressive or expansive solution; and moving away from people and becoming detached and resigned. Within the expansive solution

there are three divisions, narcissistic, perfectionistic, and arrogant-vindictive.

- What Horney terms the pride system, which includes neurotic pride, neurotic claims, tyrannical shoulds, and increased self-hate, is generated by self-idealization.
- There is a dynamic quality to Horney's theory, as conflicts follow their own cycle, causing oscillations, inconsistencies, and self-hate. Within the pride system, there is a crossfire of conflicting shoulds and a seesawing between the despised and idealized selves.
- As our energies shift from developing our real potentialities to actualizing our grandiose conception of ourselves, our behavior is marked by the formation of the idealized image. This, in turn, generates the pride system.
- Horney's theories have been applied nonclinically as well, providing a useful explanatory system in the fields of literature, culture, biography, and gender studies, as well as religion and philosophy.
- Horney tried to account for contradictory actions, attitudes, and beliefs by seeing them as part of a structure of inner conflict, and to explain behavior in terms of its function within the individual's current defenses.

Key Concepts

Arrogant-vindictive solution One of the expansive interpersonal solutions to basic anxiety. People using this strategy are motivated by a need for vindictive triumphs. Their bargain is essentially with themselves. These individuals regard life as a tough battle, with goals to be won, if they do not allow themselves to be distracted by their softer feelings or traditional morality.

Bargain with fate The belief, formed from the shoulds, that our claims will be honored, regardless of our type of solution, if we live up to our shoulds. By obeying our inner dictates, we seek magically to control external reality.

Basic anxiety Response that develops in a child when the environment is felt to be a threat to physical survival, as well as to the survival of wishes and strivings. Feeling helpless in a potentially hostile world, the child pursues power, love, or detachment as an interpersonal strategy of defense.

Basic conflict The choice of which of the three defensive moves an individual emphasizes—to become self-effacing, expansive, or detached. The selection depends on the specific combination of environmental and temperamental factors in the situation. All three will occur, though one will become predominant. The others will go underground to operate unconsciously, manifesting themselves in devious and disguised ways.

Central inner conflict The intrapsychic conflict that develops between the emerging real self and the pride system. The real self is sensed as a threat to the proud self, which turns on it with a vengeance. This conflict occurs at a relatively late stage of psychological growth.

Compliant solution Interpersonal strategy of coping with basic anxiety by controlling others through their dependency, and by gaining affection and approval. The bargain made by users of this solution is that they will be well treated by fate and other people, if they do not seek their own gain or glory and are good, humble, and loving.

Countertransference In Horney's usage, a manifestation of character structure rather than infantile reactions. In therapy it is the analyst's character structure that is engaged.

Detachment Interpersonal strategy of coping with basic anxiety by moving away from people. The bargain made by individuals who employ this solution is threefold: others will not bother them if they ask for nothing; they will not fail if they try for nothing; and they will not be disappointed if they expect little of life.

Expansive solutions Interpersonal strategies of coping with basic anxiety by moving against people and adopting an aggressive stance. Not love, but mastery, appeals to the individuals who use this solution. Because they are ashamed of suffering, helplessness is anathema to them. There are three distinct divisions within this solution: narcissistic, perfectionistic, and arrogant-vindictive.

Idealized image A self-conception based on our predominant interpersonal defense and the attributes it exalts. Imaginatively created to compensate for feelings of inadequacy, worthlessness, and weakness, it is endowed with expansive powers and exaggerated faculties. Its creation produces the search for glory, neurotic claims, neurotic pride, tyrannical shoulds, and self-hate.

Masculinity complex The constellation of feelings and fantasies built around the woman's feeling of being discriminated against, envy of the male, and the wish to discard the female role. Horney believed that the conflict is the product of particular kinds of family dynamics in a male-dominated culture.

Narcissistic solution One of the expansive interpersonal solutions to basic anxiety. Narcissists seek to master life by the exercise of charm and self-admiration. Their bargain is that life is bound to give them what they want if they hold to their dreams and their exaggerated claims for themselves.

Neurotic claims Our demands, based on our pride, to be treated in accordance with our grandiose conception of ourselves. Permeated with an air of magic, these claims intensify our vulnerability.

Neurotic pride Pride in the attributes of the idealized self, which replaces realistic self-confidence and self-esteem.

Penis envy Feelings of inferiority, competitiveness toward men, and vindictiveness, said to arise in women when their lack of a penis is realized, in classical psychoanalytic theory.

Perfectionistic solution One of the expansive interpersonal solutions to basic anxiety. The very high intellectual and moral standards of perfectionists provide the vantage point from which they look down on others. Being just, fair, and dutiful, according to their bargain, entitles them to fair treatment by life in general and specifically by other people.

Pride system A product—consisting of neurotic pride, tyranny of the shoulds, and self-hate—of our idealized image. It affects how we work with others, poisons all one's relationships, and makes it highly unlikely for them to be a source of growth or healing. It is generated by the idealized self-image, is a logical outgrowth of early development, and has its own dynamic largely independent of external events.

Real self The possible self, in contrast to the idealized self. It is a set of intrinsic potentialities—which include temperament, capacities, talents, and predispositions—that are part of our genetic makeup and need a favorable environment in which to develop. Actualized through interactions with the external world, it is not impervious to external influence. It is not a product of learning, however, as one cannot be taught to be oneself.

Search for glory A pursuit whose object is the actualization of our idealized self. It follows the formation of the idealized image. Our particular neurosis will determine the rules of this private religion. Every culture has its own featured glory systems.

Self-hate The rage that the idealized self feels toward the self we actually are for not being what it "should" be. As a despised image develops and becomes the focus for self-contempt when we inevitably fall short of being our idealized image, additional inner conflict arises and self-hate increases.

Sense of justice Our expectation determined by the bargain associated with our predominant solution.

Transference In Horney's conception, the idea that patients behave toward analysts as their character structure directs, rather than transferring onto the analyst feelings from childhood.

Tyranny of the shoulds Our compulsions to live up to our grandiose conception of ourselves. Self-destructive by their very nature, they aim at the complete eradication of individuality. They are determined largely by the values and character traits associated with our predominant solution.

Vicious circles A situation in which the defensive strategies employed to alleviate anxiety instead tend to increase it.

Womb envy The male envy of pregnancy, childbirth, and motherhood, which results in the unconscious depreciation of women. Men's impulse toward creative work may be an overcompensation for their small role in procreation.

Annotated Bibliography

(Note: Most of Horney's books, unlike her articles, were written for the layperson. All of Horney's books are in print and available in paperbound editions.)

Horney, K. (1937). *The neurotic personality of our time.* New York: Norton.

Argues for the influence of culture on personality and sets up a new paradigm for the structure of neurosis.

———. (1939). *New ways in psychoanalysis.* New York: Norton.

Systematic critique of Freud's theory, especially its emphasis on biological factors and infantile origins. Stresses environmental factors, current character structure, and self-realization as the object of therapy.

———. (1942). *Self-Analysis.* New York: Norton.

Describes the possibilities, techniques, and difficulties of both dyadic analysis and self-analysis. Contains Horney's most fully developed case history, that of Clare, which is highly autobiographical.

———. (1945). *Our inner conflicts.* New York: Norton.

Focuses on the interpersonal strategies of compliance (moving toward), aggression (moving against), and detachment (moving away from) and the conflicts between these strategies (the basic conflict). A good place to start reading Horney.

———. (1950). *Neurosis and human growth.* New York: Norton.

Focuses on the intrapsychic strategies of self-idealization, the search for glory, neurotic pride, neurotic claims, and tyrannical shoulds, all of which simultaneously defend against and increase self-hate. Integrates the interpersonal strategies into a complete system, but in an occasionally confusing manner. Horney's most complex and important book. Written for fellow analysts but lucid and accessible to laypersons.

———. (1967). *Feminine psychology.* (H. Kelman, Ed.). New York: Norton.

Essays on women's problems and the relations between the sexes. In their emphasis on the cultural construction of gender, these essays were decades ahead of their time.

Paris, B. (1994). *Karen Horney: A psychoanalyst's search for self-understanding.* New Haven, CT: Yale University Press.

Combines biography with a full account of Horney's theories. Argues that the evolution of her ideas is a product of her lifelong effort to solve her problems by understanding herself. More a character portrait of Horney than a conventional biography.

Quinn, S. (1987). *A mind of her own: The life of Karen Horney.* New York: Summit Books.

The best account of Horney's social and cultural context and the events of her life. Less good on her inner life and her ideas, especially her mature theory.

Weiss, F. (1991). Karen Horney: A bibliography. *The American Journal of Psychoanalysis, 51,* 343–347.

Quinn and Paris also contain much bibliographic information.

Westkott, M. (1986). *The feminist legacy of Karen Horney.* New Haven, CT: Yale University Press.

The most sustained effort to show how Horney's mature theory illuminates feminist issues.

References

Breuer, J., & Freud, S. (1936). *Studies in hysteria.* New York: Nervous and Mental Disease Monograph No. 61. (Originally published, 1895.)

Brown, J. F. (1939, September 23). Review of *New ways in psychoanalysis. The Nation,* pp. 328–329.

Chodorow, N. (1989). *Feminism and psychoanalytic thought.* New Haven, CT: Yale University Press.

Clinch, N. (1973). *The Kennedy neurosis.* New York: Grosset & Dunlap.

De Rosis, H., & Pelligrino, V. (1976). *The book of hope: How women can overcome depression.* New York: Macmillan.

Dowling, C. (1981). *The Cinderella complex: Woman's hidden fear of independence.* New York: Summit Books.

Glad, B. (1966). *Charles Evans Hughes and the illusions of innocence.* Urbana: University of Illinois Press.

———. (1973). Contributions of psychobiography. In J. N. Knutson (Ed.), *Handbook of political psychology* (pp. 296–321). San Francisco: Jossey-Bass.

———. (1980). *Jimmy Carter.* New York: Norton.

Hirsch, H. N. (1981). *The enigma of Felix Frankfurter.* New York: Basic Books.

Horney, K. (1935). Conceptions and misconceptions of the analytical method. *Journal of Nervous and Mental Disease, 81,* 399–410.

———. (1937). *The neurotic personality of our time.* New York: Norton.

———. (1939). *New ways in psychoanalysis.* New York: Norton.

———. (1942). *Self-analysis.* New York: Norton.

———. (1945). *Our inner conflicts.* New York: Norton.

———. (1950). *Neurosis and human growth.* New York: Norton.

———. (1967). *Feminine psychology.* (H. Kelman, Ed.). New York: Norton.

———. (1980). *The adolescent diaries of Karen Horney.* New York: Basic Books.

———. (1987). *Final lectures.* (D. Ingram, Ed.). New York: Norton.

———. (1991). The goals of analytic therapy. *The American Journal of Psychoanalysis, 51,* 219–226. (Originally published, 1951.)

Huffman, J. (1982). A psychological critique of American culture. *The American Journal of Psychoanalysis, 42,* 27–38.

———. (1989). Young man Johnson. *The American Journal of Psychoanalysis, 49,* 251–265.

Mullin, H. (1988). Horney's contribution to a rational approach to morals. *The American Journal of Psychoanalysis, 48,* 127–137.

Paris, B. (1974). *A psychological approach to fiction: Studies in Thackeray, Stendhal, George Eliot, Dostoevski, and Conrad.* Bloomington: Indiana University Press.

———. (1978). *Character and conflict in Jane Austen's novels: A psychological approach.* Detroit: Wayne State University Press.

———. (Ed.). (1986). *Third force psychology and the study of literature.* Rutherford, NJ: Fairleigh Dickinson University Press.

———. (Ed.). (1989). Special issue of *The American Journal of Psychoanalysis, 49* (3), on interdisciplinary applications of Horney.

———. (1991a). *Bargains with fate: Psychological crises and conflicts in Shakespeare and his plays.* New York: Insight Books.

———. (1991b). *Character as a subversive force in Shakespeare: The History and Roman Plays.* Rutherford, NJ: Fairleigh Dickinson University Press.

———. (1991c). A Horneyan approach to literature. *The American Journal of Psychoanalysis, 51,* 319–337.

———. (1994). *Karen Horney: A psychoanalyst's search for self-understanding.* New Haven, CT: Yale University Press.

Potter, D. (1954). *People of plenty: Economic abundance and the American character.* Chicago: University of Chicago Press.

Quinn, S. (1987). *A mind of her own: The life of Karen Horney.* New York: Summit Books.

Rubins, J. (1978). *Karen Horney: Gentle rebel of psychoanalysis.* New York: Dial Press.

———. (1980). Discussion of Barry G. Wood: The religion of psychoanalysis. *The American Journal of Psychoanalysis, 40,* 23–26.

Sheehy, D. (1986). The poet as neurotic: The official biography of Robert Frost. *American Literature, 58,* 393–410.

Symonds, A. (1974). The liberated woman: Healthy and neurotic. *The American Journal of Psychoanalysis, 34,* 177–183.

———. (1976). Neurotic dependency in successful women. *Journal of the American Academy of Psychoanalysis, 4,* 95–103.

———. (1978). The psychodynamics of expansiveness in the success-oriented woman. *The American Journal of Psychoanalysis, 38,* 195–205.

———. (1991). Gender-issues and Horney's theory. *The American Journal of Psychoanalysis, 51,* 301–312.

Thompson, L. (1966). Robert Frost: *The early years 1974–1915.* New York: Holt, Rinehart and Winston.

———. (1970). *Robert Frost: The years of triumph 1915–1938.* New York: Holt, Rinehart and Winston.

Thompson, L., & Winnick, R. H. (1976). *Robert Frost: The later years 1938–1963.* New York: Holt, Rinehart and Winston.

Tigner, J. (1985). An analysis of Spinoza's pride and self-abasement. *The American Journal of Psychoanalysis, 45,* 208–220.

Trotter W. (1916). *Instincts of the herd in peace and war.* London: T. Fischer Unwin.

Tucker, R. (1973). *Stalin as revolutionary, 1897–1929: A study in history and personality.* New York: Norton.

———. (1977). The Georges' Wilson reexamined: An essay on psychobiography. *American Political Science Review, 71,* 606–618.

———. (1985). A Stalin biographer's memoir. In S. H. Baron & C. Pletsch (Eds.), *Introspection in biography: The biographer's quest for self-awareness* (pp. 249–271). Hillsdale, NJ: Analytic Press.

———. (1990). *Stalin in power: The revolution from above, 1928–1941.* New York: Norton.

Wachtel, P. (1977). *Psychoanalysis and behavior therapy: Toward an integration.* New York: Basic Books.

——— (1989). *The poverty of affluence: A psychological portrait of the American way of life.* Philadelphia: New Society Publishers.

———. (1991). The preoccupation with economic growth: An analysis informed by Horneyan theory. *The American Journal of Psychoanalysis, 51,* 89–103.

Weiss, F. (1991). Karen Horney: A bibliography. *The American Journal of Psychoanalysis, 51,* 343–347.

Westkott, M. (1986). *The feminist legacy of Karen Horney.* New Haven, CT: Yale University Press.

———. (1989). Female relationality and the idealized self. *The American Journal of Psychoanalysis, 49,* 239–250.

Wittels, F. (1939). The neo-Adlerians. *American Journal of Sociology, 45,* 433–445.

Wolcott, J. (1996, June 3). Letterman Unbound: Dave's No. 2 and Trying Harder, *The New Yorker,* pp. 80–92.

Wood, B. (1980). The religion of psychoanalysis. *The American Journal of Psychoanalysis, 40,* 13–22.

Zabriskie, C. (1976). A psychological analysis of biblical interpretation pertaining to women. *Journal of Psychology and Theology, 4,* 304–312.

CHAPTER 7

Erik Erikson and the Life Cycle

Erik Erikson is the most widely read and influential post-Freudian theorist, both in psychology and in the popular press. His books have sold hundreds of thousands of copies, and, in 1970, Erikson was featured on the covers of both *Newsweek* and *The New York Times Magazine*. His book on Mohandas Gandhi (1969) was awarded the Pulitzer Prize and the National Book Award.

Erik Erikson has extended the insights of psychoanalysis through cross-cultural studies of child rearing, psychological biographies of great men and women, and analyzing the interaction of psychological and social dynamics. Erikson's life-span theory of ego development has had enormous influence within psychology and related fields. He is also the founder of modern psychohistory.

Erikson's work is solidly based on psychoanalytic theory; no one else since Freud has done as much to elaborate on and apply the principles of psychoanalysis to new fields and to the problems of today's world. In the process, Erikson developed an original theory rooted in psychoanalytic understanding, yet significantly different in scope, concept, and emphasis. He has been called a "nondogmatic, emancipated Freudian." Erikson's concepts of identity and identity crisis have had major professional influence throughout the social sciences. They have also become household words.

Erikson is a brilliant, insightful theorist and an elegant writer. At the core of his work is his theory of the human life cycle, a model that integrates human growth and development from birth to old age. He made three major contributions to the study of personality: (1) that along with Freud's psychosexual developmental stages, the individual simultaneously goes through psychosocial and ego-development stages, (2) that personality development continues throughout life, and (3) that each stage of development can have both positive and negative outcomes.

Personal History

Erikson has unusual, even obscure, roots. He was born on June 15, 1902. His Danish Jewish mother left Denmark for Germany while pregnant, and married a German Jewish physician, Dr. Homburger. Erikson considered himself German in spite of his Danish parentage, yet his German classmates rejected him because he was Jewish. At the same time, his Jewish friends called him the *goy* (the non-Jew) because of his blonde, Aryan appearance.

Erikson grew up as Erik Homburger and first published under that name. Later he wrote under the name Erik Homburger Erikson, and eventually settled on Erik Erikson (literally, Erik, son of Erik—although Erikson was not the name of his biological father). A Dane by parentage and a German by upbringing, he later became an American by choice. Raised as a Jew, he married a Christian and converted to Christianity.

Erikson's formal academic education lasted until he was 18, when he graduated from a classical *gymnasium*. There he had studied Latin, Greek, German literature, and ancient history. He was not a particularly devoted student. After graduation, Erikson began traveling through Europe. Along with many of his generation, Erikson was trying to "find himself." After a year of travel, he returned home and enrolled in art school. He studied art in Munich, then went to live in Florence. The artist's life was good for a young man as yet unwilling to settle down; it gave him great latitude and time for self-exploration.

Erikson returned home at the age of 25, intending to settle down and teach art. He was invited to Vienna to teach at a new school for the children of families that had come to Vienna for psychoanalysis. He taught art, history, and various other subjects. Erikson was given a free hand to create an ideal educational program.

The psychoanalytic community was much less formal in the 1920s. Analysts, patients, and their families and friends attended picnics and other social events together. At these affairs, Erikson became acquainted with Anna Freud and other prominent psychoanalysts. Erikson was screened informally and judged to be a suitable candidate for analytic training. In 1927, Erikson began daily analysis with Anna Freud in the house she shared with her father.

When he expressed doubts about the possibility of an artist becoming a psychoanalyst, Anna Freud replied that psychoanalysis would need people who help others *see*. Much of Erikson's long and rich career can be viewed as an attempt to do just that: drawing exquisite word pictures of new concepts and perspectives.

To be surprised belongs to the discipline of a clinician. (Erikson, 1963, p. 100)

Erikson also studied the Montessori system and was one of only two men who graduated from the Montessori Teachers' Association at that time. His interest in play therapy and child analysis came from his ongoing teaching, influenced by his Montessori education.

In 1929, at a Mardi Gras masked ball in a Viennese castle, Erikson met a young woman, Joan Serson, and fell in love almost immediately. They were married several months later. Serson's interests were similar to Erikson's. A teacher of modern dance, she had received a bachelor's degree in education and a master's degree in sociology, and had been in psychoanalysis with one of Freud's early followers.

Erikson finished his analytic training in 1933 and was accepted as a full member of the Vienna Psychoanalytic Society. Because of the growth of fascism in Europe, Erikson, as well as many other psychoanalysts, decided to leave for the United States. The move was made easier by his wife's Canadian-American ancestry. The Eriksons settled in Boston, where he became the city's first child psychoanalyst. He was offered positions at Harvard Medical School and at the prestigious Massachusetts General Hospital. In addition, he began private practice and became associated with Harvard's Psychological Clinic, run by Henry Murray. During these years, he had contact with a variety of brilliant and influential thinkers, including Murray, the anthropologists Ruth Benedict and Margaret Mead, and the social psychologist Kurt Lewin.

In 1936, Erikson accepted a position at Yale Medical School. While at Yale, he took his first anthropological field trip to observe Sioux Indian children in South Dakota. His paper on the Sioux combines the cultural richness of an anthropological field report with the psychologically rich perspective of a highly trained clinician. Among the Sioux, Erikson observed a new phenomenon. He noticed psychological symptoms, including the lack of clear self-image or identity, that were related to a sense of loss of cultural tradition. Erikson later observed a similar confusion of identity among emotionally disturbed World War II veterans.

The Eriksons moved to California in 1939, and spent ten years in the San Francisco area. Erikson continued his analytic work with children and conducted research projects at the University of California at Berkeley.

In 1950, Erikson's best-known book, *Childhood and Society,* was first published. This book contains the fundamental formulations of virtually all of Erikson's major contributions: identity, the life cycle, cross-cultural studies, and psychobiography. *Childhood and Society* has been translated into a dozen languages and is used as a textbook at psychiatric training centers and in psychology courses, and serves as a text in many other disciplines, at the undergraduate and graduate levels.

That same year Erikson left Berkeley because he would not sign a state loyalty oath. Erikson, along with many other liberal scholars, refused to sign because he felt that the mandatory oath represented a kind of communist witch-hunt in an era of hyperpatriotism and paranoia. The Eriksons returned to Massachusetts to the Austin Riggs Center, a leading institution for psychoanalytic training and research. While at Austin Riggs, Erikson did a psychological study of Martin Luther, entitled *Young Man Luther* (1958). An exciting and innovative combination of psychoanalysis, biography, and history, the book stirred great interest among psychoanalysts, psychologists, historians, and other social scientists.

In 1960, Erikson was appointed a professor at Harvard. Two years later, he visited India and met a number of Indians who had known Gandhi and who had been personally involved, on both sides, in his first nonviolent protest in India. Erikson became deeply interested in Gandhi, the spiritual leader and political revolutionary who transformed a negative Indian identity of powerlessness into an active, effective political technique. It was in 1969, while at Harvard, that Erikson published his study of Gandhi.

After retiring from Harvard, Erikson and his wife moved back to the San Francisco area in 1975. Their writing and research, which they continued until his death in 1994, focused primarily on old age and the last stage of the life cycle.

Intellectual Antecedents

Two principal influences on Erikson that shaped his theories were psychoanalysis and his study of life and child raising in other cultures.

Psychoanalysis

Psychoanalysis is unique. It is *the* treatment situation in which intellectual insight is forced to become emotional insight under very carefully planned circumstances defined by technical rules. But outside of that situation, interpretations cannot do what they can do within a disciplined setting. (Erikson in Evans, 1969)

Throughout his career, Erikson viewed himself as a psychoanalyst. In his application of psychoanalysis to new areas and his incorporation of recent advances in anthropology, psychology, and other social sciences, Erikson inevitably developed ideas that were significantly different from Freud's basic theories. However, Erikson's writings reveal his indebtedness to Freud. Rather than label himself *neo-Freudian,* Erikson preferred the more neutral term *post-Freudian.*

Erikson's work on in-depth psychological biographies and on child and adult development was essentially psychoanalytic in nature. "I spoke of 'insight,' rather than knowledge or fact, because it is so difficult to say in the study of human situations what you can really call knowledge" (Erikson in Evans, 1969, p. 89). As he dealt with new material, Erikson reshaped and expanded his psychoanalytic understandings.

> When I started to write about twenty-five years ago, I really thought I was merely providing new illustrations for what I had learned from Sigmund and Anna Freud. I realized only gradually that any original observation already implies a change in theory. An observer of a different generation, in a different scientific climate, cannot avoid developing in a field if it is a vital one. Even a great breakthrough like Freud's is characterized by a passionate concern to bring order into data which "haunted him," to use Darwin's phrase, for very complex reasons of his own and of his time. One can follow such a man only by doing likewise, and if one does so, one differs. I say this because some workers want to improve on Freud, as if his theories were opinions, and because they prefer nicer or nobler ones. (Erikson in Evans, 1969, p. 13)

In a sense, Erikson developed psychoanalytic theory for the second half of the twentieth century.

Other Cultures

In 1937 Erikson traveled to South Dakota to investigate the cause of apathy among Sioux schoolchildren. He discovered that they were caught between conflicting value systems: the traditional tribal values they learned in early childhood and the white middle-class values taught in school. In Sioux culture neither property nor competition was valued. The Sioux had been buffalo hunters, and successful hunters traditionally shared freely with their villages.

Several years later, Erikson visited the Yurok Indians, who lived by the Klamath River in northern California. He was particularly interested in comparing the childhood training and personality styles in this relatively sedentary fishing society with the lifestyles of the Plains hunters he had studied earlier. Erikson found that acquisition of possessions was a continuing preoccupation among the Yuroks. Acquisitiveness was learned early in childhood, as Yurok children were taught to be frugal, to value long-term gain over immediate impulses, and to engage in fantasies of catching salmon and accumulating money. The Yurok were very different from the Sioux, much closer to middle-class American values.

Erikson's work with the Sioux and the Yurok Indians had an important influence on his thinking. His field studies also reveal his remarkable ability to enter the worldviews and modes of thinking of cultures far different from his own. On both field trips, Erikson was accompanied by anthropologists who had developed long-standing friendships with the older people of the tribes. The assistance of these anthropologists gave him access to informants and rich, firsthand information never before available to a psychoanalyst. Before going into the field, he read anthropological reports on both tribes. Erikson found virtually no details on childhood training in these reports. A good part of his field research consisted of asking the grandmothers, "Before the white men came, how were your children brought up?" He found they loved to talk about the subject; they had wondered why no one ever asked.

Erikson's later theoretical developments evolved partly from his cross-cultural observations. He found that Freud's theories of pregenital stages of development were intrinsically related to the technology and worldview of Western culture. Erikson's own theoretical focus on healthy personality development was strongly influenced by firsthand knowledge of other cultures.

Major Concepts

The core of Erikson's work is his eight-stage model of human development, a model that extends psychoanalytic thinking beyond childhood to cover the entire human life cycle. Each stage has psychological, biological, and social components, and each stage builds on the stages that precede it.

Another significant contribution of Erikson's was his pioneering work on psychohistory and psychobiography, which extended his clinical insight to the study of major historical personalities and their impact on their societies.

An Epigenetic Model of Human Development

With each passage from one stage of human growth to the next we must shed a protective structure. We are left exposed and vulnerable—but also yeasty and embryonic again, capable of stretching in ways we hadn't known before. (Sheehy, 1977, p. 29)

Erikson's model of the stages of human development—a model he called *epigenetic*—is the first psychological theory to detail the human life cycle from infancy to adulthood and old age. According to Erikson, the psychological growth of the individual proceeds in a manner similar to that of an embryo. *Epigenesis* suggests that each element develops *on top of* other parts (*epi* means "upon" and *genesis* means "emergence"). Erikson's model is structurally similar to that of embryonic growth in that the emergence of each successive stage is predicated on the development of the previous one.

Each organ system of the body has its own special time for growth and development, which follows a predetermined sequence. Erikson explains the epigenetic principle as "anything that grows has a *ground plan,* and that out of this ground plan the *parts* arise, each part having its *time* of special ascendancy, until all parts have arisen to form a *functioning whole*" (Erikson, 1980a, p. 53).

Erikson's scheme of human development has two basic underlying assumptions:

> (1) That the human personality in principle develops according to steps predetermined in the growing person's readiness to be driven forward, to be aware of, and to interact with a widening social radius; and (2) that society, in principle, tends to be so constituted as to meet and invite the succession of potentialities for interaction and attempts to safeguard and to encourage the proper rate and the proper sequence of their unfolding. (1963, p. 270)

Each stage is characterized by a specific developmental task, or crisis, that must be resolved in order for the individual to proceed to the next stage. The strengths and capacities developed through successful resolution at each stage affect the entire personality. They can be influenced by either later or earlier

TABLE 7.1 Erikson's Eight Stages and Related Virtues

VIII Old Age								Integrity vs. Despair WISDOM
VII Adulthood							Generativity vs. Stagnation CARE	
VI Young Adulthood						Intimacy vs. Isolation LOVE		
V Adolescence					Identity vs. Identity Confusion FIDELITY			
IV School Age				Industry vs. Inferiority COMPETENCE				
III Play Age			Initiative vs. Guilt PURPOSE					
II Early Childhood		Autonomy vs. Shame, Doubt WILL						
I Infancy	Basic Trust vs. Basic Mistrust HOPE							
	1	2	3	4	5	6	7	8

Source: From Erikson, 1982, pp. 56–57.

events. However, these psychological capacities are generally affected most strongly during the stage in which they emerge. Each stage is systematically related to all the others, and the stages must occur in a given sequence.

Table 7.1 is taken from Erikson's first discussion of the eight stages, in *Childhood and Society.* It illustrates the progression from one stage to another over time. Also, each attribute exists in various forms before and after its critical stage. *Trust,* for example, takes one form in adolescence and yet another in old age; both are based on a sense of trust developed in infancy.

Crises in Development Each stage has a period of **crisis** in which the strengths and skills that form essential elements of that stage are developed and tested. By crisis, Erikson means a turning point, a critical moment, such as the

In Chinese, the word for *crisis* is composed of two characters, *danger* and *opportunity.*

crisis in a fever. When it is resolved successfully, the fever breaks and the individual begins to recover. Crises are special times in the individual's life, "moments of decision between progress and regression, integration and retardation" (Erikson, 1963, pp. 270–271). Each stage is a crisis in learning—allowing for the attainment of new skills and attitudes. The crisis may not seem dramatic or critical; often, the individual can see only later that a major turning point was reached and passed.

Erikson has pointed out that successful resolution of the crisis at each stage of human development promotes a certain psychosocial strength or virtue. Erikson uses the term *virtue* in its old sense, as in the *virtue* of a medicine. It refers more to potency than morality. Ideally, the individual emerges from each crisis with an increased sense of inner unity, clearer judgment, and greater capacity to function effectively.

Eight Stages of Human Development Erikson's first three stages are essentially an amplification of Freud's work. Freud discussed four major stages: oral, anal, phallic, and genital, which are tied to specific organs or specific cultures. Erikson expands these to universal issues of human development.

Babies control and bring up their parents as much as they're controlled by them. (Erikson, 1963, p. 69)

1. Basic Trust Versus Basic Mistrust The first stage, **basic trust versus basic mistrust,** occurs at a time when we are the most helpless and dependent on others for physical and emotional nourishment. When infants begin life, they develop a relative sense of trust and mistrust of the world around them. Crucial to this balance between security and insecurity is the infant's experience with the mother. Development of a strong sense of basic trust "implies not only that one has learned to rely on the sameness and continuity of the outer providers, but also that one may trust oneself and the capacities of one's own organs to cope with urges" (Erikson, 1963, p. 248). If a mother, or primary caregiver, is sensitive and responsive to her child, the infant's sense of security increases and the frustrations of hunger and discomfort are tolerable.

The relationship between mother and child is focused around the mouth and the experience of nursing. This relationship is tested during the biting stage, which is the beginning of the infant's ability to cause pain. The capacity to express anger and rage as well as the desire to harm is also connected to the pain of teething, a pain the infant must learn to endure because it cannot be alleviated as simply as can hunger. According to Erikson, this inner discomfort and the growing ability to inflict pain are the child's first experiences of a sense of evil and malevolence.

A sense of trust develops not so much from the relief of hunger or from demonstrations of love as from the quality of maternal care. Mothers who feel secure in their ability to care for their babies and who trust that their babies will develop into healthy children communicate their feelings, creating the infant's sense of trust in self and in the world.

The virtue or strength that results from achieving a balance between basic trust and mistrust is *hope*. "Hope is the enduring belief in the attainability of fervent wishes, in spite of the dark urges and rages which mark the beginning of existence" (Erikson, 1964, p. 118). Hope lays the foundation for the development of faith.

Hope is established as a basic strength, relatively independent of specific

Personal Reflection

■ Trust

Share a "trust walk" with a classmate or friend. Blindfold yourself and have your partner guide you for at least 15 to 20 minutes. Your partner should try to give you a variety of experiences—different surfaces to walk on, objects to touch, smell, and even taste. Then switch roles.

After you have both finished, take a little time to discuss your experiences. Was it difficult to trust your partner at times? How did it feel to be so dependent on another person?

expectations, goals, and desires. As the individual continues to mature, this strength is verified at each stage; rewarding experiences inspire new hopefulness. At the same time, the individual attains a capacity for renunciation and an ability to cope with disappointment. Also, the individual develops realistic dreams and expectations.

The strength of hope emerges from three essential sources. First is the mother's relation to her own childhood—her desire and need to pass on the hope transmitted from her mother and from her culture. Second is the mother-child relationship itself, the mutuality and sensitivity that can grow when this bond is healthy. Finally, the infant's hope is maintained through social institutions that confirm and restore it, by religious ritual, inspired advice, or otherwise. The mature form of an infant's hope is faith. The rituals and practices of religion are designed to support, deepen, and restore faith.

2. Autonomy Versus Shame and Doubt The next stage, **autonomy versus shame and doubt,** occurs at the time of muscular maturation and the accompanying ability to hold on or let go. At this stage, children rapidly acquire a variety of mental and physical abilities. They begin to walk, climb, hold on, and communicate more effectively. The child interacts with the world in new ways—in grasping and dropping objects and in toilet training. The child starts to exert control over self and also over parts of the outside world.

The basic modalities of this stage are to hold on and to let go. Freud focused on one aspect of this in his writings on the anal stage. Holding on and letting go have both positive and negative aspects. Holding on can become cruel restraint or it can be a pattern of caring. Letting go can be a release of destructive forces or it can be a relaxed allowing, a letting be.

A sense of autonomy develops with the sense of free choice. It is promoted by a feeling of being able to choose what to keep and what to reject. The infant's basic faith in existence, a lasting result of the first stage, is tested in sudden and stubborn wishes to choose—to grab demandingly or to eliminate inappropriately. Parenting experts have called this age the *terrible twos.* The two-year-old's favorite word is *no,* a clear bid for increased autonomy.

Some children turn this urge to control against themselves by developing a rigid, demanding conscience. Rather than mastering the outer environment,

Personal Reflection

■ Autonomy

Make an agreement with a partner that, for at least half a day, you will follow his or her directions in whatever you are told to do. In a sense, your partner gets to play "parent" and you agree to be an obedient "child." (Make some clear limits. For example, you will not be made to do anything that is illegal, unethical, or embarrassing to yourself or someone else.)

How does it feel to have someone tell you what to do—what to eat, when to sit down or stand up, how to act, and so on? In many ways, you are duplicating the experience of the average 2-year-old, who has very little say in his or her life.

Discuss your experience with your partner when you are done. It may be better *not* to switch roles afterward. Knowing that you are going to switch may inhibit your partner from being really creative in ordering you around. (And, after all, very few parents anticipate switching roles with their children.)

they judge and manipulate themselves, which often results in a strong sense of shame or self-doubt.

Shame stems from a sense of self-exposure, a feeling that one's deficiencies are visible to others and that one is, in colloquial terms, "caught with one's pants down." Shame is also associated with the child's first experience of standing upright, in which the child feels small, wobbly, and powerless in an adult world.

Doubt is more closely related to the consciousness of having a front and a back. Our front is the acceptable face that we turn toward the world. The child cannot see the back part of his or her body. It is unknown and unexplored territory and yet, at the stage of toilet training, the child's backside can be dominated by the will of others. Unless the split between front and back is reduced, the child's feelings of autonomy will become tinged with doubt.

The strength acquired at this stage is *will.* To have will does not mean to be willful but to control one's drives with judgment and discrimination. The individual learns to make decisions and to act decisively in spite of inevitable frustration. "Will, therefore, is the unbroken determination to exercise free choice as well as self-restraint, in spite of the unavoidable experience of shame and doubt" (Erikson, 1964, p. 119).

Infant will develops into the adult ability to control drives and impulses. Ideally, the individual's will joins with others in a way that permits both self and others to retain a sense of power, even when restrained by rules and reason.

Will forms the basis of our acceptance of law and external necessity. It is rooted in an appreciation that parental training is guided and tempered by a spirit of justice. The law is a social institution that gives concrete form to our ego's control of our drives. We surrender our willfulness to the majesty of the law with ambivalence and inevitable small transgressions.

Personal Reflection

■ Initiative

This exercise is very much like the previous autonomy experience. Again, with a partner, agree to follow his or her directions. Only this time, you can say *no.* Your partner gets to make all the suggestions about possible activities. You can respond with a *yes* or *no,* but you cannot suggest any ideas on your own.

For instance, if the two of you are in a restaurant, your partner can suggest various foods that you might like. You can accept or refuse, but you cannot make any suggestions on your own. Or, if the two of you are going out to a movie, your partner can suggest films to go to. You can agree or disagree, but you cannot suggest any specific films on your own.

After you have finished, discuss what it felt like to be deprived of a sense of initiative.

3. Initiative Versus Guilt At this stage, identified as **initiative versus guilt,** the child experiences greater mobility and inquisitiveness, significant growth in language and imagination, and an expanding sense of mastery and responsibility. Play is the most basic activity of this stage. The child is "into everything," finding joy in attack and conquest over the environment. This stage is analogous to Freud's phallic stage. The child is eager to learn and to perform well. The favorite word at this stage is *why?* There is tremendous curiosity and openness to new learning. The child learns the value of planning ahead and starts to develop a sense of direction and purpose.

This new sense of mastery is tempered by feelings of guilt. The child's new freedom and assertion of power almost inevitably create anxiety. The child develops a conscience, a parental attitude that supports self-observation, self-guidance, and also self-punishment. At this stage, the child can do more than ever before and must learn to set limits.

Purpose, the virtue of this stage, is rooted in play and fantasy. Play is to the child what thinking and planning are to the adult. It provides the rudiments of purpose: focus and direction given to concerted activity. "Purpose, then, is the courage to envisage and pursue valued goals uninhibited by the defeat of infantile fantasies, by guilt and by the foiling fear of punishment" (Erikson, 1964, p. 122). Purpose provides aim and direction, fed by fantasy yet rooted in reality, limited but not inhibited by guilt. The development of fantasy forms the roots of dance, drama, and ritual in adult life.

4. Industry Versus Inferiority At this stage, **industry versus inferiority,** the child makes his or her entrance into life outside the family. This period corresponds to Freud's latency stage. In our culture, school life begins. In other social systems, the child may become an apprentice or a working assistant to the father or mother.

The adult once was child and a youth. He will never be either again; but neither will he ever be without the heritage of those former states. (Erikson, 1987, p. 332)

This is a stage of systematic instruction, a shift from play to a sense of work. Earlier, the child could *play at* activities. No attention was given to the quality of results. Now the child needs to achieve and to derive a sense of satisfaction from a job well done. At this stage, children are expected to master tasks and skills that are valued in society. The attitudes and opinions of others are particularly important. Children who don't achieve—and thus don't earn the respect of their parents, teachers, and peers—may develop a sense of inferiority or inadequacy.

The virtue of this stage is *competence,* which is based on a sense of workmanship, the development of practical skills, and general capacities. "Competence, then, is the free exercise of dexterity and intelligence in the completion of tasks, unimpaired by infantile inferiority" (Erikson, 1964, p. 124). Competence is the psychological basis for technology. At this stage, we have started to become productive members of our culture; we have just begun to master our culture's technology.

For most of those in the twenties, a fantastic mystery story waits to be written over the next two decades. It races with excitement and jeopardy . . . and leads us down secret passageways in search of our missing personality parts. (Sheehy, 1977, p. 166)

5. Identity Versus Identity Confusion As childhood ends, adolescents enter the stage known as **identity versus identity confusion,** in which they integrate their past experiences into a new whole. They question role models and identifications from childhood and try out new roles. The great question of this stage is "Who am I?" A new sense of ego identity develops.

This sense of identity includes the individual's ability to integrate past identifications and present impulses, aptitudes, and skills, as well as opportunities offered by society. "The sense of ego identity, then, is the accrued confidence that the inner sameness and continuity prepared in the past are matched by the sameness and continuity of one's meaning for others, as evidenced in the tangible promise of a 'career' " (Erikson, 1963, pp. 261–262).

Because adolescence is the transition between childhood and adulthood, it is a crucial stage, Erikson believes. Often at this point in life, a psychological moratorium is called, as the adolescent takes "time out" to devote to role experimentation. During this period, social limitations and pressures can have a strong impact. The adolescent, who is likely to suffer from some role confusion, may have difficulty envisioning an appropriate occupational role or finding a meaningful place in society. Doubts about sexual attractiveness and sexual identity are also common. An inability to "take hold" and develop a sense of identification with an individual or cultural role model who provides inspiration and direction can lead to a period of floundering and insecurity. Another common reaction is overidentification (to the point of apparent loss of identity) with youth-culture heroes or clique leaders. The individual often feels isolated, empty, anxious, or indecisive. Under pressure to make important life decisions, the adolescent feels unable, even resistant, to do so.

The basic strength of this stage is *fidelity.* At the threshold of adulthood, the individual faces a need for commitment to a career and a lasting set of values. "Fidelity is the ability to sustain loyalties freely pledged in spite of the inevitable contradictions of value systems" (Erikson, 1964, p. 125). Fidelity is the cornerstone of identity; it requires the validation of acceptable social ideologies and the support of peers who have made similar choices.

It is during this stage that we incorporate our culture's ethical values and belief systems. At the same time, the culture itself is renewed by the affirmation of each generation; it is revitalized as adolescents selectively offer their loyalties and energies, supporting some traditions and changing others. Those who cannot pledge their loyalties either remain deviant or commit themselves to revolutionary goals and values.

Personal Reflection

■ Erikson's Stages: A Personal Assessment

Which of Erikson's stages is the most significant (or powerful, or difficult) for you?

What combination of factors makes this stage so important for you? What are the personality elements, family events, environmental influences, societal forces, and so on, that are the most significant in your experience?

How is your own experience of this stage related to your earlier and later development? How is it related to the stage and the growth crisis you find yourself in now?

6. Intimacy Versus Isolation This stage, **intimacy versus isolation,** generally occurs in young adulthood. It is a time for achieving a sense of independence from parents and school, establishing friendships and intimate relationships, and developing a sense of adult responsibility.

Only after we have established a relatively firm sense of identity are we capable of developing a close and meaningful relationship with another. Only then can we think of committing ourselves to partnership, affiliation, and intimacy with another person. The critical commitment that generally occurs at this stage is based on true mutuality with a love partner. This level of intimacy is significantly different from the earlier sexual exploration and intense search for sexual identity.

Without a sense of intimacy and commitment, we may become isolated, unable to sustain nourishing personal relationships. If our sense of identity is weak and threatened by intimacy, we may turn away from or even attack whatever encroaches.

The virtue developed in this stage is *love*. Erikson (1964) argues that this is the greatest virtue. "Love, then, is mutuality of devotion forever subduing the antagonism inherent in divided functions" (Erikson, 1964, p. 129). He points out that it takes many forms. Early in life, it is the infant's love for its mother, the child's love for parents, and adolescent infatuation. When real intimacy develops between adults, love includes a shared identity and the validation of each partner in the other. This virtue can manifest itself in a romantic, sexual relationship, but also in deep ties developed in joint service to ideals, home, or country. It includes true mutuality and intimacy.

7. Generativity Versus Stagnation This stage, **generativity versus stagnation,** generally spans most of our adult years. Intimate commitment to others widens to a more general concern for guiding and supporting the next generation. Generativity includes concern for our children and for the ideas and products we have created. It includes productivity and creativity in work and in our personal lives.

We are teaching as well as learning beings. Creation is important, as is ensuring the ongoing health and maintenance of our creations, ideals, and principles. Unless the sphere of our care and productivity widens, we fall prey to a sense of boredom and stagnation.

The mere fact of having and wanting children does not achieve generativity. (Erikson, 1963, p. 267)

Personal Reflection

■ The Later Stages of the Life Cycle

Rent a videotape of the Ingmar Bergman classic motion picture *Wild Strawberries* (Wilmette, IL: Janus Films, 1957). Give your own analysis of Dr. Borg's dream, and look at the events in the film from the perspective of the stages of the life cycle, especially the last three life stages—intimacy/isolation, generativity/stagnation, and integrity/despair.

Compare your analysis with Erikson's, which is published as a chapter in *Vital Involvement in Old Age* (Erikson, Erikson, & Kivnick, 1986). This is a unique chance to compare your own analysis of a case study with that of a gifted clinician. You are using the same data, as presented in the film. (For many years, Erikson assigned this exercise to his own students in his Harvard course the Human Life Cycle.)

Erikson (1982) writes that social institutions tend to reinforce the function of generativity. They provide a continuity of knowledge and structure from one generation to another. Those with a healthy sense of generativity actively participate in these institutions, seeking to maintain and enhance future generations.

The strength developed at this stage is *care*. "Care is the widening concern for what has been generated by love, necessity, or accident; it overcomes the ambivalence adhering to irreversible obligation" (Erikson, 1964, p. 131). The nurturing of children is at the core of this virtue. It includes the care not only of offspring but also of the children of our minds and hearts—our ideas, ideals, and creations. Unique to our species is the fact that care for and education of the young extends over a very long period.

As adults, we need to be needed, or else we suffer from narcissism and self-absorption. In terms of human psychosocial evolution, we are essentially a teaching species. We must teach to fulfill our identity and to keep alive our skills and knowledge.

8. Integrity Versus Despair The final stage of life, the period of **integrity versus despair,** comes with old age. It is a time of dealing with what Erikson has called *ultimate concerns*. The sense of ego integrity, which includes our acceptance of a unique life cycle, with its own history of triumphs and failures, provides a sense of order and meaning, in our personal lives and in the world around us, as well as a new and different love of parents. With a sense of ego integrity comes an awareness of the value of many other lifestyles, including those that differ widely from our own. Integrity brings with it a perspective of wholeness—an ability to see our lives as a unity and to view human problems in a comprehensive way. In Sheehy's words (1995), ego integrity is the development of the capacity for "postnarcissistic love."

If we have not gained a measure of self-acceptance, we are likely to plunge into despair over the feeling that time is short—too short to start over. Those who end up in despair may become bitter over what might have been, con-

Personal Reflection

■ Examples of Erikson's Stages

Think of three people who you feel are in different Eriksonian stages. You may wish to include a parent, yourself, and someone much younger. Does each person seem to fit his or her designated stage? What is the central issue that you see in the life of each? What are the major strengths? Major weaknesses? Can you see how the current life of each person is related to the past? How has each evolved from past strengths and past issues?

In what ways does framing the concerns, strengths, and critical issues for the three people help you understand these individuals, their differences, and possible difficulties in communication?

stantly lamenting "if only. . . ." Despair may manifest itself in fear of death or may result in contempt and rejection of other values, institutions, and lifestyles.

Erikson (1982) noted that the role of old age has been changing. When *Childhood and Society* was first published, in 1950, the cultural view of old age was very different from what it is today. Then the predominant model was that of the *elders,* those few who lived to a relatively decrepit old age but embodied the values of dignity, wisdom, and integrity. Today, as life expectancy increases, we have an ever-growing population of healthy and active elderly. Our model of old age will evolve as the parameters of aging continue to change. One of Erikson's most significant contributions has been to help develop a new theory of aging (Weiland, 1994).

The strength of *wisdom* develops out of encounters with both integrity and despair as the individual is confronted with ultimate concerns. "Wisdom, then, is detached concern with life itself, in the face of death itself" (Erikson, 1964, p. 133). Wisdom maintains the integrity of the individual's accumulated knowledge and experience. Those who have developed wisdom are models of wholeness and completeness. They are inspirational examples to younger generations who have adopted similar values and lifestyles. This sense of wholeness and meaning can also alleviate the feelings of helplessness and dependence that mark old age.

Table 7.2 (p. 206) summarizes the various dimensions of Erikson's eight stages. Each stage is associated with a particular crisis, social environment, strength, and various other dimensions.

Modes of Relating to the Environment Whereas Freud based his description of the stages of human development on specific organ-related experiences, Erikson's stages are based on more general styles of relating to and coping with the environment. Although, according to Erikson, these styles of behavior are often initially developed through a particular organ, they refer to broad patterns of activity. For instance, the mode learned in the first stage, basic trust versus basic mistrust, is *to get*—that is, the ability to receive and to accept what is given. (This stage corresponds to Freud's oral stage.) At this time, the mouth is

The infant may equally absorb the milk of wisdom where he once desired more tangible fluids from more sensuous containers. (Erikson, 1963, p. 62)

TABLE 7.2 Eight Stages of Human Development

Stages	Psychosexual Stages and Modes	Psychosocial Crises	Radius of Significant Relations	Basic Strengths	Core Pathology: Basic Antipathies	Related Principles of Social Order	Binding Ritualizations	Ritualism
I Infancy	Oral-Respiratory, Sensory-Kinesthetic (Incorporative Modes)	Basic Trust vs. Basic Mistrust	Maternal Person	Hope	Withdrawal	Cosmic Order	Numinous	Idolism
II Early Childhood	Anal-Urethral, Muscular (Retentive-Eliminative Modes)	Autonomy vs. Shame, Doubt	Parental Persons	Will	Compulsion	"Law and Order"	Judicious	Legalism
III Play Age	Infantile-Genital, Locomotor (Intrusive, Inclusive Modes)	Initiative vs. Guilt	Basic Family	Purpose	Inhibition	Ideal Prototypes	Dramatic	Moralism
IV School Age	"Latency"	Industry vs. Inferiority	"Neighborhood," School	Competence	Inertia	Technological Order	Formal (Technical)	Formalism
V Adolescence	Puberty	Identity vs. Identity Confusion	Peer Group and Outgroups; Models of Leadership	Fidelity	Repudiation	Ideological Worldview	Ideological	Totalism
VI Young Adulthood	Genitality	Intimacy vs. Isolation	Partners in Friendship, Sex, Competition, Cooperation	Love	Exclusivity	Patterns of Cooperation and Competition	Affiliative	Elitism
VII Adulthood	(Procreativity)	Generativity vs. Stagnation	Divided Labor and Shared Household	Care	Rejectivity	Currents of Education and Tradition	Generational	Authoritism
VIII Old Age	(Generalization of Sensual Modes)	Integrity vs. Despair	"Mankind," "My Kind"	Wisdom	Disdain	Wisdom	Philosophical	Dogmatism

Source: From Erikson, 1982, pp. 32–33.

the primary organ of interchange between the infant and the environment. However, an adult who is fixated on *getting* may exhibit forms of *dependency* unrelated to orality.

In the second stage, autonomy versus shame and doubt, the modes are *to let go* and *to hold on*. As with Freud's anal stage, the modes are fundamentally related to retention and elimination of feces; however, the child also alternates between possessing and rejecting parents, favorite toys, and so on.

The mode of the third stage, initiative versus guilt, Erikson calls *to make*. In one sense, the child is "on the make," focused on the conquest of the environment. Play is important, from making mud pies to imitating the complex sports and games of older children.

The fourth stage, industry versus inferiority, includes the modes *to do well* and *to work*. There is no single organ system associated with this stage; rather, productive work and accomplishment are central.

Erikson does not discuss in detail the modes involved in the remaining stages. These later stages, not as closely related to Freud's developmental stages, seem less rooted in a particular activity or organ mode.

Identity

Erikson developed the concept of identity in greater detail than the others concepts he incorporated in the eight stages. He first coined the phrase **identity crisis** to describe the mental state of many of the soldiers he treated at Mt. Zion Veterans Rehabilitation Clinic in San Francisco in the 1940s. These men were easily upset by any sudden or intense stimulus. Their egos seemed to have lost any shock-absorbing capacity. Their sensory systems were in a constant "startled" state, thrown off by external stimuli, as well as by a variety of bodily sensations, including hot flashes, heart palpitations, intense headaches, and insomnia. "Above all, the men felt that they 'did not know who they were': There was a distinct loss of ego identity. The sameness and continuity and the belief in one's social role were gone" (Erikson, 1968, p. 67).

Approaches to Identity The term **identity** brings together the theories of depth psychology with those of cognitive psychology and ego psychology (Erikson, 1993). Early Freudian theory tended to ignore the important role of the ego as, in Erikson's terms, "a selective, integrating, coherent and persistent agency central to personality function" (Erikson, 1964, p. 137). The concept of identity also provides a meeting place for psychology, sociology, and history. Because of its complexity, Erikson has wisely avoided giving the term *identity* a single definition:

> I can attempt to make the subject matter of identity more explicit only by approaching it from a variety of angles. . . . At one time, then, it will appear to refer to a conscious *sense of individual identity;* at another, to an unconscious striving for *a continuity of personal character;* at a third, as a criterion for the silent doings of *ego synthesis;* and, finally, as a maintenance of an *inner solidarity* with a group's ideals and identity. (1980a, p. 109)

Erikson spells out these aspects of identity as follows (adapted from Evans, 1969, pp. 218–219):

1. *Individuality*—a conscious sense of one's uniqueness and existence as a separate, distinct entity.
2. *Sameness and continuity*—a sense of inner sameness, a continuity between what one has been in the past and what one promises to be in the future, a feeling that one's life has consistency and meaningful direction.
3. *Wholeness and synthesis*—a sense of inner harmony and wholeness, a synthesis of the self-images and identifications of childhood into a meaningful whole that produces a sense of harmony.
4. *Social solidarity*—a sense of inner solidarity with the ideals and val-

Personal Reflection

■ Identity

To get an idea of how your identity develops, try this exercise.

1. Relax and think of a time when you felt you had a strong sense of identity. Describe that time. What were the components of that identity (for example, captain of the high school football team, oldest daughter in a large family, good student)?
2. List ten words that describe you then—your sense of self, crucial life issues, and so on.
3. How would you describe your *present* identity? Make a second list.
4. Have there been significant changes? What continuity do you notice in your sense of self over this period of time? What changes?
5. Was the transition from one sense of identity to another smooth and gradual or abrupt?
6. Do you feel that your present identity will remain relatively stable, or do you foresee major changes? If you foresee major changes, why might these occur?

> ues of society or a subgroup within it, a feeling that one's identity is meaningful to significant others and corresponds to their expectations and perceptions.

Further, in the following excerpt, Erikson describes identity in the transition from childhood to adulthood:

> Like a trapeze artist, the young person in the middle of vigorous motion must let go of his safe hold on childhood and reach out for a firm grasp on adulthood, depending for a breathless interval on a relatedness between the past and the future, and on the reliability of those he must let go of, and those who will "receive" him. Whatever combination of drives and defenses, of sublimations and capacities has emerged from the young individual's childhood must now make sense in view of his concrete opportunities in work and love . . . [and] he must detect some meaningful resemblance between what he has come to see in himself and what his sharpened awareness tells him others judge and expect him to be. (Erikson, 1964, p. 90)

The concept of identity has become particularly popular because it is generally recognized as the major life crisis in the United States today—and perhaps in all of modern society. Our cultural emphasis on extended education, as well as the complexity of most contemporary vocations, makes the development of a sense of identity especially difficult in our society. The struggle to gain a healthy, clear sense of identity frequently continues beyond adolescence, erupting later in midlife crises.

Years ago, most children took on their parents' roles. Children began to learn adult skills, attitudes, and functions early in life; their parents' vocations were generally integrated into family life. Today, given our changing values and social roles, not only are children unlikely to assume their parents' roles, but there may not be any clear adult role models available to them. The adolescent's childhood identifications and experiences are clearly inadequate for the task of anticipating a career and making a major vocational commitment.

Erikson has pointed out that a sense of negative identity may be mixed with the sense of positive identity. Negative identity may include the behavior and attitudes the individual has been punished or made to feel guilty for. There may also be a role model for a negative identity—for example, an uncle or a friend who is labeled an alcoholic or a failure in some way. (For more on negative identity, see Obstacles to Growth in this chapter.)

Erikson found that the development of a sense of identity is frequently preceded by a "psychosocial moratorium," a period of time out in which the individual may be occupied with study, travel, or a clearly temporary occupation. This provides time to reflect, to develop a new sense of direction, new values, new purpose. The moratorium may last for months or even years.

Identity Development Erikson (1980a, pp. 120–130) has stressed that the development of a sense of identity has both psychological and social aspects:

1. The individual's development of a sense of personal sameness and continuity is based, in part, on a belief in the sameness and continuity of a worldview shared with significant others.
2. Although many aspects of the search for a sense of identity are conscious, unconscious motivation may also play a major role. At this stage, feelings of acute vulnerability may alternate with high expectations of success.
3. A sense of identity cannot develop without certain physical, mental, and social preconditions (outlined in Erikson's developmental stages). Also, achievement of a sense of identity must not be unduly delayed, because future stages of development depend on it. Psychological factors may prolong the crisis as the individual seeks to match unique gifts to existing social possibilities. Social factors and historical change may also postpone adult commitment.
4. The growth of a sense of identity depends on the past, present, and future. First, the individual must have acquired a clear sense of identification in childhood. Second, the adult's choice of vocational identification must be realistic in light of available opportunities. Finally, the adult must retain a sense of assurance that his or her chosen roles will be viable in the future, in spite of inevitable changes, both in the individual and in the outside world.

Erikson has pointed out that problems of identity are not new, though they may be more widespread today than ever before. Many creative individuals have wrestled with the question of identity as they carved out new careers and social roles for themselves. Some especially imaginative people were responsible for major vocational innovations, thus offering new role models for others. Freud, for example, began his career as a conventional doctor and neurologist. Only in midcareer did he devise a new role for himself (and for many others) by becoming the first psychoanalyst.

Table 7.3 (p. 210) illustrates the role of earlier life cycle stages as develop-

TABLE 7.3 Identity and the Eight Stages of Development

VIII Old Age								INTEGRITY vs. DESPAIR, DISGUST
VII Adulthood							GENERATIVITY vs. STAGNATION	
VI Young Adulthood						INTIMACY vs. ISOLATION		
V Adolescence	Temporal Perspective vs. Time Confusion	Self-Certainty vs. Self-Consciousness	Role Experimentation vs. Role Fixation	Apprenticeship vs. Work-Paralysis	IDENTITY vs. IDENTITY CONFUSION	Sexual Polarization vs. Bisexual Confusion	Leadership and Fellowship vs. Authority Confusion	Ideological Commitment vs. Confusion of Values
IV School Age				INDUSTRY vs. INFERIORITY	Task Identification vs. Sense of Futility			
III Play Age			INITIATIVE vs. GUILT		Anticipation of Roles vs. Role Inhibition			
II Early Childhood		AUTONOMY vs. SHAME, DOUBT			Will to Be Oneself vs. Self-Doubt			
I Infancy	BASIC TRUST vs. BASIC MISTRUST				Mutual Recognition vs. Autistic Isolation			

Source: Identity, Youth and Crisis (p. 94) by E. Erikson, 1968, New York: Norton. Copyright 1968 by Norton. Reprinted by permission.

mental precursors to a healthy sense of identity (the vertical dimension). It shows, also, how each of the stages of development is engaged during the period of identity crisis (the horizontal dimension).

Psychohistory

Erikson expanded psychoanalysis by studying major historical personalities. By analyzing their psychological growth and development, he came to understand the psychological impact they had on their generation.

This interest in combining psychoanalysis and history began when Erikson left Europe for the United States as Hitler came to power. On the ship to America he wrote of the central reasons that German youths turned toward Hitler. Because of his own background, Erikson was deeply affected by developments in Germany. Although born a Dane, he grew up in Germany and considered it his home. But some of his German friends had become Nazis and were killing other friends and classmates who shared Erikson's Jewish roots. He analyzed what was happening in Germany without writing off the Nazis as "others," as depraved criminals essentially different from the rest of humanity. These notes led to Erikson's first work of **psychohistory,** which appeared as a chapter on Hitler in *Childhood and Society.*

> Psychohistory, essentially, is the study of individual and collective life with the combined methods of psychoanalysis and history. . . . Bridgeheads must be built on each side in order to make a true span possible. But the completed bridge should permit unimpeded two-way traffic; and once this is done, history will be simply history again, but now a history aware of the fact that it has always indulged in a covert and circuitous traffic with psychology which can now be direct, overt, and aware. By the same token, psychoanalysis will have become conscious of its own historical determinants, and *case history* and *life history* will no longer be manners of speaking. (Erikson, 1974, p. 13)

Psychobiography Erikson made a major contribution to historical research by applying the methods used in psychoanalytic case histories to a reconstruction of the life of historical figures. He combined clinical insight with historical and social analysis in developing the new form of **psychobiography.** Erikson realized that in making the transition from case history to life history, the psychoanalyst must broaden his or her concerns and take into account the subject's activities in the context of the opportunities and limitations of the outside world. This appreciation of the interaction of psychological and social currents in turn affected Erikson's theoretical work. In addition to his books on Martin Luther and Mohandas Gandhi, Erikson's psychobiographies included studies of Maxim Gorky, Adolf Hitler, George Bernard Shaw, Sigmund Freud, Thomas Jefferson, and Woodrow Wilson.

There is one major difference between psychological biographies and case histories. In a case history, the therapist usually tries to understand why the patient has developed mental or emotional problems. In a life history, the investigator tries to understand the subject's creative contributions, which are often made in spite of conflicts, complexes, and crises.

The Study of "Great Individuals" In his psychobiographical work, Erikson brought the insights of a trained psychoanalyst to the careful study of critical periods in the lives of influential individuals. He was particularly interested in men and women whose identity conflicts mirrored the conflicts of their era and whose greatness lay in their finding a personal solution to their own identity crisis, a solution that became a model for others. Often they were individuals who had deep personal struggles. The crisis of the age seemed to be intensified in each of them; each brought a special urgency and focus to the solution of the crisis.

And then, there are the great adults who are adult and are called great precisely because their sense of identity vastly surpasses the roles foisted upon them, their vision opens up new realities, and the gift of communication revitalizes actuality. (Erikson, 1987, p. 335)

In his first major psychobiography, Erikson laid out his fundamental approach to the study of great men and women. To Erickson, Luther should be admired most for his struggle "to lift his individual patienthood to the level of a universal one and to try to solve for all what he could not solve for himself alone" (Erikson, 1958, p. 67).

In studying Gandhi, Erikson returned, in a sense, to his early reverence for Freud. He felt that Gandhi and Freud both sought to liberate others, that both men created new social forms, new roles and identities, and both were deeply motivated by their love of truth.

Although they all were creative, energetic, and powerful people, they were not without fear, anxiety, and unhappiness. Their lives were often dominated by a sense, stemming from childhood, that they needed to *settle* or *live down* something. They were generally tied to their fathers in a way that precluded overt rebellion; they also learned a great deal from and felt needed and chosen by their fathers. These individuals frequently had early, highly developed consciences and paid early attention to ultimate values, sometimes convinced they carried special responsibility for part of humankind. These productive men and women might have simply become misfits and cranks except for their ability, energy, concentration, and spiritual devotion.

Dynamics

Positive Growth

The focus on positive characteristics developed at each stage distinguishes Erikson's schema from Freud's and from those of many other personality theorists. Erikson views basic strengths, or virtues, as more than psychological defenses against mental illness or negativity and more than simply as attitudes of nobility or morality. These virtues are *inherent* strengths and are characterized by a sense of potency and positive development. As mentioned earlier in the chapter, *hope* is the virtue of the first stage, trust versus mistrust. *Will* is the strength that arises from the crisis of autonomy versus shame and doubt. *Purpose* is rooted in the initiative versus guilt stage. *Competence* is the strength resulting from the stage of industry versus inferiority. *Fidelity* comes from identity versus identity confusion. *Love* is the virtue that develops from intimacy. *Care* originates in generativity. *Wisdom* is derived from the crisis of integrity versus despair.

Obstacles to Growth

The individual can successfully resolve the crisis at each stage, or leave the crisis unresolved in some ways. Erikson points out that successful resolution is always a dynamic balance of some sort. A clear example of an unsuccessful resolution is the formation of a sense of negative identity.

Ratio and Balance At each stage there is a dynamic ratio between two poles. Erikson's terms for these opposite poles tend to be misleading because, inevitably, one seems extremely desirable and the other extremely undesirable. However, both poles at each stage are *undesirable* from the very fact that they are extreme, as Figure 7.1 shows.

Erikson has been frequently misunderstood as advocating only the positive pole for each stage. He has pointed out that "people often take away mistrust

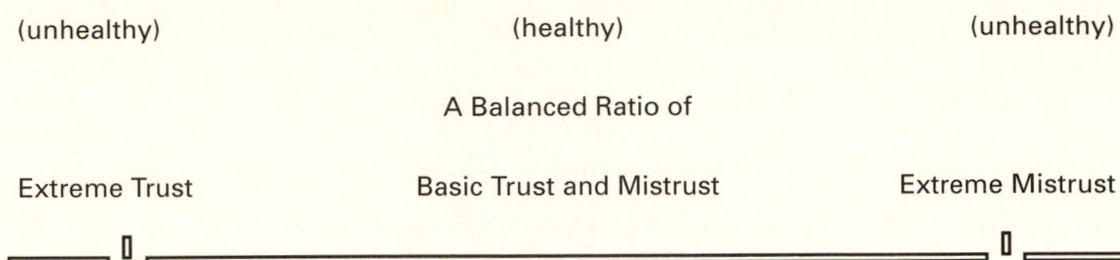

FIGURE 7.1 Balanced Ratio in Erickson's Stages

and doubt and shame and all of these not so nice, 'negative' things and try to make an Eriksonian achievement scale out of it all, according to which in the first stage trust is 'achieved' " (Erikson in Evans, 1969, p. 15). However, an individual who develops an unbalanced sense of trust can become a Pollyanna, as out of touch with reality as the individual paralyzed with extreme mistrust. We must be able to discriminate between situations in which we can trust and those in which some mistrust, or anticipation of danger or discomfort, is appropriate. Healthy ratios vary widely from relative trust to relative suspicion, but in every case elements of both trust and mistrust are present.

Similarly, unbalanced autonomy can become unreasonable stubbornness. Unbalanced initiative is a self-centered preoccupation with one's own goals and concerns. A sense of industry without a sense of limitation leads to an inflated appreciation of one's abilities. An overdeveloped sense of identity is rigid and inflexible and is likely to clash with external reality, and so on.

Negative Identity Our sense of identity always comprises positive and negative elements. These elements include things we want to become and others we do not want to be or know we should not be. Under extremely negative social conditions, it may be impossible for the majority of healthy young men and women to become committed to anything positive and large scale. The Nazi era in Germany is an example.

Lack of a healthy sense of identity may be expressed in hostility toward available social goals and values. This hostility can include any role aspect: one's sexuality, nationality, class, or family background. Children of immigrant families may display contempt for their parents' backgrounds, and descendants of established families may reject everything American and overestimate everything foreign.

Many conflicted adolescents would rather be someone bad than a nobody. Thus the choice of a negative identity is based on those roles that have been presented as undesirable or dangerous. If the adolescent feels unable to make a commitment to more positive roles, the negative ones become the most real. These may include the drug dealer, prostitute, or any model that represents failure in the eyes of society.

Structure

Body

Experience is anchored in the ground-plan of the body. (Erikson, 1963, p. 108)

The role of the bodily organs is especially important in Erikson's early stages. Later in life, the development of physical as well as intellectual skills helps determine whether the individual will achieve a sense of competence and an ability to choose demanding roles in a complex society. For example, healthy children derive a sense of competence as their bodies becomes larger, stronger, faster, and more capable of learning complex skills.

As a psychosocial theorist, Erikson is aware of the constant interaction of body, psychological processes, and social forces. He acknowledges the classical Freudian view of biological drives as fundamental but insists that these drives are also socially modifiable.

Social Relationships

A stage has a new configuration of past and future, a new combination of drive and defense, a new set of capacities fit for a new setting of tasks and opportunities, a new and wider radius of significant encounters. (Erikson, 1964, p. 166)

Erikson's basic epigenetic principle states, "Personality . . . can be said to develop according to steps predetermined in the human organism's readiness to be driven toward, to be aware of, and to interact with a widening radius of significant individuals and institutions" (1968, pp. 92–93).

Social relationships are central in virtually every stage of development. Interaction with one's parents, family, and peers is crucial in the first five stages. The emergence of a sense of identity is strongly affected by the presence of affirming peers. The stage of intimacy brings opportunities for deeper social relationships. Another qualitative change occurs during the stage of generativity, when individuals learn to care for and nurture those who are younger, weaker, and less knowledgeable.

Will

Erikson details the development of will in his discussion of autonomy versus shame and doubt. The development of a healthy and balanced will (and goodwill) continues throughout life. Crucial to the attainment of a healthy sense of identity is the belief that "I am what I can *will* freely."

Traditional psychoanalysis deals primarily with the examination of an individual's conception of reality, focusing on thoughts, emotions, and essentially private behavior. Erikson emphasizes, in addition, the importance of will and action in the world. One of the goals of psychoanalysis is to restore "a productive interplay between psychological reality and historical actuality" (1964, p. 201)—that is, to integrate inner, subjective experiences with external actions and events. According to Erikson, reality refers to "the world of phenomenal experience, perceived with a minimum of distortion." Although distortion and misunderstanding are inevitable, Erikson stresses the need for an understanding of actuality, "the world of participation, shared with other participants" (1964, p. 165).

Reassessing Freud's classic case study of Dora, Erikson points out that although Freud made a brilliant analysis of Dora's personality dynamics and distortions, he failed to consider her powerlessness as a young girl in a middle-class Viennese family. Dora initially saw Freud for three months, when she was 19 years old. She had been propositioned at the age of 16 by Mr. K, a friend of the family. Her father had asked Freud to "bring her to reason." It turned out that Dora's father was having an affair with Mr. K's wife, and he seemed willing to allow Mr. K's advances to his daughter. To further complicate matters, everyone seemed to make Dora a confidante—her father and mother, Mr. K. and Mrs. K.

Dora tried to confront her parents with the situation. Freud saw this as acting out, but Erikson disagrees. To him, Dora was actively searching for honesty and fidelity, qualities that the adult role models in her life sorely lacked.

Successful action requires both social and historical possibilities and will. To see accurately does not guarantee that one can act effectively.

Emotions

As a psychoanalyst, Erikson stresses the emotional component of psychological processes. His awareness of the role emotions play is implicit throughout his theories. As a theorist, he focused on incorporating new cognitive, historical, and social findings into a psychoanalytic framework. However, Erikson does not discuss explicitly the emotions as a distinct aspect of psychological processes.

Intellect

Like emotion, the intellect is seen as an essential element in psychological processes. Erikson does not pay specific attention to the role of intellectual capacities. He does point out, however, that the development of intellectual skills is critical in the formation of a sense of competence, if the individual is to master the tasks of a technological society, form a sense of identity, and choose an acceptable vocation and social roles.

Self

For Erikson, sense of identity includes both the development of ego identity and the flowering of a sense of self:

> The ego, if understood as a central and partially unconscious organizing agency, must at any given stage of life deal with a changing Self. . . . What could consequently be called the *self-identity* emerges from experiences in which temporarily confused selves are successfully reintegrated in an ensemble of roles which also secure social recognition. Identity formation, thus, can be said to have a self-aspect and an ego aspect. (1968, p. 211)

Self-identity results from the integration of our past and present social roles and self-images.

Therapist

Psychoanalysis is the first systematic and active "consciousness-expansion," and such expansion may be necessary as man concentrates on the conquest of matter and is apt to overidentify with it. (Erikson in Evans, 1969, p. 98)

Erickson has pointed out that a competent therapist has a strong sense of the patient's potential for growth and development. The therapist's job is to foster that growth rather than impose his or her own future expectations or past experience on the patient. This focus is implicit in the requirement that the practitioner undergo training analysis and in the stress on the role of *transference* and *countertransference* in psychoanalysis. Transference refers to the positive or negative feelings that patients develop for their therapists. These feelings are often strong, irrational, and rooted in childhood relationships with parents. Conscious understanding of the dynamics of transference can be an extremely valuable part of psychotherapy. Countertransference refers to the positive or negative feelings that therapists frequently develop for their patients. Jung had said that every patient who came to him took his life in his own hands. In response, Erikson commented, "This is true, but one must add that he came to *me,* and not to somebody else, and after that he will never be the same—and neither will I" (Erikson in Evans, 1969, p. 103).

Erikson reformulated the Golden Rule in light of modern psychological understanding. He writes that truly worthwhile, moral acts strengthen the doer even as they strengthen the other, and enhance the relationship between the two individuals. In therapy, this version of the Golden Rule implies that the therapist will

> *develop as a practitioner and as a person, even as the patient is cured as a patient and as a person.* For a real cure transcends the transitory state of patienthood. It is an experience which enables the cured patient to develop and to transmit to home and neighborhood an attitude toward health, which is one of the most essential ingredients of an ethical outlook. (Erikson, 1964, pp. 236–237, emphasis his)

Every therapist must be prepared to understand and identify with a variety of alternative lifestyles. Issues of values and morality are central to therapy. The notion of the impersonality of the classical analyst is, according to Erikson, a misunderstanding of the role of impartial acceptance of the patient's free associations and past history. The therapist is always there as an individual, with the freedom to express whatever he or she wishes, ideally without distortion from irrational countertransference.

Evaluation

Erikson has been criticized for his vagueness. He is an artist with words rather than a logician. His beautiful and brilliant formulations can appear to dissolve into conceptual sketches rather than develop into linear, logical analysis. For example, Erikson's discussion of identity consists of a diverse collection of ideas that are often more confusing than clarifying. As one reviewer has commented,

> Reading Erikson is like walking in a dense and beautiful forest with a thousand paths leading through it. The very richness of the forest can be con-

> fusing. There is so much there. . . . Erikson has never watered down or simplified his writing. Thank God! They [his books] are written with a kind of magnificent obscurity. . . . His work needs to be read and reread; his books need to be outlined and meditated on. They have a lasting quality. (Gross, 1987, p. 3)

On the other hand, Hamachek pointed out that "most of Erikson's conclusions are based on highly personal and subjective interpretations that lack the hard empirical data to support intuitions about their correctness" (1988, p. 36). Hamachek (1988, 1990) attempted to connect each of Erikson's stages to observable behaviors, as a first step in developing the empirical study of Erikson's theory.

Other critics (for example, Appadurai, 1978; Roazen, 1976) raised questions about the universality of Erikson's theories. Can his epigenetic model be applied as successfully to non-Western cultures both past and present? For example, viewing adolescence as a distinct developmental stage is a relatively new phenomenon. Also, issues like autonomy, initiative, and identity may not be central in cultures such as those in India or in tribal societies.

Other questions have been raised about the applicability of Erikson's developmental model even in the West. For example, Erikson proposes that generativity begins with parenthood. That this is not necessarily true is proven by teenage pregnancy. Young mothers and fathers, as yet uneducated in the responsibilities of generativity, are often dragged kicking and screaming into parenthood. Also, Erikson's work has been criticized as being focused primarily on the male, and relatively unclear about the particular issues of female maturation (Gilligan, 1982).

Erikson was limited by psychoanalysis. His tools are those of a clinician, intended for the treatment of unwell patients. Application of these tools to the exploration of the healthy personality is not always satisfactory. This drawback is evident in Erikson's studies of great individuals. In his analysis of Gandhi, for example, Erikson skillfully applies the tools and insights of the psychoanalyst. He does not, however, address seriously the role of Gandhi's spiritual ideals and spiritual discipline. The dynamics of Gandhi's life and thought are seen largely in terms of dysfunction rather than of psychological and spiritual transformation. Gandhi's inner state may have been qualitatively different from that of the average patient in therapy. Also, Erikson has been criticized for underestimating the role of Indian culture and the social context of many of the key events in Gandhi's life (Appadurai, 1978).

Erikson's psychoanalytic tools were not always adequate for the tasks he took on. By using these tools, he expanded psychoanalysis while at the same time revealing its limitations. In a sense, Erikson smuggled the concept of the human spirit into psychoanalytic theory. This is one of the secrets of his great appeal.

Erikson provides a stimulating, relevant reformulation of psychoanalysis. He successfully brought Freud's compelling system of thought into a new era. Erikson's concern for social and cultural determinants of behavior and his integration of psychology, sociology, and anthropology with the insights of psychoanalysis predict the future of the psychology of personality.

The Theory Firsthand

Excerpts from *Childhood and Society*

In this passage, Erikson, revealing his keen psychoanalytic skills, provides a real-life example of a young boy in a crisis of role identification.

During the last war a neighbor of mine, a boy of five, underwent a change of personality from a "mother's boy" to a violent, stubborn, and disobedient child. The most disquieting symptom was an urge to set fires.

The boy's parents had separated just before the outbreak of war. The mother and the boy had moved in with some women cousins, and when war began the father had joined the air force. The women cousins frequently expressed their disrespect for the father, and cultivated babyish traits in the boy. Thus, to be a mother's boy threatened to be a stronger identity element than to be a father's son.

The father, however, did well in war; in fact, he became a hero. On the occasion of his first furlough the little boy had the experience of seeing the man he had been warned not to emulate become the much-admired center of the neighborhood's attention. The mother announced that she would drop her divorce plans. The father went back to war and was soon lost over Germany.

After the father's departure and death the affectionate and dependent boy developed more and more disquieting symptoms of destructiveness and defiance, culminating in fire setting. He gave the key to the change himself when, protesting against his mother's whipping, he pointed to a pile of wood he had set afire and exclaimed (in more childish words), "If this were a German city, you would have liked me for it." He thus indicated that in setting fires he fantasied being a bombardier like the father, who had told of his exploits.

We can only guess at the nature of the boy's turmoil. But I believe that we see here the identification of a son with his father, resulting from a suddenly increased conflict at the very close of the Oedipus age. The father, at first successfully replaced by the "good" little boy, suddenly becomes both a newly vitalized ideal and a concrete threat, a competitor for the mother's love. He thus devaluates radically the boy's feminine identifications. In order to save himself from both sexual and social disorientation, the boy must, in the shortest possible time, regroup his identifications; but then the great competitor is killed by the enemy—a fact which increases the guilt for the competitive feeling itself and compromises the boy's new masculine initiative which becomes maladaptive.

A child has quite a number of opportunities to identify himself, more or less experimentally, with habits, traits, occupations, and ideas of real or fictitious people of either sex. Certain crises force him to make radical selections. However, the historical era in which he lives offers only a limited number of socially meaningful models for workable combinations of identification fragments. Their usefulness depends on the way in which they simultaneously meet the requirements of the organism's maturational stage and the ego's habits of synthesis.

To my little neighbor the role of the bombardier may have suggested a possible synthesis of the various elements that comprise a budding identity: his temperament (vigorous); his maturational stage (phallic-urethral-locomotor); his social stage (Oedipal) and his social situation; his capacities (muscular, mechanical); his father's temperament (a great soldier rather than a successful civilian); and a current historical prototype (aggressive hero). Where such synthesis succeeds, a most surprising coagulation of constitutional, temperamental, and learned reactions may produce exuberance of growth and unexpected accomplishment. Where it fails, it must lead to severe conflict, often expressed in unexpected naughtiness or delinquency. For should a child feel that the environment tries to deprive him too radically of all the forms of expression which permit him to develop and to integrate the next step in his identity, he will defend it with the astonishing strength encountered in animals who are suddenly forced to defend their lives. And indeed, in the social jungle of human existence, there is no feeling of being alive without a sense of ego identity. Deprivation of identity can lead to murder.

I would not have dared to speculate on the little bombardier's conflicts had I not seen evidence for a solution in line with our interpretation. When the worst of this boy's dangerous initiative had subsided, he was observed swooping down a hill on a bicycle, endangering, scaring, and yet deftly avoiding other children. They shrieked, laughed, and in a way admired him for it. In watching him, and hearing the strange noises he made, I could not help thinking that he again imagined himself to be an airplane on a bombing mission. But at the same time he gained in playful mastery over his locomotion; he exercised circumspection in his attack, and he became an admired virtuoso on a bicycle. . . .

Our little son of a bombardier illustrates a general point. Psychosocial identity develops out of a gradual integration of all identifications. But here, if anywhere, the whole has a different quality from the sum of its parts. Under favorable circumstances children have the nucleus of a separate identity early in life; often they must defend it even against the necessity of overidentifying with one or both of their parents. These processes are difficult to study in patients, because the neurotic self has, by definition, fallen prey to overidentifications which isolate the small individual both from his budding identity and from his milieu. (Erikson, 1963, pp. 238–241)

Chapter Highlights

- Erikson's model of the human life cycle integrates human growth and development from birth to old age, in eight stages.
- Positive and negative outcomes may occur at each stage. Personality development continues throughout life.
- Each successive stage is predicated on the development of the previous one; the process occurs in a manner similar to that of the growth of an embryo.
- The human personality develops according to predetermined steps, or stages, in the growing person's readiness to be aware of, and interact with, a widening social radius. Each stage is related systematically to the others and must develop in the sequence given.
- A specific psychological crisis or developmental task characterizes each stage and must be resolved in order for the individual to continue to the next.
- The strengths and skills essential to each stage are developed and tested in a period of crisis. This process, in turn, allows for the development of new attitudes and skills. Following the successful resolution of each cri-

sis, an increased sense of judgment, inner unity, and capacity to function effectively is available to the individual.

- Erikson's model is distinguished by his focus on the positive attributes, or virtues, that are acquired at each stage. Characterized by a sense of positive development and potency, these virtues are considered inherent strengths.
- Each stage holds a dynamic ratio between two poles, e.g., trust versus mistrust. Both poles are extremes, and the healthy middle ground lies in the space between these two, where elements of each pole are dynamically present.
- The concept of identity brings together theories of cognitive and ego psychologies. Some aspects of identity include a sense of individuality, a sense of continuity and sameness, a sense of synthesis and wholeness, and a sense of social solidarity.
- The development and flowering of a sense of self results in a sense of identity.
- Lack of a healthy sense of identity may result in hostility toward available values and social goals. A conflicted adolescent who feels unable to commit to a positive social role may choose a negative role instead.
- The sense that "I am what I can *will* freely" is crucial to the development of a healthy sense of identity.
- Psychobiography and psychohistory combine the methods of psychoanalysis and history in the study of individual and collective life.

Key Concepts

Autonomy versus shame and doubt The second stage, in which the child interacts with the world in new ways and a sense of autonomy develops with the sense of free choice. The virtue acquired at this stage is *will,* which develops into the basis for adult acknowledgment of a spirit of justice, manifest in the social institution of the law.

Basic trust versus basic mistrust The first stage, in which an infant's sense of trust in self and in the world develops from the quality of primary care. It results in the virtue or strength of *hope,* which lays the foundation for the development of faith.

Crisis in development The turning point, occurring at each stage of development, in which the skills and strengths of that stage are developed and tested.

Generativity versus stagnation The seventh stage, including concerns with creativity and productivity in work and in personal life, for children as well as for ideas, products, and principles. *Care* is the strength developed at this stage.

Identity A term that includes a sense of individuality, a sense of continuity and sameness, a sense of synthesis and wholeness, and a sense of social solidarity. The concept has both social and psychological aspects.

Identity crisis The loss of ego identity—a state in which the continuity, sameness, and belief in one's social role has diminished or disappeared.

Identity versus identity confusion The fifth stage, a time when the adolescent questions past role models and identifications. During this period of transition between childhood and adulthood, the question of "Who am I?" is primary. *Fidelity* is the basic strength of this stage, as the individual faces the need to commit to a set of values and a career, forming a cornerstone of his or her identity.

Industry versus inferiority The fourth stage, involving a shift from focus on play to a sense of work. The virtue of this stage is *competence,* based on the development of practical skills, general capacities, and a sense of workmanship.

Initiative versus guilt The third stage, in which the most basic activity is play. The virtue of this stage, *purpose,* is rooted in fantasy and play, which form the roots of drama, dance, and ritual in adult life.

Integrity versus despair The eighth stage. A time of dealing with ultimate concerns. Development of the ability to see one's life as a whole and an increased sense of perspective. Despair may result if one has not attained some sense of self-acceptance. *Wisdom* is the strength which develops out of encounters with both despair and integrity, in the light of ultimate concerns.

Intimacy versus isolation The sixth stage, in which a sense of adult responsibility develops, along with independence from parents and school. Intimate relationships with others are established. True mutuality with a love partner forms the basis for the critical commitment that generally occurs at this stage. *Love* is the virtue that is associated with this stage; it manifests itself in true intimacy and mutuality.

Psychobiography The study of the life of a historical figure from the perspective of psychoanalysis. This approach differs from a case history, in which the therapist is looking for why the patient developed problems. The life history focuses on understanding how a person managed to make creative contributions, often in spite of complexes, conflicts, and crises.

Psychohistory A study that combines the methods of history and psychoanalysis to examine individual and collective life.

Annotated Bibliography

Erikson, E. (1963). *Childhood and society* (2nd ed.). New York: Norton.

Erikson's first and most seminal book. It includes his most detailed description of the eight stages of human development, papers on his work with the Sioux and Yurok, and psychobiographies of Hitler and Gorky, which provide a look at the psychological implications of German and Russian culture.

———. (1964). *Insight and responsibility.* New York: Norton.

A brilliant set of essays, including a psychobiographical look at Freud, an analysis of psychosocial strengths, psychological reality, and historical actuality, and a discussion of the Golden Rule today.

———. (1969). *Gandhi's truth.* New York: Norton.

An epic psychobiography of Gandhi, which provides a model for looking at a great figure in history through psychological eyes. It also serves as a useful example of the limits of psychoanalysis, in its lack of focus on the spiritual and transpersonal aspects of Gandhi's life.

Erikson, E., Erikson, J., & Kivnick, H. (1986). *Vital involvement in old age.* New York: Norton.

A remarkable portrait of the experience of old age, based on interviews with octogenarians who have been studied for over 50 years. A review of the life cycle from the perspective of old age.

References

Appadurai, A. (1978). Understanding Gandhi. In P. Homans (Ed.), *Childhood and selfhood.* Cranbury, NJ: Associated University Presses.

Coles, R. (1970). *Erik Erikson: The growth of his work.* Boston: Little, Brown.

Cote, J., & Levine, C. (1987). A formulation of Erikson's theory of ego identity formation. *Developmental Review, 7,* 273–325.

Erikson, E. (1958). *Young man Luther.* New York: Norton.

———. (1963). *Childhood and society* (2nd ed.). New York: Norton.

———. (1964). *Insight and responsibility.* New York: Norton.

———. (1965). *The challenge of youth.* New York: Doubleday Anchor Books.

———. (1968). *Identity, youth and crisis.* New York: Norton.

———. (1969). *Gandhi's truth.* New York: Norton.

———. (1974). *Dimensions of a new identity.* New York: Norton.

———. (1975). *Life history and the historical moment.* New York: Norton.

———. (1977). *Toys and reasons.* New York: Norton.

———. (1978). *Adulthood.* New York: Norton.

———. (1979) Report to Vikram. In S. Kakar (Ed.), *Identity and adulthood.* Delhi, India: Oxford University Press.

———. (1980a). *Identity and the life cycle.* New York: Norton.

———. (1980b). *On the generational cycle: An address.* New York: Norton.

———. (1981). *The Galilean sayings and the sense of "I."* New York: Norton.

———. (1982). *The life cycle completed.* New York: Norton.

———. (1983). Reflections: On the relationship of adolescence and parenthood. *Adolescent Psychiatry,* 2, 9–13.

———. (1985). Reflections on the last stage—and the first. *The Psychoanalytic Study of the Child,* 39.

———. (1987). *A way of looking at things: Selected papers from 1930 to 1980.* New York: Norton.

———. (1993). The problem of ego identity. In G. Pollock (Ed.), *Pivotal papers on identification.* Madison, CT: International Universities Press.

Erikson, E., Erikson, J., & Kivnick, H. (1986). *Vital involvement in old age.* New York: Norton.

Evans, R. (1969). *Dialogue with Erik Erikson.* New York: Dutton.

Gilligan, C. (1982). *In a different voice.* Cambridge, MA: Harvard University Press.

Gross, F. (1987). *Introducing Erik Erikson: An invitation to his thinking.* Lanham, MD: University Press.

Hamachek, D. (1988). Evaluating self-concept and ego development within Erikson's psychosocial framework: A formulation. *Journal of Counseling and Development, 66,* 354–360.

———. (1990). Evaluating self-concept and ego development in Erikson's last three psychosocial stages. *Journal of Counseling and Development, 68,* 677–683.

Homans, P. (Ed.). (1978). *Childhood and selfhood: Essays on tradition, religion, and modernity in the psychology of Erik Erikson.* Cranbury, NJ: Associated University Presses.

Levene, M. (1990). Female adolescent development: Reflections upon relational growth. *Melanie-Klein-and-Object-Relations, 8,* 31–42.

Roazen, P. (1976). *Erik Erikson: The power and limits of a vision.* New York: Free Press.

Sheehy, G. (1977). *Passages.* New York: Basic Books.

———. (1995). *New passages.* New York: Ballantine.

Weiland, S. (1994). Erik Erikson: Ages, stages, and stories. In D. Shenk & W. Achenbaum (Eds.), *Changing perceptions of aging and the aged.* New York: Springer.

CHAPTER 8

Wilhelm Reich and Somatic Psychology

> The body's life is the life of sensations and emotions. The body feels real hunger, real joy in the sun or the snow, . . . real anger, real sorrow, real tenderness, real warmth, real passion, real hate, real grief. All the emotions belong to the body and are only recognized by the mind. (D. H. Lawrence, 1955)

Reich, perhaps more consistently than anyone else, worked out the critical and revolutionary implications of psychoanalytic theory. (Robinson, 1969, p. 10)

In this chapter, we will discuss the work of Wilhelm Reich, the founder of what might be called *somatic psychology* and *body-oriented psychotherapy*. He is the godfather of all current therapies that work with the emotional life of the body.

Wilhelm Reich was a member of the psychoanalytic inner circle in Vienna and led the technical training seminar for young analysts. In his therapeutic work, Reich gradually came to emphasize the importance of dealing with the physical manifestations of an individual's character, especially the patterns of chronic muscle tension that he called **body armor.** He was also concerned with the role of society in creating instinctual—especially sexual—inhibitions in the individual.

Reich's unique contributions to psychology include (1) his insistence on the unity of mind and body, (2) his inclusion of the body in psychotherapy, and (3) his concept of *character armor*. Each patient, Reich believed, should be approached as an *organism,* whose emotional difficulties could be explained only upon consideration of the total being. Reich was also a pioneer in sex education and hygiene, in the psychology of politics and social responsibility, and in the interfacing of psychology, biology, and physics. Reich was a courageous and stubborn innovator whose ideas were far ahead of the time.

Personal History

Wilhelm Reich was born on March 24, 1897, in Galicia, a German-Ukrainian area in Austria. He was the son of a middle-class Jewish farmer, a jealous, authoritarian man who dominated his wife and children. The father provided no religious upbringing for his children and insisted that only German be spoken at home. Consequently, Wilhelm was isolated from both the local Ukrainian peasant children and the Yiddish-speaking Jewish children. He had one brother, three years his junior, who was both companion and competitor.

Reich idolized his mother. She committed suicide when he was 14 years old, apparently after Reich revealed to his father that she was having an affair with the boys' tutor. Reich's father was devastated by his wife's death. He contracted pneumonia that developed into tuberculosis and died three years later. Reich's brother also died of tuberculosis, at the age of 26. Reich was severely affected by this series of family tragedies.

After his father's death, Reich managed the family farm but continued his studies. In 1916, when war spread throughout his homeland, the family property was destroyed. Reich joined the Austrian army. He fought as an officer in Italy. In 1918, Reich entered medical school at the University of Vienna. Within a year he became a practicing member of the Vienna Psychoanalytical Society. He received his medical degree in 1922, at the age of 25.

Reich was involved in politics as a student and subsequently sought to reconcile the theories of Freud and Marx. At the university Reich met a medical student, Annie Pink, who became his patient and later his first wife; she then became a psychoanalyst herself (Reich, 1990).

In 1922, when Freud established a psychoanalytic clinic in Vienna, Reich was his first clinical assistant and subsequently vice director. In 1924, Reich became the director of the Seminar for Psychoanalytic Therapy, the first training institute for psychoanalysts. Many young analysts came to him for personal analysis as well as for training. In 1927, as a result of his interest in social change, Reich reduced his individual treatments as he became more involved in political-community activities. Freud encouraged him to do so (Mann & Hoffman, 1980).

Reich underwent personal analysis at different times with several different psychoanalysts, but for various reasons he broke off from each one. In 1927, Reich sought analysis with Freud, who refused to make an exception to his policy of not treating members of the psychoanalytic inner circle. At this time, Reich developed a serious conflict with Freud. It stemmed partly from Freud's refusal to analyze Reich and partly from their theoretical differences. Freud was at odds with Reich's uncompromising insistence that neurosis was rooted in sexual dissatisfaction. Reich developed tuberculosis at this time and spent several months recovering in a sanitarium in Switzerland.

[W]here and how is the patient to express his natural sexuality when it has been liberated from repression? Freud neither alluded to nor, as it later turned out, even tolerated this question. And, eventually, because he refused to deal with this central question, Freud himself created enormous difficulties by postulating a biological striving for suffering and death. (Reich, 1973, p. 152)

When he returned to Vienna after his illness, Reich assumed his previous duties. He also became extremely active politically and, in 1928, joined the Communist Party. The following year Reich helped found the first sex hygiene clinics for workers, which provided free information on birth control, child rearing, and sex education.

In 1930 Reich moved to Berlin, mainly because he sought personal analysis with Sandor Rado, a leading psychoanalyst. He found an analyst outside Vienna because Viennese psychoanalysts had grown uncomfortable with his political activities. In Berlin, Reich became more deeply involved in the communist-oriented hygiene movement. He traveled throughout Germany, lecturing and helping to establish hygiene centers.

Before long, as a result of his politics, on the one hand, and his radical sex education programs, on the other, Reich was unpopular with both the psychoanalysts and the Communists. In 1933 Reich was expelled from the German Communist Party. Then, in 1934, he was expelled from the International Psychoanalytical Association.

[T]he life process is identical with the sexual process—an experimentally proven fact. . . . In everything living, sexual vegetative energy is at work. (Reich, 1961, p. 55)

After Hitler's rise to power, Reich emigrated to Denmark in 1933. He separated from his wife when they left Berlin, because of personal, political, and professional differences. A year earlier, Reich had met Elsa Lindenberg, a ballet dancer and a member of his Communist Party cell. She joined Reich in Denmark, where they were married. His controversial theories led to his expulsion from Denmark and Sweden.

Within a period of six months, Reich had been expelled from his two major affiliations—the Communist Party and the psychoanalytic movement—and from three countries. It is not surprising that his subsequent writing is somewhat defensive and polemical. In Reich's case, a certain amount of paranoia was not irrational or unjustified but represented a fairly realistic assessment of his situation.

Later in his career, Reich rejected communism and socialism, because he felt that both were committed to an ideology at the expense of human considerations. He came to think of himself more as an individualist and was deeply suspicious of politics and politicians.

5. Training of doctors, teachers, and others in all relevant matters of sexual hygiene.
6. Treatment of, rather than punishment for, sexual offenses.

Reich stressed the free expression of sexual and emotional feelings within a mature, loving relationship. He emphasized the essentially sexual nature of the energies with which he dealt, and he found that the pelvic area of his patients was the most blocked. For Reich, the goal of therapy was to free all the blocks in the body, to enable the patient to attain full capacity for orgasm, which he felt was blocked in most people.

Reich's radical views concerning sexuality resulted in misunderstanding, distortion, and vicious (and unfounded) attacks on all areas of his work, as well as on him personally.

Character

The "how" . . . the form of the behavior and of the communications, was far more important than what the patient told the analyst. Words can lie. The expression never lies. (Reich, 1973, p. 171)

The concept of character was first discussed by Freud in 1908. Reich elaborated on this concept: he was the first analyst to treat patients by interpreting the nature and function of their character, not their symptoms.

According to Reich, the character is composed of a person's habitual attitudes and pattern of responses to various situations. It includes psychological attitudes and values, style of behavior (shyness, aggressiveness, and so forth), and physical attitudes (posture, habits of holding and moving the body). Reichian character analysis continues to be an important tool in psychotherapy (Josephs, 1995).

The patient's behavior (manner, look, language, countenance, dress, handshake, etc.) not only is vastly underestimated in terms of its analytic importance but is usually completely overlooked. (Reich, 1976, p. 34)

Character Armor Reich felt that the character structure forms as a defense against the child's anxiety over intense sexual feelings and the accompanying fear of punishment. The first defense is repression, which temporarily restrains the sexual impulses. As ego defenses become chronically active and automatic, they develop into stable character traits that combine to form the individual's system of character armoring. **Character armor** includes all repressing defensive forces, which form a coherent pattern within the ego.

Character traits are not neurotic symptoms. The difference, according to Reich, lies in the fact that neurotic symptoms (such as irrational fears or phobias) are experienced as alien to the individual, as foreign elements in the psyche, whereas neurotic character traits (extreme orderliness or anxious shyness, for example) are experienced as integral parts of the personality. One may complain about being shy, but this shyness does not seem to be meaningless or pathological, as are neurotic symptoms. The character defenses are difficult to eradicate because they are well rationalized by the individual and experienced as part of the individual's self-concept.

A conflict which is fought out at a certain age always leaves behind a trace in the person's character . . . revealed as a hardening of the character. (Reich, 1973, p. 145)

Reich continually attempted to make his patients more aware of their character traits. He frequently imitated their characteristic gestures (a nervous smile, for example) and postures, or had patients themselves repeat and exaggerate them. As patients ceased taking their character makeups for granted, their motivation to change was enhanced.

Genital Character Freud used the term *genital character* to refer to the final level of psychosexual development. Reich applied the term to persons with **or-**

Personal Reflection

■ Body Awareness

Early in his career, Reich stressed the importance of awareness of our habitual postures and styles of moving. Do not move or shift your posture as you continue to read this.

You are probably either sitting or lying down right now. Are you aware of how you are holding the book, of the way your fingers and your arms are taking the weight of the book? How are you sitting or lying? Is the weight of your body more on one side than the other? How are you holding your arms? Is there excess tension in your chest, shoulders, and forearms, or throughout your body?

Do you feel that you want to shift to a more comfortable position? Shift now, and notice the changes you are experiencing. How does this new position feel? How long do you think you held your former, less comfortable, position?

Your habits of using your body are probably not as efficient or effective as they could be. Because of these habits and our lack of body awareness, we tend to sit and move in ways that are less than optimally comfortable or useful. It is not until we get back in touch with our own bodies that we can recognize this.

gastic potency: "Orgastic potency is the capacity to surrender to the flow of biological energy, free of any inhibitions; the capacity to discharge completely the dammed-up sexual excitation through involuntary, pleasurable convulsions of the body" (1973, p. 102). Reich found that as his patients relinquished their armoring and developed orgastic potency, many areas of neurotic functioning changed spontaneously. In place of rigid neurotic controls, individuals developed a capacity for *self-regulation*. Reich described self-regulated individuals as naturally rather than compulsively moral. They act in response to their own inclinations and feelings rather than following external codes or demands prescribed by others.

After Reichian therapy, many patients who had been neurotically promiscuous developed greater tenderness and spontaneously sought more lasting and fulfilling relationships. Those in loveless marriages found that they could no longer have sex with their spouses merely as a duty.

I say on the basis of ample clinical experience that only in a few cases in our civilization is the sexual act based on love. The intervening rage, hatred, sadistic emotions and contempt are part and parcel of the love life of modern man. (Reich in Rycroft, 1971, p. 81)

Individuals whom Reich viewed as genital characters were not imprisoned in their armor and psychological defenses. They were able to shield themselves, when necessary, against a hostile environment. However, they did so fairly consciously and could dispense with the armor when it was no longer needed.

Genital characters, Reich wrote, have worked through their Oedipus complex, so that the Oedipal material is no longer highly charged or repressed. The superego has become "sex-affirmative," and thus id and superego are generally in harmony (Reich, 1976). Genital characters are able to experience orgasm freely, discharging all excess libido. For them, the climax is characterized by surrender to sexuality and uninhibited, involuntary movement, as opposed to the forced or even violent movements of the armored individual.

Dynamics

Psychological Growth

It is solely our *sensation* of the natural process inside and outside ourselves, which holds the keys to the deep riddles of nature. . . . Sensation is the sieve through which all inner and outer stimuli are perceived; sensation is the connecting link between ego and outer world. (Reich, 1961, p. 275)

Reich defined growth as the process of dissolving one's psychological and physical **armoring,** gradually becoming a more free and open human being, capable of enjoying full and satisfying orgasm.

Muscular armoring, in Reich's system, is divided into seven major segments, composed of muscles and organs with related expressive functions. These segments form a series of seven roughly horizontal rings, at right angles to the spine and torso. They are centered in the eyes, mouth, neck, chest, diaphragm, abdomen, and pelvis. Reich's seven armor segments are closely related to the seven chakras of kundalini-yoga discussed in Chapter 14, although the fit is not a perfect one. It is interesting to note that Reich moves from the top down; the patient is finished once the pelvis, the most important armor segment, is opened and energized. In kundalini-yoga, the movement is from the base of the spine upward, and the yogi is "finished" once the thousand-petaled lotus of the brain, the most important chakra, is opened and energized. Boadella (1987) offers a more complete discussion of this relationship.

According to Reich, orgone energy naturally flows up and down the body, parallel to the spine. The rings of armor are formed at right angles to this flow and interrupt it. It is no accident, Reich points out, that in Western culture we have learned to say *yes* by moving our heads up and down, in the direction of energy flow in the body, whereas we say *no* by moving our heads from side to side, the direction of the armoring.

It is possible to get out of a trap. However, in order to break out of a prison, one first must confess to *being in a prison. The trap is man's emotional structure, his character structure.* There is little use in devising systems of thought about the nature of the trap if the only thing to do in order to get out of the trap is to know the trap and to find the exit. (Reich, 1961, p. 470)

Armoring restricts the flow of energy and stops the free expression of emotion. What begins as a defense against overpowering anxiety becomes a physical and emotional straitjacket.

> In armored human organisms, the orgone energy is bound in the chronic contraction of the muscles. The body orgone does not begin to flow freely as soon as the armor ring has been loosened. . . . As soon as the first armor blocks have been dissolved, the movement expressive of "surrender" appears more and more, along with the orgonotic currents and sensations. However, its full unfolding is hindered by those armor blocks that have not yet been dissolved. (Reich, 1976, pp. 411–412)

The primary goal of Reichian therapy is to dissolve the armor in each of the seven segments, beginning with the eyes and ending with the pelvis. Each segment is more or less an independent unit and must be dealt with separately (see Figure 8.1).

The spasm of the musculature is the somatic side of the process of repression, and the basis of its continued preservation. (Reich, 1973, p. 302)

Muscular Armor In Reich's system, each character attitude has a corresponding physical attitude expressed in the body as muscular rigidity or muscular armoring. Reich became aware of this connection as a result of acute observation of his patients' habitual postures and movements, combined with detailed analysis of their character structure. He examined in detail his patients' posture and physical habits. Reich would have patients concentrate on particular sources of tensions to become more aware of them and to elicit the emotion

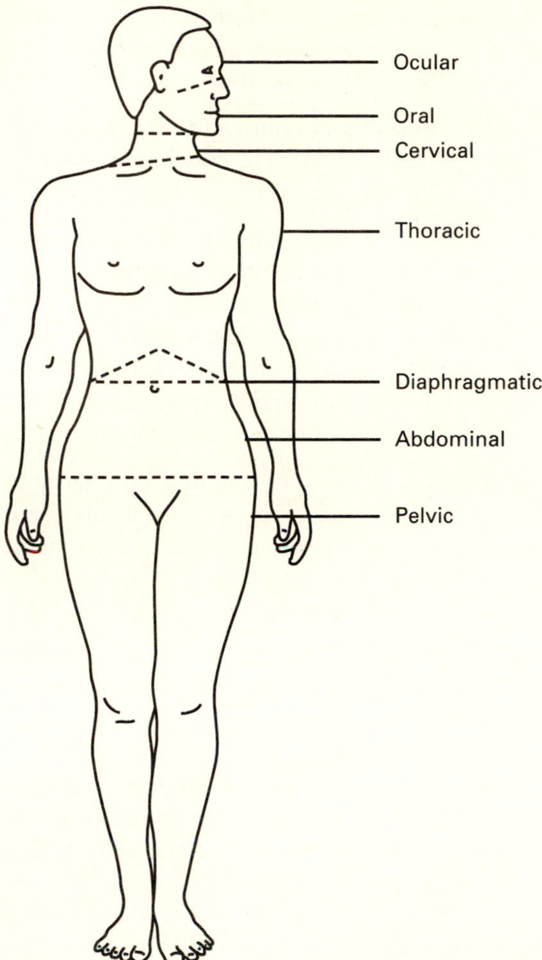

FIGURE 8.1 The Seven Segments of the Body
Source: Baker (1967), p. 71.

that had been constrained in that part of the body. Only after the bottled-up emotion was expressed, he felt, could the chronic tension be fully abandoned.

Reich began to work directly on the muscular armoring in conjunction with his therapeutic sessions. He found that loosening the muscular armor freed libidinal energy and aided the process of psychoanalysis. Reich's psychiatric approach was increasingly based on freeing the emotions (pleasure, rage, anxiety) through work with the body. The process, he discovered, led to the patient's intense experiencing of the psychological material uncovered in analysis.

> In the final analysis, I could not rid myself of the impression that somatic rigidity represents the most essential part in the process of repression. All our patients report that they went through periods in childhood in which, by means of certain practices . . . (holding the breath, tensing the abdominal muscular pressure, etc.), they learned to suppress their impulses of hate, anxiety, and love. . . . It never ceases to be surprising how the loosening of

Personal Reflection

■ Armor in Your Life

Read over the description of armoring in the text. Which is your most *important* armoring segment? How has this part of your body functioned in your life? How has your strong armoring affected your experience? (Be as specific as possible.) Has this armoring segment made you particularly vulnerable or, instead, particularly rigid and unfeeling?

Armoring Armoring is the major obstacle to growth, according to Reich.

> The armored organism is incapable of breaking down its own armor. But it is equally incapable of expressing its elemental biological emotions. It is familiar with the sensation of tickling but has never experienced orgonotic pleasure. The armored individual cannot express a sigh of pleasure or consciously imitate it. When he tries to do so, the result is a groan, a suppressed, pent-up roar, or even an impulse to vomit. He is incapable of venting anger or of banging his fist in an imitation of anger. (Reich, 1976, p. 402)

Boadella (1987) has pointed out that almost everyone suffering from maladjustment lives as though in a permanent state of emergency. Only by changing this state of chronic tension can individuals approach their environment rationally and healthfully.

I found that people reacted with deep hatred to every disturbance of the neurotic balance of their armor. (Reich, 1973, p. 147)

Reich felt that the process of armoring has created two distorted intellectual traditions that form the basis of civilization: Mechanistic science and mystical religion. Individuals whose personalities are linked to the first tradition, the mechanists, are so well armored that they have no real sense of their own life processes or inner nature. They have a basic fear of deep emotion, aliveness, and spontaneity. They tend to develop a rigid, mechanical conception of nature and are interested primarily in external objects and in the natural sciences.

> A machine has to be *perfect*. Hence the thinking and acts of the physicist must be "perfect." *Perfectionism* is an essential characteristic of mechanistic thinking. It tolerates no mistakes; uncertainties, shifting situations are unwelcome. . . . But this principle, when applied to processes in nature, inevitably leads into confusion. *Nature is inexact. Nature operates not mechanically, but functionally.* (Reich, 1961, p. 278, emphasis his)

It was only the mystics who—far removed from scientific insight—always kept in contact with the function of the living. Since, thus, the living became the domain of mysticism, serious natural science shrank from occupying itself with it. (Reich, 1961, pp. 197–198)

In contrast to the mechanists, the religious mystics have not developed their armoring so completely, according to Reich; they remain partly in touch with their life energy and are capable of great insight because of the partial contact with their innermost nature.

> In the disruption of the unity of body feeling by sexual suppression, and in the continual longing to re-establish contact with oneself and with the world, lies the root of all sex-negating religions. "God" is the mysticized idea of the vegetative harmony between self and nature. (Reich, 1973, p. 358)

Reich believed that this insight was distorted, however. Ascetic and antisexual religions lead us to reject our physical natures and to become alienated from our bodies. They deny the origin of the life force in the body and locate it in a hypothetical soul that has only a tenuous connection with the body.

Sexual Repression Another obstacle to growth is the social and cultural repression of the natural impulses and sexuality of the individual. Repression, Reich asserted, is the major source of neurosis and occurs during three principal phases of life: early infancy, puberty, and adulthood (Reich, 1973).

Infants and young children are confronted with an authoritarian, sex-suppressing family atmosphere. Reich reaffirms Freud's observations concerning the negative effects of parental demands for early toilet training, self-restraint, and "good" behavior.

The destructiveness which is bound up in the character is nothing but anger about frustration in general and denial of sexual gratification in particular. (Reich, 1973, p. 219)

During puberty, young people are kept from attaining an active, open sexual life; masturbation is still prohibited by most parents. Even more important, our society generally makes it impossible for adolescents to obtain meaningful work. As a result of this unnatural lifestyle, it is especially difficult for adolescents to outgrow infantile attachments to their parents.

Finally, as adults (and this was more true in Reich's time), many people become trapped in unsatisfying marriages for which they are sexually unprepared because of demands for premarital continence. Reich also points out that, in our culture, there are built-in conflicts within marriage.

> Marriages fall to pieces as a result of the ever deepening discrepancy between sexual needs and economic conditions. The sexual needs can be gratified with one and the same partner for a limited time only. On the other hand, the economic tie, moralistic demand, and human habit foster the permanency of the relationship. This results in the wretchedness of marriage. (Reich, 1973, p. 202)

The family situation creates the same neurotic environment for the next generation.

Reich felt that individuals who are brought up in an atmosphere that negates life and sex develop a fear of pleasure, represented in their muscular armoring. "This characterological armoring is the basis of isolation, indigence, craving for authority, fear of responsibility, mystic longing, sexual misery, and neurotically impotent rebelliousness, as well as pathological intolerance" (Reich, 1973, p. 7).

The life process is inherently "rational." It becomes distorted and grotesque when it is not allowed to develop freely. (Reich, 1973, p. 19)

> A teaching of living Life, taken over and distorted by armored man, will spell final disaster to the whole of mankind and its institutions. . . . By far the most likely result of the principle of "orgastic potency" will be a pernicious philosophy of 4-lettering all over the place everywhere. Like an arrow released from the restraining, tightly tensed spring, the search for quick, easy and deleterious genital pleasure will devastate the human community. (Reich, 1961, pp. 508–509)

Reich was not optimistic about the possible effects of his discoveries. He believed that most people, because of their strong armoring, would be unable to understand his theories and would distort his ideas.

Structure

Body

In a sense, all Reich's work is body-oriented. The body, he insisted, is an essential dynamic in *all* psychological functioning. For Reich, the body plays a critical role in storing and channeling bioenergy, which is the basis of human existence and experience.

Reich viewed mind and body as a unit. His work is a precursor to the field of holistic medicine. He also anticipated the interest in nonverbal communication that has developed in psychology, anthropology, and sociology.

As described earlier, Reich gradually moved from analytic practice, relying solely on language, to examination of both the physical and psychological aspects of character and character armor. At that point, he emphasized the dissolving of muscular armor to allow the free flow of orgone energy.

Social Relationships

In Reich's view, social relationships are determined by the individual's character. Most individuals see the world through the filter of their armoring, which cuts them off both from their inner natures and from satisfying social relationships. Only genital characters, having loosened their rigid armoring, can react openly and honestly to others.

> Nature and culture, instinct and morality, sexuality and achievement become incompatible as a result of the split in the human structure. The unity and congruity of culture and nature, work and love, morality and sexuality, longed for from time immemorial, will remain a dream as long as man continues to condemn the biological demand for natural (orgastic) sexual gratification. Genuine democracy and freedom founded on consciousness and responsibility are also doomed to remain an illusion until this demand is fulfilled. (Reich, 1973, p. 8)

Reich strongly believed in the ideals, enunciated by Marx, of "free organization, in which the free development of each becomes the basis of the free development of all" (Boadella, 1973, p. 212). Reich formulated the concept of work-democracy, a natural form of social organization in which people cooperate harmoniously to further their mutual needs and interests, and he sought to actualize these principles in the Orgone Institute.

Will

You do not strive to make your heart beat or your legs move, and you do not, by the same token, "strive" for or seek truth. Truth is in you and works in you just as your heart or your eyes work, well or badly, according to the condition of your organism. (Reich, 1961, p. 496)

Reich did not concern himself directly with the will, although he stressed the role of meaningful action in work and in family life.

> You don't have to do anything special or new. All you have to do is to continue what you are doing. . . . All you have to do is to continue what you have always done and always want to do: your work, to let your

> children grow up happily, to love your wife. (Reich, in Boadella, 1973, p. 236)

Reich would agree with Freud that the sign of a mature human being is capacity for love and work.

Emotions

Chronic tensions, according to Reich, block the energy flow that underlies powerful emotions. The armoring prevents the individual from experiencing strong emotions; it limits and distorts the expression of feeling. Emotions that are blocked are never eliminated, because they can't be fully expressed. According to Reich, only by fully experiencing a blocked emotion can an individual become free of it.

Reich also noted that the frustration of pleasure often leads to anger and rage. These negative emotions must be dealt with in Reichian therapy before the positive feelings (which underlie the negative emotions) can be completely experienced.

Intellect

The intellect, Reich believed, also operates as a defense mechanism. "The spoken word conceals the expressive language of the biological core. In many cases, the function of speech has deteriorated to such a degree that the words express nothing whatever and merely represent a continuous, hollow activity on the part of the musculature of the neck and the organs of speech" (1976, p. 398).

Intellectual activity can be structured and directed in such a way that it looks like a most cunningly operating apparatus whose purpose is precisely to avoid cognition, i.e., it looks like an activity directing one away from reality. In short, the intellect can operate in the two fundamental directions of the psychic apparatus: toward the world and away from the world. (Reich, 1976, p. 338)

Reich opposed any separation of intellect, emotions, and body. He pointed out that the intellect, which is actually a biological function, may have an energetic charge as strong as any of the emotions. "The hegemony of the intellect not only puts an end to irrational sexuality but has as its precondition a regulated libido economy. Genital and intellectual primacy belong together" (1976, p. 203). According to Reich, full development of the intellect requires the achievement of true genitality.

Self

For Reich, the self is the healthy, biological core of each individual. Most individuals are not in touch with the self; they are too armored and defended.

> What was it that prevented a person from perceiving his own personality? After all, it is what he is. Gradually, I came to understand that it is the entire being that constitutes the compact, tenacious mass which obstructs all analytic efforts. The patient's whole personality, his character, his individuality resisted analysis. (Reich, 1973, p. 148)

In penetrating to the deepest depth and the fullest extent of emotional integration of the Self, we not only experience and feel, we also learn to *understand,* if only dimly, the meaning and working of the cosmic orgone ocean of which we are a tiny part. (Reich, 1961, pp. 519–520)

According to Reich, the repressed impulses and repressing defensive forces together create a layer of contactlessness. *Contactlessness* is an expression of the concentrated interplay of the two (Reich, 1973). Contact requires free movement of energy. It becomes possible only as the individual, dissolving his or her armor and becoming fully aware of the body and its sensations and needs, comes in contact with the core, the primary drives. Where blocks are present, energy flow and awareness are restricted, and self-perception is greatly diminished or distorted (Baker, 1967).

Therapist

In addition to undergoing training in therapeutic technique, the therapist should progress in his or her personal growth. In working both psychologically and physically with a client, the therapist must have overcome any fears of overtly sexual sounds and of "orgastic streamings"—the free movement of energy in the body.

Elsworth Baker, one of the leading Reichian therapists in the United States, cautions that "no therapist should attempt to treat patients who have problems he has not been able to handle in himself nor should he expect a patient to do things he cannot do and has not been able to do" (1967, p. 223). Another eminent Reichian has written that

> the indispensable prerequisite for whatever methods the therapist uses to release the emotions held in the musculature is that he is in touch with his own sensations and able to empathise fully with the patient and to feel in his own body the effect of particular constrictions on the patient's energies. (Boadella, 1973, p. 120)

Nic Waal, one of the foremost psychiatrists in Norway, wrote about her experiences in therapy with Reich:

> I could stand being crushed by Reich because I liked truth. And, strangely enough, I was not crushed by it. All through this therapeutic attitude to me he had a loving voice, he sat beside me and made me look at him. He accepted me and crushed only my vanity and falseness. But I understood at that moment that true honesty and love both in a therapist and in parents is sometimes the courage to be seemingly cruel when it is necessary. It demands, however, a great deal of the therapist, his training and his diagnosis of the patient. (Boadella, 1973, p. 365)

Reich was well-known as a brilliant and tough-minded therapist. Even as an orthodox analyst, he was extremely honest, even brutally direct, with his patients.

Evaluation

Reich was the leading practitioner of somatic psychology and body-oriented therapy. In fact, only a small minority of psychologists have seriously concerned themselves with somatic psychology. However, the appreciation of physical habits and of tensions as diagnostic cues is steadily growing. Many therapists have been influenced by the work of Fritz Perls, who was in analysis with Reich and owes much to Reich's theories.

Reich's focus on muscular armoring and emotional release through body work has attracted less interest than it deserves. The encouragement of the expression of suppressed emotions, such as rage, fear, and aggression, is still a controversial issue in psychology.

Leonard Berkowitz (1973), who studied violence and aggression experimentally for many years, attacked what he calls the *ventilationist* approach to therapy, in which emphasis is placed on releasing bottled-up emotions. Berkowitz cites a number of experimental studies showing that encouraging the expression of aggression can increase aggression or hostility. According to behaviorist theory, encouraging the release of a given emotion serves to reward that behavior, making it more likely that the emotion will be vented in the future.

This criticism represents a shallow understanding of Reich's work, in which emotional release is never simply encouraged for its own sake. It may be true that the discharge of strong emotions often leads to recurrence. However, Reich's emphasis was always on dissolving the armoring, the blocks to feeling that distort an individual's psychological and physical functioning.

A more cogent criticism of Reich's theories concerns his depiction of the genital character as an achievable ideal state. Kelley (1971) pointed out that Reich developed a system that seems to promise a cure-all. A successful treatment is supposed to leave the individual free of all armor, a "finished product" with no need for further growth or improvement.

The underlying concept is a medical model in which the patient comes to the doctor in order to be "cured." This model pervades much of therapy, but it is given credibility by the assumption that the therapist is healthy (unarmored) and the patient is ill. Patients stay "one down" to the therapist; they are generally placed in a passive role, relying on the omnipotent, "perfected" healer for some sort of dramatic or magical cure. This model also places a tremendous strain on the therapist, who must always appear superior to patients and is permitted no mistakes or fallibility.

Learning to free ourselves from inappropriate blocks to feeling is only one aspect of our growth. Self-discipline and goal-directed behavior are also essential, and they require a certain amount of control over our emotions.

> The blocks to feeling that Reich calls "the armor" . . . are a product of the capacity of man to control his feelings and behavior, and so to direct his life along a path he has chosen. One aspect of this is protection of the self from incapacitating emotions, a second the channeling of behavior towards goals. (Kelley, 1971, p. 9)

Thus, the individual never can or should become totally "unarmored." Reich did not consider how to balance self-control and free expression as part of a continual process of growth.

With his emphasis on dissolving blocks to emotion, Reich tended to overestimate the role of armoring and resistance in the individual. He defined character almost solely in terms of armoring. "Character operates to produce almost constant resistance in psychoanalysis. For him [Reich] character is an armor formed through chronic 'hardening' of the ego. The meaning and purpose of this armor is protection from inner and outer dangers" (Sterba, 1976, p. 278). Yet character certainly consists of more than rigidity and defenses.

Reich's theories concerning therapy and psychological growth are generally clear and straightforward, as are his therapeutic techniques (West, 1994). He has provided considerable clinical as well as experimental evidence for his work, although, to date, his ideas have been too controversial to gain widespread acceptance. Interest in Reich's conception of the body is increasing, and the growth of body-oriented research is one of the more exciting possibilities in the future of psychology.

Other Approaches to Somatic Psychology

Reich's pioneering efforts to include the body as an element in psychology paved the way for the systems that followed. His work has led to greater acceptance of the role of the body and the possibility of improving physical conditions through systematic discipline.

The body-oriented systems covered in this section are by no means the only ones available. Dozens of excellent systems work primarily with the body to improve psychological and physical functioning. The disciplines and techniques mentioned in this section are perhaps better known and more accessible than some others. They also have theoretical significance for somatic psychology.

Bioenergetic Analysis

Everybody is seeking aliveness, everybody wants to be more alive. What we don't consider is that you have to *learn* to bear being more alive, to assimilate it, to permit an energetic charge to go through your body. (Keleman, 1971, p. 39)

Bioenergetics might be called neo-Reichian therapy. Founded by two of Reich's students, Alexander Lowen and John Pierrakos, it focuses on the role of the body in character analysis and in therapy. Lowen has used more easily acceptable terms than Reich—*bioenergy* for *orgone energy,* for example—and his work has generally met with less resistance than Reich's. There are many more bioenergetic practitioners than Reichians in the United States.

Lowen (1989) has summarized the major changes introduced by bioenergetic analysis:

1. Pleasure is emphasized more than sexuality, without denying the importance of sexuality.
2. The concept of grounding is added to Reich's original concepts. In traditional Reichian work, patients lie on a bed. In bioenergetic analysis, other positions are used, including an emphasis on standing and the role of the legs in supporting the individual when standing.
3. Physical exercises are taught, and patients can practice many of them at home.

Bioenergetics includes Reichian breathing techniques and many of Reich's emotional release techniques, such as allowing patients to cry, scream, and hit. Lowen also utilizes various exercises and stress postures in order to energize parts of the body that have been blocked. In these postures, stress is increased in chronically tense body parts until the tension becomes so great that the individual is forced to relax his or her armoring. These exercises include bending down to touch the floor, arching back with the fists at the base of the spine, and bending backward over a padded stool.

Personal Reflection

Stress Postures

Try these exercises. According to bioenergetic theory, they are designed to bring energy to parts of the body that are chronically tense.

Stand with legs about shoulder width apart and knees slightly bent; without straining, bend over to touch the floor. Let your body stay loose and your head hang down freely. Hold this posture for several minutes. You may find that your legs begin to shake or quiver, or you may notice other changes in your body. Keep breathing freely and naturally, and don't try to *make* anything happen.

Slowly come up from this position, feeling your spine gradually come to a vertical position, vertebra by vertebra.

Next, try a position that will curve the spine the other way. Stand with feet apart and your knees pointing slightly out. Put your fists in the small of your back and bend backward (be *very careful* not to strain your back). Again, keep your neck relaxed and your head hanging back freely, and breathe freely.

Any muscle quivering that might accompany these two postures is an indication of the relaxing and energizing of armored parts of the body.

Lowen found that Reich's approach to reducing armoring through muscular relaxation could be supplemented by the opposite process: encouraging patients to mobilize the feelings expressed by tense muscles. For example, encouraging a patient's aggression also helps the individual to surrender to tender feelings. But if the focus is chiefly on letting go and "giving in," therapy often results in feelings of sadness and anger exclusively. In order to avoid this outcome, Lowen found that the two approaches are best used alternately.

Bioenergetics can have a powerful spiritual or transpersonal dimension. John Pierrakos, the cofounder of bioenergetics, has made the transpersonal a central feature of his newer system of core energetics:

> After many years of bioenergetics work, I came to feel that something was lacking. Though bioenergetics provided a beautiful clinical approach to resolving blocks, difficulties, and neurotic symptoms, it lacked a fundamental philosophy because it did not incorporate the spiritual nature of human beings. (1987, p. 276)

Lowen and his colleagues have continued to write influential and thoughtful books and articles (Cranmer, 1994; Keleman, 1976, 1979; Lowen, 1975, 1980, 1984, 1992; Pierrakos, 1976, 1987) and also to train many others in the techniques of bioenergetic analysis.

It delights me to say that I am my body, with full understanding of what that really means. It allows me to identify with my total aliveness, without any need to split myself. (Keleman, 1971, p. 28)

The Alexander Technique

[Alexander] established not only the beginnings of a far-reaching science of the apparently involuntary movements we call reflexes, but a technique of correction and self-control which forms a substantial addition to our very slender resources in personal education. (George Bernard Shaw in Jones, 1976, p. 52)

The Alexander technique is designed to improve awareness of one's habits of movement. Alexander students learn how they use their bodies improperly and inefficiently and how they can avoid doing so when active or at rest. By *use*,

Alexander refers to our habits of holding and moving our bodies, habits that directly affect the way we function physically, mentally, and emotionally.

F. Mathias Alexander was an Australian Shakespearean actor who originated this system in the late nineteenth century. He suffered from recurring loss of voice, for which there seemed to be no organic cause. Alexander spent nine years of painstaking self-observation and self-study in a three-way mirror; he discovered that his loss of voice was related to the backward and downward pressing movement of his head. By learning to inhibit this tendency, Alexander found that he no longer developed laryngitis, and, in addition, the inhibition of pressure on the back of his neck had positive effects throughout his body. Out of this self-study, Alexander developed a technique for teaching integrated movement based on a balanced relationship between the head and the spine.

Alexander believed that a prerequisite for free and efficient movement is the lengthening of the spine. He did not mean a forced stretching but a gentle *upward lengthening*. Alexander students work primarily with the following formula: Let the neck be free to let the head go forward and up, to let the back lengthen and widen. The aim is not to engage in muscular activity; it is to allow the body to adjust automatically while the individual concentrates on repeating the formula and responding to the guiding touch of the teacher. The movements covered in the lesson are taken from common activities, and the student learns gradually to apply the Alexander principles. The balance between head and spine promotes the release of physical tensions, improved alignment, and better muscular coordination. On the other hand, interference with this relationship results in tension, misalignment of the body, and poor coordination.

Mr. Alexander has demonstrated a new scientific principle with respect to the control of human behavior, as important as any principle which has ever been discovered in the domain of external nature. (John Dewey in Jones, 1976, p. 104)

The Alexander work has been especially popular with actors, dancers, and other performing artists. It has also been shown to be highly effective for people with physical disabilities and for individuals suffering from chronic physical illnesses.

The Feldenkrais Method

The Feldenkrais method is designed to help people recover the natural grace and freedom they enjoyed as children. Feldenkrais students work with patterns of muscular movement that enable them to find the most efficient way of moving, eliminating the muscular tension and inefficient habits they have learned over the years.

I read a lot of physiology and psychology and to my great astonishment I found that in regard to using the whole human being for action, there was ignorance, superstition, and absolute idiocy. There wasn't a single book that dealt with *how* we function. (Feldenkrais, 1966, p. 115)

Moshe Feldenkrais received a doctorate in physics in France and worked as a physicist until 1944, when he was 40 years of age. He became deeply interested in judo and founded the first judo school in Europe, eventually developing his own judo system. Feldenkrais also worked with Alexander and studied Yoga, Freud, Gurdjieff, and neurology. After World War II, he devoted himself to work with the body.

The Feldenkrais method uses a tremendous variety of exercises, which differ from lesson to lesson. The exercises generally begin with very small movements; they are gradually combined into larger patterns. The aim is to develop ease and freedom of movement in every part of the body.

Feldenkrais often quoted the Chinese proverb "I hear and I forget, I see and I remember, I do and I understand." Because his work focuses on understanding through doing, he calls his exercises "awareness through movement."

Personal Reflection

■ Turning the Head

To get a general idea of how the Feldenkrais method operates, try this exercise.

Sit on the floor or in a chair and slowly turn your head to the right, without straining. Note how far your head will turn, and how far to the rear you can see. Turn your head back to the front.

Turn your head to the right again. Leave your head in place, and move your eyes to the right. See if your head can move further to the right. Repeat this three to four times.

Turn your head to the right. Now move your shoulders to the right and see if you can turn your head further to the rear. Repeat this three to four times.

Turn your head to the right. Now move your hips to the right and see if you can turn your head further to the rear. Repeat this three to four times.

Finally, turn your head to the right, and, leaving your head in its right-turned position, move your eyes, shoulders, and hips to the right. How far can you see now?

Now turn your head to the *left*. How far can you see? Continuing with the left side, repeat each step of the exercise you did with the right side, but *mentally only*. Visualize the movement of your head and visualize your eyes to the left. Visualize each step three to four times. Then turn your head to the left and move your eyes, shoulders, and hips to the left. How far can you turn now? What do you think happened?

Your range of movement increased because you broke up old movement patterns. You improved by loosening up your brain rather than loosening up your muscles.

For Feldenkrais, growth is the gradual acquisition of more effective action patterns. Rather than abandon old habits, the goal is to increase our repertoire; for example, when we begin to type, most of us use just two fingers. Then we learn touch-typing with ten fingers, a skill that takes time to develop. Touch-typing is easier and faster than the old two-finger method, and we come to prefer the new way.

If new habits are no longer useful or reliable (because of injury or other damage), old habits are available. Feldenkrais recommends gradual and natural change that does not threaten to destroy useful patterns.

Feldenkrais often said, "If you know what you are doing, you can do what you want." The aim of his exercises is to get you to do what you want, to understand the easiest patterns of movement for you in each new situation.

> To learn we need time, attention, and discrimination; to discriminate we must sense. This means that in order to learn we must sharpen our powers of sensing, and if we try to do most things by sheer force we shall achieve precisely the opposite of what we need. (Feldenkrais, 1972, p. 58)

Feldenkrais exercises work to reestablish efficient connections between the motor cortex and the musculature, connections that have been distorted by habits, tension, or trauma. According to Feldenkrais, increased awareness and flexibility can be achieved through balancing and quieting the motor cortex. The more active the cortex, the less we are aware of subtle changes. One of the fundamental principles of his work is **Weber's Law,** which states that our sensitivity to change is proportional to our current level of stimulation. If you are carrying a piano, for example, you cannot feel a matchbook added to the load.

Personal Reflection

■ The Centrality of Relationships

To better understand the importance of relationships in your life, try this exercise.

1. Think of five to seven important relationships or relational contexts in your life (for example, parents, grandparents, siblings, friends, teachers, groups, classes, clubs, or teams).
2. Describe how each relationship has affected your development. How have you changed through each relationship, either positively or negatively? How have you contributed to each relationship?
3. How do you think these relationships will contribute to shaping your future? Specifically, how do you predict they will shape your sense of self, self-esteem, career development, relational capacities, and personal values?

1. we grow in, through, and toward relationship;
2. for women, especially, connection with others is central to psychological well-being;
3. movement toward relational mutuality optimally occurs throughout life, as a result of mutual empathy, responsiveness, and contribution to the growth of each individual and to the relationship. (Jordan, 1983; Miller, 1984, 1986; Stiver, 1984; Surrey, 1985)

The need for connection and emotional joining is a primary need; much human suffering arises from disconnection and isolation. Miller has used the phrase *condemned isolation* (1986) to capture the sense of immobilization and self-blame that characterizes the pain of being disconnected from others. Jordan has described the feeling of being cut off from empathic possibility; that is, one cannot imagine that another person will be able to join one in empathic mutuality (1989). When people are unable to move from disconnection to connection, the resulting combination of immobilization and isolation may in fact become like a prison and contribute to psychological anguish. Often it is accompanied by a sense of shame, a feeling that one is unworthy of connection at the same time that one experiences a deep yearning to connect. The desire to bring oneself fully into relationship just when one fears the impossibility of such a move creates tension, distortion of one's ability to represent feelings, and thoughts of inauthenticity and fragmentation (Jordan, 1989). Women's relational style is increasingly apparent in other arenas as well. For example, in the workplace, the collaborative approach of women managers is drawing considerable attention (Godfrey, 1992; Helgesen, 1990; Rosener, 1990).

Pathways to Growth Miller's third theme acknowledges women's relational qualities and activities as potential strengths that provide pathways to healthy growth and development. This theme stands in stark contrast to the prevailing view that interpreted many of women's most valuable qualities as defects or deficiencies. In traditional theory, women's ability to express emotions more freely, and their greater attention to relationships, often led to pathologizing women with labels like *hysterical* or *too dependent* (Chesler, 1972; Houck, 1972). A review of the criteria for diagnosis of "mental illness" in psychiatry's official *Diagnostic and Statistical Manual of Mental Disorders* demonstrates how biased against women these categories really are. Taking issue with this bias, Kaplan humorously suggests adding two new characterizations more applicable to male psychopathology, the *independent personality disorder* and the *restricted personality disorder* (1983).

More recently, we have begun to explore the ways in which traditional theories of development also misinterpret men's experience. Bergman (1991) observes that society pressures boys to move away from a more connected and empathic relational context into one of competition, power, and disconnection.

Gilligan notes that women's sense of self and morality revolves around issues of responsibility for, and care of, other people. It is embedded in a compelling appreciation of context. While women's orientation is toward relationships, men's tends toward separation. Gilligan also portrays the woman's dilemma of trying to find a way to include her perspectives and desires in her relationships.

Gilligan's work has expanded over the years to explore the importance of relationships for women at many ages (Brown & Gilligan, 1992; Gilligan, Lyons, & Hammer, 1990). In particular, her research highlights the crisis girls face at adolescence. She demonstrates how hard it is for girls to maintain a strong sense of self and inner "voice," when doing so means risking disconnection in a world that does not honor women's relational desires and needs.

A Paradigm Shift

Since the early 1980s, a number of theorists have been developing a relational model of women's psychology, which has grown out of the contributions of Miller, Gilligan, and others. This is a "theory in progress." Many people have been contributing new parts to it each year. The basic model affirms the power of connection and the terrors of disconnection for women at all ages. As a result, this approach requires a paradigm shift that has led to the reframing of key concepts in psychological development, theory, and practice.

Reframing the central ideas in the psychology of women has broader implications for understanding women and women's place in our societal institutions—especially in the workplace and in the family. Women's experiences in work settings often reflect the tensions between their relational style and the focus on independence and hierarchy that dominates most work environments (Stiver, 1991c). In the family, women's relationships with their mothers is another example of a misunderstood area. Although conflict often arises in the mother-daughter relationship, mothers and daughters nevertheless exhibit strong yearnings for connection. This area has not been adequately explored. Originally, this struggle was formulated in terms of Freud's female Oedipus complex. Today, the psychology of women offers a novel way of looking at this and other family relationships (Lewis & Herman, 1986; Stiver, 1991a).

Personal Reflection

■ Exploring Parental Relationships

Try these exercises as a means of exploring parental relationships.

1. Describe to another person a recent interaction you had with your mother (or father). Now describe the interaction again, but this time imagine that your parent is in the room listening to you. Does your description change? How? What accounts for the differences?
2. With a partner or in a small group, role-play one of your parents. Tell the story of that parent's life from his or her perspective, noting in particular the major events and transitions. Reflect on your presentation. How did the events and transitions you described affect your feelings and your understanding of your mother or father?

When you cease to make a contribution, you begin to die. (Eleanor Roosevelt)

Another misunderstood area in the psychology of women is the struggle for power. Miller (1982) observed the extent to which women feel that they are not supposed to have power. Yet, she notes, women exert enormous power in their role of fostering the growth of others. For women, empowering others is seen as enhancing the growth of others in addition to the self. This is a counterpoint to the notion that power means "power over," the controlling and directing of others (Jordan, 1991a). In other words, in empowering another, we seek to assist that person in developing a sense of confidence and self-worth, which will allow him or her to move into the world with vitality and a personal sense of creativity.

When individuals exercise "power over" others, they seek to ensure their position of dominance and control. We are interested in attaining only our own self-defined goals, with little consideration or respect for the values and goals of others. Often this position is predicated on the use of force—social (silencing and shaming minority opinions), psychological (creating self-doubt or fear), or physical (threatening or actually using physical force or starting war).

In this relational approach to the psychology of women, every prior description of women requires reexamination. For example, the diagnosis of *dependent personality disorder,* and the more general use of the word **dependent** as pejorative and often pathological, are recast (Stiver, 1991b). Women's search for connection, and the relative ease with which they express their vulnerabilities and needs, are often mislabeled as *dependent*—and, thus, *neurotic, regressed,* and *infantile.* As the empowering value of relationships for women is recognized, dependency is seen as a positive movement along the path of healthy growth and development. This reframing moves us out of a value-laden and blaming mode into an empowering mode. The blaming mode originates in overvaluing independence and self-sufficiency and devaluing relationships, which are collaborative and mutually empowering.

Model of Self

This reexamination, an essential task in its own right, serves to reconceptualize notions of the self, not just in women but in all people. Traditional theories of development have emphasized the growth of an autonomous self with firm boundaries, separated from context and moving toward greater use of abstract logic and self-sufficiency. Miller (1976), Gilligan (1982), and Jordan et al. (1991) have posited a contextual, relational paradigm for the study of what has traditionally been called *self-experience.* Rather than focus on the "bounded" and contained self, these approaches emphasize the connected and relationally emergent nature of human experience. The movement of relating, of mutual initiative and responsiveness, is the ongoing, centrally organizing dynamic in women's lives. Because of this shift in paradigm, the self is no longer the primary target of interest and study. Instead, we increasingly turn to relational development: people engaged in relationships (Jordan, 1989).

Mutual empathy and mutual empowerment are at the core of growth-enhancing relationships. **Empathy** involves a motivational component (the desire to know the other), a perceptual component (the ability to perceive verbal and nonverbal signals), an affective component (the capacity to resonate with another person's feelings), and a cognitive component (the ability to make sense of this joining resonance).

Empathy always involves a movement toward understanding; it is never a perfect matching, or "mirroring," of another person's experience. ***Mutuality*** is another characteristic of "good" connection; it involves openness to change and growth in both people. Each person is respectful of the other's experience (Jordan, 1986). It is the movement of relationship, not just the development of self, that provides the focus for our interest.

Other theorists have built upon these insights. For example, they have found a relational approach helpful in understanding broader cultural contexts. The reframing of the concept of dependency has suggested an explanation of certain characteristics of the Japanese culture (Kobayashi, 1989). Turner (1987) explored the ways in which the relational approach reflects and validates African American women's experience. It also illuminates some of the specifics of lesbian development. For instance, the relational model offers a new perspective on the concept of *fusion* when applied to lesbian women as well as other issues in lesbians' lives. In lesbian relationships *fusion* has been pathologized and viewed pejoratively, in models of human development that emphasize the separation of the individual; however, the intense intimacy, sense of equality, value placed on communication, and emotional support by both partners—which have been seen as indications of fusion—seem to contribute to high levels of satisfaction in such relationships (Mencher, 1990). Mencher suggests that these indications of fusion point to intense relational engagement, a sign of health rather than of pathology.

Connections

The experience of **connection** and disconnection is the central issue in personality development. It is necessary to describe further what these terms really mean.

Extending the concept of empathy is basic to this new understanding that the human connection is fundamental to psychological development. In the late 1970s, Jordan, Kaplan, and Surrey (1982) elaborated on the concept of empathy, describing it as a complex cognitive-affective ability rather than as the mysterious, intuitive, and even regressive experience that others have suggested. Jordan later developed its implications for psychological maturation, along with an extension of the concept of mutuality (1986). Mutual empathy experientially alters the sense of a separate self in profound ways. In true empathic interaction, each person is engaged in affecting and being affected, knowing and being known, assisting the other in coming more fully into clarity and relatedness. Working along similar lines, Surrey (1991b) suggested that the underlying processes of psychological development are mutual engagement, mutual empathy, and mutual empowerment. The goal of psychological development is participation in mutually empathic and mutually empowering relationships rather than separation from others.

This vignette of two women interacting illustrates the process and consequences of mutual empathy and mutual empowerment.

> Ann has just heard from her friend Emily that Emily may have a serious illness. Ann is telling another friend, Beth, about this. Tears are in Ann's eyes and her voice sounds sad and fearful. Beth says, "Oh, how sad." Ann then adds, "Yes, sad, but I have this other awful feeling—like fear. Like I'm scared—as if it could happen to me." Beth replies, "Me, too. It is frightening to hear this. Maybe we all feel as if it's happening to us when we hear things like this."

As they continue, both Ann and Beth feel more in touch with what they suspect Emily may be feeling. They come to a deep appreciation of Emily's feelings and will do whatever is possible for and with Emily.

This example may sound ordinary, as if it describes an experience that people frequently have. Such communication *does* take place often, especially among women, but it is not ordinary in terms of its value. Furthermore, the valuable actions Ann and Beth demonstrate are often unrecognized. We believe that these interactions contain the key features that make for psychological growth and development in children and adults. This topic is examined in more detail in the next section.

Dynamics

Key Features in Psychological Growth and Development

First, the *process* of psychological growth requires the participants to respond empathically to each other. This is mutual empathy. Because each feels this empathic response, each is able to "take off" from this empathic base and add thoughts and feelings as they arise. These additions create the interplay, the flow. This mutually empathic interplay is created by both people and builds new psychological experience—that is, growth, for both.

The result of this process is that both people develop psychologically in at least five important ways (Miller, 1986):

1. Both feel a connection with the other that gives them a sense of increased *zest,* or energy. This is familiar to those who know the feeling of a sense of connection to another person. Its opposite is also familiar, the *down* sort of feeling that follows when one has been unable to connect with another person.
2. Both are active in the immediate relationship, and they feel more empowered to act beyond the relationship.
3. Each person has a bit more self-knowledge as well as knowledge of the other person; more is learned about feelings and thoughts and how they are for each person.
4. Because these processes have occurred, both people feel a greater sense of self-worth.
5. As a result, both desire more connection beyond this one.

It is important to note that in mutual interactions it is not a question of giving or getting, of helping or being helped, or of being dependent or depended upon. It is a question of whether both people *participate,* whether both people grow, and whether both therefore want more of the same.

Mutual empathy in the process of psychological growth can be seen in relational contexts, particularly with women. They become energized and empowered; they feel greater self-worth and greater clarity of their feeling-thoughts. This process also provides a baseline against which one can identify those circumstances and nonrelational contexts that lead to disconnections and thus to pathological development.

Disconnections

Because women rely so heavily on relationships in the process of psychological growth, **disconnections** can lead to serious consequences in their lives. Disconnections occur whenever a child or adult is prevented from participating in a mutually responsive and mutually enhancing relationship. Clearly, disconnections exist when a child or an adult suffers mistreatment, such as sexual and/or physical abuse, or when the individuals who play an important role in the child or adult's life are grossly unresponsive. However, many disconnections occur throughout childhood and adult life. Most do not lead to serious trouble, especially if there are sufficient empowering connections. The key ingredients that allow for growth when there is a threat of disconnection are the possibilities (1) that the child or adult can take action within the relationship to represent her experience, and (2) that the others in the relationship can respond in a way that leads back toward a reconnection (Miller, 1988).

To take a familiar example, suppose a 9-month-old infant is playing and suddenly, for no apparent reason, starts to scream and cry. The parents don't deal with this behavior well initially and respond with angry rebukes. The infant may now feel startled and afraid, in addition to the original distress. However, if the infant can reach out again to the parents and, in this second effort, find that they are more responsive to the expression of distress, the infant will feel more

to evoke some of the "forbidden" thoughts and feelings that threaten narrowly constructed images of herself and others. One feeling that threatens these images is anger. No one can withstand violations of her experience and long-term threats to connection without eventually feeling intense anger.

Most important, this process leads to a major contradiction, the **paradox of connection-disconnection.** In order to connect in the only relationships available, the child keeps more and more of her authentic self out of her relationships. She maintains relationships at the cost of failing to represent her own experience in them. In this process, she is moving further and further away from connection with her own experience—and she is losing the main source of psychological growth: interactions within relationships. The parts of herself that she has excluded are unable to change from experience. That is, her construction of a sense of herself and of others cannot benefit from the interchange provided by relationships—precisely the source of knowledge and clarity needed for the development of an accurate image of self and of others. She is constructing images of relational possibilities—and impossibilities—with less and less learning from events within relationships. It is striking to note that in studying girls moving into adolescence, Gilligan (Brown & Gilligan, 1992) described a very similar paradox.

This process of repeated disconnections sometimes (though not always) leads to anxious, depressive immobilization and complete disconnection (Hamilton & Jensvold, 1992). This immobilizing path probably exists for almost all women in patriarchal societies to some degree. It underlies many of women's psychological troubles, including phobias, addictions, eating disorders, depression, dissociative states, and paranoid ideas, as well as many of the problems labeled as personality disorders (Brown, 1992). In each of these situations, the woman elaborates specific images of herself and others, and specific forms of behavior, that come to seem the only ones possible in the framework of the relationship she has constructed.

Implications for Personality Development

We have found that framing psychological development and problems in terms of this central paradox helps us to understand both sexes better, and also helps us to explain how psychological troubles arise. Most important, it helps us to find ways to work that are clarifying and empowering. That is, *psychological problems represent the mechanisms people construct that keep them out of connection while they simultaneously seek connection.*

Stiver (1990c) has shown how this paradox develops in families labeled *dysfunctional* (for example, alcoholic, incestuous, and Holocaust-survivor families). Several theorists have elucidated other problems with this paradox in mind. Surrey (1991a), Steiner-Adair (1991), and Mirkin (1990) have reported on adolescents' development of eating disorders and have illustrated how this connection-disconnection construct unfolds in individual and family therapy. In the same way, Jack (1991), Kaplan (1984), and Stiver and Miller (1988) have described a relational understanding in the treatment of depression. Saunders and Arnold (1990) have recast the major characteristics and treatment of women who are diagnosed with borderline personality disorders. They have depicted ways of working that differ from the pejorative and destructive treatment methods that have formerly been applied.

Kilbourne and Surrey (1991) and Gleason (1992) have discussed the origins and prevention of, and recovery from, addictions using this more relational approach. They also offer an understanding of the currently popular *codependency* formulation by noting a lack of mutuality in women's available relationships, rather than by viewing women as engaged in pathological struggles to make connections when mutuality is not possible. Kaplan and Klein (1990) have examined women's suicides and suicide attempts as they differ from men's and have suggested explanations for these findings in the contrasting relational experiences of women and men.

Beyond specific clinical formulations, a relational model alters our perception of numerous overarching concepts, such as conflict, anger, and shame. Conflict and anger are seen as necessary features occurring in the movement of all relationships (Jordan, 1990; Miller & Surrey, 1989). Jordan (1989) describes shame as the feeling of being excluded from connection and the sense of *loss of empathic possibility*. For all of these authors, a relational approach leads to a reframing of central concepts in women's therapy (Miller & Stiver, 1991).

Relational Therapy

To understand how the paradox of connection-disconnection operates, we can examine the conditions in families that impede rather than foster growth-enhancing connections.

Many kinds of family systems have been characterized as dysfunctional, including, as noted earlier, alcoholic, incestuous, and Holocaust-survivor families. In these families, secrecy, inaccessibility to parents, and parentification of children contribute to sustained disconnections among family members. Children develop a range of strategies—including emotional disengagement, role-playing, and replication—to make connections, while keeping important parts of themselves out of connection. Sensitivity to these family dynamics can help therapists attend empathically to the ways in which children learn to stay disconnected in the face of their longing for connection (Stiver, 1990b).

For example, a woman who grew up in an alcoholic home recalls how, as a child, she was aware that her father drank too much and that he would upset her mother and frighten her and her siblings. When she tried to tell her father that he shouldn't drink so much, he would become enraged with her. He would insist that his drinking was not a problem and that she was a troublemaker. Her mother was also angry at her for upsetting her father. She learned very early on to keep silent about what she saw, which led her to begin doubting her own experience. While growing up, she became quite diplomatic in her dealings with others. She was careful to avoid offending anyone or causing trouble. Her early memory of confronting her father and the family's response to her were pivotal to an understanding, in therapy, of her deep sense of isolation, despite her apparently well-developed social skills.

This paradox of connection-disconnection becomes the framework for

Personal Reflection

■ A Relational Inventory

Take a relational inventory by making a special appointment with a friend or lover to discuss the qualities of your relationship.

Thinking of particular examples in your relationship, discuss the following relational concepts described in this chapter: empathy, authenticity, mutual empathy, mutual empowerment, connection, disconnection, reconnection, anger, conflict, isolation.

guiding the therapist. The therapist cues her listening, her understanding of the material that emerges, and her emotional attunement to the context of how connected or disconnected both the therapist and the patient are.

We are all familiar with some of the ways our patients move out of connection—for example, the person who talks most of the session, leaving no room for exchange, or the person who appears very compliant, although nothing moves in the process. But we had not previously thought of everything that happens in therapy as reflections of movement toward or away from connection.

Strategies for disconnection are important to patients' connection as well as their need to disconnect. The therapist holds this tension as the patient begins to develop the necessary sense of safety to relinquish these previously life-saving strategies of disconnection.

Without a rigorous and consistent evaluation of what kind of a future we wish to create, and a scrupulous examination of the expressions of power we choose to incorporate into all our relationships, including our most private ones, we are not progressing, but merely recasting our own characters in the same old weary drama. (Audre Lourde)

We are making the bold statement, then, that we see *all* of the problems that emerge in therapy to be, on one level or another, reflections of this central paradox. The focus on connection-disconnection as the central guide in therapy can develop only in a setting of safety and mutuality. Such a setting becomes defined by the therapist's empathic participation in the relationship. It is the therapist's authenticity and presence, rather than the *neutral,* nonengaged stance advocated by Freudians and other psychoanalysts, that makes an enlarged sense of connection possible. Through this relationship, therapist and patient are empowered to grow and change. For the therapy to become a relationship of *mutual empathy,* the patient must see that the therapist is *moved* or affected by the patient; when this mutual engagement occurs, movement toward expanded connection occurs.

The emphasis on building empowering connections has led to new conceptions of group therapy (Fedele & Harrington, 1990). It has also become the basis for the creation of mental health services—for example, women's inpatient psychiatric and alcoholism programs (Fedele & Miller, 1988).

Evaluation

Feminism must be on the cutting edge of real social change if it is to survive as a movement in any particular country. (Audre Lourde)

The emphasis on connection and disconnection in a relational approach speaks to the core of the human condition, a core that has remained out of focus in traditional psychodynamic approaches. Traditional theories *have* spoken about relationships. However, the core of these theories remains obscure, because they emerge from an underlying preoccupation with individual gratification and power, disguised by terms like *separation* and *individuation*. Such a preoccupation, which could arise only from the thinking of a dominant group, distorts the *total* human condition. Once we examine more accurately the lives of all people, we find ourselves moving toward a recognition of the need for human connection and of the sources and consequences of disconnection.

This model is not about *self-development*. We suggest instead that human behavior is about *relational development*, a constant movement of energy and meaning between people, a deeply contextual experience of personhood. In this perspective the enhancement of relatedness may constitute a greater goal than individual gratification and, ironically, may lead to greater individual fulfillment (Jordan, 1987). Stated more strongly, perhaps the most basic human need is the *need to participate in relationship*.

The Theory Firsthand

Excerpt from *Women's Growth in Connection*

The following excerpt, taken from Women's Growth in Connection[1] *by Jordan, Kaplan, Miller, Stiver, and Surrey, illustrates how the maintenance of distance between patient and therapist is a masculine model that does not work well.*

At first blush the connection between caring and psychotherapy seems obvious, and yet for many of us trained in the traditional model of therapy, caring about one's patients often is seen as something that may get in the way of effective treatment. The maintenance of distance between therapist and patient as well as general prohibitions against the expression of caring can be attributed to two major assumptions underlying this traditional model. The first assumption is tied to a broader model of treatment in which the treatment of the patient requires that the treater be objective, nonemotional, and relatively impersonal in order to be most helpful to the patient. . . .

The second assumption is that growth and change can occur only if the therapist does not gratify the patient. The experience of frustration and learning how to tolerate and respond to deprivations in therapy are seen as valuable and therapeutic. . . .

. . . I believe that this model is essentially a masculine model, since it reflects a style much more congenial and familiar to men than to women, that is, objective, nonemotional, impersonal attitudes, and so forth. For precisely this reason, this model does not seem to work very well with women, and perhaps not with some men either. The need to erect barriers to create distance from patients may also then reflect countertransference reactions among male therapists toward their female patients, who are different from them in important ways. . . .

[1]From "The Meaning of Care: Reframing Treatment Models" (pp. 250, 251, 255–257, 266, 267) by I. P. Stiver in *Women's Growth in Connection* by J. V. Jordan, A. G. Kaplan, J. B. Miller, I. P. Stiver, and J. L. Surrey. New York: Guilford Press.

. . . Such terms as *manipulative, seductive, controlling, needy, devouring, frigid, castrating, masochistic* and *hysterical* have been used pervasively, primarily to describe female patients, with the clear implications that such patients are hard to tolerate, and almost impossible to treat and that if one does not manage them carefully one will be taken over, fused with, devoured, and so forth. Even when the perception of the patient is more benign, the labels of "dependent," "seductive," and so forth are at best patronizing. The end result of such labeling is that the patient is not understood and not cared about.

Let me share with you a brief clinical example. I was asked to consult about a young woman who had become anxious and depressed enough to require rehospitalization after a period of fairly good adjustment. She is a young, attractive 19-year-old honor student at an Ivy League college, and is highly intelligent, very sensitive, and articulate. She talked readily to me on several occasions about the anguish she often experienced in a world that felt unreal to her. When I approached one of the administrative psychiatrists to discuss the case, he told me immediately that she was "very manipulative" and was going to be "a handful." I was a bit surprised, since she was always well mannered and quite cultivated with me and I asked him what he meant. "Oh, when we do rounds, if you look around at the group talking to her, everyone looks tense and uncomfortable." As I mused about this curious definition of "manipulative," I thought about what her major concerns were—she was always afraid that her ability to put up a good facade, to be so well socialized and so successful at academic pursuits, and so forth, would hide what she called her "true self," the self that was so terrified, so uncertain, and so confused. Her concern was that she would be misunderstood. I was often very moved in her presence by her unusual capacity to communicate the power of her frustration and pain. I could imagine her "performing" at rounds, while at the same time being vigilant about how others would respond to her, and feeling helpless and even desperate if they did not see what was underneath the facade. I also know that once she felt the other person did not understand her, she gave up trying, with a deep sense of disappointment and underlying rage. That her anxiety and anger at being misunderstood were communicated to those conducting rounds must have contributed to feelings of discomfort among them; I also believe they needed to ward off the intensity of her underlying feelings. The labeling of her as manipulative also created a climate that kept her at a distance and cut off the possibility of understanding her or of engaging with her in a meaningful way.

Male patients certainly may be misunderstood, but I am focusing here on the specific kinds of language that affect women. I would like to suggest that when the language is pejorative and serves to maintain distance between the therapist and the patient, women are more likely to be victimized in the process than are men. We know that the greater number of patients in therapy are women and, among therapists, men represent a significantly higher proportion than women. But it is not even that simple. Women who enter this profession have largely been taught by men (and treated by men) and in order to survive in their careers have often needed to adapt to the standards and values that have been associated with their professions; thus most therapists, male or female, may be very much influenced by those standards classifying mental health and illness that reflect the masculine model of therapy described above. . . .

It is most important to note that styles of caring in therapy do not seem linked in a simple one-to-one fashion with sex of the therapist. That is, some women therapists have in a sense overconformed with the distancing, "masculine model" of therapy as a result of trying to survive, to be successful and adept in this field. On the other hand, I have known "caring" male therapists who are able to be flexible and responsive to both their male and female patients in a genuine, empathic, and nonauthoritarian fashion. We are all aware that selective factors operate that make it more likely that such men, rather than, if you will, hypermasculine, unemotional men, will enter this field. However, what I have also noticed is that often these men are apt to apologize for or hide this style lest they be criticized and devalued by their male colleagues.

Let me close with an example that nicely illustrates this curious dilemma. A woman psychiatrist told me about her termination with a female patient in her last year of training. She was leaving the clinic setting and moving to another city. Because she felt connected to this patient and sad about terminating, when the patient asked where she was going and if she could contact her, she told her, and added that she would be glad to hear from her. When she reported this to her supervisor, a male psychoanalyst, he told her she had been very seductive, had behaved inappropriately and was too involved with her patient. She felt bad and accepted his criticism. She was also terminating her own therapy with a senior male analyst. When asked if she could see him again when she visited Boston he said, "Certainly, I would love to hear from you." She felt vindicated and said, "What goes on behind closed doors! There are all these analysts secretly acting like human beings but nobody is supposed to know it!" I do believe that good caring treatment does go on behind closed doors, but it is time to take it out of the closet. Let us give legitimacy and value to a model of therapy that takes into account the unique aspects of female experience and development and that also allows a more egalitarian "caring about" our patients to become a matter of prime importance.

Chapter Highlights

- The relational approach presented by Jean Baker Miller has three related themes: the impact of the cultural context on the lives of women, the importance of relationships for women, and the legitimate strength of women's activities and relational qualities.
- Women grow in, through, and toward relationship.
- For women, especially, connection with others is central to psychological well-being.
- Care of, and responsibility for, other people provides the focus for women's sense of morality and of self. Men's orientation tends toward separation, while women's is toward relationships, embedded in context.
- Traditional theories of development have also done disservice to men's experience, as boys are pressured to move toward competition, disconnection, and power, away from a more empathic and connected relational context.
- A relational model of the psychology of women affirms the powers of connection and the terrors of disconnection for women at all ages. This has implications for understanding women's role in the workplace and in the family.
- Dependency is seen as a positive movement along the path of healthy development and growth. This reframing, in turn, allows movement into an empowering mode, out of a blaming mode, which originates in overvaluing self-sufficiency and independence.

- Relationships, not the individual self, are the focus. The relationally emergent nature of human experience and the importance of the connection are respected, rather the contained and bounded self.
- The centrally organizing dynamic in women's lives is the ongoing movement of relating, of mutual responsiveness and initiative.
- A person's sense of zest, clarity, capacity for action, and worth increases in a growth-fostering relationship. In such a relationship each person feels more connected to the other person and experiences a greater motivation for connections with other people beyond those in the specific relationship.
- The central issues in personality development are the experiences of connection and disconnection. Basic to this new understanding of the importance of the human connection is the concept of empathy.
- Rather than separation from others, participation in mutually empowering and empathic relationships is considered the goal of psychological development.
- Being prevented from participating in such relationships, as a child or as an adult, can result in disconnections.
- The paradox of connection-disconnection, on one level or another, is reflected in, and underlies, all the problems that emerge in therapy.
- Psychological problems represent mechanisms people construct that keep them out of connection while they simultaneously seek connection.
- Concepts such as anger, shame, and conflict are given a different framing in a relational model. Anger and conflict are seen as a necessary part of movement in relationship. Shame is described as the sense of loss of empathic possibility and the feeling of being excluded from connection.
- Children from what are typically characterized as dysfunctional families develop a range of strategies to make connections, including role-playing, replication, and emotional disengagement, while holding important parts of themselves out of connection. Parentification of children, secrecy, and inaccessibility to parents contribute to sustained disconnections among family members.
- A setting of safety and mutuality is required for therapy. This situation comes about through the therapist's empathic, authentic, and engaged participation in the relationship, rather than the neutral stance advocated by classical Freudians, among others.
- Relational being rather than a *separate self* is at the core of experience.

Key Concepts

Connection The experience of participating with others for the benefit of all. Connection is fundamental to psychological development. The extended concept of *empathy* is basic to this understanding. Connection also includes increased mutuality, engagement, and empowerment.

Cultural context The unequal and essentially nonmutual power dynamics of patriarchal societies as they impact the lives and development of personality of men and of women alike.

Dependence A positive characteristic helping to promote healthy development and growth.

Disconnection An experience that occurs whenever a child or adult is prevented from participating in a mutually enhancing and mutually responsive relationship. Repeated disconnections can have major impact, as the individual moves further and further away from connection with his or her own experience.

Empathy A sensitivity to others that involves motivational, perceptual, affective, and cognitive components, and always has a movement toward understanding, rather than a mirroring, or matching, of another's experience.

Paradox of connection-disconnection The contradictory situation in which a child or adult, in order to connect in available relationships, withholds the authentic self. On one level or another, this paradox is reflected in, and underlies, all the problems that emerge in therapy.

Relationships Women's search for ways of connection with others. It is the central organizing feature in their development. A relational model differs from most developmental models, which are characterized by an emphasis on the struggle for autonomy and independence.

Annotated Bibliography

Belenky, M., Clinchy, B., Goldberger, N., & Tarule, J. (1986). *Women's ways of knowing.* New York: Basic Books.

This book explores the basic patterns of knowing and interacting with the world that characterize women's experience. Based on interviews with 100 women, the book also delineates the ways in which women are silenced by male standards of knowing and learning.

Brown, L. M., & Gilligan, C. (1992). *Meeting at the crossroads: Women, psychology and girls' development.* Cambridge, MA: Harvard University Press.

Delineated are the dilemmas faced by adolescent girls when they feel that they must withhold their true selves in order to participate in relationships. Also described is the idea that the authenticity and vitality available to young girls in relationships is often lost as girls attempt to meet standards of femininity that silence their real knowledge of the world of relationships.

Gilligan, C. (1982). *In a different voice.* Cambridge, MA: Harvard University Press.

Already a classic in the rethinking of the psychology of women, this book reexamines the differing paths of moral development in girls and boys. It explores the differences between a morality of justice and a morality of care. It is a must for anyone interested in new understandings of women's development.

Jordan, J. V., Kaplan, A. G., Miller, J. B., Stiver, I. P., & Surrey, J. L. (1991). *Women's growth in connection.* New York: Guilford Press.

A collection of the early papers out of the Stone Center at Wellesley College. This book introduces the reader to core concepts of a relational model of development: mutuality, empathy, mutual empowerment, the sense of self in women, and dependency.

Jordan, J. (Ed.). (1997). *Women's growth in diversity.* New York: Guilford Press.

This book continues the theory building begun in *Women's Growth in Connection* but also focuses on questions of diversity in women's development.

Miller, J. B. (1976). *Toward a new psychology of women.* Boston: Beacon Press.

A groundbreaking work that has been described as revolutionary, this book forms the core of the Stone Center's approach to understanding women. It addresses the societal forces that have shaped women's development and notes the considerable, although often devalued, strengths that women bring to relationships and the culture. Essential reading for anyone who wishes to understand women and the cultural dynamics shaping women's lives.

Stone Center Working Paper Series (1982–1997). Stone Center Works in Progress (Nos. 1–78). (Available from Stone Center, Wellesley College, Wellesley, MA 02181-8268.)

A wide-ranging series of papers covering the issues of power, courage, lesbian perspectives, developmental pathways of women of color, psychotherapy, and more. Considered by many to be at the cutting edge of approaches to the psychology of women.

References

Belenky, M., Clinchy, B., Goldberger, N., & Tarule, J. (1986). *Women's ways of knowing.* New York: Basic Books.

Bergman, S. (1991). Men's psychological development: A relational perspective. *Work in progress* (No. 48). Wellesley, MA: Stone Center Working Paper Series.

Brown, L. M., & Gilligan, C. (1992). *Meeting at the crossroads: Women, psychology and girls' development.* Cambridge, MA: Harvard University Press.

Brown, L. S. (1992). A feminist critique of the personality disorders. In L. S. Brown & M. Ballou (Eds.), *Personality and psychopathology: Feminist reappraisals* (pp. 206–228). New York: Guilford Press.

Chesler, P. (1972). *Women and madness.* New York: Doubleday.

Fedele, N., & Harrington, B. (1990). Women's groups: How connections heal. *Work in progress* (No. 47). Wellesley, MA: Stone Center Working Paper Series.

Fedele, N., & Miller, J. B. (1988). Putting theory into practice: Creating mental health programs for women. *Work in progress* (No. 32). Wellesley, MA: Stone Center Working Paper Series.

Gianino, A., & Tronick, E. (1985). The mutual regulation model: The infant's self and interactive regulation and coping defensive capacities. In P. Field, P. McCabe, & N. Schneiderman (Eds.), *Stress and coping.* Hillsdale, NJ: Lawrence Erlbaum.

Gilligan, C. (1982). *In a different voice.* Cambridge, MA: Harvard University Press.

Gilligan, C., Lyons, N., & Hammer, T. J. (Eds.). (1990). *Making connections.* Cambridge, MA: Harvard University Press.

Gleason, N. (1992). *Towards a model for preventing alcohol abuse by college women: A relational perspective.* Washington, DC: U.S. Dept. of Education (Fund for the Improvement of Post-secondary Education).

Godfrey, J. (1992). *In our wildest dreams.* New York: HarperCollins.

Hamilton, J. A., & Jensvold, M. (1992). Personality, psychopathology and depression in women. In L. S. Brown & M. Ballou (Eds.), *Personality and psychopathology: Feminist reappraisals* (pp. 116–143). New York: Guilford Press.

Helgesen, S. (1990). *The female advantage: Women's way of leadership.* New York: Doubleday.

Houck, J. H. (1972). The intractable female patient. *American Journal of Psychiatry, 129,* 27–31.

Jack, D. J. (1991). *Silencing the self: Women and depression.* Cambridge, MA: Harvard University Press.

Johnson, K., & Ferguson, T. (1990). *Trusting ourselves: The sourcebook on psychology of women.* New York: Atlantic Monthly Press.

Jordan, J. (1983). Women and empathy: Implications for psychological development and psychotherapy. *Work in progress* (No. 2). Wellesley, MA: Stone Center Working Paper Series.

Jordan, J. V. (1984). Empathy and self boundaries. In J. V. Jordan, A. G. Kaplan, J. B. Miller, I. P. Stiver, & J. L. Surrey, *Women's growth in connection* (pp. 67–80). New York: Guilford Press, 1991.

Jordan, J. (1986). The meaning of mutuality. In J. V. Jordan, A. G. Kaplan, J. B. Miller, I. P. Stiver, & J. L. Surrey, *Women's growth in connection* (pp. 81–86). New York: Guilford Press, 1991.

———. (1987). Clarity in connection: Empathic knowing, desire and sexuality. *Work in progress* (No. 29). Wellesley, MA: Stone Center Working Paper Series.

———. (1989). Relational development: Therapeutic implications of empathy and shame. *Work in progress* (No. 39). Wellesley, MA: Stone Center Working Paper Series.

———. (1990). Courage in connection: Conflict, compassion, creativity. *Work in progress* (No. 45). Wellesley, MA: Stone Center Working Paper Series.

———. (1991a). The movement of mutuality and power. *Work in progress* (No. 53). Wellesley, MA: Stone Center Working Paper Series.

———. (1991b). The relational self: A new perspective for understanding women's development. In J. Strauss & G. Goethals (Eds.), *The self: Interdisciplinary approaches.* New York: Springer-Verlag.

Jordan, J. V., Kaplan, A. G., Miller, J. B., Stiver, I. P., & Surrey, J. L. (1991). *Women's growth in connection.* New York: Guilford Press.

Jordan, J. V., Kaplan, A. G., & Surrey, J. L. (1982). Women and empathy. *Work in progress* (No. 2). Wellesley, MA: Stone Center Working Paper Series.

Kaplan, A. G. (1984). The "self-in-relation": Implications for depression in women. *Work in progress* (No. 14). Wellesley, MA: Stone Center Working Paper Series.

Kaplan, A. (1991). Some misconceptions and reconceptions of a relational approach. *Work in progress* (No. 49). Wellesley, MA: Stone Center Working Paper Series.

Kaplan, A., & Klein, R. (1990). Women and suicide: The cry for connection. *Work in progress* (No. 46). Wellesley, MA: Stone Center Working Paper Series.

Kaplan, M. (1983). A woman's view of DSM III. *American Psychologist, 38,* 786–792.

Kilbourne, J., & Surrey, J. (1991). Women, addiction, and codependency. *Colloquium Presentation.* Stone Center, Wellesley College.

Kobayashi, J. S. (1989). Depathologizing dependency: Two perspectives. *Psychiatric Annals, 19,* 653–658.

Lewis, H. B., & Herman, J. L. (1986). Anger in the mother-daughter relationship. In T. Bernay & D. W. Cantor (Eds.), *The psychology of today's woman: New psychoanalytic visions* (pp. 139–163). Hillsdale, NJ: Lawrence Erlbaum.

Mencher, J. (1990). Intimacy in lesbian relationships: A critical re-examination of fusion. *Work in progress* (No. 42). Wellesley, MA: Stone Center Working Paper Series.

Miller, J. B. (1976). *Toward a new psychology of women.* Boston: Beacon Press.

———. (1982). Women and power. In J. V. Jordan, A. G. Kaplan, J. B. Miller, I. P. Stiver, & J. L. Surrey, *Women's growth in connection* (pp. 197–205). New York: Guilford Press, 1991.

———. (1984). The development of women's sense of self. *Work in progress* (No. 12). Wellesley, MA: Stone Center Working Paper Series.

———. (1986). What do we mean by relationships? *Work in progress* (No. 22). Wellesley, MA: Stone Center Working Paper Series.

———. (1988). Connections, disconnections and violations. *Work in progress* (No. 33). Wellesley, MA: Stone Center Working Paper Series.

Miller, J. B., & Stiver, I. P. (1991). A relational reframing of therapy. *Work in progress* (No. 52). Wellesley, MA: Stone Center Working Paper Series.

Miller, J. B., & Surrey, J. L. (1989). Revisioning women's anger: The personal and the global. *Work in progress* (No. 43). Wellesley, MA: Stone Center Working Paper Series.

Mirkin, M. (1990). Eating disorders: A feminist structural family therapy perspective. In M. Mirkin (Ed.), *The social and political contexts in family therapy.* Boston: Allyn & Bacon.

Rosener, J. (1990). Ways women lead. *Harvard Business Review, 90,* 119–125.

Saunders, E. A., & Arnold, F. (1990). Borderline personality disorder and childhood abuse: Revisions in clinical thinking and treatment approach. *Work in progress* (No. 51). Wellesley, MA: Stone Center Working Paper Series.

Steiner-Adair, C. (1991). New maps of development, new models of therapy: The psychology of women and treatment of eating disorders. In C. Johnson (Ed.), *Psychodynamic treatment of anorexia nervosa and bulimia.* New York: Guilford Press.

Stern, D. (1985). *The interpersonal world of the infant.* New York: Basic Books.

Stiver, I. (1984). The meaning of "dependency" in female-male relationships. *Work in progress* (No. 11). Wellesley, MA: Stone Center Working Paper Series.

———. (1990a). Dysfunctional families and wounded relationships, Part I. *Work in progress* (No. 41). Wellesley, MA: Stone Center Working Paper Series.

———. (1990b). Dysfunctional families and wounded relationships, Part II. *Work in progress* (No. 44). Wellesley, MA: Stone Center Working Paper Series.

———. (1991a). Beyond the Oedipus complex: Mothers and daughters. In J. V. Jordan, A. G. Kaplan, J. B. Miller, I. P. Stiver, & J. L. Surrey, *Women's growth in connection* (pp. 97–121). New York: Guilford Press.

———. (1991b). The meanings of "dependency" in female-male relationships. In J. V. Jordan, A. G. Kaplan, J. B. Miller, I. P. Stiver, & J. L. Surrey, *Women's growth in connection* (pp. 143–161). New York: Guilford Press.

———. (1991c). Work inhibitions in women: Clinical considerations. In J. V. Jordan, A. G. Kaplan, J. B. Miller, I. P. Stiver, & J. L. Surrey, *Women's growth in connection* (pp. 223–236). New York: Guilford Press.

Stiver, I. P., & Miller, J. B. (1988). From depression to sadness in the psychotherapy of women. *Work in progress* (No. 36). Wellesley, MA: Stone Center Working Paper Series.

Surrey, J. L. (1985). Self-in-relation. *Work in progress* (No. 13). Wellesley, MA: Stone Center Working Paper Series.

———. (1991a). Eating patterns as a reflection of women's development. In J. V. Jordan, A. G. Kaplan, J. B. Miller, I. P. Stiver, & J. L. Surrey, *Women's growth in connection* (pp. 237–249). New York: Guilford Press.

———. (1991b). The "self-in-relation": A theory of women's development. In J. V. Jordan, A. G. Kaplan, J. B. Miller, I. P. Stiver, & J. L. Surrey, *Women's growth in connection* (pp. 51–66). New York: Guilford Press.

Turner, C. (1987). Clinical applications of the Stone Center theoretical approach to minority women. *Work in progress* (No. 28). Wellesley, MA: Stone Center Working Paper Series.

the direction for the discipline until the inclusion of experimental and behavioral psychology became equally important.

Intellectual Antecedents

James grew up as a member of a remarkable and gifted family. His father, Henry James, a prominent follower of the Swedish scientist-mystic Emanuel Swedenborg, was one of the most controversial writers on politics and religion in the nineteenth century (Habegger, 1994). Their home was a hotbed of new ideas. William James became a passionate and skilled speaker in a family that rewarded and demanded such skills. His brother, Henry James Jr., more introspective than William, gained prominence as one of the great masters of fiction. The brothers were in constant communication and remained devoted fans and thorough critics of each other's works (Matthiessen, 1980).

James was familiar with most of the leading philosophers, researchers, writers, and educators of the day and corresponded with a number of them. He frequently acknowledged his debt to this or that thinker but did not seem to be a disciple of any. A single exception may be the French philosopher Charles-Bernard Renouvier, whose ideas on free will sparked James's recovery. Renouvier's approach to other thorny metaphysical problems influenced James's own brand of pragmatism. In psychology, he was impressed with the experimental work of Wilhelm Wundt and Hermann Helmholtz, of Germany; the research on children by Alfred Binet, and on mental patients by Jean-Martin Charcot of France; the ideas about the nature of the self of Alexander Bain of Scotland and Frederic Myers of England; as well as the analysis of religious experiences by the Canadian Maurice Bucke. James read extensively and peppers his work with long quotes from hundreds of writers.

Tymoczko (1996) asserts, convincingly, that from a very early and unsigned review (James, 1874) to his last essay (James, 1910), James's interest in nonordinary states of consciousness and his arguments in support of the efficacy of beliefs rather than their absolute validity was the result, in part at least, of his personal experience with, and reflections on, the effects of nitrous oxide (laughing gas) on his own mental state.

Major Concepts

James explored the full range of human psychology, from brain-stem functioning to religious ecstasy, from the perception of space to ESP research. He could argue both sides of a controversy with equal brilliance. There seemed to be no limit to James's curiosity and no theory, however unpopular, that he was unwilling to consider (MacLeod, 1969). He pursued most vigorously the task of understanding and explaining the basic units of thought. Fundamental concepts, including the nature of thought, attention, habit, will, and emotion, held James's interest.

For James, personality arises from the continual interplay of instincts, habits, and personal choices. He viewed personal differences, developmental stages, psychopathology, and the rest of personality as arrangements and rearrangements of the basic building blocks supplied by nature and slowly refined by evolution.

In Jamesian theory, there are some contradictions. And James was keenly aware of this state of affairs, knowing full well that what holds for one aspect of his approach may not apply to others. Instead of attempting to create a grand and unified scheme, he indulged in what he called *pluralistic thinking*—that is, holding to more than one theory at a time. James acknowledged that psychology was an immature science, lacking sufficient information in its formulation of consistent laws of sensation, perception, or even the nature of consciousness. Thus he was at ease with a multitude of theories, even with those that contradicted his own. In an introduction to a book that attacked James's theories, he wrote: "I am not convinced of all of Dr. Sidis's positions, but I can cordially recommend this volume to all classes of readers as a treatise both interesting and instructive, and original in a high degree" (Sidis, 1898, p. vi).

It seems to me that psychology is like physics before Galileo's time—not a single elementary law yet caught a glimpse of. (James, 1890)

In the conclusion to *Psychology: The Briefer Course* (1892a), which is the abridged edition of his famous textbook, he admits to the limits of psychology—limits that still exist today.

> When, then, we talk of "psychology as a natural science," we must not assume that means a sort of psychology that stands at last on solid ground. It means just the reverse; it means a psychology particularly fragile, and into which the waters of metaphysical criticism leak at every joint. A string of raw facts; a little gossip and wrangle about opinions; a little classification and generalization on the mere descriptive level; a strong prejudice that we *have* states of mind, and that our brain conditions them. This is no science, it is only the hope of a science. (pp. 334–335)

James considered many different, even opposing, ideas to be basic to an understanding of psychology. In this section, the discussion of major concepts is highly selective. The topics include, first, the self, then the elements of consciousness, and, finally, how consciousness selects.

The Self

The *self* is that personal continuity that we all recognize each time we awaken. It is more than personal identity; it is the place from which all our mental processes originate and through which all our experiences are filtered. James described several layers of the self, which, like consciousness, he saw, paradoxically, to be simultaneously continuous and discrete (Knowles & Sibicky, 1990).

The Material Self The **material self** is the layer that includes those items with which we personally identify. The material self encompasses not only our bodies but also our home, possessions, friends, and family.

> *In its widest possible sense, however, a man's Self is the sum total of all that he CAN call his,* not only his body and his psychic powers, but his clothes and his house, his wife and children, his ancestors and friends, his reputation and works, his lands and horses, and yacht and bank-account. All these

Personal Reflection

■ Who Am I?

Test James's proposition about the material self. Imagine that someone is ridiculing some person, idea, or thing that matters to you. Are you objective in evaluating the merits of the attack, or do you react as if you yourself were under attack? If someone insults your brother, your parents, your hairstyle, your country, your jacket, or your religion, are you aware of the investment that you have in each? Some of the confusion between ownership and identification is clarified by understanding this expanded concept of the self.

> things give him the same emotions. If they wax and prosper, he feels triumphant; if they dwindle and die away, he feels cast down,—not necessarily in the same degree for each thing, but in much the same way for all. (James, 1890, Vol. 1, pp. 291–292)

To the extent that a person identifies with an external person or object, it is part of his or her self. Teenagers in gangs, for example, will even kill one another to protect a piece of clothing or a street corner that they see as part of themselves.

The Social Self

A man's social self is the recognition which he gets from his mates. (James, 1890, Vol. 1, p. 293)

We willingly or unwillingly accept any and all roles. A person may have few or many **social selves.** These may be consistent or inconsistent. But whatever they are, we identify with each in the proper setting. James suggests that the proper course of action is to pick a self that seems admirable and to act like that self in as many situations as possible. "All other selves thereupon become unreal, but the fortunes of this self are real. Its failures are real failures, its triumphs real triumphs" (1890, Vol. 1, p. 310). This phenomenon is what James called the *selective industry of the mind* (Suls & Marco, 1990). Some researchers have reduced this idea to the distinction between private and public selves (Baumgardner, Kaufman, & Cranford, 1990; Lamphere & Leary, 1990), but that is an oversimplification of James's original observations.

The social self constitutes patterns of personal habit that form the mainstay of our relationships. James viewed it as a shifting, malleable, surface personality, often little more than a set of masks, changed to suit different audiences. He argued that social habits are necessary; they make life orderly. Habit is a cushion; it renders relationships safe and predictable. To James, the constant interplay between cultural conformity and individual expression was beneficial to both.

To give up pretensions is as blessed a relief as to get them gratified. . . . How pleasant is the day when we give up striving to be young—or slender! Thank God! we say, *those* illusions are gone. Everything added to the self is a burden. (James, 1890, Vol. 1, pp. 310–311)

The Spiritual Self The **spiritual self** is the individual's inner and subjective being. It is an active element in all consciousness.

According to James, it is "the most enduring and intimate part of the self" (1890, Vol. 1, p. 296). It is not where we experience pleasure or pain but that part of us that pleasure and pain affect. It is the source of effort, attention, and the will.

What James struggled to explain was a "felt" sense that we are more than personalities, and certainly more than the objects we call our own. The spiritual self is of a different order of feeling from the other selves, and, while it is hard to define, it can be experienced. One expression of this self is exemplified in religious experiences, which James saw as coming from a region more central than the area of ideas or of intellect. James remained undecided on the reality of a personal soul; however, he was convinced that there is something greater than individual identity. "Out of my experience . . . one fixed conclusion dogmatically emerges. . . . There is a continuum of cosmic consciousness, against which our individuality builds but accidental fences, and into which our several minds plunge as into a mother-sea or reservoir" (James in Murphy & Ballou, 1960, p. 324).

Characteristics of Thought

While most of the other theorists in this book are interested primarily in the contents of thought, James insists that we take one step back and look at the actual nature of thought. Until we do that, he argues, we will miss the chance to see how the mind itself functions.

Personal Consciousness There is no such thing as individual consciousness independent of an owner. Every thought is personal. Therefore, says James, there is only the process of thought as experienced or perceived by an individual. Consciousness always exists in relation to a person; it is not a disembodied or an abstract event.

Changes in Consciousness We can never have exactly the same thought twice. Our consciousness may repeatedly encounter the sight of a certain object, the sound of a specific tone, or the taste of a particular food, but how we perceive these sensations differs with each encounter. What seems upon cursory inspection to be repetitious thought is actually a changing series of thoughts. Each thought within a series is unique and each is partially determined by previous modifications of the original thought.

The only thing which psychology has a right to postulate at the outset is the fact of thinking itself. (James, 1890, Vol. 1, p. 224)

> Often we are ourselves struck at the strange differences in our successive views of the same thing. We wonder how we ever could have opined as we did last month about a certain matter. . . . From one year to another we see things in new light. What was unreal has grown real, and what was exciting is insipid. The friends we used to care the world for are shrunken to shadows; the women, once so divine, the stars, the woods, and the waters, how now so dull and common;. . . as for the books, what *was* there to find so mysteriously significant in Goethe, or in John Mill so full of weight? (James, 1890, Vol. 1, p. 233)

James astutely highlighted a central fact about consciousness: its inevitable changeableness—in fact, the impossibility of its being any other way.

Within each personal consciousness thought is always changing. (James, 1890, Vol. 1, p. 225)

The Continuity of Thought and the Stream of Consciousness Observing our thoughts leads us to the seeming paradox that while thoughts are continually changing, there is an equally obvious felt sense of personal continuity. James suggested a resolution: each thought affects the one that follows it.

> Each passing wave of consciousness, each passing thought is aware of all that has preceded in consciousness; each pulse of thought as it dies away transmits its title of ownership of its mental content to the succeeding thought. (Sidis, 1898, p. 190)

What is present at the moment, conscious or not, is the personality. (Carl Rogers, the Perls, B. F. Skinner, and Zen Buddhism come to different conclusions derived from similar observations.)

Each emerging thought takes part of its force, focus, content, and direction from preceding thoughts.

> Consciousness, then, does not appear to itself chopped up in bits. Such words as "chain" or "train" do not describe it fitly. . . . It is nothing jointed: it flows. A "river" or a "stream" are the metaphors by which it is most naturally described. *In talking of it hereafter, let us call it the stream of thought, of consciousness, or of subjective life.* (James, 1890, Vol. 1, p. 239)

Stream of consciousness, a method of spontaneous writing that attempts to mimic the flow and jumble of thought, arose in part from James's teaching. Gertrude Stein, a major exponent of this genre, was a student of James at Harvard.

In consciousness, the stream is continuous. James (as did Freud) based many of his ideas about mental functions on the assumption of continuous thought. There are gaps in feelings; there are gaps in awareness; but even when there are perceived gaps in consciousness, there is no accompanying feeling of discontinuity. For example, when you awaken in the morning, you never wonder who it is who is waking up. You feel no need to rush to a mirror to verify, to see, if it is *you.* You need no convincing that the consciousness you awoke with is the same as the one you took to sleep.

How Consciousness Selects: The Role of the Fringe, Attention, Habit, and Will A basic attribute of consciousness for James is its incessant selectivity: "It is always interested more in one part of its object than in another, and welcomes and rejects, or chooses, all the while" (1890, Vol. 1, p. 284). What and how an individual chooses and what determines those choices is the subject matter of much of the rest of psychology.

The Fringe Almost all contemporary theories of consciousness have taken up the model, proposed by Freud, of the mind unevenly divided between an aware conscious and a complex and less aware unconscious. James independently suggested a different way to explain how it is that thoughts and feelings move continually in and out of awareness. For him, awareness has two aspects: the definite portion and the vague portion, or the *nucleus* and the *fringe* (1890, Vol. 1, pp. 258–261).

What we attend to is what we are aware of at any particular moment; what is on the fringe is the *context,* or the web of associations and feelings that give

Personal Reflection

■ Stream of Consciousness

Try one or all of these stream-of-consciousness exercises. In order to get the greatest benefit from them, share and discuss your findings with other students.

1. Sit quietly and let your thoughts wander for five minutes. Afterward, write down as many of your thoughts as you can recall.
2. Allow your thoughts to wander for one minute. When the minute is over, recall what thoughts you had during that minute. Write down, if possible, the whole series. Here is an example of such a series:
   I will do this one-minute exercise:
      pencil to write thoughts down
      my desk has pencils
      bills on my desk
      do I still want to buy fluoridated spring water?
      Yosemite last year
      lakes frozen at the edge in the morning
      my sleeping bag zipper stuck that night, freezing cold
3. Try to control your thoughts for one minute, keeping them on a single track. Write down those thoughts.

Does it seem realistic to consider your consciousness as a stream? When you controlled your thoughts, did they seem actually under your control, or did they continue to "flow," moving from one idea or image to another?

meaning to the content. Some common experiences of the fringe include the following:

- The feeling of almost knowing. When we say, it's on the "tip of my tongue," we know that we know something but we can't yet express it.
- The feeling of being "on the right track." Research on creative problem-solving groups shows that when a group feels it is moving toward a solution, it is correct much of the time *even though almost no elements of the actual solution have surfaced yet* (Gordon, 1961; Prince, 1969).
- The intention to act before you know exactly what action you are going to take. Some people report that when dealing with a new situation, they "know" that they will know what to do as it develops.

Instead of imagining your mind as an iceberg, with a tip of consciousness above the surface and the bulk of it below the surface (or unconscious), imagine instead that your consciousness is a lake and that you are in a glass-bottom boat. You see clearly everything in whatever part of the lake you find yourself. The parts close by are the near fringe; all of the lake is potentially available for your inspection.

Long neglected, this model, based initially on subjective observation, has been revived by a number of cognitive psychologists as an alternative model of mental experience (Baars, 1993; Galen & Mangan, 1992; Gopnik, 1993; Mangan, 1993).

The mind is at every stage a theatre of simultaneous possibilities. Consciousness consists in the comparison of these with each other, the selection of some, and the suppression of the rest. (James, 1890, Vol. 1, p. 288)

Attention Philosophers before James (John Locke, David Hume, Robert Harley, Herbert Spencer, and others) assumed that the mind is initially passive and that experience simply rains upon it. The personality then develops in direct proportion to the amounts of various experiences received. James considered this idea naive and the conclusions patently false. Before experience can be *experienced,* it must be attended to. "*My experience is what I agree to attend to.* Only those items which I *notice* shape my mind—without selective interest, experience is an utter chaos. Interest alone gives accent and emphasis, light and shade, background and foreground—intelligible perspective, in a word" (1890, Vol. 1, p. 402). Although the capacity to make choices is restricted by conditioned habits, it is still possible—and for James essential—to make real and meaningful decisions from moment to moment.

Mind engenders truth upon reality. . . . Our minds are not here simply to copy a reality that is already complete. They are here to complete it, to add to its importance by their own remodeling of it, to decant its contents over, so to speak, into a more significant shape. In point of fact, the use of most of our thinking is to help us to change the world. (James in Perry, 1935, Vol. 2, p. 479)

Intellect and the Sentiment of Rationality There are two levels of knowing: knowing through direct experience and knowing through abstract reasoning. James calls the first level **knowledge of acquaintance.** It is sensory, intuitive, poetic, and emotional.

> I know the color blue when I see it, and the flavor of a pear when I taste it; I know an inch when I move my finger through it: a second of time when I feel it pass . . . but *about* the inner nature of these facts or what makes them what they are, I can say nothing at all. (1890, Vol. 1, p. 221)

The higher level of knowledge James calls **knowledge about.** It is intellectual, focused, relational; it can develop abstractions; it is objective and unemotional.

> When we know about it, we can do more than merely have it; we seem, as we think over its relations, to subject it to a form of *treatment* and *operate* upon it with our thought. . . . Through feelings we become acquainted with things but only with our thoughts do we know about them. (James, 1890, Vol. 1, p. 222)

Different ways of knowing can lead to different social consequences.

A man who thought he was dead was talking to a friend. Unable to convince him otherwise, the friend finally asked, "Do dead men bleed?" "Of course not," replied the man. The friend took a needle and jabbed it into the man's thumb. It began to bleed. The man looked at his thumb and then turned to his friend. "Hey, dead men do bleed!"

Why does a person accept one rational idea or theory and reject another? James suggests that it is partly an emotional decision; we accept the one, because it enables us to understand the facts in a more emotionally satisfying way. James describes this emotional satisfaction as "a strong feeling of ease, peace, rest. The feeling of sufficiency of the present moment, of its absoluteness—this absence of all need to explain it, account for it, or justify it—is what I call the **sentiment of rationality**" (1948, pp. 3–4). Before a person will accept a theory (any of the theories expounded in this book, for example), two separate sets of needs must be satisfied. First, the theory must be intellectually palatable, consistent, logical, and so on. Second, it must be emotionally palatable; it must encourage us to think or act in ways that we find personally acceptable and gratifying.

Consider the way we seek advice. If, for instance, you wanted to learn more about the effects of smoking marijuana, who would you go to for such advice?

Could you predict the kinds of information and suggestions you would be offered by your parents, friends who do not smoke marijuana, friends who do, someone who sells marijuana, a police officer, a psychiatrist, a member of the clergy, or a person working in a college counseling center? You probably could predict the kind and quality of information that each might offer, as well as your willingness to accept the information.

Often we are not consciously aware of this aspect of decision making. We like to believe that we can make decisions based entirely on rational thinking. Yet there is another critical variable that enters into the process: the desire to find facts that resolve our emotional confusion, that make us more comfortable. The sentiment of rationality involves emotionally embracing an idea *before* we can turn to the business of decision making.

Habit Habits are actions or thoughts that are seemingly automatic responses to a given experience. They differ from instincts in that habits can be created, modified, or eliminated by conscious direction. They are valuable and necessary. "Habit simplifies the movements required to achieve a given result, makes them more accurate and diminishes fatigue" (James, 1890, Vol. 1, p. 112). In this sense, habits are one facet of the acquisition of skills. On the other hand, "habit diminishes the conscious attention with which our acts are performed" (1890, Vol. 1, p. 114). Whether a habitual response is advantageous or not depends on the situation. Withdrawing attention from an action makes the action easier to perform but also makes it resistant to change.

Who can decide offhand which is better, to live or understand life. (James, 1911)

> The fact is that our virtues are habits as much as our vices. All our life, so far as it has definite form, is but a mass of habits—practical, emotional, and intellectual—systematically organized for our weal or woe, and bearing us irresistibly toward our destiny, whatever the latter may be. (James, 1899a, p. 33)

James was struck by the complexity of acquired habits as well as by their resistance to extinction. The following is one example:

> Houdin [a stage magician who was the namesake of the famous Houdini] early practiced the art of juggling with balls in the air; and having, after a month's practice, become thorough master of the art of keeping up four balls at once, he placed a book before him, and, while the balls were in the air, accustomed himself to read without hesitation. "This," he [Houdin] says, "will probably seem extraordinary; but . . . though thirty years have elapsed and . . . though I have scarcely once touched the balls during that period, I can still manage to read with ease while keeping three balls up." (1890, Vol. 1, p. 117)

Habits of learning As an educator of students and teachers, James was concerned with the formation of proper habits, for instance, the habit of attending to our actions instead of performing them automatically. He suggested that the systematic training of students to develop the habit of attention was far more important in education than the rote learning that was still so popular. "Continuity of training is the great means of making the nervous system act infallibly right" (1899a, p. 35). Although much of our lives is determined by habit, we still have the ability to choose which habits to cultivate.

The only things which we commonly see are those which we preperceive. (James, 1890, Vol. 1, p. 444)

Personal Reflection

■ A Useless Task

To get a sense of how a useless task might strengthen your will, try this exercise.

Obtain a small box of matches, paper clips, pushpins, or candies. Place the box on a table in front of you. Open the box. Take out the items inside one by one. Then close the box. Open it again. Put the items back into the box, one by one. Close the box. Repeat this cycle for five minutes.

Write down the feelings this exercise engenders. Pay special attention to any reasons you thought of for not completing the task.

If you were to repeat this task over several days, each time you might discover a host of new reasons for quitting. Although you would find the task difficult at first, it would gradually become easier to complete. You also would feel a sense of personal power and self-control.

The reasons you might invent for not doing this exercise represent a partial list of the elements in your own personality that inhibit your will. You have only your will to counter these many (and excellent) reasons. There is no "good reason" to continue the exercise beyond your decision to do so.

Psychological Growth: Emotion and Pragmatism

James rejected absolutes, such as *God, truth,* or *idealism,* in favor of personal experience—especially the individual's discovery of the means to self-improvement. A recurrent theme in his writings is that personal evolution is possible and that everyone has an inherent capacity to modify or change his or her attitudes and behaviors.

Emotions According to the James-Lange theory of emotion, an emotion depends on feedback from one's own body. The theory was so called because the Danish psychologist Carl Lange published a similar theory at about the same time James did (Koch, 1986). It is a biological theory of emotion that includes a psychological component. James says that we perceive a situation in which an instinctual physical reaction occurs, and then we are aware of an emotion (e.g., sadness, joy, surprise). The emotion is based on the recognition of the physical feelings, not of the initial situation.

> Were this bodily commotion suppressed, we should not so much *feel* fear as call the situation fearful; we should not feel surprise, but coldly recognize that the object was indeed astonishing. One enthusiast [James himself] has even gone so far as to say that when we feel sorry it is because we weep, when we feel afraid it is because we run away, and not conversely. (1899a, p. 99)

Personal Reflection

■ Body and Emotion

James says his theory of emotion is easiest to observe with the "grosser" emotions—love, anger, and fear. You can experience the interplay between physical sensations and feelings as follows:

Part 1

1. Allow yourself to become angry. Visualize a person, situation, or political figure you do not like. Let the emotion build: allow your posture to change, your hands to tighten into fists, your teeth to clench, your jaw to come forward and up slightly. Be aware of these or any other physical changes. If you work in pairs, have your partner take notes as to your posture and the way your muscles change.
2. Relax: move around, shake yourself, take a few deep breaths. Let the emotion go.
3. Allow yourself to feel lonely, withdrawn, isolated. (This is probably easier to do lying down.) Curl up your body; draw your knees and head close to your chest. Notice what your hands do.
4. Now, relax as before.

Part 2

Now evoke the same feelings—that is, anger and then loneliness while sitting comfortably and relaxed, without any physical tension. Compare how it feels to experience emotion with or without the attendant physical changes.

This interpretation seems contrary to the popular conception. Most of us assume that we perceive a situation, begin to have feelings about it, and then have physical responses—we laugh, cry, grit our teeth, run away, and so on. If James is correct, we should expect different emotions to arise from different physical reactions. Evidence that sensory feedback contributes to the awareness of emotions continues to be verified experimentally (Hohman, 1966; Laird, 1974; Laird & Bresler, 1990) and clinically (Bandler & Grinder, 1979).

In short, there is considerable theoretical agreement with, and empirical support for, the assumption that the experience of emotion is basically an interpretation of behavior. (Averill, 1980, p. 161)

Criticism of the theory centers on the assumption that there is no clear-cut connection between emotional states and patterns of physiological arousal (Cannon, 1927). According to James, however, "the emotions of different individuals may vary indefinitely," and he quotes Lange: "We have all seen men dumb instead of talkative, with joy. . . . [W]e have seen grief run restlessly about lamenting, instead of sitting bowed down and mute; etc., etc." (1890, Vol. 2, p. 454). Thus what current researchers are finding is that emotion does not exist without arousal (Schacter, 1971) and that the pattern of arousal is individual, repeatable, and predictable (Shields & Stern, 1979).

Work by Schacter and Singer (1962) has demonstrated that when subjects do not understand the real cause for their emotional arousal, they will label their feelings to fit the external cues. Rather than rely on their internal prompts, they are swayed by social and environmental influences, which may actually conflict with their own visceral feelings. So-called misattribution research—in which subjects are given false information about a drug that is administered to them or a procedure that is conducted on them—follows James's lead and Schacter's model (Winton, 1990). If subjects are aware of why they are aroused (informed that their feelings result from side effects of a drug, for example), they are less likely to label their own feelings inappropriately. The event *plus* the individual *plus* the setting will determine what emotion is experienced. Our emotions are based on our physical reactions plus our perception of the situation, not on our physical sensations alone.

James's general position also seems to be partially borne out by developments in psychopharmacology. Increasingly, specific emotional responses can be evoked by inhibiting or stimulating physiological processes through the ingestion of certain medications. Groups of drugs are commonly categorized by the changes in moods they produce. The emotional difficulties experienced by mental patients can be controlled or even eliminated through daily doses of these drugs. Clearly, James's insights are at the core of a number of research studies of emotion and arousal (Berkowitz, 1990; Blascovich, 1990; Buck, 1990).

Nonattachment to Emotional Feelings It was James's contention that a balance between detachment and the expression of feelings serves the organism best. He quotes Hannah Smith:

> Let your emotions come or let them go . . . and make no account of them either way. . . . They really have nothing to do with the matter. They are not the indicators of your spiritual state, but are merely the indicators of your temperament or of your present physical condition. (1899a, p. 100)

Emotional Excitement Although detachment is a desirable state, there are advantages to being overwhelmed by feelings. Emotional upset is one means by which long-standing habits can be disrupted; it frees people to try new behaviors or to explore new areas of awareness. James himself experienced and researched psychological states arising from mystical experiences, hypnosis, faith healing, mediumship, psychedelic drugs, alcohol, and personal crisis. He concluded that the precipitating event was not the critical factor; rather, the response the individual made to the arousal formed the basis for change.

Healthy-Mindedness For James, a state of healthy-mindedness meant that if the individual acted as though things were well, they would be. Idealism was more than a philosophic concept to James; it was an active force. His own return to mental health began with his decision to hold fast to the ideal of free will. James argued that a positive attitude was more than useful; it was necessary. "I do not believe it to be healthy-minded to nurse the notion that ideals are self-sufficient and require no actualization to make us content. . . . Ideals ought to aim at *the transformation of reality*—no less!" (James in H. James, 1926, Vol. 2, p. 270). He also saw it as the vital element, a dividing line between religious experiences, those that tend toward happiness and those that tend toward despair (1902/1985).

Pragmatism **Pragmatism,** originally developed by James to clarify or eliminate unnecessary considerations about issues in one's life or one's thought, became a school of philosophy in its own right. "Grant an idea or belief to be true, . . . what concrete difference will its being true make in any one's actual life?" (1909, p. v). If no practical differences exist whether an idea is true or false, then, James suggests, further discussion is pointless. From this he proposes a pragmatic, or useful, definition of truth. "True ideas are those we can assimilate, validate, corroborate, and verify. False ideas are those that we cannot" (1907, p. 199). He understands that there are truths that cannot be assimilated and so on, but he points out that this second class of truths (which he sees as useless) may be cast aside when one is faced with a personal choice or a real decision. Although this point of view may appear obvious to some, it was roundly criticized at its inception. James writes:

> I fully expect the pragmatist's view of truth to run through the classic stages of a theory's career. First, you know, a new theory is attacked as absurd; then it is admitted to be true, but obvious and insignificant; finally it is seen to be so important that its adversaries claim that they themselves discovered it. (1948, p. 159)

By now, most of us think that pragmatism is part of normal, everyday thinking. We can add a final stage to James's analysis of a "theory's career": Eventually the theoretical view becomes so ingrained in the culture that no one is given credit for it.

Obstacles to Growth

Since James was not a therapist, the obstacles he noted are those that all of us have experienced: unexpressed emotions, too much of an emotion, and misunderstandings among people.

Unexpressed Emotions Long before the rise of modern psychotherapy as well as the encounter movement and 12-step groups, James recognized the need to release emotional energy. He felt that blocked or bottled-up emotion can lead to mental and physical illness. Although the specific emotion doesn't have to be expressed—especially if doing so might hurt the individual or others—some outlet for the arousal should be found. Moreover, he believed that it is as necessary to express noble feelings as to express hostile ones. If one is feeling brave or charitable or compassionate, those feelings ought to be translated into action rather than be allowed to subside.

Errors of Excess It is common practice to label some personal characteristics as beneficial and others as detrimental. We say that being loving is a virtue, being stingy is a vice. James was convinced that this simple dichotomy was valid only for moderate displays of feeling. For instance, an excess of love becomes

Personal Reflection

■ Testing the Validity of an Idea

Test the validity of regenerative phenomena in this exercise. Start by taking testing one of James's propositions (Taylor, 1981).

James says:

> The way to success is by surrender to passivity, not activity. Relaxation, not intentness should be now the rule. Give up the feeling of responsibility, let go your hold. . . . It is but giving your private convulsive self a rest and finding that a greater self is there. . . . The regenerative phenomena which ensue on the abandonment of effort remain firm facts of human nature. (1890)

Choose a time when you are engaged in long, difficult activity, either intellectual or physical. If you are a coffee drinker or a candy muncher, pick a time when you really want such a stimulant. Instead of having a stimulant, lie flat on the floor for five minutes, breathe slowly and fully. Do not try to do anything; simply allow your muscles to relax, your thoughts to wander, and your breathing to slow down.

After five minutes, get up and check yourself. Are you refreshed? How does this inactivity compare with getting something to eat? Have you experienced James's *regenerative phenomena*?

possessiveness, an excess of loyalty becomes fanaticism, and an excess of concern becomes sentimentality. Each virtue can diminish a person if allowed to assume its extreme form.

Personal Blindness In an essay that was a favorite of his, James describes a "certain blindness," in which he discusses the inability of people to understand one another. Our failure to be aware of this **blindness** is a major source of unhappiness. Whenever we presume we can decide for others what is good for them or what they should be taught or what their needs are, we experience a certain kind of blindness.

Hands off: neither the whole of truth nor the whole of good is revealed to any single observer, although each observer gains a partial superiority of insight from the peculiar position in which he stands! (James in McDermott, 1977, p. 645)

The blindness we have in relation to one another is only a symptom of a more pervasive blindness, a blindness to an inner vision of reality. For James, this vision was not at all mysterious; it was tangible in the immediacy of experience itself. Our blindness prevents us from being aware of the intensity and the perfection of the present moment. Like Whitman and Tolstoy before him, James advocated grasping nature directly, without the filters of habit, manners, or taste. "Wherever it is found, there is the zest, the tingle, the excitement of reality; and there is 'importance' in the only real and positive sense in which importance ever anywhere can be" (1899a, p. 115).

> Life is always worth living, if one has such responsive responsibilities. We are trained to seek the choice, the rare, the exquisite exclusively, and to overlook the common. We are stuffed with abstract conceptions and glib with

> verbalities and verbosities. . . . [T]he peculiar sources of joy connected with our simpler functions often dry up, and we grow stone-blind and insensible to life's more elementary and general goods and joys. (1899a, p. 126)

Symptoms of our blindness may include the inability to express our feelings, the lack of awareness that leads to errors of excess, and the willing acceptance of habits that restrict consciousness.

Structure

The Mind Is in the Body

James's own bouts with illness caused him to reexamine continually the relationship between the body and consciousness. He concluded that even the most spiritual person must be concerned with and aware of physical needs, because the body is the initial source of sensation. However, consciousness can transcend any level of physical excitement for a limited period of time. The body, necessary for the origin and maintenance of personality, is subservient to the activities of the mind. For example, intellectual concentration can be so tightly focused "as not only to banish ordinary sensations, but even the severest pain" (James, 1890, Vol. 1, p. 49). There are numerous reports of soldiers in battle who suffer severe wounds but do not notice them until the intensity of the fighting abates. Common also are cases of athletes who break a wrist, a rib, or a collarbone but are unaware of the break while engaged in physical activity. Examining this evidence, James concludes that it is the focus of attention that determines whether external physical sensations will affect conscious activity. The body is an expressive tool of the indwelling consciousness, rather than the source of stimulation itself.

My experience is only what I agree to attend to. (James, 1890, Vol. 1, p. 402)

Good physical health, although rare in James's own life, had, for him, its own inner logic "that wells up from every part of the body of a muscularly well-trained human being, and soaks the indwelling soul of him with satisfaction. . . . [It is] an element of spiritual hygiene of supreme significance" (1899a, p. 103). Although James wrote that the body is not more than the place where consciousness dwells, he never lost sight of the importance of the body.

Personal Reflection

■ Daily Exercise

Decide to exercise for one week, 15 to 20 minutes each day. Choose the kind of exercise you will do: running, swimming, riding a bike, or whatever appeals to you. Do it as well as you can.

Observe: Does anything interfere with your carrying out the activity? What do you feel each time you complete the exercise you have set out for yourself? Does your body have a mind of its own?

his student John Dewey and Dewey's followers) and on philosophy—not only on pragmatism but on phenomenology as well (Edie, 1987). While various of James's ideas have come in and out of fashion in academic psychology, no one (including his most severe critics) ever suggested that the way he portrayed his findings and ideas was anything less than inspiring.

The Psychology of Consciousness

The whole drift of my education goes to persuade me that the world of our present consciousness is only one of many worlds of consciousness that exist, and that those other worlds must contain experiences which have a meaning for our life also; and that although in the main their experiences and those of this world keep discrete, yet the two become continuous at certain points and higher energies filter in. (James, 1902/1958, p. 391)

James, in laying out the scope of psychology, said that the discipline would consider any and all "mental states" as its data and would investigate their origins and their linkages to physical and physiological data in order to be useful for education, medicine, religion, and any other activity that needs to consider the control of the mind (1892b). He studied a wide range of states of consciousness and, in so doing, did not draw a fixed line between abnormal and normal experience. Portions of his work on altered states, religious states, hypnosis, and paranormal states were ignored. However, as psychology has evolved new methods of investigation, these areas are once again being actively researched. "The study of consciousness . . . is emerging as a field of study because of the ardent interest of people scattered throughout the many arms of psychology and well beyond" (Goleman & Davidson, 1979, p. xvii). Professional associations such as the Biofeedback Research Society and the Association for Transpersonal Psychology publish journals and support new lines of inquiry. There has been corresponding popular interest, as articles and best-selling books about consciousness appear regularly. The growing interest in consciousness research across a host of disciplines has not yet yielded any definitive answers. One reason may be that, as Nobel Prize winner Roger Sperry describes it, there is a dynamic interweaving between the riddle of consciousness and the changing scientific worldview (1995).

A few areas have particular implications for personality theory. Research findings on psychedelic substances, biofeedback, meditation, and hypnosis has challenged some basic assumptions about consciousness and the nature of reality. New methods, new instruments, and a renewed willingness to investigate subjective phenomena are providing a scientific foundation for James's philosophical speculations.

We cannot yet answer the question of what consciousness is—because it may not be answerable within our usual ways of explanation—but we are learning more about the contents of consciousness and the forms that it takes. Ornstein (1972) argues, as have many others over the centuries, that consciousness can never be understood using an objective approach alone. "There is no way to simply write down the answer, as we might give a textbook definition. The answers must come personally, experientially" (p. ix).

> Altered states of consciousness can be triggered by hypnosis, meditation, psychedelic drugs, deep prayer, sensory deprivation, and the onset of acute psychosis. Sleep deprivation or fasting can induce them. Epileptics and migraine sufferers often experience an altered awareness in the aura that precedes attacks. Hypnotic monotony, as in solo high-altitude jet flight, may bring on an altered state. Electronic stimulation of the brain (ESB), alpha

> or theta brain-wave training, clairvoyant or telepathic insights, muscle-relaxation training, isolation (as in Antarctica), and photic stimulation (light flicker at certain speeds) may bring on a sharp change in consciousness. (Ferguson, 1973, p. 59)

The research has shifted from how to induce states of consciousness to a better understanding of what can be learned from the experiences themselves.

Psychedelic Research

Most cultures, tribal or civilized, have used herbs, seeds, or plants to alter body chemistry, emotional outlook, and levels of awareness (Bravo & Glob, 1989; McKenna, 1991). James, himself, as has been noted, experimented with nitrous oxide (laughing gas) and was deeply impressed by his experiences (Tymoczko, 1996).

> With me, as with every other person of whom I have heard, the keynote of the experience is the tremendously exciting sense of an intense metaphysical illumination. Truth lies open to the view in depth beneath depth of almost blinding evidence. The mind sees all the logical relations of being with an apparent subtlety and instantaneity to which its normal consciousness offers no parallel; only as sobriety returns, the feeling of insights fades, and one is left staring vacantly at a few disjointed words and phrases, as one stares at a cadaverous-looking snow-peak from which the sunset glow has just fled, or at the black cinder left by an extinguished brand. (James, 1969, pp. 359–360)

It appears that some of the distinctions we maintain between ourselves and the outer world are arbitrary and are alterable. Our usual perceptions may be partially a function of the state of consciousness we are in. We see a world of many colors, but colors are only a small part of the spectrum that exists. The finding that a person may lose what he or she calls "personal" identity without feeling a loss of identity (now hard to define) leads us back to James, who described the self not as a stable, fixed structure but as a constantly fluctuating field.

When James wrote *The Varieties of Religious Experience* in 1902, he observed that experiencing so-called mystical consciousness was a rare and unpredictable event. The widespread use and continued availability of psychedelics have made experiencing such states—or at least the subjective impression of having experienced such states—more possible. Subjects regularly have what they call religious, spiritual, or transpersonal experiences. Determining the value as well as the validity of these reported experiences, now that they are more common, has become crucial (Bennett, Osburn, & Osburn, 1995; Weil & Rosen, 1993).

This issue is of concern to the religious community as well. Religious conversion, experiences during prayer, visions, and talking in tongues—all these occur during altered states of consciousness. The validity of these experiences is the foundation of a number of diverse religious doctrines. The discovery and examination of substances used in religious rituals, which have proved to be active psychedelic agents, have revived interest among theologians in the origin and meaning of chemically induced religious experience (Doblin, 1991) as well as the ethics involved in having access to such experiences (Clark, 1985; Smith, 1988). The term *entheogen* (realization of the divine within) has been coined to differentiate such use from psychotherapeutic or recreational use (Jesse, 1997; Ott, 1993).

Consciousness, time, and space appear to interact. Modern physicists and ancient mystics are sounding more and more alike in their attempts to define the known universe (LeShan, 1969). Reports of psychedelic experiences suggest that the nature and genesis of consciousness may be more realistically described by mystics and modern physics than by contemporary psychology (Capra, 1975; Zukav, 1979).

Research into various states of consciousness (Lukoff & Lu, 1989; Valle & von Eckartsberg, 1981) suggests that any theory of personality that does not take into account altered states is an incomplete portrayal of fundamental human experience. Consciousness may best be described as a spectrum (Wilber, 1977) in which our normal awareness is only a small segment. This normal awareness—unaltered consciousness—seems to be a special case (Bentov, 1977; Tart, 1975) with its own rules and limitations. Although this is an underlying assumption of the Eastern philosophies described in this book, it is a relatively undeveloped idea in most of Western psychology.

Biofeedback Research

James's theory that emotion depends on feedback from one's body has been expanded in a variety of ways through biofeedback research. Biofeedback is an application of the engineering concept of *feedback*—the mechanical principle controlling most equipment that operates automatically. A furnace and its thermostat, for instance, form a self-contained feedback system. *Biofeedback* is a means of monitoring a biological process. For example, when you use your fingers to feel your pulse, you are getting feedback concerning your heart rate.

Given immediate feedback, researchers found, subjects could control a wide range of physical parameters that included heart rate, blood pressure, skin temperature, and brain-wave frequency (Barber, Dicara, Kamiya, Shapiro, & Stoyva, 1971–1978). It is safe to say that almost any bodily process that can be monitored can be consciously modified and controlled. The fact that people are not aware of how they are controlling a bodily process does not limit their capacity to do so. People and animals can actually *think* their temperatures up and down, slow down or accelerate their heart rates, or shift from one brain-wave frequency to another.

A monkey has learned to fire a single nerve cell to obtain a reward. At Queen's University in Kingston, Ontario, John Basmajian trained human subjects to discharge a single motor nerve cell, selected from the brain's ten billion cells. Miller's rats [Neal Miller of Rockefeller University] learned to form urine at greater or lesser rates, to redden one ear and blanch the other, and increase or decrease the blood in their intestinal lining. (Ferguson, 1973, pp. 32–33)

Research has spawned a host of clinical applications. Among the conditions that respond to treatment based on biofeedback are tension and migraine headaches, Raynaud's disease (cold hands and feet), asthma, epilepsy, Parkinson's disease, ulcers, bed-wetting, hypertension, and cardiac abnormalities, including fibrillation. Additional experiments, often paired with other relaxation methods, have demonstrated improvements in metastatic cancer (Gruber, Hall, Hersh, & Dubois, 1988), test anxiety (Hurwitz, Kahane, & Mathieson, 1986), rheumatoid arthritis (Lerman, 1987), and post-traumatic stress disorder (Hickling, Sison, & Vanderploeg, 1986), as well as a range of phobia, hysteria, and impotence problems (Clonini & Mattei, 1985). It appears that any physical process that can be brought into sustained awareness can be treated effectively through biofeedback training.

Implications The capacities of the nervous system have been redefined. Scientists used to believe that along with the consciously controllable voluntary nervous system, humans had an autonomic, or involuntary, nervous system, which they could not consciously control. However, this distinction has all but vanished. Now it is more accurate to speak of the *gross* nervous system, which is open to conscious control with little or no training, and the *subtle* nervous system, which is open to conscious control with specialized training.

Images from Eastern religions of apparently incredible feats—yogis resting on beds of nails, saints being buried alive, devotees walking slowly over hot coals—were feats used by adepts to demonstrate the range of human possibilities. Since some of these behaviors can be replicated in the laboratory, it behooves researchers to look again at the implications of such capabilities (Brown, 1974; Karlins & Andrews, 1972; Rama, Ballentine, & Weinstock, 1976). The evidence for "human transformative capacity" (Murphy, 1992) is so extensive that Western science should let go of the definitions of mind-body interaction that were suitable for a far less scientific era.

We may need to redefine what it means to be *in control.* Physical control may be closely linked to, or may lead to, emotional control. If so, there could be advantages to teaching children or disturbed adults basic biofeedback techniques to increase their awareness and their ability to control their own reactions. Kamiya and Kamiya (1981) and Peper and Williams (1981) were among the first to demonstrate positive and lasting results from this training.

James defined will as the combination of attention and volition (wishing). Kimble and Perlmuter (1970) conclude that the will is critical in successful biofeedback training. They note, as well, that the role of attention is important in the willing process. They present an engaging example of what can occur if you wish to do something but do not pay close attention.

Are You Paying Attention?

QUESTION: *What do you call the tree that grows from acorns?*
ANSWER: *An oak.*
QUESTION: *What do we call a funny story?*
ANSWER: *A joke.*
QUESTION: *The sound made by a frog?*
ANSWER: *A croak.*
QUESTION: *The white of an egg?*
ANSWER: . . . (From Kimble & Perlmuter, 1970, p. 373)

Only if you are very attentive will you escape the pattern established in the series, which tends to elicit the incorrect answer *yolk.* You may wish to give the correct answer, but it is the combination of your wish (volition) plus your attention that makes it possible to do what you will. (If you wish to verify this point, try reading these questions to a friend and asking him or her to respond.)

Passive volition is defined as the willingness to let things happen. It refers to the particular state of consciousness that people learn to use in successful biofeedback training. It is attention without effort. A task in biofeedback training might be, for example, to learn to lower the temperature in the right hand. At first, people will "try"; the temperature in their right hands will rise. Then many people will "try not to." This usually results in their temperatures rising as well. Eventually, over the course of training, people learn to stop "trying" and to "allow" their temperatures to fall. Passive volition has not been part of our cultural training. We are brought up to be assertive, to succeed, to resist those forces that oppose us. James's distinctions between passive and active willing turn out to be important ones.

Most theories of personality that seek to treat mental illness specify the genesis of and contributing factors to mental disorders. Biofeedback research has shown an alternative treatment that focuses on "psychological" symptoms and ignores the psychological origins of the symptoms. As Green and Green (1972) suggest, because we can become physically ill in responding to psychological stress, perhaps we can eliminate the illness by learning to control the physiological response.

Perhaps some aspects of our personalities can be modified by biofeedback, a form of external, mechanistic, nonpsychological training. Areas usually associated with psychotherapy that are now targeted for biofeedback include alcoholism, chronic anxiety, drug abuse, learning disabilities, insomnia, obsessive phobic-depressive syndrome, and writer's cramp (O'Regan, 1979). James did the initial research into what was then called *mind cure* close to a century ago (Meyer, 1980). One might conclude that biofeedback training is still but one application of James's pioneering investigations.

Meditation

Research is beginning to demonstrate that physiological behaviors are affected by meditation (Shapiro & Walsh, 1981). *Meditation* can be defined as the directing, stilling, quieting, or focusing of one's attention in a systematic manner. It may be practiced either in silence or in the presence of noise, with eyes open or shut, while sitting or standing, and even while walking. There are hundreds of techniques, practices, and systems of meditation. Most of the early laboratory work was done on one system, transcendental meditation (Kanelakos & Lukas, 1974). Apparently, the data obtained are also valid for other systems (Benson, 1975). Later work draws more heavily from research on Buddhist mindfulness practices (Epstein, 1990; Sweet & Johnson, 1990). Most of the research continues to focus on stress management; fewer studies investigate its utility as a self-exploration strategy, and fewer still explore its original use as a way for self-liberation in a host of religious traditions (Shapiro, 1994).

With the widespread acceptance of meditation, organizations offering training can be found in many large cities and on most college campuses. Interest in the practical application of meditation in psychotherapy (Carrington, 1978; Delmonte, 1990), and evidence of its utility in the treatment of cancer (Simonton, Mathews-Simonton, & Creighton, 1978) and drug abuse (Benson

& Wallace, 1972), ensure its continued use as a therapy technique that is subject to further evaluation (Delmonte & Kenny, 1985; Kenny & Delmonte, 1986).

Implications What are the contents of consciousness? James proposed that we consider consciousness as if it were a stream or a river. Research reports indicate that a more complete description might portray consciousness as having many tracks or streams, all flowing simultaneously. Awareness may move from track to track like a searchlight playing over different tracks in a train depot.

What is there in consciousness besides discrete thoughts? Reports from meditators suggest something more than the varied thought forms that float to the surface of the mind. As one explores consciousness, there are changes in the content and in the structure and form of thought itself.

Tart (1972) encouraged researchers to consider that specialized training may be necessary in order to enter and observe these specific states. Just as dentists must have special training to detect tiny irregularities in X rays of the teeth, or astronauts need special training to work in antigravity situations, so should investigators working in *state-specific* science have appropriate training. James's complaint that the insights generated under nitrous oxide "fade out" may reflect his own lack of training, not just the fleeting effects of the gas.

Of all the hard facts of science, I know of none more solid and fundamental than the fact that if you inhibit thought (and persevere) you come at length to a region of consciousness below or behind thought . . . and a realization of an altogether vaster self than that to which we are accustomed. (Edward Carpenter, 1844–1929)

What effects does meditation have on personal values, lifestyle, and motivation? Ram Dass (1974) comments that his previous beliefs, developed while teaching Western motivational psychology, were severely threatened by his experiences in meditation. Some of the meditation systems he worked with did not even suggest that the so-called basic drives for affiliation, power, or achievement—or even the biologically rooted drives for food, water, or survival—were necessary for personal well-being. From the writings of Ram Dass (1978), Sayadaw (1954), and others, it is evident that models of personality exist that are based on suppositions beyond those considered here.

Hypnosis

Although hypnosis has been an area of research for over a hundred years, it is still not a well-defined phenomenon. Some of its applications include psychotherapy, athletic training, techniques for modulating pain, and even nightclub entertainment. Subjective reality and the responses of the subject to external stimuli are markedly changed in hypnosis. Tart (1970) described some of the range of effects.

Within the province of the mind, what I believe to be true is true or becomes true, within the limits to be found experientially and experimentally. These limits are further beliefs to be transcended. (Lilly, 1973)

> One of the standard tests we use, for instance, is to tell someone they can't smell and then you hold a bottle of ammonia under their nose and say, "take a good deep breath." They sit there with a blank face if they're a good subject. (It horrifies me every time I see it done, but it works beautifully.) You can induce total analgesia for pain for surgical operations, for instance. You can have people hallucinate. If you tell them there's a polar bear in the corner, they'll see a polar bear in the corner. You can tamper with their memory in certain ways. . . . You can take them back in time so

discovered that certain respondent behaviors can be conditioned. In his classic experiment, he conditioned the salivation response in dogs by pairing a bell with the arrival of food. Dogs naturally salivate at the sight or smell of food. After Pavlov had accompanied the presentation of food with the ringing of a bell, the dogs would salivate to the sound of the bell in the absence of food. He achieved this change in the dogs' behavior after only a few pairings. The dogs were conditioned to respond to a stimulus that previously had evoked no response reaction. Like Pavlov's dogs, we can be conditioned to salivate when we enter a restaurant or hear a dinner bell. Respondent conditioning is readily learned and exhibited. Advertisers who link an attractive person with a product are seeking to form an association and elicit a certain response. They hope that, through the pairing, consumers will respond positively to the product.

Operant conditioning is not pulling strings to make a person dance; it is arranging a world in which a person does things that affect that world, which in turn affects him. (Skinner, 1972b, p. 69)

Operant Conditioning Operant behaviors are behaviors that occur spontaneously. "Operant behavior is strengthened or weakened by the events that *follow* the response. Whereas respondent behavior is controlled by its antecedents, operant behavior is controlled by its consequences" (Reese, 1966, p. 3). The conditioning that takes place depends on what occurs after the behavior has been completed. Skinner became fascinated by operant behaviors, because he could see that they can be linked to far more complex behaviors than is true of respondent behaviors. Skinner concluded that almost any naturally occurring behavior in an animal or in a human can be trained to occur more often, more strongly, or in any chosen direction.

The following example illustrates some facets of operant conditioning: I am attempting to teach my daughter to swim. She enjoys the water but is unwilling or afraid to get her head or face wet or to blow bubbles under water. This has hindered her progress considerably. I have agreed to give her a piece of candy if she wets her face. Once she can freely wet her face, I will give her a piece of candy but only if she ducks her whole head. After she is able to do that, she will get a piece of candy only for blowing bubbles underwater. Stage by stage, she will modify her behaviors, rewarded, or *reinforced,* by the candies, leading to her learning how to swim.

Operant conditioning is the process of shaping and maintaining a particular behavior by its consequences. Therefore, it takes into account not only what is presented before the response but what happens after the response. With my daughter, I am conditioning her behavior by giving her a piece of candy *after* she performs certain acts. The candy is used to reinforce certain of her behaviors in the water. "When a bit of behavior is followed by a certain kind of consequence, it is more likely to occur again, and a consequence having this effect is called a reinforcer" (Skinner, 1971, p. 25).

Extensive research on the variables that affect operant conditioning have led to the following conclusions:

1. *Conditioning can and does take place without awareness.* Numerous demonstrations illustrate that what we perceive depends, in large measure, on our past perceptions, which have been partially conditioned. For example, the way we perceive the optical illusions used by Ames (1951) were thought to be a function of the physiology of vision (see Figure 11.1). However, when illusions like the

FIGURE 11.1 "Ames" Illusion

This is not a rectangle at an angle. It is a trapezoid looked at straight on. Seeing a rectangle is a conditioned, not an innate, response.

"rectangle" in the figure were shown to people from cultures in which the dwellings and windows do not contain right angles, they did not see the illusion. Perception, in part, is culturally conditioned. A summary of research concludes that conditioning can take place "in human beings . . . in the state of sleep, and in the waking state while the subject is entirely unaware of the fact that he is learning to respond to a conditioned stimulus" (Berelson & Steiner, 1964, p. 138).

2. *Conditioning is maintained in spite of awareness.* It is disconcerting to realize that you can be conditioned even when you know that the process is happening and you may be resisting it. One experimenter trained subjects to lift a finger at the sound of a tone paired with a shock to the finger. The subjects continued to raise their fingers even after they had been told that the shock had been turned off. They continued to raise their fingers even when asked by the experimenter not to do so. Only after the electrodes had been removed from their fingers could they control their own recently conditioned responses (Lindley & Moyer, 1961).

3. *Conditioning is most effective when the subject is aware and cooperative* (Goldfried & Merbaum, 1973). Efficient conditioning is a collaboration. There is an inherent instability in conditioning when it is not undertaken with full cooperation. The following story illustrates what can happen when cooperation is not obtained:

> A half dozen old and tattered alcoholics in a Midwestern Veterans hospital a few years ago were given an alcohol treatment. [They were administered a drug that induced vomiting anytime they drank alcohol. Eventually, the men were conditioned so that drinking alcohol without taking the drug caused vomiting.] The men were thoroughly conditioned, and just the thought of drinking made them shake.
>
> One afternoon, the old men started talking about their new lives and each discovered that the others hated it. They decided they would rather be in danger of being drunkards again than be terrified of the bottle.
>
> So they plotted an evening to escape. They sneaked out to a bar, crowded together on their barstools, and through their sweating, shaking

Personal Reflection

Observing and Modifying Behavior

Observing behavior and recording what you observe is the cornerstone of behavior modification. Try this exercise in observing and modifying your own behavior. Use tally sheets or graph paper to record your observations.

Keep a record of the time you spend working on each of your courses. A simple bar graph, marked off in hours, with different bars for each subject would be appropriate. Keep records for a week to establish a baseline. Then decide which class you need to spend the most study time on.

For the next week, each time you study for that class, give yourself positive reinforcement; read a chapter of a novel, eat some candy, spend time with a friend, make a phone call, or do whatever appeals to you. *Make sure the reinforcement is something that you really enjoy.* Keep a record of the reinforcers and when you gave them to yourself.

Do you find the amount of time you are spending on the course increasing? What are the possible causes for this increase?

> and vomiting, they bolstered and chided one another to down drink after drink. They downed enough so their fears left them. (Hilts, 1973)

Thus it would appear that conditioning, while a powerful, insistent system to prevent spontaneous action, is not without its limits.

When I was a Freudian somebody would say, "I've been thinking about my mother's vagina," and I'd write down "mother's vagina" you know, and pretty soon I've got the patient reinforced so that every time I pick up my pencil he gets a flash . . . [H]e's winning my attention and love . . . [and] pretty soon he's talking about his mother's vagina 15 minutes of the hour. And then I think, "Ah, we're getting some place." (Ram Dass, 1970, p. 114)

Reinforcement A **reinforcer** is any stimulus that follows the occurrence of a response and increases or maintains the probability of that response. In the example of the child learning to swim, candy was the reinforcer offered after she correctly or successfully exhibited a specific behavior.

Reinforcers may be either positive or negative.

> *A positive reinforcer* strengthens any behavior that *produces* it: a glass of water is positively reinforcing when we are thirsty, and if we then draw and drink a glass of water, we are more likely to do so again on similar occasions. A *negative reinforcer* strengthens any behavior that *reduces or terminates* it: when we take off a shoe that is pinching, the reduction in pressure is negatively reinforcing, and we are more likely to do so again when a shoe pinches. (Skinner, 1974, p. 46)

Negative reinforcers are aversive in the sense that they are stimuli that a person or an animal turns away from or tries to avoid.

Positive and negative consequences regulate or control behaviors. This is the core of Skinner's position; he proposes that all behavior can be understood to be conditioned by a combination of positive and negative reinforcers. Moreover, he asserts, it is possible to explain the occurrence of any behavior if one has sufficient knowledge of the prior reinforcers.

Skinner's original research was done on animals; the reinforcers he used included food, water, and electric shocks. The connection between the reinforcers and the animals' needs was straightforward. For example, a hungry animal learned to do a task, such as open a hatch or push a lever, and was rewarded. The reinforcements are more difficult to perceive when one investigates more complex or abstract situations. What are the reinforcers that lead to overeating? What reinforces a person who volunteers for a life-threatening job? What keeps students doing the work in courses when they have no interest in the subject?

Primary reinforcers are events or stimuli that are innately reinforcing. They are unlearned, present at birth, and are related to physical needs and survival. Examples are air, water, food, shelter. *Secondary* reinforcers are neutral stimuli that become associated with primary reinforcers so that they eventually function as reinforcers. Money is one example of a secondary reinforcer; it has no intrinsic value, but we have learned to associate it with many primary reinforcers. Money or the eventual promise of money is one of the most widely used and effective reinforcers in our culture.

The effectiveness of money as a secondary reinforcer is not limited to humans. It has been shown that chimpanzees can learn to work for tokens. They have been trained to spend the tokens in vending machines that dispense bananas and other rewards. When they were denied access to the machines for a time, they would continue to work, hoarding their tokens until the machines were once again available.

Schedules of Reinforcement How often or how regularly a new behavior is reinforced affects how quickly the behavior is learned and how long or how often it will be repeated (Ferster & Skinner, 1957). *Continuous* reinforcement will increase the speed at which a new behavior is learned. *Intermittent* or *partial* reinforcement will produce more stable behavior—that is, behavior that will continue to be produced even after the reinforcement stops or appears very rarely. Thus researchers have found that, to change or maintain behaviors, the scheduling is as important as the reinforcement itself (Kimble, 1961). A slot machine, for example, works on an intermittent reinforcement schedule. It rewards the player only now and then but often enough so that the act of playing the machine is learned quickly and is very hard to extinguish.

Reinforcing a correct response improves learning. It is more effective than punishment (aversive control), because reinforcement selectively directs behavior toward a predetermined goal. The use of reinforcement is a highly focused and effective strategy for shaping and controlling desired behaviors.

Behavioral Control While many psychologists are concerned with predicting behavior, Skinner is interested in the control of behavior.

> We are all controlled by the world in which we live . . . The question is this: Are we to be controlled by accident, by tyrants, or by ourselves in effective cultural design?
>
> The danger of the misuse of power is possibly greater than ever. It is not allayed by disguising the facts. We cannot make wise decisions if we continue to pretend that human behavior is not controlled, or if we refuse to engage in control when valuable results might be forthcoming. Such measures weaken only ourselves, leaving the strength of science to others. The first step in a defense against tyranny is the fullest possible exposure of controlling techniques. . . .

> It is not time for self-deception, emotional indulgence, or the assumption of attitudes which are no longer useful. Man is facing a difficult test. He must keep his head now, or he must start again—a long way back. (Skinner, 1955, pp. 56–57)

If one can make changes in the environment, one can begin to control behavior. Freedom, for Skinner, means controlling one's behavior.

What Supports or Impedes Personal Growth?

Growth, in Skinner's terms, refers to the ability to minimize adverse conditions and to increase the beneficial control of our environment. By clarifying our thinking, we can make better use of the available tools for predicting, maintaining, and controlling our own behavior.

Ignorance Skinner defines *ignorance* as lack of knowledge about what causes a given behavior. The first step in overcoming ignorance is to acknowledge it; the second is to change the behaviors that have maintained the ignorance. One way to eliminate ignorance is to stop using words that are nondescriptive, mental terms. In the following example, Skinner illustrates how an individual's portrayal of behavior can reveal the way that person views the causes of the behavior being observed:

> A hungry pigeon was conditioned to turn around in a clockwise direction by reinforcing successive approximations with food. Students who had watched the demonstration were asked to write an account of what they had seen. Their responses included the following: (1) The organism was conditioned to *expect* reinforcement for the right kind of behavior. (2) The pigeon walked around, *hoping* that something would bring the food back again. (3) The pigeon *observed* that a certain behavior seemed to produce a particular result. (4) The pigeon *felt* that food would be given it because of its action; and (5) the bird came to *associate* his action with the click of the food-dispenser. The observed facts could be stated respectively as follows: (1) The organism was reinforced *when* it emitted a given kind of behavior. (2) The pigeon walked around *until* the food container again appeared. (3) A certain behavior *produced* a particular result. (4) Food was given to the pigeon when it acted in a given way; and (5) the click of the food-dispenser *was temporarily related* to the bird's action. These statements describe the contingencies of reinforcement. The expressions "expect," "hope," "observe," "feel," and "associate" go beyond them to identify effects on the pigeon. The effect actually observed was clear enough; the pigeon turned more skillfully and more frequently; but that was not the effect reported by the students. (Skinner in Wann, 1964, pp. 90–91)

This example is one of many Skinner has used to show people how their determination to think in "fictions" prevents them from being in touch with the actual, vital, and concrete world.

Functional Analysis **Functional analysis** is an examination of cause-and-effect relationships. It treats every aspect of behavior as a *function* of a condition that can be described in physical terms. Thus the behavior and its causes can be defined without explanatory fictions.

> When we see a man moving about a room, opening drawers, looking under magazines, and so on, we may describe his behavior in fully objective terms. "Now he is in a certain part of the room; he has grasped a book between the thumb and forefinger of his right hand; he is lifting the book and bending his head so that any object under the book can be seen." We may also interpret his behavior or "read a meaning into it" by saying "he is looking for something" or, more specifically, that "he is looking for his glasses." What we have added is not a further description of his behavior but an inference about some of the variables responsible for it. This is so even if we ask what he is doing and he says, "I am looking for my glasses." This is not a further description of his behavior but of the variables of which his behavior is a function; it is equivalent to "I have lost my glasses," "I shall stop what I am doing when I find my glasses," or "When I have done this in the past, I have found my glasses." (Skinner in Fabun, 1968, p. 18)

Precise descriptions of behavior help us make accurate predictions of future behaviors and improve the analysis of the reinforcements that led to the behavior. To understand ourselves, we must recognize that our behavior is neither random nor arbitrary but is a purposeful process that can be described by considering the environment in which the behavior is embedded.

Skinner says that explanations that depend on terms such as *will, imagination, intelligence,* or *freedom* are not functional. They obscure rather than clarify the causes of behavior, since they do not truly describe what is occurring.

Punishment Punishment does not provide information about how to do something correctly. It neither meets the demands of the person inflicting the punishment nor benefits the person receiving it. Thus it inhibits personal growth. People who make mistakes want to learn how to correct their error or how to come to the correct solution next time. Often, when students have tests returned to them, they learn which answers they got wrong. No further explanation is given; the correct solutions are not forthcoming. In such situations, people may feel that they are actually being prevented from learning. Skinner, although often misunderstood, is solidly against punishment in families, in schools, and in social institutions—not on moral grounds but on practical ones.

Punishment does not work—that is to say, punished behaviors usually do not go away. Unless new learning is available, the punished responses will return, often disguised or coupled with new behaviors. The new behaviors may be attempts to avoid further punishment, or they may be retaliation against the person who administered the original punishment. The more a teacher uses punishment, the more discipline problems he or she will have. The effects of a prison term illustrate the ineffectiveness of punishment. Prison life punishes inmates for their prior behaviors but rarely teaches the individuals more socially acceptable ways to satisfy their needs. Prisoners who have not learned behaviors to replace those that landed them in jail will, once released—and exposed to the same environment and still subject to the same temptations—probably repeat

Personal Reflection

Punishment Versus Reinforcement

Part 1. Punishment

Write down a behavior of your own that you wish to modify. You might choose coming to class late, writing letters during class, eatin g too much, going to sleep late, or being rude. If you are married, if you live with someone, or if you have a roommate, you can each pick a habit and help each other.

Punish yourself or have your partner punish you each time the behavior occurs. The punishment might be an insult ("Hey, piggy, you're overeating again"), forfeiture of some treat, or some other deprivation. An easy punishment is to fine yourself a given amount of money each time the behavior occurs. The accumulated fines can be given to charity. (A variation of this is to give the fines to your partner so that he or she is rewarded every time you are punished. This will make your partner more alert.)

After a week, review your progress.

Part 2. Positive Reinforcement

Now choose a behavior that you would like to perform more often, such as exercising.

Begin to reinforce yourself every time you perform the desired behavior. Give yourself, or have your partner give you, small gifts: praise, gold stars, or some other reward. Being noticed is among the most effective rewards, so be sure that both you and your partner note the desired behavior when it occurs.

After a week, review your behavior pattern. Have there been any changes? How do you feel about this way of modifying your behavior? Consider the different effects punishment and reward (reinforcement) could have in your life.

those behaviors. The high proportion of criminals returning to prison underscores the accuracy of these observations.

A related problem is that punishment selectively reinforces and encourages the punisher.

> Thus, a slave driver induces a slave to work by whipping him when he stops; by resuming work the slave escapes from the whipping (and incidentally reinforces the slave driver's behavior in using the whip). A parent nags a child until the child performs a task; by performing the task the child escapes nagging (and reinforces the parent's behavior). The blackmailer threatens exposure unless the victim pays; by paying the victim escapes from the threat (and reinforces the practice). A teacher threatens corporal punishment or failure until his students pay attention; by paying attention the students escape from the threat of punishment (and reinforce the teacher for threatening it). In one form or another intentional aversive control is the pattern of most social coordination—in ethics, religion, government, economics, education, psychotherapy, and family life. (Skinner, 1971, p. 26)

Skinner concluded that although punishment may be used briefly to suppress a behavior that is highly undesirable or could cause injury or death, a far more useful approach is to establish a situation in which a new, competing, and more beneficial behavior can be learned and reinforced.

Structure

Body

In a system based solely on observable data, the role of the body is of primary importance. However, one does not need to know neuroanatomy or the physiological processes in order to predict how people will behave. In fact, since *personality,* as we normally use the term, is for Skinner an explanatory fiction, all there is, is the body.

The body never interested Skinner. He treats a person as an unopened, but certainly not empty, box. "Rather than hypothesize the needs that may propel a particular activity, they try to discover the events that strengthen its future likelihood, and that maintain or change it. Thus they search for the conditions that regulate behavior rather than hypothesize need states inside the person" (Mischel, 1976, p. 62). Thus later behaviorists emphasize the inputs and outputs, because, in their terms, these are the only observable elements.

Relationships and the Psychology of Women

Skinner's interest is in the forces that shape and control individuals from outside themselves. For Skinner, social behavior is not special or distinct from other behavior. Social behavior is a series of interactions between two or more people.

Relationships Skinner devotes considerable attention to verbal behavior (1957) and to the importance of the verbal community's role in shaping behavior, especially early language development and other behavior in children. For Skinner, verbal behavior includes speaking, reading, writing: any activity that uses words. The **verbal community** is defined as the people who respond to the verbal behavior of others in the same community. For example, a child listens to parents, siblings, other children, and teachers. He or she responds by changing or maintaining various behaviors. This is common sense, even when expressed in behavioral terms; but Skinner goes on to say that there are no other relevant variables for behavior beyond a person's history, genetic endowment, and events in the immediate environment.

The reinforcements you receive in a social situation depend partly on your behavior and partly on how others react to your behavior. In a conversation, you say something and then you receive feedback. The feedback you receive, however, is based not only on what you said but also on how the other person behaved after hearing it. For example, you say something as a joke. The other person takes it seriously and becomes upset. You modify your behavior and add, "I was only kidding." Thus we modify our behaviors in interpersonal relationships as much on the basis of others' reactions as on our own perceptions. This is the verbal community in action.

Personal Reflection

■ Modifying Someone Else's Behavior

Many experiments have established that verbal behavior can be conditioned by selectively rewarding types of words or phrases (Berelson & Steiner, 1964). You can experiment with rewarding certain verbal behaviors by simply nodding your head or saying "mmm-hmmm" or "yeah."

Try this exercise. In conversations, indicate agreement by nodding every time a particular behavior is expressed (for example, the use of long, complex words, swear words, or emotional statements). Notice if the number of such expressions increases as you continue to reinforce them.

Although Skinner, writing as a psychologist, did not discuss social relationships, his characters in *Walden Two* discuss them at length. Frazier, the designer of the utopian community, describes the place of the conventional family.

> The significant history of our times is the story of the growing weakness of the family. . . . A community must solve the problem of the family by revising certain established practices. That's absolutely inevitable. The family is an ancient form of community, and the customs and habits which have been set up to perpetuate it are out of place in a society which isn't based on blood ties. Walden Two replaces the family, not only as an economic unit, but to some extent as a social and psychological unit as well. What survives is an experimental question. (1948, p. 138)

The Psychology of Women Skinner, in keeping with his atheoretical outlook, did not describe a psychology of women per se. According to Skinner, "a self is a repertoire of behavior appropriate to a given set of contingencies. . . . The identity conferred upon a self arises from the contingencies responsible for the behavior" (Skinner, 1971, pp. 189–190). Thus a woman's identity is unique and different from a man's identity only insofar as the contingencies responsible for women's and men's behaviors differ. To the extent, then, that a society indeed offers different contingencies to men than it does to women (in terms, say, of roles and behaviors reinforced as culturally appropriate), the "psychologies" of men and women will differ. In the society that Skinner has envisioned in *Walden Two,* for example, the contingencies determining behavior are in fact quite different from those prevalent in contemporary Western society, and conceptions of femininity and masculinity differ accordingly. Skinner did not distinguish, for instance, between jobs on the basis of sexual stereotypes but suggests that individuals will find jobs and develop skills best suited to them as they respond to the general needs of the group.

Emotions

Skinner advocates an essentially descriptive approach to emotions. Instead of treating emotions as vague inner states, he suggests that we learn to observe associated behaviors. "We define an emotion—insofar as we wish to do so—as a particular state of strength or weakness in one or more responses" (1953, p. 166). He points out also that even a well-defined emotion like anger will include different behaviors on different occasions, even with the same individual.

The "emotions" are excellent examples of the fictional causes to which we commonly attribute behavior. (Skinner, 1953, p. 160)

> When the man in the street says that someone is afraid or angry or in love, he is generally talking about predispositions to act in certain ways. The "angry" man shows an increased probability of striking, insulting, or otherwise inflicting injury and a lowered probability of aiding, favoring, comforting, or making love. The man "in love" shows an increased tendency to aid, favor, be with, and caress and a lowered tendency to injure in any way. "In fear" a man tends to reduce or avoid contact with specific stimuli—as by running away, hiding, or covering his eyes and ears; at the same time he is less likely to advance toward such stimuli or into unfamiliar territory. These are useful facts, and something like the layman's mode of classification has a place in a scientific analysis. (1953, p. 162)

Skinner feels that the current difficulties in understanding, predicting, and controlling emotional behaviors could be reduced by observing behavioral patterns, not by referring to unknown internal states.

James and others were on the right track. . . . We both strike *and* feel angry for a common reason, and that reason lies in the environment. (Skinner, 1975, p. 43)

Thinking and Knowing

Descriptions of thinking, for Skinner, are as unreliable and vague as descriptions of emotional states.

> "Thinking" often means "behaving weakly," where the weakness may be due, for example, to defective stimulus control. Shown an object with which we are not very familiar, we may say, "I think it is a kind of wrench," where "I think" is clearly opposed to "I know." We report a low probability for a different reason when we say, "I think I shall go," rather than "I shall go" or "I know I shall go."
>
> There are more important uses of the term. Watching a chess game, we may wonder "what a player is thinking of" when he makes a move. We may mean that we wonder what he will do next. In other words, we wonder about his incipient or inchoate behavior. To say, "He was thinking of moving his rook," is perhaps to say, "He was on the point of moving it." Usually, however, the term refers to completed behavior which occurs on a scale so small that it cannot be detected by others. (Skinner, 1974, p. 103)

Skinner defines knowledge as a *repertoire of behavior*. "A man 'knows his table of integrals' in the sense that under suitable circumstances he will recite it, make corresponding substitutions in the course of a calculation, and so on. He 'knows his history' in the sense of possessing another highly complex repertoire" (1953, pp. 408–409).

Personal Reflection

■ Modifying a Professor's Behavior

This is a popular stunt designed by behavioral psychology students. Try it. Choose as your subject a professor who ambles about during lectures. The experimenters in this study will be comprised of as many of the class members as agree to participate. Experimenters can begin by reinforcing the professor's walking toward one side of the room. This can be done as follows: As the professor turns or moves to one side of the classroom, the experimenters should lean forward, write notes diligently, and appear to pay very close attention to what he or she is saying. When the professor moves to the other side of the classroom, experimenters should relax and become much less attentive.

Many classes have found that after several lectures, they can keep their professors in a corner for most of the class. You might do well to restrict this exercise to professors of psychology, so that, when it is explained to them, they will not misunderstand your intentions but will reinforce you with behavioristic goodwill.

But if a behavioristic interpretation of thinking is not all we should like to have, it must be remembered that mental or cognitive explanations are not explanations at all. (Skinner, 1974, p. 103)

Knowledge is the behavior displayed when a particular stimulus is applied. Other theorists tend to consider behaviors such as naming the major character in *Hamlet* or explaining the influence of German silver-mine production on medieval European history as "signs" or evidence of knowledge; Skinner regards these behaviors as knowledge itself. Another way he defines knowledge is the probability of skilled behavior. To say that a person "knows how to read" means, to Skinner, that the occasions upon which reading is reinforced tend to produce the behavioral repertoire called reading. Skinner feels that the conventional ways of teaching suffer when the tools of behavioristic analysis are not employed. His concern moved him to devise learning situations and devices that accelerate the pace and enlarge the scope of established learning.

Self-knowledge

Skinner does explore the repertoire of behaviors known as *self-knowledge*. In so doing, he describes a number of cases in which self-knowledge is lacking. "A man may not know that *he has done something* . . . may not know that *he is doing something* . . . may not know that *he tends to*, or *is going to, do something* . . . may not recognize *the variables of which his behavior is a function*" (Skinner, 1958, pp. 288–289). These cases are of intense interest to nonbehaviorists because they are said to be manifestations of various internal states (e.g., complexes, habit patterns, repressions, or phobias). Skinner labels these incidents simply as behaviors for which there has been no positive reinforcement for noticing or remembering them. "The crucial thing is not whether the behavior which a man fails to report is actually observable by him, but whether he has ever been given any reason to observe it" (Skinner, 1953, p. 289). It is not what has happened to you that counts but whether you were given a reward for noticing.

Therapy

Skinner views therapy as a controlling agency of almost unlimited power. Since the therapist is designated as a highly likely source of relief, any promised or actual relief becomes positively reinforcing, increasing the therapist's influence.

Since Skinner's theory includes no *self,* the goal of therapy cannot be to make the client feel better, be better adjusted, or achieve insight or self-understanding. From the behaviorist's position, the goal of therapy must be to modify the shape or order of behaviors—that is, to prevent undesirable behaviors from recurring and to have desirable behaviors occur more often.

Operating from this premise, behavior therapists have successfully treated problems including some not readily improved by psychodynamic therapies. An extensive review of behavior therapies (Rachman & Wilson, 1980) described a number of well-designed studies with generally favorable results. These studies explore such areas as sexual dysfunction, sexual deviance, marital conflict, psychotic disorders, and addictive disorders, including alcoholism, smoking, and obesity.

Although there are a number of different approaches to behavior therapy, it is generally accepted that a behavior therapist is primarily interested in actual behaviors, not in inner states or historical antecedents. According to behaviorists, *the symptom is the disease,* not a manifestation of an underlying illness. The "symptom"—such as a facial tic, premature ejaculation, chronic drinking, or a fear of crowds—is dealt with directly. Symptoms are not used as an entrée to an investigation of early memories or of the patient's existential perspective.

For the patient, the therapist is a nonthreatening audience, which is also true of the psychodynamic therapies. In behavior therapy terms, the client is therefore free to express previously unexpressed behaviors, such as weeping, hostile feelings, or sexual fantasies. However, the behavior therapist is intent upon withholding reinforcement in the face of these expressions. The therapist is interested in teaching, training, and rewarding behaviors that can effectively compete with and eliminate behaviors that are uncomfortable or disabling. For example, progressive relaxation may be taught as a means to lessen specific anxiety reactions, or assertiveness training may help a patient overcome timid behaviors.

The following statements describe the special nature of behavior therapy, as well as what it shares with other forms of therapy.

1. Behavior therapy helps people respond to life situations the way they would like to respond. This includes increasing the frequency and/or range of a person's desired behaviors, thoughts, and feelings; and decreasing or eliminating unwanted behaviors, thoughts, and feelings.
2. Behavior therapy does not try to modify an emotional core of attitudes or feelings within the personality.

Personal Reflection

■ Desensitization

This exercise is not intended to show you how a therapist would actually work. It is a way for you to experience some of the dynamics that occur when you focus on a single item of behavior.

One procedure used by behavior therapists is *desensitization,* which is a method that serves to decrease gradually a person's sensitivity to a disturbing stimulus.

Part 1. Identify a Symptom

Think of a fear you have had for some time, perhaps a phobia (phobias are the easiest to work with). Fears of snakes, worms, blood, or heights are good examples. If you cannot think of or are unwilling to consider a phobia, choose a negative emotional reaction you have to a given situation. For example, you may become anxious every time a police car drives behind you, you may get defensive whenever someone mentions your religion, or you may panic just before you begin an exam. Look for a response that seems repetitive and disturbing.

Part 2. Relaxation

Sit in a comfortable chair or lie down. Let your whole body relax. Concentrate on one part of your body after another, telling it to relax and noticing the relaxation. Let your toes relax, your feet, your ankles, knees, legs, and so forth. This will take a few minutes. Practice this progressive relaxation a few times. If you cannot tell whether or not a part of your body has relaxed, tense the muscles in that area and then relax them.

Part 3. Desensitization

After completing the relaxation exercise in Part 2, while you are relaxed, think of something that has a very distant relationship to the phobia or habit you are working with. If you have a fear of snakes, think of reading about a small, harmless snake that is found only in a distant country. If you have a fear of police officers, think about a clown dressed like a police officer, giving away balloons at a circus.

Try to maintain an image in your mind related to the anxiety-provoking stimulus, while you stay physically relaxed. If you start getting tense ("Yuck, a snake!"), stop concentrating on the image and focus on relaxing, going back to the relaxation exercise until you are once again relaxed. Repeat this procedure until you can hold the image in your mind while still remaining fully relaxed.

All the following steps build on one another. Think of an image or situation that is a little more vivid, and closer to the real object or situation of fear. Visualize or imagine it while you maintain a state of relaxation. Then visualize an image that is closer still to the actual one, as you continue to be relaxed. For a snake phobia, for example, the remaining successive steps in the desensitization process could include actually reading about snakes, then looking at pictures of snakes, followed by having a snake in a cage across the room from you, then having a snake in the same cage next to you, and finally holding the snake in your hand.

Do not skip steps. Do not go to a later image or situation until you are relaxed in all the earlier ones.

3. Behavior therapy takes the posture that a positive therapeutic relationship is a necessary, but not sufficient, condition for effective psychotherapy.
4. In behavior therapy, the complaints of the client are accepted as the primary focus of psychotherapy—not as symptoms for some underlying problem.
5. In behavior therapy, the client and the therapist come to an explicit understanding of the problem presented in terms of the actual behavior (e.g., actions, thoughts, feelings) of the client. They decide mutually on specific therapeutic goals, stated in such a way that both client and therapist know when these goals have been attained. (Jacks, 1973)

Beyond Behaviorism

The strict, or radical, behaviorism of B. F. Skinner is at the core of behavior therapies; however, significant liberalization of his position has allowed behavior therapies to become the fastest-growing and most eclectic group of therapies in the English-speaking world.

While it is historically correct to credit Skinner with the founding of cognitive psychology, it is an honor that appalled him (Skinner, 1978c). In a review of the first century of psychological science, Anastasi (1992) says, "The cognitive revolution has not overthrown behaviorism; it has greatly expanded and enriched the kinds of learning investigated." Skinner—who found cognitive psychology to be a hotbed of murky thinking, revived mentalism, and explanatory fictions—argued passionately that almost all the descriptive words used by cognitive psychologists meant nothing, described nothing, and retarded rather than advanced psychological science (1989). When he offered alternatives, he was disappointed by the grudging acceptance by other psychologists (1987b).

In this textbook, partly to respect Skinner's position, we devote a separate chapter to cognitive psychology and the theories of George Kelly. In spite of Skinner's pronouncements, most people, including behaviorists, persist in their belief that thinking, although not easily measured, must be examined nonetheless. The task of the cognitive behavior therapist is to modify behaviors and emotional expressions, but to do so *while* considering the patient's thoughts.

Applied Behavioral Analysis

Skinner suggested that it is better to modify contingencies in people's environments than to blame and punish them for deviant behavior. If behavior is the result of selective reinforcement, then deviant behavior is a function of the environment. In *applied behavioral analysis,* attention is paid to the total environment rather than to the psychodynamics of the deviant's behavior.

Skinner did some of the first work in modifying the behavior of persons in institutions. He demonstrated that if one could control the environment, one could then control behavior (Lindsley, Skinner, & Solomon, 1953; Skinner, 1984b).

If the reinforcers are changed so that the deviant behavior is no longer reinforced, it should pass out of the behavioral repertoire and stop occurring. Furthermore, the environment can be adjusted to reinforce whatever new behaviors are deemed more desirable (Goodall, 1972a, 1972b). In *behavior modification,* the focus is on extinguishing behaviors that are in themselves deviant or lead to deviant or criminal activities. These ideas have been and continue to be applied in educational and custodial institutions that include hospitals, prisons, juvenile probation departments, and schools (Gilbert and Gilbert, 1991).

Critics of behavioral analysis have argued that the amount of control necessary to eliminate the undesirable behaviors is often excessive—for example, withholding food from highly disturbed mental patients until they comply with institutionally approved behaviors. Advocates point out that the approach is simply a more comprehensive and formal presentation of what the institutions are set up to do. The university's role is to educate students, but it operates inefficiently. The prison is mandated to deter and to reform persons who display criminal behavior, but it often fails. Mental hospitals exist to help return people to adequate functioning, but they frequently do not succeed. The long-standing ineffectiveness of such institutions makes it easier to suggest implementing behavioral models that impose tighter controls over more of the environment. If, for example, a back ward catatonic can be reinforced into speaking, feeding, and getting dressed, the achievement is clearly an improvement for the patient as well as a relief to the staff. It is evident that control can change behavior. But critics worry about the ethics of control: how much is too much?

From Programmed Learning to Computer Games

Skinner's most distinctive achievement, derived from his animal experiments, was the development of **programmed learning.** In its original form, a student sat before a *teaching machine.* A single frame or statement (drawing or problem) was presented to the student. The student *actively* responded (wrote, pressed a button, and so on). After completing a response, the student was shown the correct response and was invited to check if his or her answer was correct. This feedback occurred *before* the next statement was presented. In every case, the student was shown the correct response. In the early, more simple programs, students moved from statement to statement, having opportunities from time to time to redo or review their errors (Skinner, 1958). Skinner's research showed that people learn more easily and quickly when they are given instant and accurate feedback on their progress. The basic hypotheses in programmed learning are as follows:

1. *Learning is accelerated if discrete units of material are presented.* In programmed learning, simpler units are presented first. Each unit of content is given as a distinct entity, which is embedded in a larger and more complex learning program. Thus, although 4 multiplied by 7 equals 28 is a single equation (unit), it is part of the 4 multiplication table and the 7 multiplication table. These tables are part of a larger group: methods used in performing mathematical calculations.

2. *The learner must make a response.* Content is most likely to be retained if the learner actively participates in the learning process. In pro-

grammed instruction, the student chooses an answer, writes a response, presses a button, opens a slide, or makes some other response. If the student is not interested enough to respond to the item in the program, then the program stops until the student decides to continue.

3. *Punishment does not lead to learning.* Skinner once remarked that drugstores were less likely to be vandalized than schools, because drugstores do not engage in punishment. Programmed learning allows students to reinforce their own rate of learning.

> Programmed instruction is perhaps most successful in attacking punitive methods by allowing the student to move at his own pace. The slow student is released from the punishment which inevitably follows when he is forced to move on to material for which he is not ready, and the fast student escapes the boredom of being forced to go too slow. (Skinner, 1978a, p. 146)

In the preface to their programmed-learning text, Holland and Skinner (1961) argue that programmed learning has many advantages: (1) Students go at their own rate. (2) The student deals with advanced materials only after mastering the basics necessary to understand them. (3) Because the material increases in difficulty gradually, the student, who also receives "hints and prompts," almost always chooses the right answer. (4) Learning is interactive. (5) The answers are right only if the student understands the actual concept—no lucky guesses. (6) Concepts are repeated in many different variations as the student goes through the program. (7) Students have an accurate, updated, instant record of their progress.

Augmented Learning

The development of interactive computer learning is a step beyond simple programmed learning. The learner still works with discrete units, still must respond, and still gets immediate feedback; but the computer feedback is much more detailed, individual, and complex than with the teaching machine. The learning experience becomes a dialogue between student and computer. The students are not simply informed whether their response is right or wrong. They may receive encouragement, pictures, suggestions, alternative approaches, reminders of previous successes with similar items, or displays of the question in another form. While some programmed texts and teaching machines have failed to maintain student interest, this has not been a problem in computer-augmented situations.

In the light of our present knowledge a school system must be called a failure if it cannot induce students to learn except by threatening them for not learning. (Skinner, 1958, p. 977)

The computer's flexibility has other implications as well:

> We recognize still another aspect of machine teaching that in time will become the most important of all. The child, in intimate dialog with the machine, finds himself in a unique psychological situation. The computer becomes a nonjudgmental reflector of his thoughts. He is encouraged to open up his imagination, to try some of the unlikely possibilities, and to follow his curiosity and see what happens. A wrong answer is as valuable as the right one when the alternatives can be explored and he is shown *why* it is wrong. (Brown & El-Ghannam, 1971, p. 2)

There have been numerous objections to programmed learning. First of all, it was deemed to be socially isolating; students were encapsulated in their own private world while learning. The benefits of group experience and the utilization of group energy and enthusiasm were missing (but so were the negative effects of group pressure and competition). Also, students had no opportunity to disagree with the program writer's bias. However, with newer programs, students can work in groups or on group projects, sharing their work across a classroom or across the world. Moreover, interactive programs are now being written that allow users to disagree with the assumptions of the program itself.

In a truculent paper, Skinner, disappointed with the slow acceptance of teaching machines, criticized many defects of contemporary education. "With teaching machines and programmed instruction, one could teach what is now taught in American schools in half the time with half the effort" (1984b, p. 948).

This kind of learning is not limited to factual material. The following is part of a program first developed for first-year writing courses at Stanford University. The student, in this case, describes herself as "someone who doesn't ever write poetry."

> COMPUTER: Hi! What shall I call you today?
>
> STUDENT: Gail.
>
> COMPUTER: O.K. Gail, this time we're going to talk about what you can and can't see, hear, touch, taste and feel. You just touched the computer terminal. How does it feel?
>
> STUDENT: Like plastic and steel, gray and growling.
>
> COMPUTER: Fine. Now say it in a different way. It feels like . . .
>
> STUDENT: strings of steel licking at my finger bottoms.
>
> COMPUTER: Good. Even more far out? It feels as if . . .
>
> STUDENT: a noise from nowhere beating into an empty room.
>
> COMPUTER: Believe it or not, you've just written a poem. Here it is:
>
> *Like plastic and steel, gray and growling.*
> *Like strings of steel licking at my finger bottoms.*
> *Just as if a noise from nowhere beating into empty rooms.*

COMPUTER: Do you want to change the poem to make it better?
STUDENT: You bet I do.
COMPUTER: Good. Use the next three lines to type in your changes.
STUDENT: *Gray and growling, the terminal nips at my fingers.*
Strings of steel, gloved in gray.
Noises from nowhere sing into empty rooms.
COMPUTER: That's the way! Now, Gail, would you like to take an imaginary walk in the woods?
STUDENT: Sure would.
COMPUTER: Good. It's autumn, and as you're walking through the woods, what colors do you see?
STUDENT: Yellow, brown, dashes of rose and red, blue sky.
COMPUTER: What do yellow, brown, dashes of rose and red, blue sky remind you of?
STUDENT: A paintpot drawn by a chariot of the sun.
COMPUTER: Walking in the woods can lead to thoughts of abstract ideas such as death, change, beauty or cycles. Can you think of more? Type them in.
STUDENT: Renewal, quiet, wonder, silence.
COMPUTER: How do you feel when you think about renewal, quiet, wonder, silence?
STUDENT: In awe of the perfect beauty of the unknown.
COMPUTER: Would you like to write a short poem, Gail?
STUDENT: Sure.
COMPUTER: O.K., a suggestion is to type three lines using the colors yellow, brown, dashes of rose and red, blue sky which you mentioned, renewal, quiet, wonder, silence, your abstract ideas, and the feelings you have about renewal, quiet, wonder, silence . . .
STUDENT: *Yellow wheat dies—renewed in bread.*
Brown of the earth—alive in silence.
Stillness broken. The whir of falling red leaves.
COMPUTER: Nice, Gail. (from Nold, 1974)

Skinner did not predict the next step in computer-based learning: the presentation of material in game form. For example, one game teaches typing skills. The student types words that become missiles, which repel enemy space attackers. As the student types more quickly and more accurately, the only missiles that will work take the form of longer and longer words typed in the same amount of time. Not only does this next generation of programmed-teaching devices minimize punishment, but it also appears to be extremely positively reinforcing. A multi-billion-dollar industry has emerged, partially derived from Skinner's rat and pigeon research funded by the defense department during World War II, when Skinner worked with homing pigeons in the effort to develop "smarter" bombs. It is ironic, therefore, that Skinner's development of programmed learning has led to the creation of shoot-seek-and-destroy video games.

Evaluation

Skinner's behaviorism has been applied to create new modes of therapy and instruction. The impact of his ideas has led to modifications of programs in universities, jails, mental hospitals, clinics, and primary schools. Several experimental communities have attempted to make the visions of *Walden Two* a reality (Ishaq, 1991; Kinkade, 1973; Roberts, 1971).

I think the main objection to behaviorism is that people are in love with the mental apparatus. If you say that doesn't really exist, that it's a fiction and let's get back to the facts, then they have to give up their first love. (Skinner, 1967b, p. 69)

As Skinner extended his interests into the workplace, the classroom, and the home, he attracted a horde of admirers as well as critics. His treatment of freedom, creativity, and the self, and his unswerving belief in a world dominated by external forces, were chilling and compelling. In 1984 Skinner allowed six of his seminal papers to be sent to a group of professionals who had a stake in behavioral psychology. One hundred seventy-four of them responded. Their detailed comments dissected every facet of Skinner's ideas: ideological, experimental, and philosophical. Skinner then wrote a response to each and every commentator.

Of all contemporary psychologists, B. F. Skinner is perhaps the most honored and the most maligned, the most widely recognized and the most misrepresented, the most cited and the most misunderstood. (Catania, 1984, p. 473)

These critiques of Skinner's papers, along with his replies, filled an entire issue of *Behavioral and Brain Sciences* (1984). Skinner's response to almost all of his critics was that they were either misinformed, misaligned, or just plain wrong. Having discovered that the more he stood his ground, the more his ideas would continue to attract serious attention, he chose to stand firm on all of his positions, even those that dated back more than 30 years. In his final summation, Skinner writes, "In my experience, the skepticism of psychologists and philosophers about the adequacy of behaviorism is an inverse function of the extent they understand it" (1984c, p. 723).

In his last years, Skinner continued undaunted. In a radio interview conducted a few months before his death, he remarked, with amusement, "I will die before my critics can come at me for this last work" (NPR, 1990).

I am a radical behaviorist simply in the sense that I find no place in the formulation for anything which is mental. (Skinner, 1964, p. 106)

In his determination to render life more understandable, Skinner proposed a view of human nature that is inherently appealing in its compactness, its directness, and its dismissal of all metaphysical speculation. Firmly rooted in the methodology of modern science, it offers the hope of understanding ourselves without recourse to intuition or divine intervention.

Skinner presented himself as a psychologist whose basic ideas originated in laboratory findings with rats and pigeons. However, with the writing of *Walden Two,* he made a "critical transition, from laboratory scientist . . . to outspoken public advocate for a behavioristic science of human behavior" (Elms, 1981, p. 478). Skinner's own thrust for the past 30 years was best stated in his own words: "I am proceeding on the assumption that nothing less than a vast improvement in our understanding of human behavior will prevent the destruction of our way of life or of mankind" (1975, p. 42).

Just as Freud's suggestion that we are immoral and driven by lust and greed scandalized a generation of Victorians, Skinner's assertions that we are amoral and are pushed and turned by our external environment has disturbed a generation brought up to admire and value self-generated choices and personal independence.

In a late paper titled "What Is Wrong with Daily Life in the Western

World?" (1986), he cites the alienation of many individuals from their work. He points to examples of people helping those who would rather help themselves, controlling others by punishment instead of by reinforcements, and "reinforcing looking, listening, reading, gambling and so on while strengthening very few other behaviors" (p. 568). He suggested that the solution to these quality-of-life issues is to apply what we already know, what has already worked—the extensions and applications of behavioral research. He insisted that differences should be resolved on the basis of actual evidence, not abstract speculations. By forcing the argument back to science and away from purely emotional discussions, Skinner forged a systematic approach to understanding human behavior that exerts considerable influence on current cultural practices and beliefs.

The Theory Firsthand

Excerpt from "Humanism and Behaviorism"[2]

There seem to be two ways of knowing, or knowing about, another person. One is associated with existentialism, phenomenology, and structuralism. It is a matter of knowing what a person is, or what he is like, or what he is coming to be or becoming. We try to know another person in this sense as we know ourselves. We share his feelings through sympathy or empathy. Through intuition we discover his attitudes, intentions, and other states of mind. We communicate with him in the etymological sense of making ideas and feelings common to both of us. We do so more effectively if we have established good *interpersonal* relations. This is a passive, contemplative kind of knowing: If we want to predict what a person does or is likely to do, we assume that he, like us, will behave according to what he is; his behavior, like ours, will be an expression of his feelings, state of mind, intentions, attitudes, and so on.

He sought a parsimonious, elegant, and useful path to a science of psychology. Most of his efforts were steps in the right direction. (Gilbert & Gilbert, 1991)

The other way of knowing is a matter of what a person *does*. We can usually observe this as directly as any other phenomenon in the world; no special kind of knowing is needed. We explain why a person behaves as he does by turning to the environment rather than to inner states or activities. The environment was effective during the evolution of the species, and we call the result the human genetic endowment. A member of the species is exposed to another part of that environment during his lifetime, and from it he acquires a repertoire of behavior which converts an organism with a genetic endowment into a person. By analyzing these effects of the environment, we move toward the prediction and control of behavior.

But can this formulation of what a person *does* neglect any available information about what he *is*? There are gaps in time and space between behavior and the environmental events to which it is attributed, and it is natural to try to fill them with an account of the intervening state of the organism. We do this when we summarize a long

[2]From July/August 1972, *The Humanist*. Copyright 1972 by *The Humanist*. Reprinted by permission.

evolutionary history by speaking of genetic endowment. Should we not do the same for a personal history? An omniscient physiologist should be able to tell us, for example, how a person is changed when a bit of his behavior is reinforced, and what he thus becomes should explain why he subsequently behaves in a different way. We argue in such a manner, for example, with respect to immunization. We begin with the fact that vaccination makes it less likely that a person will contract a disease at a later date. We say that he becomes immune, and we speak of a state of immunity, which we then proceed to examine. An omniscient physiologist should be able to do the same for comparable states in the field of behavior. He should also be able to change behavior by changing the organism directly rather than by changing the environment. Is the existentialist, phenomenologist, or structuralist not directing his attention precisely to such a mediating state?

A thoroughgoing dualist would say no, because for him what a person observes through introspection and what a physiologist observes with his special techniques are in different universes. It is at this point that a behavioristic analysis of self-knowledge becomes most important and, unfortunately, is most likely to be misunderstood. Each of us possesses a small part of the universe within his own skin. It is not for that reason different from the rest of the universe, but it is a private possession: We have ways of knowing about it that are denied to others. It is a mistake, however, to conclude that the intimacy we thus enjoy means a special kind of understanding. We are, of course, stimulated directly by our own bodies. The so-called interoceptive nervous system responds to conditions important in deprivation and emotion. The proprioceptive system is involved in posture and movement, and without it we would scarcely behave in a coordinated way. These two systems, together with the exteroceptive nervous system, are essential to effective behavior. But knowing is more than responding to stimuli. A child responds to the colors of things before he "knows his colors." Knowing requires special contingencies of reinforcement that must be arranged by other people, and the contingencies involving private events are never very precise because other people are not effectively in contact with them. In spite of the intimacy of our own bodies, we know them less accurately than we know the world around us. And there are, of course, other reasons why we know the private world of others even less precisely.

The important issues, however, are not precision but subject matter. Just what can be known when we "know ourselves"? The three nervous systems just mentioned have evolved under practical contingencies of survival, most of them nonsocial. (Social contingencies important for survival must have arisen in such fields as sexual and maternal behavior.) They were presumably the only systems available when people began to "know themselves" as the result of answering questions about their behavior. In answering such questions as "Do you see that?" or "Did you hear that?" or "What is that?" a person learns to observe his own responses to stimuli. In answering such questions as "Are you hungry?" or "Are you afraid?" he learns to observe states of his body related to deprivation and emotional arousal. In answering such questions as "Are you going to go?" or "Do you intend to go?" or "Do you feel like going?" or "Are you inclined to go?" he learns to observe the strength or probability of his behavior.

Do I mean to say that Plato never discovered the mind? Or that Aquinas, Descartes, Locke, and Kant were preoccupied with incidental, often irrelevant by-products of human behavior? Or that the mental laws of physiological psychologists like Wundt, or the stream of consciousness of William James, or the mental apparatus of Sigmund Freud have no useful place in the understanding of human behavior? Yes, I do. And I put the matter strongly because, if we are to solve the problems that face us in the world today, this concern for mental life must no longer divert our attention from the environmental conditions of which human behavior is a function. . . .

Better forms of government are not to be found in better rulers, better educational practices in better teachers, better economic systems in more enlightened management, or better therapy in more compassionate therapists. Neither are they to be found in better citizens, students, workers, or patients. The age-old mistake is to look for salvation in the character of autonomous men and women rather than in the social environments that have appeared in the evolution of cultures and that can now be explicitly designed.

Chapter Highlights

- Skinner felt that only behavior can be studied. Distinct from an inner life, behavior is observable, measurable, and perceivable with data-collecting instrumentation. If observable behavior is the basis for defining the self, then to discuss the inner working of the personality or the self becomes unnecessary.
- He formulated distinct ways of observing, measuring, predicting, and understanding behavior. His distrust for subjective, mental, intervening, or fictional explanations led him to base his ideas on the observable behavior of animals and people.
- Skinner spoke of studying the organism itself. His propositions rest upon the accumulation of measurable behavioral data and careful laboratory experimentation.
- Although Skinner worked from observable data alone, contending that his position was a nontheoretical one, his impact on society and psychology grew from extrapolation of his data into theories stretching far beyond the boundaries of animal research.
- Rather than considering individuals as creating, initiating agents, Skinner held that genetic and environmental histories control a person's behavior.
- Future events are assumed to be predictable, given observation of past events.
- Explanatory fictions are employed when people do not understand the behavior involved, or when the pattern of reinforcements that preceded or followed the behavior is unknown. According to Skinner, it is incorrect to use any of these terms to explain behavior—*freedom, dignity, autonomous man, will,* or *creativity.*
- Skinner concluded that almost any naturally occurring behavior in a human or in an animal can be trained to occur more often and more strongly in any chosen direction.
- Research on the variables that affect operant conditioning indicates that conditioning can take place without awareness, that conditioning is maintained in spite of awareness, and that conditioning is most effective when the subject is aware and cooperative.

- Positive and negative consequences control or regulate behaviors. If one has sufficient knowledge of the prior reinforcers, it is possible to explain the occurrence of any behavior.
- How quickly a behavior is learned, and how often it will be repeated, depend on how regularly and how often the behavior is reinforced. The speed at which new behavior is learned is increased by continuous reinforcement.
- Learning is improved when a correct response is reinforced. Because reinforcement selectively directs behavior toward a predetermined goal, it is more effective than aversive control, or punishment.
- One can begin to control behavior if one can make changes in the environment. Controlling one's behavior means freedom.
- For Skinner, personal growth refers to the capacity to increase the beneficial control of our environment and to minimize adverse conditions. Functional analysis is useful in framing behavior as a cause-and-effect relationship.
- Skinner considers personality, as the term is normally used, to be an explanatory fiction. Mind and body are not separate.
- Rather than treat emotions as vague inner states, Skinner suggests that a descriptive approach be used. Individuals should learn to observe associated behaviors.
- The symptom is the disease, according to behaviorists, not a manifestation of an underlying illness, and it is to be dealt with directly.
- Derived from his animal experiments, Skinner's most original achievement was the development of programmed learning. His research showed that when people are given instant and accurate feedback on their progress, they learn more quickly.

Key Concepts

Autonomous man An explanatory fiction, in this case described as an inner person or indwelling agent, who is moved by vague inner forces independent of the behavioral contingencies.

Behaviorism The philosophy of the science of human behavior.

Canon of parsimony A formulation proposed by Lloyd Morgan. It states that, given two explanations, a scientist should always accept the simpler one.

Contingencies The antecedents of the behavior, the response to it, and the results or consequences of the response. Contingencies include an organism's genetic endowment and previous behaviors.

Explanatory fictions Those terms that nonbehaviorists use to describe behavior. For Skinner, examples include *freedom, dignity, autonomous man,* and *creativity.* To use any of these terms as explanation for behavior is simply incorrect, according to the behaviorists.

Functional analysis An examination of cause-and-effect relationships. Each aspect of behavior is treated as a function of a condition that can be described in physical terms. Explanations that depend on terms such as *will, intelligence, imagination,* or *freedom* obscure the causes of behavior, as they do not describe what is actually occurring.

Programmed learning An instructional method in which learning is accelerated as discrete units of material are presented and the learner makes a response. Students reinforce their own learning, at their own pace.

Reinforcer Any stimulus that follows the occurrence of a response and maintains or increases the probability of that response. A positive reinforcer strengthens any behavior that produces it. A negative reinforcer strengthens any behavior that reduces or terminates it. Primary reinforcers are stimuli or events that are innately reinforcing (air, water, food, shelter). Secondary reinforcers are neutral stimuli that come to function as reinforcers through association with primary reinforcers (money is one example).

Respondent behavior Reflexive behavior, in which an organism responds automatically to a stimulus.

Verbal community The people who respond to the verbal behavior of others. Verbal behavior is any activity that uses words—reading, speaking, or writing.

Annotated Bibliography

Bjork, D. (1993). *B. F. Skinner: A life.* New York: Basic Books.

Far superior to Skinner's own tedious biography, Bjork's work helps the reader see how Skinner's ideas arose from his upbringing. His radical stance is depicted as an extension of his early social and personal isolation.

Catania, C., & Harnad S. (Eds.). (1988). *The selection of behavior: The operant behaviorism of B. F. Skinner. Comments and consequences.* New York: Cambridge University Press.

Six of his seminal papers and comments on each from a number of authors, as well as Skinner's replies. More than most people would ever want to know about the pros and cons of his basic ideas.

Mahoney, M. (1974). *Cognition and behavior modification.* Cambridge, MA: Ballinger.

A thoughtful, solid examination of behaviorism and its development from laboratory experiments to field studies to clinical applications.

Nye, R. (1979). *What is B. F. Skinner really saying?* Englewood Cliffs, NJ: Prentice-Hall.

A well-written summary of Skinner's ideas, presented without much recourse to Skinnerian jargon.

Skinner, B. F. (1948, 1976). *Walden two.* New York: Macmillan.

A novel about a full-blown utopian community that is designed and managed by a behaviorist. No plot to speak of, but all facets of the culture are fully described and discussed, from child raising to work schedules to planned leisure.

———. (1953). *Science and human behavior.* New York: Macmillan.

The most complete exposition of Skinner's basic ideas.

———. (1971). *Beyond freedom and dignity.* New York: Knopf.

An examination of contemporary culture, especially its failure to apply behavioral analysis to personal understanding. A powerful, popular book on the folly of thinking the way most of us still do.

———. (1972). *Cumulative record: A selection of papers* (3rd ed.). New York: Appleton-Century-Crofts.

Skinner's choice of what he considers to be his most important papers; covers a number of areas that are not included in this chapter.

———. (1974). *About behaviorism.* New York: Knopf.

A direct answer to Skinner's critics. It explores the popular misconceptions that people have about behaviorism. It is a scaled-down version of *Science and human behavior,* written for the general public.

References

Ames, A., Jr. (1951). Visual perception and the rotating trapezoidal window. *Psychological Monographs, 65,* 324.

Anastasi, A. (1992). A century of psychological science. *American Psychologist, 47*(7), 842.

Behavioral and Brain Sciences. (1984). The canonical papers of B. F. Skinner, *7*(4). (Later reprinted: Catania, C., & Harnad, S. [Eds.]. [1988]. *The selection of behavior: The operant behaviorism of B. F. Skinner. Comments and consequences.* New York: Cambridge University Press.)

Berelson, B., & Steiner, G. A. (1964). *Human behavior: An inventory of scientific findings.* New York: Harcourt Brace Jovanovich.

Bjork, D. (1993). *B. F. Skinner: A life.* New York: Basic Books.

Brown, D., & El-Ghannam, M. A. (1971). *Computers for teaching.* Transcript of a series of talks presented at the Second Specialized Course on New Technologies in Education at the Regional Center of Planning and Administration of Education for the Arab Countries, Beirut, Lebanon.

Catania, C. (1984). The operant behaviorism of B. F. Skinner. *Behavioral and Brain Sciences, 7,* 473–475.

Cohen, D. (1977). *Psychologists on psychology.* New York: Taplinger, pp. 262–290.

Davison, G., & Valins, S. (1969). Maintenance of self-attributed and drug-attributed behavior change. *Journal of Personality and Social Psychology, 11,* 25–33.

Elms, A. (1981). Skinner's dark year and *Walden Two. American Psychologist, 36*(5), 470–479.

Erickson, M. H. (1939). Experimental demonstrations of the psychopathology of everyday life. *The Psychoanalytic Quarterly, 8,* 338–353.

Evans, R. (1968). *B. F. Skinner: The man and his ideas.* New York: Dutton. (Edited dialogues with Skinner.)

Fabun, D. (1968). On motivation. *Kaiser Aluminum News, 26*(2).

Ferster, C. B., & Skinner, B. F. (1957). *Schedules of reinforcement.* New York: Appleton-Century-Crofts.

Gilbert, M., & Gilbert, T. (1991). What Skinner gave us. *Training, 28*(9), 42–48.

Goldfried, M. R., & Merbaum, M. (Eds.). (1973). *Behavior change through self-control.* New York: Holt, Rinehart and Winston.

Goodall, K. (1972a). Field report: Shapers at work. *Psychology Today, 6*(6), 53–63, 132–138.

———. (1972b). Margaret, age ten, and Martha, age eight: A simple case of behavioral engineering. *Psychology Today, 6*(6), 132–133.

Goodell, R. (1977). B. F. Skinner: High risk, high gain. In *The visible scientists* (pp. 106–119). Boston: Little, Brown.

Hall, C., & Lindzey, G. (1978). *Theories of personality* (3rd ed.). New York: Wiley.

Hilts, P. J. (1973, May 3). Pros and cons of behaviorism. *San Francisco Chronicle.* (Originally printed in *The Washington Post.*)

Holland, J. G., & Skinner, B. F. (1961). *The analysis of behavior: A program for self-instruction.* New York: McGraw-Hill.

Ishaq, W. (Ed.). (1991). *Human behavior in today's world.* New York: Praeger, pp. 249–256.

Jacks, R. N. (1973). *What therapies work with today's college students: Behavior therapy.* Paper presented at the annual meeting of the American Psychiatric Association, Honolulu, Hawaii.

Kimble, G. A. (1961). *Hilgard and Marquis' conditioning and learning.* New York: Appleton-Century-Crofts.

Kinkade, K. (1973). *A Walden two experiment: The first five years of Twin Oaks Community.* New York: Morrow. (Excerpts published in *Psychology Today,* 1973, *6*[8], 35–41, 90–93; *6*[9], 71–82.)

Krippner, S., Achterberg, J., Bugenthal, J., Banathy, B., Collen, A., Jaffe, D., Hales, S., Kremer, J., Stigliano, A., Giorgi, A., May, R., Michael, D., & Salner, M. (1988). Whatever happened to scholarly discourse? Reply to B. F. Skinner. *American Psychologist, 43*(10), 819.

Lefcourt, H. M. (1973). The function of the illusions of control and freedom. *American Psychologist, 28,* 417–426.

———. (1980). Locus of control and coping with life's events. In E. Staub (Ed.), *Personality: Basic aspects and current research* (pp. 201–235). Englewood Cliffs, NJ: Prentice-Hall.

Lindley, R., II, & Moyer, K. E. (1961). Effects of instructions on the extinction of conditioned finger-withdrawal response. *Journal of Experimental Psychology, 61,* 82–88.

Lindsley, O. R., Skinner, B. F., & Solomon, H. C. (1953). *Studies in behavior therapy.* (Status Report 1.) Waltham, MA: Metropolitan State Hospital.

Mahoney, M. (Ed.). (1981). *Cognitive Therapy and Research,* 5(1).

Mahoney, M., & Thoresen, C. E. (1974). *Self control: Power to the person.* Monterey, CA: Brooks/Cole.

Mischel, W. (1976). *Introduction to personality.* New York: Holt, Rinehart and Winston.

National Public Radio. (1990, July 27). *All Things Considered.* Interview with B. F. Skinner.

Natsoulsas, T. (1978). Toward a model for consciousness in the light of B. F. Skinner's contribution. *Behaviorism, 6*(2), 139–197.

———. (1983). The experience of a conscious self. *Journal of Mind and Behavior, 4*(4), 451–478.

———. (1986). On the radical behaviorist conception of consciousness. *Journal of Mind and Behavior, 7*(1), 87–116.

Nold, E. (1974). Stanford University Library of Creative Writing Programs, Palo Alto, CA.

Pavlov, I. P. (1927). *Conditioned reflexes.* London: Oxford University Press.

Rachman, S. J., & Wilson, G. T. (1980). *The effects of psychological therapy* (2nd ed.). Elmsford, NY: Pergamon Press.

Ram Dass, B. (1970). Baba Ram Dass lecture at the Menninger Clinic. *Journal of Transpersonal Psychology, 2,* 91–140.

Reese, E. P. (1966). The analysis of human operant behavior. In J. Vernon (Ed.), *General psychology: A self-selection textbook.* Dubuque, IA: Brown.

Roberts, R. E. (1971). *The new communes: Coming together in America.* Englewood Cliffs, NJ: Prentice-Hall.

Sagal, P. (1981). *Skinner's philosophy.* Waltham, MA: University Press of America.

Skinner, B. F. (1938). *The behavior of organisms: An experimental analysis.* New York: Appleton-Century-Crofts.

———. (1945, October). Baby in a box. *Ladies Home Journal.* (Also in *Cumulative record: A selection of papers* [3rd ed.]. New York: Appleton-Century-Crofts, 1972, pp. 567–573.)

———. (1948). *Walden two.* New York: Macmillan.

———. (1950). Are theories of learning necessary? *Psychological Review, 57,* 193–216.

———. (1953). *Science and human behavior.* New York: Macmillan.

———. (1955). Freedom and the control of men. *The American Scholar, 25,* 47–65.

———. (1956). A case history in scientific method. *The American Psychologist, 11,* 211–233.

———. (1957). *Verbal behavior.* New York: Appleton-Century-Crofts.

———. (1958). Teaching machines. *Science, 128,* 969–977.

———. (1959). *Cumulative record.* New York: Appleton-Century-Crofts.

———. (1961). *Cumulative record* (2nd ed.). New York: Appleton-Century-Crofts.

———. (1964). Behaviorism at fifty. In W. T. Wann (Ed.), *Behaviorism and phenomenology: Contrasting bases for modern psychology* (pp. 79–108). Chicago: University of Chicago Press.

———. (1967a). Autobiography. In E. G. Boring & G. Lindzey (Eds.), *History of psychology in autobiography* (Vol. 5) (pp. 387–413). New York: Appleton-Century-Crofts.

———. (1967b). An interview with Mr. Behaviorist: B. F. Skinner. *Psychology Today, 1*(5), 20–25, 68–71.

———. (1968). *The technology of teaching.* New York: Appleton-Century-Crofts.

———. (1969). *Contingencies of reinforcement: A theoretical analysis.* New York: Appleton-Century-Crofts.

———. (1971). *Beyond freedom and dignity.* New York: Knopf.

———. (1972a). *Cumulative record: A selection of papers* (3rd ed.). New York: Appleton-Century-Crofts.

———. (1972b). Interview with E. Hall. *Psychology Today, 6*(6), 65–72, 130.

———. (1972c, July 15). On "having" a poem. *Saturday Review,* pp. 32–35. (Also in *Cumulative record: A selection of papers* [3rd ed.]. New York: Appleton-Century-Crofts, 1972.)

———. (1972d). "I have been misunderstood. . . ." An interview with B. F. Skinner. *The Center Magazine, 5*(2), 63–65.

———. (1972e, July/August). Humanism and behaviorism. *The Humanist, 32*(4), 18–20.

———. (1974). *About behaviorism.* New York: Knopf.

———. (1975). The steep and thorny way to a science of behavior. *American Psychologist, 30,* 42–49.

———. (1976a). Walden two revisited. *Walden two.* New York: Macmillan.

———. (1976b). *Particulars of my life.* New York: Knopf.

———. (1977a). A conversation with B. F. Skinner. *Harvard Magazine, 79*(8), 53–58.

———. (1977b). Hernstein and the evolution of behaviorism. *American Psychologist, 32,* 1006–1016.

———. (1978a). *Reflections on behaviorism and society.* Englewood Cliffs, NJ: Prentice-Hall.

———. (1978b). Why don't we use the behavioral sciences? *Human Nature, 1*(3), 86–92.

———. (1978c). Why I am not a cognitive psychologist. *Reflections on behaviorism and society.* Englewood Cliffs, NJ: Prentice-Hall, pp. 97–112.

———. (1979a). *The shaping of a behaviorist.* New York: Knopf.

———. (1979b). Interview. *Omni, 1*(12), 76–80.

———. (1980). *Notebooks* (Robert Epstein, Ed.). Englewood Cliffs, NJ: Prentice-Hall.

———. (1983). Intellectual self-management in old age. *American Psychologist, 38*(3) 239–244.

———. (1984a). *A matter of consequences.* New York: New York University Press.

———. (1984b). The shame of American education. *American Psychologist, 39*(9), 947–954.

———. (1984c). Reply to Harnad's article, "What are the scope and limits of radical behaviorist theory?" *Behavioral and Brain Sciences, 7,* 721–724.

———. (1986). What is wrong with daily life in the Western world? *American Psychologist, 41*(5), 568–574.

———. (1987a). Whatever happened to psychology as the science of behavior? *American Psychologist, 42*(8), 780–786.

———. (1987b, July/August). A humanist alternative to the A.A.'s twelve steps. *The Humanist,* p. 5.

———. (1989). The origins of cognitive thought. *American Psychologist, 44*(1), 13–18.

———. (1990a). Can psychology be a science of mind? *American Psychologist, 45*(11), 1206–1210.

———. (1990b). To know the future. In C. Fadiman (Ed.), *Living philosophies* (pp. 193–199). New York: Doubleday.

Skinner, B. F., & Vaughan, M. E. (1985). *Enjoy old age: Living fully in your later years.* New York: Warner Books.

Smith, L. D. (1992). On prediction and control: B. F. Skinner and the technological ideal of science. *American Psychologist, 47*(2), 216–223.

Wann, W. T. (Ed.). (1964). *Behaviorism and phenomenology: Contrasting bases for modern psychology.* Chicago: University of Chicago Press.

Watson, J. B. (1913). Psychology as the behaviorist views it. *Psychological Review, 20,* 158–177.

———. (1928a). *The ways of behaviorism.* New York: Harper & Row.

———. (1928b). *Psychological care of infant and child.* New York: Norton.

CHAPTER 12

The Personal Construct Theory of George Kelly and Cognitive Psychology

Kaisa Puhakka

George Kelly's work affirms the basic premise of this book: In the study of human personality, theory tends to reflect the theorist much as a mirror reflects an image. For Kelly, both the person as the theorist and the person as the subject of the theory are in a constant process of change and growth. A theory of the human personality should therefore remain essentially flexible and open-ended.

Central to Kelly's approach is the notion of **personal construct,** or the idea that people *construe* events by anticipating them on the basis of past experience and learning. By **construing,** Kelly means "placing an interpretation" (1955, p. 50). The objective circumstances and conditions of the world matter less than how people interpret them. All experience comes through the tinted glasses of personal constructs; there is no such thing as pure experience apart from its construed meaning.

Kelly viewed human behavior as a quest for understanding. However, *understanding* in this context ranges from a complex, well-formulated theory to a simple feeling of security and satisfaction with the way things are. For Kelly, trying to understand people through a preconceived scientific discipline or methodology is putting the cart before the horse.

Personal construct theory . . . is a notion about how man may launch out from a position of admitted ignorance, and how he may aspire from one day to the next to transcend his own dogmatisms. It is, then, a theory of man's personal inquiry—a psychology of the human quest. It does not say what has or will be found, but proposes rather how we might go about looking for it. (Kelly, 1966/1970, p. 1)

In Kelly's theory, then, the individual takes the center stage as an active construer of the world. Psychology's task is to study how people construe their worlds and their sense of self. Kelly's work is infused with a great respect for the person as well as a remarkably undogmatic spirit. He was more interested in making positive contributions than in engaging in controversy or polemics. His was an invitation for "any adventuresome soul who is not one bit afraid of thinking unorthodox thoughts about people who dares peer out at the world through the eyes of strangers, who has not invested beyond his means in either ideas or vocabulary" (1955, p. xi).

In the three decades after Kelly, cognitive psychology has risen to prominence as an academic field and also as a popular trend in psychotherapy. Representing diverse theoretic perspectives, these later developments differ in both aims and methods from Kelly's theory. For example, they are concerned with specific cognitive functions or therapeutic techniques rather than with a comprehensive theory of personality such as Kelly's. Nevertheless, cognitive psychologists share Kelly's belief that how people understand themselves and the world significantly influences their personalities and lives. Many, especially among cognitive therapists, also share Kelly's faith in the human capacity for adaptation, self-regulation, and healing. The discussion of Kelly and his personal construct theory is followed by a review of cognitive psychology and cognitive therapy.

Personal History

George Alexander Kelly was born on April 28, 1905, in Kansas. The only child of his devoutly religious Protestant parents, Kelly grew up in an atmosphere of hard work and somewhat puritanical attitudes. He was sent away to school when he was 13 years of age. From this point on, he lived away from home most of the time. The self-confidence and down-to-earth practicality that characterize Kelly's later outlook no doubt reflect his early independence as well as rural midwestern roots (Sechrest, 1977, p. 233).

Although he started college as a physics and mathematics major, his interest soon shifted to social problems. He obtained a master's degree in educational sociology from the University of Kansas, and then held a variety of teaching jobs in Minnesota and Iowa. In 1929 Kelly went to the University of Edinburgh in Scotland, where he earned another bachelor's degree, in education. When he returned to the United States, he enrolled as a graduate student in psychology at the University of Iowa. After only one year of study, he completed a dissertation on the common factors in speech and reading disabilities, and received his doctorate in psychology in 1931 (Maher, 1969).

A remarkable feature in Kelly's background is the apparent absence of significant persons or ideas that would influence his subsequent thinking and theorizing about the human personality. None stand out from his brief course of graduate studies. The behavioristic, or *stimulus-response,* psychology to which he was exposed in his undergraduate days neither inspired him nor made sense to him. His first encounter with Freud's theories, some three years later, only added to his disillusionment with psychology (Kelly, 1963).

The major sources from which Kelly drew ideas and inspiration for his theories were not his formal psychological studies but a multitude of activities during and between periods of formal study. Kelly trained labor organizers in soapbox oratory, engaged in public speaking for the American Bankers Association, and taught acting in a junior college. He also "dabbled academically in education, sociology, economics, labor relations, biometrics, speech pathology, and cultural anthropology, and had majored in psychology for a grand total of nine months" (Kelly, 1963, p. 48). The breadth and variety of Kelly's educational experience is rarely matched by students today, but neither is the meagerness of his formal studies in the discipline in which he taught and wrote during most of his life.

In 1931, in spite of the depression, he landed a job in his home state, at Fort Hays Kansas State College. This was a small college serving a rural population in the plains of western Kansas, 250 miles from the nearest metropolitan area. Kelly remained at Fort Hays for 12 years, and it is to this period that the origins of his two major contributions, personal construct theory and fixed-role therapy, can be traced. Cordial but distant in his relations with academic colleagues, Kelly developed his theory and approach to clinical practice in collaboration with students whom he personally trained (Zelhart & Jackson, 1983).

Immediately upon arrival at Fort Hays College, he took over the clinical program of the psychology department and began to develop innovative programs in research and clinical services. Perhaps the best known of these were the traveling clinics that provided services to the rural counties across Kansas. Kelly also established a highly successful satellite system of four or five permanent branch clinics throughout Kansas. Thirty years later, a mental health center model, similar in structure and operation to Kelly's clinic system, was adopted nationally (Zelhart & Jackson, 1983).

Kelly's students had a great deal of respect and affection for him. They "remarked on his humor, energy, concern for professional conduct, and intelligence. Many described him as charismatic or inspiring. Clearly George Kelly was a positive and powerful force in the lives of his students and his personality was a key element in the success of his programs" (Zelhart & Jackson, 1983, p. 145).

During World War II, Kelly served in the navy as an aviation psychologist in charge of training local civilian pilots. In 1946 he was appointed professor and director of clinical psychology at Ohio State University. The first task he undertook upon arrival at Ohio State was to organize the graduate program in clinical psychology. This he accomplished with his characteristic excellence, and, within a few years, this program became one of the leading graduate training programs in the country (Maher, 1969).

At Ohio State, Kelly completed his major contributions to psychology. In 1955 the two-volume work *The Psychology of Personal Constructs* was published and gained immediate national and international recognition as a unique, major development in the study of personality (Maher, 1969). In 1965 he took a position at Brandeis University, outside Boston. He died suddenly of a heart attack only months later, in March 1966, leaving incomplete his work on a book in which he planned to collect and edit the papers he had presented and published in the previous decade.

Kelly's work has been carried on by his students in this country and in England. His personality assessment and therapy techniques continue to inspire research, and many cognitively oriented psychotherapists use his innovations in their daily practice.

Intellectual Antecedents

More than most psychologists, perhaps, George Kelly's papers are themselves an autobiography of the man. In them, the reader will find the warmth, humor, and tolerance that characterized him so well to those who knew him best. (Maher, 1969, p. 3)

Widely read in the various disciplines and well versed in classical philosophy, Kelly integrated, in a highly personal manner, all the influences that came to bear upon him. One can truly say that the psychology of personal constructs is an invention of George Kelly (Sechrest, 1977). Nevertheless, there were a number of thinkers whose writings Kelly found inspiring, if not because they opened up entirely new horizons for him, then because they resonated with and encouraged the development of his own thinking.

Moreno and Psychodrama

From his early work with drama students, Kelly had observed the powerful influence that taking on a role can have on a person's experience and behavior. Kelly was also familiar with Jacob Moreno's (1972) work in *psychodrama,* a method of psychotherapy in which patients enact emotionally significant events in their lives instead of simply talking about them (Blatner, 1988; Kahn, 1964). Moreno viewed spontaneous action as a major factor in bringing about new learning and integration (Blatner, 1988).

In his own work with students, Kelly observed that taking on a role allows individuals to act with a spontaneity that their self-image often does not permit. Once when coaching a cast for the play *The Enemy,* Kelly chose an extremely shy, inhibited, and socially awkward young man to play the part of a shell-shocked Austrian soldier. To everyone's surprise, the young man did exceedingly well in this role. He seemed to become another person, someone intimately familiar with the trauma of shell shock. Kelly wondered whether the young man had had traumatic experiences of his own that "needed to be elaborated within the protective limits of a rehearsal situation" (1955, p. 363).

Kelly's observations, backed by Moreno's work, led him to reject the notion of the human personality as a fixed, substantial entity that predisposes and sets limits to what the individual can do. The opposite seemed to be true: What a person *does* determines what he or she *is.* Trying a new role enables individuals to explore ways of behaving, which in turn open up ways of experiencing and being. The concept of role became central to Kelly's theory of how people construe themselves in relation to others.

The Philosophy of Pragmatism

Kelly was familiar with the writings of the great American philosophers Charles Sanders Peirce, William James, and John Dewey. These three names are associated with the uniquely American brand of philosophy known as *pragmatism.* Pragmatism emphasizes the practical, experiential nature of truth and eschews abstract, metaphysical speculation. John Dewey's notion that understanding is a matter of anticipating events that might confirm one's belief especially appealed to Kelly.

The Conduct of Scientific Inquiry

Kelly had a great appreciation for the disciplined manner of scientific inquiry. The systematic, rigorous bent of the scientific approach resonated with the logical, rational style that characterized his own thinking and writing. But his respect for the scientific did not confine him to a narrowly conceived notion about what constitutes scientific method. More generally, it was the scientist's quest for knowledge and understanding that appealed to Kelly. He saw in this quest a profound expression of the human personality. For him, the methods of science were the scientist's constructs. As such, they could never fully explain the personality of the scientist, nor could they fully account for the personality of the research subject, who has his or her own constructs. However, for Kelly, this peculiar state of affairs was no cause for alarm. On the contrary, it presented psychology with an important caveat: It cautioned psychology to remain flexible and open in both theory and approach—a position that Kelly regarded as the hallmark of good science.

> Both arguments and evidence have been presented in recent years to leave little doubt that almost all methods of psychological enquiry—interviewing, testing, experimentation—are forms of human *relationships.* . . . [W]hat is implied is that we come to regard people who take part in our experiments as human beings *just like us,* the experimenters, *even while they are helping us with our research.* This really can be alarming because it means accepting that subjects, like experimenters, can and do continuously think, theorize, anticipate, experiment, react, create, rebel and comply just like everyone else—and what is more, they can and often do all these things in any experiment the psychologist designs. (Mair, 1970, pp. 157, 158–159)

Major Concepts

Kelly's is a theory of the human being's personal inquiry—"a psychology of the human quest," as he put it (1966/1970, p. 1). In this quest, individuals have an active role in construing their world and personality. The notion of *construing* is unique to Kelly and central to his theory. In what follows, we will explore the meaning of *construing* and *constructs* through related major concepts.

Constructive Alternativism

Kelly rejected the notion that there are absolute, final truths about events in the world. Instead, he thought, there are various interpretations of events, and none have a monopoly on truth, because no person can access truth or reality without viewing or *construing* it in some fashion. Kelly called this position **constructive alternativism.** This notion does not mean that constructions of truth or reality are arbitrary, or that people are locked up in their own subjective worlds, disconnected from other people. Rather, people relate to the world and to other people precisely by way of their personal constructs, and some constructs accomplish this more effectively than others.

One implication of constructive alternativism is that all interpretations are subject to revision. This point applies to the constructs of individuals coping with their lives as much as to those of scientists trying to make sense of the world. It is a sobering realization that calls for humility and open-mindedness in assessing any views or theories, one's own as well as those of others.

Another implication of constructive alternativism is that an individual has virtually unlimited options for construing his or her life in ways that allow for change and growth. Constructive alternativism conveys a spirit of confident optimism and faith in human capabilities. Individuals are capable of changing or replacing their constructions of events and of themselves. In this capacity lies the possibility of freedom: A person's behavior is free to the extent that his or her constructs are flexible or permeable enough to permit new ways of construing events.

Man-the-Scientist and Reflexivity

We take the stand that there are always some alternative constructions available to choose among in dealing with the world. No one needs to paint himself into a corner; no one needs to be completely hemmed in by circumstances; no one needs to be the victim of his biography. (Kelly, 1955, p. 15)

According to Kelly, ordinary people and scientists are alike in that both try to make sense of the world by forming hypotheses about how it works, and then test their hypotheses and revise them if they do not work. He considered human behavior to be essentially a question, an anticipation, or a hypothesis about what any given situation might hold (Kelly, 1969a).

The psychological study of personality, according to Kelly, is the study of how individuals construe their lives. Like subjects being studied, psychologists construe the human personality in an open-ended way, always ready to revise or replace their constructs as needed. When psychologists remember that they are first and foremost individuals engaged in constructing, the openness to alternative constructions comes naturally to them. Perhaps because he saw the flexibility of constructive alternativism as a fundamental feature of reality, Kelly was undogmatic and not given to polemics in defense of his own particular constructs about personality.

Kelly's notion of what he called **man-the-scientist** highlights a peculiar feature of the scientific method when it is directed to the psychological study of personality. This feature is called **reflexivity,** which assumes that the psychologist is a person who is engaged in the same kind of activity as is the person who is being studied.

Kelly's heresy was to allow the psychologist's subject all the capacities of his investigators. (Sotter, 1970, p. 229)

The problem that arises from this notion can be illustrated by the analogy of a hand trying to grab itself, or of the eye trying to see itself. The usual solution to this challenge has been to devise methods or theories that are presumed to be objective, in the sense of not being dependent on the personal constructs of the psychologist (i.e., an artificial contraption of some kind is set up to grab the hand). Kelly views this solution as misguided and doomed to failure, since it attempts to comprehend the human personality from the outside without coming to terms with the reflexivity of the endeavor. The reflexivity cannot be avoided, because of the inescapable fact that psychologists, in the final analysis, are engaged in construing just as much as the individuals being studied. Rather than viewing reflexivity as a problem, Kelly embraces it wholeheartedly as a feature of great interest and relevance to psychological inquiry.

Personal Construct Theory in 12 Statements

Kelly was meticulous in the articulation of his theory and developed his own terminology with original definitions. The theory of personal constructs is stated in 12 densely packed statements, consisting of a *fundamental postulate* and 11 *corollaries*, which are partly derivatives of and partly elaborations on the postulate. The rest of Kelly's theoretical writings constitute further delineation and expansion of these 12 statements. Kelly's (1955) statements are presented verbatim, accompanied by a brief interpretation, as follows.

1. Fundamental Postulate

> *A person's processes are psychologically channelized by the ways in which he anticipates events* (p. 46).

This is the fundamental postulate for the psychology of personal constructs. It begins by placing the individual at the center of things. But what does Kelly mean by *person?* Rather than proposing a definition of his own, he takes *person* to mean simply whatever people ordinarily mean by it when they say, for example, "I know this person" or "I would like to know that person." The person is viewed by Kelly as an event or a process that expresses his or her personality in unique ways of being, by talking and acting in the world. How the personality expresses itself through these myriad ways is psychology's task to understand. According to Kelly, theorizing about biological, social, or unconscious factors outside of the expression of personality sheds little light on how personality is conveyed and is therefore irrelevant to the task of psychology.

The term *channelized* in the basic postulate recognizes that once a process is acknowledged to be in motion, its direction needs to be specified. Because the process here is channelized in ways the individual "anticipates events," it is thus directed toward the future. People are forever attempting to get a preview of what the world has in store for them. "Anticipation is both the push and pull of the psychology of personal constructs" (1955, p. 49). Usually, individuals' subsequent experiences either confirm or disconfirm the ways in which they anticipated the events. The anticipation of events is, in a sense, a search for confirmation or disconfirmation. Superficially, this looks like the behavioristic theory of reinforcement, in which confirmation of anticipated events works as positive reinforcement and disconfirmation as punishment. But Kelly emphatically rejects the existence of any parallel between personal construct theory and behaviorism. Human beings seek confirmation of even the most feared and seemingly punitive events, and, by the same token, they seek disconfirmation of their most cherished dreams. In such cases, punishment would seem to shape behavior in unexpected ways, providing grounds for reconstruction and creative, new endeavors. Kelly's postulate envisions the nature of life "in its outreach for the future, and not in its perpetuation of its prior conditions or in its incessant reverberation of past events" (1970, p. 11).

2. Construction Corollary

A person anticipates events by construing their replications (p. 50).

Since life is a process, no two events are exactly the same. What is anticipated are events that are like the ones that have happened in the past. But an event that is like another is also *different* from various others. Here, Kelly is stating the basic principle of construing, the process whereby something is perceived as similar to some things and different from others. "Under a system that provides only for the identification of similarities the world dissolves into homogeneity; under one that provides only for differentiation it is shattered into hopelessly unrelated fragments" (1966, p. 11). Identification by both similarity and differentiation is necessary.

3. Individuality Corollary

Persons differ from each other in their construction of events (p. 55).

It is highly unlikely that two individuals would construct events in exactly the same way. Kelly doubts that any two people's construction systems are alike even in terms of employing the same logical relationships. But far from finding this to be a cause for worry, Kelly considers it an intriguing possibility, "for it seems to open the door to more advanced systems of thinking and inference. . . . Certainly, it suggests that scientific research can rely more heavily on individual imagination than it usually dares" (1970, p. 12).

4. Organization Corollary

Each person characteristically evolves, for his convenience in anticipating events, a construction system embracing ordinal relationships between constructs (p. 56).

Somehow, the numerous constructs a person has must fit into a reasonably coherent whole that enables the person to function and meet life's challenges. The organization corollary states that this process involves assigning priorities to the constructs. Some constructs are more fundamental than others. But the doubts, confusions, and deep existential dilemmas that are the common fare of human experience suggest that logic is not all that goes into establishing priorities among the constructs.

Specifically, commitments may take priority over opportunities, political affiliations may turn a person from compassion to power, or moral imperatives may render a person insensitive to the plight of the petty criminal. These, notes Kelly, "are the typical prices men pay to escape inner chaos" (1970, p. 12).

5. Dichotomy Corollary

A person's construction system is composed of a finite number of dichotomous constructs (p. 59).

The dichotomy corollary addresses a key feature of a construct. Namely, it draws a black-and-white distinction that admits no degrees or shadings of gray.

This, according to Kelly, is the most frequently misunderstood construct of his theory, because it appears to suggest rigidly categorical thinking. The dichotomy corollary, however, does not describe thinking but instead defines the structure of a construct that may be employed in thinking. A helpful analogy might be a fork in a road on a map, indicating a right turn and a left turn. Looking at the map for direction, motorists find no degrees of left turn or degrees of right turn. The drivers must choose one way or the other. Conceivably, they could decide to move off the road altogether, a choice that amounts to construing the situation in a new way. Constructs serve as guidelines for discriminating, identifying, understanding, and anticipating events. They are contrasts that individuals perceive among events, ways of seeing one element as similar to another and different from the rest. (Construing and the nature of constructs will be discussed at greater length in a later section.)

6. Choice Corollary

> *A person chooses for himself that alternative in a dichotomized construct through which he anticipates the greater possibility for extension and definition of his system* (p. 64).

The choice here refers to the alternatives expressed in the dichotomy construct—or, in the earlier analogy, the right or left fork of the road. The choice, therefore, has to do with the person's behavior, not with the events that follow once the choice has been made. Only after changing themselves, which means altering their constructs, can people change events around them. Of course, changing one's construct is no guarantee that one's objectives in the world will be automatically accomplished.

7. Range Corollary

> *A construct is convenient for the anticipation of a finite range of events only* (p. 68).

No single construct covers everything that happens in a person's experience. Surprise, puzzlement, bewilderment, and wonder are possible precisely because, as Kelly says, the geometry of the mind is an incomplete system. A construct is a distinction that has the effect of distributing objects or events impermanently by way of two associations. It has a *focus* of convenience—a set of objects with which it works especially well. It also has a *range* of convenience, which is somewhat large, over which it can work reasonably well.

8. Experience Corollary

> *A person's construction system varies as he successively construes the replications of events* (p. 72).

Constructs are not necessarily fixed but can be modified as they are repeatedly imposed upon events in a person's experience. But the modification of constructs is not something that happens automatically or through mechanisms like conditioning or reinforcement, as the behaviorists would suggest. To change or not to change one's constructs is ultimately a matter of personal choice. This could not be otherwise, in Kelly's theory, because the person, rather than some outside mechanism, is the originator of constructs. How this choice is exercised, or whether it is exercised at all, has far-reaching consequences for the individual.

If constructions are never altered, a person's life may amount to merely a sequence of parallel events that have no psychological impact on his or her life. But if a person engages in what is perceived as the most intimate event of all—unwavering investment in the enterprise—then the outcome, to the extent that it differs from his or her expectation or enlarges upon it, dislodges the person's self-construction. In recognizing the inconsistency between people's anticipation and the outcome, individuals concede a discrepancy between what they were and what they are. A succession of such investments and dislodgements constitutes the human experience (Kelly, 1970, p. 18).

9. Modulation Corollary

> *The variation in a person's construction system is limited by the permeability of the constructs within whose range of convenience the variants lie* (p. 77).

While people are capable of revising their construction systems, this capacity has limitations. *Permeability* refers to the ease with which a construct can be applied to new events or can be used as a referent for new events. In Kelly's terms, an *impermeable* construct that addresses, for example, the notion of God spells out all things holy in a concrete and literal fashion. Any novel ideas that emerge are likely to be excluded from this notion. In a *permeable* construct, this notion of God maintains a focus on all things holy, but the specific targets of that focus—the holy things per se—are open to interpretation. The more permeable the construct, the better it can accommodate new events and allow the person to remain open to experience. On the other hand, an excessively permeable construct is like a sieve that lets through everything and catches hold of nothing. A person who thinks in vague, global terms has excessively permeable constructs, and therefore has difficulty being clear and precise.

10. Fragmentation Corollary

> *A person may successively employ a variety of construction subsystems which are inferentially incompatible with each other* (p. 83).

This corollary simply acknowledges the fact that logic usually plays a rather minor role in the lives of people. A person's responses to events are not necessarily consistent or inferable from other responses he or she has made. Love can unexpectedly turn to jealousy and from jealousy to hate. This kind of irrationality, Kelly notes, is not necessarily a bad thing. People who are wholly integrated are always just themselves, holding surprises for neither themselves nor others who know them. However, it is often the incompatible fragments of people's construction systems that make them great (Kelly, 1970, p. 20).

11. Commonality Corollary

> *To the extent that one person employs a construction of experience which is similar to that employed by another, his psychological processes are similar to those of the other person* (p. 90).

This corollary refers to the construction of *experience,* rather than events. It addresses the possibility that two people who may have confronted quite different events nevertheless end up with similar constructions of their experiences. This accounts for the kind of meeting of the minds that sometimes occurs between people and may become a basis for a lasting friendship or the feeling of being kindred spirits.

12. Sociality Corollary

To the extent that one person construes the construction processes of another, he may play a role in a social process involving the other person (p. 95).

The sociality corollary establishes the basis for Kelly's view of empathy and social relationships. Behavioral psychologists, and often ordinary people as well, construe other people's observable behavior and respond to them on the basis of such constructions. Other people are then regarded as automatons, or puzzles to be pieced together. On the other hand, to recognize the humanity of another person as being no different from one's own is to view the other as a construer of his or her own experience. Relating meaningfully to other people is a matter of understanding how they construe themselves and their world. This has something to do with empathy, the capacity to put oneself in the shoes of another person, or assume the *role* of another. In Kelly's theory, the notion of role has far-reaching implications to the construction of self and social relationships and the issue of guilt.

Constructs and Construing

The fundamental postulate and the corollaries describe how construction works in people's experience of the world and of themselves. But what exactly are constructs and what is meant by construing? Let us now take a closer look at these key concepts.

Construing involves interpretation, or "erecting a structure within the framework of which the substance takes shape or assumes meaning" (1955, p. 50). Regularity or predictability is an important feature of meaning that has to do with repetition and familiarity. "To construe is to hear the whisper of the recurrent themes in the events that reverberate around us" (1955, p. 76). But the emphasis in Kelly's theory is on the anticipation of events, not on their containment. A meaningful construct embraces the future rather than merely cataloging the past. In this way, constructs connect the past with the future and provide a sense of temporal continuity.

Constructs form the bridge between the private psychological world and the public world of behavior and interaction with others. Kelly (1955) describes constructs as patterns or templates that a person creates and then attempts to superimpose or fit over the world. They are not representations or symbolizations of events but ways of coping with events.

Events do not tell us what to do, nor do they carry their meanings engraved on their backs for us to discover. For better or worse we ourselves create the only meaning they will ever have during our lifetime. (Kelly, 1970, p. 3)

Constructs are ways in which individuals organize experiences according to similarities and differences. *Aggressiveness-gentleness* is Kelly's own illustration that describes a typical construct. The construct has two poles, the *likeness end* and the *contrast end.* The things or events that are abstracted by the construct are *elements.* For example, when a person makes a judgment that Mary and

as its current possibilities (Epting & Amerikaner, 1980). Satisfaction or even self-fulfillment cannot adequately define the goal of human life, for these are themselves subject to construction and hence revision and reconstruction. Kelly never loses sight of the fact that for the person as the construer of his or her life and goals, the possibilities for change and growth are always exceeded by the range of the constructs.

Aggressiveness Personal construct theory celebrates the spirit of inquiry and adventure that turns adversity into opportunity. The theory revises and expands constructs when events fail to confirm them, rather than discard the constructs. Kelly defines aggressiveness as the active elaboration of one's perceptual field (1955, p. 508). As such, it connotes a positive quality in one's approach to life and something that is essential to a person's growth. Unlike psychodynamic theorists, Kelly does not associate aggressiveness with any negative connotations, such as destructiveness, hostility, or a drive toward death.

Each person is more aggressive in some ways than in others. And the ways in which people are aggressive depend on the anxieties that are associated with these various forms of aggression. In their aggressive moments, people may actually seek out certain aspects of their anxiety and fuss about them, testing out constructs one after another, rapidly abandoning those that do not fit until perhaps eventually finding one that does. But when the anxiety mounts to an intolerable intensity, the person may completely abandon the construction process and retreat into what seem secure and unchallenged areas. According to Kelly, "the areas of one's aggression are those in which there are anxieties he can face" (1955, p. 509).

People taking on a difficult challenge can serve to illustrate Kelly's point about aggression and anxiety. For example, two friends are trying out for a college sports team. Waiting for the coach, they wrestle and banter with each other. They might say that they are "just warming up," but they eventually respond with excessive aggression, the result of the anxiety they are experiencing.

Loosening, Tightening, and the Creativity Cycle The **creativity cycle** precipitates change in a person's construction system. The cycle begins with *loosened* construction and ends with *tightened* and validated construction (1955, p. 528). Loose construction is like a rough sketch that may be preliminary to a carefully drafted design. The sketch permits flexible interpretation because particular features are not yet precisely placed. Dreaming exemplifies loose construction. An example of tight construction would be the carefully drafted design in which each feature is precisely placed, leaving little room for ambiguity or alternative interpretation.

According to Kelly, people who always use tight construction may be productive but cannot be creative. They cannot produce anything that has not already been blueprinted.

Creativity always arises out of preposterous thinking. If the creative person mumbles the first part of a Creativity Cycle out loud, he is likely to get sharp criticism from everyone who is within earshot. (Kelly, 1955, p. 529)

If people who use only tight constructions cannot be creative, neither can people who use only loose constructions. Such people, according to Kelly, would never get past the preliminary stage of mumbling to themselves, let alone progress to the level at which their ideas could be put to the test. In creativity, as in other kinds of human activity, optimal functioning is a matter of balance. The creative person must have the capacity to move from loosening to tightening.

Creativity is not the exclusive possession of those who have, or aspire to have, accomplishments in arts, literature, or other imaginative fields. Creativity abounds in human growth of all kinds, for it is the process whereby individuals can free themselves from rigid, narrow ways of construing and open themselves up to new horizons and ways of being in the world.

Obstacles to Growth

The obstacles to growth are usually manifested in the very situations that are opportunities for growth. Such situations call for a change in a person's construction system. According to Kelly, the diagnostic constructs of threat, fear, and anxiety all essentially have to do with the transitions in one's construction system.

Threat and Fear *Threat* is the awareness of a comprehensive change about to take place in one's core structures. Facing one's imminent death, the loss of someone who is construed as essential to one's own survival or well-being, or the loss of wealth or social status that is construed as vital to one's identity, is an example of a serious threat to one's core structures.

Fear is like threat, except that fear is a transient, incidental construct rather than a lasting, comprehensive one that seems to take over. An example of the distinction between threat and fear might be the case of a woman who, while driving, indulges in wild daydreaming and impulsive thoughts. She may feel threatened by the prospect of acting on them. But if suddenly she narrowly misses crashing into another car, she is confronted with a specific situation that arouses fear in her. In both cases, there is the prospect of imminent restructuring of a core structure, but in the second example, it is incidental, and passes once the likelihood of a crash recedes. The intensity of the fear may, in this incident, be the same as that of the threat, but what distinguishes it from a threat is the short-lived, narrow character of the events involved.

Anxiety Kelly defines *anxiety* as "the recognition that the events with which one is confronted lie outside the range of convenience of one's construct system" (1955, p. 495). This recognition brings with it a sense of loss of control.

Loosening is a way in which people can protect themselves against anxiety. As one's constructs become looser, they can be stretched to cover a wider variety of events. Of course, one eventually pays the price if the loosening results in vagueness and incoherence. A person who is aware of the price he or she is paying becomes increasingly anxious; this then means that the protective maneuver is not working. On the positive side, such a person is likely to seek help for the anxiety and benefit from psychotherapy. However, a person who is not aware of the impaired functioning of his or her loosened construction system may seem free of anxiety. In extreme cases, this lack of awareness leads to serious communication problems and can ultimately result in a diagnosis of schizophrenia.

Tightening can also be used as a defense against anxiety. Rather than stretching one's constructs, one may go the route of excluding events that do not fit and developing the precision and detail of one's construction system to such an extent that it "covers all situations." Therefore, one feels in control without having to deal with the nebulous and undefined events of life. A compulsive person whose life follows carefully worked-out procedures and is excessively organized, as if every element of life could fit into compartments, is using tight construction to an extreme as a defense against anxiety.

Hostility Kelly's interpretation of hostility is unique and has significant implications for psychotherapy. Hostility, for Kelly, has nothing to do with aggression or even with the intent to do harm to others. Rather, it is defined as "the continued effort to extort validational evidence in favor of a type of social prediction which has already proven itself a failure" (1955, p. 510). Hostile individuals may insist on being right about something in the face of circumstances that show them to be wrong. But more than insist, they attempt to enforce their constructs upon the world by altering the circumstances to fit their constructs. In trying to change these circumstances, they may employ either overt force or covertly undermining tactics. Usually the circumstances involve another person whose behavior does not fit the hostile person's constructs. "The other person is the victim, not so much of the hostile person's fiendishly destructive impulses, as of his frantic and unrealistic efforts to collect on a wager he has already lost" (1955, p. 511).

Spouses who abuse their partners and children are obviously hostile individuals. There are also subtler forms of hostility. Kelly's example of "loving" hostility, for example, is a mother who treats her son as if he were her doll, and when the child behaves in an undoll-like manner, she mildly and sweetly reproaches him, shaping, through her overprotectiveness, the child's doll-like behavior.

Structure

Psychologists and nonprofessional people alike tend to think of the body, mind, and emotions as the parts that make up the human personality. In Kelly's theory, the structural components of personality—such as body, mind, and emotions—are viewed as something that individuals construe in their experience and in their encounters with the social world.

Body and Mind

Personal construct theory thus focuses on the viewpoint of the individual—specifically, how the individual construes himself or herself in relation to the world. Therefore, the body as a substantial entity outside such a construction does not enter into the theory. On the other hand, how individuals construe their own bodies as, say, *healthy-sick* or *strong-weak* can be important to a person's outlook and well-being.

Nothing which happens in the brain can be described except in terms supplied by the mind. (Mumford, 1967)

Just as Kelly refuses to view the body as a physical entity outside the person's construction of it, he also refrains from theorizing about the mind as a psychological entity or domain that exists independently of personal constructions. Theorizing about how the human mind works or how it relates to the body would amount to nothing more and nothing less than indulging in one's own personal construction. However, personal construct theory is concerned with how people view their minds and bodies. In this way, personal construct theory is similar to the phenomenological approach in psychology.

Kelly would say, to find the seat of the mind do not look into the brain, look at those responsible for it. (Sotter, 1970, p. 237)

Social Relationships

Social relationships are a vital part of a person's construction system, as is the testing out of one's constructs within the social system. The communality and sociality constructs reflect Kelly's view of people as essentially social beings who not only respond to one another's misfortunes but are capable of deep and empathic feelings for one another. Relationships based on the intimate understanding of how other people experience the world should be the basis for society, according to Kelly.

Will

True to his holistic approach, Kelly does not treat will as a distinct attribute or entity that by itself accounts for the construction process. Will is usually understood as some kind of motivating force that sets a process in motion or keeps it going, sometimes even in the face of greater obstacles. For Kelly, the construction process is already in motion and is intrinsically active, because this is what it means to be alive. There is no need to posit a separate factor or process to explain how the anticipation of events begins or what keeps it going. One might say that life itself keeps it going. Engagement in the world and the commitment to enacting one's anticipation of events, which is essential for the expansion of constructions and hence for the growth of the individual, is manifested in an integral component of the construction process called *will.*

Emotions

Like will, emotions are integrally involved in the anticipation of events and their construction. The construction process is not exclusively, nor perhaps even primarily, cognitive but incorporates emotional components. Some constructions are felt and acted on without ever coming to conscious awareness.

Intellect

Like emotion and will, the intellect is another integral component of the construction process. Accordingly, Kelly is highly critical of attempts to measure intelligence as a distinct trait. The IQ test, in Kelly's view, is a psychologist's diagnostic construct that has little utility for adults and might even hamper learning in children. Rather than provide data that could enhance learning, Kelly believes, IQ test results encourage teachers to pigeonhole their students.

Self

In the theory of personal constructs, the construer of events is central. But Kelly does not think in terms of a construing entity outside the construction system. Kelly envisions the self as construer.

The self is a construct. Perhaps more than any other, this construct has a controlling effect on the person, as witnessed by the remarkable variations in people's behavior and experience. This behavior has little to do with circumstance and everything to do with how individuals view themselves. The controlling effect of the self is a testimony to the power of construction, not an indication that some kind of substantial entity or mechanism acts to determine the construct. This view of Kelly's is reminiscent of the Buddhist conception of the self as a process, consisting of a series of perceptions and notions that are devoid of substance.

The self construct has to do with one's core role. Even though the construction of this role goes very deep, it is not static or unchangeable. For Kelly, the role, even the core role that one identifies with, refers to an ongoing activity. Thus the self is fluid and changeable, not something that binds the person to biology, any more than it does to immutable, unconscious dynamics.

Clinical Applications and Therapy

Gradually my clients taught me that a symptom was an issue one expresses through the act of being his present self, not a malignancy that fastens itself upon a man or woman. (Kelly, 1969b, p. 19)

Personal construct theory views most forms of psychological suffering and maladjustment as involving faulty or no-longer-relevant role constructs of oneself and other people. That people are often not clearly aware of how they construe their own roles or the roles of their significant others complicates the situation. Kelly devised innovative applications of his theory to help identify existing roles and develop more adaptive and creative ways of construing self and others.

The Rep Test

The *Role Construct Repertory test,* or *Rep test,* elicits and measures personal constructs in the clinical setting. An extension of this test that came to be more widely used for research purposes is the Rep Grid test (Bannister & Mair, 1968).

In the procedure, test takers receive a list of role titles. The list may be tailored to the test takers, so that they can readily identify significant people in their lives to fit each role title. The ways in which the test takers have assigned individuals to the roles are then unraveled and analyzed through a systematic procedure.

The role title list, according to Kelly, represents the cast of characters in the person's life, and the test reveals the person's casting of the parts in the play in which he or she enacts the leading role (Kelly, 1955, p. 237). This test can help clients gain insight into their important relationships. It is also a tool for exploring the nature of a client's constructs (e.g., finding how permeable or impermeable they are).

Fixed-Role Therapy

Fixed-role therapy is an approach based on the notion that revising or replacing less-than-optimal role constructs can lead to improvement in the client's sense of well-being and relationship with others. The purpose of the therapy is to help devise better role constructs and provide a safe environment for trying them out.

In their daily lives, people are reluctant to try out new ways of being with themselves and with others, for a number of reasons. They may have a realistic fear of the punitive consequences of failing to live up to other people's expectations. This disconfirmation of their self construct undermines their sense of identity and can be highly threatening. But enacting a role that both the client and the therapist know to be a fabrication can have a positive impact. The protective mask of make-believe is crucial for the success of fixed-role therapy. According to Kelly, the treatment provides the safety of a controlled laboratory environment in which the client, like the scientist, can test out his or her hypotheses without fear of the consequences should the experiment fail.

The **fixed-role sketch** is a vital element in the therapy. It consists of a written piece, several paragraphs in length, containing a description of a character the client is to portray as his or her new role. Before the description is produced by the therapist, the client is asked to provide a character sketch written in the third person. The therapist then carefully analyzes the client's character sketch and, based on the analysis, composes the fixed-role sketch.

The following considerations are important in writing the sketch.

1. *Development of a major theme other than correction of minor faults.* After some experimentation with the fixed-role sketch, Kelly came to the conclusion that the client derived more therapeutic benefit from playing out a role that alters a major theme in the individual's construct of self than from attempts to correct only minor faults.

2. *The use of sharp contrast.* It is easier for clients to play roles they believe to be highly dissimilar to their own personality than it is to assume roles that differ slightly from the way they perceive themselves.

3. *The setting of ongoing processes in motion rather than the creation of a new state.* The task of fixed-role therapy is to prepare the client to resume the natural developmental processes of which he or she is capable. As much as possible, the role to be played out should encourage movement within the client's existing constructs, making the client an agent of change.

4. *Testable hypotheses for the client.* The new role should not be merely an academic exercise but should clearly take into account the anticipated events in the client's everyday life, thus allowing him or her to test the new role against reality.

[We] are looking for bridges between the client's present and his future. Moreover, we expect to take an active part in helping the client select or build the bridges to be used in helping him cross them safely. (Kelly, 1955, p. 775)

5. *Emphasis upon role perceptions.* The role should be constructed so that it enables the client to incorporate other people's construction systems, deepening and facilitating the client's interpersonal relationships.

6. *Use of the protective mask.* This point only indirectly affects the writing of the sketch. The client is to be given the full protection of make-believe. Kelly notes that "this is probably man's oldest protective screen for reaching out into the unknown" (1955, p. 373).

Izard, C. E. (1978). On the ontogenesis of emotion and emotion-cognition relationships in infancy. In M. Lewis & L. Rosenblum (Eds.), *The development of affect* (pp. 389–413). New York: Plenum Press.

———. (1984). Emotion-cognition relationships in human development. In C. E. Izard, J. Kagan, & R. B. Zajonc (Eds.), *Emotions, cognition and behavior* (pp. 17–37). New York: Cambridge University Press.

Johnson-Laird, P. N. (1977). Procedural semantics. *Cognition, 5,* 189–214.

Kahn, S. (1964). *Psychodrama explained.* New York: Philosophical Library.

Karst, T. O. (1980). The relationship between personal construct theory and psychotherapeutic techniques. In A. W. Landfield & L. M. Leitner (Eds.), *Personal construct psychology: Psychotherapy and personality* (pp. 166–184). New York: Wiley.

Kelly, G. A. (1955). *The psychology of personal constructs* (Vol. 1). New York: Norton.

———. (1963). *A theory of personality.* New York: Norton.

———. (1969a). An autobiography of a theory. In B. Maher (Ed.), *Clinical psychology and personality: The selected papers of George Kelly* (pp. 46–65). New York: Wiley.

———. (1969b). Ontological acceleration. In B. Maher (Ed.), *Clinical psychology and personality: The selected papers of George Kelly* (pp. 7–45). New York: Wiley.

———. (1970). A brief introduction to personal construct theory. In D. Bannister (Ed.), *Perspectives in personal construct theory* (pp. 1–29). New York: Academic Press. Written in 1966.

Labouvie-Vief, G., Hakim-Larson, J., DeVoe, M., & Schoeberlein, S. (1989). Emotions and self-regulation: A life-span view. *Human Development, 32,* 279–299.

Lachman, R., Lachman, J. L., & Butterfield, E. C. (1979). *Cognitive psychology and human information processing.* Hillsdale, NJ: Lawrence Erlbaum.

Lazarus, R. S. (1966). *Psychological stress and the coping process.* New York: McGraw-Hill.

———. (1982). Thoughts on the relations between emotion and cognition. *American Psychologist, 37,* 1019–1024.

———. (1984). On the primacy of cognition. *American Psychologist, 39,* 124–129.

———. (1991a). Cognition and motivation in emotion. *American Psychologist, 46*(4), 352–367.

———. (1991b). *Emotion and adaptation.* New York: Oxford University Press.

Lazarus, R., & Folkman, S. (1984). *Stress, appraisal and coping.* New York: Springer.

Leventhal, H., & Scherer, K. (1987). The relationship of emotion to cognition: A functional approach to a semantic controversy. *Cognition and Emotion, 1,* 3–28.

Maher, B. (1969). Introduction. George Kelly: A brief biography. In B. Maher (Ed.), *Clinical psychology and personality: The selected papers of George Kelly* (pp. 1–3). New York: Wiley.

Mair, J. M. M. (1970). Psychologists are human too. In D. Bannister (Ed.), *Perspectives in personal construct theory* (pp. 157–183). New York: Academic Press.

Mayer, R. E. (1981). *The promise of cognitive psychology.* San Francisco: Freeman.

McMullin, R. E. (1986). *Handbook of cognitive therapy techniques.* New York: Norton.

McMullin, R. E., & Casey, B. (1975). *Talk sense to yourself: A guide to cognitive restructuring therapy.* New York: Institute for Rational Emotive Therapy.

Miller, G. A., Galanter, E., & Pribram, C. (1960). *Plans and the structure of behavior.* New York: Henry Holt.

Moreno, J. (1972). *Psychodrama* (Vol. 1) (4th ed.). Boston: Beacon House.

Mumford, L. (1967). *The myth of the machine.* London: Secker & Warburg.

Neisser, U. (1967). *Cognitive psychology.* New York: Appleton-Century-Crofts.

———. (1976a). *Cognition and reality.* San Francisco: Freeman.

———. (1976b). General, academic, and artificial intelligence. In L. B. Resnick (Ed.), *The nature of intelligence.* Hillsdale, NJ: Lawrence Erlbaum.

———. (1990). Gibson's revolution. *Contemporary Psychology, 35,* 749–750.

Newell, A., Shaw, J. C., & Simon, H. (1958). Elements of a theory of human problem solving. *Psychological Review, 65,* 151–166.

Newell, A., & Simon, H. (1961). The simulation of human thought. In W. Dennis (Ed.), *Current trends in psychological theory.* Pittsburgh: University of Pittsburgh Press.

———. (1972). *Human problem solving.* Englewood Cliffs, NJ: Prentice-Hall.

Perris, C. (1988). *Cognitive therapy with schizophrenics.* New York: Guilford Press.

Puhakka, K. (1993). Review of Varela, F. J., Thompson, E., & Rosch, E. (1991). *The embodied mind: Cognitive science and human experience. The Humanistic Psychologist, 21*(2), 235–246.

Quillian, M. R. (1969). The teachable language comprehender: A simulation program and theory of language. *Communications of the ACM, 12,* 459–476.

Schank, R. C., & Abelson, R. B. (1977). *Scripts, plans, goals and understanding.* Hillsdale, NJ: Lawrence Erlbaum.

Scheff, T. J. (1985). The primacy of affect. *American Psychologist, 40,* 849–850.

Sechrest, L. (1977). Personal-constructs theory. In R. J. Corsini (Ed.), *Current personality theories* (pp. 203–241). Itasca, IL: F. E. Peacock.

Shepard, R. N. (1984). Ecological constraints on internal representation: Resonant kinematics of perceiving, imagining, thinking, and dreaming. *Psychological Review, 91,* 417–447.

Sotter, J. (1970). Men, the man-makers: George Kelly and the psychology of personal constructs. In D. Bannister (Ed.), *Perspectives in personal construct theory* (pp. 223–253). New York: Academic Press.

Stein, N., & Levine, L. (1987). Thinking about feelings: The development and organization of emotional knowledge. In R. E. Snow & M. Farr (Eds.), *Aptitude, learning and instruction. Vol. 3: Cognition, conation, and affect* (pp. 165–197). Hillsdale, NJ: Lawrence Erlbaum.

Stenberg, C. R., & Campos, J. J. (1990). The development of anger expressions in infancy. In N. Stein, B. Leventhal, & T. Trabasso (Eds.), *Psychological and biological approaches to emotion* (pp. 247–282). Hillsdale, NJ: Lawrence Erlbaum.

Stroufe, L. A. (1984). The organization of emotional development. In K. R. Scherer & P. Ekman (Eds.), *Approaches to emotion* (pp. 109–128). Hillsdale, NJ: Lawrence Erlbaum.

Turing, A. M. (1950). Computing machinery and intelligence. *Mind, 59* (236). In R. P. Honeck, T. J. Case, & M. J. Firment (Eds.), *Introductory readings in cognitive psychology* (pp. 15–24). Guilford, CT: Dushkin, 1991.

Varela, F. J., Thompson, E., & Rosch, E. (1991). *The embodied mind: Cognitive science and human experience.* Cambridge, MA: MIT Press.

Waldrop, M. M. (1985, March). Machinations of thought. *Science 85,* pp. 38–45.

Webber, R., & Mancusco, J. C. (Eds.). (1983). *Applications of personal construct theory.* New York: Academic Press, pp. 137–154.

Weizenbaum, J. (1976). *Computer power and human reason: From judgment to calculation.* San Francisco: Freeman.

Zajonc, R. B. (1980). Feeling and thinking: Preferences need no inferences. *American Psychologist, 35,* 151–175.

———. (1984). On the primacy of affect. *American Psychologist, 39,* 117–123.

Zelhart, P. F., & Jackson, T. T. (1983). George A. Kelly, 1931–1943: Environmental influences. In J. Adams-Webber and J. Mancusco (Eds.), *Applications of personal construct theory* (pp. 137–154). New York: Academic Press.

CHAPTER 13

Carl Rogers and the Person-Centered Perspective

Carl Rogers has had an indelible influence on psychology and psychotherapy, as well as on education. He created and fostered client-centered therapy, pioneered the encounter-group movement, was one of the founders of humanistic psychology, and was the pivotal member of the first person-centered groups working to resolve international political conflicts.

Throughout his working life, while his interests changed and grew to include not only individual psychotherapy and group therapy but also educational, social, and governmental systems, Rogers's philosophical viewpoint remained consistently optimistic and humanitarian.

> I have little sympathy with the rather prevalent concept that man is basically irrational, and thus his impulses, if not controlled, would lead to destruction of others and self. Man's behavior is exquisitely rational, moving with subtle and ordered complexity toward the goals his organism is endeavoring to achieve. The tragedy for most of us is that our defenses keep us from being aware of this rationality, so that consciously we are moving in one direction, while organismically we are moving in another. (1969, p. 29)

Unwilling to be limited by the popularity and acceptance of his earlier works, Rogers continued to modify his ideas and to change his approach. He encouraged others to test his assertions but discouraged the formation of a "Rogerian school," which would only mimic or repeat his discoveries. Outside of formal psychology his work has been, in Rogers's own words, "one of the factors in changing concepts of industrial (even military) leadership, of social work practice, of nursing practice, and of religious work. . . . It has even influenced students of theology and philosophy" (1974a, p. 115).

It will have been evident that one implication of the view I have been presenting is that the basic nature of the human being, when functioning freely, is constructive and trustworthy. (Rogers, 1969, p. 290)

> What started for me in the 30's as a changing but supposedly well-accepted way of working therapeutically with individuals, was clumsily articulated as my own view in the early 1940's. . . . One might say that a "technique" of counseling became a practice of psychotherapy. This in turn brought into being a theory of therapy and of personality. The theory supplied the hypotheses which opened a whole new field of research. Out of this grew an approach to all interpersonal relationships. Now it reaches into education as a way of facilitating learning at all levels. It is a way of conducting intensive group experiences, and has influenced the theory of group dynamics. (1970)

Through the 1970s and early 1980s, Rogers's interest shifted away from therapy with clients to an international involvement in team building and large-scale community development. He also became more aware of and tolerant of spiritual and mystical experiences. His determination to expand his ideas and his belief in the power of individuals to help themselves continue to influence counselors and psychologists worldwide (Caspary, 1991; Macy, 1987).

Personal History

Carl Rogers, the fourth of six children, was born on January 8, 1902, in Oak Park, Illinois, into a prosperous and strictly fundamentalist Protestant home. His childhood was restricted by the beliefs and attitudes of his parents and by his own interpretation of their ideas:

These conditions are the basic obstacles to accurate perception and realistic thinking. They are selective blinders and filters, used by a needy child to help ensure a supply of love from parents and others. As children, we adopt certain attitudes and actions in order to be worth loving and to retain love. We learn that the adoption of certain conditions, attitudes, or actions is essential to our remaining worthy of love. To the extent that these attitudes and actions are contrived, they are areas of personal incongruence. In the extreme, conditions of worth are characterized by the belief that "I must be loved or respected by everyone I come in contact with." Conditions of worth create a discrepancy between the self and the self-concept.

I feel warmed and fulfilled when I can let in the fact, or permit myself to feel that someone cares for, accepts, admires, or prizes me. . . . [I]t has been very difficult for me to do this. (Rogers, 1980a, p. 19)

If you have been told, for example, "You must love your new baby sister or Mommy and Daddy won't love you," the message is that you must deny or repress any genuinely negative feelings you have for your sister. Only if you manage to hide your ill will, your desire to hurt her, and your normal jealousy will your mother and father continue to love you. If you admit such feelings, you risk the loss of your parents' love. A solution (which creates a condition of worth) is to deny such feelings whenever they occur, blocking them from your awareness. This means that the feelings, because they must come to the surface in some form, will likely find an inappropriate outlet of expression. You may begin responding in such ways as, "I really do love my little sister; I hug her until she screams," or "My foot slipped under hers. That's why she tripped," or the more universal "She started it!"

This author can still recall the enormous joy that my older brother exhibited when he was given an opportunity to hit me for something I had done. My mother, my brother, and I were all stunned by his violence. In recalling the incident, my brother remembers that he was not particularly angry with me, but he understood that this was a rare occasion and wanted to unload as much accumulated ill will as possible while he had permission. Admitting such feelings and expressing them as they occur is healthier, says Rogers, than denying or disowning them.

The Growth of the False Self-image As the child matures, the problem may persist. Growth is impeded to the extent that a person is denying inputs that differ from the artificially "nice" self-concept. In order to support the false self-image, a person continues to distort experiences—the greater the distortion, the greater the chance for mistakes and the creation of additional problems. The behaviors, errors, and confusion that result are manifestations of the initial distortions.

The situation feeds back on itself. Each experience of incongruence between the self and reality leads to increased imbalance, which in turn leads to increased defensiveness, shutting off experiences and creating new occasions for incongruence.

Sometimes the defensive maneuvers do not work. The person becomes aware of the obvious discrepancies between behaviors and beliefs. The results may be panic, chronic anxiety, withdrawal, or even psychosis. Rogers has observed that psychotic behavior often seems to be the acting out of a previously denied aspect of an individual's experience. Perry (1974) corroborates this, presenting evidence that the psychotic episode is a desperate attempt by the personality to rebalance itself and allow satisfaction of frustrated internal needs.

Client-centered therapy strives to establish an atmosphere in which detrimental conditions of worth can be set aside, thus allowing the healthy forces, which Rogers sees as inherent in a person, to regain their original dominance.

Structure

Body

Rogers does not give special attention to the role of the body. As he points out, "My background [referring to his strict upbringing] is not such as to make me particularly free in this respect" (1970, p. 58). Even in his own encounter settings, he did not promote or facilitate physical contact or work directly with physical gestures, until much later in his life.

Social Relationships

For Rogers, relationships are fundamental. Early relationships can be congruent and supportive, or they can create conditions of worth and personality constriction. Later relationships can restore congruence or diminish it. Interactions with others are crucial to developing awareness and the capacity for high congruence.

Relationships Are Necessary to Discover the Self Rogers believes that relationships enable an individual to directly discover, uncover, experience, or encounter his or her actual self. *Our personalities become visible to us through relating to others.* In therapy, in encounter situations, and in daily interactions, the feedback from others offers us opportunities to experience ourselves.

I would like to propose . . . that the major barrier to mutual interpersonal communication is our very natural tendency to judge, to evaluate, to approve or disapprove, the statement of the other person, or the other group. (Rogers, 1952a)

For Rogers, relationships offer the best opportunity to be fully functioning, to be in harmony with the self, others, and the environment. Through relationships, the basic organismic needs of the individual can be fulfilled. The desire for fulfillment motivates people to invest incredible amounts of energy in relationships, even in those that may not appear to be healthy or fulfilling.

Marriage Marriage is a special relationship; it is potentially long term, it is intensive, and it carries with it the possibility of sustained growth and development.

All our troubles, says somebody wise, come upon us because we cannot be alone. And that is all very well. We must all be able to be alone. Otherwise we are just victims. But when we are able to be alone, then we realize that the only thing to do is to start a new relationship with another—or even the same—human being. That people should all be stuck up apart, like so many telegraph poles, is nonsense. (D. H. Lawrence, 1960, pp. 114–115)

Rogers believes that marriage follows the same general laws that hold true for encounter groups, therapy, and other relationships. Better marriages occur between partners who are congruent themselves, have fewer impeding conditions of worth, and are capable of genuine acceptance of others. When marriage is used to sustain incongruence or to reinforce existing defensive tendencies, it is less fulfilling and less likely to endure.

Rogers's conclusions about any long-term, intimate relationship, including marriage, are based on four basic elements: ongoing commitment, expression of feelings, avoidance of specific roles, and the capacity to share one's inner life. He summarizes each element as a pledge, an agreed-upon ideal, for a continuing, beneficial, and meaningful relationship.

Dedication of Commitment Each member of a marriage should view "a partnership as a continuing process, not a contract. The work that is done is for *personal* as well as mutual satisfaction." Rogers suggests that this commitment be expressed as follows: "We each commit ourselves to working together on the changing process of our present relationship, because that relationship is currently enriching our love and our life and we wish it to grow" (1972, p. 201). A relationship is work; it is work for separate as well as common goals.

Communication—the Expression of Feelings Rogers insists on full and open communication. "I will risk myself by endeavoring to communicate any persistent feeling, positive or negative, to my partner—to the full depth that I understand it in myself—as a living part of *me*. Then I will risk further by trying to understand, with all the empathy I can bring to bear, his or her response, whether it is accusatory and critical or sharing and self-revealing" (1972, p. 204). Communication has two equally important phases: the first is to express the emotion; the second is to remain open and experience the other's response.

Is not marriage an open question when it is alleged, from the beginning of the world, that such as are in the institution wish to get out, and such as are out wish to get in? (Ralph Waldo Emerson, 1803–1882)

Rogers is not simply advocating the acting out of feelings. He is suggesting that one must be concerned about how one's feelings affect one's partner. And one must be equally concerned about the feelings themselves. This is far more difficult than simply "letting off steam" or being "open and honest." Both partners must be willing to accept the real risks involved: rejection, misunderstandings, hurt feelings, and retribution.

Nonacceptance of Roles Numerous problems develop from trying to fulfill the expectations of others instead of determining our own. "We will live by our own choices, the deepest organismic sensings of which we are capable, but we will not be shaped by the wishes, the rules, the roles which others are all too eager to thrust upon us" (1972, p. 260). Rogers reports that many couples suffer severe strain attempting to live up to the inappropriate images that their parents and society have thrust upon them. A marriage laced with too many unrealistic expectations and images is inherently unstable and potentially unrewarding.

Becoming a Separate Self This commitment represents a profound attempt to discover and accept one's total nature. It is the most challenging of the commitments, a dedication to removing masks as soon as and as often as they are created.

> Perhaps I can discover and come closer to more of what I really am deep inside—feeling sometimes angry or terrified, sometimes loving and caring, occasionally beautiful and strong or wild and awful—without hiding these feelings from myself. Perhaps I can come to prize myself as the richly varied person I am. Perhaps I can openly be more of this person. If so, I can live by my own experienced values, even though I am aware of all of society's codes. Then I can let myself be all this complexity of feelings and meaning and values with my partner—be free enough to give of love and anger and tenderness as they exist in me. Possibly then I can be a real member of a partnership, because I am on the road to being a real person. And I am hopeful that I can encourage my partner to follow his or her own road to a unique personhood, which I would love to share. (1972, p. 209)

This set of suggestions is difficult for the best of couples to maintain, but is one which, if held to, eventually defines an excellent long-term relationship.

Emotions

The healthy individual is aware of his or her emotions, whether or not they are expressed. Feelings that are denied expression distort perception of and reactions to the experience that triggered them.

Yet, if we are truly aware, we can hear the "silent screams" of denied feelings echoing off of every classroom wall and university corridor. And if we are sensitive enough, we can hear the creative thoughts and ideas that often emerge during and from the open expression of our feelings. (Rogers, 1973b, p. 385)

For example, one might feel anxiety without knowing why. The initial cause of the anxiety was *not admitted to awareness,* because it was perceived as threatening to the self-image. The unconscious reaction (McCleary & Lazarus, 1949) alerts the organism to possible danger and causes psychophysiological changes. These defensive reactions are one way the organism maintains incongruent beliefs and behaviors. A person can act on these beliefs but be unaware of why he or she is acting. For instance, a man might become uncomfortable at seeing overt homosexuals. His self-report would include the discomfort but not the cause. He cannot admit his own unresolved sexual identity, or (perhaps) the hopes and fears concerning his own sexuality. Distorting his perceptions, he may in turn react with open hostility to homosexuals, treating them as an external threat instead of admitting his internal conflict.

Intellect

Rogers values intellect as a tool that may be used effectively in integrating one's experience. He is skeptical of educational systems that overemphasize intellectual skills and undervalue the emotional and intuitive aspects of full human functioning.

In particular, Rogers finds graduate training in many fields excessively demanding, demeaning, and depressing. The pressure to churn out limited and unoriginal work, coupled with the passive and dependent roles forced on graduate students, effectively stifles or retards their creative and productive capabilities. He quotes Albert Einstein as a student: "This coercion had such a deterring effect [upon me] that, after I had passed the final examination, I found the consideration of any problem distasteful for me for an entire year" (1969, p. 177).

We all know the effects on children of compulsory spinach and compulsory rhubarb. It's the same with compulsory learning. They say, "It's spinach and the hell with it." (Rogers, 1969)

If intellect, like other freely operating functions, tends to direct the organism toward more congruent awareness, then forcing the intellect into specified channels may not be beneficial. Rogers's contention is that people are better off deciding what to do for themselves, with support from others, than doing what others decide for them.

Knowing

Rogers describes three ways of knowing, of determining what is real, that are used by psychologically mature people. These are subjective knowing, objective knowing, and interpersonal knowing.

Who can bring into being this whole person? From my experience I would say the least likely are university faculty members. Their traditionalism and smugness approach the incredible. (Rogers, 1973b, p. 385)

Most important is **subjective knowing**—the knowledge of whether one loves, hates, is disdainful of, or enjoys a person, an experience, or an event. One improves the quality of subjective knowing by getting more in touch with one's inner emotional processes. By paying attention to "gut" feelings, to inner indications, a person perceives that one course of action feels better than another.

It is the capacity to know enough that allows a person to act without verifiable evidence. In science, for example, such ability enables one to follow hunches in solving specific problems. Research in creative problem solving indicates that a person "knows" that he or she is on the right track long before discovering what the solution will include (Gordon, 1961).

Objective knowing is a way of testing hypotheses, speculations, and conjectures against external frames of reference. In psychology, reference points may include observations of behavior, test results, questionnaires, or the judgments of other psychologists. The idea that the sharing of information with colleagues can be very valuable is based on the notion that people who are trained in a given discipline can be relied upon to apply similar methods of judgment to a given event. Expert opinion may be objective, but it may also be a collective misperception. Any group of experts can exhibit rigidity and defensiveness when asked to consider data that contradict axiomatic aspects of their own training. It is Rogers's experience that theologians, communist dialecticians, and psychoanalysts exemplify this tendency in particular.

It has been considered slightly obscene to admit that psychologists feel, have hunches, or passionately pursue unformulated directions. (Rogers, 1964)

Rogers is hardly alone in questioning the validity of so-called objective knowledge, especially in attempting to understand someone else's experience. Polanyi (1958), a philosopher of science, has clarified the different uses and limitations of personal, or subjective, knowledge and public, or objective, knowledge. Both types of knowledge are helpful in describing and understanding various kinds of experiences. According to Tart (1971, 1975), different types of training are necessary for the sake of simply perceiving, not to mention evaluating, different kinds of subjective experiences.

Do not judge another man's road until you have walked a mile in his moccasins. (Pueblo Indian saying)

The third form of knowledge, **interpersonal knowing** or *phenomenological knowing,* is at the core of Rogerian psychotherapy. It is the practice of empathic understanding: penetrating the private, unique, subjective world of the other to check on one's understanding of the other's views. The goal is not merely to be objectively correct, not just to see if someone else agrees or disagrees with one's point of view, but to comprehend the other's experience as the other experiences it. Empathic knowing is tested by asking the other person if he or she has been understood. One might say, for example: "You seem depressed this morning, are you?" "It seems to me that you are telling the group that you need their help." "I wonder if you are too tired to finish this right now." The capacity to truly know another's reality is the foundation for forming genuine relationships.

The Fully Functioning Person

Textbook writers generally class Rogers as a "self" theorist (Hall & Lindzey, 1978; Krasner & Ullman, 1973). In fact, Rogers is more concerned with perception, awareness, and experience than with the hypothetical construct, the "self." As we have already described Rogers's definition of the self, we can now turn to a description of the **fully functioning person:** a person who is completely aware of his or her ongoing self.

> "The fully functioning person" is synonymous with optimal psychological adjustment, optimal psychological maturity, complete congruence, com-

> plete openness to experience. . . . Since some of these terms sound somewhat static, as though such a person "had arrived," it should be pointed out that all the characteristics of such a person are *process* characteristics. The fully functioning person would be a person-in-process, a person continually changing. (Rogers, 1959, p. 235)

The fully functioning person has several distinct characteristics, the first of which is an *openness to experience.* There is little or no use of the early warning signals that restrict awareness. The person is continually moving away from defensiveness and toward direct experience. "He is more open to his feelings of fear and discouragement and pain. He is also more open to his feelings of courage, and tenderness, and awe. . . . He is more able fully to live the experiences of his organism rather than shutting them out of awareness" (Rogers 1961, p. 188).

A second characteristic is *living in the present*—fully realizing each moment. This ongoing, direct engagement with reality allows "the self and personality [to] emerge *from* experience, rather than experience being translated or twisted to fit a preconceived self-structure" (1961, pp. 188–189). An individual is capable of restructuring his or her responses as experience allows or suggests new possibilities.

A final characteristic is *trusting in one's inner urgings and intuitive judgments,* an ever-increasing trust in one's capacity to make decisions. A person who is able to take in and utilize data is more likely to value his or her capacity to summarize those data and respond. This activity involves not only the intellect but the whole person. Rogers suggests that, in the fully functioning person, mistakes that are made will result from incorrect information, not from incorrect processing.

This self-trust is similar to the behavior of a cat dropped upside down to the ground from a significant height. The cat does not consider wind velocity, angular momentum, or the rate of descent, yet on some level these factors are taken into account—as can be assumed from the cat's success in responding. The cat does not reflect on who dropped it from such a height, what the motives might have been, or what is likely to occur in the future. The cat responds to the immediate situation, the most pressing problem. The animal turns in midair and lands upright, instantly adjusting its posture to cope with the next event.

The good life is a *process,* not a state of being. It is a direction, not a destination. (Rogers, 1961, p. 186)

"The person who offers the most hope in our crazy world today, which could be wiped out, is the individual who is most fully aware—most fully aware of what is going on within himself" (Rogers in Kirschenbaum & Henderson, 1989, p. 189). Thus fully functioning persons are free to respond and free to experience their response to situations. They represent the essence of what Rogers calls living the good life. Such individuals are continually furthering their self-actualization (1959).

Person-Centered Therapy

Rogers was a practicing therapist through most of his professional career. His theory of personality arises from and is integral to his methods and ideas about therapy. Rogers's theory of therapy went through a number of developmental phases and shifts in emphases, yet there are a few fundamental principles that Rogers first articulated in 1940 and found still valid 30 years later. His approach was based on the individual's drive toward growth, health, and adjustment. Therapy was a way to free the client to resume his or her normal development. It stressed feeling more than the intellect, and the immediate life situation more than the past. Finally, it saw the relationship that existed in therapy as a growth experience (1970).

Rogers initially used the word *client* and later the word *person* rather than the traditional term *patient*. A patient is usually defined as someone who is ill, needs help, and seeks treatment by trained professionals, whereas a client desires a service but feels unable to perform that service alone. Clients, although they may have problems, are still viewed as inherently capable of understanding their own situation. An equality of relating is implied in the person-centered model that is not present in the doctor-patient relationship.

The therapy assists a person in unlocking his or her own dilemma with minimum intervention. Rogers defined *psychotherapy* as "the releasing of an already existing capacity in a potentially competent individual, not the expert manipulation of a more or less passive personality" (1959, p. 221). The therapy is called person-centered because it is the person who does whatever directing is necessary. Rogers felt strongly that "expert interventions" of any sort are ultimately detrimental to a person's growth.

The Client-Centered, or Person-Centered, Therapist

The individual has within him the capacity, at least latent, to understand the factors in his life that cause him unhappiness and pain, and to reorganize himself in such a way as to overcome those factors. (Rogers, 1952b)

The client holds the keys to recovery, but the therapist should have certain personal qualities, in addition to professional tools, that aid the client in learning how to use these keys. "These powers will become effective if the therapist can establish with the client a relationship sufficiently warm, accepting and understanding" (Rogers, 1952b, p. 66). By understanding, Rogers meant "the willingness and ability to understand the client's thoughts, feelings, and struggles from the client's point of view; the ability to see completely through the client's eyes and his frame of reference" (1950, p. 443). In order to work with clients, therapists must be authentic and genuine. Therapists must avoid playing a role—especially that of a therapist—when they are with clients.

> [This] involves the willingness to be and to express in my words and my behavior, the various feelings and attitudes which exist in me. This means that I need to be aware of my own feelings, in so far as possible, rather than presenting an outward facade of one attitude, while actually holding another. (1961, p. 33)

Therapists in training often ask, "How do you behave if you don't like the patient or if you are bored or angry? Won't this genuine feeling be just what he gets from everyone else whom he offends?"

The client-centered response to these questions involves several levels of understanding. At one level, the therapist serves as a model of a genuine person. The therapist offers a relationship in which clients can test their own reality. If clients are confident of getting an honest response, they can discover whether anticipation or defensiveness is justified. Clients can learn to expect real—not distorted or diluted—feedback from their inner searching. This real-

Personal Reflection

■ The Client-Centered Therapist

This is a challenging exercise, involving the client-centered approach. It is not intended to give you an idea of what client-centered therapy is like but to give you an inkling of its complex demands, which Rogers viewed as necessary to effective counseling or therapy.

Choose a partner to work with. One of you can choose to be the therapist, the other, the client. You will switch roles so that you both experience both positions. To begin, the client tells the therapist an embarrassing incident from his or her own life that might be hard to relate. For example, you might want to share a time when you lied or cheated; or a time when you were accused of being unjust or unkind.

As the therapist, you make every effort to understand what you are being told, listening so that you can repeat what you have been hearing. Repeat to the "client" what you are hearing. You want to understand exactly what is said. As a Rogerian therapist, you do not take a stand on the rightness or wrongness of behavior, you do not offer advice, and you do not criticize. Continue to appreciate the client as another human being, no matter what he or she tells you.

This is a difficult exercise. Notice the times when you want to comment, when you have a tendency to judge, feel sorry for, or be disturbed by your client's story. Notice the difficulties in simultaneously being aware of your own experience, remaining empathic, and maintaining positive regard. Be aware of your actual feelings. You may find it is easy to *play* as if you were behaving this way, but it is much more difficult to possess genuine empathy and positive regard in such a relationship.

Reverse roles. The therapist is now the client. Follow the same procedure. As the client, become aware of what it feels like to be listened to without judgment.

ity testing is crucial if the clients are to let go of distortions and to experience themselves directly.

At another level, client-centered therapists are helpful to the extent that they are accepting and able to maintain **unconditional positive regard.** Rogers defines this as "caring which is not possessive, which demands no personal gratification. It is an atmosphere which simply demonstrates, 'I care,' not 'I care for you *if* you behave thus and so' " (1961, p. 283). For the therapist, it is "experiencing a positive, nonjudgemental, acceptant attitude" (1986a, p. 198). *It is not a positive evaluation,* because any evaluation is a form of moral judgment. Evaluation tends to restrict behavior by rewarding some things and punishing others; unconditional positive regard allows the person to be what he or she actually is, no matter what it may be.

When the therapy relationship is egalitarian, when each takes responsibility for himself in the relationship, independent (and mutual) growth is much more rapid. (Rogers, 1978, p. 287)

It is close to what Abraham Maslow called *Taoistic* love, a love that does not prejudge, does not restrict, does not define. It is the promise to accept someone simply as he or she turns out to be. (This concept also resembles

Christian love, described by the Greek word *agape;* see I Cor. 13 and I John 4:7–12, 18–21.)

To show unconditional positive regard, a client-centered therapist must keep in sharp focus the self-actualizing core of the client, while tending to overlook the destructive, damaging, or offensive behaviors. A therapist who can concentrate on an individual's positive essence can respond constructively, avoiding boredom, irritation, and anger at those times when the client is less likable. The client-centered therapist is certain that the inner, and perhaps undeveloped, personality of the client is capable of understanding itself. Rogerian therapists admit, however, that they often are unable to maintain this quality of understanding as they work.

Genuine Understanding

When I am at my best as a group facilitator or a therapist, I find I am closest to my inner, intuitive self . . . when perhaps I am in a slightly altered state of consciousness in the relationship. Then whatever I do seems to be full of healing. (Rogers, 1984)

Accepting the client means going beyond mere tolerance, which is a nonjudgmental stance that may or may not include real understanding. Tolerance is inadequate; unconditional positive regard must also include "empathic understanding . . . to sense the client's private world as if it were your own, but without ever losing the 'as if' quality" (Rogers, 1961, p. 284). This added dimension allows clients more freedom to explore inner feelings. Clients are assured that the therapist will do more than accept them; the therapist will actively try to feel whatever the clients are feeling.

The final criterion for a good therapist is to have the ability to convey genuine understanding to the client. The client needs to know that the therapist is authentic, does care, does listen, and does understand. The therapist must maintain an empathic posture in spite of the selective distortions of the client, the defensive reactions, and the crippling effects of misplaced self-regard. Once this bridge between client and therapist is established, the client can begin to work in earnest.

The foregoing description may sound static and perhaps mechanistic, as if the therapist aims for a certain plateau, reaches it, and then engages in a kind of therapy that is confined by this plateau; the process is nevertheless an ongoing dynamic that continually renews itself. The therapist, like the client, is always striving for higher congruence.

In an early book, *Counseling and Psychotherapy* (1942, pp. 30–44), Rogers outlined characteristic steps in the helping process:

- The client comes for help.
- The situation is defined.
- Free expression is encouraged.
- The counselor accepts and clarifies.
- Positive feelings are gradually expressed.
- Positive impulses are recognized.
- Insight is developed.
- Choices are clarified.
- Positive actions are taken.
- Insight increases.
- Independence increases.
- The need for help decreases.

This suggested series of events displays Rogers's belief that clients determine their own path, with the therapist's encouraging and supporting efforts.

Necessary and Sufficient Conditions

Some aspects of Rogerian therapy can be learned easily and in fact are used by many therapists. However, the personal characteristics that are necessary to be an effective therapist cannot be readily learned. The capacity to be truly present for another human being—empathic to that person's pain and confident of that person's growth—is a difficult personal demand.

Later, Rogers formulated what he called the *necessary and sufficient conditions* for successful therapy. His hypothesis, composed in an if/then format was as follows:

> IF
> 1. a client is experiencing psychological pain or dissatisfaction
> 2. and is in contact with a therapist
> 3. and the therapist is congruent in the relationship
> 4. and the therapist experiences unconditional positive regard for the client
> 5. and the therapist has empathic understanding of the client's frame of reference and communicates that to the client
> 6. and the client perceives the unconditional positive regard and the empathic understanding, even to a minimal degree,
>
> THEN
> Positive therapeutic change will occur. (Rogers, 1957)

There is a considerable body of research that seems to support the basic assumptions of what makes a therapist effective (Mitchell, Bozarth, & Krauft, 1977; Rogers, 1967; Traux & Mitchell, 1971). While Rachman and Wilson

Personal Reflection

■ Listening and Understanding

This exercise is adapted from one created by Rogers (1952a). He suggests it is a way to assess how well you understand another person.

The next time you get into an argument with your roommate, a close friend, or a small group of friends, stop the discussion for a moment. Then institute this rule:

Each person can state his or her argument only after he or she has accurately restated the ideas and feelings of the previous speaker to that speaker's satisfaction. Before presenting your point of view, you must truly understand the opposition's thoughts and feelings well enough to summarize them.

When you try this exercise, you may discover it to be difficult. Once you are able to see the other points of view, you may find that your own opinion has changed drastically. Differences get reduced with understanding. Any differences that remain will be more clear to everyone.

(1980), who have a strong behavioristic bias, reviewed major schools of psychotherapy and concluded that the prior research was limited by an inability to define and measure the relevant therapist variables, additional work (Farber, Brink, & Raskin, 1996; Paterson, 1984; Raskin, 1986) continues to demonstrate a direct relationship between an emphatic therapist-to-client connection and resulting positive personality change for the client.

While the debate may continue among researchers, Rogers's fundamental prerequisites for being a therapist have been absorbed into most counseling training programs, including those organized by laypeople working on hot lines or in local crisis centers; members of the clergy; social workers; marriage, child, and family counselors; and psychologists of many different persuasions.

Rogers's own research moved him away from teaching a "method" to stressing that therapy is not a science, perhaps not even an art; instead, it is a relationship that depends partially on the mental health of the therapist to plant and nurture the seed of mental health in the client (Rogers, 1977).

Encounter Groups

Because Rogers asserted that people, not experts, have inherent therapeutic skills, it was perhaps inevitable that he would eventually become involved in encounter groups. When he moved to California, he devoted time to participating in, establishing, and evaluating this form of group experience.

History

Apart from group therapy, the encounter group has a history that predates its popularity during the 1950s and 1960s. Within the American Protestant tradition and, to a lesser extent, within Hassidic Judaism, there have been group experiences engineered to alter people's attitudes toward themselves and to change the way they interact with others. Techniques have included working in small peer groups, insisting on honesty and disclosure, focusing on the here and now, and maintaining a warm, supportive atmosphere (Ogden, 1972).

Modern encounter groups originated in Connecticut in 1946 with a training program for community leaders. This program included evening meetings for the trainers and observers to evaluate the day's events. Participants came to listen and eventually to take part in these extra sessions. The trainers realized that giving feedback to participants enhanced everyone's experience.

Some of the trainers of the Connecticut groups joined with others to establish National Training Laboratories (NTL) in 1947. NTL helped to expand and further develop the T-group (training group) as a tool in government and industry. Participation in these groups gave people experience in observing their own functioning and in learning how to respond to direct feedback about themselves.

What was striking in the T-group experiences was that a few weeks of working with peers in a relatively supportive setting could lead to major personality changes previously associated only with severe trauma or long-term psychotherapy. In a review of 106 studies, Gibb (1971) concluded that "the evidence is strong that intensive group training experiences have therapeutic effects" (in Rogers, 1970, p. 118).

While NTL was forming and developing primarily on the East Coast, Esalen Institute in California was exploring more intense, less structured group processes. Dedicated to understanding new trends that emphasize the potentialities and values of human existence, Esalen hosted a series of workshops in the 1960s that came to be called *encounter,* or *basic encounter,* groups. Rogers's group work, which evolved independently, resembled the basic encounter form developed by Esalen; however, Rogers's groups were more inhibited. His groups reflected some of the structural components (including the unobtrusive role of the leader) of the NTL format.

All encounter groups tend to provide a climate of psychological safety and encourage the immediate expression of feelings, as well as the reactions to these feelings. The leader, whatever his or her orientation, is responsible for setting and maintaining the tone and focus of a group. In this role, the therapist creates an atmosphere that can range from very businesslike to emotional and sexual, fearful and angry, or even violent. The psychological literature offers up groups of all descriptions (Howard, 1970; Maliver, 1973).

The encounter group . . . is one of our most successful modern inventions for dealing with the feeling of unreality, of impersonality and of distance and separation that exists in so many people. (Rogers in Smith, 1990, p. 12)

The basic theoretical concepts that Rogers applied to individual therapy also applied to group work. In *Carl Rogers on Encounter Groups* (1970) he describes the major phenomena that occur in groups extending over several days. Although there are many periods of dissatisfaction, uncertainty, and anxiety in the group process, each of these gives way to a more open, less defended, more exposed, and more trusting climate. The emotional intensity and the capacity to tolerate this intensity appear to increase the longer the members of a group work together.

The Process of Encounter

A group begins **the process of encounter** with *milling around;* that is, members wait to be told how to behave, what to expect, how to deal with other members' expectations about the group. There is growing frustration as the group realizes that the members themselves will determine the way the group will function.

The following descriptions apply to groups Rogers either led or observed.[1]

There is *initial resistance* to personal expression or exploration. "It is the public self that members tend to show each other, and only gradually, fearfully, and ambivalently do they take steps to reveal something of the private self" (1970, p. 16). This resistance is visible in most social situations—cocktail parties, dances, or picnics—where there usually is some activity other than self-exploration available to participants. An encounter group discourages seeking any other outlet.

As people continue to interact, they share *past feelings.* These are feelings associated with people in their past. Although the expression of these feelings is

[1]Other styles of group leadership lead to other kinds of effects. See Egan (1970); Lieberman, Miles, and Yalom (1973); and Schutz (1971, 1973) for alternative ways of describing, as well as running, group process.

important for the individual, the act of sharing them nevertheless represents initial resistance. Past experiences and the feelings connected to them are safer, and, because these experiences have a distant quality, they have the advantage of being less emotionally charged.

When people begin to express their feelings in relation to other members in the context of the group, most often the first *expressions are negative:* "I don't feel comfortable with you." "You have a bitchy way of talking." "I don't believe you really mean what you said about your wife."

"Deeply positive feelings are much more difficult and dangerous to express than negative ones. If I say I love you, I am vulnerable and open to the most awful rejection. If I say I hate you, I am at best liable to attack, against which I can defend" (1970, p. 19). Inability to understand this characteristic of encounter-group interaction has led to a number of failures. For example, the air force developed race-relations programs, including black-white encounter sessions conducted by trained leaders. The result of these encounters, however, often seemed to be an intensification of hostile racial feelings on both sides. Because of the complications in organizing encounter groups within the military, the sessions lasted no more than three hours—just enough time for the negative feelings to be expressed and not long enough for the rest of the process to unfold.

As the negative feelings are expressed and the group manages not to crumble, or split apart, *personally meaningful material* emerges. Not all members of the group are necessarily comfortable with these circumstances, but "climate of trust" develops and people start to take real risks.

As meaningful material emerges, members begin to express *immediate feelings* to one another, both positive and negative. "I like that you could share that with the group." "Every time I say something, you look as if you'd like to strangle me." "Funny, I thought I'd dislike you. Now I'm sure of it."

As more and more emotions surface and the group reacts to them, Rogers notes the *development of a healing capacity.* People begin to take steps that seem to be helpful, that assist others in becoming aware of their own experience in nonthreatening ways. What the well-trained therapist has been taught to do through years of supervision and practice emerges spontaneously from the group itself.

> This kind of ability shows up so commonly in groups that it has led me to feel that the ability to be healing or therapeutic is far more common in human life than we suppose. Often it needs only the permission granted—or freedom made possible—by the climate of a free-flowing group experience to become evident. (1970, p. 22)

It's all right to be me with all my strengths and weaknesses. My wife told me that I seem more authentic, more real, and more genuine. (In Rogers, 1970, p. 27)

One of the effects of the group's feedback and acceptance is that *people can accept themselves.* This self-acceptance can be seen in statements such as these: "I guess I really do try to keep people from getting close to me." "I am strong, even ruthless at times." "I want so much to be liked that I'll pretend half a dozen different things." Paradoxically, this acceptance of oneself, even one's faults, signals one's readiness to change. Rogers notes that the closer one is to congruence, the easier it is for one to become healthy. It is not until a person can admit to being a certain way that he or she can consider alternatives to current behavior patterns. "Acceptance, in the realm of psychological attitudes, often brings about a change in the thing accepted. Ironic, but true" (Nelson, 1973).

As the group continues its work, there is an increasing *impatience with defenses.* The group seems to demand the right to help, to heal, to open up people who appear constricted and defensive. Gently at times, almost savagely at others, the group *demands* that individuals be themselves—that is, that they do not hide their current feelings. "The expression of self by some members of the group has made it very clear that a deeper and more basic encounter is *possible,* and the group appears to strive intuitively and unconsciously toward this goal" (Rogers, 1970, p. 27).

Most of us consist of two separated parts, trying desperately to bring themselves together into an integrated soma, where the distinctions between mind and body, feelings and intellect, would be obliterated. (Rogers, 1973b, p. 385)

Within every exchange or encounter there is *feedback,* through which the leader is continually being told of his or her effectiveness or lack of it. Each member who reacts to another may, in turn, get feedback about his or her reaction. This feedback may be difficult for a person to accept, but a person in a group cannot avoid for very long being confronted with the group opinion.

Rogers calls the extreme form of feedback *confrontation:* "There are times when the term feedback is far too mild to describe the interactions that take place—when it is better said that one individual *confronts* another, directly 'leveling' with him. Such confrontations can be positive, but frequently they are decidedly negative" (1970, p. 31). Confrontation builds feelings to such a pitch that some kind of resolution is demanded. This is a disturbing and difficult time for a group and, potentially, far more disturbing to the individuals involved.

For each surge of negative feelings, for each eruption of a fear, there also seems to be a following expression of support, of positive feelings, and closeness. Rogers, quoting a group member, says: "The incredible fact experienced over and over by members of the group was that when a negative feeling was fully expressed to another, the relationship grew and the negative feeling was replaced by a deep acceptance for the other" (1970, p. 34). It would appear that each time the group successfully demonstrates that it can accept and tolerate negative feelings without rejecting the person expressing them, the group members grow more trusting and open to one another. Many people describe their group experiences as the most positive, empathic, and accepting experiences of their lives. The popularity of encounter groups lies as much in the emotional warmth they generate as in their capacity to facilitate personal growth.

Evaluation of Encounter Groups

Are there dangers in the encounter experience? As with any intense form of interaction, there can be and have been unfortunate results. There have been psychotic breaks, suicides, and depressions that were perhaps precipitated by participation in an encounter group. In most cases, the encounter experience seems to foster the kind of underlying mechanisms that allow human beings to help one another. That such positive results do not inevitably occur in all cases should come as no surprise. But because of the work of Rogers and others, small-group experiences are now understood as one way of developing personal skills and of counseling, motivating, and helping people. Such groups afford members the opportunity to have an unusually intense personal experience.

Conflict Resolution: The International Workshops

In the last decade of his life, Rogers decided to apply his ideas about the healing power of open communication to national and international groups separated by race, ethnic orientation, war, or long-simmering hatred. He demonstrated that methods designed to aid individuals in personal growth could, with skilled facilitation, be applied to divided peoples, by improving communication, developing real trust, and encouraging them to work together despite their opposing cultures or ideologies.

The groups thus facilitated by Rogers and other staff members of the Center for the Study of the Person included Catholics and Protestants in Northern Ireland, blacks and whites in South Africa, and members of warring nations throughout Central America. He also worked with thousands of Russians in the former Soviet Union, where his person-centered techniques were even shown on national television.

Even imperfect attempts to create a climate of freedom and acceptance and understanding seem to liberate a person to move toward social goals. (Rogers in a dialogue with Paul Tillich, in Kirschenbaum & Henderson, 1989, p. 68)

These international workshops, unlike the formlessly structured traditional encounter groups, were organized around specific agendas that were understood to be political rather than personal.

The results were encouraging. In every group, inevitably, the level of rhetoric declined and trust increased. Afterward, participants reported major shifts in their thinking about those whom they had been "against." Many formed new groups, applying the same format to other political and social settings (O'Hara, 1989; Rogers, 1986b, 1987a; Swenson, 1987).

Rogers took the therapeutic principles demonstrated by clinicians and academic journals to be invaluable in individual practice and used these concepts to make a positive and distinct contribution to world peace and international understanding (Caspary, 1991).

Evaluation

During a conversation in 1966, Rogers described his status:

> I don't have very much standing in psychology itself, and I couldn't care less. But in education and industry and group dynamics and social work and the philosophy of science and pastoral psychology and theology and other fields my ideas have penetrated and influenced in ways I never would have dreamt. (1970, p. 507)

By the time of his death, his work was accepted worldwide (Macy, 1987). In fact, he had established an extensive network for client-centered therapy in Japan (Hayashi, Kuno, Osawa, Shimizu, & Suetake, 1992; Saji & Linaga, 1983). More recently, his influence in Japan has included ongoing community groups and corporate training (Murayama & Nakata, 1996; Ikemi & Kubota, 1996).

Critics focus on Rogers's positive view of the human condition, suggesting he is glossing over the dark side of humanity. To base therapy and learning on the innate capacity of a person for self-actualization is spoken of as hopelessly naive by a number of writers (Ellis, 1959; Thorne, 1957). They argue that Rogers did not take into account the ingrained patterns of psychopathology that can preclude improvement. Also, his theory is criticized for its resistance to rigorous testing.

> Whether human nature, unspoiled by society, is as satisfactory as this viewpoint leads us to believe is certainly questionable. And it will be difficult either to confirm or to disconfirm this proposition, on empirical grounds. . . . The emphasis on self-actualization . . . suffers, in our opinion, from the vagueness of its concepts, the looseness of its language, and the inadequacy of the evidence related to its major contentions. (Coffer & Appley, 1964, pp. 691–692)

Others suggest that self-actualization is neither an innate characteristic nor a learned desire in human development but derives from a more primary drive, the need for stimulation (Butler & Rice, 1963). At the heart of these criticisms is a distrust of Rogers's steadfast optimism. His unbending belief in the innate goodness of human beings does not echo the experience of those who deride his work or his research. People who do not believe in essential human goodness rarely see it exhibited. They would say that it appears to be present in everyone but that it is latent. Maslow saw human goodness as easily muffled by personal and cultural pressures. And Rollo May says, "The Rogerian agenda hides the power drives of the therapist and not judging is not real." Walt Anderson insists, "Not judging, not manipulating. This was not taking into account full humanness" (Arons & Harri, 1992). Nevertheless, a careful and impartial reading of the results of Rogers's conflict resolution work suggests that treating people as he treated them leads to the results he predicted.

Reading the emotional as well as the sensible critics of Rogers, one tends to conclude that either they have seen different kinds of patients or they simply do not accept the Rogerian ideas of trusting others to find their own way (Rogers & Skinner, 1956). Karl Menninger feels that Rogers's insistence on the indwelling thrust toward health is an expression of, at best, a half truth. "Many patients whom we see seem to have committed themselves, consciously or unconsciously, to stagnation or slow spiritual death" (Menninger, 1963, p. 398).

The argument continues with neither side referring to data or research anymore, but obviously relying on their individual experience. Thus Quinn (1993) is of the opinion that "the practice of psychotherapy in the person-centered approach overemphasizes empathy and caring to the detriment of genuineness and this fault is grounded in an overly optimistic belief" (p. 7). Let us allow Rogers, in an article discovered and published after his death, the last word.

> I would not want to be misunderstood on this. I do not have a Pollyanna view of human nature. I am quite aware that out of defensiveness and inner fear individuals can and do behave in ways which are horribly destructive, immature, regressive, antisocial, hurtful. Yet, one of the most refreshing and invigorating parts of my experience is to work with such individuals and to discover the strongly positive directional tendencies which exist in them, as in all of us, at the deepest levels. (Rogers, 1995, p. 21)

You [Rollo May] never seemed to care whether the evil impulses in man are genetic and inherent or whether they are acquired at birth. . . . For me their origin makes a great deal of difference. (Rogers, 1982b)

This new world will be more human and humane. It will explore and develop the richness and capacities of the human mind and spirit. It will produce individuals who are more integrated and whole. It will be a world that prizes the individual person—the greatest of our resources. (Rogers, 1980a, p. 356)

The image of humanity described by Rogers seems to make little sense to his critics. It is therefore doubtful that further research and solid evidence of a Rogerian humankind would make any difference to them. For Rogers, the test of the validity of his position does not depend on theoretical elegance but on general utility. Rogers's works are constantly gaining in importance and are more widely read each year; and his popularity within and beyond clinical psychology continues to increase.

Although it is clearly an oversimplification, it can be said that just as Freud's ideas met a growing need to understand aspects of human nature, so too do Rogers's ideas, only his fulfill a need that can be seen as particularly American. Rogers's philosophy "fits snugly into the American democratic tradition. The client is treated as an equal who has within him the power to 'cure' himself with no need to lean heavily on the wisdom of an authority or expert" (Harper, 1959, p. 83). Rogers's close alignment to the American worldview has facilitated the widespread acceptance of his ideas, his ways of doing therapy, and his affirmation of the individual's capacity and desire to be whole.

His intense focus on the person is well expressed in a series of statements Rogers calls *significant learnings*. They are the summation of "the thousands of hours I have spent working intimately with people in personal distress" (1961, p. 16). The following are some of his conclusions:

> 1. In my relationships with persons, I have found that it does not help in the long run to act as though I am something that I am not.
> 2. I find that I am more effective when I can listen acceptantly to myself, and can be myself.
> 3. I have found it of enormous value when I can permit myself to understand another person.
> 4. I have found it enriching to open channels whereby others can communicate their feelings, their private perceptual worlds, to me.
> 5. I have found it highly rewarding when I can accept another person.
> 6. The more I am open to the realities in me and in the other person the less do I find myself wishing to rush in to "fix things."
> 7. I can trust my experience. (pp. 16–22)

His work in conflict resolution led to a set of similar axioms, some of which Rogers stated as follows:

> I am most satisfied politically:
>
> When every person is helped to become aware of his or her own power and strength.
>
> When group members learn that the sharing of power is more satisfying than endeavoring to use power to control others.
>
> When each person enforces the group decisions through self-control of his or her behavior.
>
> When every member of the group is aware of the consequences of a decision, on its members and the external world. (1984)

Rogers concludes his list by saying, "I'm sure many of you regard this list as hopelessly idealistic. But in my experience, especially when a facilitative climate is provided for a group, the members choose to move in somewhat the ways that I have described." Rogers remained convinced of humanity's ultimate goodness from his first years doing therapy with disturbed families to his last years working with disturbed nations. Whether he was right or misguided is not to be decided by scholarship but by one's personal observations and experience.

With the best of leaders
When the work is done
The Task is accomplished
The people all say
"We did it ourselves"
(Lao-tze in the *Tao Te Ching.*
Carried by Rogers in his wallet)

The Theory Firsthand:

Rogers's Ideas[2]

This selection illustrates Rogers's ideas about client-centered therapy.

The theoretical concepts that have been defined and the brief, formal statements of the process and outcomes of client-centered psychotherapy are astonishingly well illustrated in a letter written to the author by a young woman named Susan who has been in therapy with an individual who has obviously created the conditions for a therapeutic climate. The letter appears below, followed by an explanation of the way the theoretical statements have operated in her case.

Dear Dr. Rogers: I have just read your book, *On Becoming a Person,* and it left a great impression on me. I just happened to find it one day ands started reading. It's kind of a coincidence because right now I need something to help me find me. Let me explain. . . . [She tells of her present educational situation and some of her tentative plans for preparing herself for a helping vocation.] I do not feel that I can do much for others until I find me. . . .

I think that I began to lose me when I was in high school. I always wanted to go into work that would be of help to people but my family resisted, and I thought they must be right. Things went along smoothly for everyone else for four or five years until about two years ago, I met a guy who I thought was ideal. Then nearly a year ago I took a good look at us, and realized I was everything that he wanted me to be and nothing that I was. I have always been emotional and I have had many feelings. I could never sort them out and identify them. My fiancé would tell me that I was just mad or just happy and I would say okay and leave it at that. Then when I took this good look at us I realized that I was angry because I wasn't following my true emotions.

I backed out of the relationship gracefully and tried to find out where all the pieces were that I had lost. After a few months of searching had gone by I found that there were many more pieces than I knew what to do with and I couldn't seem to separate them. I began seeing a psychologist and am presently seeing him. He has helped

[2]From *Comprehensive Textbook of Psychiatry* by A. M. Freedman, H. I. Kaplan, and B. J. Sadock, 1975, Baltimore: Williams & Wilkins. Copyright 1975 by Williams and Wilkins. Reprinted by permission.

me to find parts of me that I was not aware of. Some parts are bad by our society's standards but I have found them to be very good for me. I have felt more threatened and confused since going to him but I have also felt more relief and more sure of myself.

I remember one night in particular. I had been in for my regular appointment with the psychologist that day and I had come home feeling angry. I was angry because I wanted to talk about something but I couldn't identify what it was. By 8 o'clock that night I was so upset I was frightened. I called him and he told me to come to his office as soon as I could. I got there and cried for at least an hour and then the words came. I still don't know all of what I was saying. All I know is that *so much hurt* and *anger* came out of me that I *never really knew existed.* I went home and it seemed that an *alien* had taken over and I was hallucinating like some of the patients I have seen in a state hospital. I continued to feel this way until one night I was sitting and thinking and I realized that this alien was the *me* that I had been trying to find.

I have noticed since that night that people no longer seem so strange to me. Now it is beginning to seem that life is just starting for me. I am alone right now but I am not frightened and I don't have to be doing something. I like meeting me and making friends with my thoughts and feelings. Because of this I have learned to enjoy other people. One older man in particular—who is very ill—makes me feel very much alive. He accepts everyone. He told me the other day that I have changed very much. According to him, I have begun to open up and love. I think that I have always loved people and I told him so. He said, "Were they aware of it?" I don't suppose I have expressed my love any more than I did my anger and hurt.

Among other things, I am finding out that I never had too much self-respect. And now that I am learning to really like me I am finally finding peace within myself. Thanks for your part in this.

The Linkage to Theory

By summarizing some of the key portions of Susan's letter, the relationship between her statements and the theoretical ones will be evident.

"I was losing me. I needed something to help find *me.*" As she looks back, she realizes that she felt a vague discrepancy between the life she was experiencing and the person she believed herself to be. This kind of vague awareness of discrepancy or incongruence is a real resource for the person who becomes aware of it and attends to it. She also gives clues as to some of the reasons for her loss of contact with her own experiencing.

"My inner reactions meant to me that I wanted to do a certain type of work, but my family showed me that was not their meaning." This certainly suggests the way in which her false self-concept has been built. Undoubtedly, the process began in childhood or she would not have accepted the family's judgment now. A child experiences something in his organism—a feeling of fear, or anger, or jealousy, or love, or, as in this case, a sense of choice, only to be told by parents that this is not what he is experiencing. Out of this grows the construct "Parents are wiser than I and know me better than I know myself." Also, there grows an increasing distrust in one's own experiencing and a growing incongruence between self and experiencing. In this case, Susan distrusts her inward feeling that she knows the work she wants to do and accepts the judgment of her family as right and sound. . . .

"Things went along smoothly for everyone else." This is a marvelously revealing statement. She has become a very satisfactory person for those whom she is trying to please. This false concept of self that they have unwittingly built up is just what they want. . . .

"I left me behind and tried to be the person my boyfriend wanted." Once more, she has denied to her awareness (not consciously) the experiencing of her own organism, and is simply trying to be the self desired by her lover. It is the same process all over. . . .

"Finally, something in me rebelled and I tried to find me again. But I couldn't, without help." Why did she at last rebel against the manner in which she had given herself away? This rebelling indicates the strength of the tendency toward actualization. Although suppressed and distorted for so long, it has reasserted itself. . . . She was fortunate in finding a counselor who evidently created a real and personal relationship, fulfilling the conditions of therapy.

"Now I am discovering *my* experiences—some of them bad, according to society, parents and boyfriend—but all constructive as far as I am concerned." She is now reclaiming as her own the right to evaluate her own experiences. The "locus of evaluation" now resides in herself, not in others. It is through exploring her own experiencing that she determines the meaning of the evidence being provided within her. When she says, "some parts are bad by society's standards but I have found them good for me," she might be referring to any of several feelings—her rebellion against her parents, against her boyfriend, her sexual feelings, her anger and bitterness, or other aspects of herself. At least as she trusts her own valuing of her experience, she finds that it is of worth and significance to her.

"An important turning point came when I was frightened and upset by unknown feelings within me." When aspects of experiencing have been denied to awareness, they may, in a therapeutic climate, come close to the surface of awareness with resulting strong anxiety or fright. . . .

"I cried for at least an hour." Without yet knowing what she is experiencing, she is somehow preparing herself to come in contact with these feelings and meanings which are so foreign to her concept of self.

"When the denied experiences broke through the dam, they turned out to be deep hurts and anger of which I had been *absolutely* unaware." Individuals are able completely to deny experiencings that are highly threatening to the concept of self. Yet, in a safe and nonthreatening relationship, they may be released. Here, for the first time in her life, Susan is *experiencing* all the pent-up feelings of pain and rage that have been boiling under the facade of her false self. To experience something *fully* is not an intellectual process; in fact, Susan cannot even remember clearly what she said, but she did feel, in the immediate moment, emotions that for years had been denied to her awareness.

"I thought I was insane and that some foreign person had taken over in me." To find that "I am a person full of hurt, anger and rebellion," when formerly she had thought, "I am a person who always pleases others, who doesn't even know what her feelings are," is a very drastic shift in the concept of self. Small wonder that she felt this was an alien, a frightening someone she had never known.

"Only gradually did I recognize that this alien was the real *me*." What she has discovered is that the submissive, malleable self by which she had been living, the self that tried to please others and was guided by their evaluations, attitudes, and expectations is no longer her self. This new self is a hurt, angry self, feeling good about parts of herself which others disapprove, experiencing many things, from wild hallucinatory thoughts to loving feelings. . . . Her self is becoming much more firmly rooted in her own organismic processes. Her concept of herself is beginning to be rooted in the spontaneously felt meanings of her experiencing. She is becoming a more congruent, a more integrated, person.

"I like meeting me and making friends with my thoughts and feelings." Here is the dawning self-respect, self-acceptance, and self-confidence of which she has been deprived for so long. She is even feeling some affection for herself. Now that she is much more acceptant of herself, she will be able to give herself more freely to others and to be more genuinely interested in others.

"I have begun to open up and love." She will find that as she is more expressive of her love she can also be more expressive of her anger and hurt, her likes and dislikes, her "wild" thoughts and feelings, which later may well turn out to be creative impulses. She is in the process of changing from a person with a false facade, a false self-concept, to a more healthy personality with a self that is much more congruent with experiencing, a self that can change as her experience changes.

"I am finally finding peace within myself." She has discovered a peaceful harmony in being a whole and congruent person—but she will be mistaken if she thinks this is a permanent reaction. Instead, if she is really open to her experience, she will find other hidden aspects of herself that she has denied to awareness, and each such discovery will give her uneasy and anxious moments or days until they are assimilated into a revised and changing picture of herself.

Chapter Highlights

- Rogers's philosophical viewpoint remained humanitarian and optimistic, as his interests evolved from individual psychotherapy and group therapy, to work in social, educational, and governmental systems.
- In client-centered therapy, the client should be the major directing force in the therapeutic relationship, not the therapist. Rogers moved from a client-centered to a person-centered approach, influenced in part by his experiences in different educational settings. He saw that his work had broad implications for many kinds of social and political systems.
- People define themselves through observing and evaluating their own experiences. Realities are private affairs and can be known only by the individuals themselves.
- The self is a fluid process rather than unchanging and stable. Rogers believed that people are capable of growth and personal development, and that positive change is a natural and expected progression.
- To the extent that the ideal self varies from the actual or real self, it hampers personal health and development. A person may become dissatisfied, uncomfortable, and even experience neurotic difficulties if the discrepancy is too great.
- A tendency toward greater health or "self-actualization" is part of human nature. It is a major motivating factor in individuals who are not hampered by past difficulties or current restrictive beliefs.
- The terms *congruence* and *incongruence* refer to the degree of accuracy between communication, experience, and awareness. An external observer's observations and one's own observations would be consistent in

a situation of high congruence. Most of the symptoms described in the literature on psychopathology may be better understood in terms of incongruence.

- Once an individual becomes aware of incongruence between self-concept and experience, there is a natural movement to resolve the discrepancy.
- Rogers considers the need for positive regard, or for love, to be universal. Conditions of worth are basic obstacles to realistic thinking and accurate perception. They create a discrepancy between the self-concept and the self.
- Four basic elements provide the foundation for beneficial and meaningful relationships: ongoing commitment, expression of feelings, avoidance of specific roles, and the capacity to share one's inner life.
- Whether or not they are expressed, a healthy individual is aware of her or his emotions. When they are not brought into awareness, perception of and reactions to the experience that prompted them may be distorted.
- A person-in-process, one continually changing, is a fully functioning person. Free to respond and free to experience his or her response to situations, such a person would be engaged in ongoing self-actualization.
- In person-centered therapy, there is an implied equality of relating not found in the conventional doctor-patient relationship. It is the person in therapy who does whatever directing is necessary to unlock his or her own dilemma, with minimum intervention.
- Therapy, for Rogers, is a relationship that depends in part on the mental health of the therapist to nurture the growth of mental health in the client.
- Basic theoretical concepts used in individual therapy can be applied to group work. Many periods of uncertainty, anxiety, and dissatisfaction in the group process occur before members open up into a more trusting climate. The longer the members work together, both emotional intensity and tolerance for emotional intensity will increase.
- Rogers applied his ideas about the healing power of open communication in group work to national and international settings; he used these sessions to seek conflict resolution on a national and international level.

Key Concepts

Conditions of worth Behaviors or attitudes that deny some aspect of the self. The individual sees these conditions as necessary to obtain love and to gain a sense of worth. Behavior, maturation, and awareness are inhibited by these self-imposed restrictions. They lead to incongruence, and eventually to rigidity of one's personality.

Congruence The degree of accuracy between communication, experience, and awareness. If what one is expressing (communication), what is occurring (experience), and what one is noticing (awareness) are all nearly equal, there is a high degree of congruence.

Empathic understanding The ability to accurately sense the feelings of others. A necessary element in the self-correcting and self-enhancing cycle to help people overcome obstacles and facilitate psychological growth.

Field of experience An entity, unique to each individual, that contains all that is occurring and is available to awareness. The field may or may not correspond to observed, objective reality. A personal, private world, it is subjective, selective, and incomplete.

Fully functioning person An individual who is completely aware of his or her ongoing self. The person has several distinct characteristics: an openness to experience, living in the present, and trusting in one's intuitive judgments and inner urgings. Trust in one's capacity to make decisions involves the whole person, not just one's intellect.

Ideal self The self-concept that the individual would most like to possess. Like the self, it is constantly being redefined. It may function as a model to strive toward but may also inhibit the capacity to develop, if it is significantly at odds with one's actual values and behavior.

Incongruence The unwillingness or inability to communicate accurately, or the inability to perceive accurately, or both. It occurs when there are differences between experience, communication, and awareness.

Interpersonal knowing In Rogerian psychotherapy, the practice of empathic understanding. The goal is to comprehend the other's experience as the other experiences it, rather than to be objectively correct.

Objective knowing Knowledge in the public domain. It is a way of testing speculations, hypotheses, and conjectures against external frames of reference.

Personal power The person-centered approach found in society at large. It is concerned with the locus of decision-making power and control.

Process of encounter The following sequence applied to groups Rogers either led or observed. A group begins with milling around, displaying initial resistance to personal exploration or expression. People share past feelings. The first feelings expressed are often negative. Personally meaningful material emerges, if the group manages to stay together. As meaningful material emerges, both positive and negative immediate feelings are expressed. A healing capacity develops as more emotions surface and are reacted to. Out of the group feedback and acceptance comes people's acceptance of themselves.

Self-actualizing tendency A part of the process of all living things. In humans, it is the drive to activate and express all the capacities of the organism. Self-actualization is the only motive postulated in Rogers's system.

Subjective knowing The knowledge of whether one hates, loves, enjoys, or is disdainful of a person, event, or experience. Such awareness may be improved by getting more in touch with one's private, or "gut," feelings. It is the capacity to know enough to act on hunches, or to follow one's intuition, without verifiable evidence.

Unconditional positive regard Caring that demands no personal gratification and is not possessive. It invites the person to be what he or she actually is, regardless of what that may be. It is not a positive evaluation that can restrict behaviors by punishing some and rewarding others.

Annotated Bibliography

Kirschenbaum, H., & Henderson, V. (Eds.). (1989). *The Carl Rogers reader.* Boston: Houghton Mifflin.

An excellent selection of Rogers's most important writing. Includes personal papers as well as excerpts from his more influential books. If you read only one Rogers book, this should be your choice.

Raskin, N. J., & Rogers, C. (1989). Person-centered therapy. In R. Corsini & D. Wedding (Eds.), *Current psychotherapies* (4th ed.) (pp. 155–194). Itasca, IL: F. E. Peacock.

Finished after Rogers's death, it is a substantial, well-written summary of his ideas as they relate to psychotherapy.

Rogers, C. R. (1951). *Client-centered therapy: Its current practice, implications and theory.* Boston: Houghton Mifflin.

The core volume for what is called Rogerian therapy. Rogers himself saw some of the material here as too rigid. Still a useful and important book.

———. (1959). A theory of therapy, personality, and interpersonal relationships, as developed in the client-centered framework. In S. Koch (Ed.), *Psychology, the study of a science. Vol. 3: Formulations of the person and the social context* (pp. 184–225). New York: McGraw-Hill.

The only time Rogers laid out his work in a formal, detailed, and organized theory. He succeeds, but this essay remains one of his least read works. The obscurity is undeserved. If you stick with Rogers, eventually you will want to read this.

———. (1961). *On becoming a person: A therapist's view of psychotherapy.* Boston: Houghton Mifflin.

A personal, practical, and extensive consideration of the major themes in Rogers's work. A book that is still lucid and useful to those in the people-helping professions.

———. (1969). *Freedom to learn.* Columbus, OH: Merrill.

A set of challenges to educators. According to Rogers, most teaching is set up to discourage learning and encourage anxiety and maladjustment. More strident than his gentler, therapy-oriented volumes.

———. (1970). *Carl Rogers on encounter groups.* New York: Harper & Row.

A sensible discussion of the ups and downs of the encounter group. Most of the discussion is drawn from groups that Rogers has run or observed, so the material is both representative and explicit. Probably the best introduction to this form of interpersonal gathering in print. Not sensational and not critical.

———. (1972). *Becoming partners: Marriage and its alternatives.* New York: Dell (Delacorte Press).

Rogers interviews a number of couples who have taken varying approaches to marriage. He points out the strengths and weaknesses of the relationships. Mainly reporting, he calls attention to those forces that lead to successful or unsuccessful long-term relationships. Useful.

———. (1978). *Carl Rogers on personal power.* New York: Dell.

The first book in which Rogers considers the wide social implications in his work. It is subtitled accurately: "Inner strength and its revolutionary impact. The extension of ideas developed in therapy to educational and political systems."

———. (1980). *A way of being.* Boston: Houghton Mifflin.

A collection of essays and speeches that serves as a small autobiography and illustrates Rogers's growing realization of the social impact of his work beyond psychology. Moving and optimistic, this is his most intimate and gentle book.

———. (1983). *Freedom to learn for the 80's.* Columbus, OH: Merrill.

A revision and expansion of the earlier edition. He spends considerable time describing his own work in classrooms, facilitating "responsible freedom."

Rogers, C. R., & Stevens, B. (1967). *Person to person.* Walnut Creek, CA: Real Peoples Press (New York: Pocket Books, 1971).

A collection of articles, mostly by Rogers, with fascinating commentaries on them by Barry Stevens.

References

Ansbacher, H. (1990). Alfred Adler's influence on the three leading cofounders of humanistic psychology. *Journal of Humanistic Psychology, 30*(4), 45–53.

Arons, M., & Harri C. (1992). Conversations with the founders. Manuscript submitted for publication—*unpublished.*

Bandler, R., & Grinder, J. (1975). *The structure of magic* (Vols. 1, 2). Palo Alto, CA: Science and Behavior.

Boy, A. V., & Pine, G. J. (1982). *Client-centered counseling: A renewal.* Boston: Allyn & Bacon.

Butler, J. M., & Rice, L. N. (1963). Audience, self-actualization, and drive theory. In J. M. Wepman & R. W. Heine (Eds.), *Concepts of personality* (pp. 79–110). Chicago: Aldine.

Campbell, P., & McMahon, E. (1974). Religious type experiences in the context of humanistic and transpersonal psychology. *Journal of Transpersonal Psychology, 6,* 11–17.

Caspary, W. (1991). Carl Rogers—values, persons and politics: The dialectic of individual and community. *Journal of Humanistic Psychology, 31*(4), 8–31.

Coffer, C. N., & Appley, M. (1964). *Motivation: Theory and research.* New York: Wiley.

Dreher, D. (1995). Toward a person-centered politics: John Vasconcellos. In M. M. Suhd (Ed.), *Carl Rogers and other notables he influenced* (pp. 339–372). Palo Alto, CA: Science and Behavior.

Egan, G. (1970). *Encounter: Group processes for interpersonal growth.* Monterey, CA: Brooks/Cole.

Ellis, A. (1959). Requisite conditions for basic personality change. *Journal of Consulting Psychology, 23,* 538–540.

Evans, R. I. (Ed.). (1975). *Carl Rogers: The man and his ideas.* New York: Dutton.

Farber, B., Brink, D, & Raskin, P. (1996). *The Psychotherapy of Carl Rogers: Cases and commentary.* New York: Guilford Press.

Freedman, A. M., Kaplan, H. I., & Sadock, B. J. (1975). *Comprehensive textbook of psychiatry.* Baltimore: Williams & Wilkins.

Fuller, R. (1982). Carl Rogers, religion, and the role of psychology in American culture. *Journal of Humanistic Psychology, 22*(4), 21–32.

Gibb, J. R. (1971). The effects of human relations training. In A. E. Bergin & S. L. Garfield (Eds.), *Handbook of psychotherapy and behavior change* (pp. 2114–2176). New York: Wiley.

Gordon, W. (1961). *Synectics.* New York: Harper & Row.

Hall, C., & Lindzey, G. (1978). *Theories of personality* (3rd ed.). New York: Wiley.

Harper, R. A. (1959). *Psychoanalysis and psychotherapy.* Englewood Cliffs, NJ: Prentice-Hall.

Hayashi, S., Kuno, T., Osawa, M., Shimizu, M., & Suetake, Y. (1992). The client-centered therapy and person-centered approach in Japan: Historical development, current status and perspectives. *Journal of Humanistic Psychology, 32*(2), 115–136.

Holden, C. (1977). Carl Rogers: Giving people permission to be themselves. *Science, 198,* 31–34.

Howard, J. (1970). *Please touch: A guided tour of the human potential movement.* New York: McGraw-Hill.

Ikemi, A., & Kubota, S. (1996). Humanistic psychology in Japanese corporations: Listening and the small steps of change. *Journal of Humanistic Psychology 36*(1), 104–121.

Kirschenbaum, H. (1980). *On becoming Carl Rogers.* New York: Dell (Delacorte Press).

———. (1995). Carl Rogers. In M. M. Suhd (Ed.), *Carl Rogers and other notables he influenced* (pp. 1–104). Palo Alto, CA: Science and Behavior.

Kirschenbaum, H., & Henderson, V. (Eds.). (1989). *The Carl Rogers reader.* Boston: Houghton Mifflin.

Kramer, R. (1995). The birth of client-centered therapy: Carl Rogers, Otto Rank, and "the beyond." *Journal of Humanistic Psychology, 35*(4), 54–110.

Krasner, L., & Ullman, L. (1973). *Behavior influence and personality: The social matrix of human action.* New York: Holt, Rinehart and Winston.

Lawrence, D. H. (1960). *The ladybird together with the captain's doll.* London: Harborough.

Lieberman, M. A., Miles, M. B., & Yalom, I. D. (1973). *Encounter groups: First facts.* New York: Basic Books.

Macy, F. (1987). The legacy of Carl Rogers in the U.S.S.R. *Journal of Humanistic Psychology, 27*(3), 305–308.

Maliver, B. L. (1973). *The encounter game.* New York: Stein and Day.

McCleary, R. A., & Lazarus, R. S. (1949). Autonomic discrimination without awareness. *Journal of Personality, 19,* 171–179.

Menninger, K. (1963). *The vital balance: The life process in mental health and illness.* New York: Viking Press.

Mitchell, K., Bozarth, J., & Krauft, C. (1977). A reappraisal of the therapeutic effectiveness of accurate empathy, nonpossessive warmth and genuineness. In A. Gurman & A. Razin (Eds.), *Effective psychotherapy.* Oxford: Pergamon Press.

Murayama, S., & Nakata, Y. (1996). Fukuoka human relations community: A network approach to developing human potential. *Journal of Humanistic Psychology, 36* (1), 91–103.

Nelson, A. (1973). *A conversation with Carl Rogers.* Unpublished manuscript.

Nitya, Swami. (1973). Excerpts from a discussion. *Journal of Transpersonal Psychology, 5,* 200–204.

Ogden, T. (1972). The new pietism. *Journal of Humanistic Psychology, 12,* 24–41. (Also appears in *The intensive group experience: The new pietism.* Philadelphia: Westminster Press, 1972.)

O'Hara, M. (1989). Person-centered approach as conscientizaçao: The works of Carl Rogers and Paulo Friere. *Journal of Humanistic Psychology, 29*(1), 11–35.

Paterson, C. H. (1984). Empathy, warmth, and genuineness in psychotherapy: A review of reviews. *Psychotherapy, 21,* 431–438.

Perry, J. W. (1974). *The far side of madness.* Englewood Cliffs, NJ: Prentice-Hall.

Polanyi, M. (1958). *Personal knowledge.* Chicago: University of Chicago Press.

Quinn, R. (1993). Confronting Carl Rogers: A developmental-interactional approach to person-centered therapy. *Journal of Humanistic Psychology, 33*(1), 6–23.

———. (1959). *The study of man.* Chicago: University of Chicago Press.

Rachman, S. J., & Wilson, G. T. (1980). *The effects of psychological therapy* (2nd ed.). Oxford: Pergamon Press.

Raskin, N. (1986). Client-centered group psychotherapy. Part II: Research of client-centered groups. *Person-Centered Review, 1,* 389–408.

Raskin, N. J., & Rogers, C. (1989). Person-centered therapy. In R. Corsini & D. Wedding (Eds.), *Current psychotherapies* (4th ed.) (pp. 155–194). Itasca, IL: F. E. Peacock.

Rogers, C. R. (1939). *The clinical treatment of the problem child.* Boston: Houghton Mifflin.

———. (1942). *Counseling and psychotherapy.* Boston: Houghton Mifflin.

———. (1950). A current formulation of client-centered therapy. *Social Service Review, 24,* 440–451.

———. (1951). *Client-centered therapy: Its current practice, implications and theory.* Boston: Houghton Mifflin.

———. (1952a). Communication: Its blocking and its facilitation. *Northwestern University Information, 20*(25).

———. (1952b). Client-centered psychotherapy. *Scientific American, 187*(5), 66–74.

———. (1957). The necessary and sufficient conditions of therapeutic personality change. *Journal of Consulting Psychology, 21,* 95–100.

———. (1959). A theory of therapy, personality, and interpersonal relationships, as developed in the client-centered framework. In S. Koch (Ed.), *Psychology, the study of a science. Vol. 3: Formulations of the person and the social context* (pp. 184–256). New York: McGraw-Hill.

———. (1961). *On becoming a person: A therapist's view of psychotherapy.* Boston: Houghton Mifflin.

———. (1964). Towards a science of the person. In T. W. Wann (Ed.), *Behaviorism and phenomenology: Contrasting bases for modern psychology* (pp. 109–133). Chicago: University of Chicago Press.

———. (1967). Carl Rogers. In E. Boring & G. Lindzey (Eds.), *History of psychology in autobiography* (Vol. 5). New York: Appleton-Century-Crofts.

———. (1969). *Freedom to learn.* Columbus, OH: Merrill.

———. (1970). *Carl Rogers on encounter groups.* New York: Harper & Row.

———. (1972). *Becoming partners: Marriage and its alternatives.* New York: Dell (Delacorte Press).

———. (1973a). My philosophy of interpersonal relationships and how it grew. *Journal of Humanistic Psychology, 13,* 3–16.

———. (1973b). Some new challenges. *The American Psychologist, 28,* 379–387.

———. (1974a). In retrospect: Forty-six years. *The American Psychologist, 29,* 115–123.

———. (1974b). The project at Immaculate Heart: An experiment in self-directed change. *Education, 95*(2), 172–189.

———. (1975a). Empathic: An unappreciated way of being. *The Counseling Psychologist: Carl Rogers on Empathy* (special topic), *5*(2), 2–10.

———. (1975b). The emerging person: A new revolution. In R. I. Evans (Ed.), *Carl Rogers: The man and his ideas.* New York: Dutton.

———. (1977). A therapist's view of personal goals. *Pendle Hill Pamphlet 108.* Wallingford, PA: Pendle Hill.

———. (1978). *Carl Rogers on personal power.* New York: Dell.

———. (1980a). *A way of being.* Boston: Houghton Mifflin.

———. (1980b). Growing old—or older and growing. *Journal of Humanistic Psychology, 20*(4), 5–16.

———. (1982a). A psychologist looks at nuclear war: Its threat, its possible prevention. *Journal of Humanistic Psychology, 22*(4), 9–20.

———. (1982b). Reply to Rollo May's letter to Carl Rogers. *Journal of Humanistic Psychology, 22*(4), 85–89.

———. (1983). *Freedom to learn for the 80's.* Columbus, OH: Merrill.

———. (1984). *A client-centered, person-centered approach to therapy.* Unpublished manuscript.

———. (1986a). Client-centered therapy. In I. L. Kutash & A. Wolf (Eds.), *Psychotherapists casebook: Therapy and technique in practice* (pp. 197–208). San Francisco: Jossey-Bass.

———. (1986b). The Rust workshop. *Journal of Humanistic Psychology, 26*(3), 23–45.

———. (1987a). Inside the world of the Soviet professional. *Journal of Humanistic Psychology, 27*(3), 277–304.

———. (1987b). On reaching 85. *Person Centered Review, 2*(2), 150–152.

———. (1995). What understanding and acceptance mean to me. *Journal of Humanistic Psychology, 35*(4), 7–22.

Rogers, C. R., Gendlin, E. T., Kiesler, D. J., & Truax, C. G. (1967). *The therapeutic relationship and its impact: A study of psychotherapy with schizophrenics.* Madison: University of Wisconsin Press.

Rogers, C. R., & Haigh, G. I. (1983). Walk softly through life. *Voices: The Art and Science of Psychotherapy, 18,* 6–14.

Rogers, C. R., with Hart, J. (1970a). Looking back and ahead: A conversation with Carl Rogers. In J. T. Hart & T. M. Tomlinson (Eds.), *New directions in client-centered therapy* (pp. 502–534). Boston: Houghton Mifflin.

Rogers, C. R., & Ryback, D. (1984). One alternative to nuclear planetary suicide. *Counseling Psychologist, 12*(2), 3–12.

Rogers, C. R., & Skinner, B. F. (1956). Some issues concerning the control of human behavior. *Science, 124,* 1057–1066.

Saji, M., & Linaga, K. (1983). *Client chushin rycho* [Client-centered therapy]. Tokyo: Yuhikaku.

Schutz, W. C. (1971). *Here comes everybody.* New York: Harper & Row.

———. (1973). *Elements of encounter.* Big Sur, CA: Joy Press.

Smith, M. B. (1990). Humanistic psychology. *Journal of Humanistic Psychology, 30*(4), 6–21.

Swenson, G. (1987). When personal and political processes meet: The Rust workshop. *Journal of Humanistic Psychology, 27*(3), 309–333.

Tart, C. T. (1971). Scientific foundations for the study of altered states of consciousness. *Journal of Transpersonal Psychology, 3,* 93–124.

———. (1975). Some assumptions of orthodox, Western psychology. In C. T. Tart (Ed.), *Transpersonal psychologies* (pp. 59–112). New York: Harper & Row.

Thorne, F. C. (1957). Critique of recent developments in personality counseling therapy. *Journal of Clinical Psychology, 13,* 234–244.

Truax, C., & Mitchell, K. (1971). Research on certain therapist interpersonal skills. In A. Bergin & S. Garfield (Eds.), *Handbook of psychotherapy and behavior change* (p. 299). New York: Wiley.

Van Belle, H. A. (1980). *Basic intent and the therapeutic approach of Carl Rogers.* Toronto, Canada: Wedge Foundation.

CHAPTER 14

Abraham Maslow and Transpersonal Psychology

Abraham Maslow believed that an accurate and viable theory of personality must include not only the depths but also the heights that each individual is capable of attaining. He is one of the founders of humanistic psychology and transpersonal psychology, two major new fields that evolved as alternatives to behaviorism and psychoanalysis. The concepts of both Skinner and Freud, and their followers, have tended to ignore or to explain away the cultural, social, and individual achievements of humanity, including creativity, love, altruism, and mysticism. These were among Maslow's greatest interests.

The conclusions of one reviewer in 1983 are still true today:

> Abraham Maslow has done more to change our view of human nature and human possibilities than has any other American psychologist of the past fifty years. His influence, both direct and indirect, continues to grow, especially in the fields of health, education, and management theory, and in the personal and social lives of millions of Americans. (Leonard, 1983, p. 326)

Maslow was a pioneer, interested in exploring new issues and new fields. His work is a collection of thoughts, opinions, and hypotheses rather than a fully developed theoretical system. More a theorist than a research scientist, Maslow rarely came up with final answers. His genius was in formulating significant questions—questions that many social scientists today consider critical.

Personal History

Abraham Maslow was born in Brooklyn, New York, in 1908, of Russian Jewish immigrant parents. His father, a barrel maker by trade, had moved to the United States from Russia as a young man. He later sent for the woman who would be his wife. In his youth, Abe was extraordinarily shy and highly neurotic. A bright, unhappy, and lonely boy, he was so convinced he was ugly he would ride deserted subway cars to spare others the sight of him.

Maslow entered the City College of New York at the age of 18. His father wanted Abe to become a lawyer, but the son could not stand the thought of law school. When his father asked what he intended to do instead, Abe said he wanted to go on studying "everything."

As a teenager, Maslow fell in love with his first cousin and found excuses to spend time with her family, often gazing lovestruck at her but not daring to touch her. At the age of 19, when he finally embraced his cousin, he experienced his first kiss. Maslow later described this moment as one of the *peak experiences* of his life. Her acceptance of him, instead of the rejection he had feared, was a tremendous boost to his shaky self-esteem. A year later they were married; she was 19 and he was 20. Marriage and his immersion in psychology represented a period of renewal in Maslow's life.

In his first year in college, Maslow discovered music and drama. He fell in love with both. It was a love that would remain with him throughout his life. Maslow transferred to the University of Wisconsin, where his interest focused on psychology. He was captured by J. B. Watson's vision of behaviorism as a powerful tool for affecting human life. Maslow trained in the experimental method at Wisconsin and worked in the psychology laboratory there, conducting research using rats and other animals. He received his bachelor's degree in 1930 and his doctorate in 1934, at the age of 26.

After graduation, Maslow returned to New York to work with Edward Thorndike, an eminent Columbia University psychologist. Thorndike was particularly impressed with Maslow's performance on the intelligence test that Thorndike developed. By scoring 195 on the test, Maslow had received the second highest IQ score thus far recorded. Eighteen months later, Maslow found a teaching job at Brooklyn College, where he remained for 14 years. New York at that time was a stimulating intellectual center, attracting many of the finest scholars who had fled Nazi persecution. Maslow studied with a number of psychotherapists, including Alfred Adler, Erich Fromm, and Karen Horney. He was most strongly influenced by Max Wertheimer, one of the founders of Gestalt psychology, and by Ruth Benedict, a brilliant cultural anthropologist.

Maslow's involvement in the practical applications of psychology dates back to the beginning of his career. Even as a behaviorist graduate student, Maslow was convinced that Freud was right in his emphasis on sexuality. Maslow chose for his dissertation research the relationship between dominance and sexual behavior among primates. After leaving Wisconsin, he began an extensive investigation of human sexual behavior. Maslow believed that any advance in our understanding of sexual functioning would lead to improvements in human adjustment.

Human nature is not nearly as bad as it has been thought to be. (Maslow, 1968, p. 4)

During World War II, when he realized the insignificance of psychology's contribution to reducing international conflict, Maslow's work shifted from experimental psychology to social and personality psychology. He wanted to devote himself to "discovering a psychology for the peace table" (Hall, 1968, p. 54).

In addition to his professional work, Maslow became involved with the family barrel-manufacturing business during a prolonged illness. His interest in business and in applied psychology eventually resulted in *Eupsychian Management* (1965), a compilation of thoughts and articles related to management and industrial psychology. He wrote these pieces during the summer that he spent as Visiting Fellow at a small electronics plant in Del Mar, California.

In 1951, Maslow accepted a position near Boston, at Brandeis University, which had just been established, and remained there until 1968. He was chair of the first psychology department and was instrumental in the development of the university as a whole.

Throughout his career, Maslow's pioneering work was generally dismissed as unscientific and considered outside the mainstream of psychology. He was personally liked by his colleagues, and his ideas gradually became better appreciated. Much to his own surprise, Maslow was elected president of the American Psychological Association in 1967 and served for one year.

To Maslow, the labels used for the various schools of psychology were highly limiting. "We shouldn't have to say humanistic psychology. The adjective should be unnecessary. Don't think of me as being antibehavioristic. I'm antidoctrinaire. . . . I'm against anything that closes doors and cuts off possibilities" (Maslow in Hall, 1968, p. 57).

In January 1969 Maslow left Brandeis to accept a fellowship that allowed him to write full time. In June 1970, at the age of 62, he died of a heart attack.

Intellectual Antecedents

I am a Freudian, I am behavioristic, I am humanistic. (Maslow, 1971, p. 144)

The most important influences on Maslow's thinking were psychoanalysis, social anthropology, Gestalt psychology, and the work of the neurophysiologist Kurt Goldstein.

Psychoanalysis

To oversimplify the matter somewhat, it is as if Freud supplied to us the sick half of psychology and we must now fill it out with the healthy half. (Maslow, 1968, p. 5)

In the 1950s, when clinical psychology was a relatively new field, Maslow believed that psychoanalysis provided the best system for analyzing psychopathology and also the best form of psychotherapy available. However, he found the psychoanalytic system unsatisfactory as a general psychology applicable to all of human thought and behavior.

> The picture of man it presents is a lopsided, distorted puffing up of his weaknesses and shortcomings that purports then to describe him fully. . . . Practically all the activities that man prides himself on, and that give meaning, richness, and value to his life, are either omitted or pathologized by Freud. (Maslow in Goble, 1971, p. 244)

Psychoanalytic theory significantly influenced Maslow's life and thought. Freud's sophisticated description of the neurotic and maladaptive aspects of human behavior inspired Maslow to develop a scientifically grounded psychology relevant to the full range of human behavior. Maslow's own personal analysis profoundly affected him and demonstrated the substantial differences that exist between intellectual knowledge and actual, gut-level experience.

Social Anthropology

As a student at Wisconsin, Maslow seriously studied the work of social anthropologists, such as Bronislaw Malinowski, Margaret Mead, Ruth Benedict, and Ralph Linton. In New York he studied with leading figures in the field of culture and personality, in which psychoanalytic theories are applied to the examination of behavior in other cultures. In addition, Maslow was fascinated by William Sumner's book *Folkways* (1940). According to Sumner, human behavior is largely determined by cultural patterns and prescriptions. Maslow was so inspired by Sumner that he vowed to devote himself to the same areas of study.

Gestalt Psychology

Maslow was also a serious student of Gestalt psychology, which investigates perception, cognition, and other sophisticated human activities in terms of complex, whole systems. He admired Max Wertheimer, whose work on productive thinking is closely related to Maslow's writings on cognition and to his work on creativity. For Maslow, as for Gestalt psychologists, an essential element in effective reasoning and creative problem solving is the ability to perceive and think in terms of wholes or patterns rather than isolated parts.

Kurt Goldstein

Another important influence on Maslow's thinking was the work of Kurt Goldstein, a neurophysiologist who emphasized the unity of the organism—what happens in any part affects the entire system. Maslow's work on self-actualization was inspired partly by Goldstein, who was the first to use the term. Maslow dedicated *Toward a Psychology of Being* (1968) to Goldstein. In the preface, he stated:

> If I had to express in a single sentence what Humanistic Psychology has meant for me, I would say that it is an integration of Goldstein (and Gestalt Psychology) with Freud (and the various psychodynamic psychologies), the whole joined with the scientific spirit that I was taught by my teachers at the University of Wisconsin. (1968, p. v)

A neurophysiologist whose main focus was brain-damaged patients, Goldstein viewed self-actualization as a fundamental process in every organism, a process that may have negative as well as positive effects on the individual. In Goldstein's view, every organism has one primary drive: "[The] organism is governed by the tendency to actualize, as much as possible, its individual capacities, its 'nature,' in the world" (1939, p. 196).

Goldstein argued that tension release is a strong drive but only in sick organisms. For a healthy organism, the primary goal is "the *formation* of a certain level of tension, namely, that which makes possible further ordered activity" (1939, pp. 195–196). A drive such as hunger is a special case of self-actualization, in which tension reduction is sought to return the organism to optimal condition for further expression of its capacities. However, only in an extreme situation does such a drive become overwhelming. A normal organism, Goldstein asserts, can temporarily put off food, sex, sleep, and so forth, if other motives, such as curiosity or playfulness, are present.

According to Goldstein, successful coping with the environment often involves uncertainty and shock. In fact, the healthy self-actualizing organism invites such shock by venturing into new situations in order to utilize its capacities. For Goldstein (and for Maslow also), self-actualization does not rid the individual of problems and difficulties; on the contrary, growth may bring a certain amount of pain and suffering. Goldstein wrote that an organism's capacities determine its needs. For instance, the possession of a digestive system

Capacities clamor to be used, and cease their clamor only when they are used sufficiently. (Maslow, 1968, p. 152)

makes eating a necessity; muscles require movement. A bird *needs* to fly just as an artist *needs* to create, despite the fact that creation may require painful struggle and great effort.

Major Concepts

The most influential part of Maslow's theory was his model of the hierarchy of needs, which includes the full range of human motivations. His most important concept was self-actualization, the highest level of human need. Maslow also investigated peak experiences, special moments in each individual's life. He distinguished between two basic kinds of psychology, deficiency psychology and being psychology, and pioneered in the development of the latter. Maslow was also deeply interested in the social implications of his theory, especially with *eupsychia,* his term for a Utopian society, and synergy, or cooperation within a society.

Hierarchy of Needs

The fact that most of what we know about human motivation comes from the analysis of patients in therapy troubled Maslow. Although we have learned a great deal from these patients, their psychological drives clearly do not reflect the motivations of the population at large. In his theory of the **hierarchy of needs** (see Figure 14.1), Maslow accomplished an intellectual tour de force. He managed to integrate in a single model the approaches of the major schools of psychology—behaviorism, psychoanalysis and its offshoots, and humanistic and transpersonal psychology. He illustrated that no one approach is better or more valid than another. Each has its own place and its own relevance.

Maslow defined neurosis and psychological maladjustment as *deficiency diseases;* that is, they are caused by deprivation of certain basic needs, just as the absence of certain vitamins causes illness. The best examples of basic needs are the physiological ones, such as hunger, thirst, and sleep. Deprivation clearly leads to illness, sooner or later, and the satisfaction of these needs is the only

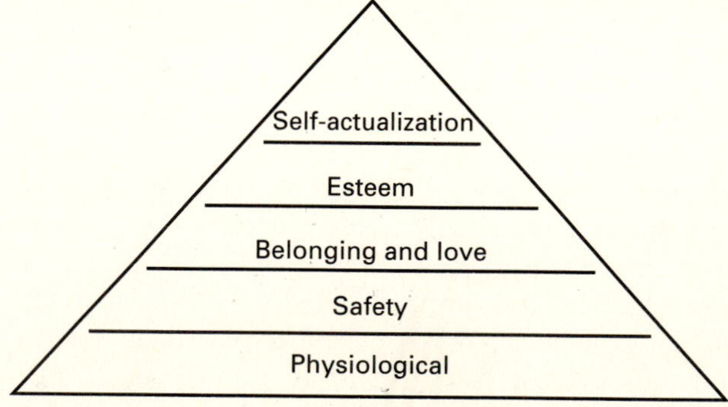

FIGURE 14.1 Maslow's Hierarchy of Needs

treatment. Basic needs are found in all individuals. The amount and kind of satisfaction varies among societies, but basic needs (like hunger) can never be ignored.

Physiological needs include the need for food, drink, oxygen, sleep, and sex. For many people in our culture, these needs can be satisfied without difficulty. However, if biological needs are not adequately met, the individual becomes almost completely devoted to fulfilling them. Maslow argues that a person who is literally dying of thirst has no great interest in satisfying any other needs. But once this particular overwhelming need is met, it becomes less important, allowing other drives to surface.

Certain **psychological needs** must also be satisfied in order to maintain health. Maslow includes the following as basic psychological needs: the need for safety, security, and stability; the need for love and a sense of belonging; and the need for self-respect and esteem. In addition, every individual has growth needs: a need to develop one's potentials and capabilities and a need for self-actualization.

Living at the higher need level means greater biological efficiency, greater longevity, less disease, better sleep, appetite, etc. (Maslow, 1948)

By *safety* needs, Maslow is referring to the individual's need to live in a relatively stable, safe, predictable environment. We have a basic need for structure, order, and limits. People need freedom from fear, anxiety, and chaos. As with physiological needs, most people take a smoothly running, stable, protective society for granted. In modern Western society, the need for safety usually becomes dominant only in real emergencies, such as natural disasters, epidemics, and riots.

All people have *belonging and love* needs. We are motivated to seek close relationships with others and to feel part of various groups, such as family and groups of peers. These needs, Maslow wrote, are increasingly frustrated in our highly mobile, individualistic society. Further, the frustration of these needs is most often found at the core of psychological maladjustment.

Maslow (1987) described two kinds of *esteem* needs. First, there is a desire for competence and individual achievement. Second, we need respect from others—status, fame, appreciation, and recognition. When these needs are not met, the individual tends to feel inferior, weak, or helpless. In Maslow's view, the esteem needs were stressed by Adler and relatively neglected by Freud, but there has been growing awareness of their importance. Healthy self-esteem comes from personal effort resulting in achievement and deserved respect from others.

Even if all these needs are satisfied, Maslow points out, individuals still feel frustrated or incomplete unless they experience *self-actualization*—utilize their talents and capacities. The form that this need takes varies widely from person to person. Each of us has different motivations and capacities. To one person, becoming an excellent parent may be a primary goal; another may feel impelled to achieve as an athlete, painter, or inventor.

According to Maslow, the more basic needs must be fulfilled before the less critical needs are met. For example, both physiological and love needs are essential to the individual; however, when one is starving, the need for love (or any other higher need) is not a major factor in behavior. On the other hand, Maslow argues, even when frustrated in love, we still need to eat (romantic novels to the contrary).

Man's higher nature rests upon man's lower nature, needing it as a foundation and collapsing without this foundation. That is, for the mass of mankind, man's higher nature is inconceivable without a satisfied lower nature as a base. (Maslow, 1968, p. 173)

Self-actualization

Maslow loosely defined **self-actualization** as "the full use and exploitation of talents, capacities, potentialities, etc." (1970, p. 150). Self-actualization is not a static state. It is an ongoing process in which one's capacities are fully, creatively, and joyfully utilized. "I think of the self-actualizing man not as an ordinary man with something added, but rather as the ordinary man with nothing taken away. The average man is a full human being with dampened and inhibited powers and capacities" (Maslow in Lowry, 1973b, p. 91).

Most commonly, self-actualizing people see life clearly. They are less emotional and more objective, less likely to allow hopes, fears, or ego defenses to distort their observations. Without exception, Maslow found that self-actualizing people are dedicated to a vocation or a cause. Two requirements for growth seem to be commitment to something greater than oneself and success at one's chosen tasks. Creativity, spontaneity, courage, and hard work are all major characteristics of self-actualizing people.

Maslow deliberately studied only those who were relatively free of neurosis and emotional disturbance. He found that his psychologically healthy subjects were independent and self-accepting; they had few self-conflicts and were able to enjoy both play and work. Although only one of Maslow's subjects belonged to an orthodox religious faith, virtually all believed in a life that could be called spiritual. The self-actualizing subjects, Maslow found, took pleasure in life, despite pain, sorrow, and disappointment. They had more interests and less fear, anxiety, boredom, or sense of purposelessness. Whereas most other people had only occasional moments of joy, triumph, or peak experience, self-actualizing individuals seemed to love life in general.

One of Maslow's main points is that we are always desiring something and rarely reach a state of complete satisfaction, one without any goals or desires. His need hierarchy is an attempt to predict what kinds of desires will arise once the old ones are sufficiently satisfied and no longer dominate behavior. There are many individual exceptions, especially in a culture such as ours, in which most basic needs are partially satisfied and still serve to motivate without becoming overwhelming. Maslow developed his hierarchy as part of a general theory of motivation, not as a precise predictor of individual behavior.

> It is quite true that man lives by bread alone—when there is no bread. But what happens to man's desires when there is plenty of bread and when his belly is chronically filled? *At once other (and higher) needs emerge,* and these, rather than physiological hungers, dominate their organism. And when these in turn are satisfied, again new (and still higher) needs emerge, and so on. (Maslow, 1987, p. 17)

Growth is theoretically possible *only* because the "higher" tastes are better than the "lower" and because the "lower" satisfaction becomes boring. (Maslow, 1971, p. 147)

Metamotivation **Metamotivation** refers to behavior inspired by growth needs and values. According to Maslow, this kind of motivation is most common among self-actualizing people, who are by definition already gratified in their lower needs. Metamotivation often takes the form of devotion to ideals or goals, to something "outside oneself." *Metaneeds* share a continuum with basic needs; frustration of these needs brings about *metapathologies*—a lack of values, meaningfulness, or fulfillment in life. Maslow argues that a sense of identity, success in a career, and commitment to a value system are as essential to one's psychological well-being as security, love, and self-esteem are.

Grumbles and Metagrumbles In Maslow's system, there are different levels of complaints that correspond to the levels of frustrated needs. In a factory situation, for example, low-level *grumbles* might be a response to unsafe working conditions, arbitrary and authoritarian supervisors, or a lack of job security. These complaints address deprivations of basic needs, for physical safety and security. Complaints of a higher level might be inadequate recognition of accomplishments, loss of prestige, or lack of group solidarity—that is, complaints based on threats to belonging needs or esteem needs.

Metagrumbles speak to the frustration of metaneeds, such as perfection, justice, beauty, and truth. This level of grumbling is a good indication that everything else is going fairly smoothly. When people complain about the unesthetic nature of their surroundings, for example, it probably means that their more basic needs have been relatively well satisfied.

To have committees . . . heatedly coming in and complaining that rose gardens in the parks are not sufficiently cared for . . . is in itself a wonderful thing because it indicates the height of life at which the complainers are living. (Maslow, 1965, p. 240)

Maslow assumes that we should never expect an end to complaints; we should only hope to move to higher levels of complaint. When grumblers are frustrated over the imperfection of the world, the lack of justice, and so on, it is a positive sign. It means that, despite a high degree of basic satisfaction, people are striving for still greater improvement and growth. In fact, Maslow suggests, a good measure of the degree of enlightenment of a community is the number of metagrumblers among its members.

Research on Self-actualization Maslow's investigations of self-actualization were first stimulated by his desire to understand more completely his two most inspiring teachers, Ruth Benedict and Max Wertheimer. Although Benedict and Wertheimer were dissimilar personalities and were concerned with different fields of study, Maslow felt they shared a level of personal fulfillment in their professional and private lives that he had rarely seen in others. In Benedict and Wertheimer, Maslow saw more than two eminent scientists. He saw deeply fulfilled, creative human beings. He began a private research project to discover what made them so special, and he kept a notebook filled with whatever data he could accumulate about their personal lives, attitudes, values, and so forth. Maslow's comparison of Benedict and Wertheimer set the stage for his lifelong study of self-actualization.

Self-actualizing people are, without one single exception, involved in a cause outside their own skin, in something outside of themselves. (Maslow, 1971, p. 43)

Maslow argued that it was more accurate to generalize about human nature from studying the best examples he could find than from cataloging the problems and faults of average or neurotic individuals.

> Certainly a visitor from Mars descending upon a colony of birth-injured cripples, dwarfs, hunchbacks, etc., could not deduce what they *should* have been. But then let us study not cripples, but the closest approach we can get to whole, healthy men. In them we find qualitative differences, a different system of motivation, emotion, value, thinking, and perceiving. In a certain sense, only the saints are mankind. (Maslow in Lowry, 1973a, p. 90)

By studying the best and healthiest men and women, researchers can explore the limits of human potential. In order to determine how fast human beings can run, for example, one should work with the finest athletes and track

Eleanor Roosevelt

performers available. It would make no sense to test an average sample from the general population. Similarly, Maslow argued, to study psychological health and maturity, one should investigate the most mature, creative, and well-integrated people.

In looking for subjects for a study of "good human beings," Maslow found only one clearly usable subject among 3000 undergraduates. Two criteria for including people in his initial study had been established. First, all subjects had to be relatively free of neurosis or other major personal problems. Second, all those studied had to be making the best possible use of their talents and capabilities.

For his study, Maslow was finally forced to rely on personal acquaintances as well as public figures. This group consisted of 18 individuals: 9 contemporaries and 9 historical figures, including Abraham Lincoln, Thomas Jefferson, Albert Einstein, Eleanor Roosevelt, Jane Addams, William James, Albert Schweitzer, Aldous Huxley, and Baruch Spinoza. It is noteworthy that Maslow's list includes intellectual giants and social reformers but no spiritual teachers or mystics; his interest in transpersonal psychology emerged later in his career. Obviously, Maslow's bias toward active, successful, intellectual personalities as the "best" people has strongly affected his writing on self-actualization. Another psychologist, who valued introverted, artistic, and spiritual qualities in people, would have formulated a different theory.

[Self-actualization] is not an absence of problems but a moving from transitional or unreal problems to real problems. (Maslow, 1968, p. 115)

Maslow lists the following characteristics of self-actualizers (1970, pp. 153–172):

1. more efficient perception of reality and more comfortable relations with it
2. acceptance (self, others, nature)

3. spontaneity; simplicity; naturalness
4. problem centering [as opposed to ego-centered]
5. the quality of detachment; the need for privacy
6. autonomy; independence of culture and environment
7. continued freshness of appreciation
8. mystic and peak experiences
9. *Gemeinschaftsgefühl* [a feeling of kinship with others]
10. deeper and more profound interpersonal relations
11. the democratic character structure
12. discrimination between means and ends, between good and evil
13. philosophical, unhostile sense of humor
14. self-actualizing creativeness
15. resistance to enculturation; the transcendence of any particular culture

> *There are no perfect human beings!* Persons can be found who are good, very good indeed, in fact, great. There do in fact exist creators, seers, sages, saints, shakers and movers. This can certainly give us hope for the future of the species even if they are uncommon and do not come by the dozen. And yet these very same people can at times be boring, irritating, petulant, selfish, angry, or depressed. To avoid disillusionment with human nature, we must first give up our illusions about it. (Maslow, 1970, p. 176)

I very soon had to come to the conclusion that great talent was not only more or less independent of goodness or health of character but also that we know little about it. (Maslow, 1968, p. 135)

Maslow pointed out that the self-actualizers he studied were not perfect or even free of major faults. Their strong commitment to their chosen career and values may even lead self-actualizers to be ruthless at times in pursuing their goals; their work may take precedence over others' feelings or needs. In addition, self-actualizers can carry their independence to extremes. Self-actualizers also share many of the problems of average people: guilt, anxiety, sadness, conflict, and so on.

Albert Einstein

Personal Reflection

■ Self-actualization

Think of four or five self-actualizing people you have known personally or have heard about. What do these people have in common? What are some of their outstanding qualities? Are they different from your own personal heroes and heroines, or are they the same people? In what ways do these people bear out Maslow's theories? In what ways does each differ from Maslow's model of self-actualization?

Self-actualization Theory In his last book, *The Farther Reaches of Human Nature* (1971), Maslow describes eight ways in which individuals self-actualize, or eight behaviors leading to self-actualization. It is not a neat, clean, logically tight discussion, but it represents the culmination of Maslow's thinking on self-actualization.

1. Concentration "First, self-actualization means experiencing fully, vividly, selflessly, with full concentration and total absorption" (Maslow, 1971, p. 45). Usually, we are relatively unaware of what is going on within or around us. (Most eyewitnesses recount different versions of the same occurrence, for example.) However, we have all had moments of heightened awareness and intense involvement, moments that Maslow would call self-actualizing.

One cannot choose wisely for a life unless he dares to listen to himself, his own self, at each moment in life. (Maslow, 1971, p. 47)

2. Growth Choices If we think of life as a series of choices, then self-actualization is the process of making each decision a choice for growth. We often have to choose between growth and safety, between progressing and regressing. Each choice has its positive and its negative aspects. To choose safety is to remain with the known and the familiar but to risk becoming stultified and stale. To choose growth is to open oneself to new and challenging experiences but to risk the unknown and possible failure.

3. Self-awareness In self-actualizing we become more aware of our inner nature and act in accordance with it. This means we decide for ourselves whether we like certain films, books, or ideas, regardless of others' opinions.

4. Honesty Honesty and taking responsibility for one's actions are essential elements in self-actualizing. Rather than pose and give answers that are calculated to please another or to make ourselves look good, Maslow says, we should look within for the answers. Each time we do so, we get in touch with our inner selves.

5. Judgment The first four steps help us develop the capacity for "better life choices." We learn to trust our own judgment and our own instincts and to act accordingly. Maslow believes that following our instincts leads to more accurate judgments about what is constitutionally right for each of us—better choices in art, music, and food, as well as in major life decisions, such as marriage and a career.

6. Self-development Self-actualization is also a continual process of developing one's potentialities. It means using one's abilities and intelligence and "working to do well the thing that one wants to do" (Maslow, 1971, p. 48). Great talent or intelligence is not the same as self-actualization; many gifted people fail to use their abilities fully, while others, with perhaps only average talents, accomplish a great deal.

Self-actualization is not a *thing* that someone either has or does not have. It is a never-ending process of making real one's potential. It refers to a way of continually living, working, and relating to the world rather than to a single accomplishment.

7. Peak Experiences "Peak experiences are transient moments of self-actualization" (Maslow, 1971, p. 48). We are more whole, more integrated, more aware of ourselves and of the world during peak moments. At such times we think, act, and feel most clearly and accurately. We are more loving and accepting of others, have less inner conflict and anxiety, and are better able to put our energies to constructive use. Some people enjoy more peak experiences than others, particularly those Maslow called transcending self-actualizers. (See the following sections: "Peak Experiences" and "Transcendence and Self-actualization.")

8. Lack of Ego Defenses A further step in self-actualization is to recognize our ego defenses and to be able to drop them when appropriate. To do so, we must become more aware of the ways in which we distort our images of ourselves and of the external world—through repression, projection, and other defenses.

Peak Experiences

Peak experiences are especially joyous and exciting moments in the life of every individual. Maslow notes that peak experiences are often inspired by intense feelings of love, exposure to great art or music, or the overwhelming beauty of nature. "All peak experiences may be fruitfully understood as completions-of-the-act . . . or as the Gestalt psychologists' closure, or on the paradigm of the Reichian type of complete orgasm, or as total discharge, catharsis, culmination, climax, consummation, emptying or finishing" (Maslow, 1968, p. 111).

> The term peak experiences is a generalization for the best moments of the human being, for the happiest moments of life, for experiences of ecstasy, rapture, bliss, of the greatest joy. (Maslow, 1971, p. 105)

Virtually everyone has had a number of peak experiences, although we often take them for granted. One's reactions while watching a vivid sunset or listening to a moving piece of music are examples of peak experiences. According to Maslow, peak experiences tend to be triggered by intense, inspiring occurrences: "It looks as if any experience of real excellence, of real perfection . . . tends to produce a peak experience" (1971, p. 175). These experiences may also be triggered by tragic events. Recovering from depression or a serious illness, or confronting death, can initiate extreme moments of love and joy. The lives of most people are filled with long periods of relative inattentiveness, lack of involvement, or even boredom. By contrast, peak experiences, understood in

Personal Reflection

■ Your Own Peak Experiences

Try to recall clearly one peak experience in your life—a joyous, happy, blissful moment that stands out in your memory. Take a moment to relive the experience. Now consider the following questions.

1. What brought about this experience? Was anything unique about the situation that triggered it?
2. How did you feel at the time? Was this feeling different from your usual experience—emotionally, physically, or intellectually?
3. Did you seem different to yourself? Did the world about you appear different?
4. How long did the experience last? How did you feel afterward?
5. Did the experience have any lasting effects (on your outlook or your relations with others, for example)?
6. How does your own experience compare with Maslow's theories concerning peak experiences and human nature?

To get a clearer sense of peak experiences, compare your experiences with others'. Look for differences as well as similarities. Are the differences the result of dissimilar situations or perhaps of variations in personality or background? What do the similarities imply about Maslow's ideas or about human potential in general?

the broadest sense, are those moments when we become deeply involved, excited by, and absorbed in the world.

The most powerful peak experiences are relatively rare. For Maslow, the highest peaks include "feelings of limitless horizons opening up to the vision, the feeling of being simultaneously more powerful and also more helpless than one ever was before, the feeling of great ecstasy and wonder and awe, the loss of placing in time and space" (1970, p. 164). They have been portrayed by poets as moments of ecstasy; by the religious, as deep mystical experiences.

Plateau Experiences A peak experience is a "high" that may last a few minutes or several hours, but rarely longer. Maslow also discusses a more stable and long-lasting experience that he refers to as a **plateau experience.** The plateau experience represents a new and more profound way of viewing and experiencing the world. It involves a fundamental change in attitude, a change that affects one's entire point of view and creates a new appreciation and intensified awareness of the world. Maslow experienced this himself late in life, after his first heart attack. His intensified consciousness of life and sense of death's imminence caused him to see the world in a wholly new way. (For a more complete description in Maslow's own words, see The Theory Firsthand in this chapter.)

Transcendence and Self-actualization Maslow found that some self-actualizing individuals tend to have many peak experiences, whereas other people have them rarely, if ever. He came to distinguish between self-actualizers who are psychologically healthy, productive human beings, with little or no experience of transcendence, and those for whom transcendence is important or even central. The first group is generally pragmatic in orientation. "Such persons live in the world, coming to fulfillment in it. They master it, lead it, use it for good purposes, as (healthy) politicians or practical people do" (1971, p. 281).

At the highest levels of development of humaneness, knowledge is positively rather than negatively correlated with a sense of mystery, awe, humility, ultimate ignorance, reverence, and a sense of oblation. (Maslow, 1971, p. 290)

Transcending self-actualizers are more often aware of the sacredness of all things, the transcendent dimension of life, in the midst of daily activities. Their peak or mystical experiences are often valued as the most important aspects of their lives. They tend to think more holistically than "merely healthy" self-actualizers; they are better able to transcend the categories of past, present, and future, and good and evil, and to perceive a unity behind the apparent complexity and contradictions of life. They are more likely to be innovators and original thinkers than systematizers of the ideas of others. As their knowledge develops, so does their sense of humility and ignorance, and they may come to regard the universe with increasing awe.

Because transcenders generally regard themselves as the carriers of their talents and abilities, they are less ego-involved in their work. A transcender is honestly able to say, "I am the best person for this job, and therefore I should have it"; or, on the other hand, to admit, "You are the best one for this job, and you should take it from me."

Not everyone who has had a mystical experience is a transcending self-actualizer. Many who have had such experiences have not developed the psychological health and the productiveness Maslow considered to be essential aspects of self-actualization. Maslow also found as many transcenders among business executives, managers, teachers, and politicians as among poets, musicians, ministers, and the like, for whom transcendence is almost assumed.

Deficiency Psychology and Being Psychology

Maslow distinguished between two basic kinds of psychology. Most psychology in his day was what he called *deficiency psychology,* concerned with human behavior in the realm of basic need satisfaction. *Being psychology,* in contrast, examines human behavior and experience during the highest states of awareness and in pursuit of self-actualization needs. Peak experiences are generally related to the being realm, and being psychology tends to be most applicable to self-actualizers.

Deficiency Motivation and Being Motivation Maslow pointed out that most psychologies address only *deficiency motivation;* that is, they concentrate on behavior whose goal is to fulfill a need that has been unsatisfied or frustrated. Hunger, pain, and fear are prime examples of deficiency motivations.

However, a close look at human or animal behavior reveals another kind of motivation. When an organism is not hungry, in pain, or fearful, *being motivations* emerge, such as curiosity and playfulness. Under these conditions, activities can be enjoyed as ends in themselves, not pursued solely as a means to gratify certain needs. **Being motivation** refers primarily to enjoyment and satisfaction in the present or to the desire to seek a positively valued goal (growth motivation or metamotivation). On the other hand, **deficiency motivation** involves a need to change the present state of affairs because of a feeling of dissatisfaction or frustration.

Deficiency Cognition and Being Cognition In **deficiency cognition,** objects are seen solely as need fulfillers, as means to ends. This type of cognition occurs most often when needs are strong. According to Maslow (1970), strong needs tend to channel thinking and perception; therefore, the individual is aware only of those aspects of the environment related to need satisfaction. A hungry person tends to see only food, a miser only money.

Being cognition is a more accurate and effective awareness of the environment. Individuals whose basic drives have been satisfied are less likely to distort their perceptions in response to needs or desires. Being cognition is nonjudgmental, without comparison or evaluation. The fundamental attitude is one of appreciation of what is. Stimuli are exclusively and fully attended to, and perception seems richer, fuller, and more complete.

A section of cancer seen through a microscope, if only we can forget that it is a cancer, can be seen as a beautiful and intricate and awe-inspiring organization. (Maslow, 1968, p. 76)

The perceiver in a state of being cognition remains somewhat independent of what is perceived. External objects are valued in and of themselves rather than for their relevance to personal concerns. In fact, the individual tends to remain absorbed in contemplation or appreciation, and active intervention is seen as irrelevant or inappropriate. One advantage to deficiency cognition is that the individual may feel compelled to act, in order to alter existing conditions.

Deficiency Values and Being Values Maslow does not explicitly address **deficiency values,** though he discusses **being values** in detail. Being values are intrinsic to every individual. "The highest values [exist] within human nature itself, to be discovered there. This is in sharp contradiction to the older and more customary beliefs that the highest values can come only from a supernatural God, or from some other source outside human nature itself" (1968, p. 170).

Maslow has listed the following as being values: truth, goodness, beauty, wholeness, dichotomy transcendence, aliveness, uniqueness, perfection, necessity, completion, justice, order, simplicity, richness, effortlessness, playfulness, and self-sufficiency.

Deficiency Love and Being Love **Deficiency love** is love of others because they fulfill a need. The more one is gratified, the more this kind of love is reinforced. This kind of love arises out of a need for self-esteem or sex, out of fear of loneliness, and so forth.

Being love is love for the essence, the "being" of the other. It is nonpossessive and concerned more with the good of the other than with selfish satisfaction. Maslow often wrote of being love as demonstrating the Taoist attitude of noninterference or letting things be, an appreciation of what is without concern for change or improvement. In love of nature, for example, an individual prompted by being love might express appreciation for the beauty of flowers by watching them grow and then leaving them in the garden. Someone acting from deficiency love is more likely to pick the flowers and make an arrangement of them. Being love is also the ideal, unconditional love of a parent for a child, which includes loving and valuing the child's small imperfections.

Personal Reflection

■ An Exercise in Being Love

For Maslow, being love is selfless; it demands nothing in return. The very act of loving, appreciating the essence and beauty of the object of love, is its own reward. In our daily experience, we usually feel a mixture of being love and deficiency love. We generally expect and receive something in return for our feelings of love.

This exercise is derived from an old Christian practice designed to develop feelings of pure love. Sit in a darkened room in front of a lit candle. Relax and gradually get in touch with your body and your surroundings. Allow your mind and body to slow down, to become calm and peaceful.

Gaze at the candle flame. Extend feelings of love from your heart to the flame. Your feelings of love for the flame are unrelated to any thought of the worthiness of the flame itself. You love for the sake of loving. (It may seem strange at first to love an inanimate object, a mere flame, but that is just the point—to experience the feeling of loving in a situation in which there is no return, no reward aside from the feeling of love itself.) Expand your feelings of love to include the entire room and everything in it.

How do these feelings compare with other experiences of love you have had—feelings of love for family, friends, lovers?

Maslow argues that being love is richer, more satisfying, and longer lasting than deficiency love. It stays fresh, whereas deficiency love tends to grow stale with time. Being love can be a trigger for peak experiences and is often depicted in the same exalted terms used for describing deeply religious experiences.

Eupsychia

Maslow coined the term **eupsychia** (yu-psī-kē-a) to refer to ideal, human-oriented societies and communities. He preferred it to utopia, which Maslow felt was overused and whose definition suggests impracticality and ungrounded idealism. The development of an ideal society by psychologically healthy, self-actualizing individuals was quite possible, he believed. All members of the community would be engaged in seeking personal development and fulfillment in their work and in their personal lives.

There is a kind of a feedback between the Good Society and the Good Person. They need each other. (Maslow, 1971, p. 19)

But even an ideal society will not necessarily *produce* self-actualizing individuals.

> A teacher or a culture doesn't create a human being. It doesn't implant within him the ability to love, or to be curious, or to philosophize, or to symbolize, or to be creative. Rather it permits, or fosters, or encourages, or helps what exists in embryo to become real and actual. (Maslow, 1968, p. 161)

Maslow preferred eupsychian, or enlightened, management practices to authoritarian business management. Authoritarian managers assume that workers and management have basically different, mutually incompatible goals—that workers want to earn as much as possible with minimal effort and therefore must be closely watched.

Enlightened managers, however, assume that employees *want* to be creative and productive and that they should be supported and encouraged rather than restricted and controlled. The enlightened approach works best with stable, psychologically healthy employees. Some hostile, suspicious people might function more effectively in an authoritarian structure and might take unfair advantage of greater freedom. Because eupsychian management works only with people who both enjoy and can handle responsibility and self-direction, Maslow suggested that eupsychian communities be composed of self-actualizing people.

Synergy

The term **synergy** was originally used by Maslow's teacher Ruth Benedict to refer to the degree of interpersonal cooperation and harmony within a society. *Synergy* means cooperation (from the Greek word for "work together"). *Synergy* also refers to a combined action of elements resulting in a total effect that is greater than all the elements taken independently.

As an anthropologist, Benedict was aware of the dangers of making value judgments in comparing societies and evaluating another civilization by how closely it conforms to our own cultural standards. However, in her study of other civilizations, Benedict observed that people in some societies are clearly happier, healthier, and more efficient than in others. Some groups have beliefs and customs that are basically harmonious and satisfying to their members, whereas other groups have traditions that promote suspicion, fear, and anxiety.

Under conditions of low social synergy, the success of one member brings about loss or failure for another. For example, if each hunter shares the daily catch with only the immediate family, hunting is likely to become strongly competitive. Hunters who improve their techniques or discover a new source of game may try to hide their achievements from others. Whenever one hunter is highly successful, there is that much less food available for other hunters and their families.

Under high social synergy, cooperation is maximized. An example would be a hunting society similar to the one just described, but with a single important difference—the communal sharing of the catch. Under these conditions, each hunter benefits from the success of the others. In high social synergy, the cultural belief system reinforces cooperation and positive feelings between individuals and helps minimize conflict and discord.

Maslow also writes of synergy in individuals. Identification with others tends to promote high individual synergy. If the success of another is a source of genuine satisfaction to the individual, then help is freely and generously offered. In a sense, both selfish and altruistic motives are merged. In aiding another, the individual is also seeking his or her own satisfaction.

Synergy can also be found within the individual as unity between thought and action. To force oneself to act indicates some conflict of motives. Ideally, individuals do what they should do because they *want* to do so. The best medicine is taken not only because it is effective but also because it tastes good.

Dynamics

Psychological Growth

The pursuit of self-actualization cannot begin until the individual is free of the domination of the lower needs, such as needs for security and esteem. According to Maslow, early frustration of a need may fixate the individual at that level of functioning. For instance, someone who was not very popular as a child may crave attention, recognition, and praise from others throughout life to counter feelings of low self-esteem.

The pursuit of the satisfaction of higher needs is in itself one index of psychological health. Maslow argues that fulfillment of higher needs is intrinsically more satisfying and that metamotivation is an indication that the individual has progressed beyond a deficiency level of functioning.

As the person becomes integrated, so does his world. As he feels good, so does the world look good. (Maslow, 1971, p. 165)

Self-actualization represents a long-term commitment to growth and to the development of capabilities to their fullest. Self-actualizing work involves the choice of worthwhile, creative goals. Maslow writes that self-actualizing individuals are attracted to the most challenging and intriguing problems, to questions that demand their best and most creative efforts. They are willing to cope with uncertainty and ambiguity and prefer challenges to easy solutions.

Obstacles to Growth

In Maslow's view, growth motivation is less basic than the drive to satisfy physiological needs and needs for security, esteem, and so on. The process of self-actualization can be limited by (1) negative influences from past experience and resulting habits that keep us locked into unproductive behaviors; (2) social influence and group pressure that often operate against our own taste and judgment; and (3) inner defenses that keep us out of touch with ourselves. Because self-actualization is at the top of the need hierarchy, it is the weakest need and is easily inhibited by frustration of more fundamental needs. Also, most people avoid self-knowledge, which is at the heart of the process of self-actualization, and are afraid of the changes in self-esteem and self-image that self-knowledge brings.

There are two sets of forces pulling at the individual, not just one. In addition to the pressures forward toward health, there are also fearful-regressive pressures backward, toward sickness and weakness. (Maslow, 1968, p. 164)

Poor habits often inhibit growth. For Maslow, these include addiction to drugs or alcohol, poor diet, and other behaviors that adversely affect health and efficiency. A destructive environment or rigid, authoritarian education can easily lead to unproductive habits based on a deficiency orientation. Also, any deep-seated habit tends to interfere with psychological growth, because it diminishes the flexibility and openness necessary to operate most effectively in a variety of situations.

Group pressure and social propaganda also tend to limit the individual. They act to reduce autonomy and stifle independent judgment, as the individual is pressured to substitute external, societal standards for his or her own taste or judgment. A society may inculcate a biased view of human nature as seen, for example, in the Western belief that most human instincts are essentially sinful and must be controlled or subjugated. Maslow argued that this negative attitude often frustrates growth and that the opposite is in fact true; our instincts are essentially good and impulses toward growth are the major sources of human motivation.

Ego defenses, Maslow felt, are internal obstacles to growth. The first step in dealing with ego defenses is to recognize them and to see clearly how they operate. Then the individual should attempt to minimize the distortions created by the defenses. Maslow adds two new defense mechanisms—*desacralization* and the *Jonah complex*—to the traditional psychoanalytic listing of projection, repression, denial, and the like.

Desacralization **Desacralization** refers to the act of impoverishing one's life by the refusal to treat anything with deep seriousness and concern. Today, few cultural or religious symbols are given the care and respect they once enjoyed; consequently, they have lost their power to thrill, inspire, or even motivate us. Maslow often referred to modern values concerning sex as an example of desacralization. Although a more casual attitude toward sex may lessen frustration and trauma, Maslow believed that sexual experience has lost the power it once had to inspire artists, writers, and lovers.

Though, in principle, self-actualization is easy, in practice it rarely happens (by my criteria, certainly in less than 1% of the adult population). (Maslow, 1968, p. 204)

The Jonah Complex The **Jonah complex** refers to the refusal to realize one's full capabilities. Just as Jonah attempted to avoid the responsibilities of becoming a prophet, many people avoid responsibility because they are actually afraid of using their capacities to the fullest. They prefer the security of undemanding goals over ambitious ones that require them to extend themselves fully. This attitude is not uncommon among students who "get by," utilizing only a fraction of their talents and abilities. In the past, many women were taught that a successful career was somehow incongruent with femininity or that intellectual achievement might make them less attractive to men. (See, for example, Horner, 1972.)

This "fear of greatness" may be the largest barrier to self-actualization. Living fully is more than many of us feel we can bear. At times of deepest joy and ecstasy, people often say, "It's too much," or, "I can't stand it." The root of the Jonah complex is seen in the fear of letting go of a limited but manageable existence, the fear of losing control, being torn apart, or disintegrating.

Structure

Body

The fact is that people are good, if only their fundamental wishes [for affection and security] are satisfied. . . . Give people affection and security, and they will give affection and be secure in their feelings and behavior. (Maslow in Lowry, 1973b, p. 18)

Maslow does not discuss in detail the role of the body in the process of self-actualization. He assumes that once physiological needs are met, the individual is free to deal with needs that are further up in the hierarchy. However, he writes that it is important that the body be given its due. "Asceticism, self-denial, deliberate rejection of the demands of the organism, at least in the West, tend to produce a diminished, stunted, or crippled organism, and even in the East, bring self-actualization to only a very few, exceptionally strong individuals" (1968, p. 199).

Maslow mentions the intense stimulation of the physical senses in peak experiences, which are often triggered by natural beauty, art, music, or sex. He also indicates that training in dance, art, and other physical forms of expression can provide an important supplement to traditional, cognitively oriented education and that physical and sense-oriented systems of instruction require the kind of active, participatory learning that should be included in all types of education.

Social Relationships

According to Maslow, love and esteem are basic needs and take precedence over self-actualization in the need hierarchy. He deplored the failure of most psychology textbooks even to mention the word *love,* as if psychologists considered love unreal, something that must be reduced to concepts like libido projection or sexual reinforcement.

Will

Will is a vital ingredient in the long-term process of self-actualization. Maslow found that self-actualizing individuals strive hard to attain their chosen goals. "Self-actualization means working to do well the thing that one wants to do. To become a second-rate physician is not a good path to self-actualization. One wants to be first-rate or as good as he can be" (Maslow, 1971, p. 48). Because of his faith in the essential health and goodness of human nature, Maslow placed little emphasis on the role of willpower in the process of overcoming unacceptable instincts or impulses. For Maslow, healthy individuals are relatively free from internal conflict, except perhaps for bad habits that must be broken. Will can be employed to develop their abilities still further and to attain ambitious, long-range goals.

If you deliberately plan to be less than you are capable of being, then I warn you that you'll be deeply unhappy for the rest of your life. (Maslow, 1971, p. 36)

Emotions

Positive emotions, Maslow maintained, play a role in self-actualization. He encouraged other psychologists to begin serious research on happiness, calmness, joy, and to investigate fun, games, and play. He believed that negative emotions, tension, and conflict drain energy and inhibit effective functioning.

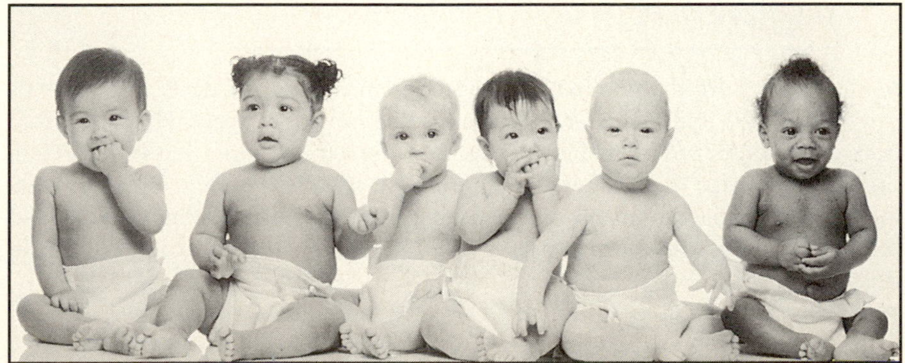

We begin life filled with joy and creativity.

What happened?

For Maslow, maturity includes "being able to give oneself over completely to an emotion, not only of love but also of anger, fascination" (1966, p. 38). Maslow goes on to point out that it is our fear of deep emotions that leads us to desacralize much of life or to use intellectualization as a defense against feeling. He felt that orthodox science has mistakenly taken "cool" perceiving and detached thinking as the best venues for discovering scientific truth. This limited approach has tended to banish, from scientific study, experiences of wonder, awe, ecstasy, and other forms of transcendence.

Intellect

Maslow emphasized the need for holistic thinking, which deals with systems of relationships and wholes rather than with individual parts. He found that peak experiences often contain striking examples of thinking that have broken through the usual dichotomies with which we usually experience reality. During peak experiences, individuals have often reported seeing past, present, and future as one, life and death as part of a single process, and good and evil within the same whole.

Holistic thinking is also found in creative individuals who are able to break with the past and look beyond conventional categories in investigating possible new relationships. This kind of thinking requires freedom, openness, and an ability to cope with inconsistency and uncertainty. Although such ambiguity can be threatening to some, it is part of the essential joy of creative problem solving for self-actualizers.

Maslow (1970) has written that creative people are **problem-centered** rather than **means-centered.** Problem-centered people focus primarily on the demands and requirements of the desired goals. Means-centered individuals, on the other hand, often become so concerned with technique or methodology that they may do intensely detailed work in trivial areas. Problem-centering stands in contrast to ego-centering (an example of deficiency cognition), in which individuals see what they wish rather than what actually is.

Self

Maslow defines the self as an individual's inner core or inherent nature—one's tastes, values, and goals. Understanding one's inner nature and acting in accordance with it is essential to actualizing the self.

Self-actualizng people, those who have come to a high level of maturation, health, and self-fulfillment, have so much to teach us that sometimes they seem almost like a different breed of human beings. (Maslow, 1968, p. 71)

Maslow approaches the understanding of the self by studying those individuals who are most in tune with their own natures, those who provide the best examples of self-expression or self-actualization. However, he does not discuss the self as a specific structure within the personality.

Therapist

For Maslow, as for Rogers, psychotherapy is effective primarily because it involves an intimate and trusting relationship with another human being. Along with Adler, Maslow felt that a good therapist is like an older brother or sister, someone who offers care and love. But more than this, Maslow proposed the model of the Taoist helper, a person who offers assistance without interference. A familiar example is a good coach, who works with the natural style of an athlete in order to strengthen that individual's style and improve it. A skillful coach does not try to force all athletes into the same mold. Good parents are like a Taoist helper when they resist doing everything for their child. The child develops best by means of guidance, not interference.

Although Maslow underwent psychoanalysis for several years and received informal training in psychotherapy, his interests always revolved around research and writing rather than the actual practice of psychotherapy. Maslow (1987) did make an important distinction between what he called *basic needs therapy,* designed to help people meet primary needs such as safety, belonging, love, and respect, and *insight therapy,* which is a profound, long-term process of growth in self-understanding.

It has been pointed out that a therapist can repeat the same mistakes for 40 years and then call it "rich clinical experience." (Maslow, 1968, p. 87)

Maslow viewed therapy as a way of satisfying the basic needs for love and esteem that have been frustrated in virtually everyone who seeks psychological help. He argued (1970) that warm human relationships can provide much of the same support found in therapy.

Good therapists should love and care for the being or essence of the people they work with. Maslow (1971) wrote that those who seek to change or manipulate others lack this essential attitude. For example, a true dog lover would never crop the animal's ears or tail, and one who really loves flowers would not cut or twist them to make fancy floral arrangements.

Recent Developments

Although Maslow himself did little in the way of formal research, his work has inspired a number of dedicated investigators. Shostrom (1963) developed the Personal Orientation Inventory (POI) as a measure of self-actualization. A significant body of research has been conducted using this instrument (Gray, 1986; Kelly & Chovan, 1985; Rychman, 1985). Maslow's concept of peak experience has also sparked research (Wilson & Spencer, 1990; see Mathes et al., 1982, for a literature review). Case studies of self-actualizing individuals have confirmed Maslow's theory and also related self-actualization to Dabrowski's (1967) theory of emotional development (Piechowski, 1978, 1990; Piechowski & Tyska, 1982; Brennan & Piechowski, 1991).

Maslow's work continues to have an impact on the study of religion (Fuller, 1994), education (Kunc, 1992), and business (Schott, 1992).

Evaluation

Maslow's great strength lies in his concern for the areas of human functioning that most other theorists have almost completely ignored. He is one of the few psychologists who have seriously investigated the positive dimensions of human experience.

I am a new breed—a theoretical psychologist parallel to . . . theoretical biologists. . . . I think of myself as a scientist rather than an essayist or philosopher. I feel myself very bound to and by the facts that I am trying to *perceive,* not to create. (Maslow in International Study Project, 1972, p. 63)

His major contributions might be summarized in the following three central ideas:

1. Human beings have an innate tendency to move toward higher levels of health, creativity, insight, and self-fulfillment.
2. Neurosis is basically a blockage of the innate tendency toward self-actualization.
3. Business efficiency and personal growth are not incompatible. In fact, the process of self-actualization brings each individual to greater efficiency, creativity, and productivity.

The experimental work that Maslow did was mostly inconclusive; *exploratory* might be a better term to describe it, and he was the first to acknowledge this:

> It's just that I haven't got the time to do careful experiments myself. They take too long, in view of the years that I have left and the extent of what I want to do.
>
> So I myself do only "quick-and-dirty" little pilot explorations, mostly with a few subjects only, inadequate to publish but enough to convince myself that they are probably true and will be confirmed one day. Quick little commando raids, guerrilla attacks. (Maslow in International Study Project, 1972, pp. 66–67)

Maslow never sought to experimentally "prove" or verify his ideas. His research was more a way of clarifying and adding detail to his theories. Even so, Maslow sometimes seems like a philosopher who remains aloof from the possible contradictions of new facts or experiences. He was generally clear on what he wanted to demonstrate in his research, but he rarely seemed to find any new data to alter his preconceived ideas. For example, Maslow always stressed the importance of positive triggers for peak experiences: experiences of love, beauty, great music, and so on. Negative triggers tend to be ignored in his writings, despite the fact that many people report their most intense peak experiences to be preceded by negative emotions (fear and depression, for instance) that are then transcended and transformed into highly positive states. (See, for example, William James's *The Varieties of Religious Experience,* 1943.) For some reason, Maslow's investigations seldom uncovered this kind of new information.

Maslow's greatest value is as a psychological theorist who has stressed the positive dimensions of human experience—particularly the tremendous potential that all men and women possess. Maslow has been an inspiration for virtually all humanistic and transpersonal psychologists. In his book on Maslow and modern psychology, Colin Wilson writes:

> Maslow was the first person to create a truly comprehensive psychology stretching, so to speak, from the basement to the attic. He accepted Freud's clinical method without accepting his philosophy. . . . The "transcendent" urges—aesthetic, creative, religious—are as basic and permanent a part of human nature as dominance or sexuality. If they are less obviously "universal," this is only because fewer human beings reach the point at which they take over.
>
> Maslow's achievement is enormous. Like all original thinkers, he has opened up a new way of *seeing* the universe. (1972, pp. 181–184)

Maslow has been called "the greatest American psychologist since William James" (*Journal of Transpersonal Psychology,* 1970). Although many might consider this praise somewhat exaggerated, no one can deny Maslow's central importance as an original thinker and a pioneer in human potential psychology.

Transpersonal Psychology

Maslow added transpersonal psychology to the first three forces in Western psychology—behaviorism, psychoanalysis, and humanistic psychology. For Maslow, behaviorism and psychoanalysis were too limited in scope to form the basis of a complete psychology of human nature. Psychoanalysis is derived largely from studies of psychopathology. Behaviorism has attempted to reduce the complexities of human nature to simpler principles but has failed to address fully such issues as values, consciousness, and love.

In the early 1960s humanistic psychology emerged from the work of Maslow, Rogers, and other theorists concerned with psychological health and effective functioning. Many humanistic psychologists have used Maslow's theories, especially his work on self-actualization, as the framework for their writing and research.

In 1968 Maslow called attention to the limitations of the humanistic model. In exploring the farthest reaches of human nature, he found that there were possibilities beyond self-actualization. When peak experiences are especially powerful, the sense of self dissolves into an awareness of a greater unity. The term *self-actualization* did not seem to fit these experiences.

The human being needs a framework of values, a philosophy of life . . . to live by and understand by, in about the same sense that he needs sunlight, calcium or love. (Maslow, 1968, p. 206)

Transpersonal psychology contributes to the more traditional concerns of the discipline an acknowledgment of the spiritual aspect of human experience. This level of experience has been described primarily in religious literature, in unscientific and often theologically biased language. A major task of transpersonal psychology is to provide a scientific language and a scientific framework for this material.

> I should say also that I consider Humanistic, Third Force Psychology to be transitional, a preparation for a still "higher" Fourth Psychology, transpersonal, transhuman, centered in the cosmos rather than in human needs and interest, going beyond humanness, identity, self-actualization and the like. . . . We need something "bigger than we are" to be awed by and to commit ourselves to in a new, naturalistic, empirical, non-churchly sense, perhaps as Thoreau and Whitman, William James and John Dewey did. (Maslow, 1968, pp. iii–iv)

One basic tenet of transpersonal psychology is that there is in each individual a deeper or true self that is experienced in transcendent states of consciousness. Distinct from the personality and the personal ego, it is the source of inner wisdom, health, and harmony.

Webster's Tenth New Collegiate Dictionary defines *transpersonal* as "extending or going beyond the personal or individual." The term refers to an extension of identity beyond both individuality and personality. One of the premises of transpersonal psychology is that we do not know the full range of human potential. The sense of a vast potential for growth within the individual provides a context for transpersonal psychology. Collections of basic essays and articles on transpersonal psychology include Ornstein (1973), Tart (1969, 1975), Walsh and Shapiro (1983), Walsh and Vaughan (1980, 1993). Frager (1989) and Valle (1989) have provided overviews of the field.

Approaches to Transpersonal Psychology

Major contributors to the field of transpersonal psychology differ in their approaches and interests. The following is a series of excerpts that reflect these varying approaches.

Without the transcendent and the transpersonal, we get sick, violent and nihilistic, or else hopeless and apathetic. (Maslow, 1968, p. iv)

One of the earliest formal definitions of the new discipline was published in the first issue of the *Journal of Transpersonal Psychology:*

> Transpersonal (or "fourth force") Psychology is the title given to an emerging force in the psychology field by a group of psychologists and professional men and women from other fields who are interested in those *ultimate* human capacities and potentialities that have no systematic place in positivistic or behavioristic theory ("first force"), classical psychoanalytic theory ("second force"), or humanistic psychology ("third force"). (Sutich, 1969, p. 15)

For some, transpersonal psychology is particularly important because it includes the psychological wisdom of other cultures and traditions:

> Transpersonal psychology is bringing together the insights of the individualistic psychologies of the West with the spiritual psychologies of the East and Middle East. The realization that our own training has been limited and that Western ideas are not the center of the psychological universe is disturbing at first. The feeling passes when one becomes aware of the amazing amount of work that has already been accomplished, but which awaits validation with the scientific and experimental tools of Western psychology, to be fully realized. (Fadiman, 1980, p. 181)

Another approach emphasizes the inclusion in transpersonal psychology of experiences that have been ignored or explained away in other fields of psychology:

> Transpersonal experiences may be defined as experiences in which the sense of identity or self extends beyond (*trans*) the individual or personal to encompass wider aspects of humankind, life, *psyche,* and cosmos. . . . Transpersonal psychology is the psychological study of transpersonal experiences and their correlates [which include daily lives, creativity, or spirituality inspired by such experiences]. (Walsh & Vaughan, 1993, p. 3)

In a survey of 40 definitions of the field (Lajoie & Shapiro, 1992), the authors synthesized the following: "Transpersonal psychology is concerned with the study of humanity's highest potential and with the recognition, understanding, and realization of unitive, spiritual, and transcendent experiences."

The Perennial Model

The underlying concept of human nature in transpersonal psychology is not a new one. It has always existed in human culture. It has been called the "perennial philosophy" (Huxley, 1944), the "perennial religion" (Smith, 1976), and the "perennial psychology" (Wilber, 1977). What is new is the task of bringing together ideas from many different traditions and cultures to form a modern psychological language and scientific framework (see, for example, Vaughan, 1995).

Not all transpersonal psychologists or scholars of religion agree with the assumption that there is a perennial tradition underlying the diverse forms of religion. At the other extreme is the position that there is *no* fundamental and neutral mystical experience that is subsequently interpreted by each mystic. The mystical experience itself is shaped by the mystic's tradition and cannot be taken meaningfully out of its cultural and religious context. (see, for example, Katz, 1978).

The perennial model includes the following four basic premises (Valle, 1989):

1. There is a transcendent reality or unity that binds together all (apparently separate) phenomena.
2. The ego or individual self is but a reflection of a greater, transpersonal ("beyond the personal") self or oneness. We come from and are grounded in that self. However, we have become estranged from our origins and we need to return to them in order to become fully healthy and whole human beings.

Personal Reflection

■ Transpersonal Experience

Think of a time when your experience went beyond your usual sense of self or identity. It may have been an active time of peak performance, a powerful experience of great beauty, or a deeply spiritual shift in consciousness. How did the experience affect you? Did it have a lasting impact on your life in some ways? What did you learn from it?

3. The fact that individuals can directly experience this reality or greater self is at the core of the spiritual dimensions of life.
4. This experience involves a qualitative shift in experiencing oneself and the larger world. It is a powerful, self-validating experience.

Another transpersonal theorist, Ralph Metzner (1986), has collected descriptions of transpersonal growth, or the transformation of human consciousness. These portrayals include such key metaphors as the transforming of a caterpillar into a butterfly; awakening from a dream to reality; moving from captivity to liberation; going from darkness to light; being purified by inner fire; going from fragmentation to wholeness; journeying to a place of vision and power; returning to the source; and dying and being reborn.

A New Paradigm

It should be clear by now that transpersonal psychology is based on radically different premises from those of other approaches to psychology. It is what Thomas Kuhn (1962) called a *new paradigm*.

Kuhn defined *paradigm* as a set of values and beliefs shared by the members of a scientific community. In any given community, both theory and research will conform to these fundamental beliefs and values. Critical progress in science, Kuhn points out, often comes from a paradigm shift. Unfortunately, initial resistance to the new paradigm is almost inevitable. Advocates of the new paradigm are frequently accused of using unscientific methods or studying unscientific problems.

Tart (1975) has given a detailed analysis of the ways in which the paradigm of transpersonal psychology differs from that of traditional psychology. These include the following:

1. ***Old:*** Physics is the ultimate science, the study of the real world. Dreams, emotions, and human experience in general are all derivative.
   New: Psychological reality is just as real as physical reality. And modern theoretical physics indicates that the two are not so far apart.
2. ***Old:*** The individual exists in relative isolation from the surrounding environment. We are each essentially independent creatures. (And so we can seek to control the world as if we are not part of it.)

New: There is a deep level of psychological/spiritual connection among all forms of life. Each individual is a *cosmic creature,* deeply embedded in the cosmos.

3. *Old:* Our ordinary state of consciousness is the best, most rational, most adaptive way the mind can be organized. All other states are inferior or pathological. Even "creative states" are suspect, often seen as bordering on the pathological (e.g., "regression").
   New: Higher orders of feeling, awareness, and even rationality are possible. What we call waking consciousness is really more like "waking sleep," in which we use but a small fraction of our awareness or capacities.
4. *Old:* Seeking altered states of consciousness is a sign of pathology or immaturity.
   New: Seeking to experience different states of consciousness is a natural aspect of healthy human growth.
5. *Old:* The basic development of personality is complete by adulthood, except for neurotics, people with traumatic childhoods, and the like.
6. *New:* Ordinary adults exhibit only a rudimentary level of maturity. The basic "healthy" adult personality is merely a foundation for spiritual work and the development of a far deeper level of wisdom and maturity.

In various spiritual traditions, authorities point out, our usual state of consciousness is not only limited—it is also dreamlike and illusory. From this perspective, psychotherapies that deal only with personality dynamics are superficial palliatives, just as giving candy to a sick friend is comforting though ineffective as treatment.

The Work of Ken Wilber

Ken Wilber has been an important transpersonal theorist. In his first major work, *The Spectrum of Consciousness* (1977), Wilber integrates a vast array of Eastern and Western thought into a single model. According to Wilber, growth is the healing of a series of dichotomies within the individual. First is the split between conscious and unconscious, or persona and shadow. Next is the division between mind and body. Following this is the separation of organism and environment. The final stage is the attainment of unity with the universe. Each level of consciousness, Wilber argues, has its own issues, problems, and appropriate forms of therapy or spiritual practice.

Wilber (1980) has also written about human growth and development in terms of two fundamental processes. First there is the outward arc, the process of personal, ego development. The second process is the inward arc, the process of transpersonal, spiritual development, from self-consciousness to *superconsciousness.*

> The story of the Outward Arc is the story of the Hero—the story of the terrible battle to break free of the sleep in the subconscious. . . . The story of the Outward Arc is also the story of the ego, for the ego *is* the Hero. . . . But the Outward Arc, the move from subconsciousness to self-consciousness, is only half of the story of the evolution of consciousness. . . .

> Beyond the self-conscious ego, according to mystic-sages, lies the path of return and the psychology of eternity—the Inward Arc. (Wilber, 1980, p. 4)

In the outward arc, we begin with what Wilber calls the *membership self,* as we acquire language and become socialized in a particular culture. Next comes the stage of the *mental egoic self,* in which we assume a positive self-concept and a healthy, balanced ego. The final stage of the outward arc is the *integrated self,* the stage of self-actualization, which is generally the highest level of human development identified in Western psychology.

The inner arc begins with the *low-subtle self,* which includes highly developed intuition and various kinds of extrasensory perceptions. The next stage, the *high-subtle self,* has been described by the world's great mystics as the experience of bliss and visions of divine realms. The final stages are the *low-causal self* and the *high-causal self,* portrayed in mystical literature as the highest levels of illumination and spiritual attainment.

Wilber (1995, 1996) views the course of evolution as the ongoing manifestation of Spirit. In the higher stages of spiritual development, Spirit becomes conscious of itself.

Many other transpersonal psychologists have sought to integrate insights and concepts from Asian sources (see, for example, Frager, 1989; Walsh, 1989; as well as Chapters 15 to 17 in this book). Asian psychologies generally focus more on spiritual levels of experience and much less on the pathological. They include maps of states of consciousness, discussions of developmental levels, and stages that extend beyond traditional psychological formulations. Walsh (1989) summarizes the literature on Eastern meditation and related practices as psychotherapeutic.

The Work of Stanislav Grof

Another important transpersonal theorist is Stanislav Grof, a European psychiatrist, who has written extensively on psychedelic research and altered states of consciousness. The mind, Grof (1993) says, can be compared to a hologram. One piece of a hologram retains all the information of the original whole. Grof argues that although we are all separate individuals, our minds contain universal patterns and truths in addition to our personal experience.

Grof (1975, 1993) has described the major characteristics of psychedelic experience. They include transcendence of space and time; transcendence of distinctions between matter, energy, and consciousness; and transcendence of the separation between the individual and the external world.

Grof (1975) has broken down psychedelic experiences into four categories—abstract, psychodynamic, perinatal, and transpersonal.

1. *Abstract experiences,* which are primarily sensory, including the extraordinarily vivid perception of colors or sounds.
2. *Psychodynamic experiences,* in which emotionally charged memories are relived. They also include symbolic experiences similar to dream images.
3. *Perinatal experiences,* which deal with birth and death. Grof discusses four stages of the birth process. The first begins from the time before la-

bor, the developing child resting comfortably in the womb. This stage is associated with a sense of limitlessness and with symbols like the ocean. The second stage, the onset of labor, is associated with anxiety and threat, a sense of being trapped. During the third stage, the fetus moves through the birth canal. This stage is symbolized by struggle for survival, crushing pressure, and a sense of suffocation. The fourth stage is the birth itself, the struggle that finally ends in relief and relaxation. It may include visions of light and beauty, a sense of liberation or salvation, or the experience of death and rebirth.

4. *Transpersonal experiences,* which include the sense of consciousness expanding beyond ego boundaries and beyond space and time. Among other experiences are extrasensory perception, visions of archetypal images, ancestral memories, memories of prior incarnations, or the sense of merging completely with others.

Grof has argued that these four levels are closely interrelated. He has observed that work with psychodynamic memories tends to lead to perinatal and then transpersonal experiences. Conversely, those who have had profound spiritual or transpersonal experiences find it easier to work with psychological issues.

Grof (1988) has developed the techniques of Holotropic Breathwork, which enable individuals to enter states of consciousness similar to psychedelic experiences. Many individuals have reported breathwork experiences that replicate his LSD studies.

Psychosynthesis

Another important transpersonal pioneer is Roberto Assagioli (1971). Assagioli, an Italian psychiatrist who studied with both Freud and Jung, developed the system called *psychosynthesis.*

> The fact that we have spoken of the ordinary self and the profounder Self, must not be taken to mean that there are two separate and independent 'I's, two beings in us. The Self in reality is one. What we call the ordinary self is that small part of the deeper Self that the waking consciousness is able to assimilate in a given moment. . . . It is a reflection of what can become ever more clear and vivid; and it can perhaps someday succeed in uniting itself with its source. (Assagioli in Hardy, 1987, p. 31)

If humanistic science may be said to have any goals beyond sheer fascination with the human mystery and enjoyment of it, these would be to release the individual from external control and to make him less predictable to the observer . . . even though perhaps more predictable to himself. (Maslow, 1966, p. 40)

Assagioli distinguishes two levels of work in psychosynthesis: personal and transpersonal. Personal psychosynthesis focuses on the integration of the personality around the personal self. Transpersonal psychosynthesis involves alignment of the personality with the transpersonal self. Assagioli points out that the self at the personality level is basically a reflection of the transpersonal self.

Evaluation of Transpersonal Psychology

It used to be that the transpersonal realm of human experience was the exclusive domain of the priest, shaman, or spiritual teacher. Today the transpersonal is very much the concern of psychology. When we deal with such human questions as values, meaning, and purpose, we inevitably raise issues of a spiritual, transpersonal nature.

Carl Jung has argued that it is only through the transformation of consciousness that we change and grow.

> All the greatest and most important problems of life are fundamentally insoluble. . . . They can never be solved, but only outgrown. This "outgrowing" proved on further investigation to require a new level of consciousness. Some higher or wider interest appeared on the patient's horizon. (Jung in Jacoby, 1959, p. 302)

As a field, transpersonal psychology is devoted to the study and explication of this process of growth and the investigation of these new levels of consciousness.

The Theory Firsthand

Excerpt from "The Plateau Experience"

The following quotation is taken from the Journal of Transpersonal Psychology. *These are excerpts from a discussion between Maslow and several other psychologists.*

I found that as I got older, my peak experiences became less intense and also became less frequent. In discussing this matter with other people who are getting older, I received this same sort of reaction. My impression is that this may have to do with the aging process. It makes sense because to some extent, I've learned that I've become somewhat afraid of peak experiences because I wonder if my body can stand them. A peak experience can produce great turmoil in the autonomic nervous system; it may be that a decrease in peak experiences is nature's way of protecting the body. . . .

As these poignant and emotional discharges died down in me, something else happened which has come into my consciousness which is a very precious thing. A sort of precipitation occurred of what might be called the sedimentation or the fallout from illuminations, insights, and other life experiences that were very important—tragic experiences included. The result has been a kind of unitive consciousness which has certain advantages and certain disadvantages over the peak experiences. I can define this unitive consciousness very simply for me as the simultaneous perception of the sacred and the ordinary, or the miraculous and the rather constant or easy-without-effort sort of thing.

I now perceive under the aspect of eternity and become mythic, poetic, and symbolic about ordinary things. This is the Zen experience, you know. There is nothing excepted and nothing special, but one lives in a world of miracles all the time. There is a paradox because it is miraculous and yet it doesn't produce an autonomic burst.

This type of consciousness has certain elements in common with peak experience—awe, mystery, surprise, and esthetic shock. These elements are present, but are constant rather than climactic. It certainly is a temptation to use as kind of a model, a paradigm for the peaking experience, the sexual orgasm, which is a mounting up to a peak and a climax, and then a drop in the completion and its ending. Well, this other type of experience must have another model. The words that I would use to describe this kind of experience would be "a high plateau." It is to live at a constantly high level in the sense of illumination or awakening or in Zen, in the easy or miraculous, in the nothing special. It is to take rather casually the poignancy and the preciousness and the beauty of things, but not to make a big deal out of it because it's happening every hour, you know, all the time.

This type of experience has the advantage, in the first place, that it's more voluntary than peak experience. For example, to enter deeply into this type of consciousness, I can go to an art museum or a meadow rather than into a subway. In the plateau experiences, you're not as surprised because they are more volitional than peak experiences. Further, I think you can teach plateau experiences; you could hold classes in miraculousness.

Another aspect I have noticed is that it's possible to sit and look at something miraculous for an hour and enjoy every second of it. On the other hand, you can't have an hour-long orgasm. In this sense, the plateau type of experience is better. It has a great advantage, so to speak, over the climactic, the orgasm, the peak. The descending into a valley, and living on the high plateau doesn't imply this. It is much more casual.

There are some other aspects of this experience. There tends to be more serenity rather than an emotionality. Our tendency is to regard the emotional person as an explosive type. However, calmness must also be brought into one's psychology. We need the serene as well as the poignantly emotional. . . .

The important point that emerges from these plateau experiences is that they're essentially cognitive. As a matter of fact, almost by definition, they represent a witnessing of the world. The plateau experience is a witnessing of reality. It involves seeing the symbolic, or the mythic, the poetic, the transcendent, the miraculous, the unbelievable, all of which I think are part of the real world instead of existing only in the eyes of the beholder.

There is a sense of certainty about plateau experience. It feels very, very good to be able to see the world as miraculous and not merely in the concrete, not reduced only to the behavioral, not limited only to the here and now. You know, if you get stuck in the here and now, that's a reduction.

Well, it's very easy to get sloppy with your words and you can go on about the beauty of the world, but the fact is that these plateau experiences are described quite well in many literatures. This is not the standard description of the acute mystical experience, but the way in which the world looks if the mystic experience really takes. If your mystical experience changes your life, you go about your business as the great mystics did. For example, the great saints could have mystical revelations, but also could run a monastery. You can run a grocery store and pay the bills, but still carry on this sense of witnessing the world in the way you did in the great moments of mystic perception. (Maslow in Krippner, 1972, pp. 112–115)

Chapter Highlights

- For a theory of personality to be considered viable and accurate, the heights as well as the depths that an individual might reach ought to be included. One should investigate the most creative, mature, and well-integrated people to study the upper reaches of psychological health and maturity.

- In the hierarchy of needs, physiological urges (hunger, sleep, sex, etc.) must be met before psychological needs. Basic psychological needs are safety (stability, order), love (belonging), esteem (self-respect, recognition), and self-actualization (development of capacities). Needs emerge from and build on the needs before.
- The hierarchy of needs model suggests that behaviorism, psychoanalysis, humanistic psychology, and transpersonal psychology each have their place and their relevance; no one approach is better than another.
- Deprivation of basic needs (including the need for self-actualization as well as physiological needs) can cause neurosis and maladjustment. The satisfaction of those needs is the only treatment.
- People still feel frustrated, even if all their other needs are met, unless they utilize their talents and capacities and experience self-actualization.
- Self-actualizing people are dedicated to a cause or a vocation, without exception. Commitment to something greater than oneself, and to doing well one's chosen tasks, are two requirements for growth. Major characteristics of self-actualizing people are hard work, courage, creativity, and spontaneity.
- Maslow identified eight behaviors that lead to self-actualization: concentration, growth choices, self-awareness, honesty, judgment, self-development, peak experiences, and lack of ego defenses.
- Being psychology tends to be most applicable to self-actualizers, and peak experiences are generally related to this realm as well. In deficiency cognition, objects are seen only as need fulfillers; in being cognition, perceptions are less likely to be distorted by wants or needs.
- Until the individual is free of the domination of the lower needs, such as for security and esteem, the pursuit of self-actualization cannot begin. The pursuit of higher needs is itself one index of psychological health.
- Growth motivation is less basic than physiological drives or psychological needs for security, esteem, and so forth. Self-actualization may be hindered by negative influences from past experience and resulting poor habits, social pressure and group influence, and inner defenses that keep the individual out of touch with his or her inner self.
- Ego defenses are internal obstacles to growth. To become aware of them and to see clearly how they operate is the first step in dealing with them. It is important, as well, to minimize the distortions they create. Maslow has added desacralization and the Jonah complex to the traditional psychoanalytic listing of defenses.
- According to Maslow, there are possibilities beyond self-actualization. When peak experiences are especially powerful, the sense of self dissolves into an awareness of a greater unity.
- The field of transpersonal psychology acknowledges the importance of the transcendent aspects of human experience. Maslow called this level of awareness the fourth force in Western psychology—after behaviorism, psychoanalysis, and humanistic psychology.

Key Concepts

Being cognition Thinking and perception in which external objects are fully attended to and are seen as having value in and of themselves rather than in relation to one's personal concerns. Being cognition is nonjudgmental, without comparison or evaluation; the fundamental attitude is appreciation of what is.

Being love Love for the "being" or essence of the other. It is nonpossessive and demonstrates the Taoist attitude of noninterference, of letting things be without concern for improvement or change. This type of love can be a trigger for peak experiences.

Being motivation Satisfaction and enjoyment in the present, or the desire to seek a positively valued goal (growth or metamotivation). Curiosity and playfulness are good examples.

Being values Beliefs that are intrinsic to every individual. According to Maslow, the highest values exist within human nature itself. The list includes truth, beauty, wholeness, aliveness, perfection, goodness, uniqueness, simplicity, justice, richness, order, transcendence of dichotomy, necessity, effortlessness, playfulness, completion, and self-sufficiency.

Deficiency cognition A type of thinking and perception in which objects are seen solely as means to ends, as fulfillers of needs, especially when those needs are strong.

Deficiency love Love of others because they fulfill a need. Such love is based on a need for self-esteem, fear of loneliness, and so on.

Deficiency motivation Motivation from frustration or dissatisfaction. It involves a need to change the present state of affairs.

Desacralization The act of impoverishing one's life by the refusal to treat anything with deep concern and seriousness. It may result from a fear of deep emotion.

Eupsychia Ideal, human-oriented communities and societies, composed of psychologically healthy, self-actualizing individuals.

Hierarchy of needs A model of human drives that suggests that basic physiological needs must be met before basic psychological needs can be addressed. Each level of need emerges from the one before. At the top are needs for growth and self-actualization.

Jonah complex The refusal to realize one's full capabilities. It is rooted in the fear of letting go of a familiar but limited existence, of being torn apart, disintegrating, or losing control. The complex may be a major obstacle to self-actualization.

Means-centered A characteristic of individuals who become disproportionately engaged in the techniques or methodology of a project or process, often losing sight of the goals.

Metagrumbles Level of complaints that correspond to the frustration of metaneeds, such as justice, perfection, beauty, truth. These grumbles usually indicate that more basic needs are reasonably well satisfied.

Metamotivation Behavior inspired by growth values and needs. It occurs most commonly among self-actualizing people.

Peak experiences Those exciting, joyous moments when individuals become deeply involved and absorbed in the world. Such experiences are often inspired by intense feelings of love, by the beauty of nature, or by exposure to great art and music.

Physiological needs In Maslow's hierarchy of needs, the most basic human wants. Biological needs for oxygen, food, drink, sleep, and sex are included here.

Plateau experiences A fundamental change in attitude that affects one's entire point of view and creates an intensified awareness and a new appreciation of the world. More stable and longer lasting than a peak experience, it represents a new, more profound way of experiencing and viewing the world.

Problem-centered One of the characteristics of creative people, in which the focus is on the requirements of the desired goals. This approach contrasts with ego-centering (an example of deficiency cognition), in which individuals see what they wish rather than what actually is.

Psychological needs In Maslow's hierarchy, the human drives that cannot be satisfied until the physiological needs are met. Psychological needs include (in this order) safety and security, belonging and love, self-esteem and respect, and self-actualization.

Self-actualization In Maslow's system, an ongoing process in which one's capacities are creatively, joyfully, and fully utilized. It is a way of continually working, living, and relating to the world.

Synergy The combined action of elements that results in a total effect greater than the sum of all the elements taken independently. The word also refers to cooperation among individuals.

Annotated Bibliography

Maslow, A. H. (1968). *Toward a psychology of being* (2nd ed.). New York: Van Nostrand.

Maslow's most popular and widely available book. It includes material on deficiency versus being, growth psychology, creativity, and values.

———. (1971). *The farther reaches of human nature.* New York: Viking Press.

In many ways, Maslow's best book. A collection of articles on psychological health, creativeness, values, education, society, metamotivation, and transcendence; also, a complete bibliography of Maslow's writings.

———. (1987). *Motivation and personality* (3rd ed.). New York: Harper & Row.

A psychology textbook that provides a more technical treatment of Maslow's work, including motivation theory, the needs hierarchy, and self-actualization.

References

Assagioli, R. (1971). *Psychosynthesis.* New York: Viking Press.

Benedict, R. (1970). Synergy: Patterns of the good culture. *American Anthropologist, 72,* 320–333.

Brennan, T., & Piechowski, M. (1991). A developmental framework for self-actualization. *Journal of Humanistic Psychology, 31,* 43–64.

Dabrowski, K. (1967). *Personality shaping through positive disintegration.* Boston: Little, Brown.

Fadiman, J. (1980). The transpersonal stance. In R. Walsh & F. Vaughan (Eds.), *Beyond ego.* Los Angeles: Tarcher.

Frager, R. (1989). Transpersonal psychology: Promise and prospects. In R. Valle & S. Halling (Eds.), *Existential-phenomenological perspectives in psychology.* New York: Plenum Press.

Fuller, A. (1994). *Psychology and religion.* Lanham, MD: Littlefield Adams.

Goble, F. (1971). *The third force: The psychology of Abraham Maslow.* New York: Pocket Books.

Goldstein, K. (1939). *The organism.* New York: American Book.

———. (1940). *Human nature in the light of psychopathology.* New York: Schocken Books.

Gray, S. W. (1986). The relationship between self-actualization and leisure satisfaction. *Psychology, 23,* 6–12.

Grof, S. (1975). *Realms of the human unconscious.* New York: Viking Press.

———. (1988). *Adventures of self-discovery.* New York: State University of New York Press.

———, with H. Bennett. (1993). *The holotropic mind.* New York: HarperCollins.

Hall, M. (1968). A conversation with Abraham Maslow. *Psychology Today, 2*(2), 34–37, 54–57.

Hardy, J. (1987). *A psychology with a soul: Psychosynthesis in evolutionary context.* New York: Routledge & Kegan Paul.

Horner, M. (1972). The motive to avoid success and changing aspirations of college women. In J. Bardwick (Ed.), *Readings on the psychology of women* (pp. 62–67). New York: Harper & Row.

Huxley, A. (1944). *The perennial philosophy.* New York: Harper & Row.

———. (1963). *Island.* New York: Bantam Books.

International Study Project (1972). *Abraham H. Maslow: A memorial volume.* Monterey, CA: Brooks/Cole.

Jacoby, J. (1959). *Complex, archetype, symbol in the psychology of C. G. Jung.* New York: Pantheon.

James, W. (1943). *The varieties of religious experience.* New York: Random House (Modern Library).

Journal of Transpersonal Psychology Editorial Staff (1970). An appreciation. *Journal of Transpersonal Psychology, 2*(2), iv.

Katz, S. T. (1978). Language, epistemology and mysticism. In S. T. Katz (Ed.), *Mysticism and philosophical analysis.* New York: Oxford University Press.

Kelly, R. B., & Chovan, W. (1985). Yet another empirical test of the relationship between self-actualization and moral judgement. *Psychological Reports, 56,* 201–202.

Krippner, S. (Ed.). (1972). The plateau experience: A. H. Maslow and others. *Journal of Transpersonal Psychology, 4,* 107–120.

Kuhn, T. (1962). *The structure of scientific revolutions.* Chicago: University of Chicago Press.

Kunc, N. (1992). The need to belong. In R. Villa, J. Thousand, W. Stainback, & S. Stainback (Eds.), *Restructuring for caring and effective education.* Baltimore: Paul H. Brookes.

Lajoie, D., & Shapiro, S. (1992). Definitions of transpersonal psychology: The first twenty-three years. *Journal of Transpersonal Psychology, 24,* 79–98.

Leonard, G. (1983, December). Abraham Maslow and the new self. *Esquire,* pp. 326–336.

Lowry, R. (1973a). (Ed.). *Dominance, self-esteem, self-actualization: Germinal papers of A. H. Maslow.* Monterey, CA: Brooks/Cole.

———. (1973b). *A. H. Maslow: An intellectual portrait.* Monterey, CA: Brooks/Cole.

Maslow, A. (1948). Higher and lower needs. *Journal of Psychology, 25,* 433–436.

———. (1964). *Religions, values and peak experiences.* Columbus: Ohio State University Press.

———. (1965). *Eupsychian management: A journal.* Homewood, IL: Irwin.

———. (1966). *The psychology of science: A reconnaissance.* New York: Harper & Row.

———. (1968). *Toward a psychology of being* (2nd ed.). New York: Van Nostrand.

———. (1970). *Motivation and personality* (rev. ed.). New York: Harper & Row.

———. (1971). *The farther reaches of human nature.* New York: Viking Press.

———. (1987). *Motivation and personality* (3rd ed.). New York: Harper & Row.

Maslow, A. H., with Chiang H. (1969). *The healthy personality: Readings.* New York: Van Nostrand.

Mathes, E., Zevon, M., Roter, P., & Joerger, S. (1982). Peak experience tendencies. *Journal of Humanistic Psychology, 22,* 92–108.

Metzner, R. (1986). *Opening to inner light.* Los Angeles: Tarcher.

———. (1989). States of consciousness and transpersonal psychology. In R. Valle & S. Halling (Eds.), *Existential-phenomenological perspectives in psychology.* New York: Plenum Press.

Ornstein, R. (1972). *The psychology of consciousness.* New York: Viking Press.

———. (1973). *The nature of human consciousness.* New York: Viking Press.

Piechowski, M. (1978). Self-actualization as a developmental structure: A profile of Antoine de Saint-Exupéry. *Genetic Psychology Monographs, 97,* 181–242.

———. (1990). Inner growth and transformation in the life of Eleanor Roosevelt. *Advanced Developmental Journal, 2,* 35–53.

Piechowsky, M., & Tyska, C. (1982). Self-actualization profile of Eleanor Roosevelt, a presumed nontranscender. *Genetic Psychology Monographs, 105,* 95–153.

Rychman, R. M. (1985). Physical self-efficacy and actualization. *Journal of Research in Personality, 19,* 288–298.

Schott, R. (1992). Abraham Maslow, humanistic psychology, and organization leadership. *Journal of Humanistic Psychology, 32,* 106-120.

Shostrom, E. (1963). *Personal orientation inventory.* San Diego, CA: Edits.

Smith, H. (1976). *Forgotten truth.* New York: Harper & Row.

Sumner, W. (1940). *Folkways.* New York: New American Library.

Sutich, A. (1969). Some considerations regarding transpersonal psychology. *Journal of Transpersonal Psychology 1,* 11–20.

Tart, C. (Ed.). (1969). *Altered states of consciousness.* New York: Wiley.

———. (Ed.). (1975). *Transpersonal psychologies.* New York: Harper & Row.

Timmons, B., & Kamiya, J. (1970). The psychology and physiology of meditation and related phenomena: Bibliography I. *Journal of Transpersonal Psychology, 2,* 41–59.

Timmons, B., & Kanellakos, D. (1974). The psychology and physiology of meditation and related phenomena: Bibliography II. *Journal of Transpersonal Psychology, 6,* 32–38.

Valle, R. (1989). The emergence of transpersonal psychology. In R. Valle & S. Halling (Eds.), *Existential-*

phenomenological perspectives in psychology. New York: Plenum Press.

Vaughan, F. (1995). *Shadows of the sacred.* Wheaton, IL: Theosophical Publishing.

Walsh, R. (1989). Asian psychotherapies. In R. Corsini & D. Wedding (Eds.), *Current psychotherapies* (4th ed.). Itasca, IL: F. E. Peacock.

Walsh, R., & Shapiro, D. (Eds.). (1983). *Beyond health and normality: Explorations of exceptional psychological well being.* New York: Van Nostrand Reinhold.

Walsh, R., & Vaughan, F. (Eds.). (1980). *Beyond ego: Transpersonal dimensions in psychology.* Los Angeles: Tarcher.

———. (1993). (Eds.). *Paths beyond ego: The transpersonal vision.* Los Angeles: Tarcher.

Wilber, K. (1977). *The spectrum of consciousness.* Wheaton, IL: Theosophical Publishing.

———. (1980). *The Atman project.* Wheaton, IL: Quest.

———. (1995). *Sex, ecology, spirituality: The spirit of evolution.* Boston: Shambhala.

———. (1996). *A brief history of everything.* Boston: Shambhala.

Wilson, C. (1972). *New pathways in psychology: Maslow and the post-Freudian revolution.* New York: Mentor Books.

Wilson, S., & Spencer, R. (1990). Intense personal experiences. *Journal of Clinical Psychology, 46,* 565–573.

Wittine, B. (1989). Basic postulates for a transpersonal psychotherapy. In R. Valle & S. Halling (Eds.), *Existential-phenomenological perspectives in psychology.* New York: Plenum Press.

CHAPTER 15

Yoga and the Hindu Tradition

Yoga has two aspects. First, it encompasses virtually all the religious and ascetic practices of India, including meditation, physical discipline, and devotional chanting. Second, Yoga is a specific school of Indian philosophy systematized by Patanjali and first mentioned in India's ancient, 3000-year-old Vedas, the world's oldest recorded literature. The roots of Yoga practice undoubtedly go even farther back to Indian prehistory.

Yoga is a Sanskrit word meaning "to join" or "to unite." The goal of Yoga practice is self-realization, which occurs when consciousness is turned within and united with its source, the Self. One of the classic Yoga authorities has written, "Yoga is *samadhi* (ecstasy) [or illumination]" (Feuerstein, 1989). Yoga also means "method." It embraces both the goal of union and the wide variety of yogic techniques meant to accomplish this end. In this sense, Yoga is the technology of self-realization or ecstasy.

In its broadest sense, Yoga embraces all systematic disciplines designed to promote self-realization by calming the mind and focusing consciousness on the Self, the immortal, unchanging essence in all people.

History

The roots of Yoga are ancient, going all the way back to the pre-Hindu culture of India. Yoga is an integral part of the rich and complex Hindu tradition, which encompasses hundreds of different traditions and sacred texts. These are all connected with the Vedas.

The Vedic Period

The Vedas were originally an oral transmission, handed down from teacher to disciple for many centuries. The earliest Vedas date back to 2500 B.C. There are four major sections of the Vedas. The oldest section consists of the Vedic hymns, which include the most sophisticated philosophy. The second section deals with rituals and sacrifices; perfect performance of long and complex rituals was believed essential to ensure good fortune. The third section, on contemplation and inner truth, comprises the forest treatises, written for forest-dwelling ascetics. The last section contains the *Upanishads*, or the *Vedanta*, literally "the end of the Vedas," which discuss the goal of knowing the Self. The Vedas form the basis of all subsequent Indian thought and philosophy.

Lead me from the unreal to the real. From darkness lead me to light. From death lead me to immortality. (*Brihadaranyaka Upanishad*, I:iii, 28)

In the Vedic period, Yoga was closely related to shamanism (Eliade, 1969). Early yogis placed great value on mastery of ecstatic trance and supernatural powers through the practice of severe austerities. They believed that individuals could, through superhuman self-discipline and self-mortification, compel the Hindu gods to fulfill their requests. The exercise of austerities and self-control has remained a major part of Yoga practice to this day.

Personal Reflection

■ Austerities

General Principles

The simplest, most direct, and most difficult practice of austerity is to give up satisfying your desires—for example, if you desire food, then you should fast. If you love to sleep, make yourself do with less. Giving up small pleasures and comforts can be an important self-discipline. If you usually get up at 8:00 A.M., try getting up at 6:00 or 7:00 every morning. If you like sleeping on a soft, comfortable bed, start sleeping on a thin mattress on the floor.

There are important cautions in this kind of practice. Austerities can have the side effect of strengthening pride and egotism. Pride in your accomplishments, pride in suffering, or masochistic enjoyment of austerities for their own sake are all indications of ego involvement. Another thing to watch for is excessive austerity. This is also a demonstration of ego and may actually cause you mental or physical harm.

Fasting

Short periods of fasting are an excellent practice of austerity. You can begin simply by deliberately missing one or two meals. A one-day fast is not too difficult for anyone in good health. Drink plenty of water, and drink orange juice if you feel the need for additional nourishment. Fasting for one day a week is an excellent practice. When you fast, you are confronted with the need to overcome temptation and to set your will against the desire for food.

Silence

Silence is another traditional practice. Try remaining silent for a few hours at home or around friends who understand your intention. Or spend a day in silence. Carry paper and pencil with you to communicate in writing if necessary. Observe yourself and others, as well as your reactions to conversations. Try to overcome your need to communicate actively. Learn just to *be,* in silence.

The *Bhagavad-Gita*

The *Bhagavad-Gita* (Mascaro, 1962) is the first and also the most popular work on Yoga. It is a part of the great Indian epic of the second century B.C. called *Mahabharata,* a magnificent collection of mythology, religion, ethics, and customs. It is about 100,000 stanzas long, almost eight times the length of the *Iliad* and the *Odyssey* combined. Yoga and related philosophies are key to the ideas discussed in the epic.

The *Mahabharata* revolves around the story of the five Pandava brothers, their upbringing, education, and many adventures. The *Bhagavad-Gita* can be read as a single great metaphor for the spiritual quest. According to some interpreters, the characters in the *Bhagavad-Gita* represent various psychological

He who works not for an earthly reward, but does the work to be done . . . he is a Yogi. (*Bhagavad-Gita,* VI:1)[1]

and physical qualities. The five brothers are the five senses, and the battlefield is the body and the consciousness of the individual.

The *Bhagavad-Gita* is a dialogue between Arjuna (the ego) and Krishna (the Self). Arjuna is a warrior, and Krishna, his charioteer, is an incarnation of God and a great spiritual teacher. Krishna discusses duty and the Yoga of action. He teaches Arjuna the importance of devotion, self-control, meditation, and other yogic practices, to serve as an example for others. As charioteer, Krishna symbolizes the *guru,* or spiritual teacher, who can help bring students to terms with the problems and conflicts they encounter in the process of spiritual development. However, the guru, like the charioteer, cannot fight the students' battles for them.

The following are some of the descriptions of Yoga from the *Bhagavad-Gita:*

> For the sage who desires to ascend in Yoga, action is stated to be the means. For him who has ascended in Yoga, serenity is said to be the means. (VI:3)

> When he does not cling to the sense-objects or to deeds and has renounced all desires, then he is called "one who has ascended in Yoga." (VI:4)

> When he has controlled the mind and is established in the Self only, devoid of all desires, then he is said to be a "yoked one." (VI:18)

The *Bhagavad-Gita* includes classic teachings on karma-yoga, the Yoga of action. Krishna advocates action without attachment over inaction and renunciation. The mind is the primary source of all action. The ideal is to develop a pure mind that is without attachment. Then your whole life becomes a continual Yoga.

> You must [always] do the allotted action, for action is superior to inaction; not even your body's processes can be accomplished by inaction. (III:8)

> Just as the unwise perform [their deeds] attached to action, O Bharata [Krishna], the wise should act unattached, desiring the world's welfare. (III:25)

The Classical Period

The classical era lasted from A.D. 200 until A.D. 800. It was the time of the development of six classical schools of Hindu thought: Mimamsa (the philosophy of ritualism), Nyaya (the school of logic), Vaisheshika (naturalistic philosophy), Vedanta (nondualistic metaphysics), Samkya (dualistic philosophy), and Yoga.

Vedanta, Samkya, and Yoga are the most influential schools today. There are strong links between Yoga and the other two. Vedanta teaches nondualism, which describes Reality as a single, indivisible whole. The major Vedanta philosophers also practiced various forms of Yoga for their own spiritual development.

Samkya is mainly concerned with understanding and describing various levels of existence. The goal is not so much to explain the world as to help tran-

[1]Quotes from the *Bhagavad-Gita* are taken from Mascaro (1962), Prabhavananda and Isherwood (1951), and Feuerstein (1989).

scend it by developing discrimination. Samkya and Yoga metaphysics are closely related, and in fact the two stem from the same earlier, preclassical tradition.

As one of the six schools of philosophy, Yoga refers to the work of Patanjali, scholar of the second-century B.C. and author of at least part of the *Yoga Sutras*. The major difference between Samkya and Yoga is their methodologies. Samkya stresses discrimination and renunciation. Yoga emphasizes the necessity of experiencing ecstatic states of consciousness (*samadhi*) that bring deep insight into oneself and the world. Patanjali's approach to Yoga is the main focus of this chapter.

Major Concepts

This section opens with a discussion of basic yogic metaphysical and psychological concepts—Spirit and Nature, the three principles of creation, consciousness, karma, and subconscious tendencies. Specific aspects of the yogic path are described in the sections on the guru, initiation, and schools of Yoga.

Spirit

In classical Yoga, there is a strict dualism between Spirit and Nature. Every human being is a combination of these two principles. Body and mind come from Nature, and the transcendental Self comes from Spirit. Spirit (*Purusha*) is pure consciousness. Spirit knows no limitations or qualifications. Spirit includes consciousness within and beyond the universe; the manifestation of Spirit in the individual is the Self. The Self is changeless, unaffected by physical or mental activity; however, the mind distorts our awareness of the Self.

The whole universe is filled by the Purusha (Spirit), to whom there is nothing superior, from whom there is nothing different, than whom there is nothing either smaller or greater; who stands alone, motionless as a tree, established in His own glory. (*Svetasvatara Upanishad,* III:9)

The opposite pole to Spirit is Nature (*Prakriti*). In Sanskrit, *Prakriti* means "that which brings forth" (the word is related to *procreate*). Nature is the ground from which all material forms spring. It is also the source of all nonmaterial forms, including thoughts and emotions. Nature is, like Spirit, eternal and unchanging.

The transcendental **Self** in each individual is Spirit in essence. The Self is like a wave, a form that the ocean takes on for a time. The Self is pure awareness, pure consciousness. The goal of yoga is Self-realization—by uncovering of the Self that is hidden by our identification with the forms generated by Nature, including the body and the subtle forms such as mind and emotions.

In the words of one of the great Indian sages, "Everyone is the Self and, indeed, is infinite. Yet each person mistakes his body for his Self" (Ramana Maharshi in Osbourne, 1962, p. 23).

The ideal of Yoga is to seek joy from its source—the Self within. Most people look to the world for pleasure, never realizing that the source of greatest joy is found in the Self, which lies within them. One Indian parable concerns the musk deer, whose musk glands become active when the mature deer enters the mating season. The deer is so taken with this entrancing scent that it often runs through the forest, seeking the source of the odor. The frenzied deer can lose all sense of direction and become entangled in underbrush or even plunge off a cliff. Frantically seeking the musk without, the deer will never discover the source of the odor, which is within itself.

To the seer, all things have verily become the Self: what delusion, what sorrow, can there be for him who beholds that oneness? (*Isa Upanishad,* 7)

Three Principles of Creation

Nature (*Prakriti*) has three primary constituents, or principles, the three *gunas: tamas* (inertia), *rajas* (activity), and *sattva* (clarity or light). These three principles function together to generate all activity. All the various manifestations of Nature (matter, thought, and so forth) are composed of different combinations of the three *gunas.*

In the process of creating a statue, for example, tamas can be seen in the untouched, inert stone. Rajas is the act of carving, and sattva is the image in the sculptor's imagination. All three are essential. Pure tamas alone is inert, dead matter. Pure rajas is energy without direction or goal. Pure sattva is a plan that remains unrealized.

Every individual exhibits some balance among these three qualities, although most people are dominated by one of them. Sattva is considered the most spiritual. Virtually everything can be classified in terms of the *gunas.* Rich or heavy foods are tamasic, because they are difficult to digest and cause laziness or sleepiness. Spicy, hot foods are rajasic, since they lead to activity, strong emotions, or nervousness. Fresh fruit and vegetables are sattvic and promote calmness. Certain places, such as mountains and the ocean shore, are sattvic and thus suitable for spiritual practice.

Consciousness

The mind is like a miraculous rubber band that can be expanded to infinity without breaking. (Yogananda, 1968a)

In Yoga terminology, mind, or consciousness (*chitta*), embraces all thought processes. Patanjali defines Yoga as "controlling the activities of the mind." Control stops the incessant "chatter" of mental activity and brings about a state of deep calm and inner peace. Yoga is the complete focusing of attention on whatever object is contemplated. The final goal is to focus attention on the Self. When mental processes, or waves of consciousness, are active, the Self is obscured, like a bright light suspended in churning water.

All Yoga practices work toward one end: to quiet the waves and calm the mind. Some schools of Yoga focus on control of the body and others on breathing techniques; still others teach meditation practices. In a sense, all the Yoga techniques and practices are only preliminary exercises designed to still the mind. Once mind and body are calm and disciplined, awareness of the Self is possible.

Karma

Before you act, you have freedom, but after you act, the effect of that action will follow you whether you want it to or not. That is the law of *karma.* You are a free agent, but when you perform a certain act, you will reap the results of that act. (Yogananda, 1968b)

Karma means action and also its results. The idea is based on the principle that every activity brings with it certain consequences, and every individual's life is influenced by past actions. This influence occurs in part through the creation of subconscious tendencies, in the sequence shown in Figure 15.1.

In order to avoid the formation of new subconscious tendencies or the strengthening of old ones, the yogi refrains from "acting out." In other words, anger tendencies are strengthened by angry thoughts and feelings and reinforced further by angry speech and actions. The yogic ideal is not suppression

FIGURE 15.1 Karma and Its Effects

of unacceptable tendencies but transmutation of negative action and thought into positive action and thought. One effective way of dealing with strong emotions is to look calmly and deeply at their roots. Inner awareness can transform subsequent thoughts and feelings. Through self-discipline, right action, and Yoga practice, the individual gradually changes his or her consciousness, transmuting old habits and thought patterns. The yogi learns to substitute positive, constructive actions for old, destructive habits. The results of long-term, positive change in action are positive alterations in subconscious tendencies, followed by transformation of consciousness (see Figure 15.1).

Subconscious Tendencies

Control of the waves of consciousness is possible only when the subconscious tendencies are diminished. Such tendencies (*samskaras*) shape mental activity. These subconscious patterns are created by past actions and experiences, from this life and from past lives. Tendencies are built up by the continued action of thought waves or waves of consciousness. For example, anger waves of consciousness gradually create anger tendencies, which predispose the individual to angry reactions.

You cannot achieve emancipation unless you have burned the seeds of past actions in the fires of wisdom and meditation. (Yogananda, 1968a, p. 110)

The discipline of Yoga must include a *complete* reformation of consciousness. Otherwise, the subconscious tendencies will seek to actualize themselves, sprouting suddenly like dormant seeds. Through meditation, self-analysis, and other powerful inner disciplines, it is possible to "roast" such seeds, to destroy their potential for further activity; that is, through fundamental inner change we can grow free of the influence of the past.

In this theory of the subconscious tendencies, Yoga anticipated by many centuries the modern notion of the unconscious. Further, Yoga has gone beyond the insights and goals of most schools of psychotherapy in developing techniques for complete transformation of the unconscious.

The Guru

The word *guru* comes from the Sanskrit root "to uplift." Many teachers in India are called gurus; the name connotes a spiritual teacher, one who can raise the student's consciousness. (In India, teachers of music, dance, and other traditional skills do more than instruct students in technique; they are considered masters of disciplines that affect one's whole life and character.) In Yoga a guru is thought to be essential for several reasons. The techniques taught are complex and subtle and cannot be learned from books. Also, many techniques have to be adapted by the teacher to the specific physical and mental makeup of the student.

Religion, which is the highest knowledge and the highest wisdom, cannot be bought, nor can it be acquired from books. . . . You will not find it anywhere until your heart is ready for receiving it and your teacher has come. (Vivekananda, 1978a, pp. 35–36)

The guru is a disciplinarian, who pushes the student beyond self-imposed limitations. As one who has been through the discipline already, the guru knows from experience the extent of human capacity. Thus the guru demands that students exert themselves to the limits of their capabilities. In addition, students are inspired by their teacher's living example to realize their highest potential.

A beautiful example of one role of the guru is found in the *Bhagavad-Gita*. In the great battle, Krishna, the guru, is Arjuna's charioteer. Krishna does not fight but leads Arjuna from battle to battle, testing and strengthening his disciple. At one point, a great enemy warrior throws a magic spear that can pass through all obstacles. Knowing that Arjuna cannot cope with this weapon, Krishna causes the wheels of their chariot to sink deep into the ground, so that the dreaded missile passes overhead. In this way, the guru brings the disciple from spiritual trial to spiritual trial, intervening only when the test is too great for the disciple's capabilities.

"Gurus can be had by hundreds and thousands, but Chelas (disciples) there is not one" is an ancient saying. It means that many are the persons who can give good advice, but those who follow it are few. (Ramakrishna, 1965, p. 328)

The guru also fosters the student's emotional and psychological development. The teacher is like a mirror, exposing faults and limitations of the student, but always remaining conscious of the essential purity and perfection of the Self behind such limitations. This kind of discipline can be administered only by someone who is relatively free of ego and strong personal biases or blind spots, which would distort the guru's reactions to the student.

In India the guru's most important attribute is spiritual consciousness. A teacher who has realized the Self transmits a sense of inner peace and bliss. Yogananda describes this kind of inspiration, which he received in his guru's presence: "If I entered the hermitage in a worried or indifferent frame of mind, my attitude imperceptibly changed. A healing calm descended at the mere sight of my guru. Each day with him was a new experience in joy, peace, and wisdom" (1972, pp. 137–138).

Vivekananda points out that the guru teaches from his or her state of being:

> If a man wants to teach me something of dynamics, of chemistry, or any other physical science, he may be anything he likes, because what the physical sciences require is merely an intellectual equipment; but in the spiritual sciences it is impossible from first to last that there can be any spiritual light in the soul that is impure. . . . Hence with the teacher of religion we must see first what he *is*, and then what he says. He must be perfectly pure, and then alone comes the value of his words, because he is only then the true "transmitter." What can he transmit, if he has not spiritual power in himself? . . . The function of the teacher is indeed an affair of the transference of something, and not one of mere stimulation of the existing intellectual or other faculties in the taught. Something real and appreciable as an influence comes from the teacher and goes to the taught. Therefore the teacher must be pure. . . .
>
> The teacher must not teach with any ulterior selfish motive—for money, name, or fame; his work must be simply out of love, out of pure love for mankind at large. The only medium through which spiritual force can be transmitted is love. . . . God is love, and only he who has known

> God as love, can be a teacher of godliness and God to man. (Vivekananda, 1978a, pp. 32–33)

One of the later Yoga texts, the *Kularnava-Tantra,* classifies six different types of gurus, according to basic function (Feuerstein, 1989). A teacher generally is a composite of several of these: (1) the *Impeller* motivates and inspires the prospective disciple, leading him or her to initiation; (2) the *Indicator* prescribes the most appropriate form of spiritual practice and discipline; (3) the *Explainer* interprets and clarifies the spiritual process and its goal; (4) the *Revealer* clarifies the details of the process; (5) the *Teacher* supervises the disciple's spiritual discipline; and (6) the *Illuminator* kindles in the disciple mental and spiritual understanding.

One great danger in the role of the guru is ego inflation. Feuerstein, a scholar of yoga, points out that although enlightened yogis may live out of the identity of the Self, their personalities are still intact (1993). He suggests that integration of the personality is a necessary complement to transcendence for any guru.

Initiation

Many authorities maintain that initiation is a crucial element in Yoga practice. According to *Kularnava-Tantra,* self-realization is not possible without initiation, and there can be no real initiation without a qualified guru (Feuerstein, 1989).

Initiation is primarily a form of spiritual transmission. The disciple is changed physically, mentally, and spiritually through the guru's transmission of spiritual energy. It also creates a special bond between guru and disciple. The disciple enters the guru's spiritual lineage, a chain that may go back unbroken for centuries.

Schools of Yoga

Several major schools of Yoga emerged in India, each suiting a particular personality. For example, *Karma-yoga,* the Yoga of action, is especially appropriate for those who possess a strong will or those who need to develop their will as their next stage of growth; it is also chosen by those who hold service to others as a central ideal. *Jnana-yoga,* the Yoga of knowledge, benefits those with keen minds and provides an essential discipline for those who need to develop discrimination. *Bhakti-yoga,* the Yoga of devotion, is ideal for those with a strongly emotional nature. *Hatha-yoga* is for individuals with strong self-discipline and interest in developing physical mastery. *Kundalini-yoga* generally involves meditative techniques most suited to those with potential for subtle awareness of inner processes. *Raja-yoga* fits those with the potential for deep concentration and mental control.

> My own temperament is principally devotional. It was disconcerting at first to find that my *guru,* saturated with *jnana* but seemingly dry of *bhakti,* expressed himself chiefly in terms of cold spiritual mathematics. But, as I attuned myself to his nature, I discovered no diminution but rather an increase in my devotional approach to God. A Self-realized master is fully

> able to guide his various disciples along the natural lines of their essential bias. (Yogananda, 1972, p. 145)

A sophisticated teacher may prescribe a particular form of Yoga practice that builds on a disciple's strengths or assign a specific practice that calls forth underdeveloped attributes. Less sophisticated teachers will simply assign their own practices, without considering individual differences.

Everything we do, physical or mental, is karma, and it leaves its marks on us. (Vivekananda, 1978b, pp. 3–4)

Karma-yoga, the Yoga of Action Karma-yoga teaches us to act selflessly, without attachment to gain or loss, success or failure. The karma-yogi seeks to serve other people, as well as to act according to high ideals. Learning to overcome one's selfishness, laziness, and pride demands considerable discipline.

Swami Vivekananda writes:

> This is the one central idea in the *Gita:* Work incessantly, but be not attached to it. . . . God is unattached because He loves; that real love makes us unattached. . . . To attain this nonattachment is almost a life work. But as soon as we have reached this point we have attained the goal of love and become free. (1978b, pp. 38, 45–46)

Karma-yoga can be an important discipline for all cultures—for those who live in secluded caves in the Himalayas as well as for those who have jobs and families. As long as we are alive, we must act. We all can learn to act well.

Offer all thy works to God, throw off selfish bonds, and do thy work. No sin can then stain thee, even as waters do not stain the leaf of the lotus. (*Bhagavad-Gita,* V:10)

The practitioner of karma-yoga need not believe in a particular religious doctrine, or even in God or Spirit. The karma-yogi is transformed by developing selflessness through service rather than through ostensible religious discipline.

Jnana-yoga, the Yoga of Knowledge Jnana-yoga, the Yoga of knowledge, is a discipline of rigorous self-analysis, a path for those endowed with a clear, refined intellect. It is basically a path of discrimination. The jnana-yogi seeks to understand the forces of delusion and bondage and to counter or avoid the influences of passion, sense attachment, and identification with the body.

This yogi is a true philosopher, a sage who wants to go beyond the visible, beyond the fleeting things of this world.

> Not even the teaching of thousands of books will satisfy him. Not even all the sciences will satisfy him; at the best, they only bring this little world before him. . . . His very soul wants to go beyond all that into the very heart of Being, by seeing Reality as It is; by realizing It, by being It, by becoming one with that Universal Being. (Vivekananda, 1976, p. 395)

Self-scrutiny, relentless observance of one's thoughts, is a stark and shattering experience. It pulverizes the stoutest ego. But, true self-analysis mathematically operates to produce seers. (Yogananda, 1972, p. 51)

Ramana Maharshi (1879–1950) is regarded by many as India's greatest modern sage and exemplar of jnana-yoga. He taught his followers a technique called *Self-Inquiry,* or *vicara,* for regaining identification with the Self. It is a method of continuously inquiring "Who am I?" and looking beyond the body, the thoughts, and emotions for the source of consciousness. Some of the flavor of this approach can be seen in Maharshi's responses to questions.

> "How is one to realize the Self?"
> "Whose Self? Find out."
> "Mine; but, who am I?"

"It is you who must find out."
"I don't know."
"Just think over the question, Who is it that says: 'I don't know'?"
"Who is the 'I' in your statement? What is not known? Why was I born?"
"Who was born? The answer is the same to all your questions."
"However much I may try, I do not seem to catch the *I* [italics added]. It is not even clearly discernible."
"Who is it that says that the 'I' is not discernible? Are there two 'I's' in you, that one is not discernible to the other?"
(Osbourne, 1962, pp. 121–122)

Ramana Maharshi stressed self-realization as the task of removing delusional understanding, not as a matter of acquiring something new. "Once the false notion 'I am the body' or 'I am not realized' has been removed, Supreme Consciousness or the Self alone remains and in people's present state of knowledge they call this 'Realization.' But the truth is that Realization is eternal and already exists, here and now" (Osbourne, 1962, p. 23 [see also Figure 15.2]).

By steady and continuous investigation into the nature of the mind, the mind is transformed into that to which "I" refers; and that is in fact the Self. (Ramana Maharshi in Osbourne, 1962, p. 113)

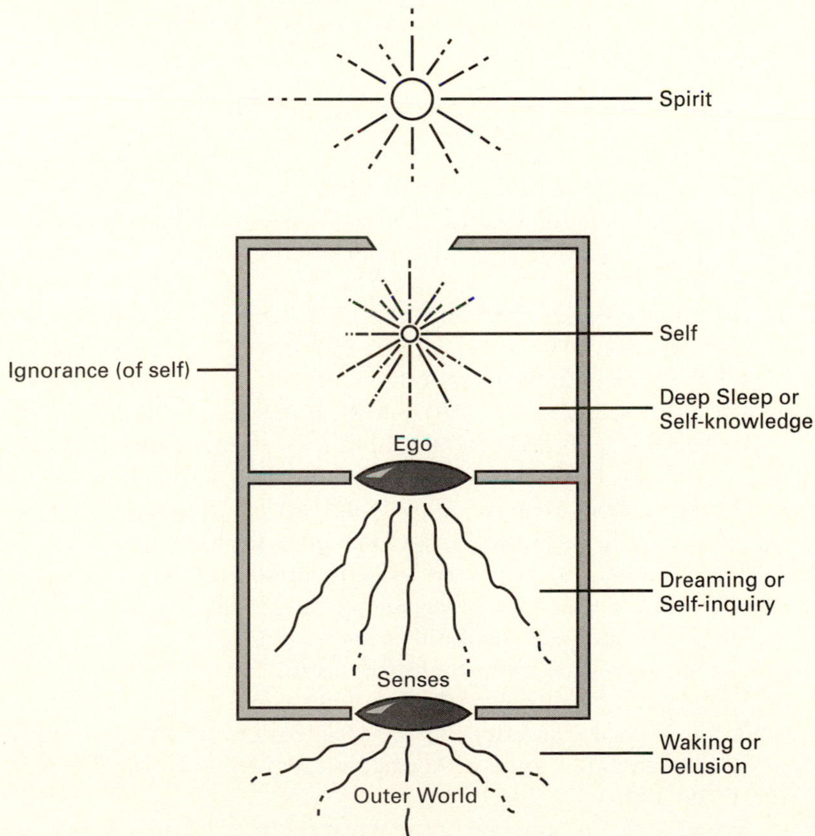

FIGURE 15.2 A Jnana-yoga Model of the Self and Consciousness

Source: Adapted from Osbourne, 1969, pp. 23–24.

The individual seeks the Self by discarding, through intelligent discrimination, all that is not the Self, all that is limiting, perishable, or illusory.

If you must be mad, be it not for the things of the world. Be mad with the love of God. (Ramakrishna, 1965, p. 187)

Bhakti-yoga, the Yoga of Devotion **Bhakti-yoga** is a way of reforming one's personality through the development of love and devotion. Its proponents argue that this simple path is most suitable to the modern era, in which few people have the time and discipline to pursue fully the other traditional paths of Yoga.

Followers of bhakti-yoga use intense devotion to concentrate the mind and transform the personality. It is easier for most people to love God personified in human form than to love abstract Spirit or consciousness. The practice of devotional Yoga is closer to traditional religion than any other form of Yoga. It includes ritual worship, chanting, and the worship of God. The great incarnations of God, such as Rama and Krishna, are a common focus of devotion in some parts of India, and the Goddess Kali, or the Divine Mother, in others.

He is the nearest of the near, the dearest of the dear. Love Him as a miser loves money, as an ardent man loves his sweetheart, as a drowning person loves breath. When you yearn for God with intensity, He will come to you. (Yogananda, 1968a, p. 1)

Long sessions of spiritual chanting typically form an important part of traditional Indian religious practice as well as a basic bhakti-yoga practice. A spiritual chant is "a song born out of the depths of true devotion to God and continuously chanted, audibly or mentally, until response is consciously received from Him in the form of boundless joy" (Yogananda, 1963, p. xiii). Chants are often simple and repetitive, inspiring concentration on one aspect of the Divine. Chanting practices can also help channel emotions, develop single-pointed concentration, and energize mind and body.

Hatha-yoga is a system of health and hygiene involving both body and mind. It aims at the whole man for his full development and self-realization. It takes into account not only the proper growth, strength and tone of the different muscles of the body but also the efficiency and function of the basic factors of constitutional health, namely, the inner organs and the glands. (Majumdar, 1964, p. 99)

Hatha-yoga, the Yoga of the Body The practices of **hatha-yoga** are designed to purify and strengthen the body for advanced meditation and higher states of consciousness. Enlightenment is a whole-body event. Through hatha-yoga, the disciple seeks to manifest the infinite Self in the finite body-mind.

The body is seen as a vehicle for vital energies, or *pranas*. Hatha-yoga disciplines strengthen these energies and bring control of them, enhancing physical, mental, and spiritual activity. Certain postures are intended to keep the body limber, exercise the spine, stimulate various nerves and organs, and increase breathing capacity. According to Yoga physiology, all functions require vital energy. The more energy that is available, the healthier and more effective is the individual.

Practice of yoga **asanas,** or postures, is only part of hatha-yoga. In fact, most hatha-yoga taught in the United States is more a form of gymnastics for physical health than a complete system of Yoga. In addition to postures, classical hatha-yoga includes strict celibacy, vegetarian diet, breathing and concentration exercises, and techniques for washing and cleansing the nasal passages and the entire alimentary canal, from the throat to the intestines. These disciplines form an integrated psychospiritual technology whose purpose is to move the practitioner toward self-realization. As the yogi masters postures, he or she is able to sit for long periods of time without physical discomfort, which would interfere with meditation.

The first principle behind the practice of Yoga postures is to accustom the body to a given pose and then gradually lengthen the time in that posture. In various postures, pressure is taken off some parts of the body and intensified in others, blood flow is increased to certain body parts, and organs are stretched

Yogi in Hatha-yoga posture

or compressed. Combinations of postures can provide balanced stimulation for the entire body. Many people in India practice routines of 15 to 20 postures daily. A given posture may have several variations, each designed to exercise different muscles or different organs. It is best to study hatha-yoga under a qualified teacher, who can correct major mistakes and also provide individualized instruction suited to a person's specific build and other physical characteristics.

Each of the classic asanas has many levels of significance. There are various physical benefits, including flexibility, strength, balance, and stimulation of the endocrine and other organ systems. Each posture also has psychological and spiritual benefits. Swami Radha's *Hatha Yoga: The Hidden Language* (1987) explains these various levels of significance for the most common classical postures.

One of the main aims of hatha-yoga is to purify and strengthen the body as a vehicle for vital energies. There are five major forms of vital energy discussed in the *Upanishads,* the ancient Indian scriptures; they are respiration, digestion, elimination, circulation, and crystallization. These and other vital energies flow through subtle channels in the body, known as *nadis.* Many hatha-yoga practices are designed to open and purify the *nadis,* which become clogged as a result of faulty diet and unhealthy living patterns. Hatha-yoga includes teachings on diet and fasting as well as breathing techniques for promoting energy flow in

Personal Reflection

■ The Corpse Pose

This pose is designed for deep relaxation. It is practiced when the yogi has completed a series of postures or when he or she desires to relax. It is best to practice on a thick carpet or pad.

Lie on your back with your arms resting on the floor, palms up. Close your eyes and consciously relax every part of your body, starting with the feet. Feel your body sinking into the floor as you relax. Imagine that you have abandoned your body completely so that it lies perfectly limp, detached from your mind. Observe your body as if you were outside of it. Observe your breath as it flows in and out, without any attempt to control it. After some time, gradually lengthen your breathing and make it rhythmical. Practice from 10 to 20 minutes.

the body. *Prana* means "breath" and "vital energy" in Sanskrit. In India, and in many other cultures as well, the two are seen as closely connected.

There are other methods of purifying the body in hatha-yoga, including techniques for washing and cleansing the nasal passages and the digestive system, and exercises for the muscles of the stomach and internal organs. Practitioners of hatha-yoga believe that psychospiritual development and growth in consciousness is possible only when the body has become transformed in order to handle higher states of consciousness.

Through hatha-yoga practice, one may develop great mental and physical abilities. However, without mental and spiritual discipline, these abilities can be used to feed the ego. One authority commented that the followers of hatha-yoga he had met "had great powers, strong healthy bodies and immense vanity . . . some more worldly than average worldly men" (Purohit, 1938, p. 30). One of the authors met a yogi of this type in India. The yogi had been a subject of considerable physiological research, demonstrating extraordinary control over his brain waves, heartbeat, and other bodily functions. However, at a major conference on Yoga, the man insisted on challenging all the other yogis present to demonstrate "scientifically" their mastery of Yoga and to determine who was the "greatest yogi."

Mantra-yoga, the Yoga of Sound A **mantra** is a sacred phrase or syllable, charged with psychospiritual power. In **mantra-yoga,** these sacred sounds are used to attain a one-pointed meditative state and to transform the individual's consciousness. According to Indian metaphysics, the universe is in constant vibration. Correct repetition of a mantra will attune the individual to that cosmic vibration.

The most important mantra in Vedic chanting was *om,* which is said to be the basic level of vibration in the universe. Om is still the most widely recognized and most frequently used mantra in India.

Personal Reflection

■ Meditation Exercises

Heartbeat

Sit with spine erect and body relaxed. Close your eyes and sink your mind into the depths of your heart. Become aware of your heart bubbling with life-giving blood, and keep your attention on your heart until you feel its rhythmic beat. With every heartbeat, feel the pulse of infinite life throbbing through you. Picture that same all-pervading life flowing through all other human beings and in billions of other creatures. Open your heart, body, mind, and feelings to receive more fully that universal life.

Expanding Love

Sit erect with eyes closed. Expand your realm of love, long limited by your love for the body and identification with your body. With the love you have given to the body, love all those who love you. With the expanded love of all those who love you, love all those who are close to you. With the love for yourself and for your own, love those who are strangers. Extend your love to those who do not love you as well as those who do love you. Bathe all beings in your selfless love. See your family, friends, all people, all beings in the sea of your love.

Peace

Sit erect, with eyes closed. Look inwardly between the eyebrows at a shoreless lake of peace. Observe the waves of peace expanding, spreading from the eyebrows to the forehead, from the forehead to the heart, and on to every cell in your body. As you watch, the lake of peace deepens and overflows your body, inundating the vast territory of your mind. The flood of peace flows over the boundaries of your mind and moves on in infinite directions.

(Adapted from Yogananda, 1967)

Traditionally, the disciple receives a mantra during an initiation ritual. Some authorities claim that the only real and effective mantras are sounds that have been received in this way. For yogis who have not received initiation, om and other sacred sounds are not truly mantras; therefore, repeating them will not be effective (Feuerstein, 1989).

It is not your passing inspirations or brilliant ideas so much as your everyday mental habits that control your life. (Yogananda, 1968b)

Laya-yoga, the Yoga of Meditation The goal of **laya-yoga** is to become totally absorbed in a state of meditation. According to one scholar, "Laya-Yoga can be understood as the higher, meditative phase of Hatha-Yoga" (Feuerstein, 1989, p. 62). Through intense contemplation, the mind gradually becomes dissolved in transcendent self-realization.

Kundalini-yoga, the Yoga of Energy The term *kundalini* means "she who is coiled." According to Yoga physiology, a subtle energy known as kundalini lies coiled at the base of the spine. All energies of mind and body are manifestations of kundalini energy, which can be consciously controlled by an accomplished yogi.

This energy is generally latent. It begins to flow freely as a result of the disciplines of **kundalini-yoga,** including meditation, visualization, breathing exercises, and the purification techniques of hatha-yoga. Once fully active, kundalini energy rises through all the levels of consciousness, leading to major physical, psychological, and spiritual changes in the individual. The psychiatrist Lee Sanella (1987) has developed a neurophysiological model that explains the kundalini process as a transformation of the electromagnetic fields of the body. Jung has discussed in detail the relationship between kundalini yoga, the chakras, and his approach to psychology (Shamdasani, 1996).

In a classic account of kundalini awakening, Gopi Krishna (1971) writes:

> Suddenly, with a roar like that of a waterfall, I felt a stream of liquid light entering my brain through the spinal cord.
>
> Entirely unprepared for such a development, I was completely taken by surprise, but regaining self-control instantaneously, I remained sitting in the same posture, keeping my mind on the point of concentration. The illumination grew brighter and brighter, the roaring louder, I experienced a rocking sensation and then felt myself slipping out of my body, entirely enveloped in a halo of light. (pp. 12–13)

Kundalini awakening occurs spontaneously in a surprising number of individuals. Some have engaged in meditation or other Yoga practices, while others have not (Greenwell, 1990; Kieffer, 1996; Ramaswami, 1989).

The Three Energy Channels There are three energy channels that run along the spine, through seven consciousness centers called **chakras.** The central channel is the *sushumna,* which is also the path for the ascending kundalini. To the left lies *ida* and to the right lies the *pingala* channel. They are represented by the moon and the sun. These two channels wind around the *sushumna* in a helical pattern (see Figure 15.3).

In most people, their **prana,** or vital energy, flows primarily in *ida* and *pingala,* as their attention is externalized. Through meditation and other inwardly focused disciplines, the yogi brings more and more energy into *sushumna.* This stimulates the dormant kundalini energy, which then rushes upward through the *sushumna* channel, leading to a state of *samadhi,* or illumination. Stimulating the kundalini energy with *prana* is like bombarding an atomic nucleus with high-energy particles in order to trigger a nuclear reaction (Feuerstein, 1989).

As kundalini reaches the higher chakras, it produces various degrees of illumination. Each chakra is associated with different physical and spiritual attributes; some are related to various senses and elements, and some to other qualities, such as form or color.

The Seven Chakras[2]

1. *Muladhara* (root-support) is located at the base of the spinal column. It is associated with the element earth, inertia, the birth of sound, the

[2] The descriptions of the chakras are taken from Eliade (1969) and Feuerstein (1989).

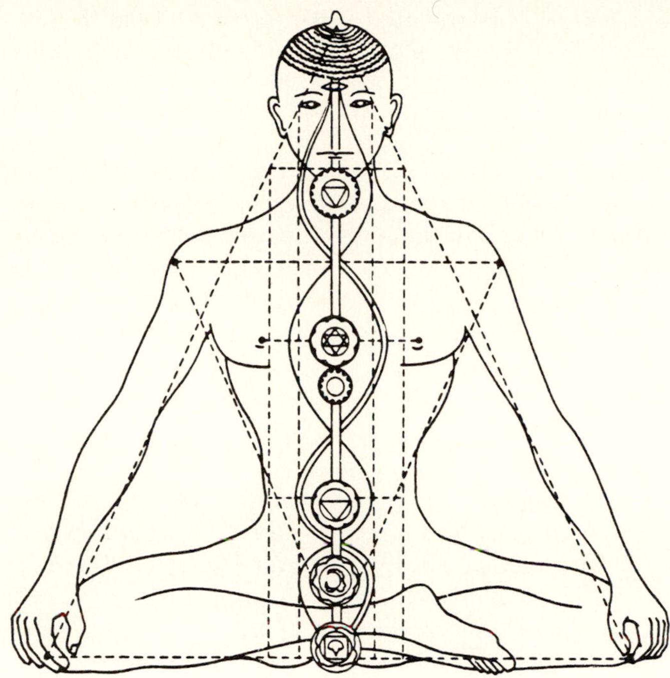

FIGURE 15.3 The Centers of Consciousness in the Body

Source: From Danilou, 1955, p. ii.

lower limbs, the mantra *lam,* the elephant (symbolizing strength), and the sense of smell. It is portrayed as a deep-red, four-petaled lotus. It is the location of the dormant kundalini.

2. *Svadisthana* (own-base) is situated several inches above the first center. It is associated with the element water, the color white, the hands, the mantra *vam,* a crocodilelike animal (fertility), and the sense of taste. It is pictured as a crimson, six-petaled lotus.
3. *Manipura* (jewel-city) is located at the level of the navel. It is related to the element fire, the sun, the anus, the mantra *ram* (fiery energy), and the sense of sight. It is depicted as a bright yellow lotus of ten petals.
4. *Anahata* (unstruck) is located at the level of the heart. The name of this chakra comes from its association with transcendental sound, which is "unstruck." It is associated with the color red, the element air, the penis, the mantra *yam,* a black antelope (swiftness), and the sense of touch. It is drawn as a blue lotus of twelve petals.
5. *Vishuddha* (pure) is located in the region of the throat. It is associated with the element ether, the color white, the mouth and skin, the mantra *ham,* a snow-white elephant (pure strength), and the sense of hearing.
6. *Ajna* (command) is situated in the brain, midway between the eyes. It is the seat of cognitive faculties, the mantra *om,* the subtle senses, and the sense of individuality. It is represented by a downward pointing triangle and a pale gray, two-petaled lotus.

7. *Sahasrara* (thousand-petaled) is located at the top of the head. It is not actually part of the chakra system. It is a body-transcending center where consciousness is connected to the human form. It is represented by a thousand-petaled lotus.

The seventh center includes the brain. When the brain is stimulated and energized by kundalini, the individual experiences a tremendous change in consciousness, an experience of bright illumination, or *samadhi*, "the blossoming of the thousand-petaled lotus."

Raja-yoga, the Yoga of the Mind and Body Raja-yoga, or *royal* yoga, emphasizes the development of mental control as the most effective and efficient discipline. Patanjali's raja-yoga has been called "psychological Yoga." Some consider it a combination of all the schools of Yoga. Others see raja-yoga as but one of the major Yoga schools.

This path is systematized by Patanjali in eight limbs of Yoga: (1) abstentions, (2) observances, (3) postures, (4) vital energy control, (5) interiorization, (6) concentration, (7) meditation, and (8) illumination. They can be thought of as successive levels of achievement, each limb building upon the one that precedes it. The eight limbs are closely interrelated branches of a single discipline; therefore, improvement in one branch tends to benefit the others.

A master bestows the divine experience of cosmic consciousness when his disciple, by meditation, has strengthened his mind to a degree where the vast vistas would not overwhelm him. Mere intellectual willingness or open-mindedness is not enough. Only adequate enlargement of consciousness by yoga practice and devotional *bhakti* can prepare one to absorb the liberating shock of omnipresence. (Yogananda, 1972, pp. 169–170)

The **abstentions** and **observances** are the moral code that serves as the foundation for Yoga practice. Abstentions include nonviolence, truthfulness, nonstealing, chastity, and nongreed. The observances are purity, austerity, contentment, study, and devotion. The abstentions and observances—which are the yogic equivalent of the Ten Commandments, the principles of right action found in all religions—are not an arbitrary system of morality. They are followed for practical reasons, to strengthen the effectiveness of the rest of Yoga practice. If a yogi does not have a calm and disciplined daily life, the concentration and peace gained from Yoga practice is soon dissipated, like water carried in a pail riddled with holes.

It is impossible to progress without developing abstentions and observances. However, we cannot expect to master them at first. Nonviolence and truthfulness, for example, are profound disciplines.

The *Yoga Sutras* teach that in the presence of one who has mastered nonviolence, no violence can occur. Obviously, the mastery of nonviolence does not take place at an elementary level. But the seeds of violence in us—arrogance, anger, rage—can be removed so that there is not a violent cell in our bodies. Violence then cannot arise in our presence, because the violence that swells in another person does not find a hook to hang on.

There is great depth to abstentions and observances. They are not simply representations of conventional morality; they are practical principles, which bring a harmony to life that is consistent with the consciousness that Yoga aims for.

Purification of mind and body also prepares the entire system to handle the higher "voltage," the greater power of the full flow of spiritual energy in samadhi.

Posture refers to the ability to remain still, in a single position, for long periods of time. The essence of posture is the stilling of both body and mind.

Personal Reflection

■ Breathing Exercises: Observing the Breath

Sit on a chair or on the floor, with your back straight and your body relaxed. Close your eyes. Exhale and then inhale calmly and deeply for as long as is comfortable without straining. Observe your breath flowing in and out, as if you were on the seashore observing the ocean waves. With each intake of breath, feel that you are breathing in fresh energy and vitality with the oxygen. With each outtake of breath, feel that you are breathing out tiredness, fatigue, and negativity as you expel carbon dioxide. Feel the fresh, vitalizing energy permeating your mind and body as you continue to do the exercise.

Then sit quietly with your mind peaceful and calm.

Patanjali writes that "posture implies steadiness and comfort. It requires relaxation and meditation on the Immovable" (*Yoga Sutras,* II:46–47).[3] In India, students of Yoga attempt to increase gradually the time they can sit in a given posture. The student masters a posture upon being able to hold that pose for three hours without stirring.

Control of vital energy is the unique, fundamental aspect of Yoga. The original Sanskrit term *pranayama* is often mistranslated as "breath control." Breathing exercises can slow the metabolism and free vital energy; however, they are only an indirect means of controlling vital energy. The breath is just one manifestation of *prana,* which is the vital force that sustains all life.

The goal is complete mastery over vital energy. It can be attained through various Yoga practices. Accomplished yogis have demonstrated this mastery by stopping their heartbeat or their breathing at will, and in the past some yogis have buried themselves alive for days or weeks (see, for example, Yogananda, 1972). Modern physiological studies have confirmed the ability of practicing yogis to control their heart rates and achieve breathlessness. (For a detailed bibliography of research on Yoga and various forms of meditation, see Timmons & Kamiya, 1970; Timmons & Kanellakos, 1974.)

Interiorization refers to the shutting off of the senses. Vital energy is withdrawn from the sense organs, and the yogi is no longer distracted by the ceaseless bombardment of outer stimuli. The yogi becomes increasingly alive within his or her own mind.

Achievement of interiorization has been verified by Indian scientists who found that brain waves of meditating yogis are unaffected by outside stimuli (Anand, Chhina, & Singh, 1961). Patanjali defines interiorization as "the restoration of sense to the original purity of mind, by renouncing its objects" (*Yoga Sutras,* II:54).

When we sit still, the outward rush of consciousness begins to subside. We learn then to slow down our breathing and to quiet our minds. During interiorization, consciousness stops flowing out through our senses into the world.

[3]Quotes from the *Yoga Sutras* of Patanjali are taken from Purohit (1938).

Personal Reflection

■ Concentration

Try this simple exercise in concentration. Look at the second hand of your watch or a clock while simultaneously remaining aware of your breathing. See how long it takes before your mind begins to wander.

Very few people can focus their concentration for even a short period of time. Like any other skill, this one improves with practice.

(Adapted from Tart, 1986)

We become aware of the source within as the energy flow turns back to the brain and consciousness.

Concentration is "attention fixed upon an object" (*Yoga Sutras,* III:1). There are two aspects of concentration: the *withdrawal* of the attention from objects of distraction and the *focusing* of attention upon one thing at a time. Concentration is a relaxed state, not a struggle or forcing of attention. Some development of interiorization must precede the practice of concentration.

Yogi doing yogic breathing exercise

When all five senses are active, it is like trying to concentrate with five telephones constantly ringing. External sensations bring thoughts that in turn produce an endless series of memories and speculations. The sound of a car prompts us to think, "Oh, there is a car going by." Then we think about cars we once owned, cars we would like to buy, and so forth.

Meditation is a term that is used loosely in the West. In Yogic terminology, meditation is a highly advanced practice in which only a single thought, the object of meditation alone, remains in the consciousness of the meditator. As concentration develops and becomes deeper and more prolonged, a natural state of meditation is achieved. In meditation, the mind is fully concentrated, completely focused on the object of meditation (see Figure 15.4).

Illumination (*samadhi*) is, in a sense, the essence of Yoga practice. It is the state that defines Yoga, and only those who have attained illumination can be regarded as true yogis. All others are students of Yoga. *Samadhi* has also been translated as "ecstasy" (Feuerstein, 1989). According to Patanjali, illumination is a state in which "union as union disappears, only the meaning of the object on which the attention is fixed being present" (*Yoga Sutras,* III:3).

Realization of the self occurs once the mind is totally calm and concentrated, reflecting the qualities of the self within. As the Self is infinite, illumination is not a final or static state. Illumination includes a variety of states of consciousness. Patanjali distinguishes two major kinds of illumination, *conscious* illumination and *supraconscious* illumination. Within conscious illumination, Patanjali describes eight distinct states. The contents in the field of consciousness become more and more subtle as meditation deepens. They progress from consciousness of a thought form, such as the image of a deity, to consciousness of abstract ideas, such as love. Eventually, there exists only consciousness of deep joy or peace, and, finally, all that remains is consciousness of the Self (see Figure 15.5).

Illumination without content defies description, as there is nothing in the field of consciousness to which words refer. Those who have reached this stage

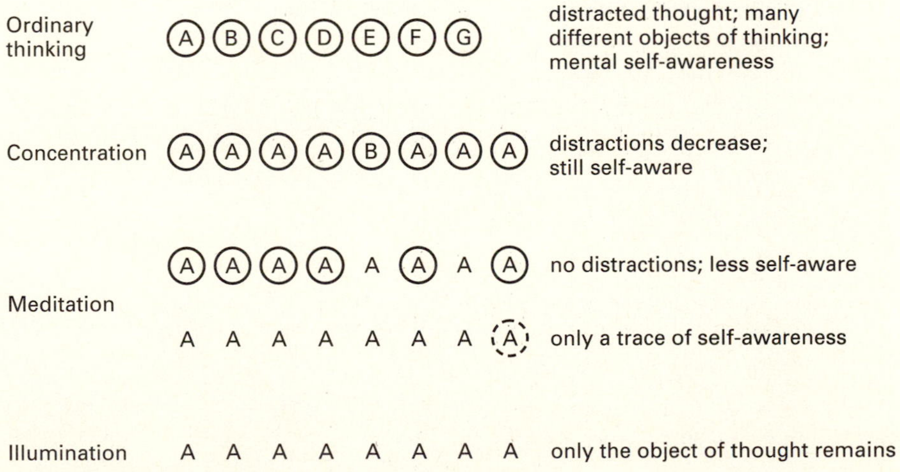

Ordinary thinking (A) (B) (C) (D) (E) (F) (G) distracted thought; many different objects of thinking; mental self-awareness

Concentration (A) (A) (A) (A) (B) (A) (A) (A) distractions decrease; still self-aware

Meditation
(A) (A) (A) (A) A (A) A (A) no distractions; less self-aware
A A A A A A A (A) only a trace of self-awareness

Illumination A A A A A A A A only the object of thought remains

FIGURE 15.4 Thought Processes in Yoga Practice

The circles indicate self-awareness. *Source:* Adapted from Taimni, 1961, p. 284.

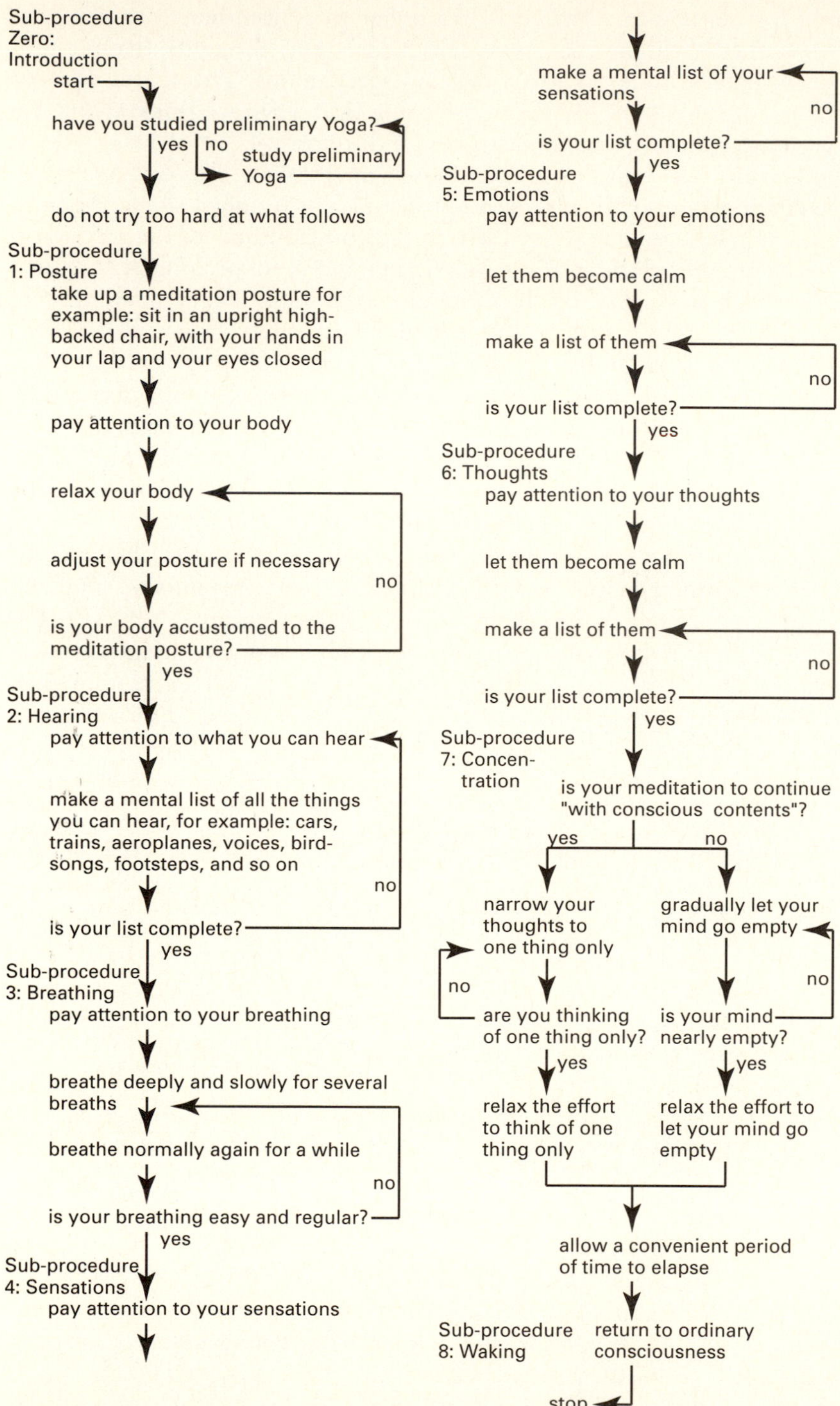

FIGURE 15.5 The Flow of Meditation

Instructions in the "Program for Patanjali," formalized by John H. Clark of Manchester University in a flow chart of the type prepared for computers. *Source:* Adapted from Clark, 1970.

are said to have become totally free of the influences of karma and of their subconscious tendencies.

Dynamics

Psychological Growth

The Yogic way of life best known in the West is that of ascetic renunciation, including celibacy, poverty, and "giving up" the world to devote oneself completely to the disciplines of Yoga. In India, there is another ideal path of spiritual growth, that of a balanced life of worldly service and responsibilities plus the practice of spiritual discipline.

The Vedas describe various types of ascetics and sages. The ascetics, who practiced austerities and other Yogic disciplines, were most likely the forerunners of the wandering Yogic ascetics of modern India. The ancient *rishis,* or sages, on the other hand, emphasized the importance of sacrifices and hymns and were more a part of the Indian social order. (For a fuller discussion, see Feuerstein & Miller, 1972.)

Four Stages of Life There are four stages in the classical, idealized Indian life cycle of the sage: *student, householder, forest dweller,* and *renunciant* (Smith, 1987). According to traditional Indian conceptions, each stage should last 25 years, as the normal life span was said to be 100 years in the more highly developed past ages.

In many classical Indian works, it is emphasized that an individual must pass through all four stages to achieve self-realization. Each stage has its own duties, and each provides certain essential lessons and experiences.

During the first stage, the **student** traditionally serves as an apprentice, living with a teacher and the teacher's family. In addition to the acquisition of occupational skills, the traditional Indian education is devoted to character building through emotional and spiritual discipline. The goal is to become a mature individual, fully equipped to live a harmonious and productive life, rather than remain a slave to one's moods, habits, and drives.

At the completion of this stage, the apprentice returns home and, after marrying, enters the stage of the **householder.** The duties of the householder include carrying on the family business and raising a family. The householder seeks satisfaction in family pleasures, in achieving vocational success, and in serving the community as an active, responsible citizen. As a result of the character training received during the first stage, the householder is able to lead a self-controlled life. He or she has disciplined the desire for sex, fame, and wealth and is able to enjoy the pleasures and duties of the householder in a moderate way.

The third stage is that of the **forest dweller.** It refers to gradual retirement from family and occupational affairs. When a husband and wife are over 50 years of age, their children have become old enough to assume the family responsibilities. The older couple might retire to a small, secluded cottage in the forest or remain in the family house after withdrawing from all duties and affairs. They remain available to the rest of the family, consulting with and advising their children when needed.

If you run after the world the world will run from you. If you run from the world, it will run after you. (Hari Dass, 1973)

The individual's last quarter century is to be devoted to the fourth stage, **renunciation.** Entrance into this stage is marked by a ritual closely resembling funeral rites. The individual is now officially dead to all social obligations and personal ties, and free to pursue self-realization without external demands or restrictions.

Self-realization The details of spiritual development vary with different branches of Yoga. For the karma-yogi, growth involves the development of self-discipline, willpower, and selfless service. For the bhakti-yogi, growth is most closely related to an increase in devotion to an aspect of God. For the jnana-yogi, growth is the development of powers of discrimination and self-analysis. In various other schools of Yoga, growth brings the ability to meditate, to withdraw one's attention from the world and the senses, and to focus, with increasing concentration, on some aspect of Self or Spirit.

The diverse branches of Yoga share certain fundamental principles. The path of Yoga is basically the process of turning the consciousness away from the activities of the external world back to the source of consciousness—the Self. The karma-yogi seeks to act with self-awareness without becoming overinvolved in the action itself or in the possible results of the action. The bhakti-yogi endeavors to keep the mind devotionally focused on a person or representation that symbolizes an aspect of Spirit or Self. The jnana-yogi seeks the Self by bringing the mind back to the roots of thought and rejecting all that is not Self.

Ramakrishna, the great devotional yogi, wrote:

> The secret is that the union with God (Yoga) can never happen unless the mind is rendered absolutely calm, whatever be the "path" you follow for God realization. The mind is always under the control of the Yogi, and not the Yogi under the control of his mind. (1965, p. 186)

The wise man beholds all beings in the Self, and the Self in all beings. (*Isa Upanishad,* 6)

As we mentioned, Yoga literally means "union," union with the Self, or illumination. One classic commentary by Vyasa (in Taimni, 1961) on Patanjali's *Yoga Sutras* states that Yoga *is* illumination. All the various paths and disciplines included in Yoga share the fundamental goal of illumination and self-realization.

Obstacles to Growth

Patanjali lists five major afflictions, or causes of suffering: *ignorance, egoism, desire, aversion,* and *fear* (*Yoga Sutras,* II:3).

The afflictions are gradually weakened by Yoga disciplines, especially austerity and self-control, scriptural study, and devotion. The yogi gradually strengthens subconscious tendencies that oppose the afflictions, weakening their influence. Afflictions have two aspects: gross and subtle. In their gross forms, the afflictions are actual thought waves (*of* fear, desires, and so forth). In their finer aspects, the afflictions are subconscious tendencies (*toward* fear, desire, and so forth) that remain until the attainment of illumination.

Ignorance **Ignorance** is the major obstacle to growth. The basis for all suffering is ignorance of our true identity. "Ignorance is the cause, the others are the effects. . . . Ignorance thinks of the perishable as imperishable, of the pure as impure, of the painful as pleasurable, of the non-Self as Self" (*Yoga Sutras,* II:4–5).

Consciousness is projected outward from the Self with such great force that it is extremely difficult to direct the mind back to its source. Concern with the external world and with continually active senses has replaced self-awareness. Ignorance is mistaking the effect for the cause; that is, attributing the qualities of the Self to the world by treating the world as the source of experience and remaining unaware of the Self as the ultimate cause.

Egoism **Egoism** results from the identification of the Self with the body and the thoughts. "Egoism is the identification of the Seer with the limitations of the eye" (*Yoga Sutras,* II:6). Identification with the body leads to fear, desire, and a sense of limitation, and identification with the thoughts leads to restlessness and emotionality.

Desire and Aversion **Desire** and **aversion** are defined by Patanjali simply and elegantly: "Desire is longing for pleasure. Aversion is recoiling from pain" (*Yoga Sutras,* II: 7–8). These afflictions tie the individual to the constant change and fluctuation of the external world, and they make deep calmness or peace impossible. One major aim of Yoga discipline is to overcome our tremendous sensitivity to pain, pleasure, success, failure, and other changes in the outer world. The yogi seeks freedom from the domination of the world, learning to be in control of physical, mental, and emotional reactions rather than being controlled by them.

Satisfying the sensory desires cannot satisfy you, because you are not the senses. They are only your servants, not your Self. (Yogananda, 1968a, p. 60)

Desire and aversion bring about **attachment** to whatever increases pleasure or reduces pain. Attachment arises from the feeling that we must have something for our own pleasure or fulfillment. Its stress on overcoming attachment does not mean, however, that Yoga is a negative, joyless self-discipline. The idea of **nonattachment** is to enjoy whatever one receives, while being ready to give it up without a sense of loss or sorrow.

A young disciple studying nonattachment was shocked to find his guru relishing a meal of exotic fruits and nuts. His teacher seemed to be deeply attached to the food he was eating, instead of being properly unconcerned with what he ate. The master explained that nonattachment does not require us to give up the experience of good food or other pleasures; rather, it is the full enjoyment of what one has and the avoidance of regret when those pleasures are no longer available. One who has mastered nonattachment enjoys the present without trying to change it by wishing for greater pleasure or less pain.

Fear **Fear** is the fifth affliction. "Fear at constant natural terror of death, that is rooted even in the minds of the learned" (*Yoga Sutras,* II:9). In his commentary on the *Yoga Sutras,* Purohit writes: "Fear of death is constant in the mind, and as desire and aversion are the result of some experience in the past, so is the fear of death the result of dying in the past" (1938, p. 48). Fear stems from identification with the perishable body instead of the imperishable Self.

The knowing Self is not born; It does not die. It has not sprung from anything; nothing has sprung from It. Birthless, eternal, everlasting, and ancient, It is not killed when the body is killed. (*Katha Upanishad,* I:ii, 18)

CHAPTER 16

Zen and the Buddhist Tradition

When asked how one should evaluate religious teachings and spiritual teachers, the Buddha replied:

> You who follow me, consider this carefully. Keep an eye open, seekers of truth. Weigh rumor, custom, and hearsay. Don't let anyone's excellence in the Scriptures mislead you. Logic and argument, supply of elaborate reasons, approval of considered opinion, plausibility of ideas, respect for the leader who guides you—beware of too much trust in them. Only when you *know,* and are sure that you know—this is not good, this is erroneous, this is censured by the intelligent, this will lead to loss and grief—only when you know, should you reject or accept it. (*The Dhammapada,* Lal, 1967, p. 17)

In Zen Buddhism, the primary concern is to lead others to a direct, personal understanding of Truth. The Buddha's teachings emphasize experience over theology or abstract philosophy. Zen is a school of Buddhism, a particular branch that stresses meditation and practice. As the Zen philosopher D. T. Suzuki has written, "The basic idea of Zen is to come in touch with the inner workings of our being, and to do this in the most direct way possible, without resorting to anything external or super-added" (1964, p. 44). In its broadest sense, Zen provides a practical, experiential approach to spirituality applicable to all religions.

History

Remember thou must go alone;
The Buddhas do but point the way. (Shakyamuni Buddha)

Buddhism is based on the teachings of Siddhartha Gautama, the Buddha. The term *Buddha* is a title, not a proper name. It means "one who is awake," or one who achieves a certain level of understanding, one who has attained full humanness. There were many other Buddhas before Gautama, and there are still Buddhas to come, according to Buddhist doctrine. The Buddha never claimed to be more than a man whose realization, attainments, and achievements were the result of his purely human capacities. He developed himself into a completely mature human being, which is such a rare achievement that we tend to look on it as somehow superhuman or divinely inspired. The central attitude in Buddhism is that every individual possesses this Buddha-nature, the capacity for developing into a complete human being and becoming a Buddha.

The life of Gautama has been recorded in the Buddhist tradition but there is little reliable evidence of specific dates and activities. His official life story can be read as an illuminating parable of Buddhist ideals and principles.

Gautama was born about 563 B.C., a prince in the Shakya kingdom in northern India (today part of Nepal). At age 16, he was married to a beautiful princess and lived in his palace surrounded by comfort and luxury. When Gautama was in his late twenties, he had occasion to slip out of his palatial prison and was suddenly confronted with the reality of life and the suffering of humankind. First, Gautama encountered an old man, worn down by a life of toil and hardship. On his second trip, he saw a man who was afflicted with a serious illness. On his third trip, Gautama watched a corpse being carried in a sorrowful funeral procession. Finally, Gautama met a religious ascetic engaged in the traditional Indian pursuit of spiritual discipline. Gautama realized that sickness, old age, and death are unavoidable endings even to the happiest and most prosperous life. The inevitability of human suffering became the central focus of Gautama's search. His present way of life, he realized, could not provide an answer to the problem of suffering, and he decided to leave his family and palace to seek a solution through mental and physical discipline.

Planners make canals, archers shoot arrows, craftsmen fashion woodwork, the wise man molds himself. (*The Dhammapada*, Lal, 1967)

At the age of 29, soon after the birth of his only son, Gautama left his kingdom and studied for six years with many teachers, including two famous Yoga teachers, engaging in severe ascetic practices. Finally, weakened by his long fast, Gautama realized that mortification of the body would never bring about enlightenment, and he accepted some food to give him strength to continue with his spiritual efforts. He then sat beneath a Bodhi tree and resolved that he would not eat or leave his seat until he reached enlightenment, even if he died in the attempt. From Gautama's experience came the Buddhist conception of the Middle Way: seeking a healthy and useful discipline without either extreme—complete indulgence of the senses or self-torture. After deep and prolonged meditation, Gautama underwent a profound inner transformation that altered his perspective on life. His approach to the questions of sickness, old age, and death changed because he changed. At age 35, he had become the Buddha.

The Buddha decided to share his understanding with others, and he taught for 45 years, walking from town to town in India with an ever-growing band of followers. He died in 483 B.C., at the age of 80.

For many centuries, Buddhism flourished in India and spread gradually throughout Asia. Between A.D. 1000 and 1200, Buddhism practically died out in India, because of the growing weakness of Indian Buddhism, the revival of Hinduism, and persecution by Muslim rulers. It is growing again in India today.

There are two major schools within Buddhism today. The Theravada or Hinayana tradition is found primarily in Southeast Asia, in Sri Lanka, Burma, and Thailand. The Mahayana school has flourished mainly in Tibet, China, Korea, and Japan. The Mahayana school, which began as a liberal movement within Theravadan Buddhism, is less strict in interpreting the traditional monastic disciplinary rules, less exclusive with regard to householders, and more willing to adopt later additions to the Buddhist scriptures. The Mahayanists have also placed high value on compassion, as opposed to the Theravada emphasis on self-discipline. Originally, these two great traditions were seen as alternative personal interpretations within Buddhism. At first, adherents of the Mahayana and Theravadan approaches lived together in the same monasteries, obeying the same basic rules.

Man's inability to control and discipline his mind is responsible for all his problems. (Dalai Lama)

Zen is one of the major schools of the Mahayana tradition. Traced back all the way to the Buddha, Zen is said to have been brought to China in the sixth century A.D. by Bodhidharma, an Indian Buddhist monk, who stressed contemplation and personal discipline over religious ritual. Under the influence of a series of great Chinese masters, Zen gradually developed as an independent school of Buddhism, with its own monasteries, monastic rules, and organization. By A.D. 1000, Zen had become the second most popular school of Buddhism in China.

In the twelfth and thirteenth centuries, two Japanese monks, Eisai and Dogen, traveled to China to study Buddhism. When they returned to Japan, these monks established temples, taught prominent disciples, and founded the two great sects of Japanese Zen Buddhism, Soto and Rinzai. According to Master Eisai (1141–1215), who introduced Rinzai Zen in Japan, enlightenment could be achieved through the use of Zen "riddles," or *koan*. Master Dogen (1200–1253), the founder of Japanese Soto Zen, stressed two major points: There is no gap between daily practice and enlightenment, and the right (correct) daily behavior is Buddhism itself.

Just as most of the chapters in this text examine the work of a particular theorist, this chapter focuses primarily on a particular school of Buddhism, Zen Buddhism, which is only one of a great number of Buddhist traditions and schools. The chapter summarizes Buddhist concepts and psychology from a Soto Zen perspective.

Basically, there is only one Buddhism. Different teachers and different schools interpret the fundamental truths of Buddhism to fit their own cultures and societies. Under "Recent Developments," we outline the major contributions of two other schools of Buddhism that are prominent in the United States, Theravadan and Tibetan Buddhism.

The Dalai Lama

Major Concepts

At the heart of Buddhist thought is the conception of existence as characterized by impermanence, lack of an imperishable Self or soul, and dissatisfaction or suffering as an essential attribute of this world. Stemming from these characteristics are the basic principles of Buddhism, the Four Noble Truths and the Eightfold Path. Zen Buddhism is based on the practice of meditation as a means of directly experiencing the principles and truths of Buddhism—that is, the experience of "enlightenment." Two conceptions of the ideal human being are found in Buddhism, the arhat and the bodhisattva.

The Three Characteristics of Existence

There are three major characteristics of existence according to Buddhist thought: *impermanence, selflessness,* and *dissatisfaction.*

Impermanence Everything is constantly changing; **impermanence** characterizes all things. Certainly nothing physical lasts forever. Trees, buildings, the sun, moon, stars—all have a finite existence; furthermore, all are in flux at any given moment.

Time flies quicker than an arrow and life passes with greater transience than dew. However skillful you may be, how can you ever recall a single day of the past? (Dogen in Kennett, 1976)

Impermanence also applies to thoughts and ideas. The concept of impermanence implies that there can be no such thing as a final authority or permanent truth. There is only a level of understanding suitable for a certain time and place. Because conditions change, what seems to be true at one time inevitably becomes false or inappropriate at others. Therefore, Buddhism cannot be said to have a fixed doctrine. To truly accept the concept of impermanence is to realize that nothing ever fully becomes Buddha, that even Buddha, or truth, is subject to change and can still progress, or that everything is an ever-changing manifestation of the same reality that is also Buddha.

The Buddhists point out that the primary feature of the universe is change. However, human beings have a strong tendency to conceive of the world as static, to see things instead of fluid and constantly changing *processes.* Although in our minds we see facets of life and nature as disconnected, these elements are actually connected, interdependent.

Perhaps the best illustration of the Buddhist concept of **interdependence** comes from Thich Nhat Hanh, a Vietnamese Zen master.

> If you are a poet, you will see clearly that there is a cloud floating in this sheet of paper. Without a cloud, there will be no rain; without rain, the trees cannot grow; and without trees, we cannot make paper. The cloud is essential for the paper to exist. . . .
>
> If we look into this sheet of paper even more deeply, we can see the sunshine in it. If the sunshine is not there, the forest cannot grow. In fact, nothing can grow. . . . And if we continue to look, we can see the logger who cut the tree and brought it to the mill to be transformed into paper. And we see the wheat. We know that the logger cannot exist without his daily bread, and therefore the wheat that became his bread is also in this sheet of paper. And the logger's father and mother are in it too. . . .

> So we can say that everything is in here with this sheet of paper. . . . Everything co-exists with this sheet of paper. . . . You cannot just *be* by yourself alone. . . . This sheet of paper is, because everything else is. (1988, pp. 3–4)

To realize that everything coexists and is in constant flux is to experience the world in a radically different way.

Selflessness Some religions have taught that the Self, or soul, is unchanging and imperishable. The Buddhist notion of impermanence, however, is applied to our innermost self as well.

The concept of **selflessness** holds that there is no immortal soul or eternal self that exists in each individual. The individual is seen as a collection of elements, all of which are impermanent and constantly changing. According to the Buddha, the individual is made up of five basic factors—body, perception, sensation, consciousness, and mental activities (i.e., ideas, intentions, and so on). The term *I* is merely a useful linguistic device to refer to an ever-changing collection of traits that comprise the individual.

In other words, our bodies and our personalities are composed of mortal, constantly changing components. The individual is not something other than the pattern formed by the temporary interaction of these component parts. When the parts perish, so does the individual. No part of ourselves goes on forever, although the consequences of our thoughts and action may continue.

All things—not only human beings—lack a separate self, including trees, mountains, plants, and animals. First, they cannot exist except in terms of interdependence or coexistence with all things. Second, all things are composites, or temporary, impermanent collections of parts.

Dissatisfaction **Dissatisfaction,** or suffering, is the third characteristic of existence. It embraces birth, death, decay, sorrow, pain, grief, despair, and existence itself. Suffering comes not from the world around us but from ourselves. It lies in the limited ego—the relative consciousness—of each individual. Buddhist teachings are designed to help us transcend our sense of self. It is only through self-transformation that we can experience a sense of real satisfaction with ourselves and with the world.

To interpret the principle of dissatisfaction to mean only that suffering is an inescapable part of existence is incorrect. The Buddha taught that the source of suffering lies within the individual and optimistically concluded that something can be done about humankind's basic dissatisfaction.

The Four Noble Truths

Gautama searched for a way to overcome the suffering and limitation he saw as an inevitable part of human life. "In what was probably the most important psychological discovery of all time, the Buddha realized the universality of suffering, its cause, its cure, and the way to attain such liberation" (Mosig, 1990, p. 53). He formulated this diagnosis and prescription as the Four Noble Truths.

We are what we think, having become what we thought. (*The Dhammapada,* Lal, 1967)

The Existence of Dissatisfaction The first Truth is the existence of dissatisfaction. Given the inner state of the average individual, dissatisfaction, or suffering, is inescapable.

Craving as the Root of Dissatisfaction The second Truth is that dissatisfaction is the result of craving or desire. Most people are caught up in attachment to the positive and pleasurable and aversion toward the negative and painful. Craving creates an unstable frame of mind in which the present is never satisfactory. If our desires are unsatisfied, we are driven by a need to change the present. If satisfied, we come to fear change, which brings about a renewal of frustration and dissatisfaction. Because all things pass, the enjoyment of fulfilled desires is tempered by the realization that our pleasure is only temporary. Therefore, we always wish things to be other than what they are. The stronger the craving, the more intense is our dissatisfaction, because we know that fulfillment will not last.

Like the spider woven in its own web is the man gripped by his craving. (*The Dhammapada,* Lal, 1967)

Elimination of Craving The third Truth is that the elimination of craving brings the extinction of suffering. According to Buddhist doctrine, it is possible to learn to accept the world as it is without feeling dissatisfaction because of its limitations. To eliminate craving does not mean to extinguish all desires. If your happiness seems to depend on the fulfillment of wants, or you are controlled by your desires, then they are unhealthy cravings and should be reined in. Other desires—like those for food and sleep—are necessary, of course, for survival. Desires also help boost our awareness. If all our wants are immediately satisfied, we can easily slip into a passive, unthinking state of complacency. Acceptance refers to an even-minded attitude of enjoying fulfilled desires without lamenting the inevitable periods when all our dreams don't come true. We learn to accept that things are as they are and cannot be otherwise. Then, by acting appropriately, in the present, we can work to make things better without becoming attached to any results.

The Eightfold Path The fourth Truth is that there is a way to eliminate craving and dissatisfaction; it is the Eightfold Path, or the Middle Way. Most people seek the highest possible degree of sense gratification. Others, who realize the limitations of this approach, tend toward the other extreme, self-mortification. The Buddhist ideal is moderation.

> Avoid these two extremes, monks. Which two? On the one hand, low, vulgar, ignoble, and useless indulgence in passion and luxury; on the other, painful, ignoble, and useless practice of self-torture and mortification. Take the Middle Path advised by the Buddha, for it leads to insight and peace, wisdom and enlightenment. (*The Dhammapada,* Lal, 1967, p. 22)

Do not sell the wine of delusion. But there is nothing to be deluded about. If we realize this there is enlightenment itself. (Diamond Sutra in Kennett, 1976)

The Eightfold Path consists of right speech, right action, right livelihood, right effort, right mindfulness, right concentration, right thought, and right understanding. The basic principle is that certain ways of thinking, acting, and so forth, tend to harm others and to injure or limit oneself.

There are three essentials in Buddhist training and discipline: ethical conduct, mental discipline, and wisdom. The divisions of the Eightfold Path fall under these three categories.

Ethical conduct is built on the fundamental Buddhist teachings of universal love and compassion for all living beings. Under ethical conduct are included right speech, right action, and right livelihood.

Right speech means abstention from (1) lies; (2) gossip, slander, or any talk that might bring about disunity and disharmony; (3) harsh, rude, or abusive language; and (4) useless and foolish chatter and gossip. We should instead speak the truth and use words that are friendly, pleasant, gentle, and useful. We should not speak carelessly but should consider what is appropriate for the time and place. If we cannot say something useful, the ideal is to keep "noble silence."

Right action means moral, honorable, and peaceful conduct. To achieve this, we should abstain from (1) destruction of life, (2) stealing, (3) dishonest actions, (4) illegitimate sexual intercourse, and (5) drugs or alcohol (which cloud the mind). Also, we should help others lead a peaceful and honorable life.

We can attain *right livelihood* if we abstain from making a living by any means that brings harm to anyone or anything, such as dealing in weapons, intoxicating drinks, drugs, or poisons; killing animals; or cheating. The ideal is to earn a living that is honorable, blameless, and harmful to no one.

Under the category of mental discipline are included right effort, right mindfulness, and right concentration.

Right effort refers to the active will, used to (1) prevent unwholesome states of mind from arising, (2) get rid of such states if they do arise, (3) facilitate and produce good and wholesome states of mind, and (4) develop and bring to perfection those good, wholesome states already present.

Right mindfulness means to be aware of and attentive to (1) the functions of the body, (2) sensations or feelings, (3) the activities of the mind, and (4) specific ideas, thoughts, and conceptions. Various types of meditation—including concentration on breathing, on sensations, and on mental activities—have been developed in different schools of Buddhism and promote right mindfulness.

Buddhist psychology distinguishes between generalized activities of the mind and its specific contents. Concerning the activities of the mind, one is to become aware of whether one's mind is given to hatred, delusion, lust, distraction, or any other negative impulses. In focusing on specific ideas and concepts, one learns how they appear and disappear, how they were developed, how they were suppressed, and so on.

If we think we hear, we no longer listen.
If we think we see, we no longer look.
If we think we know, we no longer search. (Buddhist saying)

Right concentration refers to the development of the mental "muscle" to accomplish the other aspects of the path.

Wisdom is made up of right thought and right understanding. *Right thought* includes selfless detachment, love, and nonviolence. *Right understanding* is the understanding of things as they are, which is accomplished by working deeply with the Four Noble Truths. In Buddhist psychology, there are two levels of understanding. The first is knowledge, accumulated memory, and an intellectual grasp of the subject. The second is deep understanding, in which a thing is seen in its natural form, undistorted by name and label. This type of awareness is possible only when the mind is freed from impurities and is fully developed through meditation.

Meditation

For a Zen monk the primary prerequisite for improvement is the practice of concentrated *zazen.* Without arguing about who is clever and who inept, who is wise and who foolish, just do *zazen.* You will then naturally improve. (Dogen in Kennett, 1976)

Zen comes from the Sanskrit word *dyhāna*, meaning "meditation" (which evolved to *ch'an* in Chinese and *zen* in Japanese). Meditation is a central discipline in Zen. There are two major styles of Zen meditation, or **zazen** (literally "seated zen"). One can simply sit, with concentrated awareness, or one can focus on a koan.

Meditation on a Koan

A **koan** is a question or exercise that cannot be solved by mere thinking or logic. Koans are used today in the Rinzai school of Zen to test students and to force them to go beyond the limits of thought and to contact their deeper, enlightened mind.

Many koans are found in dialogues between Zen student and Zen master. Others are taken from questions posed by a Zen master to stimulate or awaken the student's understanding. The koans vividly and immediately illustrate some aspect of the Zen master's deep understanding of Buddhism. They tend to be paradoxical and beyond logic, forcing the questioner to go beyond the inherent limitations of the categories with which he or she has viewed experience up to that point.

One of the most famous koans is known as *Mu:*

> A monk in all seriousness asked Joshu: "Has a dog Buddha-nature or not?" Joshu retorted, "*Mu!*"

The monk was deeply concerned with the Buddhist teaching that all sentient beings have Buddha-nature. (In China at that time, the dog was considered unclean, the lowest of the animals, and the monk was questioning seriously if such a low creature could be said to have the Buddha-nature.)

Joshu's answer might be translated as "nothing!" or read merely as an exclamation. It is not a simple yes-or-no answer. Joshu does not fall into the trap of accepting his questioner's assumption that there is a particular thing called Buddha-nature that can be possessed. *Mu* is a vigorous denial of dualistic thinking, a window through which the student can first glimpse Joshu's nondualistic perspective. Another Zen teacher comments, "It is clear, then, that Mu has nothing to do with the existence or nonexistence of Buddha-nature but is itself Buddha-nature" (Kapleau, 1965, p. 76).

All you have to do is cease from erudition, withdraw within and reflect upon yourself. Should you be able to cast off body and mind naturally, the Buddha Mind will immediately manifest itself. (Evening Service in Kennett, 1976)

In meditating on this koan, the individual should not indulge in intellectual speculation on the question and answer or the implications of either. The aim of the koan is to lead Zen students to see their own ignorance, to entice them to go beyond abstract conceptualizing, and to search for truth within themselves. Koan study is always done under the guidance of a qualified teacher with whom the student has regular interviews. One Zen master gave the following instructions to students working on this koan:

> Let all of you become one mass of doubt and questioning. Concentrate on and penetrate fully into Mu. To penetrate into Mu means to achieve absolute unity with it. How can you achieve this unity? By holding to Mu tenaciously day and night! . . . Focus your mind on it constantly. "Do not

> construe Mu as nothingness and do not conceive it in terms of existence or nonexistence." You must not, in other words, think of Mu as a problem involving the existence or nonexistence of Buddha-nature. Then what do you do? You stop speculating and concentrate wholly on Mu—just Mu! (Kapleau, 1965, p. 79)

In the Soto school of Zen, students are taught that the most important aspect of training concerns their daily lives and that they must learn to deal with their own personal koan, the riddle of daily life, as it manifests itself for each individual.

A personal koan has no final solution. The problem can be handled only by altering one's point of view, a process that results from changing one's personality. The problem doesn't change, but one's attitude toward it and the way one copes with it does. The individual never solves a koan but learns to respond to it at a higher level. For instance, Gautama began his religious quest in the hope of solving the koan of sickness, old age, and death. Even after he became the Buddha, these problems remained. The Buddha did not become immortal or ageless; however, his new level of understanding transcended his previous personal concern with these issues.

For some people, their personal koan involves a sense of inadequacy, a feeling of not being enough, not knowing enough, not being able to achieve enough. For others, their central koan brings a sense of complacency, a feeling that no further advancement or self-examination, leading to personal change, is needed.

As a smith removes flaws in silver, a wise man removes flaws in himself, slowly, one by one, carefully. (*The Dhammapada,* Lal, 1967)

"Just Sitting" The Soto approach to meditation can be thought of as "just sitting," without a koan or other exercise to occupy the mind. The meditator strives to maintain a state of concentrated awareness, in which he or she is neither tense nor relaxed but totally alert. The attitude is like that of someone seated by the roadside watching traffic. The meditator observes the thoughts going by, without getting caught up in them and thus forgetting to remain an aware observer.

Zazen is an expression of faith, of trust in the vastness of the universe and of our own inner nature. "Those who do not have faith will not accept zazen, however much they are taught. If you don't trust this silence and the vastness of existence, if you do not soak yourself in this realm, how can you trust yourself?" (Katagiri, 1988, p. 43).

Visions and similar experiences should not result if *zazen* is properly performed. Generally, these experiences are the result of tensions that accumulate from sitting improperly in meditation or from daydreamlike states that arise at a certain point in one's meditation. These *makyo,* or illusions, are considered valueless in one's personal growth. They are at best distractions and at worst a source of pride, egotism, and delusion. One Zen teacher has pointed out that "to see a beautiful vision of a Bodhisattva does not mean that you are any nearer becoming one yourself, any more than a dream of being a millionaire means that you are any richer when you awake" (Kapleau, 1965, pp. 40–41).

Meditation is an important discipline for developing an inner peace and calm and for learning to concentrate and stay balanced. Practicing *zazen* is like

Personal Reflection

■ *Zazen*

Try this exercise to learn something about Zen as well as about the way your mind works.

First, it is essential that your sitting posture be correct. You should be able to sit comfortably with a straight back, without becoming tense. By "straight back," Zen teachers mean that the spine should curve naturally just below the middle back.

If you wish, you may sit in a chair. Find a chair with a seat that is as flat as possible. A small, flat cushion is optional. Sit forward on the front third of the chair, with your feet flat on the floor. The lower legs should be more or less at right angles to the floor.

If you are going to sit on the floor, use a small, firm cushion to raise the buttocks. (Meditation cushions are often available at local Zen centers.) It is better to sit on a rug or blanket than on the bare floor. Sit on the edge of the cushion only, with just the tip of the bottom of the spine resting on the cushion. For most long-legged Westerners, it is more comfortable to sit Burmese style, your left foot tucked into the juncture of the right thigh and pelvis and your right leg placed immediately in front of your left leg and parallel to it. Both legs are flat on the ground, the knees resting on the ground. Knees and tailbone form a triangle.

The head should be straight, bent neither forward nor backward. The chin is tucked in. Your head should feel comfortable and almost weightless when it is positioned properly. Place your left hand over your right in your lap, with the thumbs lightly touching, and the palms up.

Sit facing a wall far enough away (about 6 feet) so that you can comfortably focus your eyes on the wall. Keep your eyes lowered to a comfortable place on the wall. Do not close them completely.

taking a shower. It cleanses the mind regularly, as a shower cleanses the body. "The reason why you have to practice zazen is that if you do not practice zazen things stick to you and you cannot let go of them" (Katagiri, 1988, personal communication to Yozan Mosig). One first learns to become peaceful and focused in meditation and then to extend that sense of calm awareness to activity. Eventually, nothing can pull an experienced meditator off center. He or she learns to cope with problems and pleasures from that calm base, with a certain amount of detached perspective. "Zazen practice is the direct expression of our true nature. Strictly speaking, for a human being, there is no other practice than this practice, there is no other way of life than this way of life" (Suzuki, 1970, p. 23).

> In Buddhist meditation we do not struggle for the kind of enlightenment that will happen five or ten years from now. We practice so that each moment of our life becomes real life. And, therefore, when we meditate, we sit for sitting; we don't sit for something else. If we sit for twenty minutes, these twenty minutes should bring us joy, life. (Hanh, 1988, p. 53)

Sway gently from side to side, backward and forward, to find the most comfortable erect posture. Lift up your rib cage slightly to take the pressure off your lower back and to allow your spine to curve naturally. Take two or three slow, deep breaths before you begin to concentrate.

Now comes the part that is easiest to describe and hardest to do. Just sit. Do not try to do anything. But do *not* try not to do anything, either. Just sit with a positive mental attitude. Try this practice at least five to ten minutes each day for a week. It will teach you something about Zen and also about the nature of your mind.

More explicit instructions regarding mental activity during meditation have been given by Kennett:

> Now don't deliberately try to think and don't deliberately try not to think; in other words, thoughts are going to come into your head; you can either play with them or you can just sit there and look at them as they pass straight through your head and out the other side. That is what you need to do—just continue to sit; don't bother with the thoughts, don't be highjacked by them and don't try to push them away—both are wrong. . . .
>
> I have often given the likeness of sitting under a bridge watching the traffic go by. You do have to watch the thoughts that travel back and forth, but not be bothered by them in any way. If you do get caught by a thought—and in the beginning it is quite likely—then OK. Right. So you got caught by a thought. Come back to the beginning again and start your meditation over. It's no good sitting there and saying, "Oh, now there, I got caught by another thought," because you will get caught over the annoyance about the other thought, and so it builds up and you never get back to the quiet within. If you get caught in that way, just come back and start again. (1974, pp. 16–17)

It is important to remember that the practice of meditation is an end in itself, not merely a technique to achieve something. To understand this chapter as more than a collection of words and ideas, you have to *experience* Zen. To do this, you must sit (as described in the Personal Reflection: *Zazen*). We cannot emphasize too strongly the importance of this kind of direct experience.

Mindfulness Zen master Thich Nhat Hanh eloquently describes the practice of mindfulness in daily life:

> You've got to practice meditation when you walk, stand, lie down, sit, and work, while washing your hands, washing the dishes, sweeping the floor, drinking tea, talking to friends, or whatever you are doing: While washing the dishes, you might be thinking about the tea afterwards, and so try to get them out of the way as quickly as possible in order to sit and drink tea. But that means that you are incapable of living during the time you are washing the dishes. When you are washing the dishes, washing the dishes must be the most important thing in your life. . . .

While you are doing zazen neither despise nor cherish the thoughts that arise; only search your own mind [or heart for] the very source of these thoughts. (Zen Master Bassui)

Personal Reflection

■ Meditation and Activity

You can learn something about applying a meditative attitude to your daily activities by doing this exercise.

Meditation can be seen primarily as a way of developing calmness and a sense of centered awareness by learning not to get caught up in your thoughts and emotions. Once you begin to understand this meditative attitude as you sit quietly, you can extend this feeling to your outward activities as well.

Begin with an hour of daily meditative activity. First, sit quietly for five to fifteen minutes, then tell yourself that you are going to remain self-aware, an observer of your thoughts, emotions, and activity for the next hour. If something does pull you off center, stop what you are doing and try to regain that sense of calmness and awareness. Initially, try this practice in silence. For most of us, talking becomes a distraction almost immediately.

It is easiest to begin with an hour of quiet physical work—gardening, cooking, and so forth. Intellectual activity is more difficult and conversation still more so. As you extend this practice to more of your daily life, you can observe where you are the most sensitive and easily disturbed. Make a list of these situations and consider what the list tells you.

> While washing the dishes one should only be washing the dishes, which means that while washing the dishes one should be completely aware of the fact that one is washing the dishes. At first glance, that might seem a little silly: why put so much stress on a simple thing? But that's precisely the point. The fact that I am standing there and washing these bowls is a wondrous reality. I'm being completely myself, following my breath, conscious of my presence, and conscious of my thoughts and actions. There's no way I can be tossed around mindlessly like a bottle slapped here and there on the waves. (1976, pp. 3–4, 23–24)

Meditation and mindfulness go together. Meditation can bring a level of inner calm and heightened awareness into our daily lives. Mindfulness prepares us to sit and meditate with calm awareness.

Enlightenment

The term **enlightenment** tends to be misleading because it seems to refer to some state that one can attain permanently; this notion would, of course, violate the Buddhist concept of impermanence. One Buddhist term related to *enlightenment* is *nirvana*. Nirvana, a state of mind in which all cravings and desires have become extinguished, is achieved through self-discipline, meditation, and realization of impermanence and selflessness.

One Japanese word that has been frequently used in Zen is *satori,* which literally means "intuitive understanding." Another term is *kensho,* which means "to see into one's own nature." Both terms refer to the individual's firsthand experience of the truth of Buddhist teachings. The experience is not static; it is a progressive, ever-changing, dynamic state of being, very much like Maslow's concept of self-actualization.

John Daido Loori, an American Zen teacher, has pointed out that the story of the ugly duckling, from a Hans Christian Andersen tale, provides a good example of the experience of *kensho*. The ugly duckling suffered because he was different from the other ducks. When he realized that he was a beautiful swan, he became overjoyed. Yet nothing had really changed. He had always been a perfect, complete swan. He simply *realized* his true nature and became liberated from the delusion of his imperfection. Realizing the perfection of our real Buddha-nature is very much the same process.

> Enlightenment is perfect peace and harmony. If you think enlightenment is something you can get, then it appears right in front of you and you rush to get it; but the more we rush to get it, the more enlightenment eludes us. We try with greater effort, and finally we become a frantic screaming warrior. Then we become exhausted. . . . But enlightenment is completely beyond enlightenment or not-enlightenment. It is just perfect peace and harmony. (Katagiri, 1988, p. 128)

Enlightenment is not some good feeling, or some particular state of mind. The state of mind that exists when you sit in the right posture is, in itself, enlightenment. (Suzuki, 1970, p. 28)

Arhat and Bodhisattva

The Theravada and Mahayana traditions contain different conceptions of the nature of the ideal human being. The Theravada ideal is the Arhat, one who has completely cut off all the limitations of attachment to family, possessions, and comfort to become perfectly free of this world. *Arhat* literally means "one who has slain the enemy," or one who has overcome all passions in the process of intensive spiritual discipline. The Arhat, basically an unworldly monastic, has achieved liberation from pride, selfishness, hate, and greed and has developed wisdom and compassion.

One Buddhist text describes the Arhat:

> He exerted himself, he strove and struggled, and thus he realized that this circle of "Birth-and-Death" . . . is in constant flux. He rejected all the conditions of existence which are brought about by a compound of conditions, since it is their nature to decay and crumble away, to change and to be destroyed. He abandoned all the "defilements" and won Arhatship. . . . Gold and a clod of earth were the same to him. The sky and the palm of his hand to his mind the same. (In Conze, 1959a, p. 94)

The Arhat seeks nirvana, or emancipation from suffering through elimination of craving. The individual who is so transformed experiences nirvana as absolute truth or ultimate reality, a state beyond this world of ever-changing phenomena.

Let others gain Enlightenment; I shall not enter Nirvana until the last blade of grass has entered Buddhahood. (Bodhisattva vow in Conze, 1959b)

The Mahayana ideal is the Bodhisattva, literally "enlightenment-being." The Bodhisattva is a deeply compassionate being who has vowed to remain in the world until all others have been delivered from suffering.

Personal Reflection

■ Walking Meditation

Meditation is not just sitting still. This exercise gives you a chance to practice meditative mindfulness in motion.

All of our physical experiences can become opportunities for mindfulness practice. Walking is a particularly good practice for maintaining awareness in our daily life.

Walk slowly in a natural setting, in a garden or along a river. Breathe normally and easily. Begin to coordinate your breathing with your footsteps. Then lengthen your exhalation by one step, without forcing your breath. See if your inhalation also naturally increases.

After 10 breaths, again lengthen your exhalation by one step. After 20 breaths, return to normal breathing. Five minutes later you can lengthen your breath again. Always return to normal if you feel the least bit tired. The point is to maintain your awareness. Any count will do as the act of counting breaths keeps you in the present. (Adapted from Hanh, 1976)

In truly understanding the principle of selflessness, the Bodhisattva realizes that he or she is part of all other sentient beings and that until all beings are freed from suffering, he or she can never attain complete liberation. The Bodhisattva vows not to enter Nirvana until every sentient being, every blade of grass is enlightened.

> As many beings as there are in the universe of beings . . . egg-born, born from a womb, moisture-born, or miraculously born; with or without form; with perception, without perception, or with neither perception nor no-perception—as far as any conceivable form of beings is conceived; all these I must lead to Nirvana. (Diamond Sutra in Conze, 1959b, p. 164)

Compassion is the great virtue of the Bodhisattva, the result of truly feeling the sufferings of all others as one's own. From the Mahayana point of view, this attitude is enlightenment. In the experience of enlightenment, the world is not transcended, but the selfish ego is.

The Bodhisattva path includes abandoning the world, but not the beings in it. The path of the Arhat emphasizes the quest for inner perfection and abandonment of the world, without the stress on service. The attitude of the Arhat is that those who desire to help others must first improve themselves. Someone who is lost in delusion is not effective in helping or teaching others; therefore self-development must naturally come first.

These two ideals can be seen as complementary rather than contradictory. The Arhat model focuses on self-discipline, whereas the Bodhisattva ideal stresses service to others; both are essential ingredients in personal growth and development.

Dynamics

One traditional way of illustrating psychospiritual growth in Zen has been through a series of ox-herding pictures. This rich group of images provides vivid examples of states of awareness beyond those usually discussed in Western psychology.

Classic Zen texts also discuss the obstacles on the path, particularly the "three fires" of greed, hate, and delusion, and also the problem of pride or egotism.

Psychological Growth

Zen masters have often discussed their students' development in terms of the ox-herding pictures, which provide clear and graphic illustrations of Zen thinking. One teacher outlined the major points of this series in counseling an advanced Zen student:

Better than a thousand vacuous speeches is one sane word leading to peace. (*The Dhammapada,* Lal, 1967)

> If you continue with zazen, you will reach the point of grasping the Ox, i.e., the fourth stage. Right now you do not, so to speak, "own" your realization. Beyond the stage of grasping the Ox is the stage of taming it, followed by riding it, which is a state of awareness in which enlightenment and ego are seen as one and the same. Next, the seventh stage, is that of forgetting the Ox; the eighth, that of forgetting the Ox as well as oneself; the ninth, the grade of grand enlightenment, which penetrates to the very bottom and where one no longer differentiates enlightenment from non-enlightenment. The last, the tenth, is the stage in which . . . one moves, as himself, among ordinary people, helping them wherever possible, free from all attachment to enlightenment. (Kapleau, 1965, p. 231)

The ox is a symbol of the Buddha-nature, and the events entailed in finding the ox refer to the internal search and inner development of the Zen student. Spiegelman and Miyuki (1985), two Jungian analysts, provide an excellent and sensitive explanation of these pictures in terms of the individuation process (see Figures 16.1 through 16.10).

Obstacles to Growth

In Buddhism, the primary obstacles to growth are basically psychological. There are three tendencies in each of us that function as major roadblocks—greed, hate, and delusion. Another serious obstacle is pride.

Greed, Hate, and Delusion Three major sources of suffering, the "three fires" of Buddhism, are *greed, hate,* and *delusion.* Some individuals are dominated by greed, others by hate, and still others by delusion. Virtually every personality contains a mixture of all three qualities, with one predominating, al-

FIGURE 16.1 Seeking the Ox

This picture represents the beginning of the spiritual quest. The man is now aware of spiritual possibilities and potentials. Having become a spiritual seeker, he has become focused on spiritual attainment. The search itself creates a new obstacle, that of seeking outside oneself for what is within. Those who are searching must eventually come to believe that they can "find" the Buddha-nature within themselves. Kakuan, the Zen master who first drew this series, added commentaries to each picture:

> The Ox has never really gone astray, so why search for it? Having turned his back on his True-nature, the man cannot see it. Because of his defilements he has lost sight of the Ox. Suddenly he finds himself confronted by a maze of crisscrossing roads. Greed for worldly gain and dread of loss spring up like searing flames, ideas of right and wrong dart out like daggers. (Kakuan in Kapleau, 1965, p. 302)

though the balance can change, depending on the circumstances. Certain situations will awaken an individual's greed, whereas others will stimulate tendencies toward anger or delusion.

Greed is a major problem for most people. We tend to want more than we have or need—more money, more food, more pleasure. Generally, children are the most obviously greedy, and it is often virtually impossible to satisfy their cravings. One piece of candy only stimulates the desire for another one. The Buddhist scriptures have described those who are dominated by greed as given to vanity, discontent, craftiness, and love of rich, sweet food and fine clothes (Conze, 1959b).

FIGURE 16.2 Finding the Tracks

The seeker has begun to study Buddhism seriously. Study of various scriptures and accounts of the lives of Buddhist sages brings an intellectual understanding of basic Buddhist truths, although the student has not yet experienced these truths firsthand.

> He is unable to distinguish good from evil, truth from falsity. He has not actually entered the gate, but sees in a tentative way the tracks of the Ox. (Kakuan in Kapleau, 1965, p. 303)

Those dominated by **hate** have sharp tempers and are quick to anger. For them, life is a continual round of fighting with enemies, getting back at others for real and imagined injuries, and defending themselves against possible attack. Those in whom hate predominates tend to hold grudges, belittle others, and suffer from arrogance, envy, and stinginess (Conze, 1959b).

Delusion refers to a general state of confusion, lack of awareness, and vacillation. Those in whom delusion is strongest find it difficult to make up their minds or to commit to anything. Their reactions and opinions are not their own but are borrowed from others. Those dominated by delusion tend to do everything inattentively and sloppily. Their behavior is characterized by laziness, obstinacy, confusion, worry, and excitability (Conze, 1959b).

At their worst, these tendencies can blossom into what Westerners term *neurosis* or *psychosis*. However, according to Buddhist thinking, even a psychosis is but a temporary intensification of one of these tendencies. It is viewed as a transient state, as are all mental and physical conditions.

FIGURE 16.3 First Glimpse of the Ox

The sight of the Ox is the first direct experience of the seeker's own Buddha-nature. The encounter with the Ox is not a result of study or abstract contemplation but is made possible through direct experience. This first glimpse is for but a moment; it is a realization that comes and goes. Further discipline is required, to expand and stabilize this experience.

> If he will but listen intently to everyday sounds, he will come to realization and at that instant see the very Source. The . . . senses are no different from this true Source. In every activity the Source is manifestly present. It is analogous to the salt in water or the binder in paint. (Kakuan in Kapleau, 1965, p. 304)

One man on the battlefield conquers an army of a thousand men. Another conquers himself—and he is greater. (*The Dhammapada*, Lal, 1967)

By working on oneself, one can transcend all three obstacles. Greed can be turned into compassion, hate into love, and delusion into wisdom. Self-discipline and the discipline of following the Buddha's precepts offer the opportunity for the individual to confront and control his or her greed. The Buddhist teachings, with their emphasis on compassion and respect for others, provide a way to overcome hate. The realization that all things *are* the Buddha is the antidote for the problem of delusion. Everything merits our deepest care and attention, because everything is a manifestation of the Buddha-nature.

Pride **Pride** can be another major obstacle to growth. It can result in a lack of respect for one's teacher and create distortions of the teachings. A Zen teacher

FIGURE 16.4 Catching the Ox

Now the Zen student must make certain that Buddhist self-discipline permeates the whole of daily life. The goal is to extend the awareness of one's Buddha-nature to all activities and to manifest that awareness in all circumstances.

The Ox here illustrates the raw energy and power of the Buddha-nature. Because of the overwhelming pressures of the outside world, the Ox is hard to keep under control. If disciplined practice is abandoned now, this power and energy may dissipate.

> Today he encountered the Ox, which had long been cavorting in the wild fields, and actually grasped it. For so long a time has it reveled in these surroundings that breaking it of its old habits is not easy. It continues to yearn for sweet-scented grasses, it is still stubborn and unbridled. If he would tame it completely, the man must use his whip. (Kakuan in Kapleau, 1965, p. 305)

The mind is restless. To control it is good. A disciplined mind is the road to Nirvana. (*The Dhammapada,* Lal, 1967)

will attempt to lead students to see and acknowledge their own pride and egotism. One of the Zen patriarchs points out, "Should the teaching you hear from a Zen master go against your own opinion, he is probably a good Zen master; if there is no clash of opinions in the beginning, it is a bad sign" (Dogen in Kennett, 1976, p. 111).

To see the self is not to be pleased with the self; not to be pleased with the self is to want to do something about the self; and to want to do something about the self is to study Buddhism. (Dogen in Kennett, 1976)

Pride can enter at virtually any point in training, even after *kensho*. Normally, the direct *kensho* experience confirms the student's understanding of Buddhism, and the student's convictions about the validity of Buddhist teachings become unshakable. However, at this stage, many students believe that they have learned everything, that they understand Buddhism fully and no longer need a teacher.

FIGURE 16.5 Taming the Ox

An effortless intimacy or friendship with the Ox is now established. The sense of struggle is gone. This is the stage of precise and perfect training. Every act, every thought begins to reflect the true self. The individual ceaselessly works to manifest Buddhism at all times, without a single interruption. Only because traces of illusion remain is there still a distinction between the seeker and the Ox.

> He must hold the nose-rope tight and not allow the Ox to roam, lest off to muddy haunts it should stray. Properly tended, it becomes clean and gentle. Untethered, it willingly follows its master. (Kakuan in Kapleau, 1965, p. 306)

A good teacher will insist that, at this point, the student continues with regular duties and training in order to ensure that pride and ambition do not distort the initial deep understanding of Buddhism. Delusion is difficult to overcome if it develops at this stage, because the student's convictions are now firmly rooted in actual experience. If training continues, students can conquer the inevitable pride and sense of holiness, or what some Zen masters have called the "smell of enlightenment" or "the stench of Zen." The student must be reminded of the doctrine of impermanence and the fact that training in Buddhism is endless.

FIGURE 16.6 Riding the Ox Home

The struggle is over. The student has now become the sage. Although the Ox is still seen as separate, the relation between man and Ox is so intimate that he can ride it effortlessly without needing to pay the slightest attention to where it is going. Life has become simple, natural, and spontaneous. Formal external training is no longer essential once one has become firmly anchored in awareness of the Buddha-nature. The discipline that was once seen as a burden is now embraced as a source of real freedom and satisfaction.

> "Gain" and "loss" no longer affect him. He hums the rustic tune of the woodsman and plays the simple songs of the village children. Astride the Ox's back, he gazes serenely at the clouds above. His head does not turn [toward temptation]. Try though one may to upset him, he remains undisturbed. (Kakuan in Kapleau, 1965, p. 307)

Structure

Body

The Buddhist concept of the Middle Way is of central importance in one's attitude toward the body. It involves neither full indulgence of all one's desires nor extreme asceticism or self-mortification.

The mealtime ceremonial recited in Zen temples affirms:

> The first bite is to discard all evil;
> The second bite is so that we may train in perfection;
> The third bite is to help all beings;

Both your life and your body deserve love and respect, for it is by their agency that Truth is practiced and the Buddha's power exhibited. (Dogen in Kennett, 1976)

FIGURE 16.7 Ox Forgotten, Self Alone

The seeker has returned home and the Ox is forgotten. The distinction between religious and worldly categories disappears, as everything is seen to possess the Buddha-nature. Training and discipline have become indistinguishable from daily life. The state of meditation is as normal now as walking or breathing and is no longer associated with any sense of motivation or separation from the goal. Everything is sacred, and there is no distinction between enlightenment and ignorance.

> In the Dharma [Teaching] there is no two-ness. The Ox is his Primal-nature: this he has now recognized. A trap is no longer needed when a rabbit has been caught, a net becomes useless when a fish has been snared. Like gold which has been separated from dross, like the moon which has broken through the clouds, one ray of luminous Light shines eternally. (Kakuan in Kapleau, 1965, p. 308)

> We pray that all may be enlightened.
> We must think deeply of the ways and means by which this food has come.
> We must consider our merit when accepting it.
> We must protect ourselves from error by excluding greed from our minds.
> We will eat lest we become lean and die.
> We accept this food so that we may become enlightened.
> (Mealtime Ceremonial in Kennett, 1976, pp. 236–237)

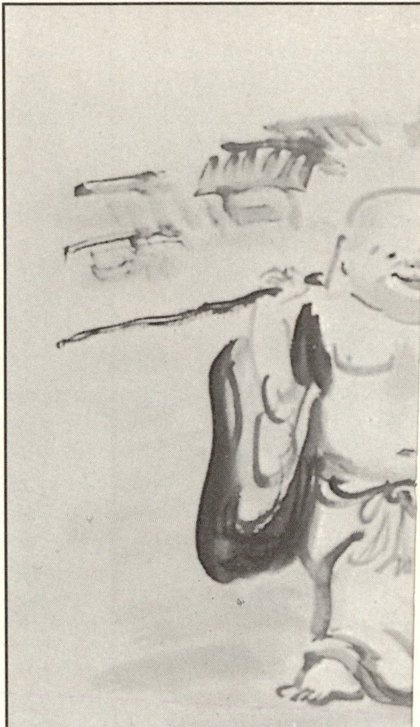

FIGURE 16.10 Entering the City wi

This is the final stage, the stage of the E
all other beings without limitation. The
secluded Zen temple or contemplation r
and a gourd of wine slung over his shoul
activities of the world, not because of
teach others.

> The gate of his cottage is closed
> panorama [concepts, opinions, and
> way, making no attempt to follow t
> he strolls into the market; leaning
> and fishmongers in the Way of the

The Zen master, who realizes that everyt
the early stages with a different perspec

Social interactions offer crucia
and principles. Someone who is in
He or she is not permitted to distu
ther. Similarly, one who behaves w
Buddha. The individual needs to
sake of revenge or cast out as evil
too is the Buddha. In addition, so
tice the calm awareness developed

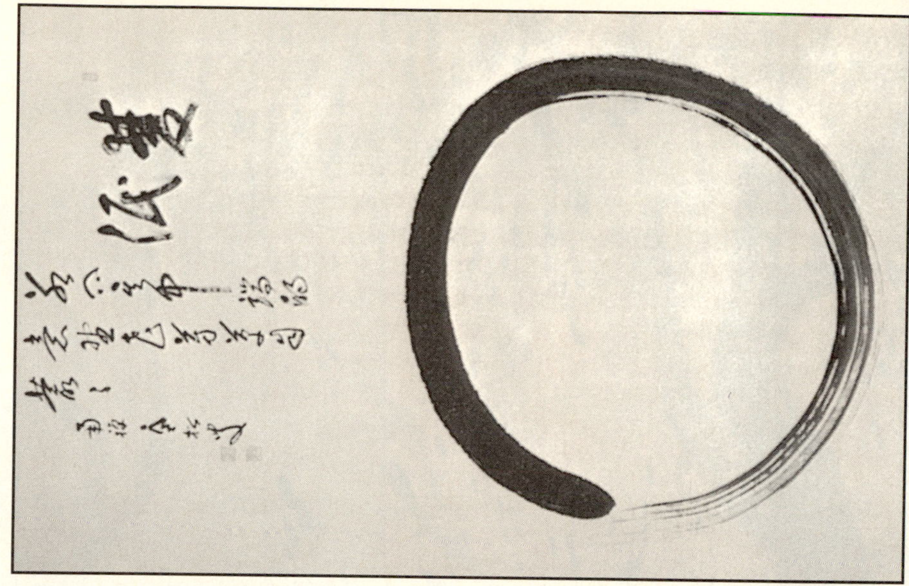

FIGURE 16.8 Both Ox and Self Forgotten

This image refers to the experience of the void, the essential nothingness of all creation. The individual nature and the Buddha-nature were transcended in the previous stage, and now it is enlightenment itself that is transcended. The perfect circle, made by the single brush stroke of the Zen master, is left open. Because the circle is not closed, further growth is possible. The process of enlightenment can go on without becoming frozen or static.

> All delusive feelings have perished and ideas of holiness too have vanished. He lingers not in "Buddha," and he passes quickly on through "not Buddha." Even the thousand eyes [of the Buddhas and patriarchs] can discern in him no specific quality. If hundreds of birds were now to strew flowers about his room, he could not but feel ashamed of himself. (Kakuan in Kapleau, 1965, p. 309)[1]

In a commentary on the Zen approach to meals, one Zen master wrote:

> If you can chant the Buddhist teachings while having a meal you are very lucky. . . . If you have breakfast to offer your body and mind to the Buddha, to the universe, how lucky you are. Offering your body and mind to the Buddha is offering your body and mind to emptiness, or in other words, to the pure sense of human action. (Katagiri, 1988, p. 9)

Hyakujo, who was the founder of Zen monastic life, always worked with his monks at manual labor, even when he was in his eighties. Although his students tried to restrain him from working as hard as they did, he insisted, saying, "I have accumulated no merit to deserve service from others; if I do not work, I have no right to take my meals" (Ogata, 1959, p. 43).

The body is a vehicle for service to others and for one's pursuit of truth. It should be cared for with this understanding.

[1]There is a legend of a Chinese Zen master who was so holy that the birds came to offer him flowers as he sat meditating in his mountain retreat. After he became fully enlightened, the birds ceased their offerings, because he no longer gave off any aura, even of devotion and holiness.

Personal Reflection

■ Mindful Housecleaning

More challenging than sitting or walking is practicing mindfulness while working. Perhaps the greatest challenge is to remain mindful while doing chores we dislike. When we do not want to do something, the tendency is to do it badly and halfheartedly. We tend to daydream or to rush through the distasteful experience. Cleaning house is an unpleasant chore for many of us.

Now take a chore like housecleaning and make it an experience in mindfulness. Divide your work into stages, such as putting things away, dusting, sweeping the floors. Allow yourself plenty of time for each stage. Move slowly, about three times more slowly than usual. Focus your attention completely on each task. For example, when putting a book back on the shelf, look at the book, be aware of what book it is, know that you are in the process of putting it back in a specific place on the bookshelf. Avoid any abrupt or rushed movement. Remain aware of your breath, especially when your thoughts wander. (Adapted from Hanh, 1976)

Will

Dogen writes, "It is by means of the will that we understand the will" (in Kennett, 1976, p. 170). Will develops through the exercise of the will. To grasp the will is to make a real commitment to your training and to take responsibility for your own actions, realizing that no one else can do your training for you.

> It is not easy for anyone, however, to cast away the chain of ignorance and discrimination all at once. A very strong will is required, and one has to search single-heartedly for his True Self, within himself. Here hard training is needed in Zen, and it never resorts to an easygoing, instant means. (Shibayama, 1970, p. 31)

There is only one thing, to train hard, for this is true enlightenment. (Evening Service in Kennett, 1976, p. 290)

One basic Buddhist principle is that daily life and activity should be brought into harmony with ideals and values. Training oneself is not merely a means to an end, but training is an end in itself. Dogen writes:

> It is heretical to believe that training and enlightenment are separable, for in Buddhism the two are one and the same. . . . [A]s this is so, the teacher tells his disciples never to search for enlightenment outside of training since the latter mirrors enlightenment. Since training is already enlightenment, enlightenment is unending; since enlightenment is already training, there can be no beginning whatsoever to training. (In Kennett, 1976, p. 121)

O Buddha, going, going, going on beyond, and always going on beyond, always becoming Buddha. (The Scripture of Great Wisdom in Kennett, 1976, p. 224)

A contemporary Zen teacher cautioned one of his disciples: "Your enlightenment is such that you can easily lose sight of it if you become lazy and forgo further practice. Furthermore, though you have attained enlightenment you remain the same old you—nothing has been added, you have become no grander" (Kapleau, 1965, p. 231).

Training is an ongoing process, because there is no end to the realization of Buddhist principles. Someone who stops and remains satisfied with an initial enlightening experience will soon be left with nothing but a beautiful memory.

Emotions

An important goal of Buddhist training is to learn to be in control of one's emotions rather than be controlled by them. There is nothing wrong with most emotions; however, few people experience their emotions properly or appropriately. They become angry or outraged over trivial matters, suppress their feelings, and carry the emotion into situations that are far removed from the source of the anger.

Through training, the Zen student gradually develops a state of meditative awareness in all daily activities. As the student becomes more aware of emotional reactions to various situations, the emotions tend to lose their hold. One Zen teacher commented that if one does show anger, the display should be like a small explosion or a thunderclap; the anger is then fully experienced and can be dropped completely afterward (Suzuki, n.d.).

The ideal Buddhist emotional state is compassion, which can be thought of as transcended emotion, a feeling of unity with all other beings, the fruit of the experience of nonduality.

Intellect

The study of Buddhist scriptures and the intellectual understanding of Buddhist teachings are important first steps in Buddhist training, as mentioned in the commentaries to the ox-herding pictures. However, reliance on the intellect alone can become a hindrance to true awareness. Ananda, the most clever and most learned of Buddha's disciples, took almost five times longer than the others to reach enlightenment. After the Buddha's passing, the other disciples went to Ananda, whose memory was so prodigious that he could recite, word for word, all the talks of the Buddha. But his love of argument, his pride in his learning, and his attachment to his teacher stood in the way of his enlightenment.

Pure intellect and abstract reasoning are useful. But intellect and reasoning alone do not enable us to comprehend ourselves and the world around us. The intellect is essentially powerless when it comes to satisfying our deepest needs. "It is not the object of Zen to look illogical for its own sake, but to make people know that logical consistency is not final, and that there is a certain transcendental statement that cannot be obtained by mere intellectual cleverness" (Suzuki, 1964, p. 67).

Buddhism distinguishes between the ordinary conscious mind and the deeper Mind:

> To live a spiritual life is to learn and to practice the Way-mind. The Way is the universal path that is complete serenity and tranquility. It is called Mind. This Mind is not ordinary mind. Mind, as serenity and tranquillity, is the original nature of human consciousness. . . .

Earth penetrates heaven whenever Zazen is truly done. (Dogen in Kennett, 1976, p. 140)

> In the study of psychology, one tries to understand the basis of consciousness, which is called the unconscious. . . . Psychology tries to understand this unconscious level, and to take things from it. When you try to take things from it, this is nothing but the functioning of ego-consciousness. . . . But whatever the ego can pick up and look at is only the surface of Way-mind. Buddhism is to learn serenity and tranquillity directly, and to practice it. (Katagiri, 1988, p. 13)

Although erudition alone is not particularly helpful, intellectual understanding plus the actual practice of that understanding is essential. Ideally, intellectual understanding deepens and becomes clarified through meditation and training in daily life, in accordance with Buddhist principles. For instance, one who reads about the concept of compassion without actually serving others knows compassion only as a shallow abstraction. Buddhist teachings are meant to be living truths, actively expressed in people's lives.

Self

In Buddhist thought, there is a distinction made between the lesser self and the greater self. The lesser self is the ego, the consciousness of one's mind and body. The lesser self remains focused on the limitations of the individual, the awareness of separateness between the individual and the rest of the world. This level of consciousness must be transcended in order to develop a sense of unity with other beings and with nature.

In one way, the lesser self is created by one's sense of inadequacy. That is, the more insecure, or inadequate, we feel, the greater the extent of our personal ego. As we become whole, integrated individuals, our lesser selves naturally diminish in strength. We never lose our egos; however, the mature person is in control of the ego, not run by it.

To study the Buddha Way is to study the self, to study the self is to forget the self, to forget the self is to be enlightened by the ten thousand things. (Dogen in Maezumi, 1978)

It is possible to identify oneself with one's greater self, which is as large as the entire universe, embracing all beings and all creation. This level of understanding is an essential element in the experience of enlightenment.

Identification with the greater self does not mean that the lesser self must be done away with. Training brings about transcendence of the lesser self so that one is no longer dominated by it. Nirvana is not annihilation of the ego, or lesser self, but transcendence of ego orientation. In Buddhist art, the Bodhisattva Monju is depicted sitting on a ferocious beast. Monju is sitting in serene meditation, although the beast is awake, with its fierce eyes open wide. The beast represents the ego, a useful tool that is not to be killed, although it must be watched and firmly sat upon.

Teacher

When you meet a Zen master who teaches the Truth, do not consider his caste, his appearance, shortcomings or behavior. Bow before him out of respect for his great wisdom and do nothing whatsoever to worry him. (Dogen in Kennett, 1976)

A true Buddhist teacher is one who not only believes in Buddhist principles but practices those teachings. Whenever a teacher fails to live up to this ideal, he or she must be ready to acknowledge it. The pupils approach their teacher as the ideal example to follow, as the living Buddha. However, genuine Zen teachers are aware of their limitations and try not to cut themselves off from their pupils by placing themselves on a pedestal. Disciples must see their teacher's humanness and shortcomings yet recognize the Buddha in the teacher in spite of his or her faults.

Originally, there were no statues of the Buddha in Buddhist temples; there were only the footprints of the Buddha. This was a reminder to the student of the principle "Thou must go alone, the Buddhas only point the way." Moreover, after seeing a concrete image, students may believe that a teacher should look like a Buddha and that only those who resemble the image are teachers. Buddhist images are symbols of mental qualities such as wisdom or compassion. Rather than icons to be worshipped, they are meant to remind us of qualities that reside within ourselves.

A teacher is involved primarily in his or her own training. Others who recognize certain exceptional qualities choose to model themselves after the teacher's example. The teacher does not try to be good for the sake of others, or to worry about whether pupils want to follow. By example, and by great patience, love, and forbearance, a teacher can serve as an inspiration for others to exert their best efforts in their own training. Trying too hard to teach inevitably creates in pupils a sense of guilt for not living up to various external ideals. The teacher can serve best as a standard against which disciples freely decide to measure their own attitudes and training.

Dogen stresses the necessity of a teacher:

> If a true teacher is not to be found, it is best not to study Buddhism at all. They who are called good teachers, however, are not necessarily either young or old but simply people who can make clear the true teaching and receive the seal of a genuine master. Neither learning nor knowledge is of much importance, for what characterizes such teachers is their extraordinary influence over others and their own will power. They neither rely on their own selfish opinions nor cling to any obsession, for training and understanding are perfectly harmonised within them. These are the characteristics of a true teacher. (In Kennett, 1976, p. 109)

To follow a Zen master is not to follow in old ways nor to create new ones; it is simply to receive the teaching. (Dogen in Kennett, 1976)

Students often judge their teacher, to decide whether the person is a "Zen master" or not. Some discrimination is, in fact, necessary, because even unprepared and unqualified people may call themselves teachers. But for a pupil to worry about the degree of realization of a qualified Zen teacher is nothing but egotism. The student is really asking, "Is this teacher worthy of teaching me?" "Does he or she conform to my standards?" Buddhist teachings hold that anything and everything can teach, if only the student has an open mind.

If you wonder "Can I trust?" you are really wondering, "Can I develop a strong enough opinion to please me?" (Bahaudin, a Sufi master)

Evaluation

One exciting and intriguing aspect of Buddhism is that it fosters a sense of a vital dialectic, the simultaneous appreciation of the real and the ideal and the recognition of the tension between the two. Besides aspiring to the ideals of Buddhism, students acknowledge the limitations of actuality. The individual must understand and live by this notion: "I am Buddha, and I am not Buddha, and I am Buddha" (Kennett-roshi, personal communication). This dialectic approach manifests itself in virtually all aspects of Buddhist life and thought. It provides a creative tension, at once a way to cope with present limitations and to move toward the ideal.

Lo! with the ideal comes the actual, like a box with its lid . . . like two arrows in mid-air that meet. (Sandokai in Kennett, 1976, p. 280)

To say flatly that "such and such is true" is to ignore the principle of impermanence. This kind of statement is misleading at best, but the opposite statement is equally misleading. It is better to say, "It is so, and it is not so, *and* it is so." Virtually every statement and every situation can be better understood by applying this dialectic.

There is great depth in the Zen notion that training is enlightenment. The trainee who maintains this attitude avoids getting caught in the trap of working for an unattainable ideal. To strive continually for a future goal or reward may mean that one is never fully involved in the present. If the path is not in harmony with the goal, how can one ever reach the goal?

This issue is made clear in a well-known Zen story about Baso, a monk who was making great efforts in meditation. Nangaku, his teacher, asked: "Worthy one, what are you trying to attain by sitting?"

> Baso replied: "I am trying to become a Buddha."
>
> Then Nangaku picked up a piece of roof tile and began grinding it on a rock in front of him
>
> "What are you doing, Master?" asked Baso.
>
> "I am polishing it to make a mirror," said Nangaku.
>
> "How could polishing a tile make a mirror?"
>
> "How could sitting in zazen [meditation] make a Buddha?"
>
> Baso asked: "What should I do, then?"
>
> Nangaku replied: "If you were driving a cart and it didn't move, would you whip the cart or whip the ox?"
>
> Baso made no reply.
>
> Nangaku continued: "Are you training yourself in zazen? Are you striving to become a sitting Buddha? If you are training yourself in zazen, [let me tell you that] zazen is neither sitting nor lying. If you are training yourself to become a sitting Buddha, Buddha has no one form. The Dharma [Teaching], which has no fixed abode, allows of no distinctions. If you try to become a sitting Buddha, this is no less than killing the Buddha. If you cling to the sitting form you will not attain the essential truth." (In Kapleau, 1965, p. 21)

Dogen has pointed out that "since Buddhist trainees do almost nothing for themselves, how is it possible that they should do anything for the sake of fame and gain? Only for the sake of Buddhism must one train in Buddhism" (in Kennett, 1976, p. 107).

The Buddhist dialectic also applies to the role of the teacher. As mentioned earlier, the ideal Buddhist teacher recognizes his or her own limitations and acknowledges these limitations to the students. This is a major point of contrast to the Indian Yoga tradition, in which the guru tends to be venerated as the perfect embodiment of all divine virtues and characteristics.

However much anyone might theoretically come to approximate these divine ideals, there is no denying the fact that all religious teachers are merely human. They all have foibles and imperfections. Attempting to maintain a role of holy perfection before one's disciples inevitably leads to a certain amount of posing and hypocrisy. Unless teachers acknowledge their limitations, they are likely to become egotistical and defensive about their slightest faults or mistakes.

Disciples who view their teacher as perfection itself avoid accepting responsibility for their own development, because they can make no connection between their own imperfections and the ostensible perfection of the master. Therefore, rather than continue the hard work of training and self-discipline, students convince themselves that their teacher is a "master" who can accomplish all kinds of things they cannot. Thus they need not even make the effort.

In Zen, Buddhist practice and daily life are not separate; they are seen as one and the same. Practical, unspectacular experience is stressed, and the esoteric and miraculous are downplayed. A Zen master once said, "My miracle is that when I feel hungry I eat, and when I feel thirsty I drink" (Reps, n.d., p. 68). Life is to be lived with full awareness by accepting and fulfilling the requirements of daily life. The Zen master Joshu was once asked for instruction by a new monk.

To live by Zen is the same as to live by an ordinary daily life. (Evening Service in Kennett, 1976)

JOSHU: "Have you breakfasted yet?"
MONK: "I have had my breakfast."
JOSHU: "Then wash out your bowl."

The monk suddenly understood the true nature of Zen.

Ramaswami and Sheikh (1989) summarize Buddhist psychology:

> The psychology of Buddhism rests on the notions of the absence of a separate self, impermanence of all things, and the fact of sorrow. Human beings suffer because of self-delusion, striving to possess that which inevitably must crumble, and because of desire. The Buddha did not stop with a mere diagnosis. He proclaimed that the cure is to reach a higher state of being, wherein self-knowledge has eradicated delusion, attachment, and desire. (p. 120)

There is no final doctrine or dogma because there can be no absolute truths, nor even an absolute Buddha, in the face of impermanence. Buddhist teachings are oriented to human realities. They are aimed at eliminating the sense of dissatisfaction and inadequacy caused by a limited, selfish ego. In the passage quoted at the beginning of this chapter, the Buddha is reported to have told his disciples not to follow any teachings in response to a particular teacher's reputation or skill with words but to rely on their own judgment and experience. The final criterion for Zen is experience. Teaching and discipline that aid people in becoming more mature, more responsible, and more complete human beings are considered to be good Buddhism.

Recent Developments: The Influence of Buddhism

Buddhist thinking has had a significant influence on different areas of psychology. Meditation may provide many of the benefits of psychotherapy. Carrington and Ephron (1975) and Engler (1986, 1993) have explored a number of ways in which psychoanalysis and meditation techniques can interact effectively. Erich Fromm (1970) believed that the goals of Zen and psychoanalysis are the same. They include insight into self, liberation from the tyranny of the unconscious, and knowledge of reality. Fromm also pointed out that Zen and psychoanalysis share the principle that knowledge leads to transformation. Zen meditation has been found to be a valuable adjunct to therapy (Boorstein, 1988; Claxton, 1986; Fuld, 1991; and Kornfield, 1988), and Eastern systems of psychotherapy inspired by Zen have enjoyed growing popularity in the West (Reynolds, 1980, 1984, 1993). Benoit (1990) has examined in detail the psychology of transformation in Zen. Soeng (1991) has interpreted Buddhist scriptures in light of modern quantum physics.

Gestalt therapy and Buddhism also share basic principles. Both stress the importance of mindful living in the present. For both, awareness is a primary tool for change. Rather than the unconscious, Perls (1969) argued that the conscious mind is our enemy. Similarly, the Buddha pointed out that it is the conscious mind that clings to cravings and to the false idea of a separate self.

A number of psychologists have begun to synthesize the insights of meditation and cognitive psychology (Brown & Engler, 1986; Goleman, 1988; Shapiro, 1980; Shapiro & Walsh, 1984). Empirical research has demonstrated significant neurological and physiological effects of Zen meditation (Hirai, 1989; Murphy & Donovan, 1988). *Zazen* and other Eastern meditative disciplines have been related to better health and ability to cope with stress and tension (Claxton, 1986; Dalai Lama et al., 1991; Kabat-Zinn, 1990, 1994; Shen-Yen, 1987).

Two other schools of Buddhism have become popular and influential in the United States—Tibetan Buddhism and Theravadan Buddhism. A number of Tibetan Buddhist teachers have emigrated to the West, where they have founded successful Buddhist centers, trained large numbers of students, and written important books. One of the best-known teachers, the late Chogyam Trungpa, established the Naropa Institute in Boulder, Colorado. His books (1975, 1988) have influenced many people interested in Tibetan Buddhism.

The most famous Tibetan teacher is, of course, the Dalai Lama (1991, 1993), who made world headlines when he received the Nobel Peace Prize in 1989. Other important Tibetan Buddhist works include Evans-Wentz (1954, 1958, 1960) and Lama Govinda (1960).

There have been a number of works based on Theravadan Buddhism. Daniel Goleman, a well-known transpersonal psychologist, has written about meditation and states of consciousness in the Theravadan tradition (Goleman, 1988; Goleman & Davidson, 1979). Another important figure is Jack Kornfield (1987, 1993), who is both a transpersonal psychologist and a Buddhist priest. One of the basic Theravadan Buddhist practices, *vipassana,* or "insight meditation," has become widespread (Dhammadudhi, 1968; Goldstein, 1976; Sayadaw, 1972).

Buddhism has grown substantially in the United States since the 1970s. It has been accepted more readily than other Eastern ways of life, because it has been viewed more as a psychology than as a religion. One Zen master has cautioned, however, that Buddhism as a psychology is limited and that Buddhism must be taught and practiced religiously:

> In a sense, Buddhism as a psychology is still part of human culture, influencing, but not exactly penetrating American life. In order to penetrate American life, Buddhism must be accepted as a religion, and zazen must be practiced as an end in itself. . . . In the nineteenth century, Western people didn't accept Buddhism as a religion because it didn't seem to have prayer; it was not what is called revealed religion. . . . Though Buddhism doesn't seem to have prayer, it does have *dhyana*. *Dhyana* means zazen (meditation), and dhyana is exactly the same as prayer. Shakyamuni Buddha says Dharma is a light you can depend on, the self is a light you can depend on, but this self is really the self based on the Dharma . . . or the Truth itself. So, Buddhism is not a revealed religion, but an awakened religion—it is awakening to the self or to the Truth. (Katagiri, 1988, p. 98)

The literature on Zen Buddhism in English continues to grow. Thich Nhat Hanh's work (1976, 1987, 1988, 1992, 1993, 1996) has had a wide influence, as has Katagiri (1988) and Deshimaru (1985, 1987, 1991).

The Theory Firsthand

Excerpts from *The Wild, White Goose*

The following excerpts are taken from the diary—called The Wild, White Goose*—of Jiyu Kennett (1977a), a British woman who studied for many years at a major Zen training temple in Japan. She founded a Zen training temple, Shasta Abbey, in Mount Shasta, California, and wrote several excellent books on Zen.*

11th. Rev. January

Rev. Hajime called me into his room early this evening so that we could get on with the translation for as long a time as possible before the bell [rang] for bed. . . .

"Shakyamuni[2] Buddha and I are one, as are all Buddhists with both him and me, and not merely all Buddhists but all people and all things both animate and inanimate. And none of us have anything to do with Shakyamuni Buddha." I paused for a moment, so that he could thoroughly digest what I had written, then I continued. "Shakyamuni Buddha is of no importance at all at the present time and Shakyamuni Buddha lives forever in me."

He was silent, simply looking deeply into my eyes; then he spoke softly.

"You should ask Zenji Sama for the Transmission," he said.

[Kennett:] "If Transmission is what I think it is I do not understand you. As I know of it, Transmission is received when all training is finished and the master wishes to give his seal of approval to a disciple before he goes out to teach. I am anything but ready for that."

[Hajime:] "That is a popular misconception. Admittedly it is the giving of the seals of the master to someone whom he knows has understood his Own Nature but

[2]In Sanskrit, *Shakyamuni* means "wise man of the Shakyas." It is one of the terms frequently used to refer to the Buddha, Siddhartha Gautama, a prince of the Shakya clan.

they are only given when the master is certain that the disciple concerned regards his training as just beginning every minute of his life and not when he thinks of it as being over. In other words, not when he thinks of himself as being enlightened and having nothing more to do. Understand the 'gyate, gyate' of the Hannyashingyo as 'going, going,' not 'gone, gone.'"

[Kennett:] "Doesn't one have to have had some great kenshō [enlightenment] before such a thing takes place? All that happened to me in October was that I realised that there was nothing more I could do but train myself constantly every day of my life and that I was the worst trainee in existence." . . .

16th January

. . . There is no part of me that can ever be chopped off. There is no emotion, no feeling, no thought, no word, no deed that does not come out of the Buddha Mind. I said this to [Reverend Hajime] and went on, "Then the sex act is part of the Buddha Nature and expresses the Buddha Nature at every turn, for it is, of itself, clean. What we have done is made it dirty with our own guilts and misuse."

"You are correct."

"Eating and going to the toilet and washing clothes and scrubbing the floor are all part of the 'with' for they are all expressions of the Buddha Nature." I stopped, amazed at myself.

"Go on," he said.

". . . and the sun and the moon and the stars and the earth; and the digging of the earth and the flowing water; these too are all expressions of the Buddha Nature, and the tongue I use to speak these words, and the food I eat, and the differences in the tastes; 'by comparing them you can'—Yes! that's what the scripture means. 'By comparing them you can distinguish one from other,'—and yet they're all the same thing; they're all expressions of the Buddha Nature and there is no way in which they can be separated off from it; and there is no way in which one can separate off any person or being or any living thing. . . ."

". . . This is the reason why it is so difficult to keep the Precepts and why the Truth can't be given to us until we have kept them and learned to make them our blood and bones. We don't *want* to know that we can be evil so where is there any need for Precepts? Thus, no-one can enter into the Truths of Buddhism until he has made the commitment of becoming a priest otherwise he could use the knowledge of his own indestructibility for all sorts of evil purposes. He would know his own true freedom and wouldn't care two hoots what he got up to with other people."

"That is completely right. You have understood the 'with' at last. You see, from now on you can carry on from there and there will be no difficulty in understanding, and you will know that you must hold everyone and everything as the 'with' aspect of the Buddha Mind and recognise that, whatever aspect of the Buddha Mind it shows, the Precepts must always hold it within themselves."

"Then making the Precepts part of my blood and bones means that the Precepts will eventually fall away because I will be their actual embodiment."

"Haven't you realised that, in your case, the early moral form of them already has? You have gone on beyond morality."

"I thought they had but . . . oh dear, there goes the bell. We'd better go to service. Can we continue this later?"

"To-morrow. I have to go out this evening."

We bowed to each other, the first time he had bowed to me fully, and I left the room.

Chapter Highlights

- Every individual has the capacity to become a Buddha, to develop into a fully mature and complete human being.
- The official life story of the Buddha may be taken as a parable of Buddhist principles and ideals. Born a prince, Gautama came to realize that even in the happiest and most prosperous life, one would encounter sickness, old age, and death.
- At the heart of Gautama's spiritual search was the problem of the inevitability of human suffering.
- Through the Buddha's own experience in religious self-discipline came the concept of the Middle Way, that of seeking a useful and healthy self-control without either extreme—of self-torture or complete indulgence in the senses.
- There are three major characteristics of existence: impermanence, selflessness, and dissatisfaction.
- Basic principles of the Four Noble Truths are these: (1) the existence of dissatisfaction is inescapable; (2) dissatisfaction is a result of desire or craving; (3) elimination of craving brings the extinction of suffering; (4) there is a way to eliminate craving, which is the Eightfold Path.
- The Eightfold Path includes right speech, right action, right livelihood, right effort, right mindfulness, right concentration, right thought, and right understanding.
- In Zen, there are two major meditation practices. One can either simply sit, with concentrated awareness, or one can focus on a koan, a Zen paradox.
- The achievement of enlightenment through the use of koans is stressed in the Rinzai school of Zen. The Soto school stresses two major points: there is no gap between daily practice and enlightenment, and right (correct) behavior is Buddhism itself.
- In the Soto school, the riddle of daily life as it is manifested for each individual is considered one's personal koan, and is the most important aspect of one's training.
- Not merely a technique to achieve something, meditation is a complete practice in itself.
- The terms *satori,* "intuitive understanding," and *kensho,* "to see into one's own nature," have often been used in Zen for *enlightenment.* Both terms refer to the experience of the truth of Buddhist teachings as a dynamic state of being, rather than as a static state that one can attain permanently.
- The Arhat is one who has become free of the world and its attachments to family, possessions, and comfort. The quest is for spiritual perfection and abandonment of the world; the focus is on self-development.
- The Bodhisattva is one who has vowed to remain in the world until all sentient beings have been delivered from suffering. Feeling the suffering of others as one's own results in compassion for all beings. The ideal stresses service to others.

- The world is not transcended in enlightenment, but the selfish ego is.
- A series of ten ox-herding pictures illustrates the path of spiritual growth in the Zen tradition. The Buddha-nature is symbolized by the ox, and the internal search and spiritual development of the Zen student is reflected in the process of finding the ox.
- Greed, hate, and delusion are seen as the major sources of suffering, or the "three fires" of Buddhism. The individual possesses a mixture of all three qualities, in a balance that changes with circumstances.
- Buddhism fosters the simultaneous appreciation of the real and the ideal, and it recognizes the tension between the two. This dialectic provides a creative tension, a way both to address present limitations and to move toward the ideal.

Key Concepts

Delusion A general state of vacillation, confusion, and lack of awareness. The behavior of one dominated by this trait is characterized by worry, confusion, obstinacy, excitability, and laziness. Delusion can be turned into wisdom through the realization that everything contains the Buddha-nature and therefore merits our deepest care and attention. Delusion is one of the "three fires," or obstacles to growth.

Dissatisfaction The belief that suffering, or dissatisfaction, comes not from the outer world but from the limited ego of each individual. The person can experience a sense of satisfaction only through self-transformation. Dissatisfaction, which encompasses birth, death, decay, pain, and existence itself, is one of the fundamental Buddhist concepts.

Enlightenment A dynamic, progressive state of mind that requires self-discipline, meditation, and realization of selflessness. It can bring about an experience of the truth of Buddha's teachings. Another approach is that "it is just perfect peace and harmony."

Greed The desire to possess more than we have or need. It is a major problem for most people. Those in whom greed is predominant are discontented, crafty, vain, and extremely fond of sweet, rich foods and fine clothes. Greed can be turned into compassion through self-discipline and obedience to the precepts. Greed is one of the "three fires," or obstacles to growth.

Hate A state in which individuals display quick anger and sharp tempers. Those dominated by hate tend to belittle others, hold grudges, and suffer from envy, arrogance, and stinginess. Hate can be turned into love by following the Buddhist teachings that emphasize respect for others and compassion. Hate is one of the "three fires," or obstacles to growth.

Impermanence The idea that nothing is everlasting, that everything is constantly in flux. The result, according to Buddhism, is that there can be no final authority or permanent truth. Impermanence is one of the three basic tenets of existence, in Buddhist thought.

Interdependence The Buddhist characterization of the world as fluid, interconnected processes. The concept of interdependence is in contrast to the human tendency to see the world as static and segmented.

Koan A question or exercise that cannot be solved by thinking or logic. Zen riddles paradoxically force one to go beyond logic and the inherent limitations of the way in which one has categorized experience up to that point. The aim of a koan is to entice Zen students to go beyond abstract conceptualizing, to see their own ignorance, and to search for truth within themselves.

Pride A state that may create a distortion of teachings, or lead to a lack of respect for one's teacher.

To counter pride, students may need to be reminded that impermanence is a fact of existence or that training in Buddhism is endless. Pride can be an obstacle to growth.

Selflessness The concept that there is no eternal self or immortal soul that exists in each individual. Impermanence is applicable to one's innermost self as well.

Zazen Zen meditation. It has been described as "just sitting."

Annotated Bibliography

Conze, E. (1959a). *Buddhism: Its essence and development.* New York: Harper & Row.

Survey of the major Buddhist traditions.

———. (Trans.). (1959b). *Buddhist scriptures.* Baltimore: Penguin Books.

Good collection of various Buddhist texts.

Kapleau, P. (Ed.). (1965). *The three pillars of Zen.* Boston: Beacon Press.

Includes lectures on training and meditation by a contemporary Zen teacher and first-person accounts of Zen training experiences.

Kennett, J. (1976). *Zen is eternal life.* Berkeley, CA: Dharma Publishing.

Includes an excellent introduction to Zen Buddhist thought, two newly translated classic Zen works, and the major Zen scriptures and ceremonials. For the serious Zen student.

———. (1977). *How to grow a lotus blossom, or how a Zen Buddhist prepares for death.* Mount Shasta, CA: Shasta Abbey Publishing.

An account of the mystical experiences of a Zen teacher, including past-life experiences and the deep transformation of mind and body.

Lal, P. (Trans.). (1967). *The Dhammapada.* New York: Farrar, Straus & Giroux.

Fine translation of a major Buddhist scripture.

Reps, P. (Ed.). (n.d.). *Zen flesh Zen bones.* New York: Doubleday (Anchor Books).

A marvelous collection of Zen stories and koans.

References

Benoit, H. (1990). *Zen and the psychology of transformation.* Rochester, VT: Inner Traditions.

Boorstein, S. (1988). Tandem paths: Spiritual practices and psychotherapy. *Inquiring Mind, 5,* 11.

Brown, D., & Engler, J. (1986). The stages of mindfulness meditation. In K. Wilber, J. Engler, & D. Brown (Eds.), *Transformations of consciousness.* Boston: Shambhala.

Burlingame, E. (1922). *Buddhist parables.* New Haven, CT: Yale University Press.

Carrington, P., & Ephron, H. (1975). Meditation and psychoanalysis. *Journal of the American Academy of Psychoanalysis, 3,* 43–57.

Claxton, G. (Ed.). (1986). *Beyond therapy: The impact of Eastern religion on psychological theory and practice.* London: Wisdom Publications.

Conze, E. (1959a). *Buddhism: Its essence and development.* New York: Harper & Row.

———. (Trans.). (1959b). *Buddhist scriptures.* Baltimore: Penguin Books.

Dalai Lama. (1993). The Nobel Peace Prize lecture. In R. Walsh & F. Vaughan (Eds.), *Paths beyond ego.* Los Angeles: Tarcher.

Dalai Lama et al. (1991). *Mind science.* Boston: Wisdom.

Deshimaru, T. (1985). *Questions to a Zen master.* New York: Dutton.

———. (1987). *The ring of the way: Testament of a Zen master.* New York: Dutton.

———. (1991). *The Zen way to martial arts.* New York: Arcana.

Dhammadudhi, S. (1968). *Insight meditation.* London: Committee for the Advancement of Buddhism.

Engler, J. (1986). Therapeutic aims in psychotherapy and meditation. In K. Wilber, J. Engler, & D. Brown (Eds.), *Transformations of consciousness.* Boston: Shambhala.

———. (1993). Becoming somebody and nobody: Psychoanalysis and Buddhism. In R. Walsh & F. Vaughan (Eds.), *Paths beyond ego.* Los Angeles: Tarcher.

Evans-Wentz, W. (1951). *Tibet's great yogi: Milarepa.* New York: Oxford University Press.

———. (1954). *The Tibetan book of the great liberation.* New York: Oxford University Press.

———. (1958). *Tibetan Yoga.* New York: Oxford University Press.

———. (1960). *The Tibetan book of the dead.* New York: Oxford University Press.

Fromm, E. (1970). Psychoanalysis and Zen Buddhism. In D. T. Suzuki, E. Fromm, & R. de Marino (Eds.), *Zen Buddhism and psychoanalysis.* New York: Harper & Row.

Fromm, G. (1992). Neurophysiological speculations on Zen enlightenment. *Journal of Mind and Behavior, 13,* 163–170.

Fuld, P. (1991, Fall/Winter). Zen and the work of a psychotherapist. *The Ten Directions,* pp. 40–41.

Glozer, G. (1974). Sitting on a chair or meditation bench. *Journal of the Zen Mission Society, 5*(3), 18–20.

Goldstein, J. (1976). *The experience of insight.* Santa Cruz, CA: Unity Press.

Goleman, D. (1988). *The meditative mind.* Los Angeles: Tarcher.

Goleman, D., & Davidson, R. (1979). *Consciousness: Brain states of awareness and mysticism.* New York: Harper & Row.

Govinda, A. (1960). *Foundations of Tibetan mysticism.* New York: Weiser.

Hanh, Thich Nhat. (1976). *The miracle of mindfulness.* Boston: Beacon Press.

———. (1987). *Being peace.* Berkeley, CA: Parallax Press.

———. (1988). *The heart of understanding.* Berkeley, CA: Parallax Press.

———. (1992). *Touching peace.* Berkeley, CA: Parallax Press.

———. (1993). *The blossoming of a lotus.* Boston: Beacon Press.

———. (1996). *Cultivating the mind of love.* Berkeley, CA: Parallax Press.

Hirai, T. (1989). *Zen meditation and psychotherapy.* New York: Japan Publications.

Kabat-Zinn, J. (1990). *Full catastrophe living.* New York: Delacorte.

———. (1994). *Wherever you go there you are.* New York: Hyperion.

Kapleau, P. (Ed.). (1965). *The three pillars of Zen.* Boston: Beacon Press.

Katagiri, D. (1988). *Returning to silence: Zen practice in daily life.* Boston: Shambhala.

Kennett, J. (1972a). The five aspects of self. *Journal of the Zen Mission Society, 3*(2), 2–5.

———. (1972b). The disease of second mind. *Journal of the Zen Mission Society, 3*(10), 13–17.

———. (1974). How to sit. *Journal of the Zen Mission Society, 5*(1), 12–21.

———. (1976). *Zen is eternal life.* Berkeley, CA: Dharma Publishing.

———. (1977a). *The wild white goose* (Vol. 1). Mount Shasta, CA: Shasta Abbey Publishing.

———. (1977b). *How to grow a lotus blossom, or how a Zen Buddhist prepares for death.* Mount Shasta, CA: Shasta Abbey Publishing.

———. (1978). *The wild white goose* (Vol. 2). Mount Shasta, CA: Shasta Abbey Publishing.

Kornfield, J. (1987). *Seeking the heart of wisdom.* New York: Shambhala.

———. (1988). Meditation and psychotherapy: A plea for integration. *Inquiring Mind, 5,* 10–11.

———. (1993). *A path with heart.* New York: Bantam.

Lal, P. (Trans.). (1967). *The Dhammapada.* New York: Farrar, Straus & Giroux.

Leggett, T. (1960). *A first Zen reader.* London: Rider.

———. (1977). *The tiger's cave.* London: Routledge & Kegan Paul.

———. (1978). *Zen and the ways.* Boulder, CO: Shambhala.

Maezumi, T. (1978). *The way of everyday life.* Los Angeles: Center.

Manne-Lewis, J. (1986). Buddhist psychology: A paradigm for the psychology of enlightenment. In G. Claxton (Ed.), *Beyond therapy.* London: Wisdom Publications.

Masunaga, R. (Trans.). (1971). *A primer of Soto Zen.* Honolulu: East-West Center Press.

Mosig, Y. (1990, Spring). Wisdom and compassion: What the Buddha taught. *Platte Valley Review,* 51–62.

Murphy, M., & Donovan, S. (1988). *The physical and psychological effects of meditation.* San Rafael, CA: Esalen Institute.

Ogata, S. (1959). *Zen for the West.* London: Rider.

Olcott, H. (1970). *The Buddhist catechism.* Wheaton, IL: Quest.

Perls, F. (1969). *Gestalt therapy verbatim*. Lafayette, CA: Real People Press.

Rahula, W. (1959). *What the Buddha taught*. New York: Grove Press.

Ramaswami, S., & Sheikh, A. (1989). Buddhist psychology: Implications for healing. In A. Sheikh & K. Sheikh (Eds.), *Eastern and Western approaches to healing*. New York: Wiley.

Reps, P. (Ed.). (n.d.). *Zen flesh Zen bones*. New York: Doubleday (Anchor Books).

Reynolds, D. (1980). *The quiet therapies*. Honolulu: University of Hawaii.

———. (1984). *Playing ball on running water*. New York: Morrow.

———. (1993). *Plunging through the clouds*. Albany: State University of New York.

Sangharakahitah. (1970). *The three jewels*. New York: Doubleday (Anchor Books).

Sayadaw, M. (1972). *Practical insight meditation*. Santa Cruz, CA: Unity Press.

Shapiro, D. (1980). *Meditation: Self-regulation strategy and altered states of consciousness*. New York: Aldine.

Shapiro, D., & Walsh, R. (Eds.). (1984). *Meditation: Classic and contemporary perspectives*. New York: Aldine.

Shen-Yen. (1987). *The advantages one may derive from Zen meditation*. Elmhurst, NY: Dharma Drum.

Shibayama, Z. (1970). *A flower does not talk*. Tokyo: Tuttle.

Soeng Mu, S. (1991). *Heart sutra: Ancient Buddhist wisdom in the light of quantum reality*. Cumberland, RI: Primary Point.

Spiegelman, J., & Miyuki, M. (1985). *Buddhism and Jungian psychology*. Phoenix, AZ: Falcon Press.

Stryl, L., & Ikemoto, T. (Eds. and Trans.). (1963). *Zen: Poems, sermons, anecdotes, interviews*. New York: Doubleday (Anchor Books).

Suzuki, D. T. (1956). *Zen Buddhism*. New York: Doubleday (Anchor Books).

———. (1959). *Zen and Japanese culture*. New York: Pantheon.

———. (1960). *Manual of Zen Buddhism*. New York: Grove Press.

———. (1964). *An introduction to Zen Buddhism*. New York: Grove Press.

Suzuki, S. (1970). *Zen mind, beginner's mind*. New York: Weatherhill.

———. (n.d.). *Teachings and disciplines of Zen*. (Lecture). San Rafael, CA: Big Sur Recordings.

Tanahashi, K., & Schneider, T. (1994). *Essential Zen*. New York: HarperSanFrancisco.

Thurman, R. (1995). *The essential Tibetan Buddhism*. New York: HarperSanFrancisco.

Trungpa, C. (1975). *Cutting through spiritual materialism*. Berkeley, CA: Shambhala.

———. (1988). *Shambhala: The sacred path of the warrior*. Boston: Shambhala.

Uchiyama, K. (1993). *Opening the hand of thought*. New York: Penguin Books.

Woodward, F. I. (1973). *Some sayings of the Buddha*. New York: Oxford University Press.

Yampolsky, P. (1971). *The Zen master Hakuin: Selected writings*. New York: Columbia University Press.

CHAPTER 17

Sufism and the Islamic Tradition

Know, O beloved, that man was not created in jest or at random, but marvellously made and for some great end. (Al-Ghazzali, 1964a, p. 17)

For thousands of years, Sufism has offered a path on which to progress toward this "great end" of self-realization. Sufism is a collection of teachings, manifested in many forms, that have a common goal: a transcendence of ordinary personal and perceptual limitations. Sufism is not simply a set of theories or propositions but has been variously described as a way of love, a way of devotion, and a way of knowledge. Through its many manifestations, Sufism is an approach that reaches beyond the intellectual and emotional obstacles that inhibit spiritual progress.

In psychology, it is both fashionable and realistic to admit how little we know and how much more research we need before we can understand human behavior. Sufism, on the other hand, explicitly asserts that there are teachers who know what is important—that is, they know how to teach their students to reawaken themselves to their natural state, to become real human beings. The objective of the Sufis is not to explain all of behavior; the task is to transmit what al-Ghazzali called useful knowledge: the knowledge that can help us to understand ourselves, our personality, and its limitations, and to experience the divine spark that lies within us.

There is no single, systematic approach to Sufi teachings, and not all teachings can be communicated in words. The wisdom of Sufism can be found in various forms, including stories, poetry, rituals, exercises, readings and study, special buildings, shrines, dance movements, and prayer.

Sufism is often described as a *path.* This metaphor suggests both an origin and a destination. Along the path, one can acquire knowledge of reality. "Real self-knowledge consists in knowing the following things: What are you in yourself and where did you come from? Where are you going and for what purpose are you tarrying here awhile? In what does your real happiness and misery consist?" (Al-Ghazzali, 1964a, pp. 19–20). Yet there are many pitfalls that render us unable, unmotivated, or even unwilling to seek this knowledge.

What we have included here is a representative selection of Sufi teachings that have been used to foster inner development. In our presentation of Sufism, we have focused primarily on a single figure whose psychological orientation is consonant with the general approach of this text. No one teacher, no one perspective, no one set of beliefs can be said to "represent" Sufism. In a growing number of Sufi writings and teachings, all different from the one presented here, a variety of approaches to Sufism have been made available. These works include the historical view (Arberry, 1970; Nicholson, 1964a); the philosophical approach (Burckhardt, 1968); the personal, contemporary approach (Meher Baba, 1967, 1972; Pir Villayat Khan, 1974; Siraj-Ed-Din, 1970); the more eclectic works by Farzan (1973, 1974) and Perry (1971); and the more traditional presentations (Nurbakhsh, 1978, 1979, 1981; Ozak, 1981, 1987, 1991a, 1991b).

A. R. Arasteh and Anees Sheikh are two psychiatrists who are also serious students of Sufism. They outline the following as some of the basic principles in Sufi practice (1989, p. 148):

1. There are as many ways to reach truth (or God) as there are individuals. All ways involve transformation of the ego and service to Creation.
2. We can live in harmony with others only if we develop an inner sense of justice. This occurs only when we have reduced our selfishness and arrogance.
3. Love is one of the underlying principles of morality. Love springs from self-work and expresses itself in service to others.
4. The cardinal truth is self-knowledge. Knowledge of self ripens into knowledge of God.

History

Historians usually describe Sufism as the mystical core of Islam and date its appearance to about the time that Islam emerged, around the seventh century A.D., as a major religious force.

Sufism is most prominent in the Middle East and in countries that embrace Islam, but its ideas, practices, and teachers are to be found in India, Europe, and the Americas as well (Shah, 1964). Sufis are scattered among virtually all nations of the world. As with any genuine mystical tradition, Sufism has changed form to fit the cultures and societies in which it has been practiced. Because Sufism has flourished in more cultures than any other spiritual tradition, it has become associated with a greater variety of outward forms. Sufi groups have existed for centuries in the Middle East, North Africa, South America, Europe, central Asia, India, Pakistan, and Indonesia.

Islam

Sufism is not different from the mysticism of all religions. . . . A river passes through many countries and each claims it for its own. But there is only one river. (Ozak, 1987, p. 1)

Islam, the Arabic word for "peace" or "surrender," is the religious system associated with its prophet, Muhammad. Muhammad had his initial revelation in the year A.D. 610. The Muslim era dates from 622, the year Muhammad fled from Mecca to the city of Medina. Islam is described in the Koran, Islam's holy book, as the original monotheistic religion revealed, in constant succession, to such teachers as Abraham, Moses, and Jesus.

In one sense, Islam has an exoteric, or outward, set of practices that support the inner practices of Sufism. "Sufism without Islam is like a candle burning in the open without a lantern. There are winds which may blow that candle out. But if you have a lantern with glass protecting the flame, the candle will continue to burn safely" (Ozak, 1987, p. 63). Islam provides a way of life that stresses honesty, charity, service, and other virtues forming a solid foundation for spiritual practice.

Five Pillars of Islam

There are five pillars of Islam: bearing witness, daily prayer, fasting, charity, and pilgrimage to Mecca.

Bearing Witness, or the Confession of Faith Entrance into Islam begins with the recitation of these basic tenets of Islamic faith: "I bear witness that there is no god but God" and "I bear witness that Muhammad is a servant and a messenger of God."

Bearing witness to something requires us to be awake, conscious. To realize the truth of the assertion "There is no god but God" is to know firsthand the unity of God. This is, in one sense, not the beginning of Islam but the pinnacle of the Islamic mystical path.

Daily Prayer Five times a day the call to prayer is sounded. Prayer times are at dawn, noon, midafternoon, dusk, and night. The prayers deliberately interrupt the community's daily activities, to reorient its members to their moral and religious concerns.

The times of prayer are visible manifestations of the doctrine that all are equal in the eyes of God, irrespective of class, social, and economic distinctions. All Muslims who come to the mosque pray together without regard to wealth or status. A king may pray beside a beggar.

Ibn 'Arabi (A.D. 1165–1240), known as the greatest of Sufi teachers, has written about prayer:

> Do everything you do in order to come close to your Lord in your worship and prayers. Think that each deed may be your last act, each prayer your last prostration, that you may not have another chance. If you do this, it will be another motivation for becoming heedful and also for becoming sincere and truthful. (Ibn 'Arabi, 1992, p. 8)

Prayer is a time to be in God's presence, a priceless opportunity for those who realize the potential of sincere prayer.

Fasting Each year, all Muslims who are able fast from dawn to sunset during the month of Ramadan. Individuals are supposed to abstain from eating, drinking, and making love, and from impure thoughts and harmful deeds, during this time. It is a difficult practice, intended to help the individual remain aware of the conflicting forces between the lower and the higher natures.

Al-Ghazzali (1986b) describes the outer and inner levels of fasting as follows:

> The fasting of the general public involves refraining from satisfying the appetite of the stomach and the appetite of the sex, as has already been discussed.
>
> The fasting of the select few is to keep the ears, the eyes, the tongue, the hands, and the feet as well as the other senses free from sin.
>
> The fasting of the elite among the select few is the fast of the heart from mean thoughts and worldly worries and its complete unconcern with anything other than God and the last day, as well as by concern over this world. (p. 20)

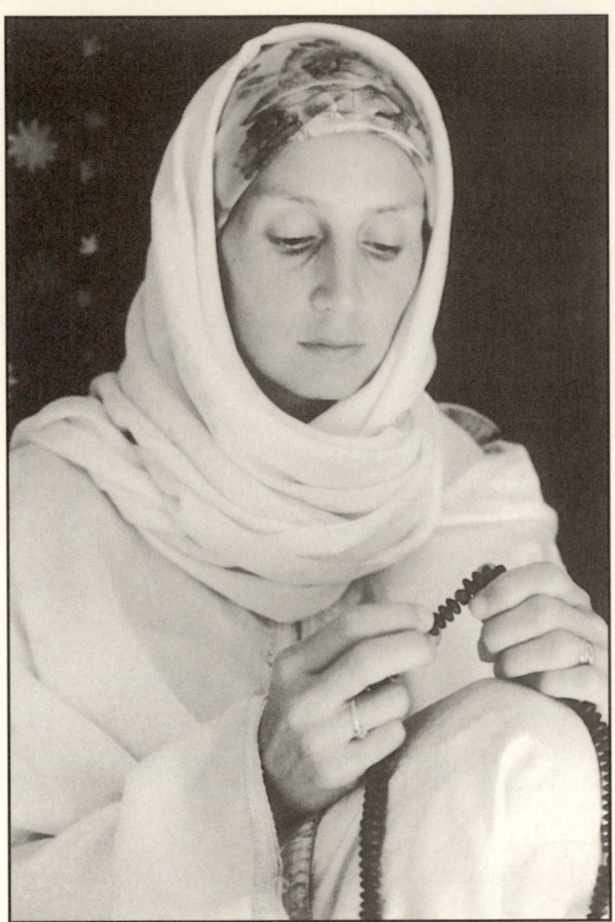

A Sufi at prayer

Fasting strengthens the will and is considered a great aid in the struggle with our lower self, or *nafs* (see "Obstacles" section).

Charity At the end of the month of Ramadan, every household is asked to give one-fortieth, or two and a half percent, of its accumulated wealth to the poor. "If God had wished he could make all creation rich, but for your trial he has created the poor that you might make gifts to them" (Al-Ghazzali, 1972, p. 16). It is said that all things originate from God; having goods and money is seen as a custodianship, in that one retains the right to possessions by returning some of them to the larger Muslim community from which they came.

Pilgrimage to Mecca The Kaaba in the city of Mecca, in Saudi Arabia, is the most holy shrine in Islam. All Muslims are required to visit it once in their lifetime, provided they can afford to do so. There are a set of rigorous observances to be followed at the time of pilgrimage, which occurs during a specified week each year. This annual ritual has kept the different Muslim peoples aware of their historical bond. The pilgrimage is a time in adult life when devotion to the spiritual completely overshadows worldly interests.

The Koran

The Koran, or Qur'an, the holy book of Islam, was revealed to Muhammad so that humankind could know God's truth. It contains essentially three levels of instruction. The first is a set of doctrines that describes reality and humanity's special role in it. The second level is a commentary on the opportunities and pitfalls that occur in life. The third level is a tangible manifestation of divinity; the words of the Koran are the direct words of God channeled through the messenger Muhammad.

It is the Merciful who has taught you the Koran. He created man and taught him articulate speech. The sun and the moon pursue their ordered course. The plants and the trees bow down in adoration. He raised the heaven on high and set the balance of all things, that you might not transgress it. Give just weight and full measure. (Koran, 55: 1)

> This is the Book:
> In it is guidance sure, without doubt,
> To those who fear [are in awe of] God
> Who believe in the Unseen,
> Are steadfast in prayer,
> And spend out of what We
> Have provided for them. (Koran, 2:2–3)

The Koran discusses religious and secular matters. It includes laws of inheritance, rules for marriage and divorce, and questions of property rights, as well as ethical and religious proscriptions. The central premise of Islam is that there can be no division of church and state; every act, every object, every relationship is part of the divine nature. The possibility of realizing the divine nature at every moment is interwoven into the daily practice of Islam. It is what the prophet preached and how he lived.

Muhammad

Muhammad, or Mohammed (A.D. 570–632), transmitted the message of the Koran to humanity. He was not divine, but he was divinely inspired. He is looked upon as the human being who comes as close as one can to living the ideal life set forth in the Koran.

When a person is reading the Koran two angels are kissing his forehead. (Al-Ghazzali, 1972, p. 17)

As the leader of the early Islamic community, Muhammad was very much involved with worldly as well as spiritual issues. He successfully settled political disputes, led armies, married and raised children, in addition to instructing his followers in the understanding of Islam. He instituted and practiced the five pillars.

After Muhammad's passing, a group of visitors came to his widow, Aisha.

They asked her, "What was the prophet, God's messenger, like?" "Have you read the Qur'an?" she replied. "He was the living Qur'an."

Sufi Teaching and Orthodox Islam

Islam is about outer, exoteric practice, whereas Sufism focuses on the inner effects of practice and subtle, esoteric truths. One story, of an encounter between a Sufi teacher and a conventionally pious man, illustrates the difference:

> One day a man came to the teacher Bayazid and said: "I have fasted and prayed for thirty years and have found none of the spiritual joy of which you speak."
>
> "If you had fasted and prayed for three hundred years, you would never find it," answered the sage.
>
> "How is that?" asked the man.
>
> "Your selfishness is acting as a veil between you and God."
>
> "Tell me the cure."
>
> "It is a cure you cannot carry out," said Bayazid. Those around him pressed him to reveal it. After a time he spoke.
>
> "Go to the nearest barbershop and have your head shaved; strip yourself of your clothes except for a loincloth. Take a nosebag full of walnuts; hang it around your neck. Go into the market place and cry out—'Anybody who gives me a slap on the neck shall have a walnut.' Then proceed to the law courts and do the same thing."
>
> "I can't do that," said the man. "Suggest some other remedy."
>
> "This is the indispensable preliminary to a cure," answered Bayazid. "But as I told you, you are incurable."
>
> (Adapted from al-Ghazzali, 1964a, pp. 128–130)

Women in Sufism and in Islam

It is often difficult to distinguish cultural, religious, and psychological ideas concerning the special status of women; nevertheless, the attempt is necessary in examining the role of women in Sufi thought.

From the early rise of Islam as a world religion, a succession of women have been regarded as saints in Sufi circles and within Orthodox Islam. From Rabia (A.D. 717–801) to the current period, these saints have been venerated and their work regarded with the same esteem as that of their male counterparts (Smith, 1977). An early Sufi teacher made it clear that in the spiritual life there could be neither male nor female (Shabistari in Smith, 1977). In contemporary Sufi teachings and groupings, women are present. The course of training is based on the capacities of the individual, not on the sex. (Irina Tweedie [1979] has written a vivid and detailed personal account of her own training and development at the hands of a contemporary Sufi teacher.)

Essentially, the rise of Islam changed the status of women, affording them "legal protections in the area of marriage, divorce and inheritance that are considered to mark a vast improvement over the situation of women in pre-Islamic society" (Smith, 1980, p. 517).

Despite their spiritual equality and their improved status through Islam, the position of women in most Islamic cultures is far from equal. As in Europe and the Americas, women have been denied equal access to education and property rights, as well as the freedom to travel and to better themselves. A growing literature in the West is sorting out the contradiction between the repressive attitudes still current in many Muslim countries and the fact that, according to serious Islamic scholars, religious and spiritual doctrines do not support this repression (Smith & Haddad, 1975).

Look not at my exterior form, but take what is in my hand. (Rumi in Shah, 1970a, p. 31)

Abu Hamid al-Ghazzali

The writings of Abu Hamid Muhammad Ibn Muhammad, known as **al-Ghazzali** (A.D. 1058–1111), are among the most widely read Sufi teachings. Because of his influence, many Islamic theologians finally accepted Sufism within formal Islam. Called the *Proof of Islam* and the *Restorer of Islam,* he is one of the dominant figures in Islamic theology. Western authorities agree that al-Ghazzali was among the few Muslim thinkers who exercised profound effects on later Christian thought.

His work altered the public view of Sufism from that of suspect, even heretical teaching, to a valued and essential part of Islam. "The accepted position of Sufism, whereby it is acknowledged by many Moslem divines as the inner meaning of Islam, is a direct result of Ghazzali's work" (Shah, 1964, p. 148).

Al-Ghazzali was born in the small town of Tus in Iran. His father died when al-Ghazzali was young, and he and his brother were raised by a Sufi who also provided for their early education. Al-Ghazzali was an excellent student; when he was old enough, he went to a larger town to study theology and canon law. He was interested in these areas, he later wrote, because they were the most direct paths to possible fame and wealth. However, his studies offered him other, more personal lessons. For example, once when he was returning to Tus, he was set upon by a band of thieves, who took all his belongings, including his lecture notes. Unable to bear the loss of the notes, he ran after the thieves, begging them to give him back his work. The leader asked him why pieces of paper should be so important. Al-Ghazzali replied that there was learning in them. "I travelled for the sake of hearing them and writing them down and knowing the science in them" (in MacDonald, 1899, p. 76). The robber laughed at al-Ghazzali and told him that knowledge that can be stolen is not knowledge at all. He returned the notes, but al-Ghazzali took the incident as a message from God; he spent the next few years learning and memorizing his scholarly notes.

After studying under a number of distinguished teachers, he was offered a position at the Nizamiya Academy at Baghdad, the most important seat of Islamic learning. He gained an international reputation as a teacher, and he also earned the respect of politicians and religious leaders. By the age of 34, he had reached the pinnacle of the Islamic intellectual world (Qayyum, 1976). By age 39, he had written 70 books.

"Do you not see," I reflected, "that while asleep you assume your dreams to be indisputably real? Once awake, you recognize them for what they are—baseless chimeras. Who can assure you, then, of the reliability of notions which, when awake, you derive from the senses and from reason?" (Al-Ghazzali, 1968a, p. 18)

In the midst of his growing fame, however, al-Ghazzali became severely depressed; he lost confidence in his teaching, his training, and his own capacities. Eventually, he grew to doubt even the experiences of his senses. Finally, he suffered a partial paralysis of his vocal cords, which prevented him from teaching. The doctors who examined him could find no physical cause for the symptoms. After two months he withdrew from the university and let it be known that he was making a pilgrimage to Mecca. Actually, he put all his property in trust, left his family, and became a dervish: a religious wanderer and seeker of truth.

He had studied the systems of formal philosophy and theology, but they seemed no longer fruitful; he had read the Sufi mystics, but knew he could not understand them. "I saw that in order to understand it [Sufism] thoroughly one must combine theory with practice" (1968a, p. 46). A desire to understand Sufi teachings led to a transformation of his own psychological structure. He was determined to become an initiate—one who has seen and experienced.

Al-Ghazzali found the principles of mysticism easy to learn but difficult to practice:

> I acquired a thorough knowledge of their research, and I learned all that was possible to learn of their methods by study and oral teaching. It became clear to me . . . that Sufism consists in experience rather than in definitions and that what I was lacking belonged to this domain, not of instruction, but of . . . initiation. (1968a, pp. 47–48)

> He proceeded straightway, hiding himself from public view into the wilderness adjoining Damascus and Jerusalem. There in solitude he sought the saints of various creeds, from whom he learnt practices of mysticism on recollection, contemplation and remembrance of the Name of the Lord, and wooed solitude and meekness, practiced the hardest austerities. This led to the development of intuition and unfoldment of hidden faculties within him. (Behari, 1972, p. xxii)

During the next 10 years, al-Ghazzali wrote his most important work, *The Revival of Religious Sciences* (1972), which aligned Sufi experiences with Islamic beliefs and practices. He established a framework in which pathological, normal, and mystical behaviors are linked in a single, unified field of human experience. He reinstated the elements of personal development and transpersonal experiences into an Islam that was rapidly becoming rigid and restrictive. In addition to various scattered works, he wrote a popular abridged version of *The Revival of Religious Sciences* titled *The Alchemy of Happiness* (1964a), which describes how one can overcome one's lower nature and find happiness through correct knowledge of the self, God, this world, and the next world.

After 11 years of wandering, he accepted, under pressure from the sultan, a teaching position at Naysabur. Several years later, he returned to his birthplace and, in the company of his disciples, lived a religious life until his death, at age 55.

Al-Ghazzali taught others to replace dogma with practice, piety with self-examination, and belief with a relentless examination of the circumstances of daily life. His books are still widely read throughout the Middle East. His ideas spread to the West, where they influenced Saint Thomas Aquinas and Saint Francis of Assisi (Shah, 1964).

Major Concepts

Sufism has been portrayed as a way of knowledge and also as a way of love. As with all mysticism, it is also a way of experiencing spiritual states beyond our limited, waking state. Those who have experienced such states describe them as a deeper knowing, a connection with ultimate truth.

Knowledge

In *The Book of Knowledge* (1966), Al-Ghazzali divides knowledge into two categories: detrimental and useful. Detrimental knowledge distracts from or retards the understanding of our inner selves. Sufism has traditionally viewed scholarly training as antithetical to true understanding, and al-Ghazzali's own legal and scholarly background made him especially sensitive to its limits. According to him, three forms of scholarship restrict our ability to learn. *Logic* is limited, especially in evaluating spiritual questions, because it does not generally allow the inclusion of novel or seemingly contradictory information. *Philosophy* does not consider realistic situations and is self-limiting because it does not validate its conclusions through actual experience. *Academic knowledge* is vain posturing; it is detrimental when it parades itself as the exclusive path to learning.

Useful knowledge furthers a person's growth. The most important form is *direct knowledge;* it cannot be described but it can be experienced. It cannot be taught but it can be received. Ibn 'Arabi called it knowledge of reality. With it, "man can perceive what is right, what is true, beyond the boundaries of thought and sense" (Shah, 1970a, p. 78). Sufi writings and teaching practices are the records of the ways in which generations of teachers have helped their students experience direct knowledge coupled with intuitive understanding. Intuition is developed to go beyond the limits of reason; therefore, it can perceive and integrate what reason alone could not accept.

A donkey with a load of books is still a donkey. (Koranic saying)

According to one of the sayings of the prophet, if you have remained the same for two days, then you are at a loss. We must learn and grow in wisdom every day; each day we should have improved from the day before.

The Four Stages of Sufism

Ibn 'Arabi (Ozak, 1988) has written that there are four stages of practice and understanding in Sufism—*sharia* (exoteric religious law), *tariqa* (the mystical path), *haqiqa* (truth), and *marifa* (gnosis). The last three are built upon the stage or stages that go before.

First is the **sharia,** which is the basic foundation for the next three stages. The **sharia** consists of teachings of morality and ethics found in all religions. It provides guidance for us to live properly in this world. Trying to follow Sufism

Personal Reflection

■ The Key and the Light

Throughout this chapter we will make use of teaching stories—stories that are told by Sufi teachers for more than just entertainment. Here is one famous story and some ways to work with it (adapted from Ornstein, 1972).

> A man is looking at Nasrudin, who is searching for something on the ground.
>
> "What have you lost, Mulla?" the man asked.
>
> "My key," said the Mulla.
>
> So they both went down on their knees and looked for it. After a time the man asked, "Where exactly did you drop it?"
>
> "In my own house."
>
> "Then why are you looking here?"
>
> "There is more light here than inside my own house."

The joke is popular in American vaudeville, as well as in Sufism. If you begin to work with it, it can be more than a joke, more than a story about a simpleton.

Read the story over a few times. Now imagine that you are searching desperately for something. Consider the following questions:

1. What are you looking for? (Allow an answer, no matter how unusual, to form in your mind.) Where are you looking? Is there a lot of light there? What kinds of associations do these questions evoke? How do you feel now?
2. Now think about a key. What is a key for? What is the key to your life right now? (Again, allow an answer, an image, or an idea to form; take your time.)
3. Now say to yourself, "I have lost my key." What does this statement evoke in you?
4. Now think, "My key is in my own house." What are your thoughts and feelings?
5. Then put the whole story together: "I am looking for my key—which I really know is in my own house—in places where I know the key is not, but where there is more light." Spend a little more time with the story.

> In addition to the personal associations called up by the story, I offer another. . . . Two areas of the mind are opposed, the light, or "day," and the dark, or "night." The key is inside the house, in the dark, unexplored area of our house, of the mind, of science. We are normally attracted and a bit dazzled by the light of the day, since it is generally easier to find objects in daylight. But *what we are looking for may simply not be there,* and often we may have to grope inelegantly in the dark areas to find it. Once we find what we are looking for in the dark, we can then bring it into the light, and create a synthesis of both areas of the mind. (Ornstein, 1972, pp. 174–175)

without following the *sharia* is like trying to build a house on a foundation of sand. Without an ordered life built on solid moral and ethical principles, no mysticism can flourish. In Arabic, *sharia* means "road." It is a clear track, a well-traveled route that anyone can follow.

Second is the **tariqa,** which refers to the practice of Sufism. *Tariqa* is the trackless path in the desert that the Bedouin would follow from oasis to oasis. This path is not clearly marked, nor is it even a visible road. To find your way in the trackless desert, you must know the area intimately, or have a guide who knows the destination and is familiar with the local landmarks. As the *sharia* refers to the outer practice of religion, the *tariqa* refers to the inner practice of Sufism. The guide you need in order to find your way is the Sufi teacher, or *sheikh*. The *sharia* makes our outsides clean and attractive; the *tariqa* makes us clean and pure from within. Each of these supports the other.

Third is **haqiqa**, or truth. It refers to the personal understanding of the inner meanings of the practices and guidance found in the *sharia* and *tariqa*. Without this understanding, we are fated to follow blindly, to imitate mechanically those who know, those who have attained the station of *haqiqa*. The attainment of *haqiqa* confirms and solidifies the practice of the first two stages. Before *haqiqa* all practice is imitation.

Fourth is **marifa**, or gnosis, a deep level of inner knowing, beyond *haqiqa*. It is the knowledge of Reality, attained by a very few—the Messengers, the Prophets, and the great sages and saints.

Ibn 'Arabi explained these four stages as follows: At the level of *sharia*, there is "yours and mine." That is, the *sharia* guarantees individual rights and ethical relations between people. At the stage of *tariqa*, "mine is yours and yours is mine." The dervishes are expected to treat each other as brothers and sisters—to open their homes, their hearts, and their purses to each other. At the level of *haqiqa*, there is "no mine and no yours." The individual realizes that all things come from God, that we are only caretakers of all that we "possess." We are expected to use the resources God has given us to benefit God's Creation. Those who attain *haqiqa* have gone beyond attachment to possessions, beyond attachment to externals in general, including fame and position. For those who reach *marifa*, there is "no me and no you." At this final stage, the individual recognizes that all is God, that nothing and no one is separate from God. This is the ultimate goal of Sufism.

What is lawful at one level of understanding may not be lawful at another. For example, only the *outer* practices of fasting are required by the *sharia*. However, according to the *tariqa*, one of the essential reasons for fasting is to develop self-discipline and to control the insatiable ego. A fast that engenders pride in those who abstain is perfectly lawful in the *sharia* but would be considered a failure in the *tariqa*.

Another example comes from the famous story of Mansur al-Hallaj, who was killed for publicly saying, "*En al Haqq*," "I am truth." One of the 99 attributes of God is truth, and, according to the *sharia*, individuals are absolutely forbidden to call themselves God. The traditional punishment for this extreme heresy was death. However, from the point of view of *haqiqa*, we each have the Divine within us, in our heart of hearts, and each person should be honored as a temple of God. As Junaid Baghdâdi replied when he was asked about Mansur, "What should he have said, 'I am falsehood'?" Perhaps if Mansur had attained the final level, *marifa,* he would have been able to speak the truth in a way that would have avoided the charge of heresy.

Annihilation and Return

Because someone has made up the word "wave," do I have to distinguish it from water? (Kabir, 1977, p. 29)

I laugh when I hear that the fish in the water is thirsty. (Kabir, 1977, p. 9)

The Sufis describe two advanced states of consciousness—annihilation and return. The first is a state of union, or annihilation—**fana**—in which individual identity seems merged with the whole of reality. In this state, a person erects no barriers between the self and God, because it is clear that no barriers exist. A person has become like a drop of water that is aware of being part of the ocean or a column of air that is conscious of the wind.

The second aspect is a state of return, or persistence—**baqa**—in which one is part of the world but not concerned about one's wordly position or rewards. The awareness of the divine element in all things is so great that personal issues become secondary to caring for the rest of God's creation (Arberry, 1966, pp. 131–145; Ibn 'Arabi, 1981). The individual is in the world but not separate from anything in it.

The following story indicates the power of a person who has realized both *fana* and *baqa,* someone who is simultaneously nothing and everything:

> At a court banquet, everyone was sitting according to his or her rank, waiting for the king to appear. A poorly dressed man came in and took a seat above everyone else. The prime minister angrily demanded that he identify himself.
>
> "Are you the vizier of a great king?"
>
> "No, I rank above a vizier."
>
> "Are you a prime minister?"
>
> "No, I also outrank a prime minister."
>
> "Are you a king in disguise?"
>
> "No, I am above that rank as well."
>
> "Then you must be the prophet," the prime minister suggested sarcastically.
>
> "No, I am above even the prophet."
>
> The prime minister shouted, "Are you then God?"
>
> "I am above that too," the man calmly asserted.
>
> "There is nothing above God!"
>
> The stranger replied, "Now you know me. That *nothing* is me."
>
> (Adapted from traditional sources)

In one sense, Sufism is essentially a path of self-transformation ending in *fana* and *baqa'*. Arasteh and Sheikh (1989) describe the states of *fana* and *baqa'* in psychological terms. *Fana* is the disintegration of one's narrow self-concept, social self, and limited intellect. *Baqa'* is the reintegration as the universal self, or the activation of one's totality.

Love

The end point of knowledge, according to al-Ghazzali, is also called love. Similarly, the end point of love leads to the state of wisdom. For al-Ghazzali, the two are the same, only the approaches are different. Each path has been taken by different Sufi teachers. The way of knowledge has been most clearly defined by al-Ghazzali; the path of love, by the Persian poet Rumi (A.D. 1207–1273).

For Rumi, love was the only force that could transcend the bounds of reason, the distinctions of knowledge, and the isolation of normal consciousness. The love he experienced was not sensual pleasure. It might be more aptly described as love for all things, for creation itself. Love is a continually expanding capacity that culminates in certainty, in the recognition that there is nothing in the world or in the spirit that is not both loved and loving.

What the eye sees is knowledge.
What the heart knows is certainty.
(Dhun'nun in Shah, 1971a, p. 195)

> Thou didst contrive this "I" and "we" in order that
> Thou mightest play the game of worship with Thyself,
> That all "I's" and "thou's" should become one soul
> and at last should be submerged in the Beloved.
> (Rumi in Arasteh, 1972, p. 146)

The perception of God as the Beloved, common to both Christian and Sufi writings, comes from mystical experience. As you channel your energy into loving God, there appears to be a response of being loved in return. Just as in a personal relationship, the act of loving brings forth or awakens love in the other. According to an old Sufi saying, if you take two steps toward God, God runs to you.

A modern Sufi master writes: "The essence of God is love and the Sufi path is a path of love. . . . Love is to see what is good and beautiful in everything. It is to learn from everything, to see the gifts of God and the generosity of God in everything. It is to be thankful for all God's bounties" (Ozak, 1987, p. 7).

> The eyes of the dervish who is a true lover see nought but God; his heart knows nought but Him. God is the eye by which he sees, the hand with which he holds, and the tongue with which he speaks. . . . Were he not in love, he would pass away. If his heart should be devoid of love for as much as a single moment, the dervish could not stay alive. Love is the dervish's life, his health, his comfort. Love ruins the dervish, makes him weep; union makes him flourish, brings him to life. (Ozak, 1981, pp. 60–61)

When we come to a certain point along the path of love, God reaches out and begins to assist us by drawing us toward God's presence. As this occurs, we stop striving and begin to surrender, to allow ourselves to be helped and be taken in.

Dynamics

Psychological Growth—Stages of Personal Development

Many Sufi teachers have described different stages in the course of personal development. Each stage trains or exposes different facets of the aspirant's character and perception. We will discuss each stage separately in order to facilitate an understanding, but no single linear pattern is typical or would be the actual experience of a Sufi student. Although other writers portray the stages differently (Arberry, 1970; Rice, 1964; Shah, 1964; Trimingham, 1971), they all acknowledge their debt to al-Ghazzali's earlier descriptions.

Initial Awakening This stage begins when a person concludes that the external world is not satisfying and decides to reevaluate his or her life. Such a realization is often preceded by a personal crisis, sometimes coupled with bewilderment about the meaning of existence. **Initial awakening,** then, marks a fundamental reorientation of personal values. What one has strived for may appear to be worthless; what one casts aside as absurd may suddenly take on great significance. In al-Ghazzali's own case, he gave up his successful career and became a dervish. Although his renunciation of worldly goods was only the first step in the process of transformation, it was the most dramatic change in his life. Rumi, too, left his academic teaching position to work with a Sufi teacher.

Patience and Gratitude At the stage of **patience and gratitude,** the individual (1) realizes that self-development takes time and (2) feels appreciation that the time is granted. Patience is not merely the passive acceptance of one's faults; it is the willingness to accept the fact that efforts at inner change are not immediately rewarded. A person reshapes his or her personality gradually, the way a tree is shaped, nourished, and pruned, again and again.

Patience, considered one of the greatest virtues, is essential for living in the present. Without patience, spiritual work is impossible. An impatient person's attention is on the future, but prayer or meditation requires present-centered, highly focused attention.

The development of patience is accompanied by a sense of gratitude that one is given the time to make progress at all. Gratitude is related to the belief that *all* things come from God. Gratitude is appreciation for everything one receives, whether it is pleasant or painful, whether it amounts to one's gaining or one's losing.

Fear and Hope Individuals seeking unity with the Divine experience **fear and hope.** Fear is fear of God. It is not fear of being punished or being sent to hell. Rather, it is the fear lovers feel when they are afraid of losing the other's love. The Sufi master Shibli stated, "Each day that I was overcome with fear, the door of knowledge and insight opened to my heart" (in Shafii, 1985, pp. 183–184).

Hope allows one to see oneself clearly and honestly, without becoming paralyzed. "The essence of Sufism is hope" (Shafii, 1985, p. 184). It is the hope that God will accept small efforts at prayer, service, and the like. The individual hopes that, in spite of very real shortcomings, he or she will progress on the spiritual path, the path that leads closer to God.

Self-denial and Poverty In pursuit of spiritual attainment, the individual may practice **self-denial and poverty.** Self-denial is service to others rather than promotion of oneself. It is service in order to please God, not to please others or to be rewarded or praised.

While poverty may be practiced in a literal sense—one may have no or few possessions—the goal is to be free of attachment. "When the heart is cleared (of all except God) poverty is not better than wealth nor is wealth better than poverty" (Hujwiri 1959, p. 24). What is significant is the loss of desire, not the loss of property. "The vacant heart [is] more important than the vacant hand" (Rice, 1964, p. 42).

Another word for Sufi is *faqir,* which comes from the Arabic root *faqr,* or poverty. Spiritual poverty is a heart empty of attachments to this world, a heart that is open and ready to be filled with God.

Trust in God Individuals who place **trust in God** have accepted the belief in the oneness of the Divine. In this stage, a person seeks neither support nor consolation from the external world; he or she seeks everything from God, not from the world.

Higher than the state of asceticism is the state wherein on the approach and departure of wealth the person remains unaffected equally. If it comes he is not glad and if it leaves him he is not sorry. (Al-Ghazzali, 1972, p. 206)

Al-Ghazzali describes three different degrees of trust. The first is the kind of trust you place in a skilled professional, such as a fine doctor or lawyer. The second is the trust of a child in its mother, a total reliance on the parent. The third is the complete submission of one's will, so that one is like a corpse in the hands of a washer of the dead. There is no resistance to whatever happens, no expectation.

> This is not like a child who calls upon the mother, but like a child who knows deeply that even if he does not call for the mother, the mother will be totally aware of his condition and look after him. This is the ultimate degree of trust in God. (Al-Ghazzali in Shafii, 1985, p. 227)

This is a period of activity, not a time of indolence, passivity, or dependency. The balance between acting for oneself and trusting in the Divine is captured in a saying of Muhammad: "Trust in God but tie your camel first." Trust arises from assuming that your efforts are part of a larger system, the details of which you are unaware.

Love, Yearning, Intimacy, and Satisfaction In this stage, of **love, yearning, intimacy, and satisfaction,** the developing personality has only one desire, which is to love God; to love anything other than God is "veiled heresy." It becomes clear that this single desire is the only desire that ever existed. The earlier stages of giving up attachments, overcoming greed, and acknowledging personal sin fade away with the all-encompassing power of this later realization.

Satisfaction comes from knowing that all things, pleasant or unpleasant, come from God. While enjoying love and a sense of intimacy with God, the individual cannot help but be satisfied with whatever comes to him or her in this world.

Intent, Sincerity, and Truthfulness The stage of **intent, sincerity, and truthfulness** is dominated by a concern for the intent, not the actual form, of action. If one's intentions are correct, then the actual practice is less important. There is less interest in observable behaviors and an ever-increasing awareness of the inner meaning of an action.

Sheikh Muzaffer used to say that someone might be walking in a poor part of town and announce, "These poor people desperately need a hospital. If I had a million dollars, I would immediately put it into a building fund for a hospital here." If the person is truly sincere in this wish—so that if he or she suddenly came into a million dollars, the money would immediately go into a hospital construction fund—then the announcement of intended generosity is equivalent to actually building the hospital. It is the sincerity of intention that counts. Whether one's actions succeed or not is God's will. It is one's inner intentions that give meaning to all actions.

Contemplation and Self-examination Al-Ghazzali considers the distractions that might prevent one from **contemplation and self-examination** and thus render one unable to perceive inner reality. His concerns are similar to those voiced in Yoga and Buddhism with regard to clearing the mind. He describes various ways of meditation and quotes incidents from the lives of teachers who were well versed in meditation.

The Recollection of Death Contemplating death can be a powerful tool in releasing one from undesirable habits and attitudes. Thinking about one's own death is an exercise in becoming more aware of one's present experiences. It is a way to begin the process of personal growth.

Al-Ghazzali suggests the following exercise to engrave the awareness of death into your consciousness:

> Remember your contemporaries who have passed away, and were of your age.
>
> Remember the honours and fame they earned, the high posts they held and the beautiful bodies they possessed, and today all of them are turned to dust.
>
> How they have left orphans and widows behind them and how their wealth is being wasted after them and their houses turned into ruins.
>
> No sign of them is left today, and they lie in the dark holes underneath the earth.
>
> Picture their faces before your mind's eye and ponder.
>
> Do not fix hopes on your wealth and do not laugh away life. Remember how they walked and now all their joints lie separated and the tongue with which they talked lightly is eaten away by the worms and their teeth are corroded. They were foolishly providing for twenty years when even a day of their lives was not left. They never expected that death shall come to them thus at an unexpected hour. (Al-Ghazzali, 1972, pp. 378–379)

In some sense, al-Ghazzali describes a cycle beginning with conversion and repentance and ending with reflection on death. It can easily go the other way: reflection on death leading to the psychological state that precedes conversion. Until recently, Western psychology has avoided the topic of death, perhaps because of our death-fearing culture.

Obstacles to Growth

The main obstacles to growth in Sufism are heedlessness and the lower self, or the *nafs*. The *nafs* is the source of most of our negative traits, including pride, greed, anger, and hypocrisy. One of the great goals of Sufism is to transform the *nafs*, to transform our negative qualities into positive ones. If habits of heedlessness or the negative traits of the *nafs* are too strong, the individual may not be capable of real Sufi practice.

Personal Reflection

■ Remembering Death

Most of us somehow believe that we will never die. We live as if death were, at best, a remote and far-distant possibility. It can help wake us up to contemplate our own death, to make the concept of our last days or hours more real.

Now imagine that you have died. You have pleaded with the Angel of Death to be allowed to return to life. There are so many things you have yet to do. The Angel of Death grants you one additional day—no more.

Imagine that tomorrow morning is the morning of that extra day. What will you do? How will you spend the day? How will you live with the awareness of your own impending death?

Reflect afterward on what this exercise evokes in you. Does it awaken powerful feelings? Does it provide you with a new perspective on life?

Heedlessness (Forgetfulness) The inability to pay attention and to remember what we know are the cardinal problems of humanity. It is the foundation that supports all other human weaknesses and psychopathology. Inherent in our makeup is the tendency to lose sight of our divine origin; even as we remember we begin to forget. The thrust of Sufi teaching is to encourage people to pay attention long enough to *develop* their capacities to remain awake.

Man, like a sleepwalker who suddenly "comes to" on some lonely road, has in general no correct idea as to his origins or his destiny. (Shah, 1972f, p. 133)

Some of those who have been influenced by Sufi teachings indicate that the initial task is to wake up enough to be aware of one's predicament. Orage (1965) writes:

> Our present waking state is not really being awake at all. . . . It is, the tradition says, a special form of sleep comparable to a hypnotic trance. . . . From the moment of birth and before, we are under the suggestion that we are not fully awake; and it is universally suggested to our consciousness that we must dream the dream of this world—as our parents and friends dream it. . . . Just as in night-dreams the first symptom of waking is to suspect that one is dreaming, the first symptom of waking from the waking state—the second awakening of religion—is the suspicion that our present waking state is dreaming likewise. To be aware that we are asleep is to be on the point of waking; and to be aware that we are only partially awake is the first conditioning of becoming and making ourselves more fully awake. (p. 89)

Man is asleep, must he die before he wakes? (Muhammad)

As Harman (1967) concludes, "We are all hypnotized from infancy. . . . The apparent corollary is that we do not perceive ourselves and the world about us as they are but as we have been persuaded to perceive them" (p. 323).

A first step in overcoming heedlessness is to learn to recognize it in one's own life. It is as mundane as misplacing one's glasses or as troubling as an incident told about Norbert Weiner, the famous cybernetic researcher. One day he was walking along a path at the Massachusetts Institute of Technology when he met a colleague. They talked for a few minutes and, as they parted, Weiner asked his friend to tell him in which direction he had been walking when they

Personal Reflection

■ Do You Know What You Like, Do You Like What You Do?

Here is an exercise to help you investigate your own heedlessness. Are you constantly aware of the choices and decisions you make?

> You wake up in the morning and propose to get up. Ask yourself whether you really wish to get up, and be candid about it.
>
> You take a bath—is it really because you like it or would you dodge it if you could?
>
> You eat your breakfast—is it exactly the breakfast you like in kind and quantity? Is it just your breakfast you eat, or simply breakfast as defined by society? Do you, in fact, wish to eat at all?
>
> You go to your office . . . or you set about the domestic and social duties of the day—are they your native tastes? Would you freely choose to be where you are and do what you are doing? Assume that, for the present, you accept the general situation. Are you in detail doing what you like? Do you speak as you please to other persons? Do you really like or only pretend to like them? (Remember that it is not a question yet of *acting* on your likes and dislikes but only of discovering what they really are.)
>
> You pass the day, every phase offering a new opportunity for self-questioning—do you really like this or not? The evening arrives with leisure—what would you really like to do? What truly amuses you: theater or movies, conversation, reading, music, games, and which ones in particular?
>
> It cannot be repeated too often that the doing of what you like comes later. In fact, it can be left to take care of itself. The important thing is to know what you like. (Orage, 1965, p. 112)

met. Weiner could not recall if he had been on his way to lunch or if he had just finished it.

Incapacity Even a person who feels ready to learn Sufism is not necessarily capable of assimilating Sufi teachings. If the student lacks the capacity to use the teachings, it is like pouring water into sand. There is a saying: "When the student is ready, the teacher appears." This does not mean when the student thinks that he or she is ready; it means instead that when the teacher decides the student is ready for learning, the teacher will attract the student. The student's opinion has little to do with his or her actual level of readiness, but the teacher's decision has everything to do with whether the student will begin.

Nafs The *nafs,* the ego or lower personality, is made up of impulses, or drives, to satisfy desires. These drives dominate reason or judgment and are defined as the forces in one's nature that must be brought under control. They prevent one from activating one's totality. The *nafs* is really a living process, rather than a static structure in the psyche. "The *nafs* is not a thing. The Arabic term is related to words for 'breath,' 'soul,' 'essence,' 'self,' and 'nature.' It refers to a process which comes about from the interaction of body and soul" (Ozak, 1987, p. 31).

The *nafs* is a product of the self-centered consciousness—the ego, the "I"—and eventually can be controlled. The *nafs* must be transformed—this is the ideal. Like a wild horse, the *nafs* is powerful and virtually uncontrollable at first. As the *nafs* becomes trained, or transformed, it becomes capable of serving the individual.

> The *nafs* is not bad in itself. Never blame your *nafs*. Part of the work of Sufism is to change the state of your *nafs*. The lowest state is that of being completely dominated by your wants and desires. The next state is to struggle with yourself, to seek to act according to reason and higher ideals and to criticize yourself when you fail. A much higher state is to be satisfied with whatever God provides for you, whether it means comfort or discomfort, fulfillment of physical needs or not. (Ozak, 1987, p. 32)

The following categories of *nafs* are derived from a number of sources (Al-Ghazzali, 1963; Arasteh, 1973; Nurbakhsh, 1992; Ozak, 1981, 1987; Shafii, 1974; Trimingham, 1971).

The Commanding Nafs This level has also been described as the "domineering self" or the "self that incites to evil." The **commanding nafs** seeks to dominate us and to control our thoughts and actions. At this level, the individual displays unbridled selfishness and no sense of morality or compassion.

Descriptions of this level of *nafs* are similar to descriptions of the id in psychoanalytic theory; the two concepts are closely linked to lust and aggression. Al-Ghazzali calls *nafs* the swine and the dogs of the soul—the sensual *nafs* behaves like swine, the ferocious *nafs* is like fierce dogs or wolves. Wrath, greed, sensual appetites, passion, and envy are examples of this stage of *nafs*. This is the realm of physical and egoistic desires. We are all dominated by these impulses at times, but it is assumed that we have moments of perspective in which we see the tyranny of the least evolved aspects of ourselves.

At this level, people are like addicts in denial. Their lives are dominated by negative urges, yet they refuse to believe they have a problem. There is no hope of change, because there is no acknowledgment of any need for change.

The Accusatory Nafs At the first level, we are unaware and unconscious. As the light of faith grows, we begin to see ourselves clearly, perhaps for the first time. We start to understand the negative effects of our self-centered approach to the world.

At the level of **accusatory nafs,** the individual is still dominated by wants and desires but repents from time to time and *tries* to follow higher impulses. This stage of inner struggle closely corresponds to the stage in the Zen picture "Taming the Ox" (see page 532).

> There is a battle between the *nafs,* the lower self, and the soul. This battle will continue through life. The question is who will educate whom? Who will become the master of whom? If the soul becomes the master, then you will be a believer, one who embraces Truth. If the lower self becomes master of the soul, you will be one who denies Truth. (Ozak, 1987, p. 4)

This level of *nafs* parallels aspects of the superego in psychoanalytic theory. There may be excessive self-accusation, self-belittlement, or defensiveness, which appears in the form of excessive vanity. Typical manifestations include an insatiable hunger for praise, for recognition, or for control of others. "In this stage it is possible for one's motives to become so distorted that it is difficult to distinguish between fantasy and reality" (Beg, 1970). One of the strongest tendencies is hypocrisy. Because they have some knowledge of higher ideals, individuals at this stage tend to pretend to what they have not yet achieved.

At this level, individuals do not yet have the ability to alter their lives significantly. However, as they see their faults more clearly, their regret and their desire for change grow. They are like addicts beginning to realize the extent of their addiction and the pain they have caused themselves and others. Because the addiction is still so powerful, change requires far stronger medicine.

The radical division into good and bad can be the sickness of the Mind. (Erikson, 1964)

The Inspired Nafs The individual who has reached the level of the **inspired nafs** takes genuine pleasure in prayer, meditation, and other spiritual activities. Only now is the individual motivated by ideals such as compassion, service, and moral values. This stage marks the beginning of the real practice of Sufism. At earlier stages, the best anyone can accomplish is superficial understanding and mechanical worship.

Though the individual is not free of the power of desires and ego, the new level of motivation significantly reduces their power for the first time. What is essential is to *live* according to these higher values; otherwise they will wither and die. Behaviors common to the inspired *nafs* include gentleness, compassion, creative acts, and moral action. Overall, a person who is impelled by the inspired *nafs* seems to be emotionally mature, respectable, and respected.

This concept is similar to the mana personality described by Jung. Someone who has touched powerful archetypes may gain great energy or mana, which can then be used in the service of the ego instead of the self. This stage can be the most dangerous in the development of the individual. If the inspiration and energy of this stage feed the ego, the person can become inflated with pride and grandiosity. A sheikh is particularly important for someone going through this stage.

The Contented Nafs The seeker is now at peace, and the struggles of the earlier stages are basically over. The old desires and attachments are no longer binding. This level—the **contented nafs**—is similar to the stage of gratitude and trust mentioned earlier; it also corresponds to the stage shown in the Zen picture "Riding the Ox Home" (see page 533). The ego-self begins to let go, allowing the individual to come closer to the Divine.

This level of *nafs* predisposes one to be liberal, grateful, trusting, and adoring. Individuals who accept difficulties with the same sense of security with which they accept benefits may be said to have attained the level of the contented *nafs*. Developmentally, these *nafs* mark a period of transition. The soul can now begin to "disintegrate" and let go of all previous concern with self-boundaries; it can "reintegrate" as an aspect of the universal self (Arasteh, 1973).

The Pleased Nafs At this stage, the individual is content not only with his or her lot but even with the difficulties and trials of life, realizing that they come from God. The state of the **pleased nafs** is quite different from the individual's usual experience of the world, in which the focus is on seeking pleasure and avoiding pain. A Sufi story illustrates this state clearly.

Sultan Mahmud of Ghazna once shared a cucumber with Ayaz, his most loyal and beloved servant. Ayaz was happily eating his half of the cucumber, but when the sultan bit into *his* half, it was so bitter he immediately spit it out.

"How could you manage to eat something so bitter?" the sultan exclaimed. "It tasted like chalk or like bitter poison!"

"My beloved sultan," answered Ayaz, "I have enjoyed so many favors and bounties from your hand that whatever you give me tastes sweet to me."

A person whose love and gratitude to God are like Ayaz's faithfulness has reached the stage of the pleased *nafs.*

The Nafs Pleasing to God Those who reach this stage—the **nafs pleasing to God**—realize that all power to act originates in God, that they can do nothing by themselves. They no longer fear anything or ask for anything.

The path of Sufism is the elimination of any intermediaries between the individual and God. (Ozak, 1987, p. 1)

These individuals have achieved genuine inner unity and wholeness. People struggle with the world because they experience multiplicity. A broken mirror creates a thousand different reflections of a single image. If the mirror could be made whole again, it would then reflect the single, unified image. Healing the multiplicity within themselves enables people to experience the world as whole and unified.

The Pure Nafs Those few who have attained this final level, that of the **pure nafs,** have transcended the self entirely. There is no ego or separate self left, only union with God. At this stage, the individual has truly realized the truth "There is no god but God." The Sufi now knows that only the Divine exists, that there is nothing other than God, and that any sense of individuality or separateness is an illusion. This is equivalent to the stage of *fana* described earlier.

The stages of the *nafs* are parallel to the stages of development described earlier. Each stage of growth has within it impulses that are contrary to the values of that stage. The conflict leads to growth, provided the *nafs* is subdued, or to regression, if the *nafs* predominates.

Structure

Body

Al-Ghazzali says that one should consider the body as the carrier and the soul as the rider. "The soul should take care of the body, just as a pilgrim on his way to Mecca takes care of his camel; but if the pilgrim spends his whole time in feeding and adorning his camel, the caravan will leave him behind, and he will perish in the desert" (1964a, p. 49). Good health is encouraged because it allows outer service as well as inner work to proceed without impediment.

Ibn 'Arabi also advocates caring for the body without becoming dominated by concern for it. He taught a middle ground that exists between asceticism and hedonism, an approach that is remarkably like that of Buddhism. "Do not sleep until you are unable to stay awake. Do not eat until you are hungry. Dress

The Body too is a great and necessary principle, and without it the task fails and the purpose is not attained. (Rumi, 1972, p. 31)

only to cover your body and to protect it from cold and from heat" (Ibn 'Arabi, 1992, p. 7).

Some Sufi schools employ exercises that entail a "fine-tuning" of the body and mind. The so-called whirling of the dervishes, a combination of music and constantly turning movement, is the most widely known. "The objective is to produce a state of ritual ecstasy and to accelerate the contact of the Sufi's mind with the world-mind of which he considers himself to be a part" (Burke, 1966, p. 10). An exercise may consist of movement, movement with music, or music alone.

The use of dance or movement to bring about the state of ecstasy is described by Burke (1975): "A dance is defined as bodily movements linked to a thought and a sound or a series of sounds. The movements develop the body, the thought focuses the mind, and the sound fuses the two and orientates them towards a consciousness of divine contact" (p. 49). This ecstatic state is a physical condition that allows certain subtle inner experiences to be felt and understood; it is not simply a joyful, hyper-aroused state.

Social Relationships

Ibn 'Arabi stressed the importance of associating with others who are also on the spiritual path:

> It is best to separate yourself from people who do not believe in what you believe, who do not do what you do, and who are against your faith. Yet at the same time you should not think badly of them or condemn them for what they are. Your intention in ignoring them should be that you prefer the company of believers. (Ibn 'Arabi, 1992, p. 10)

Al-Ghazzali discussed two special situations: the relationship of teachers to students and the relationship between close companions.

> The kernel of the human development called "Sufism" is the basic human unit: the members who meet together and carry on the studies prescribed for them by a contemporary teacher. . . . This is necessary to the realization which comes from being a Sufi. It may be called community, communion, meeting. (Foster, 1968, p. 14)

A teaching story by Sa'di (c. A.D. 1200–1291) illustrates the subtle understanding of relationships in Sufism.

> A student said to his teacher: "What am I to do? I am troubled by the people, many of whom pay me visits. By their coming and going they encroach upon my precious time." He replied: "Lend something to every one of them who is poor and ask something from every one who is rich and they will come round thee no more." (1966, p. 131)

The great Sufi saint Shibli also tested the sincerity of his students. Shibli once entered a mystical state and was locked up as a madman. Many of those who had heard him teach went to visit him.

> Shibli asked, "Who are you?"
>
> "We are some of those who love and follow you."

> Shibli began throwing stones at his visitors. They began to run away, crying, "It is true. Shibli really has gone crazy!"
>
> Then Shibli called out to them, "Didn't I hear you say that you loved me? You could not even bear a stone or two before running away. What became of that sincere love you claimed you had for me? Did your love fly away with a couple of stones? If you had really loved me, you would have patiently endured the little bit of discomfort I caused you." (Adapted from traditional sources)

The relationship between companions on the Sufi path is considered extremely important.

An explanation of the power of Sufi groups has been given by a contemporary writer.

> Our tendency is toward personal independence, but in order to know our real Self we need to abandon the ego-protective behaviors that keep us in separation. We need to open ourselves to other beings in this milieu of Love. . . . Only as we begin to open to others in love can the isolated ego be transformed. (Helminski, 1992, p. 15)

Al-Ghazzali (1975) wrote that real friendship includes the following eight responsibilities:

1. *Material aid.* You have an obligation to help your companions with food, or money, or other things they need for their own survival or development.
2. *Personal support.* "If they are sick, visit them; if they are busy, help them; if they have forgotten, remind them" (p. 33).
3. *Respect.* You should not complain of their faults to them or to others. Also, you should not give advice when you know it cannot be acted upon.
4. *Praise and attention.* You should praise the good qualities of your companions and let them know that you care for them.
5. *Forgiveness.* It is helpful to forgive others for their failings.
6. *Prayer.* You should pray for the well-being of your companions with the same fervor as you pray for your own well-being.
7. *Loyalty.* You should be firm in your friendships so that you can be depended on by those who put their trust in you.
8. *Relief from discomfort.* You should not create awkward or difficult situations that involve your companions. You should not be a burden to others.

You will not enter Paradise until you believe, and you will not believe until you love another. Let me guide you to something in the doing of which you will love one another: salute all and sundry among you. (Muhammad)

Will

Although the term *will* is used in Sufi writings, it is elusive and not subject to a single definition. "'Will,' to the Sufi, will vary in nature, quality and significance in direct relation to the stage which the aspirant has reached" (Khan, 1974). Every act is made up of the conception, the motivation, and the capacity to carry it out. There is also the question of balance between free will and divine will.

The effort of attention by which we hold fast to an idea . . . is the secret of will. (James, 1899, p. 91)

Free Will Free will is assumed to be part of human nature. Humanity is unique in its propensity and capacity to perform actions that are contrary to natural law and incompatible with physical, mental, or spiritual health. Unlike animals, we have the ability to turn away from our own best interests. One of the great goals of Sufism is to surrender our individual will to divine will.

Thy will be done
On earth as it is in heaven.
(Lord's Prayer)

Divine Will In contrast to free will, divine will is described as a fundamental law of nature. A stone falls because it is obeying the divine will manifested as gravity. One definition of *saint* might be "one whose every action is in conformity with the divine will." *Islam* means "surrender," or surrender of one's limited personal will to divine will.

One modern sheikh has explained divine will and personal will with the metaphor of an airplane trip. As an individual passenger, you can do virtually nothing that will affect the plane's arrival time. You have neither the skill nor the power to influence the flight itself. But you can decide whether or not to read or write, eat dinner, watch the movie, and so on. In short, you can use your personal will to have a pleasant and profitable time while on the plane, or not. The plane will arrive at exactly the same time in any case.

Emotions

Three things in life are destructive: anger, greed and pride. (Muhammad)

Emotions orient consciousness either toward or away from knowledge of reality. A particular emotion is less important than its overall effect on one's behavior. Al-Ghazzali (1968a) recalls times of bliss and despair, both of which he saw as instrumental in his own realization.

Awareness of one's emotions is important. This awareness is itself transformative, as Fritz Perls and other therapists have recently discovered. "What is essential from you is to be heedful at all times, to be attentive to what comes into your mind and your heart. Think about and analyze these thoughts and feelings. . . . Beware of the wishes of your ego, settle your accounts with it" (Ibn 'Arabi, 1992, p. 7).

Intellect

Al-Ghazzali's description of the intellect foreshadows the developmental models of Piaget (Inhelder & Piaget, 1958; Piaget, 1952). Al-Ghazzali distinguishes four stages of development. First there is a drive for understanding, what Western psychology calls *curiosity* or the need for competence (White, 1959). The second is *axiomatic intellect,* which is the capacity to understand logical relationships. The third element is *empirical knowledge;* it is the aspect that is concerned with external things and events. The last element to appear is the *developed intellect,* which is a higher form of the original drive for understanding. It is this quality of the intellect that guides inner development and allows a person to "conquer and subdue his appetite which hankers for immediate pleasure" (Al-Ghazzali, 1966, p. 228).

If your thought is a rose, you are a rose garden; if it is a thorn, you are fuel for the bath stove. (Rumi in Helminski, 1992, p. 34)

The developed intellect includes the heart as well as the head. It is an integrated way of understanding oneself, the world, and spiritual knowledge as well. Jelaladin Rumi (1207–1273) is a clear example of the integrated intellect.

Not only was he one of the world's greatest mystical poets; Rumi was a gifted philosopher and was the founder of the Mevlevi Order, whose members are known as the whirling dervishes.

Conventional learning can retard the developed intellect if its function is not understood. Al-Ghazzali again and again upbraids his former scholastic colleagues for their unwillingness to use their learning to reach beyond the empirical and achieve real knowledge (Watt, 1971). He recounts that he needed to pierce his own intellectual training repeatedly with ecstatic and revelatory states until he understood enough to keep his intellect in balance.

Self

There are two ways to describe the self. The first way is to see the self as a collection of socially determined, changeable roles—the self within society. The second is to see the true self, the core of one's being, distinct yet part of a larger entity. Sufi teaching is one way to learn to shift people's identification of who they are from the social self to the true self. As they identify more and more with their true selves, they do not deny or give up their own personalities. Rather, as they accept themselves for who they are, the external attributes of personality (how they speak, how they eat, and so forth) are put into a new perspective. These attributes assume their natural place in the totality of the personality.

He who knows himself knows his Lord. (Muhammad)

Sufi masters have a wide variety of personalities. Their personalities remain even after they identify with the true self. It is only the internal point of identification that has shifted. We begin by being identified and controlled by our personality. Later, the personality is a tool that can be consciously used, but the master is in charge, not the personality. An old Sufi metaphor tells of a confused peasant who is carrying his donkey on his back. He needs to learn to put down the donkey, train it, and ride it. The ordinary person, likewise, must learn that the true self is the master.

Teacher

Arasteh and Sheikh (1989) comment that although the teacher-student relationship may seem to be hierarchical and authoritarian, the inner reality is quite different. In reality, two souls are communicating. One is a channel for a higher level of energy and inspiration. The other receives and progresses. The more the dervish progresses, the less guidance he or she requires. Eventually, the student's own heart provides all the guidance necessary.

But how will you ever know him as long as you are unable to know yourself? (Sanai, 1974, p. 10)

The Necessity of a Guide Why is a guide necessary? Mohammed Shafii, a psychiatrist knowledgeable in Sufi tradition, suggests:

> The Sufis feel that maturity cannot be achieved alone. They feel there is a need for guidance and discipline. The path is unknown, the night is dark and the road is full of danger. Dangers include preoccupation with selfishness, false visions, misinterpretations of mystical states, arrest in development, fixation in a particular state, appeal to various drugs to create false

mystical experiences and not infrequently overwhelming anxiety and insanity. (1968, p. 11)

A teacher is like a doctor, a physician of the soul. Because few of us have the knowledge of medicine to cure ourselves and fewer still have the self-knowledge to diagnose ourselves correctly, we must turn to a teacher.

A Sufi sheikh is like a doctor, and a student is someone who is sick at heart. The student comes to the sheikh for healing. A real sheikh will give a certain diet and certain medications to cure the person's ills. (Ozak, 1987, p. 2)

Duties of a Teacher Al-Ghazzali (1966, pp. 145–152) describes eight duties of a teacher. Although the teaching techniques and personal styles of teachers vary widely, this is an excellent guide to understanding the complex role of the sheikh.

1. "The first duty of the teacher is to be sympathetic to students and treat them as his own children." Generally, the group of dervishes who work with a teacher form an *ihwan*, or fellowship. Their group is like a family. The dervishes are brothers and sisters and the sheikh is father and mother. In many Orders, any romantic or sexual involvement between sheikh and dervish is absolutely forbidden. It is considered a form of incest.

With a Guide you may become a real man, without one you will remain an animal. (Rumi in Shah, 1970a, p. 37)

Much of the spiritual growth in Sufism is based on the love and support of the dervishes for each other, as well as their love for the teacher, and the teacher's love and understanding of each dervish. Tremendous change is possible when the dervishes find that their teacher is fully aware of their faults and weaknesses and still loves and respects them. However, if this loving, family atmosphere is not present, little or nothing is accomplished.

2. "The second duty of the teacher is to follow the example of the Law-giver: he should seek no remuneration for his services . . . and accept neither reward nor thanks." This is related to the ancient tradition, found in both Judaism and Islam, that one does not take money for teaching God's scriptures or divine truth. Religious teaching is too important to mix with business considerations.

3. "[The teacher] should not withhold from the student any advice, or allow him to attempt work at any grade unless he is qualified for it." The teacher is openhanded with his or her teaching. At the same time, overambitious students need to be discouraged from taking on duties or practices that are beyond their capacities. To start a practice and then drop it because it is too difficult can be very disheartening and can seriously slow a student's progress. Too many students begin with unrealistically high goals and then become frustrated and drop out entirely.

If men had been forbidden to make porridge of camel's dung, they would have done it, saying that they would not have been forbidden to do it unless there had been some good in it. (Muhammad in Al-Ghazzali, 1966, p. 149)

4. "The teacher, in dissuading the student from his evil ways, should do so by suggestion rather than openly, and with sympathy rather than with odious upbraiding. . . . Open dissuasion destroys the veil of awe, invites defiance, and encourages stubbornness."

A good teacher will often point out specific rules of religious or spiritual law without specifying just who needs to hear these rules at the moment. Hopefully, certain students will realize that these rules pertain to them and will try and change, without ever having been singled out or embarrassed.

5. "The person who is teaching a certain science should not belittle or disparage the value of other sciences before his students." A wise teacher will praise the strengths and advantages of other teachers and disciplines and will say nothing about their faults. Ideally, the teacher will find something positive to

say about everyone and every tradition. In this way, the teacher models patience and tolerance.

6. "He should limit the student to what the latter is able to understand and should not require of him anything which his mind cannot grasp for fear that he would develop a feeling of dislike for the subject, and his mind would become confused." An older man came to a teacher one day and said that his doctors told him he had a terminal illness. He had not been particularly religious, but now he wanted to begin reading the Koran, and he wanted to know where to start. The teacher said, "Don't start reading the Koran now. Begin with Rumi's *Mathnawi,* which is really an extended commentary on the Koran." He knew that the man would quickly become discouraged trying to understand the Koran without a substantial period of preparation.

7. "The teacher should give his backward students only such things as are clear and suitable to their limited understanding and should not mention to them anything about the details that are apt to follow but which he deems fitting for the present to withhold. . . . Even the most foolish and most feeble-minded among men is usually the most pleased with the perfection of his mind."

The Sufi must act and speak in a manner which takes into consideration the understanding, limitations and dominant concealed prejudices of his audience. (Ibn 'Arabi in Shah, 1970a, p. 33)

The basic problem is that our imaginations distort reality. We don't see ourselves as we truly are, or the world as it truly is. The teacher's job is to lead students back to reality. At the early stages in particular, the teacher has to be fully aware of the distortions in the minds of each student.

8. "The teacher must do what he teaches and not allow his works to give the lie to his words."

One day, a teacher was asked about patience. He spoke beautifully about patience, with words full of wisdom. Just then, a scorpion stung his foot, not just once but repeatedly. However, he did not interrupt his talk, despite the pain.

When his listeners became aware of what had happened, they wondered why the teacher had not moved his foot away from the scorpion.

"I was discussing patience," he explained. "I could hardly give you any advice on that subject without setting an example of patience myself. I would have felt ashamed before God."

In the West we are often taken in by those who write or speak beautifully about great truths. To talk about the truth and not live it is hypocrisy, and it can weaken or even destroy students' faith to realize that their teacher does not practice what he or she preaches. Empty words have no weight.

Evaluation

Sufism is difficult to evaluate because it has taken so many forms and adapted its teachings to many different cultural settings. Sufism has been presented here as a theory of personality and a way to self-understanding, rather than as a religious doctrine.

Sufism is an ancient tradition; but it has not become so formal, so burdened with old ideas and practices, that it has lost its relevance. It is still responsive to new cultural demands and is still modifying its methods and its message for a new generation of students who can be taught Sufism (Shah, 1981).

There is little use in teaching wisdom. At all events wisdom cannot be taught in words. It is only possible by personal contact and by immediate experience. (Jung, 1973)

It is difficult to accept the emphasis on the need for a living, personal teacher. We have become accustomed to the idea that there is nothing we cannot do for ourselves. Bookstores bulge with shelves of do-it-yourself literature on everything from carpentry to beekeeping, Yoga to childbirth. What Sufism suggests is that we must do the work ourselves, but a teacher can help us accomplish our task. It is a common error to think that, because we are striving diligently, our efforts will lead to some personal benefit. No matter how hard we whip our horses, no matter how vigorously we kick their sides, no matter how fast they go—if we are racing around a circular track, we will not advance beyond the point at which we started.

One begins to appreciate the Sufi point of view by experiencing the distinctions between useless knowledge and useful knowledge as illustrated by the following story:

> Nasrudin sometimes took people for trips in his boat. One day a fussy pedagogue hired him to ferry him across a very wide river.
>
> As soon as they were afloat the scholar asked whether it was going to be rough.
>
> "Don't ask me nothing about it," said Nasrudin.
>
> "Have you never studied grammar?"
>
> "No," said the Mulla.
>
> "In that case, half your life has been wasted."
>
> The Mulla said nothing.
>
> Soon a terrible storm blew up. The Mulla's crazy cockleshell was filling with water.
>
> He leaned over towards his companion.
>
> "Have you ever learnt to swim?"
>
> "No," said the pedant.
>
> "In that case, schoolmaster, ALL your life is lost, for we are sinking." (Shah, 1972d, p. 18)

Not only do humorous tales contain valuable structures for understanding. Their use also helps to weed out people who lack a sense of humour. Sufis hold that people who have not developed or who have suppressed their capacity to enjoy humour are, in this deprived state, also without learning capacity. (Shah, 1981, p. 21)

This story raises some questions: What have you learned that is useful knowledge? What have you learned that is extraneous to your life? What have you learned that may, even now, be holding you back?

Sufism proposes that the more we can sift out the true from the unimportant and the false, the closer we are to being able to see the larger picture of humanity, of which our personality is such a small part.

It has been said that in the West we are able to use only very little of the Sufi teaching. It is all too new to us; it contains too many ideas that we immediately dismiss. It is for this reason that, according to some teachers, they are laying the groundwork for later, more direct teaching experiences.

One contemporary teacher has explained the point this way.

> There are different ways of "awakening." Man may be asleep, but he must wake in the right way. One necessity is that when he is awake, he will also have the means to profit by his wakefulness. It is the preparation for this profiting as well as the preparation for waking, which is our current endeavor. (Pendlebury, 1974, p. 74)

In this chapter, we have attempted to present Sufism in as cogent a way as possible, so that as Sufi ideas become more available to the West, you can more easily accept and understand them.

The Theory Firsthand

Excerpt from *Forty Days: The Diary of a Traditional Solitary Sufi Retreat*

The following passage is taken from the diary kept during a 40-day Sufi retreat. It was written by a Western woman who is not only a Muslim but also a prominent European psychologist.

The *zhikrs* [the practice of repetition of a sacred word or phrase] are becoming even deeper; in the truest sense of the word they are taking on "substance." This is where the inner peace unfolds, the peace described so beautifully by Islam as the tranquility of the heart. My head moves inside a column formed by my air body. Then I get the feeling that every back-and-forth motion of my head is spraying strings of this substance all over the room. Like water spraying from the hide of a wet dog when it shakes itself. Except that these strings have some kind of life of their own that draws them out farther and farther into the universe. Right above the heart region is where you feel it, as if pulling open curtains (veils?) on either side. With the steady, broad-stepping movements of a skater's legs—right, left, right, left. . . . So is this the "polishing of the heart"?

Sometimes it feels as if I'm penetrating directly into the syllables of the holy formulas, into the sound that echoes silently within me. The greater the awareness, the more intense the experience is. The *zhikr* is showing me how to do *zhikrs*! The old precept comes to mind: "At first you act as if you're doing the *zhikr*. Then you do the *zhikr*. Then finally the *zhikr* does you." All at once I perceive this steering process as one of the "signs" of Allah: "*He is closer to you than your jugular vein.*" Where can one perceive Him Who is immanent and transcendent if not in one's deepest insides? The signs of which the Holy Quran speaks are "*on the horizons and within yourselves.*" Is that it? "His Heaven and His Earth cannot contain Him," says Islam, "only the [shiny, polished] heart of the believer has room for Him."

Suddenly it becomes painfully clear to me. There's really only one way: absolute surrender, absolute giving-up of wanting-for-oneself. The voluntary giving-up of "whatever is dearest." In the words of Hz. Mevlâna [Rumi]: "to take the step toward the lion *in the lion's presence,*" to "jump into the fire," to "fall into the trap."

The Lion

So the reports of a lion reached every corner of the world. A man amazed by the rumors made his way to the forest from a faraway place to see the lion. For a whole year he endured the rigors of the journey, traveling from waystation to waystation. When he got to the forest and saw the lion from afar, he stood still and couldn't go a step closer. "What's this?" they said to him. "You came all this

> way out of love for this lion. This lion has the trait that if a person boldly comes up to him and strokes him lovingly, he will not hurt that person or do anything to him; but if someone is fearful and anxious, then the lion becomes furious at him; indeed he attacks some people meaning to kill them because they have a bad opinion of him. That being so, you've given yourself a year of trouble. Now that you've gotten close to the lion, you stand still. What kind of standing there is that?" No one had the courage to go a single step farther. They said, "All the steps we took up to now were easy. Here we can't take a step farther." Now, what Omar [one of the four Caliphs of Islam] meant by faith was this step, taking a step in the lion's presence toward the lion. This step is extremely rare; it is the part of the elect and God's close friends alone. It is the real step, the rest are only footprints.
>
> (Rumi)

. . . At some point, much later, . . . I experience the deepest and richest tranquility of the heart that I have ever felt. . . . Now I have given everything, I have nothing left. Will I ever be able to stop crying? Only three weeks more [to the retreat], then they'll come and get me out. I wonder whether I can get myself back together by then.

And yet these few seconds of such a qualitatively utterly different, such an indescribable feeling of the peace of the heart are enough to strengthen me in the assumption that I'm on the right track. So I go on and on, until, between the tears and the exhaustion, I no longer know for sure whether I'm asleep or still praying.

(Özelsel, 1996, pp. 54–56)

Chapter Highlights

- Not all Sufi teachings can be communicated in words, nor is there a single, systematic approach to the teachings. Sufism is often described as a path, a metaphor that suggests both an origin and a destination.
- There are four basic principles in Sufi practice: (1) There are as many ways, involving transformation of the ego and service to creation, to reach truth (or God) as there are individuals. (2) An inner sense of justice is needed if we are to live in harmony with others, and our selfishness and arrogance must be reduced for this to occur. (3) One of the underlying principles of morality is love, which springs from self-work, and expresses itself in service to others. (4) Self-knowledge is the cardinal truth, which ripens into knowledge of God.
- Sufism is usually described as the mystical core of Islam, dating from about the seventh century A.D. as a major religious force.
- Al-Ghazzali divides knowledge into the categories of detrimental and useful. Knowledge that distracts from or retards the understanding of the inner self is detrimental. (Logic, philosophy, and academic knowledge are three such limiting forms.) The most important form of useful knowledge, that which furthers a person's growth, is direct knowledge.

- According to ibn 'Arabi, there are four stages of practice and understanding in Sufism, each built upon the one before. The first is *sharia* (exoteric religious law); the second is *tariqa* (the mystical path); the third is *haqiqa* (truth); and the fourth is *marifa* (gnosis).
- Two states of advanced consciousness are described by the Sufis. The first is a state of annihilation or union (*fana*) and the second is that of persistence or return (*baqa*).
- Common to both Christian and Sufi writings, the perception of God as the Beloved comes from direct experience. It is said that if you take two steps toward God, God runs to you.
- Stages of psychospiritual growth include the following: initial awakening; patience and gratitude; fear and hope; self-denial and poverty; trust in God; love, yearning, intimacy, and satisfaction; intent, sincerity, and truthfulness; contemplation and self-examination; and the recollection of death.
- Heedlessness and the *nafs,* or lower self, are the main obstacles to growth in Sufism. The *nafs* is the source of most of our negative traits, such as pride, greed, anger, and hypocrisy. To transform the *nafs* into positive qualities is one of the great goals of Sufism.
- The *nafs* is a living process made up of impulses, or drives, to satisfy desires, which dominate reason or judgment. The process derives from the interplay of body and soul.
- The *nafs* have been categorized into the following levels: the commanding *nafs,* the accusatory *nafs,* the inspired *nafs,* the contented *nafs,* the pleased *nafs,* the *nafs* pleasing to God, and the pure *nafs.*
- It is the teacher's decision whether a student has the capacity to learn Sufism.
- The teacher is considered a physician of the soul.

Key Concepts

Accusatory nafs Second stage of the *nafs,* or ego. The individual is dominated by desires and wants but from time to time tries to follow higher impulses, as the negative effects of his or her self-centeredness become evident. This level of *nafs* is similar to the psychoanalytic concept of superego.

Al-Ghazzali One of the most important figures in Islamic theology. He established a framework in which pathological, normal, and mystical behaviors are linked in a single, unified field of human experience. He also reinstated the elements of personal development and transpersonal experience into Islam.

Baqa State of return or persistence in which the individual is part of the world but unconcerned about his or her rewards or position in it. *Baqa* is reintegration as the universal self, or the activation of the individual's totality.

Bearing witness Recitation of the basic tenets of Islamic faith. Entrance into Islam begins with the confession of faith "I bear witness that there is no god but God" and "I bear witness that Muhammad is a servant and a messenger of God."

Commanding nafs First stage of the *nafs,* or ego. The commanding *nafs,* like the id in psychoanalytic theory, seeks to dominate the individual's thoughts and behavior. At this level, there is unbridled selfishness and no sense of morality or compassion. It is the tyranny of the least evolved aspects of the individual.

Contemplation and self-examination Meditation in order to perceive inner reality. The concerns of this stage, stilling and clearing the mind, are similar to those of Yoga and Buddhism.

Contented nafs Fourth stage of the *nafs,* or ego. The individual is at peace, and old desires and attachments are no longer binding.

Fana A state of union or annihilation in which individual identity seems merged with the whole of reality. *Fana* is the disintegration of the person's narrow self-concept, social self, and limited intellect. The experience of the individual is like a drop of water aware of being part of the ocean.

Fear and hope The sense of losing God (fear) and the anticipation that one's efforts will bring one closer to God (hope). The fear is akin to what lovers feel when they worry about losing their sweetheart. Hope allows one to see oneself clearly. One hopes that in spite of personal shortcomings, progress along the spiritual path is possible.

Haqiqa Truth, the third stage of Sufism. The term refers to the personal understanding of the inner meanings of the guidance and practices of the preceding stages, *sharia* and *tariqa.* All spiritual practice is imitation prior to this stage.

Initial awakening The beginning of a fundamental reorientation of personal values. It is often preceded by a personal crisis, after which the individual concludes that the external world is not as satisfying as it had once seemed.

Inspired nafs The third stage of the *nafs,* or ego. The individual is motivated, for the first time, by ideals such as compassion, service, and moral values. The power of the desires and the ego is reduced. This stage marks the beginning of the real practice of Sufism.

Intent, sincerity, and truthfulness Concern for the aim, or intent, of an action, rather than for the action itself. The individual experiences ever-increasing awareness of the inner meaning of events and less interest in observable behaviors.

Love, yearning, intimacy, and satisfaction The stage at which the developing personality has only the desire to love God. While enjoying a sense of intimacy with God, the individual derives satisfaction from knowing that all things come from the Divine.

Marifa Gnosis, the fourth stage of Sufism. A deep level of understanding, beyond *haqiqa,* it is the station of the great sages and saints, the messengers, and the prophets.

Nafs pleasing to God The sixth stage of the *nafs,* or ego. The individual realizes that all power to act comes from God, that nothing can be done without divine help. It is the stage of genuine inner unity and wholeness.

Patience and gratitude Willingness to accept the fact that efforts toward self-improvement are not immediately rewarded (patience) and appreciation for the fact that one is given time to make progress (gratitude). Gratitude is related to the belief that *all* things, whether pleasant or painful, come from God.

Pleased nafs The fifth stage of the *nafs,* or ego. The individual is contented with whatever happens, realizing that even pain and suffering come from the Divine.

Pure nafs The final stage of the *nafs,* or ego. It is equivalent to the stage of *fana.* The sense of "I" has been dropped. The Sufi now knows that only the Divine exists.

Recollection of death A potent practice in becoming more aware of one's present experiences, and a powerful tool in letting go of undesirable habits and attitudes.

Self-denial and poverty Service to others rather than to oneself (self-denial) and freedom from attachment (poverty). Service is rendered in order to please God, not for any worldly rewards. The inner meaning of *poverty* is to be free of desire and attachment so that one may receive God.

Sharia The first of the four stages of Sufism. It consists of teachings of morality, ethics, and outer practice. The word means "road" in Arabic, and it refers to a route anyone can follow.

Tariqa The trackless path in the desert from oasis to oasis; not a visible road. The second stage of Sufism, it refers to the inner practice of the teachings.

Trust in God The stage at which the individual seeks everything from God. It is an active process, not passive or dependent. Trust arises from the assumption that one's efforts are part of a larger system, whose details are unknown.

Annotated Bibliography

Al-Ghazzali, M. (1964). *The alchemy of happiness* (C. Field, Trans.). Lahore, Pakistan: Muhammad Ashraf.

Part of his own abridgment of *The revival of religious sciences.* It is a short, vivid book with very few references to purely Islamic ideas.

———. (1971). *Ghazzali's Ihya Ulum-id-din* (Alhaj Maulana Fazlul Karim, Trans.). Dacca, Bangladesh: Mission Trust.

The only full translation of al-Ghazzali's *The revival of religious sciences* available.

———. (1972). *The revival of religious sciences* (B. Behari, Trans.). Farnham, Surrey, England: Sufi Publishing.

The best translation of the most important of al-Ghazzali's major works. Selections drawn primarily from the last half of *Ihya 'Ulum Ad-din.*

Bakhtiar, L. (1987). *Sufi: Expressions of the mystic quest.* New York: Avon.

A different approach; symbolic, geometric, and with beautiful illustrations.

Ozak, M. (al-Jerrahi). (1987). *Love is the wine.* (Edited and compiled by Sheikh R. Frager al-Jerrahi.) Putney, VT: Threshold Books.

This book is derived from talks given in the United States by a contemporary Sufi master. It presents the depths of Sufi wisdom in a modern, highly accessible form.

———. (1988). *Irshad: Wisdom of a Sufi master.* Amity, NY: Amity House.

A collection of discourses on Sufism, its practice and philosophy. For the serious student.

Shah, I. (1964). *The Sufis.* New York: Doubleday.

Shah discusses the major traditional Sufi teachers, Sufism's major influences on Western thought, and some of the central ideas of Sufi practice.

———. (1971). *The pleasantries of the incredible Mulla Nasrudin.* New York: Dutton.

A collection of short, funny stories about the mulla, a folk hero who is the subject of numerous Sufi stories.

References

Abdul-Hamid, Sufi. (1976). First statement. In L. Lewin (Ed.), *The elephant in the dark.* New York: Dutton.

Al-Ghazzali. (1952). *Mishkat al-anwar (The niche for lights)* (W. H. T. Gairdner, Trans.). Lahore, Pakistan: Muhammad Ashraf.

———. (1963). *The foundations of the articles of faith* (N. A. Faris, Trans.). Lahore, Pakistan: Muhammad Ashraf.

———. (1964a). *The alchemy of happiness* (C. Field, Trans.). Lahore, Pakistan: Muhammad Ashraf.

———. (1964b). *Ghazzali's book of counsel for kings* (F. R. C. Bagley, Trans.). London: Oxford University Press.

———. (1966). *The book of knowledge* (N. A. Faris, Trans.). Lahore, Pakistan: Muhammad Ashraf.

———. (1968a). *The confessions of al-Ghazzali* (C. Field, Trans.). Lahore, Pakistan: Muhammad Ashraf. (Also in *The faith and practice of al-Ghazzali* [correctly translated as "Deliverance from error"] [W. M. Watt, Trans.]. London: Allen & Unwin, 1953.)

———. (1968b). *The mysteries of fasting* (N. A. Faris, Trans.). Lahore, Pakistan: Muhammad Ashraf.

———. (1972). *The revival of religious sciences* (B. Behari, Trans.). Farnham, Surrey, England: Sufi Publishing.

———. (1975). *On the duties of brotherhood* (M. Holland, Trans.). London: Latimer.

———. (1976). *Letters of al-Ghazzali* (A. Qayyum, Trans.). Lahore, Pakistan: Islamic Publications.

———. (1983). *Inner dimensions of Islamic worship* (M. Holland, Trans.). London: Islamic Foundation.

Ali, S. N. (1944). *Some moral and religious teachings of al-Ghazzali* (2nd ed.). Lahore, Pakistan: Muhammad Ashraf.

Arasteh, A. R. (1965). *Final integration in the adult personality.* Leiden, Holland: Brill.

———. (1972). *Rumi, the Persian: Rebirth in creativity and love.* Tucson, AZ: Omen Press.

———. (1973). Psychology of the Sufi way to individuation. In L. F. Rushbrook Williams (Ed.), *Sufi studies: East and West* (pp. 89–113). New York: Dutton.

———. (1980). *Growth to selfhood: Sufi contribution.* London: Routledge & Kegan Paul.

Arasteh, A., & Sheikh, A. (1989). Sufism: The way to universal self. In A. Sheikh & K. Sheikh (Eds.), *Eastern and Western approaches to healing.* New York: Wiley.

Arberry, A. J. (1966). *The doctrine of the Sufis.* Lahore, Pakistan: Shri Muhammad Ashraf. (Also, Cambridge: Cambridge University Press, 1977.)

———. (1970). *Sufism: An account of the mystics of Islam.* New York: Harper & Row.

Attar, Farid Ud-Din. (1961). *The conference of the birds* (C. S. Nott, Trans.). London: Routledge & Kegan Paul.

Baba, M. (1967). *Listen, humanity.* New York: Dodd, Mead.

———. (1972). *Life at its best.* New York: Harper & Row.

Beg, M. A. (1970). A note on the concept of self, and the theory and practice of psychological help in the Sufi tradition. *Interpersonal Development, 1,* 58–64.

Behari, B. (1972). Introduction. *The revival of religious sciences* by al-Ghazzali. Farnham, Surrey, England: Sufi Publishing.

Burckhardt, T. (1968). *An introduction to Sufi doctrine.* Lahore, Pakistan: Muhammad Ashraf.

Burke, O. (1966). Travel and residence with dervishes. In R. Davidson (Ed.), *Documents on contemporary dervish communities.* London: Hoopoe.

———. (1975). *Among the dervishes.* New York: Dutton.

Chittick, W. (1983). *The Sufi path of love: The spiritual teachings of Rumi.* Albany: State University of New York Press.

———. (1989). *The Sufi path of knowledge: Ibn al-'Arabi's metaphysics of imagination.* Albany: State University of New York Press.

Dallas, I. (1973). *The book of strangers.* New York: Warner Books.

Dawood, N. J. (Trans.). (1968). *The Koran* (3rd rev. ed.). Baltimore: Penguin Books.

Deikman, A. (1980). Sufism and psychiatry. In S. Boorstein (Ed.), *Transpersonal psychotherapy* (pp. 200–216). Palo Alto, CA: Science and Behavior.

el-Qadiri, I. H. (1974). *The secret garden.* Introduction by Mahmud Shabistari (J. Pasha, Trans.). New York: Dutton.

Erikson, E. (1964). *Insight and responsibility.* New York: Norton.

Farzan, M. (1973). *Another way of laughter.* New York: Dutton.

———. (1974). *The tale of the reed pipe.* New York: Dutton.

Foster, W. (1968). *Sufi studies today.* London: Octagon.

Gurdjieff, G. I. (1950). *All and everything, the first series: Beelzebub's tales to his grandson.* New York: Dutton.

———. (1968). *Meetings with remarkable men.* New York: Dutton.

Haeri, F. (1989). *The journey of the self.* Dorset, England: Element Books.

Harman, W. W. (1967). Old wine in new wineskins. In J. Bugental (Ed.), *Challenges of humanistic psychology* (pp. 321–334). New York: McGraw-Hill.

Helminski, K. (1992). *Living presence: A Sufi way to mindfulness and the essential self.* New York: Tarcher.

Hujwiri. (1959). *Kashf al-mahjub* (R. A. Nicholson, Trans.). London: Luzac.

ibn 'Arabi, M. (1981). *Journey to the lord of power* (R. Harris, Trans.). New York: Inner Traditions.

———. (1992). *What the seeker needs* (T. Bayrak al-Jerrahi & R. Harris al-Jerrahi, Trans.). Putney, VT: Threshold Books.

Inhelder, B., & Piaget, J. (1958). (A. Parsons & S. Milgrim, Trans.). *The growth of logical thinking from childhood to adolescence.* New York: Basic Books.

James, W. (1899). *Talks to teachers on psychology and to students on some of life's ideals.* New York: Holt, Rinehart and Winston. (Unaltered republication, New York: Dover, 1962.)

Jung, C. G. (1973). *C. G. Jung's letters* (G. Adler, A. Jaffe, & R. F. C. Hull, Eds.) (Vol. 1). Princeton, NJ: Princeton University Press, pp. 1906–1950.

Kabir. (1977). *The Kabir book.* Versions by Robert Bly. Boston: Beacon Press.

Khan, Pir Villayat. (1974). *Toward the one.* New York: Harper & Row.

MacDonald, D. B. (1899). The life of al-Ghazzali, with special reference to his religious experience and opinions. *The Journal of the American Oriental Society, 20,* 71–132.

———. (1903). Al-Ghazzali. In *Development of Muslim theology, jurisprudence and constitutional theory.* Lahore, Pakistan: Premier Book House, pp. 215–242.

———. (1909). *The religious attitude and life in Islam.* Chicago: University of Chicago Press.

Nasr, S. (Ed.). (1987). *Islamic spirituality: Foundations.* New York: Crossroads.

Nicholson, R. A. (1964a). *The idea of personality in Sufism.* Lahore, Pakistan: Muhammad Ashraf.

———. (1964b). *Rumi, poet and mystic.* London: Allen & Unwin.

Nurbakhsh, J. (n.d.). *Sufism and psychoanalysis (Parts 1 and 2).* Unpublished papers, Department of Psychiatry, University of Tehran, Tehran, Iran.

———. (1978). *In the tavern of ruin.* New York: Khaniqahi-nimatullahi Publications.

———. (1979). *In the paradise of the Sufis.* New York: Khaniqahi-nimatullahi Publications.

———. (1981). *Sufism: Meaning, knowledge and unity.* New York: Khaniqahi-nimatullahi Publications.

———. (1992). *The psychology of Sufism.* New York: Khaniqahi-nimatullahi Publications.

Orage, A. R. (1965). *Psychological exercises and essays* (rev. ed.). London: Janus.

Ornstein, R. E. (1972). *The psychology of consciousness.* San Francisco: Freeman; New York: Viking Press.

Ouspensky, P. D. (1949). *In search of the miraculous.* New York: Harcourt Brace Jovanovich.

Ozak, M. (al-Jerrahi). (1981). *The unveiling of love* (M. Holland, Trans.). New York: Inner Traditions.

———. (1987). *Love is the wine.* (Edited and compiled by Sheikh R. Frager al-Jerrahi). Putney, VT: Threshold Books.

———. (1988). *Irshad: Wisdom of a Sufi master.* Amity, NY: Amity House.

———. (1991a). *The garden of dervishes* (M. Holland, Trans.). Westport, CT: Pir Publications.

———. (1991b). *Adornment of hearts* (M. Holland and S. Friedrich, Trans.). Westport, CT: Pir Publications.

Özelsel, M. (1996). *Forty days: The diary of a traditional solitary Sufi retreat.* Brattleboro, VT: Threshold Books.

Pendlebury, D. L. (1974). Afterword. *The walled garden of truth* by H. Sanai (D. L. Pendlebury, Trans.). London: Octagon.

Perry, W. N. (1971). *A treasury of traditional wisdom.* New York: Simon & Schuster.

Piaget, J. (1952). *The origins of intelligence in children.* New York: International University Press.

Qayyum, A. (Trans.). (1976). *Letters of al-Ghazzali.* Lahore, Pakistan: Islamic Publications.

Rice, C. (1964). *The Persian Sufis.* London: Allen & Unwin.

Rumi, Jalal al-Din. (1972). *Discourses of Rumi* (A. J. Arberry, Trans.). New York: Weiser.

Sa'di, M. (1966). *The gulistan or rose garden of Sa'di* (E. Rehatsek, Trans.). New York: Capricorn Books.

Salinger, J. D. (1965). *Raise high the roofbeam, carpenters and Seymour, an introduction.* New York: Bantam Books.

Sanai, H. (1974). *The walled garden of truth* (D. L. Pendlebury, Trans.). London: Octagon.

Schimmel, A. (1975). *Mystical dimensions of Islam.* Chapel Hill: University of North Carolina Press.

———. (1985). *And Muhammad is His Messenger.* Chapel Hill: University of North Carolina Press.

Shafii, M. (1968). The pir (Sufi guide) and the Western psychotherapist. *R. M. Bucke Memorial Society Newsletter 3,* 9–19.

———. (1974). *Developmental stages in man in Sufism and psychoanalysis.* Unpublished manuscript.

———. (1985). *Freedom from the self.* New York: Human Sciences Press.

Shah, I. (1964). *The Sufis.* New York: Doubleday.

———. (1970a). *The way of the Sufi.* New York: Dutton.

———. (1970b). *Tales of the dervishes.* New York: Dutton.

———. (1971a). *The dermis probe.* New York: Dutton.

———. (1971b). *The pleasantries of the incredible Mulla Nasrudin.* New York: Dutton.

———. (1971c). *The magic monastery.* New York: Dutton.

———. (1972a). Interview with Pat Williams. In L. Lewin (Ed.), *The diffusion of Sufi ideas in the West.* Boulder, CO: Keysign Press.

———. (1972b). *Caravan of dreams.* Baltimore: Penguin Books.

———. (1972c). *Wisdom of the idiots.* New York: Dutton.

———. (1972d). *The exploits of the incomparable Mulla Nasrudin.* New York: Dutton.

———. (1972e). *Thinkers of the East: Teachings of the dervishes.* Baltimore: Penguin Books.

———. (1972f). First statement. In L. Lewin (Ed.), *The diffusion of Sufi ideas in the West* (pp. 133–145). Boulder, CO: Keysign Press.

———. (1981). *Learning how to learn.* San Francisco: Harper & Row.

Shah, S. (1933). *Islamic Sufism.* London: Rider.

Shea, D. (Trans.). (1943). *The Dabistan.* London: Oriental Translation Fund.

Siraj-Ed-Din, A. (1970). *The book of certainty.* New York: Weiser.

Smith, J. (1980). Women in Islam: Equity, equality, and the search for the natural order. *Journal of the American Academy of Religion, 47*(4), 517–537.

Smith, J., & Haddad, Y. (1975). Women in the afterlife: The Islamic view as seen from Koran and tradition. *Journal of the American Academy of Religion, 43*(1), 39–50.

Smith, M. (1977). *Rabia, the mystic A.D. 717–801 and her fellow saints in Islam.* San Francisco: Rainbow Bridge. (Originally published, 1928, Cambridge University Press, England.)

Trimingham, J. S. (1971). *The Sufi orders in Islam.* New York: Oxford University Press.

Tweedie, I. (1979). *The chasm of fire.* England: Element Books.

Watt, W. M. (1971). *Muslim intellectual: A study of al-Ghazzali.* Edinburgh: University Press.

White, R. W. (1959). Motivation reconsidered: The concept of competence. *Psychological Review, 66,* 297–333.

Credits

Text

P. 89: From *Analytical Psychology: Its Theory and Practice* by C.G. Jung. Copyright © 1968 by Heirs of C.G. Jung. Reprinted by permission of Pantheon Books, a division of Random House, Inc.

P. 119: From Alfred Alder, *Social Interest: A Challenge to Mankind,* Copyright 1964, Capricorn Books.

P. 149: From R. Coles, Anna Freud, © 1992 by Robert Coles. (pages 164, 192, 193). Reprinted by permission of Addision Wesley Longman, Inc.

P. 149: Reprinted from *The Analysis of Defense: The Ego and the Mechanism of Defenses Revisited* by Joseph Sandler and Anna Freud. By permission of International Universities Press, Inc. Copyright © 1985 by International Universities Press, Inc.

P. 150: From: Frederick S. Perls, *Gestalt Therapy Verbatim,* copyright 1969 The Real People Press.

P. 183: From: *Self-Analysis* by Karen Horney. Copyright 1942 by W.W. Norton & Company, Inc., renewed © 1970 by Mariannevon Renate Mintz, and Bridgett Swarzenski. Reprinted by permission of W.W. Norton & Company, Inc.

P. 218: From: *Childhood and Society* by Erik H. Erikson. Copyright © 1950, © 1963 by W.W. Norton & Company, Inc., renewed © 1978, 1991 by Erik H. Erikson. Reprinted by permission of W.W. Norton & Company.

P. 250: Copyright © 1971 by Orson Bean from *Me and the Orgone* by Orson Bean. Reprinted by permission of St. Martin's Press, Incorporated.

P. 271: From: J.V. Jordan et al. *Women's Growth in Connection.* Copyright © 1991. Reprinted by permission of Guilford Publications, Inc.

P. 309: From: William James, *Talks to Teachers on Psychology and to Students on Some of Life's Ideals.* Copyright © 1962. Reprinted by permission of Dover Publishers.

P. 310: Reprinted with the permission of Simon & Schuster from *The Varieties of Religious Experience* by William James. Copyright © 1961 by Macmillan Publishing Company.

P. 351: From: B. F.Skinner, "Humanism and Behavorism" from *The Humanist,* July/August 1972. Copyright © 1972. Reprinted by permission of the B.F. Skinner Foundation.

P. 390: Reprinted from *Perspectives in Personal Construct Theory,* (ed.) D. Bannister, Copyright © 1970, by permission of the publisher Academic Press Limited London.

P. 390: Reprinted from *Cognitive Therapy and Emotional Disorders* by Aaron Beck. By permission of International Universities Press, Inc. Copyright © 1976 by International Universities Press, Inc.

P. 391: From: Francisco Varela, Evan Thompson, and Eleanor Rosch, *The Embodied Mind: Cognitive Science and Human Experience* (Cambridge, MA: The MIT Press, 1991).

P. 429: From: Harold I. Kaplan, *Comprehensive Textbook of Psychiatry,* 2/e. Copyright 1995.

P. 470: From: A. Maslow in Stanley Krippner, "The Plateau Experience: A.H. Maslow and Others," *Journal of Transpersonal Psychology,* Vol. 4, Number 2. Copyright © Transpersonal Institute, 1972. Reprinted by permission.

P. 505: Reprinted from *Radha: Diary of A Woman's Search* by Swami Sivananda Radha. (1981) Timeless Books, PO Box 3543, Spokane, WA 99220

P. 545: Reprinted with permission from *The Wild, White Goose* (vol. 1) by Rev. P.T.N.H. Jiyu-Kennett, Roshi (Mt. Shasta, California: Shasta Abbey Press, 1977), pp. 81–95. © 1977 Rev. P.T.N.H. Jiyu-Kennett, Roshi.

P. 581: From: M. Ozelsel, *Forty Days: The Diary of a Traditional Solitary Sufi Retreat,* copyright 1996. Originally published by Threshold Books, 139 Main Street, Brattleboro, VT 05301. Reprinted by permission.

Photographs

Unless otherwise acknowledged, all photographs are the property of Addison Wesley Educational Publishers, Inc. Abbreviations are as follows: right (R), center (C), left (L), top (T), bottom (B).

Cover: Painting by Jeanette Stobie, photographed by Francine Bernard, from the Collection of Eddy J. Louis

P. xx: Courtesy, Sundance Images

P. xxi: Courtesy, Renee Fadiman

P. 1: Painting by Jeanette Stobie, photographed by Francine Bernard, from the Collection of Eddy J. Louis

P. 16: (L) Archives of The History of American Psychology, University of Akron, Akron, Ohio; (R) AP/Wide World

P. 57: © Yousuf Karsh/Woodfin Camp & Associates

P. 68: Paul Solomon/Woodfin Camp & Associates

P. 82: UPI/Corbis-Bettmann

P. 96: UPI/Corbis-Bettmann

P. 114: AP/Wide World

P. 124: (TL) The Freud Museum/SYGMA; (TC) Wellcome Institute Library, London; (TR) British Psycho-Analytical Society Archives, London; (BL) W. W. Norton & Company; (BC) Michael Alexander; (BR) Courtesy The Estate of Laura Perls and The Gestalt Journal Press

P. 157: Courtesy Marianne Horney Eckardt, M.D.

P. 191: Archives of The History of American Psychology, University of Akron, Akron, Ohio

P. 223: UPI/Corbis-Bettmann

P. 257: (TL) Courtesy Jean Baker Miller,The Stone Center, Wellesley College; (TR) Courtesy Irene Pierce Stiver, The Stone Center, Wellesley College; (BL) Courtesy Judith Jordon, The Stone Center, Wellesley College; (BR) Courtesy Jan Surrey, The Stone Center, Wellesley College

P. 278: Culver Pictures, Inc.

P. 321: Ken Heyman/Woodfin Camp & Associates

P. 348: Dean Brown

P. 359: Courtesy The Ohio State University Archives

P. 398: Corbis-Bettmann

P. 439: Archives of The History of American Psychology, University of Akron, Akron, Ohio

P. 448: Corbis-Bettmann

P. 449: Topham/The Image Works

P. 459: Anne Nielsen/Gamma-Liaison

P. 460: Mark Antman/The Image Works

P. 477: A. Reininger/Woodfin Camp & Associates

P. 489: A. Reininger/Woodfin Camp & Associates

P. 496: R. Berriedale Johnson/Panos Pictures

P. 512: Milt & Joan Mann/Cameramann International, Ltd.

P. 515: Dean Wong/The Image Works

Pp. 528–537: Ten Ox Herding Paintings by Jikihara Gyokusei, from, "Zen-no Bokugyu Zu," Sogen-sha Inc., Publishers, Osaka, Japan.

P. 552: Jack Vartoogian

P. 556: Peter Sanders

Name Index

Subject Index